D0722190

Nathaniel Hawthorne's
The Scarlet Letter

Nathaniel Hawthorne's
The Scarlet Letter

A Critical Resource Guide
and Comprehensive Annotated Bibliography
of Literary Criticism, 1950-2000

Kimberly Free Muirhead

Studies in American Literature
Volume 73

The Edwin Mellen Press
Lewiston•Queenston•Lampeter

Library of Congress Cataloging-in-Publication Data

Muirhead, Kimberly Free.
    Nathaniel Hawthorne's The scarlet letter : a critical resource guide and comprehensive
bibliography of literary criticism, 1950-2000 / Kimberly Free Muirhead.
        p. cm. -- (Studies in American literature ; v. 73)
    Includes bibliographical references and index.
    ISBN 0-7734-6196-5
    1. Hawthorne, Nathaniel, 1804-1864. Scarlet letter. 2. Hawthorne, Nathaniel,
1804-1864. Scarlet letter--Bibliography. I. Title. II. Studies in American literature
(Lewiston, N.Y.) ; v. 73.

PS1868.M85 2005
813'.3--dc22

                                                                                    2004061070

This is volume 73 in the continuing series
Studies in American Literature
Volume 73 ISBN 0-7734-6196-5
SAL Series ISBN 0-88946-166-X

A CIP catalog record for this book is available from the British Library

Front cover: Original artwork by Matthew Clancy

The Edwin Mellen Press   The Edwin Mellen Press
Box 450   Box 67
Lewiston, New York   Queenston, Ontario
USA 14092-0450   CANADA L0S 1L0

The Edwin Mellen Press, Ltd.
Lampeter, Ceredigion, Wales
UNITED KINGDOM SA48 8LT

Printed in the United States of America

For my children

Table of Contents

Preface

No other "classic" American novel can vie with *The Scarlet Letter* for widespread readership, critical attention, and influence. Accordingly, the novel has assumed, at least nominally, as much a part of American heritage as any cultural icon that anyone would be likely to name. As Richard Brodhead and Jane Tompkins have made clear, Hawthorne achieved canonized status before the end of the nineteenth century, and *The Scarlet Letter* was the chief work to which commentators pointed as the leading cause of his elevation. That status received fresh impetus in the early 1920s, when D. H. Lawrence declared that everyone had been misreading Hawthorne, that he was not the tame, blue-eyed darling whom readers had taken to their hearts, that the ironic language and artfully concealed meanings of *The Scarlet Letter* revealed a demon in Hawthorne's soul, expressing the very demon belonging to America from the start.

To a significant extent, therefore, Lawrence inaugurated rereadings of *The Scarlet Letter* that have waxed to the present time and show no signs of waning. Since 1950, more than a thousand notes, essays, chapters in monographs, introductions, and even entire books have been devoted to the novel. In 2000, the 150-year anniversary of the novel's publication, two academic journals published essays focusing exclusively on it; and, in further commemoration of the event, the Nathaniel Hawthorne Society convened multiple sessions on *The Scarlet Letter* at three conferences. Beyond the few "casebooks" that have been published on it, a further measure of the continuing reappraisals of the novel can be observed in the fact that the Norton Critical Edition will soon appear in a fourth edition, while no other work in the Critical Edition series has exceeded two.

Finding guidance to approach and negotiate ways through the formidable amount of commentary on *The Scarlet Letter* has posed a problem for at least two decades. Numerous essays have been published in recent years bearing obvious signs that their authors have not adequately informed themselves of previous scholarship. Part of the reason for the ignorance underlying this lapse in proper attribution can be attributed to the fact that there has been no full-scale bibliography of criticism on the novel, especially a bibliography that reliably maps out the subjects and issues existing in the welter of published commentary. This problem has now been resolved.

Many are the virtues of this bibliography of criticism on *The Scarlet Letter*, and Kimberly Free Muirhead will receive for many years, if only in silence, the gratitude of students, teachers, and scholars. It would have been quite helpful had she simply chosen to compile a bibliography and left it at that, but it would appear that, from the outset, Muirhead wanted to engage in a project that would prove far more useful to anyone interested in discovering the myriad ways *The Scarlet Letter* has been interpreted and contextualized. She therefore undertook the immense task of reading all of the commentary on the novel of any potential importance, annotating that commentary, and weighing the results. One of the first things that she determined was that numerous essays or sections of essays and books were either derivative or contributed nothing new to the history of commentary on the novel. She therefore omitted them. As much as scholars can place faith in the work of their peers, I believe it safe to say, because she has done all the requisite reading that no one will likely do again, we can confidently rely on Muirhead's judgment in this respect. Thus her work will save future investigators countless hours of tracking down and reading insignificant material.

That's one virtue; but the most compelling virtue lies in the annotations themselves. Beginning with the most salient and influential criticism on *The Scarlet Letter* written in the nineteenth and first half of the twentieth centuries, and then undertaking a decade by decade sequence of commentary from 1950 to 2000, Muirhead intelligently selects and distills the theses, principal arguments and evidence, critical or theoretical approaches, and relevant collateral issues in some eight hundred entries. If read from beginning to end, these annotations permit readers to observe the emergence and sway of a host of perspectives that

Hawthorne's masterpiece has invited and continues to invite: biographical, psychological, philosophical, theological, political, sociological, scientific, New Critical, structuralist, post-structuralist, historicist, new historicist, feminist, gender, reader-response, iconographic, aesthetic, linguistic, narratival, and rhetorical—along with all of the source studies included for good measure.

Surely the merit of any bibliography depends upon its organization and accessibility, and in these respects yet another virtue of Muirhead's project becomes evident. In arranging entries alphabetically by authors' last names in a series of divisions by decades, and sub-categories within each decade, Muirhead affords opportunity for readers to observe the development of *Scarlet Letter* criticism in a historical chronology as accurate and convenient as could be managed. And yet, knowing full well that few readers will likely proceed from cover to cover, Muirhead has provided two exceedingly helpful features. First, following the annotations to most entries appear cross-reference designations germane to those entries in a variety of important ways. Second, at the end of the book appear three indexes that permit readers convenient and reliable access to entries by author's last names, to an alphabetical list of subjects and issues that have received critical and scholarly attention, and to critical and theoretical approaches that have informed analyses of the novel.

The Subject Iindex, comprising hundreds of topics and subtopics, deserves special commendation. Through key words, readers are afforded comprehensive access to works written, for example, on Hester or Dimmesdale; on Hawthorne's reading in Puritan history and its bearing upon the context of *The Scarlet Letter*; on the array of symbolic interpretations of the letter A; on motherhood and childhood; on guilt and redemption; on the relation of the novel to other works of Hawthorne or to works of writers appearing either before or after its publication; or on the perennial problem of the relation of "The Custom-House" to the scarlet letter tale. With such easy access to subjects of their interest, readers can efficiently narrow the focus of their research efforts, thereby avoiding innumerable hours of consulting materials having no immediate pertinence to their concerns.

It fairly staggers the imagination to consider the amount of work required to complete this volume. And it really is all here, helpfully organized and tabulated—all that anyone might need as a research guide to the scholarship, the persistent conversations, and both the old and new debates on American's premier novel.

Frederick Newberry
Editor, *Nathaniel Hawthorne Review*
Duquesne University

Foreword

"Doubtless the meaning of any work of art that
plumbs the mysteries of human life will be subject
to endless debate."

Roy R. Male

This project, badly needed and long overdue, provides a "selectively comprehensive" and cross-referenced record of the enormous body of scholarship on *The Scarlet Letter* from 1950 to 2000, as well as an introductory overview of the major patterns and trends in the interpretations and critical judgments of the novel over the past fifty years. The four-part study is designed for both new and seasoned readers/critics and can be used in two ways to examine the critical, theoretical, and biographical approaches to the novel: as a chronological record and historical survey of the development of ideas in criticism as they have appeared over five decades, and as a guide that can be accessed through the Author, Subject, and Critical Approach Indexes.

Part I provides a chronological, annotated listing of the ten most popular and frequently anthologized "Early Reviews" of the novel. Part II offers alphabetically arranged, full citations for "Early Influential Criticism [Pre-1950]" and is comprised of forty-one landmark commentaries that appeared between 1850 and 1950. Part III, which makes up the bulk of the project and begins with the year 1950, presents a chronologically arranged, comprehensive annotated bibliography of *Scarlet Letter* criticism that includes books, articles, special critical editions, collections of criticism, general student introductions and help books, teaching aids and guides, and biographies. The critical bibliography provides descriptive annotations for all entries, as well as classifies and cross-references all books and articles written on the novel from 1950 to 2000, in a practical effort (1) to indicate the usefulness of individual sources for specific readers and (2) to offer an accessible overview of the major patterns and trends in the interpretations and critical judgments of *The Scarlet Letter* over the past fifty years—a period of time that has seen dramatic changes in approaches to literature—so that readers may better come to terms with their own interpretations of the novel.

The six-part Resource Guide that makes up Part IV groups together special critical editions, collections of criticism, general student introductions to the novel, teaching aids and guides, bibliographies, and biographies. An Author Index, a Subject Index, and a Critical Approach Index conclude the study. The Critical Approach Index identifies fifteen dominant critical and theoretical approaches that have been used to analyze *The Scarlet Letter* over the past fifty years and classifies a significant number of the bibliography's citations to those specific methodologies: morality studies, religious/theological studies, language studies, law studies, New Criticism, archetypal/myth criticism, structuralism, semiology/semiotics, post-structuralism, deconstruction, reader-response theory, historicism, New Historicism, psychoanalytic/psychological criticism, and feminist studies (the last category of which is broken down into sub-categories of feminist studies, black feminist studies, gender studies, and family studies).

Initially intimidated by my own ignorance of the scholarship on *The Scarlet Letter*, I have designed this critical bibliography and resource guide, above all, to serve the specific purposes of enlarging readers' understanding of and appreciation for the novel. More pragmatically, it intends to assist readers in arriving at their own critically-informed assessments of the novel and in achieving a more coherent sense of its critical history. In fact, I determined to write this bibliography while I was compiling entries on Hawthorne criticism for the bibliographies that appeared in the fall issues of the *Nathaniel Hawthorne Review* in 1998 and 1999. I found myself particularly fascinated by essays that explored gender issues in the novel, especially the critical debates over whether Hester or Dimmesdale is the "true" protagonist and how one is to interpret Hester's return to New England at the end. The more these analyses conflicted with one another, the more I felt compelled to read all there was on the subject. My intention was to write a study that would describe and organize the immense body of commentary on the novel and facilitate the inquiries and studies of future readers, students, critics, teachers, and scholars.

Until now, there has been no comprehensive history of *Scarlet Letter* criticism that spans the time frame of this bibliography, nor one that offers a thorough survey of outlooks and approaches to the novel. One need only type in the title of the novel on any number of humanities indexes or databases to be staggered by the hundreds of pieces of criticism that have been published in the last few decades alone. Such an array of criticism might intimidate a student who seeks to add to the scholarship but can scarcely discern what contributions might yet be made, what subjects might still fruitfully be explored, and what topics may seem to have long-since exhausted themselves. If studies continue to be written that show scant knowledge of previous scholarship, then new scholarship itself will necessarily be repetitive and derivative, wasting critical energies. Because the novel continues to inspire a wide variety of critical approaches, it is my hope that this bibliography will serve critics and scholars who may be unaware of the weighty and valuable legacy of past criticism on *The Scarlet Letter*.

Acknowledgments

Over the past four years, I have accumulated a small list of people without whose generous help I could not have completed this project. First I would like to offer thanks to Kathy Julius and her staff in Duquesne University's Interlibrary Loan Department for processing and filling over a thousand journal and book requests for me. Kathy answered numerous inquiries over email and was patient when, early on, my organizational system for requesting and rejecting so many sources was anything but "fine tuned." The reference librarians and staff working at Duquesne's circulation desk (especially Barbara Adams and Joe Nelson) also provided much needed assistance in various capacities (answering questions, helping me locate "missing" books, double-checking publication information, facilitating my access to several confusing databases, and giving "crash course" directions when the library's computers and software were replaced with intimidating new ones), so I am grateful to them, as well. Thanks must also go to Don Luisi of Robert Morris University's Interlibrary Loan Department for processing a few hundred journal requests—and to my parents-in-law, Mary Ann and Ed Muirhead, for providing baby-sitting service for my two sons (both of whom were born during the writing of this book) so that I could occasionally go to Robert Morris's Moon campus library to work uninterrupted on annotations.

Thank you to Dr. Monika Elbert of Montclair State University and Dr. Linda Kinnahan of Duquesne University for agreeing to sit on my dissertation committee and for making helpful suggestions to improve my introduction. A special note of gratitude is due to my dissertation director, Dr. Frederick Newberry, who first suggested the idea for this project in November, 1999, and who guided me along with expert advice and excellent suggestions (via dozens of emails, many conferences, and in written comments on several drafts) so that I could not only complete the monstrous project but also turn it into something to be proud of. For his generous assistance and time, I am grateful and indebted.

I am also grateful for my husband Mike's steady support and faithful encouragement while I worked on this bibliography: for driving across town on his lunch hour to pick up books for me when I could not, for occasionally copying book chapters at work, for gaining me access to his student account at Robert Morris University to save money on journal requests, for always standing ably by (even over the phone) to fix any and all problems with the computer and/or printer, for making late night trips to Kinko's, and—most of all—for showing real interest in every phase of the project's development. Thanks also to my two little boys, William and Carter, for providing much needed perspective and comic relief—and for being patient with a mother who spends too much time at the computer.

A final note of gratitude goes to my mother, Dr. Suzanne Hamilton Free, who took painstaking care and enthusiastic interest in editing the final draft of my introduction. She inspired me to follow in her academic footsteps, and to strive for a healthy balance between professional accomplishment and private fulfillment. We nod in agreement with Goethe that "All theory is gray, dear friend / But the tree of life is green."

Introduction

"Even after all the spilled ink—after so much intense and discriminating analysis and interpretation—we still have not been able to possess [Hawthorne]."

Malcolm Cowley

"Interpretations of works of art are necessary, but no critic can formulate more than he has been able to perceive, and *The Scarlet Letter* is greater than any interpretation of it. That is why it has outlived so many and may be trusted to outlive so many more."

Edward Wagenknecht

"*The Scarlet Letter* will outlast its critics, for it is not a book that has ever required blood transfusions from fat literary histories or that has been brought back to life by a devoted coterie with artificial respiration."

Charles Child Walcutt

"Like the shamans who handle the spiritual energies at work in other cultures, we are stewards of the magic, not possessors of it, and our explanations are stillborn when they are not celebratory."

T. Walter Herbert

The Reception, Canonization, and Critical History of *The Scarlet Letter*

Gary Scharnhorst writes in his own assessment of *The Critical Response to Nathaniel Hawthorne's The Scarlet Letter* that "the history of its reception is, in fact, nothing less than a case-study in canon formation" (xiii). From the start, Hawthorne's romance had every necessary component to ensure that it would become a classic.[i] It was published by James T. Fields of Ticknor, Reed, and Fields, New England's most prominent publisher of fine literature, who encouraged Hawthorne to publish *The Scarlet Letter* and "The Custom-House" in a single volume (and to exclude other tales in a proposed collection entitled *Old-Time Legends: Together with Sketches, Experimental and Ideal*, as Hawthorne had originally intended), thus to capitalize on the nation's craze for novels. Much impressed with Hawthorne's manuscript, Fields had accepted the "germ" of the novel before it was even complete (the last three chapters had yet to be written), and he rightly anticipated that "The Custom-House" sketch alone would tweak the public's interest because it offered Hawthorne's personal account of the well-known local scandal involving his self-described political "decapitation" from the position of Surveyor at the Salem Custom House on June 8, 1849.

Fields shrewdly let word leak out to the editors of such influential newspapers as the *New York Literary World* and the *Transcript* (sending them extracts of Hawthorne's portrait of the "Old Inspector") that Hawthorne's introductory sketch contained humorous and satiric portraits of Hawthorne's Custom-House employees that would likely incite an uproarious commotion. Fields also energetically promoted *The Scarlet Letter*, advertising it as a "first rate romance" and a true work of American genius before it was released on March 16, 1850—to a young country eager to establish a national literature independent of and distinguished from England's.

The timing was especially ideal because, in addition to the country being "suffused by an American inferiority complex in regard to arts and letters" (Cohen ix), New England intellectuals were embarking "on a program to install their region as the historical fountainhead of the nation" and were "encouraging literature [novels especially] written by New Englanders, with New England subjects and themes presented in a national context" (Baym 65). Fields was well aware that "America needed a living novelist whom it could regard as this country's answer to Dickens and Thackeray, a novelist who represented both what was essentially American and what was 'best' by some universal criteria of literary value" (Tompkins 25). Hawthorne, Fields suspected, fit the bill perfectly with his "tale of human frailty and sorrow" set in Puritan Boston during the mid-seventeenth century.

Hawthorne, however, was not as optimistic as his publisher about whether the novel would be a success, reportedly telling Fields that "it is either very good or very bad—I don't know which."[ii] He was most fearful that the public would find it too tragic, too "stern and sombre" and too much "ungladdenedby genial sunshine" (43), which they did, acknowledging in a letter to friend Horatio Bridge that it was "positively a h—ll-fired story into which [he] found it almost impossible to throw any cheering light" (Charvat xv). But Hawthorne nevertheless suspected that he had a triumph on his hands, even if his tale of sin and unrelenting, oppressive guilt *was* too gloomy for a general readership that preferred light-spirited "coming-of-age" novels with happy endings.[iii] And he was right. His romance had everything to commend it, attracting the attention of a publisher who recognized both talent and opportunity when he saw it. Eager to capitalize on the notoriety Hawthorne had recently acquired over the minor public scandal involving his Custom House firing,[iv] Fields also believed Hawthorne could satisfy the country's thirst for a first-rate novelist who could sensitively treat "the humbler aspects of the American scene" and act as "a spokesman for the democratic way of life" (Tompkins 25). The first edition of 2,500 copies sold out in three days. In six months' time, *The Scarlet Letter* had gone through three printings and six thousand copies (at 75 cents each). This is not to say that the novel earned Hawthorne a great deal of money, however. His total earnings for the book, given that he earned "15 per cent on a retail price of seventy-five cents, were a little over $1,500" [Charvat xvi].

The widespread promotion of "The Custom-House" without a doubt helped to get the novel off to a good start, even if it did incite many readers in Salem and vicinity. The sketch occasioned cries of outrage from Salemites, many of whom found Hawthorne's "despicable" caricatures of fellow Custom House employees unwarranted, tasteless, and cruel. Curiously, the first critic to review the novel in Salem, Caleb Foote, made no mention of "The Custom-House" whatsoever. He writes in his cheerful review for the *Salem Gazette* that "It is indeed a wonderful book, and we venture to predict that no one will put it down before he reaches the last page of it, unless it is forcibly taken out of his hands" (Clark, Jr., 401). Most Salemites sided with the reviewer of competing Salem newspaper, the *Salem Register*, in which John Chapman venomously attacked

"The Custom-House" preface for being "so atrocious, so heartless, so undisguised, so utterly inexcusable" for its "calumnious caricatures of inoffensive men" (402). Locals generally agreed with Chapman's assessment and stirred up a frenzied storm of animosity for Hawthorne that lasted well until the twentieth century (Chandler 39).

Thrilled with the taste of literary success and the immediate fame that came with the novel's publication, however, Hawthorne was not about to apologize for attacking the political enemies who had him ousted from the Custom House; nor was he to repent of his insulting jibes at the "set of wearisome old souls" who were his subordinates. Responding immediately to incensed readers and more specifically to Chapman's review, knowing that he could never live in Salem again after having become the object of such antipathy, Hawthorne composed a preface to the second edition on March 30, which playfully denied any wrongdoing or intended offense, assuring the public that he was guiltless, and that not a word of the sketch would be changed since "The Custom-House" could not have been written "in a better or kindlier spirit," and that only "frank and genuine good-humor" filled its pages (1-2).

Outside of Salem, critical evaluations were based upon the romance itself. The earliest reviews by respected professional critics largely valued *The Scarlet Letter* "to the extent that it embodie[d] the correct moral and political values, and thus could contribute positively to the consolidation of the national character" (Kennedy-Andrews 17). Most of them, English reviewers included,[v] were enormously impressed with Hawthorne's masterful and delicate handling of the subject of adultery and rated *The Scarlet Letter* highly on a moral scale that charted the novel's ability to uphold ethical and moral standards, to promote Christianity and self-sacrifice, and to encourage decorum, virtue, and delicacy among its middle-class reading audience. A couple of reviews even made flattering comparisons between Hawthorne and more famous contemporary authors, observing his artistic likeness to Edgar Allan Poe (in ER2) and Washington Irving (in ER10).

Negative reviewers saw *The Scarlet Letter* "as evidence of national moral decay as well as of the decline of the novel" (Murfin 206). These critics, who were not so willing to declare Hawthorne a national treasure, a great man of letters, or "a model of moral and aesthetic excellence" (Tompkins 25)—such as Arthur Cleveland Coxe (see ER10), Anne W. Abott (see ER5), Orestes A. Brownson (see ER9), and even English critic and Hawthorne admirer, Henry F. Chorley (see ER4)—faulted Hawthorne's offensive choice of subject matter and questioned his fidelity to the strict principle (widely accepted in the nineteenth century) that art should be, above all, morally instructive and edifying to its impressionable audience. Orestes A. Brownson admonished Hawthorne for "perverting" his genius by writing such as loathsome tale, and Arthur Cleveland Coxe (see ER10) went so far in his assault on the romance as to call it a "dirty story" peopled with "criminals."

Defenders of *The Scarlet Letter* were quick to vindicate Hawthorne from such attacks. George B. Loring, for one, (see ER7), passionately defended Hawthorne's romance in the *Massachusetts Quarterly Review* against conservative critics on religious grounds, reassuring Christian moralists that *The Scarlet Letter* was firmly rooted in Christian precept and served as a trustworthy guide to right conduct and "to the truths of the human heart" (Tompkins 18). Writing for *Graham's Magazine*, E. P. Whipple (Hawthorne's favorite critic) also endorsed the novel, claiming that its moral purpose was so definite that "the most abandoned libertine could not read the volume without being thrilled into something like virtuous resolution" (see ER3). But as Nina Baym notes, it didn't much matter whether the critics reviewed the novel favorably or unfavorably: "They wrote about it with the expansive seriousness that salutes a major work. *The Scarlet Letter*, the classic that had been waiting to happen, had appeared"

(70), and Hawthorne was aglow with having "w[on] official acceptance as America's greatest novelist" (Brodhead 48).

Once *The Scarlet Letter* had been reviewed favorably by several important professional critics who praised the novel's moral intent (like Loring, Whipple, and Evert A. Duychinck, the latter of whom was the first critic to refer to *The Scarlet Letter* as a "psychological romance"), and once it had been discussed in the most fashionable literary periodicals and been selected by New England's well-connected, "cultivated minority" as a book that could assist in raising the level of popular taste and in refining "the impulses of the multitude" (Tompkins 25), the novel gained Hawthorne a secure place in New England's socio-cultural network, solidly assuring his prominence and establishing him as a literary giant on an international scale.[vi]

Ticknor and Fields[vii] (and then later Houghton, Mifflin), influential friends, powerful literary acquaintances, and determined family members worked cooperatively to promote Hawthorne's reputation, to create and sustain his cultural identity, and to increase his popularity.[viii] They continued to do so even after his death in 1864, by encouraging posthumous publications and republishing existing works, by writing poems, biographies, and essays, and by producing family memoirs. In 1876, for instance, George Parsons Lathrop wrote the first biography of Hawthorne, an effort that further secured his father-in-law's prominence as a literary and cultural institution. And in 1879, writing for Macmillan's English Men of Letters series, the American expatriate Henry James completed the first critical book on Hawthorne, which not only sustained Hawthorne's popularity but also provoked enormous critical response. James praised *The Scarlet Letter* (see EC15) as "the finest piece of imaginative writing yet put forth in this country," something that "might at last be sent to Europe as exquisite in quality as anything that had been received, and the best of it was that the thing was absolutely American" (James 110). Though full of reverential admiration for Hawthorne's moral tale, insisting that the "classic" book was not about adultery, and impressed with Hawthorne's delving into "deeper psychology," James was nonetheless critical of Hawthorne's "densely dark," provincial, and overly "gloomy" tale. Himself a proponent of realism, James faulted the romance's exaggerated and mechanical use of symbolism and its cold, abstract "want of reality," anticipating the critical opinion of future generations of Hawthorne scholars. So important were James's controversial assessments, and so timely were his remarks as romanticism was giving way to realism in American fiction (and debates developing over the distinctions between "idealism" and realism, romances and novels), that "his critical biography remain[ed] the most influential of the commentaries on Hawthorne during the period 1865 to 1910" (Cohen xi).

Henry James was not the only famous author to make a memorable pronouncement on Hawthorne's romance; in the same year, English novelist Anthony Trollope (see EC33) praised the "black forebodings" of Hawthorne's tragic vision as "communicating a transcendent sublimity which ennobled readers" (Cohen xii). He also commended Hawthorne's presentation of realistic characters, the "incongruous" Pearl being the exception, and detected a "vein of drollery" that lends the relentlessly dark and starkly moral tale a "touch of burlesque." And in 1901, William Dean Howells (see EC14) also praised *The Scarlet Letter*'s realistic qualities, registering his surprise that the American romance, which one would typically expect to reflect the country's "crude" landscape and thin social texture, seemed to him superior in its realistic presentation of character to any novel by Dickens. Howells found all of the characters—save Pearl (again)—to be "robust," and, like Trollope and unlike James, cited Hester as the "chief" character over the comparatively weak and cowardly Dimmesdale.

To further keep Hawthorne at the forefront of the public's attention and secure his fame, a definitive "Riverside Edition" of his works in twelve volumes appeared in 1883 by Houghton Mifflin (which took over James R. Osgood and xviii

Co., which had taken over Ticknor and Fields), edited by George Parsons Lathrop, who had married Hawthorne's youngest daughter, Rose. "And in the same year [Houghton Mifflin] established an Education Department to produce textbooks for the enormously expanding school population of the United States. This department designed a pamphlet series of what were designated as American literary classics" (Baym 71), with Hawthorne's *The Scarlet Letter* exhibited in inexpensive "classic" editions designed for high schools in the 1880s and for colleges in the 1890s. The "builders of an American national literature," the "institutional establishment" that was largely composed of "specialized experts," had judged Hawthorne's "highly moral tale of secret guilt and the psychological consequences of sin" to be of supreme cultural value. Promoting national stability and high culture (Brodhead 63), *The Scarlet Letter* at last reached a mass audience.

In an effort to cover the royalties and expenses due to Hawthorne's heirs, Houghton Mifflin began, around 1880, to repackage *The Scarlet Letter* "for every level of the market" (Brodhead 58). Literary magazines like the *Atlantic*, *Harper's*, and *Century*, which emerged between the mid and late nineteenth century, similarly reinforced and solidified Hawthorne's reputation as a "classic" author by publishing pieces about him. In short, Hawthorne was everywhere, admired by critics and readers alike, and his "exquisiteness as an artist" was asserted "with [such] monotonous regularity in the critical literature of the late nineteenth and early twentieth century" that writing a piece on him "became one of the things that a critic did to prove himself on both sides of the Atlantic Ocean" (Baym 71).

The 1904 centennial celebrations of Hawthorne's birth created a new surge in critical interest, providing "another generation of official literary eminences the chance to display themselves as eminences" (Brodhead 58). Yet the criticism on Hawthorne and *The Scarlet Letter* written in the early twentieth century was much like that of the late nineteenth century, largely subjective, impressionistic, nationalistic, and biographical. Charles Child Walcutt observed in *"The Scarlet Letter* and Its Modern Critics"* that many early readings provided little more than detailed plot summaries of the story and took up more space appreciating rather than explicating the novel (72). When studies did attempt explications, they tended to examine the novel's allegorical content and speculate about such issues as Hawthorne's historical accuracy, his didacticism and morality, and his questionable affiliation with transcendentalism. A great many also addressed Hawthorne's exceptional knowledge of psychology, use of symbolism, dark vision, and overall artistic craft.

As was the case in the commentary on "The Custom-House," early critics eagerly portrayed Hawthorne as a great artist of an emerging national literature clearly differentiated from English literature;[ix] they focused on specifically American aspects of *The Scarlet Letter*, such as its stark New England setting and weighty Puritan presence and heritage, and likewise presented Hawthorne as "the sombre heir of an austere and diseased Puritanism" (Scharnhorst xx). Early biographers such as George Parsons Lathrop (see EC17), George Woodberry (see EC41), and Herbert Gorman (see EC10) reinforced the stereotype of Hawthorne as an ultra-reserved, morbidly sensitive, physically frail and withdrawn intellectual seeker of solitude whose obsessions with sin, guilt, and his Puritan ancestors colored every aspect of his life with a tragic sense of gloom and doom.

In the early 1920s, when the canon of classic American literature was being reconstructed to reflect both the cultural reorganization of literature's place in society[x] and the modern concerns and interests of a highly-mechanized age of industrial capitalism (characterized by the collapse of traditional ideals and values, as well as by profound religious doubts and a pervading sense of alienation and despair), Hawthorne's image also underwent reconstruction. Literary scholars treated him as if he had been entirely misunderstood in his own day, finding characteristics of modernists' avant-garde artistic practices in his craft: in expressions of anxiety and contradiction, depictions of multiple perceptions of reality, moral irresolution, experimentation with narrative point of view and traditional sex roles, conspicuously unrealistic method, and interest in psychological analysis. Modernists, who broke with traditional forms of expression and were noted for their experimental representations of fragmented experience, isolation, and loss, adopted Hawthorne as a precursor of their own time, as a fellow questioner of social, religious, and moral "truths" who, as they did, subverted in his fiction the very structures he was claiming to represent.

So while Hawthorne's contemporaries were ousted from their canonized positions as "greats" in the American literary tradition (such as Irving, Longfellow, Cooper, Whittier, Lowell, and Holmes) and replaced with the darker, more complex "classic" authors still studied today (such as Poe, Melville, and Dickinson), Hawthorne remained. Interest in his social connections to the former writers gave way to curiosity about his private identity, shy nature, and relationship to "a more abstract fraternity of independent, isolated geniuses," particularly Herman Melville, as the two were thought to be kindred spirits (Baym 73).[xi] Although *The Scarlet Letter* had not been considered a characteristic work of Hawthorne's in the nineteenth century (he had been admired most, as his contemporaries were, for his "combinations of light humor, pathos, sentiment, and fancy" [Charvat xxiv]), it came to be the work most intimately associated with him in the twentieth century, because, as Richard Brodhead explains, in it Hawthorne displayed the literary virtues "around which the new American canon was largely grouped": "dividedness, subversivess, darkness, [and] demoralization" (8). In other words, Brodhead says that Hawthorne retained his canonical status not because *The Scarlet Letter* exempted him "from the ravages of time," but because the perception of him had changed, and the stereotypical view of his solitary habits and withdrawal from society matched what the specialists were looking for. Thus the canon-reformers in the early twentieth century re-evaluated Hawthorne and literally made him an expression of their new interests, adopting the "isolated genius" with the melancholy personality into their "new age's institutions of cultural conservation and transmission" (Brodhead 211).

In 1923, right around the time that the characteristics of "great" American literature were being redefined to reflect the "ache" of modernism, D. H. Lawrence's timely and revisonary *Studies in Classic American Literature* (see EC18) appeared on the scene, contributing another critical capstone to Hawthorne's already established place in the American literary canon and paving the way for future studies on the dark, subversive nature of Hawthorne's imagination. In it, Lawrence provocatively (and idiosyncratically) challenged old-fashioned views of American literature, seeing in *The Scarlet Letter* the duplicity he perceived to lie at the heart of American literature and insisting that the romance has two sides: "a tame, mindlessly conventional Victorian surface [that appealed to nineteenth-century tastes] and a wild depth of passionate subversion" that defined Hawthorne's true interests (Brodhead 9). Lawrence implied that critics had been too willing to accept the "pious as pie" conventional morality at the surface level of *The Scarlet Letter*, oblivious to the more authentic, diabolical underpinnings of the seemingly moral Puritan tale.

By the late 1930s and early 1940s, as Hawthorne studies were regularly taken up in universities[xii] and criticism was approached more systematically, Hawthorne's image underwent yet another revision, and he came to be viewed "less [as] an unworldly, isolated, brooding man and conversely as better adjusted and more in tune with fellow human beings and the life of his period" (Blair 108). The 1948 publication of Randall Stewart's highly influential, updated biography (see EC30) breathed new life into Hawthorne studies by "normalizing" him and demythologizing the events in Hawthorne's life.[xiii] With the coincident New Critical emphasis upon the close reading of literary texts, Hawthorne studies quickly gained sophistication, and scholarship began to develop into the serious academic discipline that it is today.

One of the most influential of the early critical studies was F. O. Matthiessen's 1941 *American Rensaissance: Art and Expression in the Age of Emerson and Whitman* (see EC20), which, building upon formalist criticism, emphasized Hawthorne's artistry, symbolism, coherence and symmetry, but placed Hawthorne contextually within a historical tradition of romanticism (along with Emerson, Thoreau, Melville, and Whitman) in the mid-nineteenth century. Matthiessen also pinpointed and gave name to Hawthorne's famous narrative technique of sustaining numerous symbolic references, calling it "the device of multiple choice" (referred to three years earlier by Yvor Winters as "the formula of alternative possibilities"). Generations of critics would tirelessly examine this mystifying technique as the "key" to the success and tremendous accessibility of *The Scarlet Letter*—for its ability to establish ambiguity; to create diverse interpretations of the romance; to preserve the elements of doubt, uncertainty, and mystery; or to illustrate Hawthorne's refusal or inability to resolve conflict.

One other important early study on Hawthorne worth mentioning appeared in 1944, John C. Gerber's analysis of the form and content in *The Scarlet Letter* (see EC9). Gerber's influential essay, which not only anticipated the flood of New Critical approaches in the 1950s but also helped set the stage for the psychological investigations of the 1960s, closely examined the structure of the novel (dividing it into four parts) and considered the effects of guilt on the psyches of the main characters, focusing on the psychological impact of guilt resulting from sin rather than sin itself, because—as Gerber perceived—the concept of sin in the novel is relative, not absolute, and therefore represents only the "violation of what the sinner thinks he violates."

The Reception and Critical History of "The Custom-House"

Although the majority of critics briefly acknowledge and explore the dimensions of "The Custom-House" in their discussions of *The Scarlet Letter*, many studies over the years have focused exclusively on the sketch. Because there has been so much critical commentary written on it, and because the assessments have evolved over the past fifty years—either by building on previous arguments or by trying out new critical/theoretical approaches—it is impossible to do justice to the body of scholarship on "The Custom-House" without providing a separate section on its own reception and critical history.

Legend has it that when Nathaniel Hawthorne announced to his wife on June 9, 1849, that he had been fired from his government position as Chief Executive Officer of the Salem Custom House, she took the news in stride and cheerfully replied, "Good. Now you can write your book."[xiv] Comforted and emboldened by his wife's support, as well as by a contribution of money that she had been secretly saving, and encouraged by several friends who also pledged financial help after his embarrassing dismissal from office, Hawthorne re-assumed his longed-for identity as a "literary man"[xv] and set about to earn his living exclusively (if temporarily) by the pen. Although shaken by fears of literary failure, straining under financial pressure, and deeply mourning the death of his mother (who died that summer on July 31, 1849), Hawthorne began to write. He composed *The Scarlet Letter* at a feverish pace and in apparently effortless fashion, completing his dark romance in less than six months, on February 3, 1850.[xvi]

"The Custom-House" is Hawthorne's introduction to *The Scarlet Letter*, written when the novel was just three chapters short of its final length and had already been anticipated by James T. Fields to be an enormous success. In it, Hawthorne provides for the reading public a combined fictional and autobiographical account of his "three years' experience" in the Custom House during the years 1846-1849. Knowing that the majority of local readers would be familiar with the minor political scandal that had ensued after his termination, and eager to tell his version of the story in print, Hawthorne presents an utterly blameless version of himself before the public (using language so courteous and subtle, in fact, that readers today who are unfamiliar with the sketch's history might altogether miss the satiric attack on his political enemies and Salem itself). He exonerates himself of any wrongdoing and explains that his unwarranted dismissal from public office—the result of petty partisan politics, because he was a Democrat working in a house of Whig supporters when Whig candidate Zachary Taylor was elected President of the United States—proved to be the best thing that ever happened to him. His sudden loss of a job forced him to fall back upon his own resources and to resume the calling that best suited his sensitive, intellectual nature: that of author, a profession that he had earlier set aside as unprofitable in order to pursue the spiritually stultifying and mindless—though lucrative—occupation from which he had been recently dismissed. "The Custom-House" becomes Hawthorne's triumphant victory over those who saw fit to "decapitate" him,[xvii] his opportunity to wreak revenge for his public humiliation and to affirm that he had emerged from the beheading unscathed and victorious over the dullards whose jobs remained secure in the Custom House. It also paints a portrait of its author as having taken the moral "high road" in replacing self-interest and material desire with a genuine, communal concern for the well-being of a nation whose degraded cultural heritage needed to be edified and uplifted.

Most of the early reviewers of *The Scarlet Letter* did not devote significant attention to "The Custom-House,"[xviii] and those who did address its import had mixed reactions. The most famous review attacking "The Custom-House" was that of John Chapman from the Salem *Register* (see 255, 257, 273), in which he expresses outrage on behalf of the entire Salem community and charges Hawthorne with fabricating his "heartless" and "inexcusabl[y]" vindictive portraits of "inoffensive" fellow Custom-House workers.[xix] Critics more removed from Salem who addressed "The Custom-House" naturally tended to write about the introduction more objectively than Chapman had in his emotionally charged review, but without critical sophistication. While George Ripley (see ER2) found the tone of the sketch "objectionably querulous," Anne W. Abbott (see ER5) thought it "naughty," with a "racy" and "pungeant" style. Edwin P. Whipple (see

ER3), on the other hand, found "The Custom-House" to be very funny, and he remarks on Hawthorne's inexhaustible good humor. An anonymous reviewer for *Holden's Dollar Magazine* (see 310) also found the sketch amusing, calling it a "pleasant piece of gossipry," but he also argued that it was an "encumbrance" to the novel and objected to its placement as a preface to *The Scarlet Letter* because the two pieces are so strikingly different in tone.

Many other early critics also found "The Custom-House" an "encumbrance," sometimes ignoring it altogether in their analyses of the novel, or making a point of questioning its relevance and suitability as an introduction—a point that has extended well into the twentieth century. George Woodberry writes in his 1902 biography of Hawthorne (see EC41) that, while *The Scarlet Letter* itself is a praiseworthy masterpiece, Hawthorne "stooped" in taking "literary revenge" against his Custom-House associates by ridiculing them, and he embarrasses himself by posing immodestly as an unappreciated genius. In 1934, examining the preface from an aesthetic perspective, Austin Warren (one of the first to delve beneath the autobiographical surface of the sketch) concludes (see EC38) that "The Custom-House" is still a "curiously unsuitable introduction." Even in the mid-twentieth century, critics continued to question the relatedness of the sketch to the novel it introduces. In his 1959 forward to the Signet Classic Edition (see 78), for instance, Leo Marx advises "impatient" readers to skip over "The Custom-House" because it is not "integral" to the meaning of the story.

"The Custom-House" started to be taken seriously as a crucial part of *The Scarlet Letter* in the late 1950s and early 1960s, a change that perhaps reflected the flagging popularity of New Critical approaches to the novel that generally eschewed consideration of the autobiographical sketch in order to focus strictly on the work of art itself. In 1958, Larzer Ziff wrote the first major critical essay on "The Custom-House" (see 76), extending the value of the preface beyond the fact (commonly acknowledged by critics at the time) that it contains Hawthorne's aesthetic theory of romance and arguing that it also includes Hawthorne's views on morality. Two years later, two new introductions to *The Scarlet Letter*, by David Levin (see 92) and Harry Levin (see 93), also showed critical interest in "The Custom-House," arguing that the introductory sketch is indispensable to understanding the novel. And in 1961, after determining that too many critical evaluations of *The Scarlet Letter* were still neglecting the import of the introduction, Sam S. Baskett pled for the pertinence of "The Custom House" (see 111), insisting that the preface "clarifies and extends the meaning of the romance and thus should be read as a significant part of the total work." Also emphasizing the relevance of the sketch but taking a different tack by highlighting the differences between the two pieces, Douglas Grant wrote that the semi-confessional and conversational tone of "The Custom-House" contrasts marvelously with the narrator's detachment and economy of expression in the story itself (see 166).

In the years that followed, more and more critics included examinations of "The Custom-House" in their treatments of *The Scarlet Letter*, regarding it as a crucial part of the whole, and it became relatively common (and still is today) for essays to be devoted entirely to the introduction, with some even arguing that "The Custom-House" is an important text in its own right (as in 270, 310, and 421). Many evaluations after the 1960s have several features in common, regardless of their specific critical or theoretical orientations. Critics almost always address the on-going debate over the value of "The Custom-House" and examine its relationship to the novel, "proving" that the connection exists by establishing three significant parallels between the sketch and *The Scarlet Letter*. They often cite thematic similarities between the two works that link them (such as isolation, alienation, guilt over sins of the past, and tensions between solitude and sociability, the past and the present, public and private interests, and artistic and social responsibilities); they show how Hawthorne's personal and political experiences during and after the Custom-House scandal parallel Hester's and Dimmesdale's experiences in the novel; and they frequently extend those comparisons by illustrating that Hawthorne projects his own artistic temperament, personality, or state of mind onto one or more of his primary characters.

Biographers, historicists, and New Historicists especially review the circumstances surrounding the novel's composition, with reference to two specific shaping forces that provided Hawthorne with the impetus to write: Hawthorne's financial straits after his dismissal from the Custom House and the death of his mother, both of which are frequently offered as explanations for *The Scarlet Letter*'s dark nature. The popular consensus among critics by the end of the twentieth century (and so far into the twenty-first) is that "The Custom-House" *is* a critical part of *The Scarlet Letter*, but there are a few contemporary critics with lingering doubts who still question its connection to the novel, such as Michael J. Colacurcio (see 485) and Edward Wagenknecht (see 593), the latter of whom admits that he cannot help but find it "hopelessly out of tune with the story itself" (78). And although Colacurcio and Wagenknecht are now in the vast minority in the critical debate over the value of "The Custom-House," it is still a common practice among teachers in high school English classes around the country to skip the introductory sketch and move straight to the novel (presumably so that students will not be put off by Hawthorne too quickly).

Among the more seasoned readers and scholars who defend the central importance of "The Custom-House," critical commentary is diverse. They consider it in relation to *The Scarlet Letter* itself and with reference to the circumstances surrounding the novel's composition; they examine it for its purposes, functions, and sources; for Hawthorne's aesthetic principles, literary method, and definition of romance; and in relation to his own and others' fiction. It has been described variously: as Hawthorne's declaration of independence from Salem and its oppressive, guilt-inspiring Puritan past, as a strategic and semi-confessional effort to "open an intercourse with the world," as an appeal for a sympathetic audience for his tale, as a smooth and satiric attack on Hawthorne's political enemies and fellow Custom-House officials, as a badly disguised attempt to cover his humiliation over the disgraceful dismissal from the surveyorship, as a plea to fellow countrymen to forego material success for greater personal and communal rewards, as an idealized autobiography, as an autobiographical romance, as an allegorical dramatization of the creative process, as Hawthorne's triumphant recovery of the Imagination, and as the "something" Hawthorne needed to offset or relieve the concentrated gloom of the novel.

A few of the most prominent issues or key points that have been explored and wrestled with time and again by critics regarding "The Custom-House" entail (1) Hawthorne's feelings about authorship and art, (2) his treatment of the relation of the Puritan past to the present, and (3) his aesthetic theory of romance. The first (and largest) category encompasses dozens of studies that examine Hawthorne's relationship to his readers, his editorial pose, the role of the artist in nineteenth-century America, and the commercialization of literature in the mid-nineteenth century. Hawthorne is clearly preoccupied with his readership in "The Custom-House." While self-consciously fishing for a small, "select" sympathetic audience for his tale, he anticipates an overall negative response from "the many who will fling aside his volume, or never take it up" (3). Therefore, critical interest in Hawthorne's relationship to his audience is common in *Scarlet Letter* studies, primarily since the early 1970s, and especially by reader-response critics in the eighties and nineties. Hawthorne's yearning for a sympathetic audience has been examined many times, with considerable argument over whether this yearning is sincere or feigned, out of a legitimate desire to embrace humanity and "open an intercourse with the world" or stemming from the more practical aspiration of reaping financial reward. Some critics like John G. Bayer (see 397) contend that Hawthorne's desire to reach a wide, "sympathetic" audience was monetarily motivated and that it was easier for him to blame the low-minded public for misunderstanding him than it was to come to terms with the possibility that he was a failure as an artist. Hawthorne was contemptuous of middle-class readers, Bayer proposes, an audience he now needed to reach if he wanted his book to sell; so he had to feign interest in them to win their sympathetic appreciation of his art. Other critics like Stephen Railton (see 648 and 699) argue the opposite point, insisting that Hawthorne genuinely wanted to connect to a large middle-class audience by writing in the universal language of the human heart; he seeks to win a sympathetic response from them through various artistically manipulative techniques and strategies.

Hawthorne's authorial insecurities have been cited as explanation for his editorial pose in "The Custom-House" (his insistence that he did not invent the story but came across the documents containing Hester Prynne's history in the Custom-House attic). Several explanations have been offered by critics who question Hawthorne's motivation for asserting himself as the editor and not the creator of the tale, the most common of which is that Hawthorne wanted to protect himself: that he was either fearful that he would not connect well with his audience or worried that his readers would find his story objectionable; the shocking and potentially offensive subject matter—adultery and hypocrisy—might be reason enough for Hawthorne to deny claim to it. Thus Hawthorne fabricated the story of Surveyor Pue, some critics suggest, in an effort to distance himself from potentially damaging repercussions, in much the same manner that he self-protectively concealed and guarded the "inmost Me" from the probing gaze of potentially insensitive readers among the general public. Gordon Hutner suggests (see 445) that Hawthorne's practice of confessionally revealing and evasively concealing information from his readers is his clever way of simultaneously teasing their interest and sidestepping his humiliating termination at the Custom House, perhaps indicating that Hawthorne did indeed have something to hide about the reasons for his dismissal from office. Several other possibilities have been suggested, however, including the notion that Hawthorne's editorial pose provided him the freedom and critical latitude to critique the socio-political and moral climate of nineteenth-century America without having to own up to his unpopular convictions (as argued by Harry C. West [see 299], Zelda

Bronstein [see 542], and Jon B. Reed [see 642]); or, that Hawthorne's pretense of finding the manuscript of Hester's story in the attic of the Custom House was actually a popular technique employed in historical fiction of the period (as suggested by David Levin [see 201]); or, that Hawthorne adopted the editorial pose to create the effect of factual/historical authenticity for a realism-loving audience who considered the "flights of fancy" typical of romances to be morally degrading (as Michael Davitt Bell suggests [see 482]), or, finally, that Hawthorne denied any personal connection between himself and his tale of torturous guilt and sin to conceal his doubts about the integrity of his own art (as Stephen Nissenbaum asserts [see 464]).

Just as Hawthorne adopts an editorial pose in "The Custom-House," so he also presents himself as a detached and lighthearted litterateur, a posture that many critics believe not only minimizes his humiliation over being fired from a government position which he very much wanted to keep but also masks his ambivalence about his profession as an author/artist in the mid-nineteenth-century America. The topic of Hawthorne's ambivalence about authorship and art, as well as his desire to create an indigenous American literature, has been extensively explored since the 1980s, especially among psychological, historicist, and New Historicist critics who link Hawthorne's professional anxiety to an emerging view of literature in the mid-nineteenth century as a commercialized commodity instead of an esteemed work of art produced for the cultural elite (as in Michael T. Gilmore's 1985 essay [see 488], in which Gilmore suggests that Hawthorne was "both eager for and fearful of popular success"). Several studies also consider Hawthorne's ambivalent feelings about the isolating effects of professional authorship, a private profession that removed him from everyday social relations and made him feel estranged from the daily motion and pulse of humanity. Hawthorne felt torn, these critics suggest, between his perceived public responsibility to his society (and the security that comes from belonging to a community) and his self-isolating position as a private artist committed to his work.[xx]   Some New Historicists also detect gender anxieties lurking beneath Hawthorne's lighthearted and witty rhetoric in "The Custom-House," such as Scott S. Derrick (see 512), Robert K. Martin (see 620), and Jon B. Reed (see 632), all of whom examine places in "The Custom-House" and the novel where Hawthorne appears to be uncomfortably evaluating the role of the increasingly socially-estranged male artist in the mid-nineteenth century's developing market economy—uneasy, to say the least—in a culture that defined masculinity in terms of commercial success and equated femininity with housebound economic and political powerlessness.

The second category of studies on "The Custom-House," which covers Hawthorne's treatment of the relation of the Puritan past to the present, contains numerous examinations of his ambivalent feelings about his own Puritan ancestors, his conception of the "living past," his comparison of nineteenth- and seventeenth-century New England, and his treatment and understanding of history. Critics examining the issue of the past in "The Custom-House" focus specifically on the passages in which Hawthorne evaluates his communal ties to Salem and his Puritan ancestors and expresses his difficulty with severing the "unhealthy" bond to the "worn-out" soil of a native community that no longer nourishes him or enables his family to flourish. They make much of the fact that, although Hawthorne admits to being intrinsically drawn to Salem with "oyster-like tenacity" because his noble ancestors lived and died there, he is also ashamed of his ancestral past, feeling strongly that he has in some capacity inherited the sins of his forefathers.[xxi]

Critics have pondered endlessly (and still do) Hawthorne's obsession with and ambivalence toward his ancestors,[xxii] whom he condemns for their persecuting spirit while simultaneously seeking to align himself with their stronger traits and be worthy of their respect and approval as a "mere" author. New Historicist critics especially have pointed out Hawthorne's anxieties over his chosen profession, noting that because Hawthorne recognized that living by the pen was not considered especially masculine, business-like, profitable, or "useful" in the middle of the nineteenth century, he imagines his ancestors frowning down upon him in disgrace: "A writer of story-books! What kind of a business in life,—what mode of glorifying God, or being serviceable to mankind in his day and generation,—may that be?" (10).

It is most commonly asserted that Hawthorne was deeply critical of his hypocritical, intolerant, self-righteous, and unsympathetic forebears (see the many categories under "Puritanism" and "the Puritans" in the Subject Index for specific entries), but it is also argued (with much less frequency) that Hawthorne held great respect for the Puritans, particularly first generation Puritans, whose vitality, introspective earnestness, and zeal for moral and social order were commendable when compared to his complacent, materialistic, and intellectually stunted contemporaries and the religious liberals and self-oriented transcendentalists of his own day (see 279, 348, 360, 539, and 570 for these latter arguments). For these critics, Hawthorne is perceived as something of a latter-day, enlightened, or softened Puritan, a critic of fanatical Puritanism of the past but also a social critic of the romantic libertarianism that defined many intellectuals of his day.[xxiii]

More than a few critics have observed that, while Hawthorne appears to dissociate himself from Salem and its oppressive Puritan past, he nonetheless feels inextricably bound to its culture and history; he is unable to escape from the weighty burden of a sinful past just as he refuses to let Hester break away from her own past in *The Scarlet Letter*. This observation—along with Hawthorne's (or his narrator's) assertion in "The Custom-House" that "the past was not dead"—has led many critics to conclude that Hawthorne intends to emphasize the "use" of the past in "The Custom-House" (as in 156, 210, 280, 320, and 548), suggesting that the past lives on as an integral part of the present and shaping force of the future, and that personal and national identity cannot be achieved or maintained without realizing the interconnectedness of the past and the present. Donald Pease (see 540) focuses on the issue of the past in "The Custom-House," asserting that Hawthorne establishes the vital link between seventeenth- and nineteenth-century New England in order to convince his readers that the past is continuous, that they need to acknowledge and understand their Puritan roots if they really want to know and understand their own national character, to see and recognize themselves as a united community of brethren and as a Democratic culture. For critics like Pease, it is ultimately irrelevant whether Hawthorne paints the values of the past in a more favorable light than those of the allegedly shallow, money-obsessed present or whether he favors the freer, more tolerant present over the sin-tainted, oppressive past. In either case, they contend, Hawthorne is deeply influenced by his sense of history, committed to the idea that time and human experience are continuums, and that he must therefore accept and bear the weight of his own sins as well as the sins of his predecessors. Hawthorne illustrates by his own example in "The Custom-House" and through *The Scarlet Letter* that perceiving the connection between the past and the present enables all Americans to grow in maturity and moral stature, allowing them to see and judge themselves with greater accuracy against the background of their own sin-stained pre-history.

The third grouping of criticism on "The Custom-House" treats Hawthorne's aesthetic theory of romance and encompasses studies that examine his conception and appropriation of the romance mode, his theoretical reflections on the imagination's power to spiritualize the material, and the debate over whether *The Scarlet Letter* is truly a romance (typically associated with American literature) or a novel (associated with English literature). All critics who have considered Hawthorne's aesthetic theory of romance end up in the "moon-lit room" passage in "The Custom-House" where Hawthorne describes the conditions necessary to create a romance (an art form he feels compelled to justify, though in deceptively vague terms, Michael Davitt Bell explains [see 482]; romances were considered morally dangerous to readers and were associated with deviant and antisocial behavior). He describes "the glimmering coal-fire and the moon" illuminating familiar objects in an unusual way, investing them "with a quality of strangeness and remoteness" and creating a "medium" conducive to a "romance-writer": producing "a neutral territory, somewhere between the real world and fairy-land, where the Actual and the Imaginary may meet and each imbue itself with the nature of the other" (36).

Most early critics argued that Hawthorne's description of the "neutral territory" translates to the central characteristics of nineteenth-century American romanticism, such as insularity, exploration of the subconscious, and escape from the conditions of reality. Richard Chase (see 55) and Joel Porte (see 238), for instance, use Hawthorne as their chief source and example in devising theories of American romance, specifically citing Hawthorne's disengagement from sociopolitical issues. But later critics challenged this romance theory altogether in the seventies, eighties, and nineties, arguing—as did Charles Swann (see 314) and Emily Miller Budick (see 677)—that Hawthorne was deeply concerned with issues of history and society, illustrating through Hester the inadequacy of extreme romantic individualism and even returning her to Boston at the novel's end because her hard-won personal identity is not fully meaningful even to her unless she exists within the social and historic framework of the experience—the community—that forged that identity.

Arguing similar points, John Burt (see 498) and Scott Freisner (see 615) assert that Hawthorne's deliberately vague description of romance has led critics to misperceive that he championed romanticism and preferred the self-governing, self-isolating conditions necessary to produce his art. Rather, Burt and Freisner insist, Hawthorne implies a solid commitment to the "united effort of mankind" in both "The Custom-House" and the novel, where his firm conviction that imaginative freedom should exist *within* social boundaries shines through. Hawthorne's blend of the actual and the imaginary, or the material and the spiritual, does not reflect an escapist "flight of fancy" but a reality that is deeper than realism can depict. When Hawthorne is seen to embrace the moral responsibilities associated with society and history (more concerned with revealing the "truths" of the human heart than with mimetic description of reality), his romance does not "fit" the earlier definitions of American romance enunciated by Chase and Porte, nor does it exactly fit the "requirements" for the English novel. This change in perception of Hawthorne's art—the recent insistence that his brand of romanticism is actually socially and historically grounded—coincides somewhat with altered assessments of Hawthorne's personality since the mid-twentieth century. No longer viewed as a shy, melancholy recluse, Hawthorne is now understood to have been more of a socially-oriented family man active in the public arena.

Critics who consider Hawthorne's motivation for distinguishing romances from novels, and for claiming that the romance mode suits his artistic purposes better, wonder if his self deprecating remarks (his implication that he is incapable of writing a novel) are feigned or genuine. When Hawthorne describes his creative powers as bound to ebb until he is relieved of his public office (since "lean[ing] on the mighty arm of the Republic" with the support of "Uncle Sam's gold" had dwindled or damaged his intellectual and imaginative abilities), he confesses that he is unable to "spiritualize" the "petty and wearisome incidents, and ordinary characters" of his daily life. But he senses that converting the "dull and commonplace" into something of real value would be of even "deeper import" even than the romance he has written. "A better book than I shall ever write was there," he reflects (37). Some critics, like Richard Chase (see 55) and John C. Stubbs (see 251), take him at his word as a self-proclaimed failure in the novel-writing business, citing as evidence such facts that Hawthorne presents characters and scenes artificially and unrealistically, that he orders and structures events with mechanical precision, and that his writing style highlights the contrived artifice of the romance form itself. Others, like Jesse Bier (see 40), sense that Hawthorne feigned these self-deprecating remarks, the better to flatter the integrity of his "true" motive for writing romances and not novels: because romance enabled him to write about the universal, the timeless, and the real in a way that a mannerish novel could not. Bier and several additional critics detect that Hawthorne was deeply proud of the profession he selected for himself, and that he felt vindicated when, free of the Custom House and thrown back on his own resources, he fully recovered his imagination and discovered the true power of his artistry in *The Scarlet Letter*. Ultimately, these critics assert, if "The Custom-House" and *The Scarlet Letter* are viewed as an artistic whole, they may be seen to represent the complementary connection between the "material" and the "spiritual" worlds that combine to produce the stunning "neutral territory" of Hawthorne's unique art.

Sorting the Scholarship

As *The Scarlet Letter* continues to be intensely explored and vigorously debated, with seemingly no end in sight, there can be no doubt that it remains a significant work in American literature—perhaps *the* great American novel itself. In the introduction to his 1969 collection of selected Hawthorne criticism, B. Bernard Cohen assesses that, while patterns and trends in Hawthorne scholarship vary, many of the most hotly-debated issues and judgments "reverberate through a century and a half of Hawthorne criticism" (vii). Because so much criticism duplicates (unintentionally), echoes, responds to, or builds upon previous studies of *The Scarlet Letter*, it is possible to chart the most popular topics, both then and now, that guide inquiries into the novel. These are Hawthorne's ambiguity, imagination, use of allegory, psychological realism, language, and relation to his Puritan past; his artistic identification with Hester and/or Dimmesdale; his relation to America's culture, history, and identity; his use of symbolism and irony; his condemnation or partial endorsement of Puritanism; the novel's relation to "The Custom-House" and its appropriation of the romance form; the nature of the novel's "true" subject or moral; the meaning and significance of the scarlet letter, whom Hawthorne intended the protagonist to be, and whether Hawthorne was a romantic or a realist, a subversive feminist sympathizer or conservative patriarch.

Just as popular topics can be determined by grouping individual studies, so too can popular approaches to the novel be organized. After surveying fifty years of scholarship on *The Scarlet Letter*, I have identified fifteen dominant critical and theoretical approaches in the Critical Approach Index. These are morality studies, religious/theological studies, language studies, law studies, New Criticism, archetypal/myth criticism, structuralism, semiology/semiotics, post-structuralism, deconstruction, reader-response criticism, historicism, New Historicism, psychoanalytic/psychological criticism, and feminist studies. Embracing hundreds of treatments of *The Scarlet Letter* (many of which defy classification in a single approach and so appear cross-listed when methodological boundaries overlap), these categories are intended to help contemporary readers, critics, and budding scholars in confronting the bewildering body of commentary on Hawthorne's romance.

As early as 1934, Austin Warren perceived that the "total impression" of Hawthorne scholarship "convey[ed] confusion" because of its inconsistency and need of sorting (xi). Add another seventy years of scholarship on *The Scarlet Letter* and the disorganization has become all the more entangled. Even when the scholarship is "sorted" and organized into distinguishable categories, much of it fails to reflect consistent viewpoints. It does not help that Hawthorne was himself perhaps willfully inconsistent, a characteristic that derives from his "complex artistic vision in which contrasting aspects of life emerge as essential elements of a thorough grasp of it" (Male 228). Roy R. Male suggests that the solution to the Hawthorne "dilemma" is to view his fiction through the concept of complementarity, "a mode of description in which contrasting aspects of nature are seen as equally essential to a full understanding of it" (228). This concept seems "particularly applicable" to an interpretation of Hawthorne's fiction, "with its fundamentally interdependent relationships between head and heart, organic and mechanical, romantic and Puritan, good and evil, harmony and disintegration. Instead of minimizing or discrediting one or the other of these aspects in an attempt to gain a factitious unity, we should, it seems clear, explore the richness provided by his complementary modes of describing and appreciating life—each essential but, at the same time, standing in bold contrast with each other" (229). It is this perceived sense of contradiction or creative tension that often characterizes *The Scarlet Letter*, helping to account for the galaxy of conflicting and contradictory readings about Hawthorne and the novel.

J. Donald Crowley writes in "Hawthorne Criticism and The Return to History" that, because "there have always been at least two Hawthornes," criticism has almost always tended to flow in divided streams (98). This divided stream helps to explain why, over the years, he has been described as both profoundly dark and whimsically light, as moralist and non-moralist, as realist and idealist, as devout Puritan and shrewd critic of Puritanism, and as both a staunchly conservative patriarch and radically subversive feminist—to name just a few polarities. Crowley concedes that Hawthorne's voice itself is often contradictory, "at once private and public, self-concealing and self-revealing, probing yet decorous, doubtful and assertive" (8). This voice is, above all, Crowley concludes, "a collaborative voice whose tones first invite the reader to aid in the imaginative process and then lead him gradually to explore the unfamiliar territory of the deeply ambiguous and problematic nature of experience in the New World" (8).

These characterizations translate into equally antithetical or inconsistent readings of *The Scarlet Letter*, making the only certainty about the novel its unquestionably ambiguous and elusive nature. This ambiguity and elusiveness are what most attract eager critics, and they too might be divided into two camps: those who seek to unlock its mystery and get at a solid "core" of meaning or those who admire Hawthorne's forward, modernist thinking in creating a text that encourages multiple meanings, makes single interpretations problematic, and even resists declaring the identity of the main protagonist. Of course, there exists a lesser camp that attributes Hawthorne's ambiguity to his imaginative failings as an artist, to his overblown fears of being detected as either too conservative or too radical, or to his inability to believe in anything wholeheartedly.

Therefore, *The Scarlet Letter* has been seen at various times as "both a naughty novel and a moral allegory of sin and suffering, both a burlesque and a covertly sympathetic treatment of nineteenth-century feminism and transcendentalism, both a satire of Puritanism and a reliable history of it" (Scharnhorst xxvii). While such diversity in interpretation over time is a wonderful testament to Hawthorne's achievement, to the beginner with a serious interest in the novel, the massiveness of critical materials and theoretical angles can be frustrating and even demoralizing. How do the plethora of studies range in method, scope, and significance? Are there specific critical approaches that seem to lend themselves particularly well to analysis of the novel? What dominant interpretations emerge from this vast body of critical study? And, finally, how has Hawthorne's literary reputation evolved or grown in more than a century and a half of critical debate and consideration—and what factors have contributed to varying accounts of that reputation? These are the questions that I have kept in mind for readers of this critical bibliography and resource guide while sorting the scholarship and charting trends in literary criticism on *The Scarlet Letter*.

From Artistry to Anxiety: Trends in Scholarship
in the Criticism of *The Scarlet Letter*, 1950-2000

Just as pre-1950s criticism mirrored influential tides in critical orientation and methodology, so critical studies on *The Scarlet Letter* that spanned the five decades from 1950-2000 naturally reflected waxing and waning shifts in literary scholarship from modernist to post-modern outlooks. It is therefore possible— and instructive—to enumerate proliferating trends and define the variety of critical and theoretical perspectives on Hawthorne's romance within the enormous body of scholarship over the past fifty years. In 1953, Charles Child Walcutt's "*The Scarlet Letter* and Its Modern Critics" (see 28) offered an initial aid to readers and critics by attempting such a sorting process, grouping interpretations of the novel under various taxonomies. Several critics followed Walcutt's lead by charting the historical development of critical/theoretical approaches to *The Scarlet Letter*—such as B. Bernard Cohen (234), Michael J. Colacurcio (485), David B. Kesterson (567), Ross C. Murfin (637), Gary Scharnhorst (670), Peter Shaw (727), and Elmer Kennedy-Andrews (829). In 1970, for instance, Roy Male observed with interest "the way Hawthorne's work has responded to shifting expectations" over the years. "In the fifties," he writes, *The Scarlet Letter* "rewarded the explicatory and mythic analyses of the New Critics; in the mid-sixties it survived, at the cost of some diminution, the rigorous inquest of the New Historicists and the neo-Freudians; and now his fiction seems more vital than ever for readers aware of new developments in psychology and related fields" (19-20). Also making helpful generalizations about trends in scholarship on *The Scarlet Letter* was David B. Kesterson who, in 1988, noted that the most significant critical directions of the seventies and eighties—which paved the way to criticism of the nineties—were the New Historical, the biographical, the psychological, the feminist, the deconstructionist, and post-modernist/reader-response strains (11). And Peter Bellis rounded out consideration of the century's criticism by asserting that, in *Scarlet Letter* criticism of the 1990s (and today), "revisionary critical energy has [. . .] been directed toward politicizing our view of the canon, yielding both newly historicized or ideological readings and studies of canon construction itself" (Bellis 97).

These rough estimates provide a helpful and fairly accurate breakdown of the critical history of *Scarlet Letter* studies, because the scholarship has naturally followed the "signs of the times" by adhering to changes in contemporary literary criticism and theory as they have occurred over the past fifty years; they nevertheless tend to gloss over the continuity of ideas over time, topics that are explored with consistency throughout the years. Regardless of critical or theoretical approach, the majority of studies also participate in ongoing dialogues and debates about *The Scarlet Letter* that have never been (and perhaps should never be) resolved with any degree of certainty or finality. So, while mapping trends in scholarship illustrates how readily the romance lends itself to a welter of critical perspectives, the process also reveals a fascinating oscillation in the continuity of ideas—an ever-renewing and relentless concern over the same central questions, issues, conflicts, and themes, such as the psychological effects of prolonged isolation on the individual, the consequences of dissimulation, Hawthorne's famous ambiguity, his mind and temperament (especially the correlation between his personality and his imaginative fiction), his attraction to allegory, his obsessions with guilt, inherited sin, and the past, his ambivalence about Puritanism (represented in Dimmesdale) and romanticism (represented in Hester), his views on morality and religion, his poetic style, the relationship of the individual to society and to the "magnetic chain of humanity," the redeeming power of sin and suffering, the tensions between head/heart, light/dark, town/forest, society/solitude, past/present, passion/law, Old World/New World, public/private identity, and the two most frequently asked questions of all: who the main character is and how the reader should interpret Hester's return to Boston at the novel's end. Attention to both the evolving critical/theoretical approaches and the issues explored in the criticism provides a clearer and more holistic sense of where *Scarlet Letter* scholarship has been and where it is going.

1950s

Scarlet Letter criticism in the 1950s was largely composed of New Critical and archetypal/myth studies that praised Hawthorne's artistry, unity, and achievement in their examinations of the romance's tight structure, highly symbolic language and action, image patterns, plentiful ironies, paradoxes, and ambiguities, contrasts and conflicts, and moral and religious themes. The most influential critics of the decade were Richard Harter Fogle (see 15), Hyatt H. Waggoner (see 38), Roy R. Male (see 56), Randall Stewart (see 58), Harry Levin (see 70), and Richard B. Sewell (see 80), all of whom addressed *The Scarlet Letter*'s artistry and focused on image patterns, symbolism, ambiguity, and Hawthorne's tragic/dark vision; the latter, most of them argued, was clearly at odds with transcendentalism and the generally optimistic and materialist influences of mid-nineteenth-century America. These critics were intrigued by the complex nature of Hawthorne's tragic view of life that assumed man's innately depraved and sinful nature, complicated by his insistence that lone or alienated individuals have a moral responsibility to take their place in the human community and brotherhood of sinners—which implies that Hawthorne was as critical of the romantic ideals of freedom and self-reliance as he was of Puritanism's inhumanity and crippling influence on its adherents.

In addition to considering Hawthorne's complicated tragic vision, several critics also writing in the New Critical vein picked up on John C. Gerber's interest (see EC9) in the novel's structure (Hugh N. MacLean [see 42], Darrel Abel [see 46], Robert F. Haugh [see 48]), Anne Marie McNamara [see 50], and Malcolm Cowley [see 59 and 68]), arguing that *The Scarlet Letter* is structurally divided into three, four, or five parts. A few scholars also examined archetypal patterns and cultural myths embedded in the novel, as when Donald Ringe considered the "Fortunate Fall" theme (see 6), William Bysshe Stein the Faustian myth (see 22), and R. W. B. Lewis the myth of the New World (see 37). Complementing these New Critical studies were a number of historical and source studies that grounded Hawthorne and his novel in historical, political, and social contexts, exploring such issues as history and historiography in Hawthorne's representation of the Puritans (as do Edward H. Davidson [see 11] and G. Harrison Orians [see 19]) and submitting possible historical and literary sources of characters and events (as do Alfred S. Reid [see 35 and 53] and Robert Louis Brant [see 73]).

Additionally, new types of studies from the 1950s reflected the growing interest in Hawthorne criticism and/or the widespread use of *The Scarlet Letter* in high school and college curricula, including two surveys of criticism on Pearl (by Anne Marie McNamara [see 50] and Barbara Garlitz [see 62]) two reviews of Hawthorne criticism (see 28 and 43), an instructor's manual (see 44), and several student-oriented collections of critical essays or general introductions to the novel (see 30, 45, 81, and 82).

Also considered at this time was Hawthorne's amazingly acute psychoanalytic understanding. Joseph Levi (see 26) examined the Oedipal theme in *The Scarlet Letter*, suggesting that Hawthorne projected his own sublimated desires and certain aspects of his personality onto his main characters, and Lois Atkins (see 31) studied the psychological effects of guilt and isolation on Dimmesdale, Hester, and Chillingworth. Rudolph Von Abele (see 39) read the novel as an autobiographical compendium of Hawthorne's wrestlings with art, sex, and society, regarding Dimmesdale as the character with whom Hawthorne most identified; and Marvin Laser (see 41) speculated that Hawthorne employs the scientific language of popular nineteenth-century psychological theories to create realistic psychological portraits of his three main characters, who represent imbalances of head (Chillingworth), heart (Hester), and will (Dimmesdale).

Especially prevalent in *Scarlet Letter* criticism of the 1950s and nearly every decade before and after were moral and religious studies. Critics like Leonard J. Fick (see 36), Hyatt H. Waggoner (see 38), Anne Marie McNamara (see 50), Randall Stewart (see 58 and 72), Henry G. Fairbanks (see 61), Joseph Schwartz (see 71), and Horton Davies (see 77) grappled with Hawthorne's ever elusive theological views and his treatment of the moral and religious character of man in the novel. They explored the conflict between good and evil both in and among the characters and examined the influences of Calvinism in relation to the concepts of Original Sin and Innate Depravity, visible sainthood, free will vs. predestination, the covenants of grace and good works, and the doctrines of xliv

election and damnation, as well as Puritanism (Hawthorne's attraction to and repulsion by it, in addition to its susceptibility to hypocrisy, narrowness, intolerance, and inhumanity); they also examined the issues of Confession (relating to the question of Dimmesdale's salvation or damnation) and punishment/repentance (relating to the question of Hester's own legitimate spiritual triumph or fall).

An especially noteworthy study from the 1950s was Richard Chase's 1957 book *The American Novel and Its Tradition* (see 55), significant because it used *The Scarlet Letter* to flesh out what many critics at the time perceived to be the essential differences between English "novels" and American "romances," a distinction that would be challenged later in the century as Hawthorne's historical and sociopolitical concerns were emphasized over his private creative interests, always with reference to Chase's definitions. Romances, Chase contended, are the natural fictional result of American culture's lack of a past or of class-conscious social "texture," and are more "free" and daring than their "mannerish" English counterparts, which are characterized by their realistic portrayals of everyday discourse and social experience. Although the question of whether *The Scarlet Letter* is an ideal or a naturalistic depiction of reality was not new in 1957, Chase's book influenced two generations of Hawthorne scholars with his romance theory of American fiction, establishing the groundwork for a debate that still goes on today. Like Matthiessen before him, Chase sought to define *The Scarlet Letter*'s place in literary tradition, associating the "romance-novel" with other romantic American works distinguished by their non-realistic portrayals of events, their flights from the ordinary and the actual to the realm of the ideal, and their intense concern with inward desires.

1960s

The Scarlet Letter continued to inspire debates and elicit hosts of increasingly sophisticated critical inquiries in the 1960s,[xxiv] with the centennial of

Hawthorne's death in 1964 inspiring even more critical attention. So many papers, articles, essays, and books were generated that a market quickly developed to accommodate poor readers, critics, students, and teachers who could not possibly keep up with burgeoning studies and the most "relevant" criticism on Hawthorne's most famous work. Critical and new editions of the text, collections of critical essays, resource guides, teaching aids, source books, study guides, and introductions geared toward the general reader proliferated during the sixties at an incredible rate (one that would never be matched in any later decade). Seymour Gross's *Scarlet Letter Handbook* (see 86), for instance, ushered in the decade with 36 representative selections of criticism. A year later, in 1961, two critical editions were released: the Norton Critical Edition (see 102) and Kenneth S. Lynn's sourcebook (see 103), both of which were fully annotated with sources and criticism to assist readers. And in 1962, the much anticipated and celebrated Centenary Edition of *The Scarlet Letter* appeared as the first volume in the Centenary series of Hawthorne's works (see 122, 123, and 124), becoming the standard text that most editors and scholars would use from then to the present. By my count, the rest of the decade saw an astonishing total of eight more new editions (see 88, 92, 93, 164, 166, 200, 220, and 233), seven teaching aids (see 105, 115, 117, 131, 163, 194, 199), five more collections of critical essays (see 164, 167, 186, 214, and 234), three study guides (see 153, 181, and 215), two general introductions (see 104 and 202), and one more sourcebook (see 199)— which together comprised an enormous addition to the previous decade's resource materials.

Accompanying such intense critical interest in *The Scarlet Letter* in the 1960s was attention to Hawthorne the man, with two biographies appearing before 1963—Edward Wagenknecht's *Nathaniel Hawthorne: Man and Writer* (see 107) and Hubert H. Hoeltje's *Inward Sky: The Mind and Heart of Nathaniel Hawthorne* (see 125), both of which built upon Randall Stewart's "updated" portrait of Hawthorne by emphasizing his "sunnier" side as essentially good-natured, well-adjusted, extroverted, and contented with his life's work. Not everyone endorsed this revised assessment of Hawthorne's mind and temperament, however. Several skeptical critics objected to the new image of Hawthorne as a blithe artist completely in control of his materials, especially psychoanalytically-oriented critics like Frederick Crews (see 170 and 182), who argued that the novel reveals that Hawthorne really was painfully withdrawn, introverted, and racked with sin and inherited guilt. Such critics preferred to view Hawthorne as tormented, unconsciously working out his demons by projecting repressed desires conflicts onto his characters.[xxv] Crews's 1966 book *The Sins of the Fathers: Hawthorne's Psychological Themes* (see 182), which projected such an image of Hawthorne, proved to be so monumentally influential in its exploration of Hawthorne's complex and conflicted nature that later critics defined the entire decade as belonging to psychological treatments of Hawthorne (which may now seem baffling, considering that only three other *Scarlet Letter* studies from the 1960s were psychological in orientation (those by Eugene Arden [see 109], William S. Marks III [see 174], and Leon Edel [see 183]).

Responding to the enormous critical attention Hawthorne was receiving in the sixties, Martin Green wrote an essay (that would become well known) entitled "The Hawthorne Myth: a Protest" (see 143) to launch an argument against what he perceived to be undeserved devotion to Hawthorne and to declare his work drastically overrated. Building on critical views of earlier unimpressed critics like W. C. Brownell (see EC3), Marcus Cunliffe (see 29), and Rudolph Von Abele (see 39), Green articulated what he—and others[xxvi]—perceived as Hawthorne's chief failings, such as his alleged preference for a voyeuristic life of private, isolated reflection over warm-blooded, public, lived experience, his cold and clinical treatment of characters (whose unreality reflects his lack of passion or his inability to display or project genuine emotion or warmth), his artificial rendering of events, his inconsistency in tone and point of view, his failure to represent the Puritans with historical accuracy, his relentless pessimism, and his lack of conviction that translates into what overgenerous critics (mis)interpret as "ambiguity."

Writing in a somewhat similar vein was Philip Young (in 180), who responded with playful exasperation to the 1962 Centenary Edition of *The Scarlet Letter* and the *Hawthorne Centenary Essays* that appeared in 1964, neither of which he deemed especially useful or necessary, considering that Hawthorne had already been examined from every conceivable critical angle *ad nauseum*. Like the psychoanalysts of his decade, Young also expressed mild contempt for what he termed the trendy "white myth" of Hawthorne in contemporary studies, especially since Hawthorne's "whitewashed" image clashed so spectacularly with current critical estimates of his work as darkly troubled and complex.

Although *Scarlet Letter* studies began to splinter in so many directions in the 1960s, some common associations may be ventured. In addition to producing the usual religious and morality studies (see 96, 98, 126, 133, 146, 178, 191, 192, and 206) and a few more New Critical studies (see 136, 138, 209, 210, 236, and 239), the decade saw renewed dedication to the mythic/archetypal aspects of the novel (see 106, 120, 151, 152, 179, 191, 219, 237, and 238). New to Hawthorne studies, however, was an outpouring of historical interest in Hawthorne's romance—which generated such a shower of criticism as to dominate all other critical approaches of the sixties.

Historicists examined Hawthorne within his nineteenth-century American social and political milieu, especially in relation to his contemporaries, and situated him within a literary tradition of romance writers. They investigated the historical accuracy of his recreation of the Puritan past and his implied statements on the central issues and moralistic assumptions of nineteenth-century romanticism and transcendentalism. A multitude of historical studies (see 94, 154, 158, 187, 198, 200, 201, 204, 227) and historical/literary source studies (see 109, 118, 124, 129, 166, 172, 173, 176, 188, 195, 206, 217, 224, 227, and 228) were written, as were comparative literature studies, which cited parallels to earlier works like John Bunyan's *Pilgrim's Progress* (see 188), John Gibson Lockhart's *Adam Blair* (see 132 and 166), and Sir Walter Scott's *Heart of Midlothian* (see 129 and 166), and to later works by such authors as Charles Dickens (see 248), Henry James (see 208), Harold Frederic (see 232), D. H. Lawrence (see 174), William Faulkner (see 161, 169, and 212), Robert Frost (see 171), and Arthur Miller (see 241). Considerable attention was also directed at Hawthorne's short fiction and his Notebook entries that anticipate or provide the "germinal seeds" for *The Scarlet Letter* (see 90, 99, 108, 124, 156, 164, 166, and 200).

Two other noteworthy trends that originated in the 1960s deserve mention. The first involves several studies that anticipated structuralist, post-structuralist, and deconstructionist approaches of the eighties and nineties in their attention to the novel's ambiguity, especially in their assertions of Hawthorne's awareness of the constructedness of human meaning and the limits of human knowledge, his belief in the arbitrary nature of signs, and his view of the dual nature of reality and truth—all of which contrast strikingly in *The Scarlet Letter* with Hawthorne's depiction of the Puritans' inflexible and dogmatic beliefs in absolutes. Earl Rovit (see 119), for example, posited that "The Custom-House" and the novel both concern "the meaning of meaning," attempting to answer the question of "how to find meaning in arbitrary meaninglessness." Like Gerber, who had suggested in the previous decade that Hawthorne's concept of sin is relative, Rovit asserted that the scarlet letter's meaning is also relative, dictated not by Puritan authorities who try to impose one strict meaning on it but by individual, subjective interpretations of its import over time. Marshall Van Deusen (see 196) also found that a symbolic ambiguity connects the novel and highlights the historical, epistemological, and ethical problems that Hawthorne was working through in both. Fred H. Marcus likewise provided an explanation for Hawthorne's intended ambiguity, warning (see 131) against allegorical readings of the novel because Hawthorne's complex plurality of meanings (illustrated by multiple interpretations of key events, characters, and symbols, as well as by the narrator's own contradictory assertions) implies a distrust of all "absolute" interpretations. And Austin Warren argued (see 178) that all attempts to locate the clear moral center of *The Scarlet Letter* will always be frustrated, because Hawthorne does not permit absolute truth or ultimate reality to be imparted to any of his characters, the narrator included. Arguing a comparable point, Lawrence W. Hyman (see 192) claimed that all efforts to determine the true protagonist of the novel would also be thwarted, because there is not any one character whose moral scheme is perfect. In other words, Hawthorne's belief in man's limited human perception prevented him from privileging one "true" or comprehensive view of morality over another—just as it prevented him from presenting any one interpretation of reality as inherently "truer" than any other; each one represented the subjective or arbitrary determinations of individual perception (as Arthur Mizener and Darrel Abel also suggest in 202 and 239).

The second noteworthy trend perhaps amounts to a curiosity rather than a direction that future critics would take in *Scarlet Letter* studies, and involves a theme explored with surprising regularity only in the criticism of the early 1960s: Hawthorne's treatment of love. Attention to Hawthorne's depiction of love in *The Scarlet Letter* was inaugurated in 1960 by Leslie A. Fiedler in his study of the mythic qualities of romantic American literature, *Love and Death in the American Novel* (see 89). In the fashion of Matthiessen, Chase, and Lawrence, he writes that Hawthorne's "shadowy and sterilized" treatment of erotic passion is typical of his era and that the novel is actually an "elegiac treatise on the death of love." In the same year, Seymour Gross argued (see 95) that what determines the tragic design of *The Scarlet Letter* is Hester's agonizing guilt over the knowledge that, in loving Dimmesdale on her own moral terms, she paradoxically violates every moral principle he holds sacred. And in 1961, Edward Wagenknecht wrote (see 107) that Hawthorne's presentation of Hester's abundant sexuality and

1

unquenchable love for Dimmesdale, accompanied by his insightful understanding of "the perversities of love," actually reflects his modernity.

The preeminent treatment came in 1962 with "*The Scarlet Letter* as a Love Story" (see 135), in which Ernest Sandeen contends that the novel's chief subject is love, not sin or guilt, and that the grand passion between Hester and Dimmesdale—smoldering torturously throughout the seven years that the story takes place—morally and spiritually transforms and ennobles the two suffering lovers. Also writing in 1962, Lawrence E. Scanlon (see 136) located heart imagery as key to the symbolic structure of the novel, concluding that love triumphs in the end over hate; and in 1964, Cecil L. Moffitt read the novel as "A Puritan Love Story" (see 157) that celebrates the "reckless" and "triumphant" love of Hester and Dimmesdale, and suggests, like Sandeen two years earlier, that their silent, solemn, and sacred bond remains constant throughout the story. And finally, in 1969, Katsumi Okamoto submitted that Hester's profound love for both Dimmesdale and Pearl brightens the otherwise "unmitigatedly dark" novel and provides her motivation for returning to Boston at the end. One can only speculate about the inspiration for the unusual cluster of studies appearing in the sixties that explored Hawthorne's treatment of love, whether influenced by Fiedler's important book or perhaps reflecting the "free love" movement that characterized the decade in America.

1970s

As critical methodologies continued to develop and branch into early post-modern treatments of *The Scarlet Letter* (by structuralists, post-structuralists, deconstructionists, reader-response critics, and feminists), attention to Hawthorne's ambiguity increasingly led to discussions of meaning, knowledge, reality, and language (the latter of which became an especially popular issue in the later decades). Such critics as Gabriel Josipovici (see 264) John T. Irwin (see 321), Reed Sanderlin (see 338), Henry Nash Smith (see 356), Michael Dunne (see

360), William Bysshe Stein (see 365), Marjorie Pryse (see 371), and Maureen Quilligan (see 372) emphasized Hawthorne's uncannily modern perceptions of the relativity of truth and meaning, the unreliability of human perception and judgment, problems of interpretation based on the discrepancy between illusion and reality, the inability of symbolic meaning to remain "fixed" or absolute, and the arbitrary nature of language. Henry Nash Smith (see 356), for instance, asserted that Hawthorne challenged the "solidity" of several nineteenth-century social institutions of his day by projecting ontological and epistemological uncertainties that make it impossible for his characters to attain absolute truth or certainty about anything. And Reed Sanderlin (see 338) demonstrated that the novel concerns "the meaning of meaning," or the ways meaning is generated, and that Hawthorne challenges the Puritans' symbolic mode of perception because, as Hester's letter proves, symbolic meanings change and thereby do not have intrinsic or absolute meaning in any of their forms.

These critics also observed Hawthorne's interest in multiple ways of perceiving reality, contrary to the Puritans' presumptuous insistence on their ability to interpret events, dictate laws, administer punishments, and determine God's will with self-righteous certainty—all while exhibiting a rigid intolerance of difference, paradox, ambiguity, or anything mysterious or unknown. Time and again in the novel, as William R. Manierre pointed out (see 275), "Hawthorne illustrates the limitations and unreliability of human perception," calling attention to the fallacies under which the historical Puritans labored by offering and encouraging among his readers multiple interpretations of key events, providing an equivocal, unreliable (or a reliably non-committal) narrative point of view. The narrator is characterized, as Elaine Tuttle Hansen similarly determined (see 337), by his humility before the paradoxical nature of the tale, presenting a trusted, seemingly angelic pastor as a bitter exemplum of ministerial hypocrisy and a condemned adulteress as a secular saint and Sister of Mercy, and employing a symbolic letter whose "fixed" meaning constantly changes as perceptions of its wearer alter through time.

Although analyses informed by literary theory contributed a significant portion of scholarship on the novel, historical studies still dominated all other critical approaches to *The Scarlet Letter* in the seventies (just as they did in the sixties), providing background on the history of Puritanism and transcendentalism, suggesting crucial links between the moral, intellectual, and religious climates of nineteenth- and seventeenth-century New England, locating Hawthorne's likely and probable literary and historical sources, demonstrating ways that Hawthorne diverged from the historical romance tradition (and other popular literary traditions from which he borrowed), and offering historical referents for the "The Custom-House" and for the novel's characters, themes, plot devices, and symbolic actions and events. The topics for historical discussion were as varied as they were provocative. For instance, John T. Irwin (see 321) cited the nineteenth-century fascination with recently deciphered Egyptian hieroglyphics as a likely historical source for Hawthorne's technique of ambiguity. M. X. Lesser (see 323) explained that Hawthorne does not provide specific details about the actual text of Dimmesdale's Election-Day sermon because there was no historical basis from which Hawthorne could model the sermon, given that the first New World Puritan sermon was not published until well after the period of the novel's setting. And Ursula Brumm (see 335) shed light on the connection between "The Custom-House" and the novel by providing literary and historical models that Hawthorne drew upon and blended to create his prefatory sketch.

In their own treatments of *The Scarlet Letter*, Michael Davitt Bell (see 261) and Frederick Newberry (see 348) addressed the historical dimensions of the novel's thematic tensions between the Old World and the New World, contrasting the warm-blooded, passionate, and light-spirited first-generation Puritans with their dour, emotionally repressed, and starkly practical descendents. Whereas

Bell showed that Hester adapts the "antique gentility" in her nature to the harsh conditions of the New World in order to survive, Newberry demonstrated that, despite her adaptability, Hester symbolizes English ancestry and her story illustrates the unfortunate demise of rich Old World values. Another significant contribution to *Scarlet Letter* studies was Michael J. Colacurcio's essay, "Footsteps of Anne Hutchinson: The Context of *The Scarlet Letter* (see 289), which demonstrated Hawthorne's knowledge of Puritan history and examined the likelihood that he modeled Hester and Dimmesdale after seventeenth-century historical figures Anne Hutchinson and John Cotton.

While many studies in the seventies focused on the historical dimensions of *The Scarlet Letter*, several others examined the social dimensions of the text, reconsidering the central conflict between social restriction and individual freedom and situating Hawthorne—for the first time with regularity   squarely on the side of society. Because Hawthorne was frequently singled out from his transcendentalist contemporaries for being deeply committed to social responsibility (whereas Emerson and Thoreau praised the self-governing, self-reliant individual), increased attention was once again given to Hawthorne's realist impulse, as well as to a re-evaluation of the distinction between "novels" and "romances" established earlier by Richard Chase and others.[xxvii]   Quentin Anderson (see 259) found no trace of the "American flight from culture" that supposedly accompanies romantic fiction like *The Scarlet Letter*, which he concluded is much more akin to English fiction in its embrace of society. And Michael J. Hoffman (see 281) argued that the novel's tendency toward realism belies its categorization as "romantic," given its rejection of transcendental principles and its implication that each individual's humanity depends on his recognition and acceptance of his membership in—and moral responsibility for—the larger human community that requires a certain degree of self-sacrifice for the greater good. David J. Hirsch (see 263), Harold Kaplan (see 282), Nicolaus Mills (see 307), and Arne I. Axelsson (see 309) reached similar conclusions based on

Hawthorne's evident commitment to democracy, his emphasis on the main characters' public roles rather than on their private interests, and his effort to humanize self-isolating, self-destructive sinners by bringing them closer to a sympathetic union with fellow sinners and to recognize their interdependent relations with one another.

Charles Swann voiced perhaps the most strenuous objection of the decade to critics who categorized *The Scarlet Letter* as a non-realistic romance (see 314), not only rejecting the legitimacy of the theory of American romance (as several others also did in the eighties and nineties) but also persuasively insisting that the novel exposes the social implications and moral deficiency of romantic individualism and that it ultimately concerns "the problems of man in society and his existence in history." Approaching the novel from a similar perspective, Joseph F. Doherty wrote (see 318) that *The Scarlet Letter* can scarcely be defined as a typical American romance because of its obvious interests in sociality. In privileging communal solidarity over self-interested fulfillment of personal desires, advocating commitment to society and self-sacrificing compromise for the greater good, Hawthorne is, in fact, a precursor of realist fiction.

Perhaps the most significant contribution to *Scarlet Letter* studies in the seventies that also addressed the conflict between society and the individual was Nina Baym's 1976 book *The Shape of Hawthorne's Career* (see 339), a major study that traced Hawthorne's literary development and showed that *The Scarlet Letter* boldly inaugurated the romantic phase of his writing. Baym differed from several other critics at this time by asserting that, although Hawthorne privileged the needs of society over the desires of the individual, he illustrated through the suffering, repressed figures of Hester and Dimmesdale just how devastating and costly that ranking could be for passionate, artistic, and self-expressive individuals.

While attention to the historical and social issues at stake in *The Scarlet Letter* was not new in the 1970s, budding critical interest in Hawthorne's attitude toward women *was* new, gaining so much momentum as it went along (generated by the feminist movement beginning in the late 1960s) that the topic would prove to dominate every other critical interest in *Scarlet Letter* studies for the next thirty years. Surprisingly, an essay written in 1954 by Morton Cronin entitled "Hawthorne on Romantic Love and the Status of Women" (see 32) offered a perceptive, anticipatory glimpse of the feminist and women's studies of the seventies, eighties, and nineties in its suggestion that Hawthorne created strong, intellectual "New Woman" types like Hester in an effort to work out answers to the "woman question," the debate over the proper role of women in nineteenth-century American society.

In 1972, Darrel Abel's "The Strong Division-Lines of Nature" (see 284) picked up precisely where Cronin left off, looking at Hawthorne's ambivalent feelings about strong minded "New Woman" types like Margaret Fuller who, like seventeenth-century antinomian Anne Hutchinson (both serving as models for Hester), overstepped the boundaries of women's "propriety" by advancing dangerously into the sphere of men. Ben Barker-Benfield (see 286) and Michael J. Colacurcio (see 289) also considered the rebellious Hester's resemblance to Puritan heretic Anne Hutchinson in their discussions of Hawthorne's treatment of women. Acknowledging that Hawthorne recognized that women were unnaturally and unhealthily suppressed by patriarchal institutions (Puritan theology being one of them) and was clearly sympathetic to the plight of oppressed women in his own time and in the fictionally reconstructed world of Puritan Boston, they argued that Hawthorne nevertheless hems in his unconventional heroine so that she is no longer a perceived threat to masculine authority.[xxviii]

James G. Janssen anticipated several feminist critics of later decades who would argue (in the minority) that Hester's return to Boston only appears to represent her complete submission to Puritan authority and that it actually indicates indirect renewal of her quiet rebellion, with Hawthorne subtly lvi

celebrating her radical, subversive triumph over the unfathoming Puritan community. Janssen writes (see 329) that when the self-effacing Hester becomes a sympathetic counselor of rejected or repressed women, she, in fact, ironically becomes the prophetess she once dreamed of becoming, having taking it upon herself to comfort burdened, betrayed, and heart-broken women with the assurance that the day will come when "the whole relation between man and woman" will be established "on a surer ground of mutual happiness."

Several other critics who scrutinized Hawthorne's treatment of women characters, namely Carolyn G. Heilbrun (see 303), Judith Fryer (see 340), and John Franzosa (see 361) examined Hester's androgynous characteristics, speculating that Hawthorne was critical of strictly traditional, limiting, and potentially damaging definitions of "masculinity" and "femininity" and so created a passionate, free-thinking, "fallen" heroine to challenge nineteenth-century perceptions of women. Paul Lewis came to a similar conclusion (see 384) about Hawthorne's "liberated" view of women, seeing Hester's complex, intellectual, and fascinating character as deviating strikingly from conventional heroines in nineteenth-century American Gothic fiction.

1980s

The sheer number of *Scarlet Letter* studies produced in the eighties was staggering, with a sixty-one percent increase over the previous decade, reflecting increased devotion to Hawthorne's most celebrated work of fiction and indicating that feminist criticism in particular was flourishing as a well-established and respected discipline. Hawthorne's attitude toward women took center stage in critical treatments of the novel, with studies encompassing a wide range of interests and approaches. Critics examined Hester's unusual strength, endurance, and intellectual independence as envisioned by a nineteenth-century male author (often noting her likeness to Margaret Fuller and Anne Hutchinson), scrutinized Hawthorne's reversal of traditional gender roles (portraying Hester as either masculine or androgynous and Dimmesdale as feminine), re-examined his relationship to his mother, wife, daughter, sisters, and aunts, and speculated on Hawthorne's feminist or anti-feminist leanings based on the narrator's ambivalent portrayal of Hester, which is sometimes sympathetic, sometimes stern.[xxix] All addressed the ambiguous import of Hester's return to Boston at the end of the novel, at which time she resumes wearing the scarlet letter and lives out her remaining years as a counselor to suffering and wayward women.

Several feminist critics supposed that Hester's "uncharacteristic" return and apparent conformity to Puritan society signaled Hawthorne's misogyny and/or disgust over the nineteenth-century feminist movement and the convention-thwarting "New Woman." They argued that Hawthorne intended Hester to illustrate the perils of revolutionary, radical-minded feminists and that he "saved" her by neutralizing her radical potential, returning her to her proper place as a submissive, maternal, and self-abnegating "angel of the house." One such critic, Louise DeSalvo, considered Hester's return as an illustration of Hawthorne's conservative position on women's role in society, (see 535), suggesting that *The Scarlet Letter* was not only Hawthorne's "uneasy masculine exploration" of the women's rights movement of his day but also a patriarchally committed text that exposed on several levels his misogynistic tendencies. In the same year that DeSalvo's piece arrived on the scene to expose Hawthorne's alleged allegiance to his misogynistic Puritan ancestors, Amy Schrager Lang argued (see 536) that, by modeling Hester's "dissenting" character after seventeenth-century antinomian Anne Hutchinson, Hawthorne subtly registered his intense disapproval of his heroine's errant ways. Lang compared Hawthorne's denunciation of the "unnatural" Hutchinson (as seen in his 1830 sketch "Mrs. Hutchinson," in which he criticized her for stepping out of the "feminine" role prescribed for her) to his apparent condemnation of Hester's radical individualism; she also pointed out that, in the sketch, Hawthorne likened Hutchinson's domestic failings to those of the popular sentimental novelists of his era—that "damned mob of scribbling women" whose "irregular status" as authors also originated from dangerous "feminine ambition." Two years later, Jean Fagan Yellin demonstrated (see 594) that Hawthorne specifically employed the rhetoric of contemporary nineteenth-century American antislavery feminists in order to turn the tables on them and reject their ideology; according to Yellin Hawthorne attacked their radical new definitions of womanhood through the experiment of Hester's failed rebellion and subsequent suffering—which ends with Hawthorne safely restoring Hester to the status of a "true" woman who conforms to and reaffirms existing patriarchal values.

More common to feminist studies on *The Scarlet Letter* in the eighties were arguments in favor of Hawthorne's treatment of women. In 1982, for instance, Nina Baym's pivotal essay "Thwarted Nature: Nathaniel Hawthorne as Feminist" (see 419) defended Hawthorne from the charge that *The Scarlet Letter* portrays Hester negatively.[xxx] Baym contended that Hawthorne must himself have been a feminist, because he not only takes a woman for his novel's leading character but also presents her as a powerful and intellectual pioneer who resists patriarchal oppression. What's more, he shows heartfelt sympathy for the limited, powerless resources available to women (both in Puritan times and in his own era), appearing to condemn punitive patriarchal authority—at least until the end of the novel, where Baym and several other critics (such as David Leverenz [see 447] and Myra Jehlen [515]) admit that Hester's return to Boston suggests that Hawthorne lost his nerve and ended up reinforcing his culture's predispositions about women, either intentionally or unintentionally, by returning Hester to the scene of her crime and punishment, apparently to willingly conform to the Puritan norms of "femininity" or "true womanhood."

Like Baym, Joyce W. Warren concurred (see 467) that Hawthorne goes well beyond "the stereotyped image of femininity" in his portrayal of Hester, but Warren defended Hawthorne's conservative rejection of Hester's revolutionary aspirations on the political grounds that he would not have advocated radical individualism or reactionary reform for either of the sexes. Also defending Hawthorne from the common charge that he was ambivalent about his heroine's unconventionality was David Stineback (see 505), who suggested that Hawthorne's inconsistent approach to his heroine stemmed from cultural confusion in the mid-nineteenth century regarding woman's "true" nature and her "proper place" in society. Hawthorne's apparent sympathy for Hester's suffering (despite her moral and intellectual "waywardness"), Stineback concluded, shows him to be quite liberated for his time in his views on women.

Arguing for an even more liberated view of Hawthorne, and also answering complaints lodged by some feminists who asserted that Hawthorne reversed Hester's radicalism because he was fearful of her dangerous "mind wanderings" and sexual power, Andrew J. Scheiber wrote (see 583) that Hawthorne is not so much interested in asserting masculine power over his strong, intellectual heroine as he is in critiquing a society (both in the seventeenth and nineteenth centuries) that disempowers women by undervaluing the crucial "feminine" values of passion, feeling, and sympathy that he wishes Hester—and her male counterparts—would embrace. In like fashion, Cynthia S. Jordan maintained (see 588) that Hawthorne's sympathies expand to include all marginal figures who feel labeled as "Other" in society, and that he represents through Hester the redemptive potential of feminine and maternal values in a cruelly oppressive patriarchal culture. Seeming to take Scheiber's and Jordan's arguments a logical step forward, James J. Waite argued (see 585) that Hawthorne's sympathies are not just limited to Hester but also extend to Dimmesdale, because Hawthorne's own androgynous nature, more "feminine" than society would have found "normal" in a man, led him to be critical of restrictive, socially-prescribed gender roles that debilitate both sexes.

Also examining Hawthorne's reversal of traditional gender roles was Scott S. Derrick (see 512), whose views typified the direction post-modern *Scarlet Letter* studies took in the eighties and nineties, especially in his emphasis on

Hawthorne's "anxieties" or shaky manhood rather than on his overall craft. "Anxious" became the key word in both decades for describing Hawthorne's feelings about women, authorship, and his own gender and sexual identity. Less concerned with Hawthorne's artistry (as earlier critics were) than with the psychological burdens that he either knowingly or unknowingly projected onto his characters, Derrick argued that Hawthorne anxiously worked out definitions of masculinity and femininity in *The Scarlet Letter*, reversing traditional gender roles for Hester and Dimmesdale in order to come to terms with his own uneasiness about the "feminine" profession of authorship. That Hawthorne "re-masculinizes" Dimmesdale at the end and "domesticates" Hester testified to his need to assert his own unsure masculine identity over Hester. Several other critics argued similar cases.

Myra Jehlen (see 515), David Leverenz (see 447), George Dekker (see 534) Mary Suzanne Schriber (see 541), Janis P. Stout (see 553), Leland S. Person, Jr., (see 569), and T. Walter Herbert (see 581) also contended that Hawthorne questions traditional gender role stereotypes regarding the social role and moral nature of women; but they, too, found that he became so anxiously conflicted about his strong, sexually vibrant and socially rebellious heroine that he was compelled to contain her and to assert his own masculine power over her, "forcing" her to conform to society's expectations of women and to become objectified by the punitive letter. Leland S. Person, Jr., however, went further than the critics named above had, arguing that Hawthorne's "masculine poetics" was more complicated than they were allowing, and that, although Hawthorne ultimately showed a marked ambivalence about men's and women's gender "roles" in society, he nevertheless identified with his subversive heroine outcast/artist, and thus his relegation of Hester to a domesticated, feminine role had less to do with his view of women's proper place than with what he perceived to be society's unsympathetic attitude toward artists.

Just as Charles Swann voiced an empassioned appeal in the seventies that argued for Hawthorne's anti-romantic commitment to society, so he presented an equally powerful feminist argument in 1987 (see 554) that faulted "lukewarm" feminist readings of the novel's conclusion (including Baym's). Such readings conceded that Hawthorne checks Hester's radical potential by making her conform to the expectations of her seventeenth-century patriarchal society while also affirming the existing values of Hawthorne's nineteenth-century cult of "True Womanhood." Like James G. Janssen in his 1975 essay (see 329), Swann argued strenuously that Hester is a subversive feminist to the very end, and that her prophecy about the complete restructuring of society and religion proves just how unbelievably radical Hawthorne intended his feminist heroine to be. Michael Davitt Bell (see 482) pleaded a similar case by suggesting that Hester conceals her still-subversive nature after her return, rebelling quietly and subtly in her final years by counseling oppressed women who continue to suffer under the affliction of patriarchal authority.

Also considering what Hester's return means to and about Hawthorne were the New Historicist critics of the novel, whose ideologically oriented approaches frequently appeared in the eighties and nineties. New Historicists examined *The Scarlet Letter* primarily as a cultural register that reflected the dominant ideology or the prominent ideological contradictions of Hawthorne's historical moment (often explaining away the debate over the significance of the ending by claiming that, although Hawthorne challenges cultural assumptions about women and appears to be sympathetic to their plight, he is nevertheless so imprinted by his culture's ideology on women that he cannot maintain a subversive portrayal of Hester). Two critics in particular served as spokesmen for the New Historicist view of the novel in the eighties (their works would be cited time and again as representative examples of the approach): Jonathan Arac and Sacvan Bercovitch.[xxxi] Arac (see 508) examined the "A-politics" of *The Scarlet Letter*, explaining that Hester's socialization at the end could be attributed to

Hawthorne's political passivity or intense fear of extremes, a fear that led him (just as it did in his 1852 campaign biography of Franklin Pierce) to advocate inaction and to promote a policy of progressive evolutionary gradualism to right all wrongs in society. And Bercovitch (see 560, 575, and 576) took on the issue of Hawthorne's ambiguity in his own examinations of the "A-politics" and "A-morality" at the heart of the novel, claiming that such evasiveness typified American representations of revolution, which commonly evaded conflict. That Hester "consents" to be "socialized" at the end (Bercovitch used the same terminology that Arac did and came to similar conclusions) not only reflected Hawthorne's fears of the disruptive potential of both the pre-Civil War Compromise Resolutions of 1850 and the women's rights movement but also spoke to the scarlet letter's strategic function (reflecting a plurality of meaning) as an agent of reconciliation of the novel's conflicting forces, thus reinforcing Hawthorne's political view of the merits of compromise and gradualist accommodation to progressive ideology.

Post-structuralist interest in matters of meaning, knowledge, reality, and language in the novel increased significantly in the eighties. Paula K. White's post-structuralist approach (see 432), which contained elements of deconstructionist and reader-response criticism, claimed Hawthorne's awareness of the symbolic function of language, explaining that he purposely obscured the meaning of many important events and narrative statements to unsettle the reader and to intimate that "interpretation" itself is the subject of the romance. Several other critics came to similar conclusions regarding the thematic "unknowability" that they perceived to be central to the novel. Deconstructionist Norman Bryson argued a nearly identical point to White (see 435), insisting that Hawthorne's continual efforts to inhibit or complicate interpretation was his method of calling attention to the problems inherent in the Puritans' self-righteous and simplistic judgmentalism.

Approaching *The Scarlet Letter* from a semiological point of view, Millicent Bell (see 425) examined Hawthorne's use of intentionally vague words and attended to the narrator's inconsistency and the "indeterminacy" or subjective nature of signs in the novel, concluding that Hawthorne (like his heroine) was ahead of his time, a pre-deconstructionist masquerading as a conservative moralist. Likewise, John T. Irwin (see 389) considered Hester's scarlet letter to be a hieroglyphic emblem that demonstrated that there can be no objective truth in life but only limitless individual perspectives projected on "indeterminate ground." This persistent attention to the ways that Hawthorne deconstructed the Puritan system of "absolutes" and resisted nineteenth-century political ideologies continued all the way through the 1990s, often in direct conflict or dialogue with New Historicist approaches.

The majority of post-modern studies in the1980s showed an especial concern for language and the act of writing, focusing on a variety of related topics. Michel Small (see 405), Roy R. Male (see 408), Dennis Foster (see 443), Gordon Hutner (see 445), Stephen Nissenbaum (see 464), David B. Downing (see 473), and Michael Davitt Bell (see 482) argued for Hawthorne's and Dimmesdale's deceptive, duplicitous, and/or manipulative uses of language, asserting that Hawthorne and Dimmesdale both exploit the arbitrary, ambiguous nature of language to simultaneously confess sins while protecting themselves from the threat of exposure.[xxxii] David Van Leer (see 496 and 592) examined the narrative, linguistic, and tonal contradictions in the novel that seemed to him to address Hawthorne's concern with the indeterminacy of meaning and language. Allen Lloyd Smith (see 462 and 551) contended that the scarlet letter itself—as the first letter of the alphabet—was Hawthorne's way of calling attention to the critical issues of language and the act of writing in the novel, and Michael T. Gilmore argued (see 488) that the novel foregrounds failures of communication, which are the result of ambiguous acts of speech and writing among Hawthorne's characters, willfully crafted by an author who prefers "obfuscation" over "clarity."

Michael Ragussis explored matters of speech and silence (see 431), citing "silence" as the crime in *The Scarlet Letter* that chiefly precipitates the tragedy and produces devastating effects on the characters; Leland S. Person, Jr., (see 604) argued that Hester's silences, her refusal to name Dimmesdale as her partner in sin and her willingness to hide her husband's true identity from Dimmesdale, actually empower her and serve her own interests. In her own investigation into speech and silence in *The Scarlet Letter*, Louise K. Barnett (see 440 and 690) anticipated a revisionary trend in the scholarship of the 1990s by challenging deconstructive readings that cited Hawthorne's "modern" awareness that language is an arbitrary construct that can not be trusted. Critics who used the characters' consistent failures to communicate meaningfully or truthfully to one another as proof of Hawthorne's belief in the "indeterminacy" of language were misinterpreting both Hawthorne and the novel, Barnett forcefully and pragmatically argued, because all failures to communicate can be logically attributed to characters' personal fears of censorship under strict Puritan law.

1990s

The nineties continued to invite a slew of post-structuralist studies (and a great many reader-response approaches that synthesized elements of psychoanalysis and New Historicism) and dozens of feminist interpretations (which branched into distinct new directions that warranted my creating subcategories for black feminist studies, gender studies, and family studies under "Feminist Criticism" in the Critical Approach Index[xxxiii]). The decade also welcomed modest interest in law studies that focused on issues of crime and punishment in *The Scarlet Letter*. A more significant critical direction involved a trend toward re-evaluations of previous scholarship, re-evaluations of critical approaches themselves, and re-evaluations of canonicity. In the previous two decades there had been occasional revisionary studies that addressed problems or limitations in specific approaches, as in *Out of My System: Psychoanalysis, Ideology, and Critical Method* (1975), in which Frederick Crews rethought his influential analysis of the novel (see 182); he faulted his earlier insistence on divorcing Hawthorne's moral and religious themes from his psychological themes and questioned the ability of psychoanalytic criticism to illuminate works of literature at all.[xxxiv] In the late seventies and early eighties, Nina Baym also contributed revisionary critical energy in two essays (see 339 and 406) that re-evaluated the dated "canonical" criticism on the novel by citing faults in "conservative" New Critical treatments of *The Scarlet Letter*.[xxxv] In the nineties, however, dissenting viewpoints became more common. More than a few critics in the nineties and at present are impatient with pervasive "bandwagon" approaches to literature, dissatisfied—for various reasons—with the directions that many post-modern studies of Hawthorne are leading and call for a return to earlier ranges of interpretation and types of studies. A growing number of voices appear to be going against the grain of popular discourse to register their disgust with incessant discussions of Hawthorne that remove him entirely from his nineteenth-century context, that apply current ideological trends in literary criticism to the novel, and that thus view both Hawthorne and *The Scarlet Letter* through distorting late-twentieth-century frames of reference. These exasperated critics are distressed by what they conceive to be the emotionally flat, excessively jargon-ridden, intentionally abstract readings that strike a reader as forced exercises in theoretical application rather than useful or revealing analyses of literature; they show scant knowledge of the novel's historical context and little awareness of past critical studies on Hawthorne, and commonly apply only the most current activist topics to their considerations of the novel. Such studies most frequently center on Hawthorne's gender or sexual anxieties, his unfair or neglectful treatment of marginal figures like women, slaves, or Native Americans, his lack of confidence in language to determine fixed meanings, or his belief that all perceptions of reality are arbitrary and subjective, and that all truths are plural.

Michael J. Colacurcio, for one, argued in 1985 (see 485) that such mechanical, "meta-critical" readings are unfortunately "likely to arise whenever interpreters have lost humanistic or historical interest in an author's religious or philosophical meanings, or when they have begun to doubt the possibility of 're-cognizing' an author's conscious intentions." Such efforts," he concludes, "provide a way of mastering a text at the highest level of structural or linguistic analysis—while draining it, at the same time, of the very qualities that engage most readers and baffle ordinary critics" (21). Colacurcio was certainly not alone in questioning the value of much current criticism on *The Scarlet Letter*. Another disappointed critic of post-structuralist and New Historical studies, Peter Shaw, expressed concern in *Recovering American Literature* (see 727) that recent criticism stifles free discussions of literature by "heretically" imposing distorted and distorting political agendas on such works as *The Scarlet Letter*. Shaw was also deeply critical of the way most contemporary ideological interrogations of the novel make a mockery of Hawthorne's conflict between natural impulse and repressive social force, dismissing the now unpopular view that society has any rightful claims on the individual.

Just as Louise K. Barnett had reacted specifically against deconstructionist approaches to *The Scarlet Letter* in the eighties, so several other critics of the nineties contested the validity and usefulness of contemporary post-structuralist, New Historicist, and/or feminist analyses of the novel. Janet Gabler-Hover (see 616) and Raymond J. Wilson, III, (see 766), for example, rejected deconstructive readings that affirm the unstable nature of language and the indeterminacy of meaning by returning to a consideration of the novel's aesthetics and morality, arguing that Hawthorne affirms the "truth-telling power" of language and literature.

A large number of critics debated the legitimacy of New Historical approaches especially, frequently citing Sacvan Bercovitch's1991 *The Office of The Scarlet Letter* (see 635) as problematic in its insistence that Hawthorne participated in the dominant middle-class ideology of his day by affirming social compromise and consensus over radical reform and revolution. These critics argued instead that Hawthorne radically resisted prevailing ideologies such as patriarchy, racism, and classism. Charles Swann (see 651), Emily Miller Budick (see 677), Michael T. Gilmore (see 693), Robert E. Abrams (see 728), Peter Bellis (see 746), T. Walter Herbert (see 752), Charles Lewis (see 755), Paul K. Johnston (see 782), Robert Milder (see 787), and Richard H. Millington (see 788) all contested New Historicist readings that linked Hawthorne's aesthetics to liberal ideology and social compromise, faulting such politicized interpretations of the novel for minimizing or pretending to resolve the conflicts inherent in the text by way of proof that Hawthorne contributed to a stabilized political vision and conservative view of the middle class in nineteenth-century America.[xxxvi] Richard H. Millington's essay (which cited Bercovitch as guilty of obsessive participation in current ideological trends in New Historicist literary criticism) particularly stands out in its against-the-grain return to a content-oriented reading of *The Scarlet Letter* (that with refreshing clarity and humanity addressed the emotional experience of reading the novel). Millington argued that Hester's return at novel's end results not from Hawthorne's fear of her radicalism or his hatred of women or his sexual insecurities or his artistic anxieties or his commitment to the prevailing ideology—but from Hester's own emotional commitment to Dimmesdale and her sense of loyalty to a place and community that shaped her identity and gave her life meaning.

Just as critics faulted post-structuralist and New Historical approaches, so a few other critics rallied specifically to protest what they perceived to be worn out, adolescent, or outdated feminist arguments. Two in particular condemned both literary criticism and the culture at large. In her article on feminist cinematic adaptations of *The Scarlet Letter* and *Portrait of a Lady* (see 863), Kristin Boudreau showed disdain for the contemporary feminist celebration of female sexuality and "absolute freedom" that accompanied the late twentieth-century reenactments of the novels, not only because they endorsed what she discerned to be American culture's selfish privileging of the desires of the individual over the individual's obligation to the communal good, but also because such self-oriented endorsements get further and further away from Hawthorne's central message in *The Scarlet Letter*—the importance of social responsibility and the fundamental truth that identity is historically and socially constituted. Roger Bromley came to an identical conclusion in reference to the same "liberal" film adaptation of *The Scarlet Letter* by Roland Joffé (see 833), which completely abandoned Hawthorne's central conflict of individual freedom vs. social restraint and instead reflected only America's hedonistic and shallow contemporary culture that celebrates the "sovereign self" over all other selves.

Several critics were also quick to qualify Jamie Barlowe's feminist charge (see 804 and 853) that there still existed in the late nineties an exclusionary, conservative practice in mainstream Hawthorne scholarship that privileged criticism written by men and ignored most women's scholarship on *The Scarlet Letter*. Emily Miller Budick (see 806) accused Barlowe of participating in the same exclusionary practice of "Othering" that she faulted male critics for doing— reductively separating male scholarship from female scholarship and making gross generalizations about both), and T. Walter Herbert (see 809) found Barlowe's feminist complaint to be outdated, especially since so much of the mainstream criticism on the novel, by both men and women, was feminist in orientation.

While there are relatively few critics today who question Hawthorne's entitlement to a secure placement within the revised canon,[xxxvii] there are some like Jane Tompkins (see 495), Gary Scharnhorst (see 670), and Nina Baym (see 777) who attribute his success not so much to the intrinsic quality of his work as to auspicious personal circumstances, good literary and political connections, and specific historical forces, meaning that Hawthorne and his novel were in the right place at the right time. These studies on canon formation, on the "politics" of Hawthorne's literary reputation, and on the enduring classic status of *The Scarlet Letter*, represent one of the most popular types of Hawthorne studies at the end of the 1990s—along with reader-oriented approaches and feminist studies of the novel.

Just as there are more studies today that emphasize Hawthorne's public identity, political awareness, and social interests, so there also appears to be a shift in the general consensus in the debate over *The Scarlet Letter*'s central conflict of individual freedom vs. social control. Whereas some of the earliest critics feared and condemned Hawthorne's allegiance to defiant and "natural" romantic individualism, and many modern critics "discern[ed] a celebration of human individuality and an affirmation of the heroic struggle for personal freedom at all costs" (Tompkins 21), post-modern critics argue that *The Scarlet Letter* advocates socially sanctioned behavior. J. Donald Crowley maintains that what makes Hawthorne's novel so great is his sustained tension between self and society, or, more specifically, that his "genuinely American voice" registers a "radical sound of freedom" while it "evaluate[s] even more sharply the disturbing consequences of that freedom" (8). The majority of critics seem to concur (at least for now) that the conflict is meant to go unresolved because Hawthorne accepts the tension as unreconcilable and argues for a middle way, for a balance between romantic impulse and Puritanical restraint, for the enlightened and rational compromise between individual freedom and social responsibility. This compromise is perhaps demonstrated most profoundly by Hester's return to New England at the end, a move that not only reveals Hester's tremendous strength of character and rootedness in both personal and social reality but that also recalls Dimmesdale's untimely death as the consequence of his inability to balance personal or errant desires with the weights of social and moral responsibility. As

Quentin G. Kraft concludes in his study of *The Scarlet Letter* (see 244), "The either-freedom-or-morality choice is unsatisfactory [for Hawthorne] because [he believed that] genuine human relationships require not only that freedom be qualified by moral concern but also that morality exist within a context of freedom" (422-423). Thus a "thwarted dialectic" and a complex opposition ultimately characterize and constitute the form of the novel, producing a "dialectical stalemate" that may *seem* to invite "either-or" judgments but in fact supports a "both-and" view (424).

More and more studies also tread the middle ground in the debate over who constitutes the main character of the novel, conceding (perhaps since there is no critical agreement over whether Hawthorne ultimately wants the reader to sympathize exclusively with Hester or Dimmesdale) that there may not even *be* a main character, that Hawthorne actually invests in all three (or four, if Pearl is included) of the characters, who together comprise his own complex and conflicted self-portrait (as is suggested in 392, 563, 644, 723). Having projected conflicting aspects of his own social/antisocial personality into his characters, Hawthorne is legitimately in each primary figure, Pearl included, in their strengths and weaknesses as each plays out his or her journey to moral and spiritual maturity or degradation. What conclusions are to be drawn from their experiences are left to the reader to decide. About Dimmesdale's untimely death, the narrator closes with this: "Among many morals which press upon us from the poor minister's miserable experience, we put only this into a sentence:—"Be true! Be true! Be true! Show freely to the world, if not your worst, yet some trait whereby the worst may be inferred!" (260). The lesson of this perhaps ambiguously worded moral implies that, for man to fully embrace his own humanity and the humanity of others, he must first recognize, come to terms with, and embrace the essence of his own character, his vulnerabilities, failings and triumphs. In the end, Hawthorne shows mercy to all of his erring characters,

Chillingworth included, validating social connectedness and sympathy above all in *The Scarlet Letter*, just as he does in "The Custom-House."

Highlights and Additional Perspectives:
A Final Look at a Half-Century of Scholarship

Not given their due attention in the "Trends in Scholarship" section are the examinations of Hawthorne's literary and historical sources submitted over the past five decades. The source studies in particular (references to which can be found in the Subject Index, as separate from the historical approaches listed in the Critical Approach Index) contribute some of the most valuable and intriguing pieces that have been written on *The Scarlet Letter*. Whether written to illustrate Hawthorne's literary borrowings from such sources as Sir Walter Scott's *The Heart of Midlothian*, John Gibson Lockhart's *Adam Blair*, popular nineteenth-century seduction novels, or his own earlier tales[xxxviii]—or to speculate about his historical borrowings from New England Puritan histories and law books or from contemporary "powerhouses" like Margaret Fuller and the transcendentalists— these studies enrich and inform the body of scholarship on *Scarlet Letter* while contributing provocative and elucidating historical contexts from which to examine the novel. These studies offer insights that have developed out of genuine appreciation for and curiosity about the work, or out of a desire to add something new or revelatory about *Scarlet Letter* scholarship that will illuminate future readers and potentially influence or change the direction of *Scarlet Letter* studies.

Dozens of source studies have made worthy contributions over the years, although a few stand out for being particularly engaging. Benjamin Lease revealed, for instance, that the "certain venerable personage" whom Hawthorne venomously attacks in "The Custom-House" was not C. W. Upham (as most critics had previously assumed) but Permanent Inspector William Lee (see 257). R. B. Jenkins's essay (see 292) corrected several previous misreadings by critics who had mistakenly interpreted the novel's final sentence of heraldic description, "On a Field, Sable, the Letter A, Gules," to mean that the phrase itself was etched on the tombstone shared by Hester and Dimmesdale, rather than merely a scarlet capital "A" on the dark shield. Even Robert and Marijane Osborn's note (see 313) carried some weight in its speculation that the last line of the novel was likely based on Andrew Marvell's poem, "The Unfortunate Lover": "In a Field, Sable, a Lover Gules." Also fascinating is Patricia Marks's essay (see 347) on Hawthorne's likely debt to Increase Mather's1683 study *Kometographia: Or a Discourse Concerning Comets*, in which Mather described the superstitious belief among the Puritans that comets—such as the one appearing in the midnight scaffold scene of the novel—occasionally took the color and shape of "red letters" that were believed to signify gravely serious import.

The studies that identified possible historical sources for the main characters are also intriguing. John J. McAleer's, for one, (see 118) suggested historical bases for Hester and Dimmesdale, identifying a tombstone located in the center of the King's Chapel burial ground in Boston as belonging to "Hannah Dinsdale, wife of Adam Dinsdale." Laurie N. Rozakis's (see 530) claimed that she had personally searched King's Chapel cemetery to locate a possible source for Hester, and that she happened upon a weathered plaque—never before mentioned in any other Hawthorne study—that identified Puritan adulteress Elizabeth Pain (whose tombstone is "emblazoned" with a letter "A") as Hawthorne's model for Hester. In similar types of studies, Julian Smith (see 195), Hena Maes-Jelinek (see 224), Mukhtar Ali Isani (see 291), Frederick Newberry (see 550), and Carol M. Bensick (see 702) also speculated convincingly about likely sources for Hester, Dimmesdale, and Chillingworth, lending meaning and adding historical dimensions to the fictional characters.

Far more prevalent than source studies are those pieces that trace Hawthorne's broad influence on contemporary and future authors. After reviewing Hawthorne's pervasive influence on writers of his generation and beyond, Richard Brodhead goes so far as to call Hawthorne "the establisher of the coherence and continuity of American literature" (9), including in the impressive literary line of Hawthorne followers such authors as Herman Melville, Henry James, William Dean Howells, Stephen Crane, Harold Frederic, Sarah Orne Jewett, Mary Wilkins Freeman, William Faulkner, and Flannery O'Connor. Other American authors who show their indebtedness (whether acknowledged or not) to Hawthorne through their own fiction are Harriet Beecher Stowe Louisa May Alcott Emily Dickinson, Edith Wharton, D. H. Lawrence, Tennessee Williams, Robert Frost, John Fowles, Arthur Miller, Walker Percy, John Updike, Toni Morrison, Margaret Atwood, Virginia Woolf, and Thomas Pynchon. Hawthorne's influence also extends to authors of such varied ethnic backgrounds as Maryse Condé, Anaïs Nin, Bharati Mukherjee, and Isaac Bashevis Singer.[xxxix] Such a tremendous literary following is attributed, Brodhead avers, to "Hawthorne's tradition [having] an enigma for its source." Because he is so ambiguous, critics have been equally ambiguous about pinpointing what exactly makes Hawthorne so great.

John L. Idol, Jr., and Melinda M. Ponder come to a similar assessment in their 1999 anthology that traces Hawthorne's influence on women writers, *Hawthorne and Women: Engendering and Expanding the Hawthorne Tradition* (see 831, 834, 836, 837, and 841 for anthology entries on *The Scarlet Letter*). Concluding their study is a selected bibliography of criticism devoted exclusively to the debate over Hawthorne's stance on the "Woman Question," an issue never resolved in the criticism because, again, Hawthorne is a "master of ambiguity": "appearing to some readers to present Hester as a challenge to patriarchal dominance, seeming to others to force Hester back into a role of domestic subservience" (301). Yet, as Brodhead concludes, "[Hawthorne's] indefiniteness does not prevent him from being followed" (15). Male and female authors both experimental and conservative, romantic and realist, invent their own versions of Hawthorne, just as critics have done and continue to do to suit their own purposes.

Although there is no fundamental disagreement among critics about *The Scarlet Letter*'s essential conflicts (with the tension between the individual and society as the one most recognized), interpretations of the main characters remain as open as ever—although there *are* general shifts in the critical treatment of each. Pearl and Chillingworth have most often been considered as artificial, accessory characters, as allegorical personifications or psychological/symbolic projections of the inner realities or internal torments of Hester and Dimmesdale. Serving functional purposes as instruments of punishment, intentionally or not, they lead the main characters to salvation. While early studies typically faulted the artificiality of both characters, finding Pearl too unnatural (as the personification of truth, the living symbol of sin, or the embodiment of hope for the New World) and Chillingworth too unrealistically diabolical (as the embodiment of evil and the torturer of Dimmesdale), later studies have assigned more prominent roles to the characters. Most recent critics identify Pearl as a believable child modeled after Hawthorne's own precocious daughter Una, and a growing number likewise paint a three-dimensional portrait of Chillingworth (although he has drawn significantly less critical attention than she), identifying qualities that highlight his complexity and/or his humanity and suggesting that, because the narrator shows sympathy toward him at the end,[xl] he perhaps deserves some measure of the reader's pity.

An entire book could be written about the various ways critics have attempted to prove Hester's or Dimmesdale's status as the main character, as the "one" Hawthorne wants the reader to sympathize most with. Few readers have been as interested in Dimmesdale as in Hester (much for the same reason that Satan outshines Jesus in Milton's *Paradise Lost*, because he appears more interesting), but there have been nevertheless several religious and historical studies that provide enough background on Puritan theology to argue convincingly for Dimmesdale's prominence. Harold P. Simonson's essay "Puritan Faith, Romantic Imagination, and Hawthorne's Dilemma" (see 438) takes up Hawthorne's conflict between his Calvinist and romantic selves and argues that twentieth-century readers bent on vilifying Dimmesdale—quick to dismiss him as feeble-spirited, despicably weak, and hypocritical and thus to champion Hester's romantic cause—diminish the novel's chief conflict and fail to appreciate the complex depth of Dimmesdale's suffering while he lives with the torturous paradoxical dilemma of existing as a passion-driven, rebellious sinning man and as an orthodox Puritan minister who is supposed to lead his flock by his own spotless example. Hawthorne emphasizes and reemphasizes Dimmesdale's torturous state for a reason, Simonson determines. Because Dimmesdale legitimately "adores the truth" and "reckon[s] all things shadow-like" that are not of "divine essence," he imagines himself the "dimmest of all shadows," so "utterly a pollution and a lie" (143) that the agonizing contrast between what he seems and what he thinks he *is* makes him verge on complete self-delusion and even lunacy. Many critics have pointed out that, unlike Hester, Dimmesdale requires the "iron framework" of Puritan orthodoxy to support and confine him, a difference that ultimately estranges him from her, as when he fails to acknowledge her during the Election-Day processional. When he passes her by, she believes all at once that she does not know him and that they are not compatible,[xli] not kindred after all: "Her spirit sank with the idea that all must have been a delusion, and that, vividly as she had dreamed it, there could be no real bond betwixt the clergyman and herself"(240).

Critics have also rethought Hester's role in *The Scarlet Letter*, pointing out inadequacies in countless studies that have championed Hester as a radical agent of romantic individualism, and rethinking Hawthorne's often neglected emphasis on Hester's chronic feelings of guilt, shame, and anguish, her abiding faith in God, and what she really does with her sad and lonely life, both before Dimmesdale's death and after her return to Boston to fulfil the penitent office of the scarlet letter. In the evolution of her own scholarship on the novel, revising her earlier estimates of Hester, Nina Baym points out (see 339) that "almost nothing that [Hester] does in *The Scarlet Letter* can be labeled as an example of romantic individualism" (9). John P. McWilliamscomes to a similar conclusion (see 463), arguing that critics today too frequently race to the exciting passages in the novel where Hester's subversive nature shows itself and all but ignore the vast majority of the story which consistently details her suffering, sorrow, and shame; her guilty certainty that she has destroyed Dimmesdale; and her humility as she goes about the quiet business of her life on the outskirts of Boston for seven long years, raising Pearl in the Christian faith, earning a modest wage through her skillful needlecraft, and offering her thankless services as a "self-appointed Sister of Mercy" to the poor, sick, and downtrodden in the community.

Although *The Scarlet Letter* has been—as Philip Young observes (see 180)—"explicated, allegorized, source-hunted, theologized, annotated, romanticized, de-romanticized, decoded, psychoanalyzed, and mythologized" ad nauseum (217), it remains undamaged, unreduced by all the attempts to demystify it. In the end I am struck by *The Scarlet Letter*'s remarkable resistance to every effort to pin it down. Even post-modern, canon-destabilizing skeptics who only grudgingly grant that some texts might appear to "transcend" their own time or outlast their age have to admit that *The Scarlet Letter* continues to appeal to generation after generation of readers, persisting to "reward the scrutiny of successive generations of readers, speaking with equal power to people of various persuasions" (Tompkins 35). Jane Tompkins is one such critic. She writes in *Sensational Designs: The Cultural Work of American Fiction 1790-1860* that

> The trouble with the notion that a classic work transcends the limitations of its age and appeals to critics and readers across the centuries is that one discovers, upon investigation, that the grounds of critical approval are always shifting. *The Scarlet Letter* is a great novel in 1850, in 1876, in 1904, in 1942, and in 1966, but each time it is great for different reasons. In the light of this evidence, it begins to appear that what we have been accustomed

> to think of as the most enduring work of American literature is not
> a stable object possessing features of enduring value, but an object
> that—because of its place within institutional and cultural
> history—has come to embody successive concepts of literary
> excellence (35).

Despite her qualifying remarks, Tompkins admits that *The Scarlet Letter* is worthy of its classic status. "The text itself must be deeper and broader than any of its individual concretizations, for there is no other way to explain how the same text could give rise" to such a variety of critical approaches over such a long period of time (36). Richard Brodhead claims that *The Scarlet Letter* continues to "live" because it gets reinvented each time it is examined. Or, one might simply conclude that a true classic retains its power to attract and hold attention no matter what critical angle we approach it from. The grounds of critical approval are always shifting; systems, schools, theories, and approaches flame up and pass away. The novel endures. Remarkably, *The Scarlet Letter* speaks to each generation's concerns and interests and makes itself accessible to critical and theoretical approaches that emerge over the course of time to provide new insights into old problems. "What Hawthorne will need [in order to sustain critical interest in his novel] is what every potential past needs in order to survive—for the living present to continue to make it the image of its living concerns and needs" (Brodhead 215). At least for now, because no interpretations have yet mastered *The Scarlet Letter* to the point of definitively closing debates and satisfying inquiries, critical interest goes on.

The Cultural Impact of *The Scarlet Letter*
in The Late Twentieth Century

As the bibliography demonstrates in its comprehensive survey of fifty years of *Scarlet Letter* criticism, literary critical trends have fluctuated over the decades. The only common denominator among the rich diversity of perspectives, whether social, historical, political, psychological, religious, economic, ideological, or philosophical, is agreement about Hawthorne's ambiguity and elusiveness. Perhaps these two crucial characteristics best account for the novel's staying power and its continuing attraction to new generations of admiring readers.

Surveying the vast critical responses to *The Scarlet Letter*, Gary Scharnhorst refers to the novel as an "academic shibboleth" (xxi) that has responded remarkably well to rapidly shifting expectations over the decades, and Jane Tompkins marvels at the text's capacity for being continually reinvented year after year, each time being "great for different reasons" (35). It has been examined in relation to "The Custom-House"; to Hawthorne's earlier short stories and later fiction; to his relations with contemporaries such as Ralph Waldo Emerson, Herman Melville, and Margaret Fuller; to his Puritan history, ancestors, and religion; to his attitude toward society, politics, and art; to his literary theory and practice; to his literary devices (primarily his use of symbol, allegory, and ambiguity), literary and historical sources, and influences; to his overall achievement and place in literary history. *The Scarlet Letter* has been examined not only by New Critics, mythologists, structuralists and post-structuralists, historicists and New Historicists, sociologists and psychoanalysts, deconstructionists, reader-response critics, feminists, and biographers (among others), but as Seymour L. Gross humorously notes in his 1960 handbook on the novel (see 86), even by "lawyers, psychiatrists, journalists, and clergymen" who have felt compelled to offer their impressions and critical appraisals of *The Scarlet Letter*.

Adding to Seymour Gross's list of literary laymen, one might also include medical and business professionals, politicians, poets, and fiction writers. Allusions to Hawthorne's novel—if not informed discussions—are not limited to the rarified environment of the college campus. His importance in the development of America's literary consciousness, cannot be measured or underestimated. Many medical, law, and business journals allude to *The Scarlet Letter* and thus assume readers' familiarity with the novel and presuppose its lingering and pervasive cultural influence on the American public. Such references indicate that *The Scarlet Letter* is more than a literary classic to be enjoyed for its artistic merits. It explores issues as pertinent and controversial today as they were in the nineteenth century, such as adultery, women's rights, single parenthood, corporal punishment, separation of church and state, and child custody—often highlighting two social problems in particular, as Claudia Durst Johnson discovers in her own examination of twentieth-century issues pertinent to *The Scarlet Letter*—the unwed mother and the immoral clergyman (see 741).

Certain titles of articles outside the literary community confirm a wide-ranging awareness of the controversial issues raised in *The Scarlet Letter*; two such articles relate sexuality to punishment, N. G. Osborne's "Genital Herpes Simplex Virus Infection: The Forgotten Scarlet Letter" (from the *Journal of Gynecologic Surgery* [14.1 [1998]: 47]) and June Adinah's "Norplant: The 'Scarlet Letter' of Birth Control" (in *Misdiagnosis: Woman as a Disease* [Ed. Karen M. Hicks. Allentown: People's Medical Society, 1994. 219-221]). The latter essay, the title of which does not clearly indicate its content, claims that Norplant (the reproductive method involving hormone-releasing rods surgically implanted under the skin of a woman's arm) "brands" women. "Spare me the Hester Prynne syndrome," Hicks writes in conclusion.

Other titles in non-literary journals affirm strong reactions to the novel's presentation of adultery, as in three articles that address the issue of sexual misconduct and allude unforgivingly to Dimmesdale's silence about his adultery: Alan R. Kabat's "Scarlet Letter Sex Offender Databases and Community Notification: Sacrificing Personal Privacy for a Symbol's Sake" (in *The American Criminal Law Review* [35 (1998): 333-370]), Claire M. Kimball's "A Modern Day Arthur Dimmesdale: Public Notification When Sex Offenders Are Released Into the Community" (in the *Georgia State University Law Review* [12.4 (1996):

1187-1221]), and Ann-Janine Morey's "Blaming Women for the Sexually Abusive Male Pastor" (from the *Christian Century* [105.28 (1988): 866-869]).

All of the above implicitly cast Hester in a sympathetic light and blot Dimmesdale darkly—in a manner similar to two law and literature studies within the bibliography itself, whose authors verify that Hawthorne's novel is alive and well in the contemporary public's imagination. Garry Wamser and Shira Pavis Minton, who share a background in law,[xlii] show that the treatment of women in twentieth-century America sometimes closely resembles that of the controlling, male-dominated, censurious Puritan era that persecutes Hester. In "The Scarlet Contract: Puritan Resurgence, the Unwed Mother, and Her Child" (see 776), Wamser contends that the federal government does little to aid unmarried women with children, whom he likens to adulteresses in the seventeenth century who faced condemnation and humiliating punitive sanctions. In "Hawthorne and the Handmaid: An Examination of the Law's Use as a Tool of Oppression" (see 826), Shira Pavis Minton considers the origins of misogynist law and illustrates ways in which today's society permits a sexual double standard for men, oppresses women, and attempts to control women's sexuality in a manner similar to the way Hester is dominated by the Puritan patriarchs.

Other non-literary essays steer clear of the legal and gender issues in *The Scarlet Letter* and focus instead on the effect of Hester's punitive letter. In "The Hester-Prynne Sanction," for instance (in *Business Ethics: A Philosophical Reader*. Ed. Thomas I. White. New York: Macmillan, 1993. 276-286), Peter French discusses a shame-based morality sanction that, when put into effect in corporate criminal cases, potentially proves effective in triggering significant retributive and deterrent effects on corporate offenders. This proposed punishment—with an effect similar to that of individuals forced to wear scarlet letters—threatens prestige, image, and social standing, and places a "damaging blot" on a person's or company's reputation as a mark of shortcoming, an indicator of others' disgust, and as a signal that identity must be rebuilt. French's use of the penalty inflicted on Hester Prynne in *The Scarlet Letter* assumes that a large readership—in this case corporate America—will instantly recognize and comprehend the reference.

Doctors, lawyers, and business professionals are not the only ones capitalizing today on the public's knowledge of Hawthorne's novel. Politicians likewise display their acquaintance, as in Lisa McCormack's "The Scarlet Letter" in *Campaigns & Elections* (11.2 [1990]: 26-33). Even sports writers assume reader familiarity, as in the case of *Sports Illustrated* boasting its literary prowess in an article entitled Tim Layden's "Scarlet Letter" (87.16 [1997]: 30-35).

As mentioned above, *The Scarlet Letter* has also attracted the attention of contemporary fiction writers, lending inspiration for novels such as Kathy Acker's *Blood and Guts in High School* (New York: Grove Weidenfeld, 1978), Peter De Vries' *Slouching Toward Kalamazoo* (Boston: Little, Brown, 1983), Charles R. Larson's *Arthur Dimmesdale* (New York: A & W Publishers, Inc., 1983), Christopher Bigsby's *Hester: A Romance* (London: Weidenfeld and Nicolson, 1994), and John Updike's *Scarlet Letter* trilogy.[xliii] Not all of these works of fiction have enjoyed the critical acclaim of their model, however.

While the novels are a contemporary testament to Hawthorne's staying power, indicating that Hawthorne's novel still lives and breathes through their own, most, in fact, seem to parody or make a mockery of *The Scarlet Letter*, "updating" or modernizing it much as poor movie adaptations have. Kathy Acker's *Blood and Guts* has been largely dismissed by critics for its vulgar and foul-mouthed content; DeVries's comical "modernization" mocks the seriousness of Hawthorne's tale—telling a story in which a high school teacher has an affair with a student after teaching a unit on *The Scarlet Letter* (the teacher becomes pregnant and protests being fired by standing on a balcony with a scarlet A+ emblazoned on her blouse); and Larson's retelling of *The Scarlet Letter* from the minister's point of view belittles the integrity of its model and has likewise been panned by critics.

Even more than the above-mentioned novels, the movie industry has contributed to keeping *The Scarlet Letter* at the forefront of the public's attention, having produced five feature-length films in the twentieth century (the 1926 MGM silent film starring Lillian Gish and directed by Victor Sjöström, the 1934 "slapstick talkie" directed by Richard Vignola and starring Colleen Moore, the 1972 German-language adaptation by Wim Wenders, the 1979 four-hour PBS television release by Rich Hauser, and the 1995 box-office disaster directed by Roland Joffé and starring Demi Moore). Most of the films have not been reviewed with much enthusiasm by critics (see 807 and 846 in particular), all of whom generally agree that no film adaptation of the novel has yet done *The Scarlet Letter* justice (although two [see 662 and 846] have argued that Wim Wenders's version comes the closest, even though it takes the most liberties and dramatic license).

While some critics may assert (as Michael Dunne does in 807) that *The Scarlet Letter* has tremendous cinematic potential, others (such as Larry Baker in 453) concede that the novel simply does not translate well from page to silver screen, that, even if the dialogue and script strictly follow the text, the movie still fails, because the novel is too densely packed with narrative complexity, rich texture, ambiguity, and subtlety to ever successfully transfer to visual image. If a classic work of literary art is characterized by both complexity and unity, in which every word "tells" and nothing is missing or superfluous, then, arguably, the selecting, editing, and patching processes of screen-play writing amount to little more than mutilation. Joffé's 1995 "updated" and "freely adapted" version has taken the most critical heat, being almost unanimously labeled as an "outrageous," "preposterous," "ridiculous," "disastrous" debacle, a "vulgar spectacle" and an "abomination" that would make Hawthorne groan with insult for abandoning his highly complex social message about the legitimate claims of society on the individual. The movie thus depreciates the novel's chief conflict, tiresomely portraying Hester and Dimmesdale's social situation (and inner conflicts) as so uncomplicated that they may simply, self-righteously and guiltlessly, ride away, wagon wheel grinding the scarlet letter in the dirt. They triumph over the constraints of their repressed Puritan society so airily that one forgets that they are supposedly Puritans themselves.

Without doubt the disappointing movie downplays the complex conflict between the individual and society, commercially exploiting and sugar-coating the novel so that *The Scarlet Letter* will (theoretically) appeal to late-twentieth-century audiences comfortable with two-dimensional, action-packed tales of sexual liberation and naïve, ego-driven rebels who thwart society's conventions for their own personal fulfillment. However, Sacvan Bercovitch (see 778) and Jennifer Solmes (see 852) have argued that Joffé's "freely adapted" movie is not so different from other film versions—or even from the novel itself—when one considers that all of them are strategically geared both to the concerns of their own times and to appeal to a mass audience. In this sense, the movies are all in themselves useful studies or cultural artifacts of the values and prejudices in which they were produced, each in its own way juggling commercial and artistic priorities: responding to the demands of the marketplace while trying to resist compromising the integrity of its creator's artistic vision.

Critics besides Bercovitch and Solmes who have examined one or more of the five feature-length film versions of *The Scarlet Letter* also observe that the movies are strategically geared to reflect the values, concerns, and prejudices of their times so that box office profits will be maximized[xliv], which is undoubtedly true. But they—namely Michael Dunne (see 807) and Bruce Daniels (845, 846)—fear the effects films have on general audiences who do not realize that they are witnessing inaccurate portrayals of Puritans and poor dramatizations of the novel. As directors adapt *The Scarlet Letter* to the commercial demands of the marketplace and imprint their film versions of the story with the latest trends in Hollywood "taste" and "style," the movie-going masses respond with the purchase of one ticket and two hours of attention. At best, they may seek out the novel for a richer telling; at worst (most often the case), they may avoid the novel altogether because the movie offers so little of complex and sustaining interest about the Puritans or Hawthorne's tale.

While the movie industry's interest in *The Scarlet Letter* has certainly kept Hawthorne's novel fresh in the minds of the American public, quite under its own power the novel has never gone out of print and is continually included in the curricula of middle schools (designed for young readers), high schools, colleges, and universities—sometimes without the "The Custom-House" preface.[xlv] Surely this speaks most to *The Scarlet Letter*'s importance and enduring status as a literary treasure. Few novels have appealed to so many consecutive times and audiences, outlasting generations of critics and critical perspectives in its power to engage. "*The Scarlet Letter* has had an edition almost every year and has never been out of print," Nina Baym writes in an essay on the novel's enduring classic status (62). "It is now one of the ten most frequently read novels in junior and senior high schools in the United States," Claudia Durst Johnson verifies (x). "Over two dozen editions are now available,"[xlvi] Rita Gollin confirms in her analysis of special editions of *The Scarlet Letter* (12), indicating that the novel is as safely entrenched in the canon of American masterpieces as ever—its status even expanding as perceptive readers continue to deem it worthy of attention.

Even at the present time in the early twenty-first century, at the bicentennial of Hawthorne's birth, the meaning and significance of Hawthorne's romance are still controversial and feverishly debated. Perhaps the debates continue because, as John C. Gerber proposed many years ago,

> today's reader finds Hawthorne's skeptical temperament congenial. In his doubts about the possibilities of the human mind, in his awareness of human loneliness, in his insight into the enormous complexities of the human psyche, in his great regard for human affection, in his assumptions about life that approach

those of modern existentialism, in all of these ways and others Hawthorne speaks directly to our own age. *The Scarlet Letter*, therefore, remains a book to be read not as a monument in literary history but as a work unceasingly capable of engaging the mind and the emotions (14).

Future generations of readers will doubtless be "engaged" for similar and unpredictable reasons, because *The Scarlet Letter* will continue to invite disparate readings and new approaches in accord with the concerns of successive generations— as well as to solicit calls for inquiry into issues that have never been—and probably never will be or were meant to be—solved: whether Hester or Dimmesdale is the leading character; whether Dimmesdale is damned or saved at his death; whether the ending of the novel represents Hawthorne's conservative return to patriarchal ideology or his sympathetic response to nineteenth-century feminists; whether Hawthorne is a Puritan or a romantic; or whether he promotes the needs of the individual over the welfare of the community at large. As many critics say or imply, a mystery perhaps lies at the heart of *The Scarlet Letter*. Hawthorne, crouching over his writing desk and working at a frenetic pace, seemed to find that intensity of musical pitch that Dimmesdale achieved in his last sermon: "Like all other music, it breathed passion and pathos, and emotions high or tender, in a tongue native to the human heart" (243).

Scope and Limits

While my original intention was to provide a comprehensive, annotated listing of criticism that extended all the way back to the novel's date of publication on March 16, 1850, it soon became clear that I would have to be selective. Creating such a massive bibliography was neither necessary nor practical. First, it would make the bibliography tiresomely long, cumbersome, and intimidating to any readers beyond the most devoted bibliographers. Second, my early research led me to several older published bibliographies on Hawthorne and *The Scarlet Letter* that already offered adequate coverage and summaries of the scholarship written in the nineteenth century and the first half of the twentieth century. (Refer to section E of the Resource Guide for titles of such bibliographies.) And finally, the most helpful and relevant scholarship for today's critics and readers of *The Scarlet Letter* is necessarily the most current. This is not to imply that criticism published prior to the 1950s is less worthy, but there is a marked trend in *Scarlet Letter* criticism that recognizes the advent of "serious" academic studies as coincident with the New Criticism of the 1940s and 1950s; they set off an explosion of sophisticated analyses, especially since the centennial of Hawthorne's death in 1964 (and the authoritative Centenary Edition of *The Scarlet Letter*, which appeared in 1962). Most of the work completed before the 1940s was comprised of general impressions, personal remarks, and subjective commentary that tended to focus on Hawthorne's temperament, poetic style, allegorical method, affiliation with transcendentalism, and sense of morality. Much of this is of considerable interest. Although there were notable exceptions, (see Part II, which is devoted exclusively to such exceptions), the majority of late nineteenth- and early twentieth-century studies were driven by their authors' liberal humanist, moral and religious convictions rather than by any systematic approach to literary criticism.

It seemed most logical, then, for the annotated bibliography to include all books and articles from 1950 to 2000 that dealt specifically with the novel. Yet, early into the research I soon learned that once again I would have to be selective, limiting or omitting certain pieces which seemed to be of negligible value. The number of potential sources, which originally totaled more than 1,400, I finally reduced to 867. Roy R. Male addressed the issue of deleting "clutter" from surveys of Hawthorne scholarship in the 1969 issue of *American Literary Scholarship* (in which journal a chapter on Hawthorne appears with each annual issue), writing that

> Each year roughly one-eighth of the work done on Hawthorne is of
> considerable significance. The remainder consists of dissertations

(which in distilled form may later prove to be significant), forced publications by young scholars, commercial casebooks and reprints, articles done on assignment or with their left hands by established critics, and miscellaneous bits and pieces of information or interpretation, often useful, but limited in scope (19).

A few years later, Nina Baym expressed a similar opinion in the 1971 issue of *American Literary Scholarship*, confirming that "too much of the published material [on Hawthorne] is disturbingly insubstantial—unoriginal, slight in scope, rarified in argument, and distressingly amateurish in learning, style, and critical method" (24).

While I initially felt unprepared to confidently distinguish serviceable from unserviceable scholarship given the sheer volume of materials, I knew I had to develop a system for categorizing the most useful, original, and influential sources. Therefore, I have excluded hundreds of passing references and general discussions that would litter the bibliography with plot summaries and unoriginal critical opinions. I have also omitted dozens of pieces in which *The Scarlet Letter* is briefly related to three or more other primary works (either of Hawthorne's or another author's). There are literally thousands of commentaries that briefly mention *The Scarlet Letter*. Since my fundamental interest is to provide sources that specifically treat the novel or say something groundbreaking about it, I have included only those pieces that deal exclusively with *The Scarlet Letter* or focus on it as one of no more than two other primary works.

Moreover, in the interest of keeping the project to a manageable length, I have regrettably deleted from consideration all dissertations, studies in a foreign language, reviews, and reprints. Although I do not retain reprints or later editions unless they contain significant revisions or additions, I indicate reprintings, minor revisions, and expansions under the original titles of pieces—highlighting them with asterisks—so that readers may seek out in the most convenient way either the original or its reprint. Likewise, I have noted all journal article reprints that later appeared in bound collections so that the reader might save money by ordering books through Interlibrary Loan rather than having to incur the photocopying fees that often accompany periodical requests. While omissions of dissertations, studies in a foreign language, reviews, and reprints qualify the inclusiveness of the bibliography by abbreviating the full record of scholarship, they do not compromise the overall goal of the project, which, again, aims to assist readers and critics in arriving at their own assessments of the novel by providing a "selectively comprehensive" record of past scholarship in English and an overview of the trends in *Scarlet Letter* criticism.

Abundant scholarship in so many areas over so many years makes it nearly impossible to identify individual studies that are representative of each decade's most "worthy" scholarship (although I have attempted this in the "Trends in Scholarship" section, and many specific studies throughout the bibliography itself are recommended or recognized for their significance to the literary community). As Ross C. Murfin points out in his own survey of the major critical responses to the novel from 1850 to 1990 (see 637), "A great work of literature such as *The Scarlet Letter* elicits a host of different interpretive responses, no one of which stands alone or is entirely adequate to unpack its significance" (Murfin 221). I decided that, in the interest of consistency and impartiality, the most efficient and effective method of charting *Scarlet Letter* criticism from the latter portion of the twentieth century was to break down the studies into critical approaches (see Critical Approach Index) and subject categories (see Subject Index).

Rita Gollin writes, "Anyone who undertakes to analyze the various ways in which *The Scarlet Letter* has been presented to its readers must feel the mixed emotions of a Roger Chillingworth—wonder and joy mixed with horror" (12). Indeed, the process of classifying the vast array of opinions and critical judgments on Hawthorne and his most famous romance for the Critical Approach Index was one of the most challenging and intimidating parts of the project, largely because the task of classifying critical and theoretical approaches into indexed groupings is itself problematic. Many individual works do not fit neatly into any one category or declare allegiance to any specific methodology, and some studies reflect multiple critical or theoretical orientations. (For more on the difficulties I encountered in compiling the Critical Approach Index, see "Methods and Organization.")

Perhaps the most difficult, complicated, and rewarding part was writing the "Trends in Scholarship" section of the introduction: studying the Subject Index and Critical Approach Index and re-reading the completed bibliography, entry by entry, to reach some conclusions about the general direction Hawthorne studies took in the mid-to-late twentieth century and where they are heading now, also which outlooks were most dominant and well received, which trends and topics would take (or had already taken) hold, and which would recede into obscurity and likely go unnoticed by future critics.[xlvii]

Arrangement of Materials

Critical appraisals of *The Scarlet Letter* can be traced all the way back to the publication of the earliest reviews of the novel in 1850. Social, moral, and religious critics reacted strongly to Hawthorne's first serious romance, but, as Ross C. Murfin notes, serious criticism of Hawthorne and *The Scarlet Letter* did not emerge until the fourth decade of the twentieth century: "Because literary criticism had not yet developed into the intellectual discipline that it has become since the 1940s, Hawthorne's novel was not written about—certainly it was not carefully and systematically analyzed—with the frequency that it has been in the past fifty years" (208). Yet, even though the earliest critiques lacked modern-day critical sophistication, there are many significant nineteenth-century and early twentieth-century appraisals of the romance that anticipated or influenced modern criticism—beginning with the first reviews. Part I, therefore, provides a chronological, annotated listing of the ten most popular and frequently anthologized "Early Reviews" of the novel. Citations and annotations for these reviews by Evert A. Duychinck, George Ripley, Edwin P. Whipple, Henry F. Chorley, Anne W. Abbott, Herman Melville, George B. Loring, Jane Swisshelm, Orestes A. Brownson, and Arthur Cleveland Coxe are also included because references to them appear so commonly in *Scarlet Letter* criticism, anthologies, and collections of criticism.

Part II offers alphabetically arranged, full citations for "Early Influential Criticism (Pre-1950)" and is comprised of forty-one notable commentaries that appeared between 1850 and1950. Like the ten early reviews, these pieces of early criticism are incorporated into the bibliography because they influenced later criticism or because they have been or continue to be highlighted works in anthologies and collections of criticism on *The Scarlet Letter*.

Part III, which makes up the bulk of the project and begins with the year 1950, presents a comprehensive annotated bibliography of *Scarlet Letter* criticism that includes books, articles, special critical editions, collections of criticism, general student introductions and help books, teaching aids and guides, and biographies. The numbered citations are listed chronologically to emphasize the development of scholarly or critical opinion, divided by year of publication, then alphabetically arranged within each year into three sections: Books, Essays and Studies in Books, and Journal Notes and Articles.

Within the annotations for individual citations in all three Parts, I have attempted a close paraphrase of the language of each author in an effort to present most accurately and concisely the controlling ideas of each piece. I have tried to keep the annotations roughly the same length, but there are exceptions. Where annotations are rather lengthy, the reader may generally assume that the studies are extensive, complex, or groundbreaking. Where annotations are especially brief, the reader may infer that the sources themselves are terse, brief, marginally original, or comparatively lacking in critical value. In the interest of creating a comprehensive record of scholarship, I have sought to avoid imposing my own views of what is more or less critically valuable and to omit personal evaluations or characterizations in my descriptions. When evaluative comments do appear, they are based upon the views of readers appearing in the critical record.

The six-part Resource Guide that makes up Part IV offers groupings of special critical editions, collections of criticism, general student introductions to the novel, teaching aids and guides, bibliographies, and biographies. All individual titles within these groupings include parenthetical annotation numbers that refer the reader to their placement within the larger numbering system of the bibliography (bibliographies excepted, since citations for them do not generally appear within the larger bibliography).

An Author Index, a Subject Index, and a Critical Approach Index conclude the study. The Subject Index provides instant access to dozens of key concepts (such as language, meaning, nature, sin, sympathy, and truth), terms (like ambiguity, allegory, archetype, art, gothicism, imagery, irony, metaphor, myth, structure, style, the supernatural, and technique), and topics (such as "The Custom-House" in relation to the novel, Hester's return to Boston, "the office" of the scarlet letter, the Puritans, and the moral of *The Scarlet Letter*). It includes character analyses; historical and literary source studies; comparison studies (such as between Hawthorne and Sir Walter Scott, George Eliot, Henry James, or William Faulkner); studies that evaluate Hawthorne's influence on other writers (such as Arthur Miller, John Updike, or Toni Morrison); dramatic and cinematic studies (under Drama, Opera, Play, and Movie Versions of *The Scarlet Letter*); and surveys that compare *The Scarlet Letter* to Hawthorne's other works, which are listed alphabetically by title under "Comparisons," "Influences," and "Sources."

The Subject Index also offers formal interrogations of flaws and inconsistencies in the novel; it lists primary and secondary themes and conflicts, images, patterns, and symbols; it contains subject headings for such crucial issues as feminism in the nineteenth century, Hawthorne's concept of the past, his politics, tragic vision, view of and portrayal of women, and relation to the reader; it includes analyses of the many meanings of the scarlet letter and the ambiguous ending; it cites studies on gender, imagination, history, humor, romanticism, religion, and transcendentalism; it enumerates critiques of both modern criticism and specific theoretical approaches by individual authors; and it contains an entire section on *The Scarlet Letter* itself as it has been viewed by critics, whether as an allegorical romance or as a Western novel.

The Critical Approach Index identifies the fifteen most popular critical and theoretical approaches to the romance that have been used to analyze *The Scarlet Letter* over the past fifty years and connects a significant number of the bibliography's citations to those specific methodologies: morality studies, religious/theological studies, language studies, law studies, New Criticism, archetypal/myth criticism, structuralism, semiology/semiotics, post-structuralism, deconstruction, reader-response theory, historicism, New Historicism, psychoanalytic/psychological criticism, and feminist studies (the last category of which is so large and diverse that I have broken it down into subsections of feminist studies, black feminist studies, gender studies, and family studies). In addition to furnishing a list of texts or essays on Hawthorne that examine critical approaches and trends in scholarship on *The Scarlet Letter*, the Index also provides general definitions of each theoretical approach as well as to explain— where appropriate and with examples—what characteristics about *The Scarlet Letter* make the novel conducive to these approaches.

Methods and Organization

In the interest of making the bibliography as accessible and useful to students and scholars as possible, I have followed the standard MLA procedure in compiling a bibliography of this type and length (observing the guidelines of James L. Harner's *On Compiling an Annotated Bibliography* and the *MLA Style*

Manual and Guide to Scholarly Publishing), although I have included a few slight modifications. Abbreviations for Hawthorne's name, character names, and "The Custom-House" have been avoided in the interest of keeping citations as easy to read as possible. Instead of using acronyms when citing serial articles and titles of other Hawthorne's works (*The Scarlet Letter* itself aside, which is abbreviated as *Letter*), I also spell out titles to reduce the possibility of mystifying or frustrating readers. For the same reason, I list page numbers fully (such as 250-261 as opposed to 250-61).

To further aid the reader in swift searches through the bibliography, I have chosen to number each bibliographic citation within the "main" bibliography (Part III) from first to last—from 1 to 867—and not from section to section, because, from my own experience, complicated numbering systems involving both numbers and letters can be confusing. Part I, which is composed of ten early reviews, is numbered ER1-ER10, and Part II, on early influential criticism, is numbered EC1-EC41. Entries that escaped my notice until the numbering sequence had already been established appear under "Errata." Finally, for the convenience of the reader, internal notes pertaining to individual entries are indicated with brackets directly under annotations.

Both the Author and the Subject Indexes are self-explanatory. The Critical Approach Index requires clarification, since it was not easy to organize or to assign the entries in the bibliography to the critical approaches they represent. While one may readily identify and categorize some methodologies in *Scarlet Letter* criticism, it is sometimes a complicated, imprecise, and difficult process. In the first place, most books and articles do not clearly identify or label themselves as belonging to a particular critical/theoretical camp. Second, critical/theoretical approaches themselves are often eclectic and even depend upon one another, thus making it difficult or imprudent to assign them to an exclusive school. (For example, it is not unusual to see a New Historicist essay with a feminist outlook or to find a deconstructionist who employs elements of reader-response theory). As Michael P. Spikes explains, "Contemporary theory is a complicated fabric of crisscrossing and tangled threads, no one of which can be entirely separated from the others" (19). What's more, while some essays adopt more than one critical approach, others appear to be written with no clear guiding theses or critical apparata at all. Third, to place individual works on *The Scarlet Letter* in categories also risks doing disservice not only to critics but also to the novel itself, which clearly resists single schools of thought.

I have been careful, therefore, classifying and placing individual works in categories. A great many studies are cross-listed or assigned to multiple categories (such as both psychoanalytical and historical) when they appear to cross over methodologies and approaches. Yet, despite my lingering reservations about the necessarily imprecise process, I do believe that grouping and classifying critical resources on *The Scarlet Letter* offers a useful, practical aid for readers of Hawthorne studies so that they may recognize the prominent types of scholarship that have gone before. If, for instance, critics wish to attempt a feminist approach to the novel, or if readers simply want to know how much feminist criticism is available on the novel, they can refer to "Feminist Criticism" in the Critical Approach Index and see for themselves. In a similar manner, readers may also make use of the Subject Index to look up key terms relating to their issues of interest.

As noted above in "Scope and Limits," to make the Critical Approach Index serviceable and accessible, I have organized into groupings fifteen specific methodologies that have lent themselves particularly well to analyses of *The Scarlet Letter*. I have also made an effort to define individual critical and theoretical approaches and to note characteristics of *The Scarlet Letter* that have drawn the most attention of literary critics and theorists. My intention here is not to map out the history of contemporary literary theory (see my "Works Consulted" at the end of the Critical Approach Index for books that provide such histories) but to provide helpful groupings of the most commonly used critical/theoretical approaches to *The Scarlet Letter*. Of course, not all 867 citations in the bibliography fit into or employ these approaches. Most early pieces by social, moral, and religious critics written in the late nineteenth and early twentieth century, for instance, do not readily conform to these categories because they did not approach *The Scarlet Letter* in an easily classifiable, systematic way (although some of the liberal humanist critics anticipated later criticism). In addition, several post-modern "offshoots" examine the novel from an angle that extends beyond the distinct boundaries of the fifteen approaches identified.[xlviii]

Valuable critical studies can also be located in the six-part Resource Guide (which groups Special Critical Editions, Collections of Criticism, General Student Introductions to the Novel, Teaching Aids and Guides, Bibliographies, and Biographies) and in the Subject Index (such as character studies; comparative studies; historical and literary source studies and examinations of Hawthorne's own influence on other writers; explorations of specific subjects, symbols, images, metaphors, patterns, themes, conflicts, and techniques; interrogations of flaws and inconsistencies in the novel; analyses of the multiple meanings of the scarlet letter and the ambiguous ending of the novel; critical treatments of the numerous film versions of *The Scarlet Letter*; as well as critiques of both modern criticism and specific theoretical approaches by individual authors).

Resources

In addition to consulting numerous databases to compile the bibliography (such as MLA International Bibliography, FirstSearch on WorldCat, ABELL, PCI Full Text, ArticleFirst, Humanities Index, Nineteenth-Century Reader's Guide to Periodical Literature, Reader's Guide to Periodical Literature, Book Review Digest, Books in Print, and the Arts and Humanities Citation Index), I relied heavily on the bibliographies that appear in such serial publications as the *Nathaniel Hawthorne Review*, *American Literary Scholarship*, and the *Nathaniel Hawthorne Journal*. I also consulted the annual bibliographies in *PMLA*, *American Literature*, *Studies in the American Renaissance*, and the Modern Humanities Research Association's *Annual Bibliography of English Language and Literature*. A vast number of entries were also obtained from existing, though dated, bibliographies (the complete listing of these sources appears in section E of the Resource Guide), as well as from footnotes and bibliographies that accompany numerous articles and books.

Notes

---

[i] Three studies in particular argue that strong literary and political connections and fortunate historical circumstances, in addition to Hawthorne's literary merit, account for *The Scarlet Letter*'s tremendous success: Jane Tompkins's "Masterpiece Theater: The Politics of Hawthorne's Literary Reputation" (see 495*), Richard H. Brodhead's *The School of Hawthorne* (see 511), and Nina Baym's "Hawthorne's *Scarlet Letter*: Producing and Maintaining an American Literary Classic" (see 777). In Tompkins's book, for instance, *The Scarlet Letter*'s success is attributed to "a series of quite specific documentable circumstances having to do with publishing practices, pedagogical and critical traditions, economic structures, social networks, and national needs which constitute the text within the framework of a particularly disciplinary hermeneutic" (36).

* Note that all references to numbers in the introduction (such as those above in this footnote) direct the reader to the chronologically arranged entries in the bibliography.

[ii] J. Donald Crowley believes that Hawthorne's insecurity over the quality of the book stems from his artistic isolation; "almost every aspect of [his] creativity was conditioned by his acute awareness that for over twenty years he had no sympathetic audience" (6). He had longed to be a famous and successful author since his youthful days at Bowdoin College, and although he had published several children's books and two moderately successful collections of short stories before 1849, sales had certainly never been good enough to permit him to live comfortably as a "man of letters" without also having to earn a considerable supplemental income on the side.

[iii] On finishing his romance, Hawthorne read the conclusion to his wife, Sophia, and considered it a great triumph that its dark intensity "broke her heart and sent her to bed with a grievous headache." (Crowley 151).

[iv] For the most comprehensive study on the details surrounding Hawthorne's dismissal, which includes the rarely discussed possibility that Hawthorne deserved being terminated from his position, see Stephen Nissenbaum's "The Firing of Nathaniel Hawthorne" (*Essex Institute Historical Collections* 114 [1978]: 57-86), entry 363.

[v] With the exception of Henry F. Chorley's (see ER4), early English reviews are rarely cited or reprinted, but their authors' assessments were influential to contemporary American readers. The reviews by Margaret Oliphant, Richard Holt Hutton, and Leslie Stephen generally praised the novel even more highly than the critics had in early American notices.

[vi] Gary Scharnhorst confirms that *The Scarlet Letter* was "translated into German and French within months of its original American publication and into dozens of other languages over the next hundred and forty years" (xvii).

[vii] Richard Brodhead provides a fascinating account of Hawthorne's indebtedness to Fields in chapter three of *The School of Hawthorne* (pp. 54-59), emphasizing that Hawthorne largely owed his spectacular literary success to Fields, who worked tirelessly for years to keep Hawthorne's name before the public—beginning with the promotion of *The Scarlet Letter* and ending with "orchestrating the chorus of his obituaries" when Hawthorne died.

[viii] Jane Tompkins emphasizes that Hawthorne's prominence in the post-Civil War era had a great deal to do with his "relation to the mechanisms that produced literary and cultural opinion. Hawthorne's initial connections with the Boston literati, his acquaintance with Longfellow at college, his residence next door to Alcott and a half mile from Emerson (his son and Emerson's nephew roomed together at Harvard), his marrying a Peabody, becoming fast friends with Ticknor and Lowell, being published by the indefatigable Fields, socializing with Duyckinck and Whipple—these circumstances positioned Hawthorne's literary production so that it became the property of a dynastic cultural elite which came to identify itself with him" (29-30). Hawthorne's canonization, therefore, "was

the result of a network of common interests—familial, social, professional, commercial, and national" (32).

[ix] Nineteenth-century American writers were strongly encouraged to create an indigenous literature that would shake off traces of British influence and develop a uniquely American language and voice suited to the New World experience. The argument still wages today over whether *The Scarlet Letter* is more an American "romance" or an English "novel."

[x] Richard Brodhead explains in his chapter "The Modernization of Tradition" that Modernists exploded the nineteenth-century notion that classic literature was at the center of "high" culture, creating "racier or jazzier self-expressions" that made "older forms of conduct look painfully restrained and inhibited by contrast" (202). Literary critics who advanced the project of cultural reorganization and canon reconstruction include Van Wyck Brooks, H. L. Mencken, T. S. Eliot, Waldo Frank, Lewis Mumford, D. H. Lawrence, Cleanth Brooks, and Robert Penn Warren.

[xi] Melville's image underwent similar reconstruction. Best loved in the nineteenth century for his early romantic tales of exotic sea voyages (and passing into obscurity when his works grew darker and more complex), Melville became known almost exclusively in the twentieth century for his greatest novel, *Moby-Dick*, but also for other dark works such as *The Confidence Man* and *Billy Budd*. It became commonplace—as it still is today—to cite Melville's review of *Mosses from an Old Manse* (see ER6), which extols the genius of Hawthorne's dark vision, praising the "power of blackness" that defines Hawthorne's fictive imagination. Richard Brodhead finds it ironic, however, that just at the time that Melville (who considered himself misunderstood and undervalued as an author) was aligning himself with Hawthorne and erecting him as "the patron for a fiercely oppositional [and under-appreciated] school of writing," Hawthorne was finally "winning official acceptance as America's greatest novelist" (48).

[xii] Rita Gollin explains (see 661) that college enrollments continued to expand and courses in American literature proliferated as mid century approached, making it only natural that new editions of *The Scarlet Letter* were designed for an academic audience and were thus introduced by college professors like Carl Van Doren (in 1946), Malcolm Cowley (in 1948), Newton Arvin (in 1950 [see 1]), Roy Harvey Pearce (in 1957 [see 57]), and Leo Marx (in 1959 [see 78]).

[xiii] J. Donald Crowley writes in 1974 that Hawthorne still "remains for us a largely unsolved riddle," *especially* in

> the disjunction between our biographical and our critical assessments. His contemporaries saw the man himself as a figure of mystery, hauntingly withdrawn and etherealized, and his fiction as consisting oftentimes of pleasant and endearing, because (so they thought) ultimately harmless, fantasies. In contrast, we restructured him as a well-adjusted and even dully normal citizen at exactly the same time we were discovering his tales and romances to be full of deep ambiguities and tension-ridden conflicts (5).

[xiv] It is widely accepted that this story was first advanced by Hawthorne's own son, Julian, in his 1884 biography *Nathaniel Hawthorne and His Wife*, where he claims that his father started composing the novel on the very day he was fired. Most critics today disclaim Julian as a reliable source and are skeptical that Hawthorne began writing before the early fall of 1849. See entry 65, for instance, for a brief essay by Alfred S. Reid that specifically takes up the subject of the composition date. Refer to 607, however, for Gary Scharnhorst's suggestion that Julian might actually have been right.

[xv] Although Hawthorne was well respected by the intellectual class, literary men, and professional critics, he considered himself "the obscurest man of

letters in America." His most successful works up until this time were the short story collections *Twice-told Tales* (1837) and *Mosses from an Old Manse* (1846).

[xvi] Hawthorne described the ease with which he composed the novel to his publisher, James T. Fields: "*The Scarlet Letter* being all in one tone, I had only to get my pitch, and could then go on interminably" (Charvat xxv).

[xvii] The list of Whig conspirators who worked to oust Hawthorne from his position includes Charles W. Upham, William Lee, H. L. Conolly, Richard S. Rogers, and William M. Meredith.

[xviii] Some early local reviews did not mention "The Custom-House" at all, such as Caleb Foote's for the Salem *Gazette* (see 255) and an anonymous review from the Boston *Post* (see 295)—omissions that seem strangely out of accord with today's common assertion that Hawthorne's malicious mudslinging in "The Custom-House" preface is what originally attracted curious readers and made the *The Scarlet Letter* such a success.

[xix] As Benjamin Lease explains in 257, it was in response to this particular review that Hawthorne wrote his defensive Preface to the Second Edition.

[xx] One such study is by Henry Nash Smith (see 356), who contends that, although Hawthorne was eager to accommodate his readers and be a successful author so that he could financially support his growing family, he refused to reduce or cheapen his dark artistic vision to better suit readers' "sunshiny" tastes.

[xxi] To safeguard his children from this punishing legacy, he assumes personal responsibility in "The Custom-House" for the sins of two of his direct Puritan ancestors, William Hathorne, who mercilessly persecuted the Quakers, and John Hathorne, who likewise persecuted "witches" and sentenced them to their deaths—and he seems to make his peace with the past (or perhaps deceives himself into thinking that such peace can be made) before marching triumphantly into the future as "a citizen of somewhere else." It has been suggested that Hawthorne added the "w" to the family name in an effort to dissociate himself from the atrocities of his ancestors. It has also been suggested, however, that he

added the "w" for the much more practical purpose of adding a phonetic element to aid in the proper pronunciation of his name. A third view is that Hawthorne merely reverted to the old English spelling of his family's name for purposes that are not clear.

[xxii] See Subject Index under "Ambivalence" for specific entries.

[xxiii] The criticism reflects uncertainty, however, since it is so difficult to determine whether Hawthorne's sympathies lie with his conservative Puritan ancestors or with his liberal romantic contemporaries; it is unclear whether Hawthorne's comparison of the two centuries is intended to illustrate America's historical progress or its moral and religious degeneration—or some combination of the two.

[xxiv] Rita Gollin notes that, for critics of the 1960s who were consciously trying out new methodologies, *The Scarlet Letter* "was less a cause for celebration than an opportunity for critical analysis" (20).

[xxv] See "Characters, as aspects/projections of Hawthorne's personality or state of mind" in the Subject Index and "Psychoanalytic/Psychological Criticism" in the Critical Approach Index for more on this topic.

[xxvi] For other critics who attend to Hawthorne's shortcomings in *The Scarlet Letter*, see "Flaws in novel" and "Inconsistencies" in the Subject Index. See also 76 and 541 for essays that address Hawthorne's own dissatisfaction with the novel.

[xxvii] In 314, Charles Swann names several critics whose investigations of *The Scarlet Letter* hinge on its status as a non-realistic American art form, namely Charles Feidelson, Jr., R. W. B. Lewis, Richard Chase, Leslie A. Fiedler, Daniel Hoffman, and Joel Porte.

[xxviii] For certain critics who champion Hester (especially feminists), this is one of the chief problems with the novel, that Hawthorne stifles Hester's romantic individualism at the end of the novel and disappointingly "domesticates" or returns her to the proper sphere of womanhood to conform to conventional

"womanly" values. It has been suggested that Hawthorne does this because he is fearful of Hester's lawless intellect and powerful sexuality, or that he is too socially conservative or patriarchally committed to permit Hester's radical views and free speculations; or that he is anti-feminist or a mysogynist; or that Hester's situation is meant to illustrate the perils of self-reliance and the inadequacy of self-alienating romantic individualism.

[xxix] A host of studies have been written on Hawthorne's feminist or anti-feminist leanings. For studies that view Hawthorne as feminist, see 419, 554, 827, and 858. For studies that view Hawthorne as anti-feminist/misogynist, see EC7, 216, 303, 535, 594, 716, and 827. See also studies that argue for Hawthorne's endorsing of traditional patriarchal beliefs (594, 716, 764, 804, and 827) and his rejection of patriarchal traditions (588, 614, 654, 656, 687, 720, 721, 768, 822, 858, and 859).

[xxx] Baym prefaces her argument in "Thwarted Nature" by explaining that pre-feminists and feminists writing in the seventies and early eighties, whose agendas involved either "uncover[ing] the hidden, destructive attitudes toward women" in male writing or "turn[ing] away from male authors entirely," actually tended to avoid Hawthorne in their literary re-evaluations because his stories "presented many problems to the critic who wished to define him as an orthodox espouser of patriarchal attitudes" (58).

[xxxi] Although Arac and Bercovitch are cited most frequently in discussions of Hawthorne's conservative social philosophy, Lee R. Edwards (see 458) was the first to suggest that Hester's return and conformity to conventional domestic values indicate that Hawthorne was uncomfortable with incarnating a vision that would prove antithetical to social stability.

[xxxii] Bell and Craig Milliman (see 758) extend their arguments to include Hester as a master rhetorician herself who also conceals and expresses her "deviant" impulses.

^{xxxiii} As the Critical Approach Index states under "Feminist Studies," the first subcategory of "black feminist studies" contains criticism that examines *The Scarlet Letter* in reference to issues of race and slavery and mostly in connection to African-American fiction (especially to the fiction of Toni Morrison). The second subcategory, "gender studies," examines Hawthorne's gender anxieties and/or his treatment of gender roles in the novel. The third grouping, "family studies," includes several examinations of *The Scarlet Letter* that treat the novel as a "family romance" or that concern marriage, domesticity, maternity, paternity, or the parent/child relationship.

^{xxxiv} See the note following entry 439 of the bibliography for more specifics on Crews's reassessment.

^{xxxv} Baym condemned New Critics Richard Harter Fogle, Roy R. Male, and Hyatt H. Waggoner, all of whom followed fashionable turn-of-the-century biographical criticism, which viewed Hawthorne inaccurately and anachronistically as a melancholy, pessimistic hermit haunted by his inescapable Puritan past and religion. As Baym and several newer biographical studies have pointed out since the publication of Stewart's pivotal 1948 biography, Hawthorne was more lighthearted, more secular-minded, and more society-oriented than earlier accounts had allowed. In her later feminist essay (406), Baym similarly faulted Darrel Abel for maintaining an outdated New Critical bias in his post-formalist treatment of *The Scarlet Letter*, censuring Abel's male-chauvinistic, patriarchy-endorsing estimation of Dimmesdale as the rightful protagonist of the novel—and even using Abel's New Critical method against him (by focusing strictly on the text and identifying the number of times Hester and Dimmesdale are the subjects of individual chapters) to "prove" that Hester is, in fact, the main character.

^{xxxvi} Two critics who reacted in nearly identical fashion against New Historicist readings that praised Hawthorne's "progressive" stance on political issues, Eric Cheyfitz (see 732) and Christopher Diffee (see 779), found

Hawthorne's political passivity on the issue of slavery to be inexcusable, reprehensible, and even immoral; they both concluded that what is mistaken by New Historicists for liberal "equivocal pluralist politics" in the novel is actually Hawthorne's ultra-conservative, empty, and passionless passivism.

xxxvii Two early studies that insisted Hawthorne and his literary reputation were drastically overrated and claimed that his classic status was undeserved were Rudolph Von Abele's 1955 essay "The Wages of Sin" in *The Death of the Artist: A Study of Hawthorne's Disintegration* (see 39) and Martin Green's infamous 1963 essay "The Hawthorne Myth: a Protest" (see 143). For other studies that address defects in *The Scarlet Letter*, see "Flaws" and "Inconsistencies" in the Subject Index. For two essays that speak to Hawthorne's own dissatisfaction with *The Scarlet Letter*, see 76 and 541.

xxxviii Over the decades, several critics who have examined the evolution of Hawthorne's literary development consider *The Scarlet Letter* as the culmination of his early tales, frequently noting that Hawthorne's notebook entries indicate that the idea for the novel had been brewing in his imagination for years, with "germs" of it developing in several of his short stories set in Puritan New England ("Endicott and the Red Cross" especially [written in 1837], in which a beautiful woman is publicly punished for committing adultery and is doomed to wear the letter "A" on the breast of her gown).

xxxix For critical commentary on these and other authors who were influenced by Hawthorne, refer to the Subject Index under "Influence." As a curious sidenote, Charles Dickens, George Eliot, and Elizabeth Gaskell are all occasionally identified as having been influenced by *The Scarlet Letter* (and a few critics have suggested affinities between Hawthorne and English authors Emily Brontë and Thomas Hardy); yet there is an absence of studies that trace similarities between Hawthorne and English writers who might have followed in his literary footsteps.

[xl] The narrator begs sympathy and mercy for Chillingworth when he speculates that "It is a curious subject of observation and inquiry, whether hatred and love be not the same thing at bottom" (260).

[xli] See 252 and 258 in particular for studies that examine Hester and Dimmesdale's incompatibility.

[xlii] Lawyers, it seems, find *The Scarlet Letter* ripe with legal issues, as two more titles attest: William T. Barto's "*The Scarlet Letter* and the Military Justice System" in *The Army Lawyer* (297 [1997]: 3) and Daniel L. Feldman's "The 'Scarlet Letter Laws' of the 1990s: A Response to Critics" in the *Albany Law Review* (60.4 [1997]: 1081-1125).

[xliii] Critical assessments for *A Month of Sundays, Roger's Version,* and *S.* can be found throughout the bibliography. For specifics on them, see the Author Index and/or the Subject Index under "Comparisons" and Influence."

[xliv] See 319, 325, 453, 662, 765, 767, 774, 778, 785, 807, 833, 845, 846, 852, 853, and 863 for comparisons of movie adaptations of *The Scarlet Letter* to the novel.

[xlv] It remains true that "The Custom-House" is still sometimes excluded from classroom study, especially among younger audiences, even though it is generally accepted today as a crucial link to the novel itself.

[xlvi] As one of the most popularly taught novels, *The Scarlet Letter* has generated many resources for both student and instructor alike. See "General Student Introductions to the Novel and Study Guides" in section C and "Teaching Aids and Guides" in section D of the Resource Guide for titles of such works.

[xlvii] Compiling the Subject Index was especially helpful in mapping areas of interest among scholars and critics. One need only skim it to pinpoint major issues and types of studies, popular views of Hawthorne, and recurring treatments of specific scenes, themes, conflicts, images, and symbols from the novel.

[xlviii] These include one or more essays by a lesbian/gay theorist, who identifies "gay episodes" or homoerotic encounters in *The Scarlet Letter* and

closely examines the homosexual aspects of Dimmesdale and Chillingworth's relationship (Scott S. Derrick [see 747], Karen L. Kilcup [see 784], Lora Romero [see 799], and John N. Duvall [see 857])); a Marxist, who examines the social and political circumstances in which the novel was produced, and identifies class struggles and conflicts within the story itself (Caroline Borden [see 268] and Jay Grossman [see 708]); a stylistician, who focuses on grammatical structures or other technical aspects of language and uses linguistic terms and methods in his or her analysis of the novel (Kiyoshi Ito [see 69], Arie Staal[see 345], Mary Jane Hurst [see 619], and Sylvie Mathé [see 735]); a post-colonialist, who examines the representation of different cultures and ethnic backgrounds in the novel, seeks to identify limitations in the Western outlook, and brings to the forefront neglected issues of colonialization and imperialism while also emphasizing states of marginality, plurality, and "Otherness" (Carolyn Duffey [see 780], Aleida Assmann [see 830], and Judie Newman [see 840]); and a phenomenologist, who deals with atemporal and ahistorical "criticism of consciousness," attempting to reveal the underlying nature of consciousness and phenomena in the novel and stressing the perceiver's vital and central role in determining meaning (John Carlos Rowe [see 403]).

Works Cited

Baym, Nina. "The Major Phase I, 1850." *The Shape of Hawthorne's Career.* Ithaca: Cornell UP, 123-151.

----. "Hawthorne's *Scarlet Letter*: Producing and Maintaining an American Literary Classic." *Journal of Aesthetic Education* 30 (1996): 61-75.

----. "The Significance of Plot in Hawthorne's Romances." *Ruined Eden of the Present: Hawthorne, Melville, and Poe: Critical Essays in Honor of Darrel Abel.* Ed. G. R. Thompson and Virgil L. Lokke. West Lafayette: Purdue UP, 1981. 49-70.

----. "Thwarted Nature: Nathaniel Hawthorne as Feminist." *American Novelists Revisted: Essays in Feminist Criticism.* Ed. Fritz Fleischmann. Boston: Hall, 1982. 58-77.

Bellis, Peter. "Representing Dissent: Hawthorne and the Drama of Revolt." *ESQ: A Journal of the American Renaissance* 41 (1995): 97-119.

Blair, Walter. "Hawthorne." *Eight American Authors: A Review of Research and Criticism.* Ed. Floyd Stovall. New York: Norton, 1956. 100-152.

Brodhead, Richard [H.]. *The School of Hawthorne.* New York: Oxford UP, 1986.

Chandler, Elizabeth L. "Salem Again, 1845-1850. Period of the Last Tales and *The Scarlet Letter*." *A Study of the Sources of the Tales and Romances Written by Nathaniel Hawthorne Before 1853.* Darby: Arden Library, 1926. 38-44.

Charvat, William. Introduction. *The Scarlet Letter* in *The Centenary Edition of Works of Nathaniel Hawthorne.* Vol. 1. Ed. William Charvat et al. Columbus: Ohio State UP, 1962. xv-xxvii.

Clark, Jr., C. E. Frazer. "Posthumous Papers of a Decapitated Surveyor: *The Scarlet Letter* in the Salem Press." *Studies in the Novel* 2 (1970): 395-419.

Cohen, B. Bernard. Preface. *The Recognition of Nathaniel Hawthorne: Selected Criticism Since 1828*. Ann Arbor: U of Michigan P, 1969. vii-xvii.

Colacurcio, Michael J. "The Spirit and the Sign." Introduction. *New Essays on The Scarlet Letter*. Ed. Michael J. Colacurcio. New York: Cambridge UP, 1985. 1-28.

Crowley, J. Donald. "Hawthorne Criticism and The Return to History" *Studies in the Novel* 6 (1974): 98-105.

Gerber, John C. Introduction. *Twentieth-Century Interpretations of The Scarlet Letter: A Collection of Critical Essays*. Ed. John C. Gerber. Englewood Cliffs: Prentice-Hall, 1968. 1-15.

Gibaldi, Joseph. *MLA Style Manual and Guide to Scholarly Publishing*. 2nd ed. New York: MLA, 1998.

Gollin, Rita K. *"The Scarlet Letter." From Cover to Cover: The Presentation of Hawthorne's Major Romances*. Ed. Richard C. Fyffe. *Essex Institute Historical Collections* 127.1 (1991): 12-30.

Gross, Seymour L. "Prologue to *The Scarlet Letter*: Hawthorne's Fiction to 1850." *A Scarlet Letter Handbook*. Ed. Seymour L. Gross. Belmont: Wadsworth Publishing, 1960. 1-14.

Harner, James L. *On Compiling an Annotated Bibliography*. Rev. ed. New York: MLA, 1991.

Idol, John L., Jr., and Melinda M. Ponder, eds. *Hawthorne and Women: Engendering and Expanding the Hawthorne Tradition*. Amherst: U of Massachusetts P, 1999. 301-305.

James, Henry. *Hawthorne*. 1879. New York: AMS, 1968.

Johnson, Claudia Durst. *Understanding The Scarlet Letter: A Student Casebook to Issues, Sources, and Historical Documents*. Westport: Greenwood Press, 1995.

Kennedy-Andrews, Elmer, ed. *Nathaniel Hawthorne: The Scarlet Letter*. New York: Columbia UP, 1999.

Kesterson, David B. Introduction. *Critical Essays on Hawthorne's The Scarlet Letter*. Ed. David B. Kesterson. Boston: G. K. Hall, 1988. 1-18.

Lawrence, D.H. *Phoenix: The Posthumous Papers of D.H. Lawrence*. Ed. Edward D. McDonald. New York: Viking, 1936.

Male, Roy R. "'From the Innermost Germ': The Organic Principle in Hawthorne's Fiction." *ELH: Journal of English Literary History* 20 (1953): 218-236.

Male, Roy R. "Hawthorne." *American Literary Scholarship 1969*. Durham: Duke UP, 1971. 18-35.

Minton, Shira Pavis. "Hawthorne and the Handmaid: An Examination of the Law's Use as a Tool of Oppression." *Wisconsin Women's Law Journal* 13 (1998): 45-73.

Murfin, Ross C. "Introduction: The Biographical and Historical Background." *Case Studies in Contemporary Criticism: Nathaniel Hawthorne: The Scarlet Letter*. Ed. Ross C. Murfin. Boston: Bedford Books of St. Martin's Press, 1991. 3-19.

Hawthorne, Nathaniel. *The Scarlet Letter* in *The Centenary Edition of Works of Nathaniel Hawthorne*. Vol. 1. Ed. William Charvat et al. Columbus: Ohio State UP, 1962.

Scharnhorst, Gary. Introduction. *The Critical Response to Nathaniel Hawthorne's The Scarlet Letter*. *Critical Responses in Arts and Letters, Number 2*. New York: Greenwood Press, 1992. xiii-xxx.

Spikes, Michael P. *Understanding Contemporary American Literary Theory*. Columbia: U of South Carolina P, 1997.

Tompkins, Jane. "Masterpiece Theater: The Politics of Hawthorne's Literary Reputation." *Sensational Designs: The Cultural Work of American Fiction 1790-1860*. New York: Oxford UP, 1985. 1-39.

Wagenknecht, Edward. *"The Scarlet Letter." Nathaniel Hawthorne: The Man, His Tales and Romances*. New York: Continuum, 1989. 78-95.

Walcutt, Charles Child. *"The Scarlet Letter* and Its Modern Critics." *Nineteenth-Century Fiction* 7 (1953): 251-264.

Warren, Austin. Introduction. *Nathaniel Hawthorne: Representative Selections, With Introduction, Bibliography, and Notes.* New York: American Book Co., 1934. xi-lxxiii.

Wamser, Garry. "The Scarlet Contract: Puritan Resurgence, the Unwed Mother, and Her Child." *Law and Literature Perspectives.* Ed. Bruce L. Rockwood. New York: Peter Lang, 1996. 381-406.

Young, Philip. "Hawthorne and 100 Years: A Report from the Academy." *Kenyon Review* 27 (1965): 215-232.

Errata

I created and organized the 867 entries in the bibliography, along with all cross-references and indexes, before I or my editor could scrupulously proofread and/or edit each citation. In proofreading, we discovered several errors that could not be readily corrected, because such corrections would have involved renumbering every entry and changing the hundreds of numbers within the cross-references and indexes. Attention to these errors should, therefore, be provided for the reader.

1. Entry nine should be deleted because it is a reprint.
2. Entry 134 should only appear in section E on Bibliographies in the Resource Guide (Part IV).
3. Jane Lundblad's 1964 essay (under entry 155) "Hawthorne and Gothic Romance" was originally written in 1947 and should appear in Part II under "Early Influential Criticism (Pre-1950)."
4. The note following the asterisk under entry 447, David Leverenz's 1983 essay "Mrs. Hawthorne's Headache: Reading *The Scarlet Letter*," which indicated modest revision to the original essay, should probably have been converted into its own annotated entry in 1989.
5. Entry 862 should be deleted because it is not a substantial piece of criticism.
6. All entries from the *Nathaniel Hawthorne Journal*, a hardbound collection that appeared annually 1971-1978, are incorrectly placed under "Essays and Studies in Books" instead of under "Journal Essays and Notes" for their particular years.

PART I

The Most Frequently Anthologized Early Reviews
(Listed chronologically after the novel's publication on March 16, 1850)

ER1   Duychinck, Evert A[ugustus]. *"The Scarlet Letter." Literary World* 6 (March 30, 1850): 323-325.

Distinguishes *Letter* as a fascinating "psychological romance" with a "severe" but "wholesome" moral, and not only praises Hawthorne's depiction of Puritanism but also applauds Hawthorne's "delicate" handling of adultery. *Letter* is "a sounder piece of Puritan divinity than we have been of late accustomed to hear from the degenerate successors of Cotton Mather. We hardly know another writer who has lived so much among the new school who would have handled this delicate subject without an infusion of George Sand [referring here to novels of seduction and adultery modeled after the risqué French school]. The spirit of his old Puritan ancestors, to whom he refers in the preface, lives in Nathaniel Hawthorne."

ER2   Ripley, George. *"The Scarlet Letter." New York Daily Tribune* (April 1, 1850): 2.

A Unitarian minister and transcendental liberal (who was also one of the founders of the Brook Farm experiment), Ripley praises *Letter* enthusiastically, especially for its use of Gothic elements, and compares Hawthorne's genius and enchanting art to Edgar Allan Poe's, suggesting that the former's is superior because his supernatural tales "are always motivated with wonderful insight and skill to which the intellect of Poe was a stranger." *Letter* is Hawthorne's greatest achievement, despite the "objectionably querulous" tone of "The Custom-House."

ER3   Whipple, Edwin P[ercy] *"The Scarlet Letter." Graham's Magazine* 36 (May 1850): 345-346.

Similar to Evert A. Duychinck (ER1) in his praise of *Letter*'s "very instructive and edifying" moral treatment of adultery, Whipple argues that Hawthorne "utterly undermine[s] the whole philosophy on which the French novel rests." The moral purpose of the "beautiful and touching romance" is, in fact, "made more definite" by the dark and intense treatment of his subject, so that even "the most abandoned libertine could not read the volume without being thrilled into something like virtuous resolution." This concentrated gloom is relieved only by "The Custom-

House," which reveals the exhaustless "fountain of mirth Hawthorne has at his command."

ER4 Chorley, Henry F[othergill]. *"The Scarlet Letter: A Romance."* *Athenaeum* (June 5, 1850): 634.

Rating Hawthorne "among the most original and peculiar writers of American fiction," this English review of the "more than ordinarily painful" tale, in which Hester's "painful purification through repentance is crowned by no perfect happiness," acknowledges a "lofty," pure, sympathetic, and skillful treatment of a subject that Chorley nonetheless doubts is legitimate for fiction.

ER5 Abbott, Anne W. "Hawthorne's *Scarlet Letter*." *North American Review* 71 (July 1850): 135-148.

In this very lengthy review, the first to express dissatisfaction with the questionable morality of the novel, Abbott (a fundamentalist Christian) finds fault first with the "racy and pungent" style of the "naughty" "Custom-House" sketch, although she praises the magical effect of Hawthorne's style in the novel and compares his delineation of characters with that of Dickens. She then expresses irritation over Hawthorne's speculation that love and hate are perhaps "the same thing at bottom," and casts doubt on the effectiveness of Hester's character to provoke a moral stance. Abbot confesses sympathy for Hester early in the novel when she suffers in seeming humility and self-abnegation, and "we have hope for her soul"; but "anon her humility catches a new tint, and we find it pride [. . .]. She disappoints us [. . .] when we were looking to behold a Christian." Abbott wonders why an author of such graceful skill, with such a "wizard power over language," did not choose "a less revolting subject."

ER6 Melville, Herman. "Hawthorne and His Mosses." *Literary World* 7 (Aug. 17, 1850): 125-127, 145-147.

Beginning with a review of *Mosses From an Old Manse* four years after its publication in 1846 and then briefly evaluating "Twice-told Tales" and *Letter*, Melville praises Hawthorne's exceptional genius and imaginative skill, admiring most the blackness that is "ten times black." Hawthorne's "power of blackness," Melville speculates, "derives its force from its appeals to that Calvinistic sense of Innate Depravity and Original Sin, from whose visitations, in some shape or other, no deeply thinking mind is always and wholly free." Of *Letter*, Melville writes only that it, like "Twice-told Tales," is "full of manifold, strange, and diffusive beauties."

ER7   Loring, George B[ailey]. "Hawthorne's *Scarlet Letter.*" *Massachusetts Quarterly Review* 3 (Sept. 1850): 484-500.

Devoted to the promotion of transcendental ideals (though not a transcendentalist himself), Loring eloquently and enthusiastically defends the novel against those skeptical of its moral import. He praises Hawthorne's freedom of mind as both a "speculative philosopher" and an "ethical thinker" and commends Hawthorne's nearly supernatural rendering of man's nature, going so far as to call the novel "a vehicle of religion and ethics" because it exposes Puritan dogma as intolerant and inhumane and reveals the redeeming power of sin and temptation—since untried virtue is useless. Great religious truth "bows instinctively around [Hester's isolated, cast out] life of agony," which makes her far superior to the cowardly and Calvinist-belief-bound Dimmesdale in terms of "moral and religious excellence." Guided by the power of love, Hester's open confession brings her strength and heroic courage, while Dimmesdale's failure to confess only aggravates his "false delicacy" and hypocritical nature. [For more on this important early review, see Perry Miller (3).]

ER8   Swisshelm, Jane. "*The Scarlet Letter.*" *The Saturday Visitor* (Sept. 28, 1850): 146.

"If [Hawthorne] meant to teach the sinfulness of Hester's sin [. . .], his book is the most sublime failure of the age," since Hester shines as "the most glorious creation of fiction that has ever crossed our path." As for Pearl, Swisshelm argues that, as a punishment sent to Hester, "we never saw a mother who would not be happy to be so punished." If Hawthorne meant to teach a moral lesson, "he had better try again." "For our part if we knew there was such another woman as Hester Prynne in Boston now, we should travel all the way there to pay our respects, while the honorable characters of the book are such poor affairs it would scarce be worth while throwing a mud-ball at the best of them."

ER9   Brownson, Orestes A[ugustus]. "*The Scarlet Letter.*" *Brownson's Quarterly Review* 7 (Oct. 1850): 528-532.

Attacks Hawthorne's novel of "fearful power" by referring to it as "genius perverted," enjoyable only by those with "no well defined religious belief" and "no fixed principles of virtue." Its lack of moral and religious effect, compounded by the fact that its loathsome subject is presented "with all the fascination of genius, and all the claims of a highly polished style," makes *Letter* an altogether scandalous and offensive read. Hawthorne is "wholly ignorant of Christian asceticism," evident in that both Hester and

Dimmesdale fail to repent their crime against God—which is not even presented as sinful. Hester suffers only regret and disgrace, and Dimmesdale merely repents his own hypocrisy and cowardice. Hawthorne's representation of the Puritans has its merits but is "unjust" because the Puritans' lenient treatment of Hester's adultery is far more Christian than Hawthorne gives them credit for. Thus "we should commend where the author condemns and condemn where he commends."

ER10 Coxe, Arthur Cleveland. "The Writings of Hawthorne." *Church Review* 3 (Jan. 1851): 489-511.

This lengthy and fervent attack claims to attempt an impartial review of *Letter* to show Hawthorne the deleterious effect that his immoral novel produces "on a large, but quiet portion of the community," especially on young ladies who "do injury to their young sense of delicacy" by reading such a "dirty story" that clearly sympathizes with its "criminals." That Hawthorne belongs to the insufferably self-important "Bay School of writers"* is forgivable only because he almost displays the talent of Washington Irving—lacking only tasteful discrimination and "instinctive delicacy." But viewing the novel as one in a growing trend of American imitations of George Sand, Coxe (himself an Episcopal bishop) asks two questions: "Is the French era actually begun in our literature?" and "[Must] a running undercurrent of filth [. . .] become requisite to a romance, as death in the fifth act of a tragedy?" Like Brownson (ER9), Coxe asserts that American literature—as of yet "undefiled"—should be of "moral benefit" to readers, and thus declares his astonishment over Hawthorne's choosing adultery for his subject in this "nauseous amour of a Puritan pastor [. . .] and a frail creature [. . .] whose mind is [. . .] more debauched than her body." He is morally outraged and disgusted by Dimmesdale's suggestion in the forest scene that adultery is less serious than Chillingworth's crime of revenge, and is further offended by Hester's desire for a life outside the "glorious sphere of [a woman's] duties and her joys." Hester's thinking about tearing down relations between the sexes and building them anew is "an insult and a degradation" to "the daughters of America."

*The "[Massachusetts] Bay School" that Coxe smugly refers to here is the Concord School of writers, a group commonly associated with the transcendentalist movement in New England.

Note: For the most complete collection of the early reviews and a checklist of 19 additional reviews of *The Scarlet Letter*, see *Nathaniel Hawthorne: The Contemporary Reviews*, compiled by editors John L. Idol, Jr., and Buford Jones (Cambridge: Cambridge UP, 1994. 117-155). See 725 for the complete list of reviewers in this book. For more on the early reviews (including additional ones from those cited above), see EC8, 255, 257, 273, 295, 310, 332, 361, 396, 670, and 789. For other, less comprehensive, collections of reviews (many of which in excerpted form), see 103, 164, 199, 234, 249, 250, 353, 558, 829.

PART II

Early Influential Criticism (Pre-1950)

A few of the 41 entries below may not be recognized today as having been relevant to Hawthorne studies, but they nonetheless later appeared in anthologies that collected significant criticism on *The Scarlet Letter* and have, for that reason, been retained. The vast majority of the entries were and still are considered pioneering and influential studies on the novel.

EC1   Arvin, Newton. *Hawthorne*. Boston: Little, Brown, 1929.

Arvin's brief analysis of *Letter* (pp. 187-191) demonstrates the spiritual starvation that results from the main characters losing their place in the "magnetic chain of humanity." While Dimmesdale's sin of spiritual pride is more serious than Hester's sin (which Arvin does not name), and both are "finally perverted and vitiated by the central falsity of [their lives]," it is Chillingworth's monstrous crime that lies at the very root of the tragedy and brings about his spiritual ruin: the pride of a detached intellect. Arvin also discusses *Letter*'s limitations in relation to *House of the Seven Gables* and *Blithedale Romance* (pp. 209-219), and although he finds *Letter* vastly superior to them, he reproaches Hawthorne for the "dreamlike, inelastic, ungainly, and ill-spaced" action and the "woodenness" of the narrative movement that make the novel too much like a pageant or an opera "to be a novel of the very first order." [Many critics acknowledge that this biography marks the shift to a modern psychological consideration of Hawthorne.]

EC2   Blair, Walter. "Color, Light, and Shadow in Hawthorne's Fiction." *New England Quarterly* 15 (1942): 74-94.

Hawthorne's handling of "sunlight and shadow, bright colors and black" gives "various moral significations" to his works, helping "to characterize, to mark important changes in the narrative, and to stand for moral meanings." Although the use of this symbolic device can be traced in several tales (namely "Minister's Black Veil" and "Rappaccini's Daughter") and in all of the romances, Blair limits serious consideration to *House of the Seven Gables* and *Letter*, the latter of which most symbolically exploits "manipulations of color and gleams of light" in order to illustrate the character development and moral conditions of Hester, Dimmesdale, Chillingworth, and Pearl.

EC3   Brownell, W. C. "Hawthorne: *The Scarlet Letter*." *American Prose Masters*. New York: Charles Scribner's Sons, 1909. 116-123.

Excepting his achievement in *Letter*, an imaginative and original masterpiece, Hawthorne frittered away his talents, employing not his imagination but his undisciplined fancy "to mingle bad allegory with worse symbolism." But in *Letter*, "the Puritan *Faust*," we have "a story neither of sin nor of the situation of illicit love" but of "the concealment of sin amid circumstances that make a sin of concealment itself." For once Hawthorne got it right in creating an "allegory neither vitiated by caprice nor sterilized by moralizing, but firmly grounded in reality and nature." His characters are "very real and very human," and Pearl is simply a "jewel of romance." Chillingworth, however, is "a mistake, or at most a wasted opportunity," since Hawthorne fails to "complete" the tragedy by showing how an innocent shares in the punishment of the guilty and instead wastes that character "into a mere function of malignity." Hawthorne "atones" for this error by focusing exclusively on the psychology of Hester and Dimmesdale, perhaps even increasing the "poignancy of his effect" by so "narrowing his range" to eliminate their passion and depict only the concealment of sin "rather than depicting its phenomena and its results."

EC4   Carpenter, Frederic I. "Scarlet A Minus." *College English* 5 (1944): 173-180.

Finding fault with *Letter*'s ambiguous logic and moralistic conclusion, Carpenter grants that its very imperfections illustrate "a fundamental confusion in modern thought" and make it a classic, although one of "a minor order." Three perspectives determine whether "the action symbolized by the scarlet letter" is "wholly sinful." Traditional moralists would argue "yes," since Hester's act of passion is the fatal flaw that causes the tragedy. Romantic enthusiasts would answer "no," because Hester courageously follows the natural laws of her instinctive nature, the tragedy stemming from the intrinsic evil of a tyrannical, restrictive society. Transcendentalists would answer "partly yes"—because Hester sins against both Dimmesdale's sense of morality and her own sense of "higher truth" by protecting Chillingworth's identity—and "partly no," because Hester simply does not share Dimmesdale's orthodox morality and thus attempts to transcend it to a "higher law." Each interpretation is possible, the novel being so "rich in suggestion," but, unfortunately, "Hawthorne the moralist sought to destroy this richness." The novel's "dramatically perfect" conflicting moralities are flawed by "moralistic, subjective criticism of Hester Prynne"—a transcendental character disappointingly damned for being "romantically immoral." Ultimately, Hawthorne's failure results from his "never remotely admitting the possible truth of the transcendental ideal which he had objectively described Hester Prynne as realizing." Yet the greatness of the novel still lies in Hester: "She achieved spiritual greatness in spite of her own human weakness, in spite of the prejudices of her Puritan society, and, finally, in spite of the prejudices of her creator himself."

EC5   Chandler, Elizabeth L. "Salem Again, 1845-1850. Period of the Last Tales and *The Scarlet Letter.*" *A Study of the Sources of the Tales and Romances Written by Nathaniel Hawthorne Before 1853.* Darby: Arden Library, 1926. 38-44.

Having personally interviewed Custom House employees in Salem for this book, once considered a classic on Hawthorne's life and authorship, Chandler discusses the sheer storm of animosity that Custom House employees and their successors felt toward Hawthorne after the publication of the novel until "recently." She addresses the somber nature of the novel and traces the historical origin of *Letter*'s main themes and characters to specific passages from Hawthorne's "Notebook." Chandler humorously concludes: "It would be possible to give references for Hawthorne's coming into contact with the crime of adultery; however, no man can avoid that."

EC6   Dickens, Charles. "To John Forster." July 1851. *The Letters of Charles Dickens.* Vol. 2. Ed. Walter Dexter. Bloomsbury: The Nonesuch Press, 1938. 335.

"I finished *Letter* yesterday. It falls off sadly after that fine opening scene. The psychological part of the story is very much overdone, and not truly done I think. Their suddenness of meeting and agreeing to go away together, after all those years, is very poor. Mr. Chillingworth ditto. The child out of nature altogether. And Mr. Dimmisdale [sic] certainly never could have begotten her." [For an examination of Dickens's objections to Hawthorne's novel, see Ghulam Ali Chaudhry's "Dickens and Hawthorne" (160).]

EC7   Doubleday, Neal Frank. "Hawthorne's Hester and Feminism." *PMLA* 54 (1939): 825-828.

It remains a "persistent misapprehension" among interpretive critics of the novel that Hawthorne sides with Hester and her "consecration" speech that advocates "a new standard of sex morality." Quite the contrary, Hawthorne embodies his criticism of the nineteenth-century feminist movement through his portrait of Hester and therefore "would hardly have intended an identification of her views and his own." Not "the splendid example of self-reliance some of Hester's interpreter's would have her be," the character is rather "infinitely pathetic," presented in a similar negative manner to the "type feminist" Zenobia in *Blithedale Romance*.

EC8   Faust, Bertha. *"The Scarlet Letter, The House of the Seven Gables,* and *The Blithedale Romance." Hawthorne's Contemporaneous Reputation: A Study of Literary Opinion in America and England, 1828-1864.* Philadelphia: n.p., 1939. 67-117.

With Hawthorne's publication of *Letter*, his already excellent reputation among the intellectual classes took a sudden leap in the estimation of the popular public consciousness.   Faust examines eight representative reviews (pp. 67-86) as they appeared in *Literary World*, the *New York Daily Tribune, Graham's Magazine, Athenaeum, North American Review, Massachusetts Quarterly Review, Brownson's Quarterly Review,* and *Church Review* (see Section I) to assess *Letter*'s initial impression upon the public, finding most curious that, although many critics often cite the early reviews as mixed, most of the commentators were quite satisfied with the moral import of the book and in fact argued that Hawthorne clearly vindicated conventional and moral laws in his telling of the tale.

EC9   Gerber, John C. "Form and Content in *The Scarlet Letter." New England Quarterly* 17 (1944): 25-55.

One of the first New Critical approaches to the novel, Gerber's essay argues that form and content are so intricately and effectively interwoven in the novel that their union bespeaks "a work of rather astonishing sophistication." *Letter*'s form is divided into four parts, "each of which gains its distinctiveness from the character that precipitates or is responsible for the action that takes place within its limits." First the Puritan community (chapters 1-8), next Chillingworth (chapters 9-12), then Hester (chapters 13-20), and finally Dimmesdale (chapters 21-24) successively precipitate and forcefully propel the dramatic action. While the form is four-layered, the content is tri-fold, involving sin, isolation, and reunion. Above all, *Letter* is a study of isolation, although sin and reunion play a necessary interactive part in what respectively determines and ends the term of isolation. No inherent crime is involved with "sin" itself but rather "a violation of what the sinner thinks he violates." Likewise, the reasons for Hester's isolation are less important than the psychological effects of her enforced estrangement. While she has not sinned against God, natural laws, or the Puritan community in her own mind, Hester does seem to feel guilt about violating the "law of order" with Dimmesdale, having "introduced an act of disorder in an orderly universe." [For adaptations of Gerber's thesis, see EC25, 42, 46, 95, 138, and 364. For a reading that refutes Gerber's thesis, see Robert F. Haugh (48).]

EC10 Gorman, Herbert. *Hawthorne, A Study in Solitude.* N.p.: George H. Doran, 1929. 83-90.

This early psychological study interprets *Letter* as about the results of adulterous sin as they gradually grow more and more terrible for Dimmesdale and Chillingworth; for Hester's "slow years of ridicule and the stony path of regeneration" are nothing compared to the agony Dimmesdale experiences as the secret consciousness of his sin eats into him or the torment Chillingworth feels as he, with fiendish patience, grows more and more malevolent in his desire to destroy Dimmesdale. Yet Hester and Dimmesdale both triumph whereas Chillingworth does not, since their problems are resolved with confession. Overall, the characters are not flesh and blood so much as they are composed of "moonlight and abstract qualities," but they, like the air of unreality that permeates the entire novel, are "the result of careful esthetic selectivity."

EC11 Grabo, Carl H. "The Omniscient Author—*The Scarlet Letter.*" *The Technique of the Novel.* New York: Charles Scribner's Sons, 1928. 44-53.*

Though he praises the novel for its mysterious qualities, Grabo finds fault with several things, most notably Hawthorne's method of generalizing character analysis and sparing use of an omniscient narrator. Hester is clearly the central figure of the three main protagonists, since she is the only one described with partial omniscience, but even she never becomes "flesh and blood" for the reader because of Hawthorne's overly objective presentation of her character. He "lectures to his class as though conducting a clinic. Only now and again does he seem to remember that his subject is an individual human being, not a pathological case." In the end, "we are not deeply concerned with the fates of the individual characters but with the mysteries of human destiny upon which they throw a brief and uncertain light."

*Reprinted in 1964 (Ann Arbor: Edwards Brothers).

EC12 Hawthorne, Julian. "Problems of *The Scarlet Letter.*" *Atlantic Monthly* 57 (1886): 471-485.

Although the title suggests a discussion of problems within the novel, this review by Hawthorne's son seems to answer to critics who have had problems of their own with *Letter* and offers nothing but generous praise for Hawthorne's management of his subject, for his representation of characters (none of whom are meant to elicit our sympathy, he says), and for his overall craft. The novel is "alive with the miraculous vitality of genius," combining "the strength and substance of an oak with the subtle organization of a rose." Julian specifically defends Hawthorne's status as a modern—and perhaps misunderstood—writer who reaches in *Letter* "unconventional conclusions" whose true meanings "would scarce be apprehended by one reader in twenty." "The reader may choose his depth according to his inches," he writes, "but only a tall man will touch the bottom."

EC13   Hawthorne, Julian. "The Making of *The Scarlet Letter*." *Bookman* 74 (1931): 401-411.

Discusses the "birth-pains" that Hawthorne underwent while writing *Letter*, noting most especially that Hawthorne's profound love for his enigmatic daughter Una, coupled with the pervading gloom in his house caused by the illness and impending death of his mother, induced him to write the novel as he did. Una was, according to Julian, "the key put into [Hawthorne's] hand," and he compares sketches in his father's notebooks that address Elizabeth Manning Hawthorne's anticipated death with passages in the story that describe Pearl's angelic/demonic character. *Letter*'s enduring fame results from the presence of its only unique character, Pearl, whose "quasi-miraculous" nature as a law unto herself led Hawthorne "to interrogate the essential nature of Evil as a fundamental condition of human life" and to develop the overall theme of the work as the battle between selfish and social forces. Pearl "seizes the reins, usurps authority, and becomes predominant, and the others comparatively inert."

EC14   Howells, William Dean. "Hawthorne's Hester Prynne." *Heroines of Fiction*. Vol. 1. New York: Harper and Row, 1901. 161-174.

Having been written in America's "crude" landscape, Hawthorne's romance should be "rude, shapeless, [and] provincial" when compared with a realistic novel by a master such as Dickens. Yet it is actually superior for its presentation of "rounded, whole" characters as opposed to types. In addition, "each detail of the drama, in motive [and] action, [as well as] character, is substantiated, so that from first to last it is visible, audible, tangible." In short, "it is hard to see how [*Letter*] shall ever be surpassed, or even companioned." While *Letter* has its faults (Howells cites "quaint foibles of manner" and an unrealistic quality about Pearl that places her uncomfortably amongst otherwise "robust" characters), it is nonetheless Hawthorne's "modernist and maturist" romance, written with an antiquated language and stately dialogue appropriate to Puritan conditions. Further, Hester and Dimmesdale are "no mere types of open shame and secret remorse." With "melancholy grace and somber power," Hawthorne depicts their "fall under the law of their common doom." "In all fiction one could hardly find a character more boldly, more simply, more quietly imagined" than Hester, who "owns" her sin (unlike Dimmesdale) and always remains "exterior and superior" to her sexual transgression—as if fully knowing that her Maker "apparently does not deal with [sin] like a Puritan." Her author apparently does not either, since Hawthorne seems to imply that "ceasing to do evil is, after all, the most that can be asked of human nature."

EC15 James, Henry. "The Three American Novels." *Hawthorne.* London: Macmillian, 1879. 83-115.*

"*Letter* is, par excellence, the classic American novel," James concludes after evaluating *Letter, House of the Seven Gables,* and *Blithedale Romance,* and studying them against Hawthorne's "provincial" social background. James describes it (pp. 83-96) as "densely dark, with a single spot of vivid colour in it," and views Hester as an "accessory figure" to the main character, Dimmesdale—in whose shadow lurks the vengeful Chillingworth, who himself is only "on the edge" of Hawthorne's consideration. James praises the novel for being Hawthorne's masterpiece (and lauds Hawthorne as "the most beautiful and eminent representative of a [national] literature"), but complains of a few significant shortcomings which include "a want of reality and an abuse of the fanciful element—of a certain superficial symbolism." James particularly finds fault with the drastically overused symbol of the letter "A," which becomes ridiculous and exaggerated in the midnight scaffold scene when the letter appears to glow supernaturally in the sky. Such faults stand out significantly when the novel is compared to John Gibson Lockhart's *Adam Blair* (1822), which is remarkably similar to *Letter* but far more passionate, warm, and natural. [See Terence Martin's rebuttal of James's argument (132) of the similarities between *Adam Blair* and *Letter.*]

*Reprinted in 1975 (Ithaca: Cornell UP).

EC16 Jones, Llewellyn. "Mr. Hawthorne's *Scarlet Letter.*" *Bookman* 57 (1924): 622-625.

The story of *Letter* is built upon "three main strands": a nearly Freudian psychological analysis of human feelings and motives, a Puritan disapproval of earlier Puritanism, and a "playing with Gothic romanticism that is in odd contrast to the divinatory psychology." Though the novel as a whole is contrived "artfully and naturally," two flaws in particular stick out. Artistically speaking, Pearl is a rather "hopeless loss" because an un-life-like character. And Hawthorne's interpolating moral commentary that interrupts the narrative and attempts to block readers' sympathies for the errant minister and his mistress actually seems "unhealthily Puritan and bigoted." Such intrusions reveal quite clearly that Hawthorne is "not without some of the old maidishness of American Puritanism."

EC17 Lathrop, George Parsons. *"The Scarlet Letter." A Study of Hawthorne.* Boston, 1876. 210-225.

In this first biography of Hawthorne, written by Hawthorne's son-in-law and later used by Henry James as the primary biographical source for his own study (EC15), Lathrop discusses the novel's conception and sources, its rapid sale and mixed reviews, and its foundation as "a massive argument for repentance, which is the flinging aside of concealment, and the open and truthful acknowledgment of sin." He describes Hester as the most honest of all the characters in the tragedy, the lesson of which is "that nothing is so destructive as the morality of mere appearances." [Lathrop directs this reading of Hester against Arthur Cleveland Coxe's harsh review of the novel (ER10) that aligned Hester's errant ways with Hawthorne's own belief system.]

EC18 Lawrence, D. H. "Nathaniel Hawthorne and *The Scarlet Letter." Studies in Classic American Literature.* 1923. New York: Viking Press, 1964. 83-99.

Written in a maddeningly elusive and yet masterful style that is, as Austin Warren assesses (in 178), "not for the literal-minded," this highly influential and imaginative essay on Hawthorne delves beneath the "pious as pie," "smarm"-covered surface of the didactic and Puritanical *Letter* to the "perfect duplicity" of the "inner diabolism of the symbolic meaning" of this American re-making of the myth of the Fall of Man. Hawthorne's "moral tale" is actually a "great allegory of the triumph of sin," a subversive vision (in which the "devilish" moral is that people should keep up appearances) that carefully disguises the demonism that lies beneath the American experience. It focuses on Hester—the destructive female principle—and her subversive delight (her "life work") in seducing, making a fool of, and destroying the pure-hearted Dimmesdale and raising the devilish Pearl ("perhaps the most modern child in all literature") to bring forth "a new brood of vipers." Lawrence thus views the novel as having at its dark, subversive center little to do with Hawthorne's seemingly conventional moral tale that only appears to profess the merits of sexual self-denial and self-sacrifice for the greater social good. [For an essay that evaluates the import of Lawrence's famous remark that Hawthorne "knew disagreeable things in his inner soul," see R. V. Cassill (189). For more information on Lawrence's view of *Letter*, see Charles W. Mann (306). For an essay that critiques Lawrence's negative reaction to Hester's character, see Virginia Hudson Young (556).]

EC19 Lawton, William C. "Hawthorne: A Lonely Life." *The New England Poets*. New York: Macmillan, 1898. 48-104.

This transcendental reading of Hawthorne's life and works defends the author's "deliberate mystification" (through supernaturalism, witchcraft, and allegorical symbolism) and rates him as "the most perfect artist in form, the most original creative genius, and the most consummate master of style yet born upon American soil." Lawton's discussion of *Letter* (pp. 82-88) focuses on sin as "no malignant, demoniacal power contradicting and thwarting the will of Heaven" but as "estrangement, distortion, misuse, of impulses not themselves accurst" that may "therefore through repentance, atonement, and penance [. . .] work out the blessedness even of the sinner." In this liberal view of sin, Hester and Dimmesdale's love is never actually destroyed but instead purified and spiritualized—supporting Dimmesdale in death and Hester "in the heavier trial of life."

EC20 Matthiessen, F. O. "*The Scarlet Letter*." *American Renaissance: Art and Expression in the Age of Emerson and Whitman*. Oxford: Oxford UP, 1941. 275-282.

This classic study, which explores the powerful "democratic" literature of five "American Renaissance" writers (Ralph Waldo Emerson, Henry David Thoreau, Hawthorne, Herman Melville, and Walt Whitman), briefly examines *Letter* for its "variety of symbolic reference." Matthiessen contends that the novel's success largely results from Hawthorne's development "of one of his most fertile resources, the device of multiple choice"—a device referred to as "the formula of alternative possibilities" by Yvor Winters* (EC40). More than coherent plot, symmetrical design, organic development, and excellent contrasting characters, then, these symbolic intricacies allowed Hawthorne to best develop his theme and illustrate correspondences between external events and inner significances.

*When discussing Hawthorne's notorious ambiguity and ambivalence, most critics make reference to both of these now-famous phrases by Matthiessen and Winters.

EC21   Michaud, Régis. "How Nathaniel Hawthorne Exorcised Hester Prynne."
       The American Novel Today: A Social and Psychological Study. Boston:
       Little, Brown, 1928. 25-46.

This Freudian approach to the novel argues that Hawthorne has been
mistaken by critics for a Puritan, and that, in *Letter*, what he actually
shows himself to be is "a very subtle psychologist and a precursor and
pioneer of psychoanalysis." Referring to Hawthorne as an "explorer of the
subterranean world" and "the Conan Doyle of the conscience," Michaud
expresses his admiration for what he detects as the "very modern" aspects
of the novel, especially Hawthorne's "pagan imagination" and "immoral
protagonists," despite the fact that Hawthorne "spoil[s] his masterpiece by
creating a conventional "edifying ending." Before he grows "too
timorous," however, Hawthorne "proves the dangers of the famous
Freudian inhibition and tries to cure it." Hester and Dimmesdale are both
victims of social conventions and repressed desires, while Chillingworth is
"Suppressed Hatred," sensing Dimmesdale's hidden libido. Yet
ironically, though Chillingworth is an "able practitioner," he "is a very
poor psychologist," because "he works against his own ends," not
realizing that Dimmesdale will be "freed from repression and anxiety"
once he becomes healed by Hester in the forest and can then publicly
reveal his secret to become "an amoralist and a Nietzschean."

EC22   Morris, Lloyd. "*The Scarlet Letter.*" *The Rebellious Puritan: Portrait of
       Mr. Hawthorne.* New York: Harcourt, Brace, 1927. 197-232.*

Provides a lengthy biographical account of the time period in which
Hawthorne wrote *Letter* (detailing both domestic and political
circumstances) and discusses the novel itself as Hawthorne's enunciation
of "intellectual radicalism." In the "inexorably realistic study" that was
only superficially a historical romance, Hawthorne "justifies the self-
reliant individual, and expresses his contempt for the society which hedges
that individual about with conventions devoid of spiritual validity" and
raises the question of "whether sin itself, rather than the repentance of sin,
is not a source of the highest good."

*Reprinted in 1969 (Port Washington: Kennikat Press).

EC23   Munger, Theodore T. "Notes on *The Scarlet Letter.*" *Atlantic Monthly*
       93 (1904): 521-535.

Most notable in this evaluation of the novel is its characterizing of Hester,
based upon Hawthorne's chapter, "Another View of Hester," as "the
picture of a saint." The chapter does not paint a picture of despair or

suffering, nor does it present Hester as having transcended her situation, because "to forget her past would be to defraud the soul of its heritage in life." Instead, it portrays Hester as cleansed from dedicating her life to service in the spirit of God. Her life comes to "blessed uses, with rewards of love and gratitude from others."

EC24 Rahv, Philip. "The Dark Lady of Salem." *Partisan Review* 8 (1941): 362-381.*

Argues that critics inaccurately pigeonhole Hawthorne as an ultra-moral "novelist of sin" when he was actually "haunted not only by the guilt of his desires but also by the guilt of his denial of them." This conflict between his split Puritan and romantic selves affects the "whole tone and meaning" of Hawthorne's writing and is reproduced in his rebellious and emancipatory "dark ladies" as a way of "enjoy[ing] the warmth and vitality of experience without exposing himself to its perils." Of the four dark ladies (Beatrice, Hester, Zenobia, and Miriam) who "dominate all the other characters because [they] alone personif[y] the contrary values that her author attached to experience," Hester is the most complex and "the least symbolically overladen and distorted." She is "essentially a mythic being, the incarnation of hidden longings and desires, as beautiful as she is inexpressibly terrible, a temptress offering the ascetic sons of the Puritans the treasure-trove of a great sin [. . .]. Times past are mirrored in the dark lady's harsh fate, yet in her mystic sensuality she speaks of things to come."

*This essay was reprinted in Rahv's *Image and Idea: Twenty Essays on Literary Themes* (Norfolk: New Directions, 1949. 27-50.).

EC25 Roper, Gordon. Introduction. *The Scarlet Letter and Selected Prose Works*. By Nathaniel Hawthorne. New York: Hendricks House, 1949. xxxvii-xlii.

Adapts John C. Gerber's method of structuring the novel (see EC9). To accommodate the dramatic presentation of three disparate sides of sin, which are symbolically represented by Hester, Dimmesdale, and Chillingworth, Hawthorne built a structure in four parts, with the Puritan community representing the fourth. These four "forces" shift in dominating the action of the other three forces. The initial force of the Puritan community gives way to Chillingworth, who gives way to Hester, who gets replaced by Dimmesdale as he drives the action of the narrative to its dramatic conclusion.

EC26 Schubert, Leland. *"The Scarlet Letter." Hawthorne, the Artist: Fine-Art Devices in Fiction.* Chapel Hill: U of North Carolina P, 1944. 136-161.

Largely concerned with matters of form, this study examines Hawthorne's use of "devices of the non-literary arts—structure, color, sound, line, mass, rhythm—to achieve emotional effects very similar to those achieved by other artists in a painting, or in a piece of sculpture, or in a symphony." Schubert admires the structural plan of *Letter* for its near perfect balance, repetition, and rhythm, with "The Custom-House" and "Conclusion" serving as "the frame around the story of Hester Prynne." Although the story itself is patterned and built around the scaffold scenes, which mark a distinct beginning, middle, and end, *Letter* can actually be seen to fall into a structural pattern—frame aside—of seven vibrant and fluid parts (based on the characters in the center of the stage), the division of which is supported by the "color distribution" throughout the novel. Schubert also considers several additional formal devices and Hawthorne's use of rhythmic motifs, contrast, "spots of light," and sound patterns.

EC27 Sherman, Stuart P. "Hawthorne: A Puritan Critic of Puritanism." *Americans.* New York: Charles Scribner's Sons, 1922. 122-152.

Remarking on Hawthorne's powerful skill of "reducing the insolent pretensions of circumstance to insignificance, and of giving to the moral and ideal world reality, importance, and supreme interest," Sherman expresses contempt for the new, younger generation of critics whose derogative definition of "Puritans" (as self-torturing, slavishly obedient to moral codes, morbid ascetics who display hostility to the beauties of nature and art) has little to do with the original definition that should be associated with Hawthorne's treatment of them: those who experienced "emancipation from ecclesiastical and social oppression, escape from the extortion of the sense and the tyranny of things, a consciousness at least partly liberated from the impositions of space and time, freedom from self-dominion, a hopeful and exultant effort to enter into right, noble, and harmonious relations with the highest impulse of one's fellows, and a vision, a love, and pursuit of the beauty which has its basis in the 'good and true.'" If the newer critics cannot permit the true definition, Sherman pleads, then "Let us" concede and not call Hawthorne a Puritan at all but a "transcendentalist, a subtle critic and satirist of Puritanism from the transcendental point of view."

EC28 Short, Raymond W. Introduction. *Four Great Novels.* New York: Henry Holt, 1946. xxi-xxviii.

In creating the allegory of *Letter* and focusing strictly on his obsession with the symbolic "A," Hawthorne found direction for his genius, which Short likens to a "too delicately balanced weathervane." Like Spenser and Milton before him, Hawthorne sacrificed the "humanness" of his characters to privilege transcendental values while working out his theme of "the ambiguous bounty of nature in conflict with the paradoxical cruelty of religion."

EC29   Spiller, Robert E. "The Mind and Art of Nathaniel Hawthorne." *Outlook* 149 (1928): 650-652, 676, 678.

One of the first (perhaps even *the* first) to point out that Hawthorne contributed to modern literature by anticipating both the short-story form and the genre of psychological fiction (the latter through his allegorical technique), Spiller explores "the ultimate significance of Hawthorne's work" and "its relative importance to American literature." Hawthorne is "an integral part of the Puritan tradition," as well as "the prophet of its decline." His greatest works "gave form and voice to the spirit of moral truth," and the "keynote" of his best writings is "the sense of inherited sin, either that of commission or that growing out of intolerance." Regarding *Letter* in particular, "the sin motif is introduced in the bass strings, and is sustained and tossed about by various voices forming, over all, a tone poem of rich harmony and graceful dignity."

EC30   Stewart, Randall. "Salem and *The Scarlet Letter*, 1846-1850." *Nathaniel Hawthorne: A Biography*. New Haven: Yale UP, 1948. 75-100.

Stewart is considered the first biographer to protest against the "romanticized" picture of Hawthorne as lonely, aloof, and alienated—as painted by earlier biographers like George Woodberry (EC41) and Newton Arvin (EC1). He provides a detailed account of the desperate circumstances that inspired Hawthorne's feverish writing of *Letter*, explains the outraged response of Hawthorne's fellow Salemites to "The Custom-House," and details the critical reception that secured the author's reputation for life. [This book is still regarded by a few critics as the best standard biography on Hawthorne.]

EC31   Stewart, Randall. Introduction. *The American Notebooks by Nathaniel Hawthorne*. New Haven: Yale UP, 1932. xiii-xcvi.

Divided into four parts, this introduction covers: "Mrs. Hawthorne's Revisions of the American Notebooks," "The Adaptation of Material from the American Notebooks in Hawthorne's Tales and Novels," "The Development of Character Types in Hawthorne's Fiction," and "Recurrent

Themes in Hawthorne's Fiction." Stewart divides the leading characters and four major themes (isolation of the individual, the unpardonable sin, the influence of the past, and the elixir of life) into groups and then traces a repetitive and cumulative process of development within each group. Of the chief characters in *Letter*, Stewart classifies Hester as one of Hawthorne's exotic woman types whose nature is marked by intellectual ability, physical beauty, and sinfulness. Dimmesdale develops from a sequence of characters tortured by a secret guilt and also represents the culmination of the "scholar-idealist" type that can be traced from *Fanshawe* and shares a kinship with the main characters in "Roger Malvin's Burial," "Minister's Black Veil," and "Egotism; or The Bosom-Serpent." Pearl derives primarily from Hawthorne's detailed descriptions of Una; and Chillingworth, who is not based on Hawthorne's life experience* and so is the most artificial of his villains, derives both from devils and wizards of early tales and from Hawthorne's intimate knowledge of John Milton and Edmund Spenser.

*For an essay that argues that Chillingworth's character was indeed based on Hawthorne's life experience (modeled after Salem enemy Richard S. Rogers), see Julian Smith (195).

EC32   Stoddard, Francis Hovey. "The Growth of Personality in Fiction." *The Evolution of the English Novel*. New York: Macmillan, 1900. 75-81.

Views the novel as a Greek tragedy, a medieval romance, and a modern historical tale all rolled into one, "limited to no age, belonging to all experiences, to all time." "The picture of Hester Prynne portrays a human soul not merely as a strong, demanding individuality, but as under stress of such relation to verdict of law and to the rights of fellow-mortals as to compel its development into a completed personality."

EC33   Trollope, Anthony. "The Genius of Nathaniel Hawthorne." *North American Review* 274 (1879): 209-211.

In this mercilessly moral novel of "diseased human nature," Hawthorne sees with great clarity "into the black deeps of the human heart." He tells a story of love and jealousy in which "love is allowed but little scope" while "full play is given to the hatred which can spring from injured love"—although there is yet a "vein of drollery" throughout the relentlessly punishing tale, since Hawthorne's "weird, mocking spirit" cannot help but add a "touch of burlesque."* Of the four major characters, it is only the magnificent, "pure as undriven snow" Hester with whom we are expected to sympathize, even though Hawthorne deals with her "in a spirit of assumed hardness." Although one might be compelled to pity

Dimmesdale's greater suffering, it is difficult to ignore his hypocrisy and cowardice, and he is all the more despised at the end for coming clean only when "the hand of death is upon him." Pearl, though charming, is "incongruous with all else in the story," "a drawback rather than an aid" because she is miraculously elf-life and therefore unrealistic in a story otherwise peopled with realistic characters. Hester's desolation would "have been more perfect without the child." *Letter* is Hawthorne's greatest novel because Hawthorne "had it [in his imagination] to write," while a novel like *House of the Seven Gables* "he had to write."

*Trollope may well have been the first to detect a note of humor in *Letter*, but he is not the last. See "Humor" in the Subject Index.

EC34 Van Doren, Carl. "Flower of Puritanism: Hawthorne's *Scarlet Letter*." *Nation* 111 (1920): 649-650.

Although Puritanism was in his blood, Hawthorne believed—unlike the Puritans—that sin was less a violation of God's law than of the "natural integrity of the soul." Softening its harsh doctrines, Hawthorne thus lifts Puritanism into "an enduring loveliness" in *Letter*. [See next annotation (EC35) for Van Doren's expanded discussion of this subject.]

EC35 Van Doren, Carl. "Nathaniel Hawthorne." *The American Novel*. New York: Macmillan, 1921. 65-71. 77-108.

The somber Puritan strain accounts for the fact that "the flesh go[es] unsung" in *Letter* (pp. 86-93) and that the novel overlooks "the surfaces of life." It also explains why Hawthorne's "conception of adultery [is viewed as] an affair not of the civil order but of the immortal soul" and why his three primary characters are so occupied with the conflict between good and evil. Although Hawthorne clearly inherits the stern Puritan tradition, "the novel's broader implications critically transcend the doctrines of the Puritans." Hawthorne humanizes the action, viewing the love between Hester and Dimmesdale not as blasphemous (as the Puritans would have) but as having "a consecration of its own." Hawthorne also implies that the instincts and antipathies of Dimmesdale and Chillingworth fester because the men are unnaturally repressed. Hester becomes the type "of the moving principle of life which different societies in different ways may constrain but which itself irresistibly endures."

EC36 Van Doren, Mark. "*The Scarlet Letter*." *Nathaniel Hawthorne*. New York: William Sloan, 1949. 146-156.

The themes that obsessed Hawthorne in the tales (sin, guilt, isolation, and pride) are taken up in the novel to expose both the fanaticism of the Puritans and the despised blandness of his own time. In *Letter*, which is "in a sense the last of Hawthorne's tales, and of course their climax," Hawthorne "went to the center of woman's secret, her sexual power, and stayed there." Although the three central characters are powerfully represented personalities (which accounts for the novel's greatness), Hester alone—with her majestic "passion and beauty"—dominates every other character and scene. Dimmesdale is only redeemed for us because Hester has loved him, and Chillingworth seems too unreal, too much of a caricature of a villain, to compete with Hester's great nature.

EC37 Waggoner, Hyatt H. "American Literature Re-Examined: Nathaniel Hawthorne: The Cemetery, the Prison, and the Rose." *University of Kansas City Review* 14 (1948): 175-190.

Discussing Hawthorne's "essentially moral and religious sensibility," Waggoner relates Hawthorne's works to four major influences that formed his age: New England Protestant Christianity, science and secular thought, romanticism, and democracy. Of these four influences, religion played by far the greatest—and most trusted—part in Hawthorne's thinking and writing, proving to be the foundation from which his themes of pride, isolation, human brotherhood, humility, and man's imperfections evolved. By "religion," Waggoner means Hawthorne's own unique brand of "undogmatic" religion, which stemmed from his instinct for the "catholic essence of traditional Christianity" rather than for either Puritan Calvinism or liberal modernism. *Letter* (pp. 184-190) is "nearly flawless" in conception as an allegorical romance of the most complex symbolism and structure. The novel progresses in an upward and downward movement across "lines representing nature and culture" (a diagram appears on 186). "The complexity of correspondence and contrast" of the three major symbols with which the book opens, the cemetery (as symbol of natural evil), the prison (symbol of moral evil), and the rose (symbol of natural good), all work together to create "richness and subtlety of irony and paradox." The chief flaw of the novel is its failure to offer something positive to replace the condemned system of Puritanism (such as a recapturing of traditional Christian ethics). Hawthorne's vague moral—"Be true! Be true!"—is "wholly inadequate," as is Hester's grossly unfair, lifelong punishment (since she sins the least in the novel, Chillingworth the most). Hawthorne's failure to carry the themes of *Letter* to completion can best be explained by allowing that the novel reflects "some of the hypocrisy, confusion, sentimentalism, and prudishness" of Hawthorne's Victorian age.

EC38 Warren, Austin. Introduction. *Nathaniel Hawthorne: Representative Selections, With Introduction, Bibliography, and Notes.* New York: American Book Co., 1934. xi-lxxiii.

Traces "the development of Hawthorne's religious, ethical, political, social, and literary ideas" and "interpret[s] his writing in the light of his personality and aims." Warren asserts the orthodoxy of Hawthorne's "Calvinism" and his "inveterate love of allegory," and describes Hawthorne as a solitary genius. "All sins may be reduced to versions of Pride and Sensuality" in his fiction. Warren's most noteworthy statement about *Letter* is that "The Custom-House" is a "curiously unsuitable introduction to the masterpiece."

EC39 Werner, William L. "The First Edition of Hawthorne's *The Scarlet Letter.*" *American Literature* 5 (1934): 359.

This brief note identifies four features of true, first-edition copies of the now "rare and expensive book," distinguishing between first and second edition copies. Naturally lacking the "Preface to the Second Edition," first editions contain the word "reduplicate" on page 21 of "The Custom-House" (erroneously changed by a type-setter to "repudiate" in the second edition) and the incorrect spelling of "stedfast" (corrected to "steadfast" in the second edition). The texts are otherwise identical, the only other miniscule difference lying in changes in spacing over pages 19-30 and 214-232.

EC40 Winters, Yvor. "Maule's Curse, or Hawthorne and the Problem of Allegory." *Maule's Curse: Seven Studies in the History of American Obscurantism.* Norfolk: New Directions, 1938. 3-22.

Letter is Hawthorne's only "faultless" novel because its New England Puritan background provided the perfect material to write one "pure allegory." Although the method of allegorization in the novel is identical with that of the Puritans, Hawthorne's point of view is more enlightened and "hints throughout at a richer and more detailed understanding than the Puritan scheme of life is able to contain." [This essay is most often acknowledged as having first pinpointed Hawthorne's "formula of alternative possibilities" in his narrative technique. See EC20 for F. O. Matthiessen's similar assessment.]

EC41 Woodberry, George. "*The Scarlet Letter.*" *Nathaniel Hawthorne.* Boston: Houghton Mifflin, 1902. 159-205.

Building upon materials collected from the first biographies of Hawthorne by Julian Hawthorne, Rose Hawthorne Lathrop,* and George Parsons Lathrop (EC17), this important early biography stresses, without exaggerating, the nature of his solitude. Woodberry describes Hawthorne's historic consciousness, Puritan temperament, and strong sense of New England's past that captured his imagination. Hawthorne's Custom House experience and the "disagreeable circumstances of his removal and the penniless condition in which it left him," as well as the death of his mother (his last attachment to Salem) and the material assistance provided by his wife and friends, inspired and enabled him to write the novel and, at last, establish his fame. *Letter* is a powerful and "gloomy tale of how sin stains the soul" of its characters, dealing profoundly with spiritual reality at the expense of human nature—and even seems in its stark moral intellectualism to anticipate George Eliot's scientific pessimism. In the end, there is no forgiveness for a sin against the soul, although the "human element threatens to break through the bondage of the moral scheme" to humanize Hawthorne's "stubborn, dark, harsh narrative of misery," especially in the forest scene where Hester and Dimmesdale recall that their sin had a "consecration of its own." Woodberry's only real criticism is that Hawthorne "stooped in taking his literary revenge on his humble associates by holding them up to personal ridicule" in "The Custom-House," taking immodestly upon himself the character of the unappreciated genius.

*For these first biographies written by two of Hawthorne's children, see Julian Hawthorne's two-volume "family biography" *Nathaniel Hawthorne and His Wife* (Boston, 1884) and Rose Hawthorne Lathrop's *Memories of Hawthorne* (Boston, 1897).

PART III

Comprehensive Annotated Bibliography of Literary Criticism, Scholarship, Teaching Aids, Study Guides, and Help Books, 1950-2000

1950

Essays and Studies in Books

1   Arvin, Newton. Introduction. *The Scarlet Letter.* By Nathaniel Hawthorne. 1850. New York: Harper and Brothers, 1950. v-xiii.

Reviews the notebook entries and the short story ("Endicott and the Red Cross") that foreshadow the events, motives, images, and characters in *Letter*, and then addresses the symbolic import of the scarlet letter and the novel's three-part structure. Arvin briefly extends his discussion of structure to cover contrasts of day/night, town/forest, and society/solitude, and relates these contrasts to the themes of purity and innocence.

2   Gerber, John C. Introduction. *The Scarlet Letter.* By Nathaniel Hawthorne. 1850. New York: Modern Library, 1950. vii-xxxi.

In this very similar version of his 1944 journal essay (see EC9), Gerber discusses Hawthorne's distinction between novel and romance.

3   Miller, Perry. "George B[ailey] Loring: Hawthorne's *Scarlet Letter.*" The *Transcendentalists: An Anthology.* Ed. Perry Miller. Cambridge: Harvard UP, 1950. 475-482.

Miller's anthology, which "aims to make available articles and books that by now can be found only in a few special libraries," includes Loring's review of *Letter* (ER7) to illustrate how the transcendentalists' mixed attitudes toward society had filtered by mid-century into the ideas of even non-transcendentalists of the age. Miller suggests (pp. 475-476) that Dr. Loring—not a transcendentalist but generally familiar with the ttranscendental debates over society vs. the individual—was so imbued with transcendentalist notions that he "naturally" viewed the novel as "an indictment of the social morality of the dominant classes," as "an attack upon society and convention, under the banner of self-reliance." Little did Loring realize that Hawthorne did not consider himself a transcendentalist, either. As Loring writes in his review for the *Massachusetts Quarterly Review* (the authorship for which he tried to keep secret because of his liberal attention to the lusty nature of the novel), "We see in the lives of Arthur Dimmesdale and Hester Prynne, that the severity of puritanical law and morals could not keep them from violation; and we see, too, that this very severity drove them both into a state of moral insanity." Loring concludes with the statement that readers morally outraged by the characters' crime of passion deny their own humanity by viewing the adulterous act as anything other than a "warm-hearted crime" necessary to relieve the "cold, false, vulgar, and cowardly asperity which is sometimes called chastity."

Journal Essays and Notes

4   Cowley, Malcolm. "100 Years Ago: Hawthorne Set a Great New Pattern." *New York Herald Tribune Book Review* (Aug. 6, 1950): 1, 13.

This brief note, which asserts that *Letter* brought Greek tragedy to the American novel, provides the germ for Cowley's later essay, "The Five Acts of *The Scarlet Letter*" (59).

5   Hart, John E. "*The Scarlet Letter*—One Hundred Years After." *New England Quarterly* 23 (1950): 381-395.

Re-examines *Letter*'s "symbolic action"—particularly Hawthorne's "shadow" metaphor—one hundred years after the novel's publication, arguing that attitudes and actions of characters reflect different sides of Hawthorne's personality. Through them, Hawthorne explores not only "the necessity of Art as a way of expiating his feeling of guilt toward his Past" but also "the relationship of the isolated individual to the outside world." Of the four primary characters, Pearl seems best to represent the healthy balance between intellect and passion, sin and sanctity, and isolation and affinity with community, which Hawthorne was therapeutically moving towards when he wrote the novel.

6   Ringe, Donald A. "Hawthorne's Psychology of the Head and Heart." *PMLA* 65 (1950): 120-132.

Taking a concept developed by F. O. Matthiessen (in EC20) as his starting point, Ringe considers the psychological conflict between head and heart in Hawthorne's fiction, especially in *Letter*. Hawthorne centers the conflict between these two aspects of man's character upon a critical and irreconcilable theme: "the problem of life in an evil world." Hester, Dimmesdale, and Chillingworth represent possible solutions for living in the evil Puritan society (which is evil because of its egotism), each illustrating the head/heart conflict (Chillingworth to the least degree, however, since his warped personality contains a drastic "overbalance of head"). Isolated from common humanity, Hester (heart) and Dimmesdale (head) enact one such solution by "achiev[ing] insight and ris[ing] above the moral level of the community." Whereas Dimmesdale eventually gains heart, Hester develops her mind, and both find in the end redemptive value in their respective falls as they attempt to rejoin the magnetic chain of humanity. Dimmesdale's insight and moral triumph are more profound than Hester's, although the minister is doomed to fail because his position in the community is so far above the "common horde of humanity" that he cannot hope to find happiness in "sacrific[ing] his individuality in the common anonymity of ordinary life" (a second solution). The "ideal solution" rests with Hester's return at the end (her true insight gained only after she leaves the colony and rejects the option of "los[ing] herself in the mass of men"), sacrificing her "common anonymity of ordinary life" abroad to live out her remaining years in America as a living symbol of the "omnipresence of sin." Ringe concludes, "It is only in the Hester Prynnes of the world that gradual and perhaps continuing moral progress for man can be hoped for or sought."

7   Roper, Gordon. "The Originality of Hawthorne's *The Scarlet Letter*." *Dalhousie Review* 29 (1950): 62-79.

Links Hawthorne with Charlotte Brontë, Emily Brontë, and Herman Melville, who transformed the fiction genre—which in the nineteenth century was used exclusively for popular entertainment or indoctrination—into high art by courageously expressing their personal visions. *Letter* demonstrates the way in which Hawthorne converted the conventional elements of character, motivation, setting, climax, and ending into an organic and symbolic "complex abstraction about human life." In Hawthorne's psychological study of the consequences of sin, for instance, the characters are not intended to be seen as heroine, hero, and villain, but as personifications of the three faculties that comprise human nature (according to Hawthorne's contemporary psychology), Hester standing for the Heart, Chillingworth the Head, and Dimmesdale, the spirit. Each must be true unto himself to be a "living personality," and sins committed by each are relative since acts are only sinful if they violate an individual's integrity and nature. The only salve for Hawthorne's private vision of "the darker ambiguities of life," or his "acute awareness that the individual was isolated from his fellow men, hence from his society, and finally, from his God," is the possibility of love bridging the gaps that separate people.

8   Smith, Harrison. "Hawthorne: The Somber Strain." *Saturday Review* 33 (1950): 18.

This brief, superficial revaluation of *Letter* (ninth in a series of such literary revaluations that this magazine presented) identifies Hawthorne as "a haunted and apprehensive figure" whose imaginative greatness was undervalued by his contemporaries. Hawthorne is admired most for *Letter*'s "universal and inescapable" central theme: the "sense of evil and redemption that lies, not only at the heart of man's conduct but in all religions as well, 'the sadness,' in his own words, of a contrite heart broken at last under its own weight of sin."

1951

Essays and Studies in Books

9   Zabel, Morton D., ed. "Hawthorne: *The Scarlet Letter*." By Henry James. *The Portable Henry James*. New York: Viking Press, 1951. 440-453.

Essay extracted from chapter five of James's *Hawthorne* (see EC15). Although reprints do not generally warrant a separate citation, this one is included because numerous studies refer to it instead of the original source.

Journal Essays and Notes

10   Abel, Darrel. "Hawthorne's Pearl: Symbol and Character." *ELH: Journal of English Literary History* 18 (1951): 50-66.*

Although she is "the most complex figure in the romance," a blend of romantic and Calvinist conceptions of childhood, and although she carries out a "triple role as representative of childhood, as artist presence, and as spiritual messenger," Pearl is not a true character in her own right because "her actions and symbolic gestures" sacrifice her character's individuality and credibility as the "real" child modeled after Hawthorne's daughter Una. While Pearl is similar to the pure "Romantic Child of Nature" described by Wordsworth in the Lucy poems, Hawthorne's belief that such child would lack moral awareness differs from Wordsworth's belief that Nature alone can be a spiritual teacher and moral guide. For Hawthorne, social interactions are just as crucial in the formative process. Agreeing with the Calvinist doctrine that infants inherit the moral and physical traits of their parents, Hawthorne nevertheless disagrees with the Calvinist creed that infants are born corrupted. Stuck in a pre-moral state of development (richly imaginative and insightful though she is), Pearl's "capricious disposition" can only be "regularized" when Hester and Dimmesdale fully recover their integrity. Thus Dimmesdale's "resumption of moral truth" in his dying confession enacts Pearl's humanization and ends her mission as "messenger of anguish" to her parents.

*Reprinted in Abel's *The Moral Picturesque: Studies in Hawthorne's Fiction* (see 559).

11   Davidson, Edward H. "The Question of History in *The Scarlet Letter*." *Emerson Society Quarterly* 25 (1951): 2-3.

Hawthorne's unjust representation of the Puritans in *Letter* as "limned only in unrelieved gloom, in shades of dusky somberness, and in tones of bigotry and prejudice" is largely responsible for many American readers' "warped" sense of their New England heritage. While Hawthorne offers brilliant insight into the Puritan mind, his narrative is—unbeknownst to some—an intentionally distorted act of "historical re-creation." His presentation of the first-generation Puritans' "dark, inquisitorial tendencies" is inaccurate, since historically it was two decades later in the 1690s that Puritans were somber-tempered and "deeply troubled."

12   Eisinger, Chester E. "Pearl and the Puritan Heritage." *College English* 12 (1951): 323-329.

Takes issue with D. H. Lawrence's assessment of Pearl as "perhaps the most modern child in literature" (in EC18) to argue that she is actually "an old-fashioned child [. . .] whose wayward course through the novel, culminating in a happy marriage and an apparently stable life [. . .] is based on orthodox Puritan postulates of the seventeenth century." Eisinger examines Pearl in the historical context of Puritan theories of natural/civil liberty and natural/civil law, contending that critics err in thinking that Hawthorne is a disciple of either "the eighteenth century's belief in nature's simple plan" or "the Romantic notion of living in harmony with nature." Rather, Hawthorne is "a latter-day Puritan" who "looked askance at the uncontrolled and uncontrollable realms of nature." He creates Pearl as "an airy sprite," a wild creature of nature who is "beyond the reach of divine salvation and human society" until Dimmesdale acknowledges her publicly and "restore[s] her to the jurisdiction of God and man." With her immortal soul no longer in danger of being beyond the possibility of grace, Pearl is saved from the natural realm, standing "as an apotheosis of Puritan morality."

13   Leavis, Q. D. "Hawthorne as Poet." *Sewanee Review* 59 (1951): 179-205, 426-458.

Few critics have succeeded to observe Hawthorne's achievement because they incorrectly view Hawthorne as an aloof allegorist. As "the critic and interpreter of American cultural history and thereby the finder and creator of a literary tradition from which sprang Henry James on the one hand and Herman Melville on the other," Hawthorne was deeply committed to exploring problems related to the individual and society—and was in effect a "sociological novelist," "employing a poetic technique which communicates instead of stat[es] his findings." Hawthorne's technique and theme in *Letter* are similar to Tolstoy's in *Anna Karenina* (1873). The tragedy in both "consists in the separation of the genuinely united couple by an inhuman society and originated in the false relation imposed on a girl by an unlovable husband." Given the narrow social confines in which the protagonists are trapped, death provides the only means of escape.

14   Von Abele, Rudolph. "*The Scarlet Letter*: A Reading." *Accent* 11 (1951): 211-227.

Letter illustrates Man's fall from grace, focusing on the exile of Adam (Dimmesdale) and Eve (Hester) from society and the efforts of each to come to terms with the harsh facts of expulsion in their symbolic journeys, Dimmesdale's ending in death, Hester's "never." Von Abele also argues that "the interplay of the personages of *Letter* is interpretable in terms of the relations Hawthorne conceived as existing among art, nature, religion, and science." In describing Hester as a statuesque work of art, Pearl as a child of Nature, Dimmesdale as a minister, and Chillingworth as a probing physician, Hawthorne is working out his understanding of these relationships. A too close relation between art (Hester) and science (Chillingworth) produces sterility, while a too close association between science (Chillingworth) and religion (Dimmesdale) insidiously reduces the latter. Similarly, because the "religious impulse" is "feeble and insecure in an increasingly secular age," a too close connection between art (Hester) and religion (Dimmesdale) adulterously secularizes the latter, watering it down, so to speak. While art and science are both dangerous to religion, Nature (Pearl) ultimately asserts a threatening dominance over both religion and science.

1952

Essays and Studies in Books

15   Fogle, Richard Harter. "*The Scarlet Letter*." *Hawthorne's Fiction: The Light and the Dark*. Norman: U of Oklamoma P, 1952. 104-121.*

In the method of New Criticism, this book examines Hawthorne's central images and symbols (in eight short stories and all four novels) for an overall pattern of "light" and "dark." The light in Hawthorne is his "clarity of design," his "classic balance" and "lucid language." The dark refers to Hawthorne's "tragic complexity," which involves his ambiguous use of symbolism and allegory, his tendency to cast doubt upon interpretations that at first seem clear, and the complexity of his characterization. Excellence derives from "his clarity [. . .] intermingled with subtlety, his statement interfused with symbolism, his affirmation enriched with ambiguity." In the chapter on *Letter*, which begins by disproving any "cheerful" readings of the novel, Fogle attends to the ambiguous moral meaning by focusing on four "states of being": one subhuman (nature), two human (the heart versus the head), and one superhuman or heavenly (the "sphere of absolute insight, justice, and mercy"). This superhuman state, denied to Chillingworth but accessed in the end by Dimmesdale and Hester, redeems all other signs of dreary hopelessness in the otherwise "darkly tragic" novel.

*The revised edition in 1964 reprints the original text, but includes a new preface (pp. ix-xi) and two new sections on "My Kinsman, Major Molineux" (pp. 104-116) and "The Birth-mark" (pp. 117-131). Dropped from the new edition is the list of "Suggested Readings" supplemented in the original study, now considered superfluous following Walter Blair's elaborate survey of Hawthorne criticism in 1956 (see 43). For Fogle's "supplement" to his revised edition, see *Hawthorne's Light and Imagery: The Proper Light and Shadow in the Major Romances* (236).

Journal Essays and Notes

16   Abel, Darrel. "Hawthorne's Hester." *College English* 13 (1952): 303-309.*

Modern-day champions of Hester misconstrue her place in the novel as the primary character. Hester does not function as "spokesman of Hawthorne's views favoring a 'larger liberty'" but rather demonstrates that "persons who engage our moral compassion may nevertheless merit moral censure." In following natural instinct and rejecting the authority of both God and society, Hester actually "exhibit[s] the inadequacy of [. . .] the philosophy [. . .] of romantic individualism." Her isolation from the common experience of mankind corrupts her "feminine virtues," she is "unfit for intellectual speculation," and she "fail[s] to secure even the natural satisfaction she sought." Although we may certainly sympathize with her, the fact that she is "more sinned against than sinning" is beside the point. She is morally responsible for her actions, her greatest error lying in the mistaken belief that a life of happiness is more important than a life of virtue. [See 18 for Frederic I. Carpenter's response to this article, which accuses Abel of committing the "three cardinal sins of criticism." See also 406 for Nina Baym's own harsh criticism of Abel's article.]

*Reprinted in Abel's *The Moral Picturesque: Studies in Hawthorne's Fiction* (see 559).

17   Brand, Howard. "Hawthorne on the Therapeutic Role." *Journal of Abnormal and Social Psychology* 47 (1952): 856.

Startled and amazed by Hawthorne's acute, instinctive awareness of what would become modern psychotherapy, Brand cites a lengthy quotation from *Letter* that describes Chillingworth's relationship to Dimmesdale, or "the role of the physician in relation to his patient." Brand finds it "sobering" that "Hawthorne writing over one hundred years ago states the problem of the therapeutic relationship with a sensitivity and cogency equaled by few psychologists today."

18   Carpenter, Frederic I. "Hester the Heretic." *College English* 13 (1952): 457-458.

Since Darrel Abel (in 16) names Carpenter as the most recent offender among modern critics who defend romantic readings of *Letter*, Carpenter feels compelled to set the record straight and to defend his "Scarlet A Minus" (EC4) from Abel's inaccurate reading of it—especially since he does not validate a romantic reading of the novel. Abel commits "three cardinal sins of criticism" in "Hawthorne's Hester." First, Abel "damns all critics" whose ideas conflict with his own, basically calling them heretics for sympathizing with Hester (herself a heretic, according to Abel). Second, he unfairly "ignore[s] the distinctions and qualifications made by such critics," lumping them all together as "romantic individualists." And third, he ridicules his opponents without attempting to answer their arguments.

19   Orians, G. Harrison. "Hawthorne and Puritan Punishments." *College English* 13 (1952): 424-432.

Of all the New England fiction writers from 1820 to 1860 who told "dramatic tales of the past," only Hawthorne focused upon grim Puritan punishments for misdemeanors and crimes. Through extensive historical readings of criminal cases and law controversies, Hawthorne was well aware of seventeenth-century criminal offences against Colony laws and refers to them in several places, though especially in "Endicott and the

Red Cross" and *Letter*, both of which explore the effects of wearing a penal letter. Other punishments Hawthorne was familiar with (for which Orians cites penalties and cases) were the pillory, the stocks, the cleft stick (for pinching the tongue), imprisonment, the gallows, whipping post, ear-cropping, branding, the rope penalty (where a halter of rope is placed around the neck as the wearer is viewed sitting in the gallows), the attachment of incriminating phrases or letters to the criminal's clothing, and capital punishment. Hawthorne's selection of a scarlet letter—when he had such an arsenal of punishments to choose from—best suited his interests in creating "a design into which a variety of moral and psychological themes were fitted." The letter "was a penalty with rich and multiple significance, and Hawthorne found it a symbol that turned and glowed beneath his hand until it became the center of his greatest novel."

20   Stocking, David M. "An Embroidery on Dimmesdale's Scarlet Letter." *College English* 13 (1952): 336-337.

Hawthorne's offering multiple choices to explain the "A" on Dimmesdale's chest does not indicate artistic uncertainty; rather, the four alternative explanations—that Dimmesdale carved it into his chest, that Chillingworth caused it to appear by magic or drugs, that it appeared psychosomatically, and that it did not exist at all—are "a simple yet subtle device for leading the attention away from the 'undesirable distinctness' of the symbol" and back to more basic moral issues. In other words, because Hawthorne feared that the physical horror involved with the original gory theory would distract readers from the symbol's more important spiritual significance, he offered three other theories to deflect or slightly water down the melodramatic effect of the first. These alternatives, which descend in plausibility as they ascend in order of increasing symbolic and moral importance, together "serve to submerge the symbol within its significance, to bring the attention back to Dimmesdale's guilt and its consequences."

1953

Essays and Studies in Books

21   Feidelson, Charles, Jr. "Hawthorne." *Symbolism and American Literature*. Chicago: U of Chicago P, 1953. 6-16.

In this groundbreaking book that treats Hawthorne along with Walt Whitman, Herman Melville, Edgar Allan Poe, Ralph Waldo Emerson, and Henry David Thoreau, Feidelson places Hawthorne in a literary tradition of mid-nineteenth-century American authors devoted to "the possibilities of symbolism" as opposed to idealism, materialism, romanticism, and realism.* Hawthorne was only occasionally a symbolist, however, because "the truth of that symbolism at once fascinated and horrified him," and so he most often turned to the "safety" of conventional allegory to beg the question of absolute reality. The section on *Letter* (pp. 9-12) concentrates primarily upon the relationship of "The Custom-House" to the novel. In his own way and with his own results, each character in the novel "re-enacts the 'Custom House' scene in which Hawthorne himself contemplated the letter, so that the entire 'romance' becomes a kind of exposition of the nature of symbolic perception." The subject is not only the meaning of adultery but also how meaning itself is generated so that the letter gains significance.

*Feidelson specifically argues that F. O. Matthiessen's *American Renaissance* (see EC20), which focuses on the ways that nineteenth-century writers were devoted to "the possibilities of democracy," overplays how politics and society figured into the same authors' works.

22   Stein, William Bysshe. "*The Scarlet Letter*: The New England Faust." *Hawthorne's Faust: A Study of the Devil Archetype*. Gainesville: U of Florida P, 1953. 104-122.

This study proposes to pioneer a new analytical path in Hawthorne criticism, tracking the "genetic development" and organic nature of the fiction as a whole by applying to it the devil-archetype of the Faustian myth. The story of Faust, based upon man's desire to apprehend the moral mystery of the universe, "provides Hawthorne with the medium of inquiring into the riddle of good and evil." An analysis of *Letter* reveals that "a fluid conception of the Faust myth is the dynamic principle of composition ruling Hawthorne's creative imagination." Hawthorne's Puritan Faust, represented most prominently in Chillingworth, motivates most of the action in the novel. Hester, too, is depicted as Fausta, "her desperate efforts as a Faustian tempter [. . .] designed to express the eternal philosophy of womanhood." Assigning to Dimmesdale the character of a lascivious monk (a variant of the Faust myth), "Hawthorne, with poetic justice that betrays his true feelings about the minister, rewards the latter's ignominious spiritual hypocrisy and moral cowardice. And by recourse to another Faustian phenomenon, Hawthorne ennobles Pearl's struggle to achieve identity in the human family."

23   Williams, Stanley T. "Nathaniel Hawthorne." *Literary History of the United States*. Eds. Robert E. Spiller, Willard Thorp, Thomas J. Johnson, and Henry S. Canby. Revised edition.* New York: Macmillan, 1953. 416-440.

Solitude and Puritan attitudes significantly contributed to Hawthorne's works set in New England. Of all his novels, *Letter* (pp. 425-431) is the noblest to emerge from the pessimistic and darkly skeptical author's mind, largely due to its superior presentation and inquiry of evil and isolation. Although its ideas are not particularly original or complex, and the characters of Chillingworth and Pearl lack authenticity, the romance is to be praised for its unity and "perfection of tone."

*An earlier edition appeared in 1946 and another revised edition appeared in 1981 by Simon and Schuster.

Journal Essays and Notes

24   Abel, Darrel. "The Devil in Boston." *Philological Quarterly* 32 (1953): 366-381.*

Explores Chillingworth's role in the novel as "an embodiment of certain Calvinist conceptions of the development of moral personality," asserting that the covertly vengeful character is "a Miltonic Satan" similar to "the villain of an historical romance." Chillingworth is also reminiscent of Calvinist humanism of seventeenth-century England (moreso than the transcendentalist optimism of nineteenth-century New England), because he views his own human failure as the Puritans did, as "a lapsing from excellence or from the possibility of excellence." Chillingworth, in Emersonian fashion, represents "not badness incarnate, but goodness perverted." He allows himself to nourish anger over and resentment of Dimmesdale into dehumanizing, diabolical revenge, and he uses his medical expertise and quest for forbidden knowledge—like Rappaccini—to "pervert" and tamper with spiritual nature. His claim that his vengeance is a predetermined "dark necessity" goes against Hawthorne's concept of *karma* ("the conception that a human being defines his own character continuously and progressively through the tendency of his choices"), since it is through his own free will that Chillingworth "gradually debase[s] his own character by deliberate persistence in a wrong course."

*Reprinted in Abel's *The Moral Picturesque: Studies in Hawthorne's Fiction* (see 559).

25   Abel, Darrel. "Modes of Ethical Sensibility in Hawthorne." *Modern Language Notes* 68 (1953): 80-86.

"*Letter* represents symbolically and dramatically various phases or postures of man's ethical sensibility." Symbolically represented in the Puritan jail, cemetery, scaffold, exotic gardens, forest, and weather are "traits of the Calvinist temper and way of life." Dramatically represented in the actions and speeches of characters are "modes of ethical sensibility" or the various ways characters endeavor to accommodate themselves to the "external constraints and restraints" of the world around them. Dimmesdale represents the self-abnegating pietist for whom the world is controlled by moral law; the Puritan community exemplifies the moral law-obsessed theocratic position; Chillingworth embodies the hubris-prone scientist's point of view that conforms to the laws of the physical world and presumes superior intellect; Hester represents the position of romantic individualist; Pearl embodies the morally-unconscious amoralist who lives by instinct; and Hawthorne himself represents the illusionist whose "detached, passive, speculative mind" tends to blur the boundaries between reality and fantasy.

26   Levi, Joseph.   "Hawthorne's *The Scarlet Letter*: A Psychoanalytic Interpretation." *American Imago* 10 (1953): 291-306.

Locating the source of *Letter*'s "captivating effect" in its acute psychoanalytic understanding, Levi stresses the powerful influences of Hawthorne's father's death ("at the height of Hawthorne's oedipal complex") and his mother's death, suggesting that the "oral aspects of Hawthorne's personality"—which include a penchant for asking favors, a tendency toward melancholy, and a dependency on women—determine *Letter*'s Oedipal theme.   After linking the novel thematically and structurally with Sophocles' *Oedipus Rex*, Levi goes on to show how the main characters in *Letter* project the oral sides of Hawthorne's personality: Dimmesdale representing his weak, guilt-prone ego, Chillingworth his "extremely punishing" superego, and Pearl his libidinous id.   Hester represents Hawthorne's image of the ideal mother. The novel was written, in fact, to reunite Hawthorne with his dead mother through the character of Hester.

27   Male, Roy R.   "'From the Innermost Germ': The Organic Principle in Hawthorne's Fiction."   *ELH: Journal of English Literary History*   20 (1953): 218-236.

Hawthorne shared with other American romantics "a thorough commitment to the organic principle," which, "complemented and enriched a tragic sense of the ambiguous intertexture of good and evil in human life." While consistently recurring organic and mechanical images appear in Hawthorne's fiction ("Drowne's Wooden Image," "The Birth-mark," "Feathertop," "Fire Worship," and *House of the Seven Gables*), organic/mechanical antithesis is best illustrated in *Letter* (pp. 223-228), where this "chief conflict" is introduced in the first chapter's symbolic contrast between the wild rose and the prison door. These extremes extend to the "predicament" of Hester and Dimmesdale at the heart of the novel, since Hester is torn between Pearl's (and her own) wild nature and Dimmesdale's conformist need for the "iron framework" of his faith and the Puritan social system. Hawthorne intends to advocate neither extremist position, however, but instead implies the need for a healthy balance between "organic individual development and necessarily restrictive social control."

28   Walcutt, Charles Child. "*The Scarlet Letter* and Its Modern Critics." *Nineteenth-Century Fiction* 7 (1953): 251-264.

Classifies five modern interpretations of *Letter* "to inquire how far they are justified by Hawthorne's words, and to consider whether their range and variety are due to some fundamental ambiguity in *Letter* or to the prepossessions of its readers." Of the five types, the first is the "orthodox Puritan reading" (by such critics as Austin Warren [EC38] and Frederic I. Carpenter [EC4]), which argues that the central motive of the Greek-like tragedy is the idea that sin is both inescapable and "permanently warping." The second reading, a variant of the first, views sin not only as man's tragic plight but as a "Fortunate Fall" that brings wisdom and spiritual enlightenment (Donald Ringe [6]). The third, a "romantic" reading, rests "on the premise that society is guilty of punishing individuals who have responded to a natural urge" and applauds the intellectual and spiritual growth of Hester and Dimmesdale (Newton Arvin [EC1], Lloyd Morris [EC22], F. O. Matthiessen [EC20], and Mark Van Doren [EC34, EC35]). The "transcendental" reading (George Woodberry [EC41]) insists that the true sin in the novel is not adultery but the protagonists' denial of their true selves. The fifth, a "relativist" reading (Herbert Gorman [EC10] and John C. Gerber [EC9]), focuses not on sin itself but on the psychological impact of guilt that results from committing sin. "The ultimate source of ambiguity in *Letter* [accounting for the diversity of interpretations] lies in the fact that, although Hawthorne firmly believes sin to be permanently warping, he dos not in his heart love the Providence which ordains it thus."

1954

Essays and Studies in Books

29   Cunliffe, Marcus. "New England's Day (Emerson, Thoreau, Hawthorne)." *The Literature of the United States*. Melbourne: Penguin Books, 1954. 75-104.

Demonstrates how Hawthorne differed markedly from Ralph Waldo Emerson and Henry David Thoreau in relation to nature, sin, society, the use of the past, and status as author (pp. 96-104). Hawthorne struggled with a more profound knowledge than they of man's fate in the New World, and he felt a correspondingly more difficult task as a writer in providing a new voice in American fiction. That Hawthorne is such a tentative writer results from his lack of a suitable literary guide (for coming to terms with the "Actual" and the "Imaginary") and his bringing "himself up on two of the worst possible models, [. . .] Bunyan and Spenser." The *American Notebooks* illuminate his obsession with the Imaginary that culminated in the only slightly flawed *Letter*, which, although a masterpiece, suffers from a heavy-handed presentation of tiresome symbols and "inveterate weakness of dressing up characters to exemplify a theme that is often quite incompatible with 'actuality.'"

30   Stewart, Randall, and Dorothy Bethurum. "Nathaniel Hawthorne: *The Scarlet Letter*." *Living Masterpieces of American Literature*. Vol. 2. Chicago: Scott, Foresman, 1954. 55-175.

Of the nine nineteenth-century pieces of fiction selected for their celebrations of Western ideals of democracy and freedom, only *Letter* and Henry James's *The Spoils of Poynton* (1897) anticipate the twentieth-century's gradual recognition of the social implications of individual freedom. *Letter* (pp. 55-62) is a historical novel that epitomizes Puritan ideals and the Puritan way of life. In addition to being an important historical document, *Letter* is fascinating for its presentation of a tight four-part structure, its highly symbolic language, and its abundance of "ironies, paradoxes, and ambiguities of human experience."

Journal Essays and Notes

31   Atkins, Lois. "Psychological Symbolism of Guilt and Isolation in Hawthorne." *American Imago* 11 (1954): 417-425.

As a "forerunner of the modern psychological drama," *Letter* concerns the transformation of human behavior into symbolic representations, most often concerning Hawthorne himself and the psychological processes associated with guilt and isolation. In relation to modern psychoanalytic theory, *Letter* demonstrates that Pearl represents the unsocialized id, Dimmesdale the overburdened superego, and Hester, who most rationally mediates the relation between the individual and society, the ego. Chillingworth and Hester together also represent familiar aspects of the Freudian complex, Chillingworth symbolizing the unconscious personality in its dark and mysterious levels and Hester the conscious personality that accepts and lives by the social and moral code.

32   Cronin, Morton. "Hawthorne on Romantic Love and the Status of Women." *PMLA* 69 (1954): 89-98.

Hawthorne divided his women characters "rather neatly" into three groups: fragile and obedient, self-reliant and wholesome, and larger-than-life in terms of beauty, intellect, and strength. The latter types, "fit subjects for tragedy," include Hester, Zenobia, and Miriam, used by Hawthorne to work out "the question of the proper status of women in society and the relation, whether subordinate or superior, that love should bear to the other demands that life makes upon the individual." Although many critics assume that Hawthorne's criticism of Puritanism means that he embraces the romantic ideal of freedom, Hawthorne emphatically disapproves of Hester's romantic justification for committing adultery (her assertion of the omnipotence of love). Hawthorne does not intend for his appealing portrayal of Hester to overshadow his "moralizing" about the dangers of romanticism. While Hawthorne was fascinated by "New Women" types (and favors more freedom for women than the Puritans certainly would have), he found the "half-tints" of his less extreme female characters more "congenial" than "the primary colors of the New Woman."

33   Hoeltje, Hubert H. "The Writing of *The Scarlet Letter.*" *New England Quarterly* 27 (1954): 326-346.

Records what is known about the political, economic, and social circumstances under which *Letter* was written, specifically Hawthorne's financial straits at the time, his Custom-House appointment, and the ultimately providential "petty political conspiracy" involving Charles W. Upham, H. L. Conolly, Richard S. Rogers, and William M. Meredith that led to his dismissal from the Surveyorship. Also discussed are the counter efforts of friends such as G. S. Hillard and J. L. O'Sullivan to get Hawthorne's position back and to defend him from his enemies' charges.

1955

Books

34   Gannon, Fred A. *Hawthorne and the Custom House*. Salem: Salem Books, 1955. 9 pp.

Prints Gannon's conversation with a tour guide as the two walked through Salem's old Custom House together to peruse rooms, charts, legal records, financial ledgers and to discuss Hawthorne's brief but financially comfortable career there.

35   Reid, Alfred S. *The Yellow Ruff and The Scarlet Letter: A Source of Hawthorne's Novel*. Gainesville: Florida UP, 1955. 150 pp.

Exploring historical sources for *Letter* that extend beyond New England's,* Reid theorizes that Hawthorne drew details of plot, characters, setting, and style from the trial records of the Sir Thomas Overbury murder in the Tower of London in 1613 that involved an actual case of isolation, adultery, revenge, deceit, murder, and concealed sin. *Letter* contains two references to this murder. Hawthorne knew about it from his reading in *The Harleian Miscellany*, *The Loseley Manuscripts*, and *State Trials* during the summer and fall of 1849. "The numerous parallels between the novel and accounts of the murder indicate not a mere chance borrowing of a few details, but a major creative operation that assimilated a group of materials into a new and vastly superior poetic arrangement." The accounts of this murder provided Hawthorne's "story-germ" for *Letter*; for instance, Hester, Dimmesdale, Chillingworth, and Mistress Hibbins have seventeenth-century historical counterparts in Lady Frances Carr, Jervaise Helwyse, Dr. Simon Forman, and Anne Turner. Reid concludes with a discussion of Hawthorne's creative processes (his "spiritualizing" of the material) and the genesis and evolution of the novel. A bibliography of primary sources for *Letter* and works consulted conclude the study. [For a contradiction to Reid's thesis, see Hena Maes-Jelinek's essay on Chillingworth (224). For more on this subject, see also Reid's *Sir Thomas Overbury's Vision* (53).]

*See Charles Ryskamp's "The New England Sources of *The Scarlet Letter*" (85).

Essays and Studies in Books

36   Fick, Leonard J. *The Light Beyond: A Study of Hawthorne's Theology*. Westminster: Newman Press, 1955. 56-57, 82-84, 103-105.

Refuting the theory that Hawthorne was attracted to skepticism or Roman Catholicism, this study treats Hawthorne's sense of guilt and penance in terms of such constants as Augustianism, Thomism, and Arminianism, arguing that Hawthorne's theological thinking is Arminian rather than Calvinistic. *Letter* concerns the nature of both formal and material sin. Although both Hester and Dimmesdale consented to transgress a grave commandment of God, only Dimmesdale yielded to what he alone knew was a deadly sin. Dimmesdale commits a damning "formal" sin, while Hester commits a "material" sin, which brings neither guilt nor stain to her soul. Ultimately, "each of the three key personages of *Letter* is guilty of sin: Dimmesdale, of adultery (a sin of passion, not of purpose), of cowardly deception, and of a deliberate yielding to what he knew to be deadly sin; Hester, of deception; Chillingworth, of diabolical revenge. And each of them, no matter what his or her evil deed was, experienced the sense of isolation, physical and spiritual, which is the inevitable consequence of sin." [See John C. Gerber's essay (EC9), which argues that Hawthorne's concept of sin had no sense of uniformity.]

37   Lewis, R. W. B. "The Return into Time: Hawthorne." *The American Adam: Innocence, Tragedy, and Tradition in the Nineteenth Century.* Chicago: U of Chicago P, 1955. 110-126.

Explains how Hawthorne's work relates to and expresses the myth of the American Adam, commonly represented in nineteenth-century fiction as an adventurous figure of "heroic innocence and vast potentialities, poised at the start of a new history." Like Herman Melville after him, Hawthorne introduces in *Letter* (pp. 111-114)* the isolated hero "alone in a hostile, or at best a neutral universe" to replace the Adamic personality in the New World Eden. Hawthorne adds a tragic element to the New World experience to create a darker, more realistic situation that involves evil, fear, and destructiveness in the scenario that places the solitary hero against the world. Hawthorne was also the first American author to give fair play to both the hero and his inimical society in order "to set up a pattern of escape and return that is at once tragic and hopeful."

*Although treatment of *Letter* in Lewis's book is skant, many later studies on *Letter* refer to it, and two anthologies of *Letter* criticism include excerpts from it.

38   Waggoner, Hyatt H. "*The Scarlet Letter.*" *Hawthorne: A Critical Study.* Cambridge: Belknap P of Harvard UP, 1955. 118-150.*

This New Critical approach denies readings of *Letter* that pigeonhole the paradoxical Hawthorne as a transcendentalist, Puritan, or feminist, and finds that the most accurate interpretation of all of his works—since even the best biographies find little connection between the "real" man and his sketches, tales, and novels—derives from close scrutiny of their imagery and symbolism. An examination of the color and light imagery, in addition to the slightly less pervasive flower and weed imagery, "provides a chief key to the symbolic structure and intention of [*Letter*]." Waggoner discusses the relationships between the numerous images ("pure," "mixed," or "drained") and colors associated with various types of good and evil in the novel, arguing that the constant interweaving of good and evil with images and symbols prevents the novel from becoming true allegory. Also providing thematic structure to the story are its three chief symbols, the cemetery, the prison, and the rose. As manifest in the first chapter, the moral and natural values associated with the cemetery (a negative value), the prison (another negative value), and the rose (a positive value), "suggest a symbolic pattern within which nearly everything that is most important in the novel may be placed." Because of the "imbalance" between negative and positive values, death and sin overshadow life and goodness, and the rose is finally not sufficient to relieve the "darkening close of a tale of human frailty and sorrow." *Letter* ultimately seems to suggest that Hawthorne's "vision of death was a good deal stronger and more constant than his vision of life."

*See 1963 for revised edition (140). See EC37 for an earlier essay by Waggoner that takes up the symbolic value of the cemetery, prison, and rose. See also Walter Blair's even earlier study (EC2) that examines color, light, and shadow imagery in the romance.

39   Von Abele, Rudolph. "The Wages of Sin." *The Death of the Artist: A Study of Hawthorne's Disintegration*. The Hague, Netherlands: Martinus Nijhoff, 1955. 45-57.

Von Abele's overall study views Hawthorne as "an interesting failure" who does not deserve to be ranked among the nineteenth-century literary giants, and the chapter on the "minor" achievement of *Letter* explains that the novel, while too encumbered with Hawthorne's conflicts about the role of the artist in a democratic culture to be truly great, yet capitalizes upon these conflicts to create "the perfect symbolic projection of [Hawthorne's] inner life." When the novel is read autobiographically, *Letter* becomes a compendium of Hawthorne's problems about art, sex, and society, projected in terms of historical fable. Dimmesdale's situation and symbolic confession of failure parallels Hawthorne's. Hawthorne is most concerned with saving the Dimmesdale side of himself, the innocent and ethereal side capable of visions of the "beautiful," and so he situates Dimmesdale in the climax of the novel beyond the reach of Hester (sex, art) or Chillingworth (intellect).

Journal Essays and Notes

40   Bier, Jesse. "Hawthorne on the Romance: His Prefaces Related and Examined." *Modern Philology* 53 (1955): 17-24.

Relates the ideas of the "enigmatic" and "elusive" prefaces to "Rappaccini's Daughter" and the four novels to determine Hawthorne's "latent and abiding artistic principles." Bier finds Hawthorne's consistently modest, unassuming, and soft-spoken tone deceptive. The common features of the "remarkably homogeneous" prefaces—their conspicuous amount of apologetic self-evaluation and humble criticism of Hawthorne's own literary shortcomings, as well as their justification for his nonrealistic technique—relate to Hawthorne's conception of the imagination in "The Custom-House." In the crucial moon-lit room passage, the mirror reflects how the imagination functions in the artistic process to represent the reality and truth of life when it is kept "in a state of high polish." The moonlight itself becomes a metaphor for the medium by which the imagination perceives the world anew, illustrating Hawthorne's imaginative process of spiritualizing familiar objects or shaping reality into universal truth. The moon-lit room passage implies the "integrity of his motive for writing Romances and not novels," for Hawthorne "sought to get away from realism [. . .] and to get back into the universal, timeless, real 'territory' to which the essentially poetic vehicle of imagination could transport him."

41   Laser, Marvin. "'Head,' 'Heart,' and 'Will' in Hawthorne's Psychology." *Nineteenth-Century Fiction* 10 (1955): 130-140.

Discusses Hawthorne's "groping toward psychological realism" in *Letter* and *House of the Seven Gables*. The systematic application of the terms "head," "heart," and "will" to the psychological analyses of Hawthorne's characters suggests not only that he "adopted the 'scientific' language of the faculty psychology of his era, but that in doing so he was specifically indebted to the work of a now forgotten psychologist, Thomas C. Upham." Hawthorne pervasively used Upham's psychology to create scrupulously accurate psychological portraits of his characters. The central characters in *Letter*, for example, show imbalances of head, heart, and will— Chillingworth possessing an excess of will that diminishes his heart and corrupts his keen intellect, Dimmesdale possessing an overdeveloped sensibility and nonexistent volition, and Hester exhibiting strength in heart and will but an undisciplined intellection. "By the end of the novel, of course, the psychological changes in the three major characters bring about the inevitable denouement. Dimmesdale's one great effort of will, his open confession, kills him; Chillingworth, thus deprived of his revenge-object, simultaneously suffers a complete collapse of will. Hester alone survives to bring head, heart, and will back into a functioning balance."

42   MacLean, Hugh N. "Hawthorne's *Scarlet Letter*: 'The Dark Problem of This Life.'" *American Literature* 27 (1955): 12-24.

The tendency of critics to consider Hester the heroine of *Letter* has been replaced by "a tougher but more accurate interpretation" that builds on John C. Gerber's approach to the novel's structure and theme (EC9). An "artful balance" is struck between structure, use of allegory, and "levels of meaning" that illuminates the "dark necessity" of Hawthorne's theme: the "contrast between man's complete weakness (consequent on his sin) and God's complete power (revealed by His grace)." The novel's four-part progressive structure (in which mirrors act as "signposts" that illustrate the theme) interacts with the three epic quests in the novel (Dimmesdale's search for salvation, Chillingworth's quest to destroy Dimmesdale, and Pearl's desire to learn her paternity), and this interaction unifies the central theme of God's saving power and man's futility.

1956

Essays and Studies in Books

43   Blair, Walter. "Hawthorne." *Eight American Authors: A Review of Research and Criticism.* Ed. Floyd Stovall. New York: Modern Language Association, 1956. 100-152.*

This valuable and thorough review describes and evaluates critical and scholarly work on Hawthorne up to 1955. It contains sections on bibliographical materials, editions, biography, studies of ideas (including religious and philosophical concepts, social and political ideas, and literary theories), and criticism (including studies of sources, evaluations and analyses, and discussions of Hawthorne's influence).

*Reprinted with "a Bibliographic Supplement: A Selective Check List, 1955-1962" by J. Chesley Matthews (New York: Norton, 1963) and then edited and updated with additional material (up until 1969) by James Woodress (New York: Norton, 1971).

44   Butler, John F. "Hawthorne: *The Scarlet Letter*." *Exercises in Literary Understanding.* Chicago: Scott-Foresman, 1956. 18-22.

This instructor's manual includes Hawthorne among fifteen other American "greats" often taught in composition and literature courses. The chapter on *Letter* provides suggestions for planning a course and a "discussion approach" to the novel. A proposal for an in-class exercise on symbolism in *Letter* is followed by directions, questions, and answers for a second, more detailed assignment on the nature of sin—although both are designed to get students to read carefully and analytically on their own.

45 Cady, Edwin Harrison, Frederick J. Hoffman, and Roy Harvey Pearce, eds. "Notes on Reading *The Scarlet Letter*." *The Growth of American Literature: A Critical and Historical Survey.* Volume 1. New York: American Book, 1956. 463-466.

This brief introduction to *Letter* asserts that Hester, Dimmesdale, and Chillingworth come to know themselves and each other through their interdependent relations and through their coming to terms with the impact of their lives on Pearl. "The end toward which the novel's action is directed is to bring Pearl to full life, or to the possibility of full life," since she represents the future.

Journal Essays and Notes

46 Abel, Darrel. "Hawthorne's Dimmesdale: Fugitive from Wrath." *Nineteenth-Century Fiction* 11 (1956): 81-105.*

Although Dimmesdale has been "comparatively neglected" by critics for the "more interesting character" of Hester, he is nonetheless the "structural and thematic center of the romance." As a popular Puritan minister, Dimmesdale most logically illustrates Hawthorne's theme: "in every heart, even the holiest, there is a germ of evil." Indeed, the entire plot of the novel hinges on "the struggle between God and the devil" for Dimmesdale's soul or, more specifically, on the mysterious competing forces that attempt to prevent or encourage the minister to ascend the scaffold and reveal his sin. Borrowing structural principles for the novel previously established by John C. Gerber (in EC9), Abel distinguishes between four "parts" or "activating agents" that act upon Dimmesdale and advance the plot: organized society, then Chillingworth, next Hester, and finally God, who is "revealed to have been the ultimate activator in the three earlier parts which had other ostensible agents." Although some critics lack "critical sympathy" for Hawthorne and fail to perceive the sincerity of his Puritan-like belief in "universal depravity" (even though that belief is "colored by an unPuritan sympathy for the sinner"), it remains true that Dimmesdale serves "as an illustration of Puritan conceptions of sinfulness and regeneration." [See 406 for Nina Baym's critique of Abel's assertion that Dimmesdale is the novel's true protagonist.]

*Reprinted in Abel's *The Moral Picturesque: Studies in Hawthorne's Fiction* (see 559).

47   Bewley, Marius. "Hawthorne and the Deeper Psychology." *Mandrake* 2 (1956): 366-373.

Argues that Hawthorne's interest in the "deeper psychology"—as Henry James defined it (in EC15)—is a mere facet of his real focus, which is the "moral reality" of his characters: "Hawthorne was interested in the psychology of his characters only insofar as he could use it as a stage on which certain complex moral problems could be dramatically acted." His characters "dissolve" from living personalities into external, universally-understood symbols that advance his dramatization of moral problems. Thus Hawthorne "is not interested in Hester's private drama" but rather in her status as the symbolic focus of "tangled moral forces." Hawthorne's belief system recognized only one truth or reality, which grounded his sense of moral reality: the "inner sphere of reciprocal love."

48   Haugh, Robert F. "The Second Secret in *The Scarlet Letter*." *College English* 17 (1956): 269-271.

Of the three scaffold scenes, only the first two can be considered static tableaux motivated by the novel's first adulterous secret; the third scaffold scene, "tense with energy and activity," is motivated by "the second secret," the conspiracy to hide Chillingworth's true identity. This secret structures and "energizes the action of the novel," not four different motivating forces, as John C. Gerber suggests (in EC9), and "at last bring[s] all to realization of the moral consequences of their acts." For instance, it is only when Hester realizes the detrimental effect her silence has had on Dimmesdale that the first stirrings of moral and social responsibility awaken within her and compel her to "redeem her error." Likewise, the source of Dimmesdale's astonishing strength after being with Hester in the forest "is implicit in the second secret," surfacing once the "visible Satan" is pointed out to him and can be fought. Dimmesdale's confession during the dynamic third scaffold scene destroys the "energy" of the second secret and completes the major action of *Letter*, thus explaining why at this point the action of the book seems to conclude. [For a response to this essay, see Francis W. Lovett, Jr.,'s review directly below (49)].

49   Lovett, Jr., Francis W.   Review of "The Second Secret in *The Scarlet Letter*," by Robert F. Haugh. *College English* 17 (1956): 492.

Though Haugh's essay (see 48) is "convincingly presented, the conclusion correspondingly acceptable," it "overlook[s] the obvious," which is that the action of the novel clearly "takes its life from the [adulterous] deed, its movement from the consequence thereof."   Thus the novel's first and second "secrets" are really just aspects of the true theme of *Letter*: the consequences of sin.   Further, the characters are more complicated than Haugh allows.   Hester's fundamental error is not so much a refusal to see her moral responsibility, as Haugh suggests, but her "impulsively hasty" nature for which she pays dearly.   And Dimmesdale's suddenly acquired strength at the end is not the immediate result of Hester's disclosure about Chillingworth's identity, but stems from the emotional release he experiences soon after Hester makes the decision for them to flee.

50   McNamara, Anne Marie.   "The Character of Flame: the Function of Pearl in *The Scarlet Letter*." *American Literature* 27 (1956): 537-553.

Previous critical discussions of *Letter* have surprisingly neglected the significance of Pearl's role.   It is Pearl "who effects [Dimmesdale's] unexpected public confession of paternity" during the final scaffold scene. Agreeing with Henry James's assessment (in EC15) that the novel is primarily Dimmesdale's story, but rejecting Leland Schubert's view that the three scaffold scenes highlight the novel (see EC26), McNamara contends that the story of Dimmesdale "centers" in the forest scene, where the "otherworldly" Pearl, by dramatically rejecting him, provides the "missing" spiritual motivation for his later confession.   The novel is structured into four parts that lead up to Dimmesdale's redemption: Preparation   (chapters   1-16),   Communication   (chapters   17-19), Transformation (chapters 20-22), and Revelation (chapter 23).   Much more than a "passive link between her father and mother and more than a static symbol of their sin," Pearl (a figure of grace) enacts Dimmesdale's confession and salvation, and is a "powerful but hidden force urging him to good."   [See Edward C. Sampson's article, "Motivation in *The Scarlet Letter*" (66), for an argument against McNamara's reading.   For more on Pearl's function in the novel, see the Subject Index under "Characters." For an essay that assesses critical treatments of Pearl's character over time, see Barbara Garlitz's "Pearl: 1850-1955" (50)].

51   Stanton, Robert.   "Hawthorne, Bunyan, and the American Romances." *PMLA* 71 (1956): 155-165.

Examines the "more subtle" allusions to John Bunyon that have been previously overlooked by critics in *Letter*, *House of the Seven Gables*, and *Blithedale Romance*, arguing that echoes of *The Pilgrim's Progress* (1678) can be found with surprising regularity in three parallel episodes in each romance: the forest scene between Hester and Dimmesdale (chapters 16-20), "The Flight of Two Owls" in *Seven Gables* (chapter 17), and "A Modern Arcadia" (chapter 8) in *Blithedale*. In each, "two or more characters try to cast off the evil of the past, to find happiness or satisfaction by breaking free of a worn-out system of laws or conventions, and to return to a simpler, more natural life." The impulses to give in to temptation, which mimic Christian's desire to travel the easy route to the Celestial City, all fail and end in either discouragement or despair. The allusions to Bunyan provide simultaneous irony and foreshadowing by presenting the attempted escapes as optimistic, exhilarating, and even intoxicating to the reader, while at the same time "suggest[ing] the moral error and impending fall of the characters. In other words, they express, with economy and effectiveness, a detailed view of the nature of sin." Guilt cannot be cast off and the past cannot be discarded, because to do either leads to the most severe moral crimes of all: "discarding human conventions and laws" and "disregarding accepted human limits."

52   Stewart, Randall. "Hawthorne and Faulkner." *College English* 17 (1956): 258-262.

While admittedly not the first to notes similarities between Hawthorne and Faulkner (Stewart cites George Marion O'Donnell as claiming that distinction in 1939), Stewart claims to be the first to extend the comparison "beyond a sentence or two" by suggesting likenesses between Judge Pyncheon and Flem Snopes, Donatello and Benjy-Dilsey, and Dimmesdale and Joe Christmas. As for the latter comparison, "Dimmesdale is perhaps the one Hawthorne character who can be compared with Christmas, who would have understood him, and who exemplifies with something approaching Faulknerian power the destruction wrought by civil war within the soul." Of the many general similarities between Hawthorne and Faulkner, a few of the most noteworthy are a shared view of the human condition and the past as inescapable and heroic; a tendency toward symbolical and allegorical writing; and a tri-fold fascination with the problem of evil, the concept of the Fortunate Fall, and the struggle toward redemption.

1957

Books

53   Reid, Alfred S. *Sir Thomas Overbury's Vision (1616) by Richard Niccols and Other English Sources of Nathaniel Hawthorne's The Scarlet Letter.* Gainesville: Scholars' Facsimiles and Reprints, 1957. 202 pp.

Intended as a companion volume to Reid's *The Yellow Ruff and The Scarlet Letter: A Source of Hawthorne's Novel* (see 35), this collection of facsimile reprints "makes available in one convenient reference work those major documents of the Overbury murder that stimulated Hawthorne's imagination to shape into a novel the idea which had lain dormant in his mind for many years." While *The Yellow Ruff* discusses the accounts all together, this approach addresses "the distinctive flavor" and "significance of the individual sources" in Reid's introduction (v-xviii). The original documents that exerted a recognizable influence on Hawthorne include *The Loseley Manuscripts* (which offer a helpful compendium of the Overbury Case); "The Five Years of King James" (a moralistic pamphlet that "minutely" traces the murder as well as gives a chronology of events and descriptions of the *dramatis personae* and their relationships); the "Preface" to *The Narrative History of King James* by Michael Sparke (which most likely inspired Hawthorne's editorial hoax about Surveyor Pue's manuscript and suggested the idea of an article of clothing becoming infamously connected to its wearer); State Trial Records (which influenced the form of the novel); and Richard Niccols's *Sir Thomas Overbury's Vision* (which poetically "recreates the remorseful thoughts of the guilty participants"). "An intimate reading of the sources and a close analysis of Hawthorne's adaptations will give the reader a glimpse into the creative workshop of one of America's foremost literary artists."

Essays and Studies in Books

54   Bewley, Marius. "Hawthorne's Novels." *The Eccentric Design: Form in the Classic American Novel.* New York: Columbia UP, 1957. 147-186.

Enlarging upon the insights of D. H. Lawrence (see EC18), Bewley asserts that Hawthorne's fiction, like that of other nineteenth-century American novelists, is specifically shaped by tensions between solitude and society, past and present, America and Europe, and democratic faith and disillusion. Hawthorne's short stories and novels are especially concerned with "the tension between isolation and social sympathy." *Letter* (pp. 161-175) becomes "a subtle exploration of moral isolation in America" that takes for its subject the effects of the violation of the magnetic chain of humanity on the human spirit. The crime in the novel is not Hester's and Dimmesdale's adulterous act, or even the claustrophobic limitations of New England Puritanism, but the damage that Hester and Dimmesdale do to the sanctity and purity of social relationships by separating themselves from society, the result of which is a living death for both.

55   Chase, Richard. "Hawthorne and the Limits of Romance." *The American Novel and Its Tradition*. Garden City: Doubleday, 1957. 67-87.

American fiction has always tended toward the original, often melodramatic creation of "romance-novels" (which are "freer, more daring, more brilliant" than mannerish English novels). The leading characteristics of this kind of fiction are "an assumed freedom from the ordinary novelistic requirements of verisimilitude" and "a tendency to plunge into the underside of consciousness." The chapter on Hawthorne focuses mainly on *Letter* but also treats *Blithedale Romance* and briefly mentions Hawthorne's influence on Melville in writing *Moby-Dick*. Hawthorne was interested less in expressing his political or social concerns than in presenting his "art-view of the world." Conditions in America (as described in Hawthorne's prefaces) and his "Puritan scruples" (directing him to treat the "physical passions" obliquely) led Hawthorne to write romances as opposed to novels. Chase concludes that, "although Hawthorne was a superb writer of romance and a considerable novelist from any point of view, he was aware that his romances, as he himself insisted on calling them [. . .], proceeded in part from his inability to portray character and scene with novelistic fullness." [See Nicolaus Mills (307) for an argument that runs counter to Chase's.]

56   Male, Roy R. "The Tongue of Flame: *The Scarlet Letter*." *Hawthorne's Tragic Vision*. Austen: U of Texas P, 1957. 90-118.*

Explores the details of Hawthorne's tragic vision in *Letter*, beginning with an examination of several disparate critical interpretations as evidence of the novel's fundamental complexity and richness. *Letter* cannot be reduced to any single explication, but the novel's unique language pattern helps in answering some interesting questions that conventional readings of the book fail to answer. Male systematically establishes the allegorical significance of Pearl and Chillingworth, and then outlines the book's structure (divided into three equal parts that reveal "Hester's limited ascension," "the burdens of guilt," and later "Dimmesdale's complete ascension"). *Letter*'s guiding metaphor is the "Tongue of Flame," which Hawthorne derives from a description of the Holy Ghost descending upon the chosen disciples in Acts 2:3-4. This metaphor, which symbolizes the ability to address "the whole human brotherhood in the heart's native language" and which becomes identical with the scarlet letter itself, is an intuitive type of revelatory communication that deals with the ability both to "speak" and to "see" the highest truths—the combined act of which

Dimmesdale alone achieves in his "saintly" confessional gesture at the end of the novel. *Letter* ultimately concerns different kinds of vision, different ways of seeing to gain a clearer perspective of the truth, and the moral of the tale is finally the importance of being true: "one must not mean, but *be.*"

*Reprinted in 1964 (New York: W. W. Norton).

57   Pearce, Roy Harvey. Introduction. *The Scarlet Letter.* By Nathaniel Hawthorne. 1850. New York: J. M. Dent and Sons, 1957. v-x.

Only wishing to provide a brief outline that will account for *Letter*'s "moral and artistic qualities," Pearce claims to know "the secret of [the novel's] symbolic structure, its form, its technique, and its meaning, of its total grasp on its small world." In the novel (an "unrelievedly hard book"), Hawthorne "treats most fully and complexly" his major subject: the discovery, through sin, of true and authentic self, the isolation which is the consequence of that discovery, and the struggle to endure which is the consequence of that isolation." Hawthorne does not flesh out his story (more of a tale than a novel) with details, because he intends for its meaning to be "sensed" rather than lived through. He does present with absolute "sureness and clarity" the symbolic pattern that underlies his characters' lives—and all people's lives—as they work out the psychological and moral effects of their sins. It is in getting at the "deeper psychology" of life (to borrow from Henry James, EC15) that Hawthorne is interested in, the necessity of the individual sinner to acknowledge his private sin and authentic self and then to recognize his place in the community of sinners—and finally to "endur[e] the burden of being such a self living with other such selves."

58   Stewart, Randall. "The Vision of Evil in Hawthorne and Melville." *The Tragic Vision and the Christian Faith.* Ed. Nathan A. Scott, Jr. New York: Association Press, 1957. 238-263.

Hawthorne and Melville, who subscribed to the Christian concept of Original Sin and viewed human life as a battleground for the struggle of good and evil, found the promotion of extravagant individualism by their fellow romantics to be unsatisfying and overly optimistic. *Letter*, in particular (pp. 245-250), illustrates the perils of self-reliance (just as do several of Hawthorne's stories and Melville's *Moby-Dick* and *Billy Budd*). But just as *Letter* criticizes the romantic impulse, so too does it condemn Puritan tendencies—the conflict between the two comprising the chief tension in *Letter*. Stewart grants more sympathy to Dimmesdale (the Puritan) than to Hester (the romantic), however, and he ultimately sees the novel as Dimmesdale's tragedy alone because his suffering is more intense and difficult to endure than Hester's. Hester remains impenitent and unredeemed to the last, while Dimmesdale redeems himself during the "noble" climax of his public confession.

Journal Essays and Notes

59   Cowley, Malcolm. "Five Acts of *The Scarlet Letter.*" *College English* 19 (1957): 11-16.*

Hawthorne was the first author to have "by accident or design" invented a form in *Letter* "that was closer to stage drama than it was to ordinary novels." In spite of Edgar Allan Poe's feeling that "unity of effect" and "strict economy of means" cannot be achieved in a novel but only in the short story, Hawthorne succeeds in creating that effect in *Letter*. His most impressive technical innovation (later developed by Henry James and many others) involved his novelistic approach, which had hitherto essentially been a chronicle of events. Instead of creating narrative episodes, Hawthorne "dramatistically" divided *Letter* into scenes, "each of which is a posed tableau or a dramatic confrontation" that lends architectural form to the novel. He most likely modeled this method after the French dramatist Racine, whose work Hawthorne was well-acquainted with. When read as "a Racinian drama of dark necessity," the tragedy's twenty-four chapters can be roughly divided into five acts and subdivided into eight scenes. Act I, Scene I (chapters 1 to 3) is set in the marketplace of Boston; Scene 2 (chapter 4) is in a room in the prison. Act II, Scene I (chapters 7 and 8) takes place in the governor's hall; Scene 2 (chapter 10) is set in Chillingworth's laboratory. Act III (chapter 12) takes place on the scaffold. Act IV, Scene I (chapters 14 and 15) is laid on the seashore; Scene 2 (chapters 16 through 19) takes place in the forest, and Act V (chapters 20-23) is set in the marketplace. In developing the tragic drama in the framework of the novel, Hawthorne not only established his kinship with Racine, but "recaptured for New England, the essence of Greek tragedy." [See 68 for an expanded version of this essay.]

*Reprinted in Cowley's *New England Writers and Writing* (Ed. Donald W. Faulkner. Hanover: UP of New England, 1996. 43-55).

60   Douglas, Harold J., and Robert Daniel. "Faulkner and the Puritanism of the South." *Tennessee Studies in Literature* 2 (1957): 1-13.

Compares the influence of the doctrines of election and damnation on Faulkner and Hawthorne, noting an especial affinity between the two writers in their mutual hatred of "the excesses of Calvinism." A juxtaposition of the "substructures" in *As I Lay Dying* and *Letter* illustrates that similarities between Faulkner and Hawthorne are greater than those noted by critics in the past (such as "the pervasively sombre tone arising from an awareness of degeneration, the sense of doom, the absolute moral certainty"). These more significant correspondences include adulterous relations with weak ministers following loveless marriages, illegitimate children (Pearl and Jewel), and consequent experiences of isolation from "the common stream of humanity." Such "incontrovertible" likenesses prove a kinship between the two that stems from their "Calvinistic bent"— despite any objections readers might initially have regarding the authors' very different styles.

61   Fairbanks, Henry G. "Hawthorne and Confession." *Catholic Historical Review* 43 (1957): 38-45.

Hawthorne's interest in Catholic confession "as an outlet for the guilty heart" is by no means isolated to *Marble Faun*. The idea of confession was an "old theme" of Hawthorne's and can be found in "Roger Malvin's Burial," *Letter*, and the French and Italian Notebooks, as well. In *Letter*, which focuses specifically on "the necessity and blessings of confession" in the discussion between Chillingworth and Dimmesdale in chapter five, Hawthorne's original intention was for Dimmesdale to make his confession to a priest. But Hawthorne decided against featuring the Catholic confessional in the novel, yielding to "a strong sense of historical propriety" by not introducing a priest into "inhospitable seventeenth-century Boston."

62   Garlitz, Barbara. "Pearl: 1850-1955." *PMLA* 72 (1957): 689-699.

Numerous diverse and contradictory interpretations of Pearl over the past hundred years inspired this detailed survey of Pearl criticism. Garlitz illuminates the "unfathomable maze" of Pearl's character by charting evolving attitudes toward her (which to some extent reflect changing attitudes toward children over the decades) and emphasizing her complexity, which has been overlooked by critics who tend to isolate certain aspects of Pearl's personality. In general, Pearl has been viewed as more innocent in the nineteenth century than in the twentieth, and she has variously been considered as angelic/evil, moral/amoral, symbolic/realistic, and natural/unnatural. Hawthorne's exaggeration of "general characteristics" of children in Pearl becomes symbolic of Hester's "diseased moral state" (particularly Pearl's perversity, lack of sympathy, and proclivity to hate). Hawthorne tends to consider Pearl in terms of the physical inheritance of sin (not to be confused with original sin, which Garlitz insists Hawthorne did not believe in). Pearl therefore is "a microcosm of Hester's moral chaos" but also "a mixture of Hawthorne's sober observation of childhood and his continuing [nineteenth-century] belief in the sinless child. The physiological psychology of the period must have appealed to Hawthorne, for it enabled him to shift the responsibility for Pearl's evil to Hester, to make her originally innocent but the victim of an unusually faulty moral inheritance." [For more on Pearl, see Anne Marie McNamara's famous 1956 essay (50). See also the Subject Index under "Characters."]

63   Mathews, James W. "Hawthorne and the Chain of Being." *Modern Language Quarterly* 18 (1957): 282-294.

"Contrary to the views of many Hawthorne commentators," isolation or estrangement is not only an all-pervading theme in Hawthorne but also "the basic sin of mankind" that leads to other sins. Hawthorne's moralistic philosophy depended heavily on his firm belief in the "Chain of Being" theory. For example, because Hester and Dimmesdale have trouble confining themselves to their "rightful"—if limiting—boundaries in both nature and society, tragedy ensues for them and the novel ends up being a tale of their own "thwarted purposes." *Letter* as a whole enacts "the frustration that results when each of the three principal characters fails to achieve a harmonious relationship with his environment." Only when "penance and true penitence are effected" can Dimmesdale and Hester be restored to the great Chain of Being (Chillingworth failing to make a "satisfactory readjustment"). Although illustrating his thesis most fully with *Letter*, Mathews also briefly discusses several short stories ("The May-Pole of Merry Mount," "Wakefield," "The Shaker Bridal," "The Birth-mark," and "Ethan Brand"), *Blithedale Romance*, and *Marble Faun*.

64   O'Connor, William Van. "Hawthorne and Faulkner: Some Common Ground." *Virginia Quarterly Review* 33 (1957): 105-123.*

Both Hawthorne and Faulkner "lived under the spell" of their own family's and town's "gloomy wrongs," as is especially apparent in *Letter* and *Light in August* (pp. 105-113)—where the New England Puritans and North Mississippi Presbyterians are similarly presented as dark, guilt-ridden, and excessively moralized. "In each novel, human weakness and the need to sympathize and to forgive are played off against an iron-like rigidity and lack of sympathy." Similar relationships appear in *House of the Seven Gables* and *The Sound and the Fury*, *Marble Faun* and *Absalom! Absalom!*

*Reprinted in *American Literary Scene* (Bombay: Popular Book Depot, 1962) and *The Grotesque: An American Genre and Other Essays* (Carbondale: Southern Illinois UP, 1962).

65   Reid, Alfred S. "A Note on the Date of *The Scarlet Letter.*" *Furman Studies* 4 (1957): 30-39.

Speculating on when Hawthorne began writing *Letter* (having discounted the now questionable date suggested by Hawthorne's son, Julian, that composition began June 8, 1849, the day Hawthorne was fired from the Custom House), Reid provides three factors that suggest Hawthorne delayed writing until October or November: library withdrawals (source books on the Overbury murder) from the Salem Athenaeum from October 9 to December 21, Hawthorne's typical writing practice (his tendency not to write in the summer months), and the distracting personal hardships in June and July of that year (losing his job and his mother).

66   Sampson, Edward C. "Motivation in *The Scarlet Letter.*" *American Literature* 28 (1957): 511-513

Anne Marie McNamara's claim (see 50) that Pearl provides the motivation for Dimmesdale's confession ignores two points: first, Dimmesdale's guilt-ridden ethical sense when coupled with Hester's revelation of Chillingworth's identity in the forest (which motivates Dimmesdale's latent ability to act) provides a much more powerful impetus for confession; and second, Pearl plays no part in the procession following the Election-Day Sermon until after Dimmesdale has confessed—at which point, even then, he turns to Hester first.

67   Stone, Edward. "The Antique Gentility of Hester Prynne." *Philological Quarterly* 36 (1957): 90-96.

The coat-of-arms edifice on the scaffold plays an important role in the structural symmetry of *Letter* not only for its ever-central presence but also as a symbolic reminder of Hester's Old World gentility and aristocracy.   Hawthorne extends his nostalgic treatment of Old World heritage (fighting a losing battle in the "rough air and temper" of the New World) in his representations of Bellingham's mansion and Hester's magisterial letter and fantastic embroidery—all of which are "virtually aglow with symbols of Old World aristocracy."   Stone suggests that Hester's adorned letter itself is perhaps her (and Hawthorne's) way of transmuting Old World armorial bearings into a new, "wilderness form" with the letter.   After all, the letter eventually takes on heraldic significance (as does her grave's epitaph), reclaiming through "the gorgeously beautiful" her aristocratic birthright. Hawthorne similarly invests Pearl with attributes of Old World aristocracy and eventually a heraldry of her own, perhaps to project the Old World identity into the future.

1958

Essays and Studies in Books

68   Cowley, Malcolm. "Five Acts of *The Scarlet Letter.*" *Twelve Original Essays on Great American Novels.* Ed. Charles Shapiro. Detroit: Wayne State UP, 1958. 23-43.

An expansion of the original journal article that appeared in 1957 (see 59), with more historical background information from Hawthorne's several notebook entries that contain germinal ideas for the novel. Cowley further fleshes out the two major technical problems that Hawthorne faced in writing the novel, the first of which he solved by including the characters of Governor Bellingham, the Reverend John Wilson, and Mistress Hibbins (to represent society in its "essential aspects") and the second by creating an innovative novelistic approach because he knew that he lacked skill as a "chronicler of events."

69   Ito, Kiyoshi. "Similarity of Wordings in Hawthorne's Two Works." *Studies in English Grammar and Linguistics: A Miscellany in Honor of Takanobu Otsuka.* Ed. Kazuo Araki. Tokyo: Kenkyusha, 1958. 275-288.

Observes similarities in wordings in *Letter* and *House of the Seven Gables* and discusses their common "stylistic peculiarities" as clues to the artistic nature of both. Ito examines twenty "equal narrative" portions of both works and notes percentages of "classical words" (that give the impression of solemnity and formality and exhibit an artistic abstractness) and parts of speech, literally listing ratios of nouns, verbs, adjectives, and adverbs— and compares them to the classical vocabularies in *Moby-Dick, Walden,* and "The Fall of the House of Usher" (since the latter works share an "elevated, subjective, and emotional tone peculiar to writers of the Romantic school"). Both novels are written in extremely similar language, although *Letter* contains more abstract nouns and is generally more fanciful and subjective—because it is a romance—than the mannerish, more realistic novel, *House of the Seven Gables.*

70   Levin, Harry. "The Skeleton in the Closet." *The Power of Blackness: Hawthorne, Poe and Melville.* New York: Alfred A. Knopf, 1958. 68-100.

Explores Hawthorne's tragic vision, which was in direct contrast with the optimistic, popular, and materialist influences of his time. His fascination with "the power of blackness" is best revealed when one considers Hawthorne's sense of historical consciousness ("Puritanical Gloom") and his obsessive concern with both sin and human relations. While creating an atmosphere of enclosure, isolation, and secrecy in *Letter* (pp. 73-79), Hawthorne yet makes an oblique plea for the natural magnetism of society—for although the punishing scarlet letter is designed to isolate Hester from her community, it "proves to be a talisman which establishes bonds of sympathy."

71   Schwartz, Joseph. "God and Man in New England." *American Classics Reconsidered: A Christian Appraisal.* Ed. Harold C. Gardiner. New York: Charles Scribner's Sons, 1958. 121-145.

Argues that Hawthorne's chief interest lay in the moral and religious character of man, and provides background on changes in theology, philosophy, and politics in Hawthorne's time. Schwartz focuses primarily on the theological controversy involving free will between the Calvinists and Unitarians that influenced Hawthorne's thinking and made him reject both theologies (Calvinism because of its exclusiveness and smug righteousness and Unitarianism for its "mistiness") for the more "positive concept" of a beneficent, loving Deity. The issue of Hawthorne's faith is the "crucial matrix" of both *Letter* and *The Marble Faun.* "The key to *Letter* is in the character of Dimmesdale, whose fundamental weakness is not his sin, nor even his hypocrisy, but his failure to recognize that God is a God of love." Dimmesdale's indecision about the nature of God is what most defines his miserable nature—even at his death. Unlike Dimmesdale's, Donatello's spiritual problem is resolved when he triumphs through knowledge of God's love.

72   Stewart, Randall. "Guilt and Innocence." *American Literature and Christian Doctrine.* Baton Rouge: Louisiana State UP, 1958. 73-106.

Slight revision of Stewart's 1957 essay on "The Vision of Evil in Hawthorne and Melville" (see 58) that examines Hawthorne and Herman Melville as "counter-romantics" to Ralph Waldo Emerson and Walt Whitman, and discusses the tensions between Puritan (Dimmesdale) and romantic (Hester) tendencies in *Letter.*

Journal Essays and Notes

73   Brant, Robert Louis. "Hawthorne and Marvell." *American Literature* 30 (1958): 366.

Challenges previous interpretations of the last line of *Letter* by claiming that the source for the final words is from the last two lines of Andrew Marvell's poem "The Unfortunate Lover": "And he in Story only rules, / In a Field Sable, a Lover Gules." This source, which suggests an aesthetic rather than moral intention in the novel, implies "a redeeming light in the beauty of the tragedy." [See 313 for an extension of Brant's thesis.]

74   Gleckner, Robert. "James's *Madame de Mauves* and Hawthorne's *The Scarlet Letter*." *Modern Language Notes* 73 (1958): 580-586.

Finds in Henry James's nouvelle *Madame de Mauves* "not only some interesting general similarities to *Letter* but also (1) James's implicit criticism of Hawthorne's allegorical method, (2) James's unusual use of that method in Longmore's dream in the forest, and (3) the relationship between James's own presentation of certain scenes in *Madame de Mauves* and his explicit criticism (in his critical study, *Hawthorne* [EC15]) of similar scenes in *Letter*." In effect, James learned both from Hawthorne's greatness and from his own sense of Hawthorne's limitations and flaws.

75   Ryan, Pat M., Jr. "Young Hawthorne at the Salem Theater." *Essex Institute Historical Collections* 94 (1958): 243-255.

Records and letters attest to Hawthorne's "boyhood attraction to the stage," and this early interest in the Salem theater colored his writing, especially evident in the drama-indebted *Letter*, where the public square scenes are "closely patterned on the form of a play."

76   Ziff, Larzer. "The Ethical Dimension of 'The Custom-House.'" *Modern Language Notes* 73 (1958): 338-344.

While many critics have pointed out that "The Custom-House" contains Hawthorne's aesthetic theory of romance, no one has clearly outlined the crucial relationship between that theory and Hawthorne's moral "theory of the good life" ("one which blends the reveries of the past with the actions of the present" and "combines morality and materiality"). In other words, Hawthorne believed that "just as the good romance strikes a balance between the actual and the imaginary, so the man of good character strikes a balance between his inner state and the materiality of the world." Hawthorne faults his morally-stunted Custom House colleagues—save one—for attending exclusively to their outer lives and charges the isolated old General Miller for indulging too much in the reveries of his own inner life (as does Hester). Hawthorne implies that he, himself, has struck a good balance between outer/inner lives because he appreciates the present "through a consciousness of the past." Although seemingly pleased with himself, Hawthorne expresses dissatisfaction in "The Custom-House" with the overall achievement of *Letter*, finding the novel imbalanced for overdeveloping "the half of the dualism embodying the past, the inner state, and the imaginary," and thus underdeveloping "the virtues of the present, the material, and the actual." This professed "shortcoming" does not appear in Hawthorne's subsequent romances.

1959

Essays and Studies in Books

77   Davies, Horton. "Preachers and Evangelists: *The Scarlet Letter*." *A Mirror of the Ministry in Modern Novels*. New York: Oxford UP, 1959. 24-28.

Letter reflects Hawthorne's fascination with and repulsion by his Puritan Congregational ancestors, and serves as both a parable of ministerial hypocrisy and an "epitaph for Puritanism." In the promising early days of the Puritan theocracy in Colonial America, the minister was not only the preacher but also "the moral leader and exemplar of his community." Hawthorne chose a minister for the primary role of sinner to show best the flaws of Puritanism that led to its failure: hypocrisy, timidity, and lack of integrity and compassion. Despite his brilliant potential, Dimmesdale possesses the fatal flaws that led to the downfall of Puritanism, and actually ranks third in the novel (below Hester and Chillingworth) in terms of strength of character and dominance because of "the paucity of his convictions."

78   Marx, Leo. Foreword. *The Scarlet Letter*. By Nathaniel Hawthorne. Signet Classic edition. New York: New American Library, 1959. vii-xiv.

Lists *Letter* among the classics of American fiction and explores its "remarkable" qualities as a work of great economy and unity which had been in Hawthorne's brooding mental works for twenty years prior to the novel's composition. Discusses symbolic contrasts in the novel that show the essential and perpetual conflict between "restraint, order, and institutional control" and "the impulsive, passionate, and spontaneous." Marx also provides information on the landscape, setting, action, and overall moral, and speculates about how readers are to accept Hester's "defeat" at the end. He concludes by reminding the "impatient reader" that he may skip "The Custom-House" and move straight to the novel itself since the sketch "is not an integral part of the story."

79   Mauriac, François. "Hawthorne's *The Scarlet Letter*." New York: Farrar, Straus Giroux, 1959.*

In this "document of supreme importance," Hawthorne "turns a cruel caricature of Christianity into an apologia which opens a door upon the mystery of evil." What gives this "terrible story" its true significance is that the Puritans ("a republic of bitter hypocrites") "flout the very word of God" by falsifying the Gospel and refusing to admit sin as the very principle that humanizes us. Hawthorne contrasts this false pharisaism of the Puritan community of Boston with the genuine sainthood achieved by Hester and Dimmesdale after years of suffering and remorse. So in stressing "the most odious distortions of the religious spirit," Hawthorne manages miraculously to show that "sin becomes a principle of total renewal" and that "the very principle of our regeneration is to be found in what is worst in us."

*I was not able to track down a complete bibliographic citation for this source in my own research or through Interlibrary Loan. The page numbers and the exact source for the original translation of this brief essay are not listed in the acknowledgments of the collection of criticism where I found Mauriac's reprinted essay: *Transatlantic Mirrors: Essays in Franco-American Literary Relations* (Ed. Sidney D. Braun and Seymour Lainoff. Boston: Twayne Publishers, 1978. 85-89). The editors acknowledge only that Gerard Hopkins translated Mauriac's piece into English in 1960, a translation copyrighted by Eyre and Spottiswoode.

80   Sewall, Richard B. "*The Scarlet Letter*." *The Vision of Tragedy*. New Haven: Yale UP, 1959. 86-91.

Those writers who possess the tragic vision (from the author of Job to William Faulkner) see man as "questioner, naked, unaccommodated, alone, facing mysterious, demonic forces in his own nature and outside, and the irreducible facts of suffering and death." Hawthorne wrote in the true vein of tragedy and "dealt not with doctrinaire injunctions but with actions in their entirety, with special regard in *Letter* [. . .] for their consequences." Sewall juxtaposes Hawthorne with the transcendentalists, noting that Emerson did not share Hawthorne's "pure" tragic vision that encompasses the irrevocable contraries of life and the soul's perpetual struggle with conflict. If any light shines through Hawthorne's dark vision at all, it is "the tragic opposite of Emerson's triumphant gleaming sun that 'shines also today.'" Yet Hawthorne's tragic vision isn't without its reward. Hester's suffering is not in vain, since "there is wisdom to be won from the fine hammered steel of woe." This hard-won, acquired wisdom is a "major salvage" not only for Hester in her seven-year ordeal but also for her Puritan community that she humanizes and forces to reassess its severe dogmas.

81   Feidelson, Charles, [Jr.], and Paul Brodtkorb, Jr., eds. *Interpretations of American Literature*. Oxford: Oxford UP, 1959.

This student-oriented collection of reprinted, interpretive essays on major works includes Hyatt H. Waggoner's *"The Scarlet Letter"* (pp. 3-29) [38] and Q. D. Leavis's "Hawthorne as Poet" (pp. 30-50) [13].

82   Weber, J. Sherwood, Jules Alan Wein, Arthur Waldhorn, and Arthur Zeiger. "Hawthorne: *The Scarlet Letter*." *From Homer to Joyce: A Study Guide to Thirty-Six Great Books*. New York: Holt, 1959. 200-209.

Primarily provides historical background on Hawthorne and the novel, but also includes 25 questions for study and discussion, along with a listing of suggested readings in background and criticism.

Journal Essays and Notes

83   Bonham, M. Hilda. "Hawthorne's Symbols *Sotto Voce*." *College English* 20 (1959): 184-186.

Analyzes the symbolic importance of Hester's needlework, noting that each reference to her masterful artistry "adds another deft stroke to [Hawthorne's] portrait of a strong-willed, passionate, sensitive, speculative, large-hearted woman, at the same time indicating the severe limits placed on her contacts with the community." Less prominent symbols—such as Hester's rich, original, and daring needlework—contribute more to Hawthorne criticism than the more obvious symbols that have been discussed to death by critics.

84   Mann, Robert W. "Afterthoughts on Opera and *The Scarlet Letter*." *Studi Americani* 5 (1959): 339-381.

Explains the process by which Mann developed the libretto for his operatic adaptation of *Letter*, after having been struck by the novel's "operatic feel." The composition of the score came easily to Mann because of Hawthorne's already melodious and rhythmic prose. Following his "afterthoughts" is Mann's *"The Scarlet Letter*: Libretto in

Four Acts and Nine Scenes" (pp. 351-381), which concludes with Dimmesdale's death.

85   Ryskamp, Charles. "The New England Sources of *The Scarlet Letter*." *American Literature* 31 (1959): 257-272.

Adumbrates the American sources for the factual background of *Letter* that have been largely neglected.* Hawthorne's adaptations of New England historical incidents, places, and people rely on Caleb Snow's *History of Boston*, Increase Mather's *Illustrious Providences*, Cotton Mather's *Magnalia Christi Americana*, George Bancroft's *History of the United States*, Thomas Hutchinson's *History of Massachusetts*, Joseph B. Felt's *Annals of Salem*, and John Winthrop's *Journal*. Hawthorne depended most heavily on Snow's *History of Boston* in authenticating the setting and time scheme, but he had to make deliberate adjustments to develop the plot of his story, the time scheme for which Ryskamp observes is from June of 1642 to late May of 1649. [See 94 for a refutation of Ryskamp's claim in 85 that there is no historical basis for Hester's character. See also 486 for Michael J. Colacurcio's essay that posits an even earlier possible New England source for *Letter* than has been considered before. Refer to the Subject Index under "Sources" for additional studies on the origins of *The Scarlet Letter*.]

*Ryskamp credits two previous source studies as having paved the way for his research on Hawthorne's New England Sources. They are by Arlin Turner ("Hawthorne's Literary Borrowings," *PMLA* 51 [1936]: 543-562) and Edward Dawson (*Hawthorne's Knowledge and Use of New England History: A Study of Sources*, Nashville: Joint University Libraries, 1939.)

1960

Books

86   Gross, Seymour L., ed. *A Scarlet Letter Handbook*. Belmont: Wadsworth Publishing, 1960.

This anthology is divided into four parts. First, an introduction (pp. 1-14 [see 90]) discussing Hawthorne's fiction that anticipates *Letter*. Second, 36 excerpted articles and essays organized under the subject headings of theme, character, symbolism, and structure (pp. 16-140). Third (pp. 142-149), "Topics and Questions for Discussion and Student Papers"; and fourth (pp. 152-161), a helpful annotated bibliography of *Letter* criticism. Under "Theme" are excerpts from George E. Woodberry's *Nathaniel Hawthorne* (EC41), Gordon Roper's "Introduction" to *Letter* (EC25),

James W. Mathews's "Hawthorne and the Chain of Being" (63), Richard H. Fogle's *Hawthorne's Fiction: The Light and the Dark* (15), R. W. B. Lewis's *The American Adam* (37), Roy Male's *Hawthorne's Tragic Vision* (56), and Rudolphe Von Abele's "The *Scarlet Letter*: A Reading" (14). Under "Characters" are Raymond W. Short's "Introduction" to *Four Great Novels* (EC28) and Marius Bewley's "Hawthorne and 'The Deeper Psychology'" (47). Under "Hester Prynne" are Theodore T. Munger's "Notes on *The Scarlet Letter*" (EC23), Stuart P. Sherman's "Hawthorne: A Puritan Critic of Puritanism" (EC27), F. I. Carpenter's "Scarlet A Minus" (EC4), Mark Van Doren's *Nathaniel Hawthorne* (EC36), Darrel Abel's "Hawthorne's Hester" (16), William Bysshe Stein's *Hawthorne's Faust* (22), and Marius Bewley's *The Eccentric Design* (54). Under "Arthur Dimmesdale" are Rudolphe Von Abele's "*The Scarlet Letter*: A Reading" (14), Darrel Abel's "Hawthorne's Dimmesdale: Fugitive from Wrath" (46), and Joseph Schwartz's "God and Man in New England" (71). Under "Roger Chillingworth" are Darrel Abel's "The Devil in Boston" (24) and William Bysshe Stein's *Hawthorne's Faust* (22). Under "Pearl" are Julian Hawthorne's "Problems of *The Scarlet Letter*" (EC12), Chester E. Eisinger's "Pearl and the Puritan Heritage" (12), Darrel Abel's "Hawthorne's Pearl: Symbol and Character" (10), Anne Marie McNamara's "The Character of Flame: The Fuction of Pearl in *The Scarlet Letter*" (50), and Barbara Garlitz's "Pearl: 1850-1955" (62). Under "Symbolism" are Henry James's *Hawthorne* (EC15), F. O. Matthiessen's *American Renaissance* (EC20), Charles Feidelson, Jr.,'s *Symbolism and American Literature* (21), Roy Male's " 'From the Innermost Germ': the Organic Principle in Hawthorne's Fiction" (27), Hyatt H. Waggoner's *Hawthorne: A Critical Study* (38), and M. Hilda Bonham's "Hester's Needlework: Symbolism Sotto Voce" (83). Under "Structure" are Leland Schubert's *Hawthorne the Artist* (EC26), John C. Gerber's "Form and Content in *The Scarlet Letter*" (EC9), Hugh N. Maclean's "Hawthorne's *Scarlet Letter*: 'The Dark Problem of this Life'" (42), and Rudolph Von Abele's "*The Scarlet Letter*: A Reading" (14).

Essays and Studies in Books

87 Armour, Richard. "*The Scarlet Letter*—An A for Effort." *The Classics Reclassified.* New York: McGraw-Hill Book Co., 1960. 65-83.

This "irreverent telling" of Hawthorne's classic includes a prefatory section on Hawthorne, comical illustrations by Campbell Grant, and eight concluding "nonsense questions" about the novel, the answers to which summarize the action of *Letter*.

88   Bogan, Louise. Foreword. *The Scarlet Letter*. By Nathaniel Hawthorne.
       New York: Libra, 1960. ix-xiv.

Offers a very general introduction to *Letter*, providing little more than
biographical information and Henry James's impression of the romance.
Bogan grants Hester the distinction of being "the first portrayal in
American fiction of women's nature in all its complication and
contradiction," but then argues that there is "no trace of nineteenth-century
feminism in her." Hester is "not a heroine in the large sense," but merely
a sensible, industrious woman and a devoted mother who suffers great
hardship.

89   Fiedler, Leslie [A.]. *"The Scarlet Letter*: Woman as Faust." *Love and
       Death in the American Novel*. New York: Criterion Books, 1960. 485-
       519.*

One of the defining characteristics of American fiction is its inability to
deal maturely with adult heterosexual love and its consequent obsession
with death, incest, and innocent homosexuality. This "premature" or
"boyish" tendency to flee into nature or damnation from the
responsibilities associated with society and domestic life is prevalent in
classic American literature, *Letter* being no exception. Although *Letter* is
the only pre-modernist classic American text to make passion a central
theme, Hawthorne's treatment of erotic love is "shadowy and sterilized" at
best ("a seduction story without a seduction")—and may even disguise a
theme of incest under the guise of adultery. In his parable of the Fall,
Hawthorne's alienated lovers ("maternal" woman, "childlike" man—who
together form an Oedipal-like relation) commit a kind of spiritual suicide
by stepping outside the bounds of society to live in unrepented sin. Both
are doomed from the start, because just as Hawthorne leans toward a
Goethe-like justification of diabolism as an instrument of salvation
(through Hester), he also insists upon the dangers of passion (through
Dimmesdale). *Letter* may appear to be a love story, but it is essentially
Hawthorne's "elegiac treatise on the death of love" (that borrows largely
from sentimental and gothic novels) since the guilt-ridden Dimmesdale is
not capable of maintaining a Faustian stance. In the end, Dimmesdale
triumphs not only over the Devil in denying his passion, but also over the
Faustian Hester, "who considers their damnation bliss" in her proposed
flight from Boston.

*See revised edition (184).

90   Gross, Seymour L. "Prologue to *The Scarlet Letter*: Hawthorne's Fiction to 1850." *A Scarlet Letter Handbook*. Ed. Seymour L. Gross. Belmont: Wadsworth Publishing, 1960. 1-14.

"The dominant concerns of the novel—sin, love, isolation to name the most prominent—had been explored in various stories [. . .] Hawthorne wrote before coming to the composition of his finest achievement." More than twenty early tales and sketches prepare for *Letter*, clearly exhibiting a horror at the inhumanity of the Puritans ("The Gentle Boy," "Endicott and the Red Cross" and "The May-Pole of Merry Mount"); depicting dark journeys necessary for a soul's moral growth ("My Kinsman, Major Molineux," "Young Goodman Brown," "The Minister's Black Veil," "Rappaccini's Daughter," and "The Birth-mark"); and focusing on isolated individuals who exist outside the "magnetic chain of humanity" ("The Hollow of the Three Hills," "The Canterbury Pilgrims," "The Ambitious Guest," "Lady Eleanore's Mantle," and "Ethan Brand").

91   Jaffe, Adrian, and Herbert Weisinger, eds. "*The Scarlet Letter*." *The Laureate Fraternity: An Introduction to Literature*. Evanston: Row, Peterson, 1960. 261-263.

Analyzes *Letter* to determine for the student reader the "real" subject of the novel, Hester's choice to accept the judgment of the Puritan authorities as just and thus converting punishment into "a meaningful source of strength." Hester becomes so strong that "she requires [Dimmesdale] no longer." Chillingworth's and Hester's roles reverse, he emerging as ironic symbol of evil from good, she emerging as ironic symbol of good from evil. Dimmesdale is curiously ironic because his profound strength as a passionate spiritual leader develops from what is initially "astounding feebleness and lack of moral fiber."

92   Levin, David. Introduction. *The Scarlet Letter*. By Nathaniel Hawthorne. 1850. New York: Dell, 1960. 7-20.

This general introduction, which discusses *Letter* as "an extremely skillful re-creation of the Puritan past with a forceful statement on the central issues of nineteenth-century romanticism," attributes the novel's success to its blending the conventions of the popular historical romance genre of Hawthorne's day with romantic standards and vocabulary. From this "blend," Levin argues for the indispensable inclusion of "The Custom-House" in every new edition of *Letter*. The three main characters represent types of sinners: Hester as the publicly known and partially contrite sinner, Dimmesdale as the secret sinner, and Chillingworth as the

Unpardonable Sinner. Pearl illustrates Hawthorne's "skillful fusion of allegory and psychology."

93 Levin, Harry. Introduction. *The Scarlet Letter*. By Nathaniel Hawthorne. 1850. Ed. Harry Levin. Boston: Houghton Mifflin, 1960. vii-xxi.*

Provides biographical information, justifies the placement of "The Custom-House" sketch as a calculated and characteristic preamble to *Letter,* explains how employment of the romantic mode and quasi-historical setting allowed Hawthorne to "question certain moralistic assumptions with a freedom and candor which he could not have applied to a nineteenth-century subject," briefly addresses character analysis and form, and defends the novel's contradictions and inconsistencies as the logical result of the "interplay between puritanical restraints and romantic impulses." Following the introduction is a brief "Bibliographical Note" (pp. xxiii-xxvi) that reviews the differences between the first four editions of *Letter* and surveys several pertinent early pieces of criticism.

*This same introduction appears in *The Scarlet Letter and Other Tales of the Puritans*. (Boston: Houghton Mifflin Co., 1961. vii-xxi.)

Journal Essays and Notes

94 Boewe, Charles, and Murray G. Murphey. "Hester Prynne in History." *American Literature* 32 (1960): 202-204.

Refutes Charles Ryskamp's assertion (in 85) that there is no historical basis for Hester's character. Far from a fabrication of Hawthorne's imagination, Hester is a "composite picture" built from "historical scraps," a "mosaic of bits and pieces" whose character is based on historical adulteresses Goodwife Mendame of Duxbury (of Plymouth Colony) and Hester Craford of Salem.

95 Gross, Seymour L. "'Solitude, and Love, and Anguish': The Tragic Design in *The Scarlet Letter*." *College Language Association Journal* 3 (1960): 154-165.

Rejects all didactic, moralistic interpretations of *Letter* for their "inadequacy" in accounting for Hester's profound sense of guilt that Hawthorne emphasizes, arguing that the design of the novel is tragic. Gross builds on and clarifies John C. Gerber's suggestion (in EC9) that Hester "somehow" knows her act of adultery is wrong, despite her refusal to consider it a sin. Hawthorne presents Hester's position, that her and Dimmesdale's love for one another "sacramentalizes" their passionate act, as neither "romantically irresponsible" nor "gloriously liberated" but a "deliberately controlled balance of [tragic] sympathies." "What is significant in *Letter* is not that Hester is right or wrong in an absolute sense, but rather that she has integrity in her own terms, that she has fallen in love with a minister who has integrity in different terms, and that therefore their love is condemned to be mangled in the clash of their ultimately irreconcilable moralities." Thus Hester's "conflict of moralities," the "tragic paradox" that "out of love she has violated love," is the source of her guilt that shapes the tragic design of the book.

96   Hamblen, Abigail Ann. "Protestantism in Three American Novels." *Forum* 3 (1960): 40-43.

American literature is "profoundly influenced" by the weighty concept of sin and its inevitable expiation, as can be seen in three novels that reveal "what effect the Protestant church has had on the culture of the United States": *Letter*, Don Marquis's *Sons of the Puritans* (1939), and Ruth Suckow's *The John Wood Case* (1959). All depict church-centered communities, and all show that "Protestant theology has never lost the sad, unrelenting doctrine of Jonathan Edwards," that man's moral lapses are of concern not just to himself but to the group—since, by sinning, he makes them sinners, too.

97   Justus, James. "Beyond Gothicism: *Wuthering Heights* and an American Tradition." *Tennessee Studies in Literature* 5 (1960): 25-33.

Arguing that an American tradition exists that is distinct from the "Great Tradition" established by F. R. Leavis, Justus establishes "certain affinities" between Hawthorne, Herman Melville, and Emily Brontë. Like *Wuthering Heights* (1847), *Letter* and *Moby-Dick* (1851) involve each author's intensely private vision of characters whose wills clash on a larger-than-life scale that combines great tragedy and the Gothic novel. Similar "moral dialectics" and psychological realities appear in the three novels, and Chillingworth's and Ahab's dark intellects and "soul struggles" parallel Heathcliff's. But whereas Brontë's vision commands that the raging war waged between "contrarieties" subsides into harmony, her American counterparts stay "agonizingly self-involved" and grimly unresolved.

98   McCullen, Joseph T., and John C. Guilds. "The Unpardonable Sin in Hawthorne: A Re-examination." *Nineteenth-Century Fiction* 15 (1960): 221-237.

Affirms Hawthorne's traditional Christianity and argues that critics who "unduly minimize" the "necessary theological basis" of Hawthorne's conception of sin mistake ordinary sinners for unpardonable sinners. Hawthorne would have agreed with Christian theologians that the correct definition of the unpardonable sinner is one who sins against God *and* is willfully impenitent. This two-fold distinction only allows for three truly unpardonable sinners in Hawthorne: Richard Digby (from "The Man of Adamant"), Ethan Brand, and Chillingworth. Digby and Brand are unequivocally unpardonable sinners, but Chillingworth is problematic, since eternal damnation for him remains undecided in the traditional view of the definition. For even though Chillingworth accepts his diabolical nature as "a dark necessity," Hawthorne remains somewhat ambivalent about the character's "ultimate spiritual disposal" in the "Conclusion"— because Chillingworth's fiendish revenge against Dimmesdale is not necessarily spiritually unforgivable.

99   Metzger, Charles R. *"Effictio* and *Notatio*: Hawthorne's Technique of Characterization." *Western Humanities Review* 14 (1960): 224-226.

Hawthorne "modified and joined together" traits from his partially-developed short story characters to create the richly-detailed characters of the romances. The employment of the expository devices "effictio" (appearance) and "notatio" (personality) contribute to the presentation of dramatically effective characters, Hester in *Letter* most notably. Hawthorne "strikes just the right balance" in blending specific and general characteristics for his heroine (effictio) and in portraying the "polar qualities" of her complex personality (notatio)—so effectively, in fact, that Hester's dynamism anticipates Freudian insights into emotional, intellectual, and social foundations.

100   O'Donnell, Charles R. "Hawthorne and Dimmesdale: The Search for the Realm of Quiet." *Nineteenth-Century Fiction* 14 (1960): 317-332.

Hawthorne employs the civilization/wilderness dichotomy in *Letter* to illustrate the sensitive artist's dilemma of choosing to live in the community of mankind (which symbolizes social integration and lack of individuality) or in the isolated world of the mind (which Hawthorne associates with the dark unknown and the quest for self-knowledge). Hester, Dimmesdale, and Pearl represent different types of alienation from the existing pattern of civilization in their respective quests toward selfhood, the completion of which is "dependent upon a synthesis of the fragmented personalities" on the scaffold. Dimmesdale, in particular, illustrates through his parable-like death the victorious drama of the artist in creating order and form out of a defeating situation. The minister's quest for selfhood in a moral wilderness parallels Hawthorne's own in "The Custom-House," where Hawthorne suggests that art alone can bridge the gap between the world of affairs and the world of the mind.

101   Putzel, Max. "The Way Out of the Minister's Maze: Some Hints for Teachers of *The Scarlet Letter*." *Die Neueren Sprachen* 9 (1960): 127-131.

Insists that students' resistance to Hawthorne's weighty issues and "iron" logic in *Letter* must be countered, and that their temptation to side with Hester and her plan for escape be ruthlessly squashed—most especially because Hester's plan can only be accomplished by compromising Dimmesdale's integrity and chance for salvation. Hester's and Dimmesdale's violation of human laws is a sin every bit as deadly as Chillingworth's, as is made apparent by Hawthorne's refusal to justify Hester's actions or to exonerate her. Chillingworth is indispensable—albeit indirectly—in saving Dimmesdale and his faith and in contributing to Hester's own salvation through good works. Above all, students must deny the seductive rhetoric in the novel and recognize instead that "moral realities are not a worn-out illusion." Hawthorne's story is just as timely in the twentieth (and twenty-first) century as in the nineteenth, both as a guide to right conduct and for the necessity of social order.

1961

Books

102   Bradley, Sculley, Richard Croom Beatty, and E. Hudson Long., eds. *The Scarlet Letter: An Annotated Text, Backgrounds and Sources, Essays in Criticism*. Norton Critical Edition. New York: W. W. Norton, 1961. 375 pp.*

In addition to providing a brief and general introduction (pp. vii-ix) that attributes *Letter*'s continued success to its symbolic expression of "a persistent, dark riddle in the American spiritual experience," this edition includes the text of the first edition (prefixed by Hawthorne's preface to the second edition) and "an unusual group of background and source materials." This grouping is divided into selections from Hawthorne's own notebooks and journals, records based on primary sources, the scholar and the sources, nineteen previously published essays in criticism, and a select bibliography. After "Selections from Hawthorne's Own Notebooks and Journals" are listed the excerpted "Records Based on Primary Sources" (Caleb Snow's *History of Boston*, Joseph B. Felt's *Annals of Salem*, Cotton Mather's *Magnalia Christi Americana*, and Alfred S.

Reid's facsimile edition of *Sir Thomas Overbury's Vision* [53]). The next section, "The Scholar and the Sources," includes articles that illustrate the manner in which scholars have made use of the early documents (Charles Ryskamp's "The New England Sources of *The Scarlet Letter*" [85] and Charles Boewe's and Murray G. Murphey's "Hester Prynne in History" [94]) and Hawthorne's early short story, "Endicott and the Red Cross"). The last section, composed of 19 essays in criticism and a select bibliography, contains excerpts from Henry James's *Hawthorne* (EC15), Anthony Trollope's "The Genius of Nathaniel Hawthorne" (EC33), W. C. Brownell's *American Prose Masters* (EC3), Herbert Gorman's *Hawthorne, A Study in Solitude* (EC10), Régis Michaud's *The American Novel Today* (EC21), Robert E. Spiller's "The Mind and Art of Nathaniel Hawthorne" (EC29), F. O. Matthiessen's *American Renaissance* (EC20), Leland Schubert's *Hawthorne, the Artist* (EC26), Frederick I. Carpenter's "Scarlet A Minus" (EC4), Mark Van Doren's *Nathaniel Hawthorne* (EC36), Richard Harter Fogle's *Hawthorne's Fiction: The Light and the Dark* (15), Hyatt H. Waggoner's *Hawthorne: A Critical Study* (38), R. W. B. Lewis's *The American Adam* (37), Malcolm Cowley's "Five Acts of *The Scarlet Letter*" (59), Roy Male's *Hawthorne's Tragic Vision* (56), Randall Stewart's *American Literature and Christian Doctrine* (72), Harry Levin's *The Power of Blackness* (70), Seymour Gross's "'Solitude, and Love, and Anguish': The Tragic Design of *The Scarlet Letter*" (95), and Daniel Hoffman's *Form and Fable in American Fiction* (106).

*Revised editions appeared in 1962, 1978 (see 353), and 1988 (see 557).

103   Lynn, Kenneth S. *The Scarlet Letter, Text, Sources, Criticism*. New York: Harcourt, Brace, and World, 1961. 217 pp.

The goal of this sourcebook is to "suggest the diversity of interpretation that the book has inspired." In addition to the brief introduction, text, and listing of Hawthorne's sources for *Letter* (from *The American Notebooks* and "Endicott and the Red Cross"), Lynn includes what he deems the most seminal reviews from 1850 (by George B. Loring [ER7] and Orestes A. Brownson [ER9]), critical estimates of novelists Anthony Trollope (EC33) and Henry James (EC15), and three important appraisals of the novel (by D. H. Lawrence [EC18], Yvor Winters [EC40], and F. O. Matthiessen [EC20]). Appendices include suggested topics for papers and a selected bibliography.

Essays and Studies in Books

104   Bowden, Edwin T. "The Mighty Individual: Nathaniel Hawthorne, *The Scarlet Letter*." *The Dungeon of the Heart: Human Isolation and the American Novel*. New York: Macmillan, 1961. 73-89.

This non-critical study, which attempts "to satisfy the general reader's curiosity" about 12 famous American novels that represent American life (from *Of Plymouth Plantation* to *Catcher in the Rye*), limits discussion to the theme of isolation in each. Of *Letter*, it suggests that Hester's "mighty" strength and humility in the face of isolation from society enable her to move toward a life of love and Christian charity. Of the three main characters, all of whom are presented as figures in isolation, Hester alone—the only true outcast from society—accepts herself for who she is and eventually finds escape from a "blighting inner isolation from man and from God."

105   Gibson, William M. "The Art of Nathaniel Hawthorne: An Examination of *The Scarlet Letter*." *The American Renaissance: the History and Literature of an Era*. Ed. George Hendrick. Frankfurt am Main: Diesterweg, 1961. 97-106.

This general introduction to American Renaissance writers for German high school teachers contains a chapter on *Letter* that asks and answers over a dozen questions relating to multiple issues. Addressed are Hawthorne's life and career during the composition process of *Letter*; the tale's status as romance, historical novel, gothic novel, and nouvelle; sources; the function of "The Custom-House"; the subject of the novel, which is defined as "the effects of adultery and other sins, of guilty suffering and aggression, with no resolution possible for the characters' difficulties until their relationships are fully revealed"; Hester's emergence as the central figure; and plot and structure as they relate to the three "cumulative" scaffold scenes.

106   Hoffman, Daniel. "Hester's Double Providence: The Scarlet Letter and the Green." *Form and Fable in American Fiction*. New York: Oxford UP, 1961. 169-186.

Hawthorne is one of several authors closely examined in this book that traces the debt of nineteenth-century American literature to myth and folk traditions. In both his tales and romances, Hawthorne's imaginative treatments of superstitious beliefs, unfallen paganism, magic, witchcraft, myth, and the "self-transforming native character" clearly stem from his artistic need to create myth.* In *Letter*, the folklore of the supernatural is particularly appropriate to the development of Hawthorne's conflicts, especially between the amoral freedom of the green, natural world and the rigid theology of the Puritan faith. This curious intermixture of the supernatural with the real can be seen in the scarlet letter itself, which, instead of providing a fixed allegorical meaning, becomes a wondrous "supernatural providence" that produces ambiguity and fluidity of meaning on every side—and more spiritual truth than the theological absolutes of Puritanism ever could. Indeed, Hawthorne's "reliance upon the alternative interpretations [of the letter] which oral tradition gives to supernatural wonders proves to be a structural principle essential to his conception" of the novel that consistently denies the staying power of Puritan dogma. In the end, the force of popular belief is stronger "than even the force of religious law which branded Hester, for she long outlives the censure with which her letter was to have forever marked her."

*This idea is in direct opposition to F. O. Mattheissen's assertion in *The American Renaissance* (EC20) that Hawthorne did not conceive of his work in any relation to myth but remained strictly a provincial.

107 Wagenknecht, Edward. "The Fire in the Members." *Nathaniel Hawthorne: Man and Writer.* New York: Oxford UP, 1961. 131-171.

Opposed to much of the fashionable criticism of the 1950s (which tends to concentrate on Hawthorne's symbolism, ambiguity, and myth) in order to place Hawthorne in historical context with the writers of his time, this "common sense" critical biography claims to be a "psychography," "simply a study of Hawthorne's character and personality." In establishing Hawthorne's outgoing, healthy characteristics in a manner that is unapologetically "tentative, personal, and partial," Wagenknecht purposely neglects the often-overemphasized darker aspects of Hawthorne's character. His brief treatment of Hawthorne's most "voluptuous" novel acknowledges that Hawthorne is astonishingly modern not only in his treatment of Hester's abundant sexuality and rich humanity, but also in his understanding of the "perversities of love." As to whether Hester truly repents at the end, Wagenknecht is certain that "the question would not greatly have interested her," since sin and repentance are masculine conceptions. Hester's desire to flee New England with Dimmesdale has nothing to do with right or wrong in her own mind; as a woman, she is concerned only with saving the man she loves from an environment that is killing him. The only real reason that the plan for escape fails is because Dimmesdale is a man—who is not capabe of meeting Hester on her own ground in seeking "the best possible" future.

Journal Essays and Notes

108   Allen, M. L. "Hawthorne's Art in His Short Stories." *Studi Americana* 7
        (1961): 9-41.

Charts Hawthorne's development into a mature writer from the
appearance of the poorly written *Fanshawe* in 1828 to the masterpiece
Letter in 1850 by examining Hawthorne's "discoveries" in material,
method, and technique in the stories collected in *Twice-told Tales, Mosses
from an Old Manse*, and *The Snow-Image*. Of Hawthorne's stories, which
are divided into five groups ("sketches of everyday life, tales based on
contemporary anecdotes, romances and fantasies, allegories, and historical
tales"), Allen briefly discusses "Wakefield," "The Minister's Black Veil,"
"Egotism; or, The Bosom-Serpent," "Rappaccini's Daughter," "The
Celestial Railroad," "The Great Carbuncle," "Great Stone Face," "Main
Street," "The Gentle Boy," "Young Goodman Brown," "Endicott and the
Red Cross," and especially "My Kinsman, Major Molineux."
Experimentation and an increased complexity of awareness over the years
led Hawthorne to work out imperfections (such as heavy-handed
didacticism, a homiletic manner, tedious reiterations, and saccharine
sentiment) and achieve original and significant expression in *Letter*.

109   Arden, Eugene. "Hawthorne's 'Case of Arthur D.'" *American Imago* 18
        (1961): 45-55.

"A Freudian before Freud himself," Hawthorne was "clinically accurate in
his psychological insights." While modern psychiatrists (namely, early
twentieth-century doctors Clarence Obendorf and Louis Bragman) have
previously noted the "extraordinary profundity of Hawthorne's special
medical insights" into the "psychology of the unconscious," Arden claims
to advance the study of Hawthorne's uncanny, precursory knowledge of
psychosomatic illness and to clear up previous inaccuracies in tracing
Hawthorne's sources for it. The process of Chillingworth's "talking cure"
sessions with Dimmesdale (especially the passage in chapter nine that
compares Chillingworth to a "treasure-seeker in a dark cavern") "is
described by Hawthorne so accurately that he could have been writing a
twentieth-century textbook on psychotherapy." Hawthorne's sources,
however, are based less on memory and crushing personal experience (as
suggested by Obendorf—who "fatally confuses" Hawthorne's "facts of
life" with his "miracles of art") than on the result of "a very tightly
controlled transmutation from fact to art." Dr. Oliver Wendell Holmes is a
more likely source for Hawthorne's theory of psychosomatic medicine, as
is the entire "circle of Hawthorne's literary acquaintances in New
England," among whom "exciting currents" in nineteenth-century
psychology were "in the air." Further sources emerge from Hawthorne's
own avid reading of psychological and scientific journals, the influence of

classical English authors (Sir Thomas Brown, Edmund Spenser, and John Milton), and, most of all, a "power which must ever remain in part a mystery."

110   Austin, Allen. "Distortion in '*The* (Complete) *Scarlet Letter*.'" *College English* 23 (1961): 61.

Rebuttal of Baskett's essay (see 111 directly below). "Sam Baskett's point that Hawthorne compares the nineteenth century unfavorably with seventeenth-century Puritanism is contrary to the meaning of *Letter* and to Hawthorne's general attitude toward Puritans." Hawthorne "deplore[d] the cruelty and hypocrisy of the American Puritans," basing his novel on an enormous discrepancy between behavior and belief among the Puritans—that despite their belief in universal depravity, they refused to admit that an elite member of their society could be guilty of adultery. If anything, Hawthorne implies that "the further removed from [the Puritans] we are, the more fortunate we become." Hawthorne actually rejected organized religion in both time periods, so "to talk of Hawthorne's preference for Puritanism is like talking of a man's preference for death by poison to death by fire." [For Baskett's reply to Austin's rebuttal, see 112.]

111   Baskett, Sam S. "*The* (Complete) *Scarlet Letter*." *College English* 22 (1961): 321-328.

Taking issue with interpretations of "The Custom-House" that "relegate it to a precariously tangential position in relation to the principal part of the book," Baskett insists that the preface "clarifies and extends the meaning of the romance and thus should be read as a significant part of the total work." In both preface and romance, Hawthorne repeatedly contrasts and compares seventeenth- and nineteenth-century New England life. Yet far more relevant than the contrasts—which consistently paint the "ultimate values" of the past in a more favorable light than the shallow, money-obsessed present—are the comparisons that illustrate the true theme: the relation of the individual to society. No matter how the individual finds himself at cross-purposes with his own society, he must still participate in the human community. [See Allen Austin's rebuttal (110) and W. R. Moses's extension of Baskett's thesis (133). See also Baskett's reply to Austin's rebuttal (112) directly below.]

112   Baskett, Sam S. "Reply." *College English* 23 (1961): 62.

Responding to Allen Austin's charge of "distortion" (see 110), Baskett urges that Austin has mis-read his article and his thesis. Baskett is fully aware that "Hawthorne is strongly critical of the Puritan society," and restates that the main thrust of his article connects "The Custom-House" and the romance—and thus necessarily invites "as a sub-point" comparisons and contrasts between the two centuries.

113   Canaday, Nicholas, Jr. "Ironic Humor as Defense in *The Scarlet Letter.*" *South Central Bulletin* 21 (1961): 17-18.

The "flecks" of ironic humor in *Letter*—infrequent though they are (Canaday cites five instances)—serve as Hawthorne's "defense against a commitment to harsh Puritanism." "The irony permits him to express his insight into the problems of sin, guilt, and punishment without sacrificing their complexities.   Together with the ironies of character and circumstance, the symbolism, and the characteristic multiple explanations accompanying crucial events, ironic humor makes possible the moral ambiguity of the novel."

114   Casson, Allan.   "*The Scarlet Letter* and *Adam Bede.*"   *Victorian Newsletter* 20 (1961): 18-19.

"A comparison of *Adam Bede* [1859] and *Letter* reveals points of similarity of situation and common ground in technique and theme as well." After establishing George Eliot's admiration for Hawthorne and her familiarity with *Letter*, Casson cites correspondences between the two novels that include similar settings in small rural communities, likenesses in chapter titles and recurring tableaux, similar names and characteristics for heroines and heroines (Arthur Donnithorne/Arthur Dimmesdale, Hetty Sorrel/Hester Prynne), and parallel themes of "the fortunate fall, the doctrine of consequences, and the humanizing power of sorrow."

115   Josephs, Lois. "One Approach to the Puritans." *English Journal* 50 (1961): 183-187.

An effective way to approach a critical unit on the Puritans for eleventh-grade English students—and more importantly to present students an accurate picture of Puritan society—is to read Puritan writings such as Perry Miller and Thomas H. Johnson's anthology *The Puritans* (1938) and also to compare *Letter* and Arthur Miller's *The Crucible* (1953). The comparison should be discussed first to generate interest in the Puritan mind. When specific aspects of both literary works are examined (such as the evil natures of both Chillingworth and Abigail, adultery as a basis for conflict, and similarities between heroines Hester and Abigail), insights into specific facets of Puritans' lives and their inflexible religious and social rules accrue.   Critical understanding of the Puritans' cultural justification for interfering in the personal and religious lives of their neighbors in *Letter* and *The Crucible* is further stimulated by reading Puritan histories and several personal narratives of Puritan writers. Close study of these pieces all together "evokes cultural insight into the Puritans and literary insight into much of American literature."

116   Lane, Lauriat, Jr.   "Allegory and Character in *The Scarlet Letter.*" *Emerson Society Quarterly* 25 (1961): 13-16.

Professes to offer helpful formal and philosophical distinctions between "allegory" and "symbolism," terms too often used interchangeably or inaccurately by critics, Lane argues, to get at the particular problem of interpreting *Letter* as an allegory. Such an interpretation hinges on one's grasp of the major characters, Hester, Pearl, Dimmesdale, and Chillingworth (the latter whom Lane initially calls "Coverdale"). Pearl and Chillingworth play out their allegorical roles, she as "the product of sin, the scarlet letter personified," and he "as guilt personified and diabolic, obsessed revenge"; but they, as well as the external world of *Letter*, are merely "parts of a moral-psychological allegory of the state of Hester's and Dimmesdale's souls. In this sense, Hester and Dimmesdale inhabit a literal world whose actualities allegorize their own inner worlds of conscience and spirit and salvation or damnation." These two characters also participate in a second allegory, "a moral-theological, Calvinist allegory that contains [. . .] all members of the historical Puritan world of *Letter*." These two allegories together create the novel's "interesting tension" that "complicates the roles and the moral significance of the major characters."

117   Male, Roy R.   "Hawthorne's Allegory of Guilt and Redemption." *Emerson Society Quarterly* 25 (1961): 16-18.

Presents the most effective ways to combat students' inveterate dislike of Hawthorne's allegorical method: (1) discussion of how Hawthorne's mature allegoric mode evolved, (2) an explanation of Hawthorne's technique as balanced and often ironic, (3) and a focus on the complicated personifications of characters. Pearl, in *Letter* (the only work in which Hawthorne found his proper "pitch" as an allegorist), functions not just as living symbol of sin but also as "personification of truth and grace." Indeed, "the quest for truth in *Letter* is an effort to know Pearl." Chillingworth, more than leech and healer, is "an inspired personification of guilt." Male concludes by contrasting Hawthorne's method with the detective story, again noting that Hawthorne "got it right" only in *Letter*.

118   McAleer, John J. "Hester Prynne's Grave." *Descant* 5 (1961): 29-33.

The three references to King's Chapel burial ground in *Letter* serve as Hawthorne's subtle encouragement for curious "cemetery amblers" (of which there were many in Hawthorne's day) to seek out Hester's grave there. While Hester's grave is, of course, not there, Isaac Johnson's seventeenth-century monument—mentioned in one of those three references—is, and it is still distinguishable. More interesting, however, is a small broken stone in the center of the cemetery where Johnson's grave is said to be in the novel, but bearing the name of Hannah Dinsdale, wife of Adam Dinsdale. Because no other marker appears with Adam Dinsdale's name on it, the husband and wife may have shared the grave marker after the husband died, a speculation that "not improbably" influenced Hawthorne's choices of names for his lovers (the minister's last name as well as the first initial of both character's names) and may even have generated the story itself.

119   Rovit, Earl. "Ambiguity in Hawthorne's *Scarlet Letter*." *Archiv für das Studium der neueren Sprachen und Literaturen* 198 (1961): 76-88.

Grapples with the American cultural significance of *Letter*, no easy task because the novel's ambiguity has created countless problems of interpretation for critics and readers alike. To demystify *Letter* and determine its integral place in American literature, Rovit focuses on the relation of "The Custom-House" to the rest of the novel, since it concerns the relation of the past to the present and introduces the major question of "how to find meaning in arbitrary meaninglessness" which the tale dramatizes so effectively. *Letter* is actually as much about the ambiguity and impossibility of meaning as it is about meaning itself. The scarlet letter itself functions as a torturous "speculum of revelation" to each of the three principal characters, transforming them not because of its innate power to define but because of the power that each assigns to it. In this way, Hawthorne mocks his three players for banishing the infinite possibilities of their individual existences, treating the problematic condition of individualism just as he questions both the meaning of meaning itself and the significance of experience. The real human frailty of the story may not actually be sexual temptation or guilt or even pride, but man's inevitable susceptibility to assign arbitrary meanings to a letter and then live as victims within the dark necessity imposed by the design.

120   Wellborn, Grace Pleasant. "The Mystic Seven in *The Scarlet Letter*." *South Central Bulletin* 21 (1961): 23-31.

Since the days of antiquity, the number seven has been considered "a mystic and sacred number" that symbolizes wholeness or completeness.

Hawthorne borrows its legendary significance in *Letter*, where the number appears at least 48 times and symbolizes the four main characters' dreams of physical, psychological, and spiritual fulfillment. Their desires for wholeness—stemming from the "measureless potentialities" of their spiritual sides—remain thwarted, however, since their mortal imperfections doom them to fragmented existences. Hope resides only in the enduring possibility of fulfillment, or—according to Jung's psychological theory—in re-establishing the "balance of life" that can only come after penetrating the unconscious to face and reflect on past misdeeds. Because Chillingworth refuses to face his own guilt to enact the redemptive process that involves penitence, confession, and petition for forgiveness, he submits to his own evil impulses. But the transformative process of redemption enables Hester and Dimmesdale to eventually recover—at least partly—from the evils of sin and to hope for the possibility of moral rebirth or redemption, with Pearl acting the role of catalyst or regenerative force.

1962

Books

121 Scholes, James B. *Nathaniel Hawthorne's The Scarlet Letter: A Study Guide.* Ed. Walter Harding. Bound Brook: Shelley Publishing, 1962. 95 pp.

This guide includes a biographical sketch of Hawthorne, a chapter-by-chapter analysis of the novel through a terse summary and numerous questions that may prove useful both to instructors and students alike, a list of vocabulary words following each chapter analysis, brief sketches of the four major characters, a sampling of critical excerpts, and a short bibliography. The excerpts include criticism by Herman Melville (ER6), Orestes A. Brownson (ER9), Henry James (EC15), Yvor Winters (EC40), F. O. Matthiessen (EC20), Stanley T. Williams (23), Gordon Roper (7), Richard H. Fogle (15), Darrel Abel (16), Frederic I. Carpenter (EC4), and Marius Bewley (47).

Essays and Studies in Books

122 Bowers, Fredson. A Preface to the Text. *The Scarlet Letter* in *The Centenary Edition of the Works of Nathaniel Hawthorne.* Vol. 1. Ed. William Charvat et al. Columbus: Ohio State UP, 1962. xxix-xlvii.

Provides information about the Centenary Edition, which establishes the documentary and literary form of *Letter* and outlines the general procedures for arriving at this "established" text of the novel. The purpose of the edition—based on the first edition of 1850, the only authoritative copy-text—is to "establish the text in as close a form, in all details, to Hawthorne's final intentions [. . .]."

123   Bowers, Fredson. Textual Introduction: *The Scarlet Letter*. *The Scarlet Letter* in *The Centenary Edition of the Works of Nathaniel Hawthorne*. Vol. 1. Ed. William Charvat et al. Columbus: Ohio State UP, 1962. xlix-ixv.

Presents technical information primarily about the first and second editions (such as gathering and type variations, punctuation and typographical alterations, emendations, and the like), but also documents several other characteristic editions: the pirated edition of 1851, the third American edition (1850), the Little Classics edition (1875), the Riverside edition (1883), and the Autograph edition (1900). Bowers concludes by noting the need for this centennial edition, since "the history of the corruption of *Letter*['s] text [. . .] is a particularly sorry one."

124   Charvat, William. Introduction to *The Scarlet Letter*. *The Scarlet Letter* in *The Centenary Edition of the Works of Nathaniel Hawthorne*. Vol. 1. Ed. William Charvat et al. Columbus: Ohio State UP, 1962. xv-xxviii.

Attributes *Letter*'s continued success in Hawthorne's lifetime to the work of skillful promoters and conspicuous advertisements by Hawthorne's publisher, offers the history of the novel's composition, and is quick to point out that, while *Letter* is Hawthorne's finest achievement, it is not truly representative of the body of his work because Hawthorne was best known and admired in his own day for tales of "light humor, pathos, sentiment, and fancy." Charvat further discusses possible sources for historical equivalents to the main characters and mentions early stories and notebook entries that make up the germinal "seeds" of *Letter*. [For a technical review of the Centenary edition, see 148. For a humorous review of the Centenary edition that questions the edition's relevance, see 180.]

125   Hoeltje, Hubert H. "A Tale of Sorrow." *Inward Sky: The Mind and Heart of Nathaniel Hawthorne*. Durham: Duke UP, 1962. 240-296.

In this biographical survey that examines the range of Hawthorne's writing (letters, journals, fiction), Hoeltje attempts a "spiritual portrait" through an examination of Hawthorne's outward and inward lives that concludes with reference to Hawthorne's overall quiet joy and affirming "serenity" with respect to his life and work. Chapter seven, which details

Hawthorne's life before, during, and after his Custom House appointment, builds to a discussion of *Letter* (pp. 284-296). The romance is largely autobiographical—and in it can be found all the "troubled questionings following the brutal encounter with the world which Hawthorne sought vainly to blot from his memory." In addition to composing *Letter* during the period of his final residence in Salem, Hawthorne was also working on "Ethan Brand" and "Main-street," both of which were "of [the] greatest significance in preparing and shaping Hawthorne's thought for the writing of that great romance" (the former because it addresses the claims of the sympathetic "heart" over the claims of the rational "head," and the latter because it represents Hawthorne's first critical handling of the Puritans). Only in *Letter*, however, does his artistic power culminate and allow him to probe so deeply the problem of evil in an "atmosphere of strict reprehension." The novel is primarily Hester's story, dealing sympathetically with her questionings and gradual rise from despair and adversity to a redemptive state that brings peace and acceptance of the will of Providence (a kind of "Fortunate Fall" that parallels Hawthorne's experience following the Custom-House dismissal).

Journal Essays and Notes

126   Austin, Allen. "Hester Prynne's Plan of Escape: The Moral Problem." *University of Kansas City Review* 28 (1962): 317-319.

Although Hawthorne condemns Hester's plan in the forest scene to flee Boston and begin a new life abroad with Dimmesdale and Pearl, her decision is morally justified because it is based on her familiarity with Puritan bigotry and hypocrisy, as well as her concern for Dimmesdale's and Pearl's welfare. Her decision differs from Dimmesdale's "morally meaningless" confession that "can satisfy nothing except his own morbid ego." This discrepancy between the action of the forest scene—that justifies Hester's decision to flee an unhealthy environment—and Hawthorne's condemnation of that decision "is not a major weakness in the novel" but proof that "Hawthorne the novelist triumphs over Hawthorne the moralist."

127   Austin, Allen. "Satire and Theme in *The Scarlet Letter*." *Philological Quarterly* 41 (1962): 508-511.

"Hawthorne ridicules the hardheartedness, blindness, and hypocrisy of the Puritan rulers in order to point up the absolute necessity of compassion—a compassion based on a mature awareness of the imperfection common to all men." The "uninstructed multitude," Hawthorne implies, is "infinitely more perceptive" and sensitive than its selfish leaders who illogically fail to acknowledge sinful acts amongst their elite, despite a firm belief in the doctrine of Original Sin. Hawthorne satirizes the Puritan philosophy most explicitly through Chillingworth (the "major advocate" of Puritanism in the novel), who uses the Puritan tenet of predestination to justify evil and to excuse his own lack of forgiveness and compassion. Hawthorne also condemns the Puritans for being materialists because they change their attitude toward Pearl when she inherits Chillingworth's fortune.

128   Evanoff, Alexander. "Some Principal Themes in *The Scarlet Letter.*" *Discourse* 5 (1962): 270-277.

Proposes to offer "new insights into Hawthorne's understanding of Hypocrisy, Individual Harmony, and the relationship between the Individual and the State" through a brief examination of "Hawthorne's demonstration of the inter-relatedness of sin, and his exposition of three states of being." These three states entail one dominated by the heart (represented by Hester), one ruled by reason (represented by Chillingworth), and one dominated by a head/heart spiritual balance (represented by Dimmesdale). Each of the three major sinning, hypocritical characters exists in a state of disproportion and disharmony, and seeks a way to create happiness and harmony—although no harmony can be achieved in isolation or without the realization of sin's regenerative potential. Dimmesdale's confession brings him back to a true association with society, just as Hester's return to Boston reestablishes a tacit harmony with the community, both of which suggest that "Hawthorne's ultimate meaning [. . .] is that the individual's proper function is to place himself more perfectly in that relationship wherein one both takes from and gives to The Greater Whole."

129   Grant, Douglas. "Sir Walter Scott and Nathaniel Hawthorne." *University of Leeds Review* 8 (1962): 35-41.

This essay, which I was unable to acquire, explores the influence of Scott's treatment of the Puritan conscience in *Peveril of the Peak* (1823) and *The Heart of Midlothian* (1818) upon—respectively—*House of the Seven Gables* and *Letter.*

130   MacShane, Frank. "The House of the Dead: Hawthorne's Custom House and *The Scarlet Letter.*" *New England Quarterly* 35 (1962): 93-101.

Attends to "the subtler reasons" for the presence of "The Custom-House," pointing out many thematic connections between the the preface and the scarlet letter tale, namely the "major themes of isolation, guilt, decadence, and the sinister power that one person or institution can exercise over another," as well as the most important, the desire to "face life" or have the courage "to take up arms against [. . .] fate." MacShane also detects similarities in point of view, suggesting connections not only between Hawthorne and Dimmesdale (with Hawthorne, upon being dismissed from his hypocritical position, experiencing "much the same feeling of relief that Dimmesdale experienced upon his final public confession of guilt"), but also between Hawthorne and Hester, since "as Hester is given the opportunity to reconcile herself with God and to embark on a period of spiritual renewal because Society has judged her a sinner, so Hawthorne is 'saved' by being dismissed from the Custom House. Both Hawthorne and Hester make this discovery in isolation, when they are thrown upon their own resources and [are] no longer dependent on either the strong arm of the Republic or the Puritan Church."

131   Marcus, Fred H. *"The Scarlet Letter*: The Power of Ambiguity." *English Journal* 51 (1962): 449-458.

Designed for teachers as one in a series of "refresher course[s] in the technique of the novel," this article provides a basic explication of *Letter* that emphasizes the text itself over any "tools" that might be used to examine it, and primarily studies its structure, symbolism, and themes. Whereas the novel invites an allegorical view of the characters—with Pearl as Nature, Dimmesdale as Religion, Chillingworth as Science, and Hester as Art (with Art and Science viewed as incompatible, and Science and Religion as "at war")—pursuits into the allegorical implications or any other "absolutes" in the novel should be undertaken only with extreme caution. *Letter*'s ambiguities, paradoxes, and psychological probings point to a pluralism more complex than any one approach allows.

132   Martin, Terence. "Adam Blair and Arthur Dimmedale: A Lesson from the Master." *American Literature* 34 (1962): 274-279.*

Reconsiders Henry James's comparison (EC15)—well-received and accepted in the literary community—of *Letter* to John Gibson Lockhart's *Adam Blair* (1822), and examines the grounds on which James based his judgment. Although James rightly detects similarities of settings in a "rigidly theological society" and of ministers who secretly commit adultery and then later confess to it, the novels show significant differences in plot, characterization, and structure that belie James's interpretation and extend beyond his allowance of dissimilar tones in Lockhart's and Hawthorne's treatments of adultery. For starters, the first half of *Adam Blair* offers no parallels to *Letter*. While the second half of the novel does share "striking resemblances," fundamental differences between the two (involving interrelationships of characters, settings, and plot developments) prove that the novels "have very little analogy with each other." James's judgment is largely based on his erroneous presumption that Dimmesdale is the star of the tale (as Adam Blair is in his). In addition, because James objects to Hawthorne's overblown symbolism, he overlooks the crucial "scarlet letterness" of *Letter*, or the letter's centrality to the novel "in its various manifestations." The special quality of Hawthorne's achievement in *Letter* inheres in his presentation of the essential duality or ambivalence of reality and experience. To sustain his vision of the ambivalent nature of reality, Hawthorne relies on the dominating power of the scarlet letter itself, which not only encompasses and transcends all its individual meanings but also ultimately dominates every relevant scene, defines the dramatic contours of the narrative, and dramatizes the multiple natures of Hester, Dimmesdale, Chillingworth, and the Puritan community.

*A similar version of this essay, entitled "*The Scarlet Letter*," appears in Martin's *Nathaniel Hawthorne* (New York: Twayne Publishers, 1965. 108-127). See also 437 for the revised edition.

133   Moses, W. R. "Rebuttal: A Further Note on 'The Custom House.'" *College English* 23 (1962): 396.

Without denying the validity of Baskett's thesis (in 111) that *Letter* is not "complete" without "The Custom-House," Moses extends it by suggesting that the issue at stake "is wider than the opposition or parallelism of particular centuries, or even than the relation of the individual to his society." More relevant than whether the Custom House employees and the primary characters in the novel participate in the social, "united effort of mankind" is whether they take on moral responsibility—which they do. "The Custom-House" thus becomes "ironic counterpoint" to *Letter*, enunciating the higher moral responsibility of God in the seventeenth century and "the categorical imperative" in the nineteenth century.

134   Phillips, Robert. "*The Scarlet Letter*: A Selected Checklist of Criticism (1850-1962)." *Bulletin of Bibliography* 23 (1962): 213-216.

This checklist is included here because it asserts itself as a stepping-stone to a "badly needed" updated Hawthorne bibliography. For numerous other bibliographies on *Letter* (none of which are included in the body of this bibliography), see "Bibliographies" under Part IV of the Resource Guide.

135   Sandeen, Ernest. "*The Scarlet Letter* as a Love Story." *PMLA* 77 (1962): 425-435.

Considers the possibility—long overlooked by critics—that *Letter* is less a story about sin than about love, asserting that just because Hawthorne opens the tale in the aftermath of the erotic act does not mean that the lovers' grand passion for each other has terminated. When this love affair is seen as "the fixed reality" throughout the novel, "sin" becomes a "shifting, ambiguous term." Hester and Dimmesdale's love, erotic and adulterous though it may be, "matures them morally and spiritually; under its influence they grow to a tragic height of character which they otherwise would probably not have reached." That love, not guilt, is "the deep [motivating] force which moves through the story" ("A" stands for "Amor") can be seen in Hester's enduring the letter for seven years not because she is penitent but "because she is still in love." Dimmesdale's is a more complicated and central position in the novel. Not nearly as committed to their love as Hester because he is so deeply implicated in the Puritan theocracy, Dimmesdale yet suffers persistent guilt because his passion for Hester frustrates his attempts to feel truly penitent. Unable to reconcile his two conflicting selves until he comes to accept his passionate side following his forest interview with Hester, Dimmesdale is finally "united harmoniously"—with passion working *with* him and not against him—and is ready to confess both his sin and his testimony to the power of love. His confession does not repudiate but redeems passion, the proof of which is registered in Pearl's humanization. [For a similar argument, see Cecil L. Moffitt's "*The Scarlet Letter*: A Puritan Love Story" (157).]

136   Scanlon, Lawrence E. "The Heart of *The Scarlet Letter*." *Texas Studies in Literature and Language* 4 (1962): 198-213.

Although many critics have "anatomized [*Letter*] into parts, sections, divisions, stages, tableaux, acts, and scenes of varying numbers," none have demonstrated the continuous interrelations of two specific structural elements in the novel: the scaffold *and* the heart imagery. While it is clear (noted often in the past) that the scaffold is central to the structure of the novel—as "the center of Puritan intellectual-spiritual life in the novel"—it may not be so obvious that heart imagery plays just as key a structural role, and in fact works with the three scaffold scenes to create the overall unity of *Letter*. Both the scaffold and the heart references (Scanlon counts 141) possess the magnetic quality of rhythmic attraction and repulsion, and the continuous rhythm created by the movements back and forth, to and from the scaffold by characters similarly drawn to or repelled from each other, produces the overall unity of the novel. Following the first scaffold scene, images of constraint, inward movement, and darkness predominate until the second scaffold scene, which is "a kind of externalization, an acting out" that develops "like an explosion" of

85

freedom in the chapters leading up to the final scaffold scene, which is characterized by light, freedom, and sympathy. Such a conclusion shows that truth is not necessarily black or shadowy with Hawthorne. Quite the contrary, Hawthorne's ultimate position in the novel seems to suggest that, although the heart is pulled in opposite directions, light over dark and love over hate triumphs—and that "if man wishes to find sympathy, forgiveness, love, and light [. . .], he will find it eventually in the people, the community."

137   Steele, Oliver L. "On the Imposition of the First Edition of Hawthorne's *The Scarlet Letter." Library* 17 (1962): 250-255.

Discusses in the terminology of descriptive bibliography the techniques used in the hand-press printing era, to which Hawthorne's first edition of *Letter* would have belonged, and analyzes the imposition of three first-edition texts by examining the patterned edges of the novels' untrimmed leaves. Demonstrating, with numerous tables and schemes, that the quires of *Letter* were "printed from formes containing two octavo sub-formes," Steele argues that these quires were printed by "the work and turn method." He concludes that "the quires of *Letter* were printed from formes containing the inner and outer sub-formes of a single quire."

138   Tanselle, G. Thomas. "A Note on the Structure of *The Scarlet Letter.*" *Nineteenth-Century Fiction* 17 (1962): 283-285.

John C. Gerber (EC9) and Gordon Roper (EC25) argue that four successive dominant forces propel the action and divide the novel into four clear sections (the community until chapter four, Chillingworth from chapters nine through twelve, Hester from thirteen to twenty, and then Dimmesdale until the third scaffold scene), but they grant that Hawthorne breaks his pattern in the forth section (his habit of introducing each section by analyzing the activating "force" that will dominate it, concentrating briefly on a newly subordinate force from the previous section, and concluding each part with a "great scenic tableaux"). Tanselle slightly modifies this structural scheme to add "perfect symmetry to the novel" by inserting chapter twenty ("The Minister in a Maze") as the beginning of Dimmesdale's section, arguing that it is more logical and appropriate for Hester's section to conclude in the forest in chapter nineteen and more fitting to view Dimmesdale as taking charge of the action in the next chapter as he returns, shaken and changed, to town. This perfectly symmetrical form has the added advantage of correlating with the narrative movement of the plot.

1963

Essays and Studies in Books

139   Kaul, A. N. "Nathaniel Hawthorne: Heir and Critic of the Puritan Tradition." *The American Vision: Actual and Ideal Society in Nineteenth-Century Fiction*. New Haven: Yale UP, 1963. 139-213.

While the book as a whole examines the shaping influence of society on James Fenimore Cooper, Hawthorne, Herman Melville, and Mark Twain, it finds that the connection between historical reality and social ideals in *Letter, House of the Seven Gables,* and *Blithedale Romance* "represents the high-water mark of American literature." *Letter* (pp. 173-190) directly addresses how the social principles of the Puritans became a travesty of Christian aspirations in seventeenth-century New England. The novel may be seen not only as a profound "critical comment on the decisive beginnings of American civilization" but also as a suggestive commentary on "the breakdown of human relationships in the society of the seventeenth century," which "perhaps carried the seed of the dislocations more readily observable in our own." Although the ideal social intention of the Puritans was to establish a Commonwealth of brotherly love, what they actually built was a stony foundation of law and order more repressive than that left behind in England. The blame for Hester's tragic predicament falls heavily on the Puritan arbiters of her destiny who isolated her from society; and although the novel endorses her plan of withdrawing from the stern Puritan colony, Hester's eventual return to Boston at the end affirms her moral victory over her oppressors.

140   Waggoner, Hyatt H. "*The Scarlet Letter*." *Hawthorne: A Critical Study*. Revised edition. Cambridge: Belknap P of Harvard UP, 1963. 126-159.

Although the overall volume contains "many extensive revisions" of the first edition in 1955, the chapter on *Letter* (see 38) remains essentially the same, aside from a brief introductory comment referring generally to recent criticism of the novel that seems to Waggoner to "exhaust the possibilities, for our time at least, of 'interpretation.'" As in the first edition, Waggoner is less concerned with providing a new interpretation of *Letter* than with showing *why* the novel is more enigmatic than Hawthorne's other finished romances. He explores the opening chapter's light/color/vegetative imagery and three chief symbols (the cemetery, prison, and rose) that provide thematic structure to the story.

141   Ziff, Larzer. Introduction. *The Scarlet Letter*. By Nathaniel Hawthorne. 1850. Ed. Larzer Ziff. Indianapolis: Bobbs-Merrill, 1963. vii-xvii.

Addresses "Hawthorne's Preparation" (the political and social circumstances that led up to writing *Letter*); "Hawthorne's Technique" (his "corresponding" method of writing that simultaneously offers an "outside," realistic view of events and a "chamber" view that insists on a psychological and supernatural explanations of events); "The Technique of *The Scarlet Letter*" (which establishes a theory of romance in addition to a "meeting ground between the remoteness of his tale and the immediacy of his audience"), and an explanation of the ambiguous "Moral Drama of *The Scarlet Letter*."

Journal Essays and Notes

142   Davidson, Edward H. "Dimmesdale's Fall." *New England Quarterly* 36 (1963): 358-370.

Because Dimmesdale fails to come to terms with his sinful "Fall" and enter on the painful path of self-discovery to salvation, he charts a path of his own descent from grace to damnation that is "as awesome as that of a soul plummeting through Milton's chaos to hell." Dimmesdale's downfall stems from two related factors: his refusal to acknowledge the kinship of body and soul, and his imagining that his flesh can be guilty and corrupt while his soul abides in its own high realm of safety from degradation. Neither as a Puritan nor as a romantic does Dimmesdale seek salvation—thus making him "doubly damned" for neglecting the truth that the soul must necessarily experience a descent before it can recover and be redeemed. Dimmesdale's self-glorifying spiritual pride turns his world into a deadly illusion that remains until his very death, when, in the solipsistic projection of his innermost guile, he imagines himself still "a destined man whose sin could ennoble and whose suffering might spiritualize the gross, earthly part." [The question of whether Dimmesdale is damned or saved at the end of the novel has been, and still is, hotly disputed. See Dimmesdale "as damned" and "as saved" in the Subject Index under "Characters."]

143   Green, Martin. "The Hawthorne Myth: a Protest." *Essays and Studies by Members of the English Association* 16 (1963): 16-36.*

Hawthorne's work is not the "allegorical articulation of the deepest and darkest experience of the American psyche" that most critics believe it to be. Despite popular critical opinion that Hawthorne was a master craftsmen of the written word, a rare psychological genius of subtlety and irony, it is more likely that he was not an especially bright or sensitive man. Building on Newton Arvin's biographical account of Hawthorne's life (EC1), which Green finds more convincing that those of Mark Van

Doren (EC36) and Randall Stewart (EC30), Green argues that "playing with imaginary characters was much easier for him than responding to real ones." Hawthorne delighted in unreality throughout his life, and his fiction is marked by the effects of his cold temperament and self-imposed isolation from society, especially in terms of the false and ungenerous emotion that abound there. *Letter* is immensely overrated, another example of Hawthorne's irresponsible wishy-washiness (often misinterpreted as "meaningful irony" or "ambiguity"), "carping pessimism," "emotional paralysis," and "narcotic dissipation of reality." Worse is *Letter*'s "crude and unhistorical version of historicity." "Very little is actually Puritan in the novel," he argues, and "the thoughts and emotions expressed all belong to the nineteenth century." In addition, the book clearly reflects Hawthorne's inability to understand or create complex characters or emotions. Further, it is full of "crude implausibilities" and inconsistencies; it even appears to be "fundamentally confused" about the characters and incidents involved—especially in the case of Chillingworth, who does not develop but emerges from the start and remains dark and devilish. "Because of such gross oversights and shortcomings on Hawthorne's part, "we have therefore no readiness to respond to any of the book's dramatic moments," nor any "readiness to believe the critics when they construct large interpretations of them."

*Reprinted in Green's *Re-Appraisals: Some Common-Sense Readings in American Literature*. (New York: Norton, 1965. 61-85.)

144   Luecke, Jane Marie. "Villains and Non-Villains in Hawthorne's Fiction." *PMLA* 78 (1963): 551-558.

Argues for a reclassification of Hawthorne's "villains," suggesting that such two-dimensional types have been "misnamed" and that Hawthorne's only true villains—those who come closest to resembling fully developed characters, who are truly evil in character and motive, and who are guilty of unpardonable sins—are Chillingworth in *Letter* and Judge Jaffrey Pyncheon in *House of the Seven Gables*. Chillingworth is Hawthorne's "pre-eminent unpardonable-sinner-villain," the character whom Hawthorne comes as close to humanizing "as it is possible to do without engaging the reader's sympathy." Yet even though Chillingworth is his best effort, Hawthorne does not portray him realistically, because to assign Chillingworth a human dimension would perhaps "have made of sin and crime something less vile than [Hawthorne] thought it to be."

145   Parcher, Adrian. "Hawthorne's *The Scarlet Letter*." *Explicator* 21.6 (1963): Item 48.

More than the personification of her mother's sin, Pearl is "even more profoundly the child of her father's secret guilt." The fact that the spell bewitching Pearl is loosened at Dimmesdale's public confession especially points to the centrality of Dimmesdale to the novel. The final scaffold scene thus reveals that Pearl has been, throughout the novel, the symbol of Dimmesdale's—and not Hester's—inner conflict.

146   Schwartz, Joseph. "Three Aspects of Hawthorne's Puritanism." *New England Quarterly* 36 (1963): 192-208.

Various facets of Puritanism appearing in his works demonstrate that Hawthorne found neither solace nor comfort in the "gloomy, joyless, and rigid" religion of his ancestors. While he admired any sincere faith in religion and endorsed the tyranny-resisting character of the Puritans, he condemned their refusal to extend this same freedom to Puritan dissenters. Many of his short stories (such as "Main-street," "The Gentle Boy," "Alice Doane's Appeal," "The Minister's Black Veil," and "Young Goodman Brown") and two of his novels (*Letter* and *House of the Seven Gables*) negatively comment on the principal theological tenets of Puritanism, especially those involving the universal depravity of the soul and the doctrine of necessity (which flows from the concept of predestination). In *Letter*, Hester denies the concept of depravity put forth by Governor Bellingham, and corrects him by stating that she has made a conscious choice to choose good (a life of service for the good of Pearl) over evil (accompanying Mistress Hibbins into the forest to meet the "Black Man"). Hawthorne further shows the damage done to those who follow Puritan tenets in his presentation of Chillingworth and Dimmesdale. Chillingworth's moral nature is distorted because he follows the doctrine of "dark necessity" to escape personal responsibility for his sins, and Dimmesdale's fanatical belief in the righteousness of the system leads to his demise, since "the framework of his order inevitably hemmed him in."

147   Takuwa, Shinji. "Theme in *The Scarlet Letter*." *Kyushu American Literature* 6 (1963): 35-41.

Written in broken English, this essay identifies the concepts of sin, love, isolation, and self-examination as central themes of the novel.

148   Thorp, Willard. "*The Scarlet Letter* by Nathaniel Hawthorne." Review of the Centenary Edition of the Works of Nathaniel Hawthorne, Vol. 1, Columbus: Ohio State UP, 1962. *New England Quarterly* 36 (1963): 405-407.

Discusses the process by which this first volume of the Centenary Editions—which adheres closely to the text of the first edition and will henceforth be the standard edition of *Letter*—has been edited and produced, noting the names of the "rigorous" editors responsible for the "critical unmodernized reconstruction": William Charvat, Roy Harvey Pearce, Claude M. Simpson, and Fredson Bowers. Thorp also explains the methods to be followed in each successive text, which will include an introductory statement about the process of editing and publishing the Centenary Edition, historical and textual introductions, and appendices. [For more information on the Centenary Edition of *Letter*, refer to 122, 123, and 124 for citations and annotations of the three introductions to it. For a review that questions the necessity of the newly-created edition, see 180.]

149   Vogel, Dan. "Roger Chillingworth: The Satanic Paradox in *The Scarlet Letter*." *Criticism* 5 (1963): 272-280.

Most critics are too quick to point out Chillingworth's Satanic nature and therefore fail to recognize his humanity and his purgatorial role in *Letter* that illustrates the paradox of evil, or the concept that out of suffering springs ennoblement and redemption. Just as Pearl is "depersonalized" for a time in the novel and sublimated into a "cosmic agency" through Divine intervention for the sake of Hester's soul, so too is Chillingworth for the sake of Dimmesdale's.   Thus the purpose of his "unforgivable transgression" is to purify Dimmesdale's "besmirched soul." Hawthorne's working out of Chillingworth's diabolic purpose has its roots in Christian theology and humanism, illustrated time and again in works like *Job*, Calvin's *Institutes of the Christian Religion*, Jonathan Edwards's *Freedom of the Will*, Dante's *Inferno*, Bunyan's *Pilgrim's Progress*, and Milton's *Paradise Lost*. Vogel further lays claim to the "humanly tragic" status of Chillingworth by comparing him to Hawthorne's truly evil characters— the Black Man, Aylmer, Rappaccini, and Ethan Brand.

150   Warfel, Harry R. "Metaphysical Ideas in *The Scarlet Letter*." *College English* 24 (1963): 421-425.

Asserts that Hawthorne's "absolute presuppositions regarding nature, deity, and man" in *Letter* are Emersonian.   Through his characters, Hawthorne was "universalizing the social arrangements of mankind," concluding that conflicts between an individual and the state can best be resolved by rejecting social laws. Since salvation for Hester, Dimmesdale, and Pearl is achieved by their "ultimate fidelity to their own higher institutions," for Hawthorne—like Emerson—the renovation of society depends upon the individual freeing himself from man-made institutions "so that he may make the most of himself" through God-given truths about right and wrong that "correspond with the principles discernible in nature's joyous moods."

151   Wellborn, Grace Pleasant. "Plant Lore and *The Scarlet Letter*." *Southern Folklore Quarterly* 27 (1963): 160-167.

Withdrawal records from the Salem Athenaeum indicate that Hawthorne selected specific plants, flowers, and trees for their symbolic meaning and for their good and evil connotations in *Letter*. "From the first chapter onward Hawthorne used the symbols from the plant world to implement his version of the Eden story." The unsightly plants described in chapter one, burdock, pigweed, and apple peru, contribute to creating the unpleasant atmosphere of the prison area. In contrast, the wild rosebush that also thrives near the prison symbolizes (and foreshadows) moral regeneration and hints at Pearl's role in the novel—since Pearl is identified several times with the rose—as agent of grace for her parents. Other flowers with favorable implications associated with Pearl are the violet, anemone, and columbine. Plants appropriately selected to link the wicked Chillingworth with alchemy and witchcraft are nightshade, dogwood, and henbane.

152   Wellborn, Grace Pleasant. "The Symbolic Three in *The Scarlet Letter*." *South Central Bulletin* 23 (1963): 10-17.

Noting that number symbolism frequently occurs in the novel, Wellborn points out that the number three appears most often—"approximately five hundred times." Wellborn explores the possibility that Hawthorne employed the symbolic three both consciously and unconsciously (the latter use suggested by Jungian psychology) in several ways: to lend symmetrical structure to mark beginning, middle, and end (by way of the three scaffold scenes); to analyze the three-fold nature of man (body, mind, and spirit); and, most importantly, to suggest the absolute, or man's relation to the Deity. The mystic number three also advances Hawthorne's theme of the Eden story and the three-step process of man's disobedience, fall, and redemption. Pearl is especially relevant in promoting the process because she is—to borrow from Anne Marie McNamara's thesis (in 50)—the "regenerative, redemptive, disciplining power" that guides Dimmesdale and Hester to the path of moral transformation.

1964

Books

153   Leavitt, Charles. *Review Notes and Study Guide to Hawthorne's The Scarlet Letter*. New York: Thor Publications, 1964. 94 pp.

The "Monarch Literature Review Notes" for *Letter* contains an introduction; brief summaries of the four major romances; analysis of "The Custom-House"; a chapter-by-chapter summary of *Letter* that includes brief commentary and character analyses; a critical section that includes references divided in two parts (the first dealing with Hawthorne and his career and the second with specific attention to *Letter*); essay questions and answers; and a subject bibliography with a guide for research papers.

Essays and Studies in Books

154   Feidelson, Charles, Jr. "*The Scarlet Letter.*" *Hawthorne Centenary Essays*. Ed. Roy Harvey Pearce. Columbus: Ohio State UP, 1964. 31-80.

While the volume as a whole suggests the difficulties modern readers face in trying to establish an original relationship to Hawthorne, Feidelson's chapter focuses on the structure and shifting symbolic meaning of *Letter* (although Feidelson departs somewhat from his formalist method in his earlier study on Hawthorne in 1953 [see 21]). The imaginative method of the novel is not so much moral or religious as it is "distinctly historical." The story, setting, and characters themselves "are shaped by and give shape to" the meaning of seventeenth-century Boston. Yet the novel is also remarkably modern in the sense that it was written out of the "modern experience of radical solitude," which Hawthorne sought to externalize and make his true subject. He dramatized his own sense of spiritual isolation in an effort to acknowledge and escape it, and in doing so depicts America's history as the history of alienation. The spiritual history of isolation, then, is the "magnetic chain" that links Hawthorne and his fellow "isolatoes" together throughout American history. Because the Puritan community in *Letter* actually fosters a logic of "negative freedom" and encourages "an alienated individualism," the main characters are as much "sinned against as sinning" in their social isolation. Of all the characters, Hester comes closest to a positive vision by deliberately living out the symbolic existence assigned to her by the Puritan magistrates. Unlike Dimmesdale, who is unable to break free from the negative Puritan rationale, Hester ends up converting "disinheritance into freedom, isolation into individuality, and excommunication into a personal presence that is actual and communicable." Out of the negative world which she inherits, Hester—like Hawthorne—constructs an image of positive human enterprise.

155   Lundblad, Jane. "Hawthorne and Gothic Romance." *Nathaniel Hawthorne and the Tradition of Gothic Romance*. New York: Haskell House, 1964. 24-95.

Investigates the influence of Gothic Romance on Hawthorne's fiction, that influence showing itself most prominently in the employment of Gothic machinery in his first short stories and in his latest works. A brief section concentrates on the traces of the Gothic Romance to be found in *Letter* (pp. 55-61). Following a synopsis of the action of the novel appear the twelve principal traits of the Gothic novel (Manuscript, Castle, Crime, Religion, Italians, Deformity, Ghosts, Magic, Nature, Armored Knights, Words of Art/Mirrors, and Blood) and how they figure in *Letter*. For instance, "The Custom-House" provides the *manuscript*, the letter itself is an "amulet" with pronounced *magical qualities*; Governor Bellingham's medieval-style house is the *castle*, on the inside of which is found the *armor/mirrror*; the *crime* is represented by Hester's and Dimmesdale's guilt as well as Chillingworth's evil work of torturing of Dimmesdale. Further Gothic elements include Dimmesdale's position of minister (which invests the crime of adultery with the *religious character* so essential to Gothic Romance), the *magic* letter A's appearance in the sky, and Chillingworth's *magician-like* interest in alchemy and healing herbs. [Note: This essay was originally published in 1947 and should have appeared in Part II under "Early Influential Criticism (Pre-1950)."]

156   Martin, Terence. "The Method of Hawthorne's Tales." *Hawthorne Centenary Essays*. Ed. Roy Harvey Pearce. Columbus: Ohio State UP, 1964. 7-30.

Hawthorne's tales attempt to create a "neutral ground" between the real world and the imaginary, between past and present—paving the way for the composition of *Letter*. *Letter* is actually "the culmination of Hawthorne's efforts to adapt the form of the tale to the special purposes of his imagination." The novel represents the "master product" of the method of his tales with its "sustained tone and rigid economy of presentation; its use of the past and concern for the 'great warm heart of the people'; its ambivalence, mode of characterization, and exploration of the protean nature of pride; and above all, its use of a central symbol to generate narrative coherence."

157   Moffitt, Cecil L. "*The Scarlet Letter*: A Puritan Love Story." *Reality and Myth: Essays in American Literature in Memory of Richard Croom Beatty*. Eds. William E. Walker and Robert L. Welker. Nashville: Vanderbilt UP, 1964. 52-59.

Addresses the dichotomy of appearance and reality in fiction that leads to a "finer perception of truth," arguing that *Letter* is "one of the world's great love stories," one that celebrates "a sudden, reckless, and triumphant love" that prevails and redeems in defiance of iron Puritan laws. While it is true that Hawthorne deliberately refuses to supply details of the adulterous meetings of his lovers (out of deference to the moral sensibility of his age and because of his own artistic "shyness"), he does imply that Hester and Dimmesdale share a solemn, silent vow of constancy to each other that supersedes all previous vows. This sacred code remains unbroken until the novel's climactic end, at which time Dimmesdale's public confession becomes a "a canonization of a great and true love." [For a smilar argument, see Ernest Sandeen (135).]

158   Pearce, Roy Harvey. "Romance and the Study of History." *Hawthorne Centenary Essays.* Ed. Roy Harvey Pearce. Columbus: Ohio State UP, 1964. 221-244.

"The Gray Champion," "Young Goodman Brown," *Letter* (pp. 235-238), "My Kinsman, Major Molineux," and *House of the Seven Gables* are prime examples of Hawthorne's symbolic presentation and transformation of history into art. As a "historian-romancer," Hawthorne works with multiple symbolic levels of meaning and asserts his belief in the correspondence between past and present. Thus he "rejected his age's dominant mode of historical understanding and strove to put in its place a mode altogether consonant with the events of the past and the present." In other words, Hawthorne viewed history in a different way from that of his fellow writers of historical novels because he believed that Puritan history not only produces present-day Americans but also lives actively within them. Holding firmly to the idea that Americans cannot know themselves (in the present) or their common destiny (in the future) until they understand their Puritan origins, Hawthorne saw his historical fiction as a means to a moral understanding of that history.

Journal Essays and Notes

159   Arthos, John. *"The Scarlet Letter* Once More." *Ball State Teachers College Forum* 5 (1964): 31-38.

Hawthorne was influenced by the "unending questioning" typical of the Enlightenment, almost to the point that it dissipated most of his Calvinist beliefs. The tension created by the combination of the ruthless rationality of enlightened thought *and* Puritan ardor produces an ironic "hardness of heart" that characterizes the cold spirit of *Letter* (ironic because Hawthorne always considered this quality to be the greatest of sins)—not only in the characters' unsympathetic, loveless interactions with each other but also in Hawthorne's own inhumane attitude of alienation from them. Yet Hawthorne's "ingenious display of lack of sympathy"—coupled with the continual use of undisguised and obvious symbolic, allegorical, and rhetorical techniques—is the unifying element that "serves the author's conception of his characters' struggles and confusions as conflicts that lead to each individual's isolation, and, in certain instances, his monstrosity." Overall, Hawthorne's exploration of the Enlightenment's devastating effects on humanity (isolating and estranging man from his fellow man) concludes with only one moral element: 'the idea of the irremediable," which "imposes a coldness and strangeness upon the relationships of [his characters] that is qualified by a dilemma Hawthorne himself cannot find his way out of." [For another essay that considers Hawthorne's relation to Enlightenment thought, see Richard Hull (865).]

160   Chaudhry, Ghulam Ali. "Dickens and Hawthorne." *Essex Institute Historical Collections* 100 (1964): 256-273.

The relationship between Dickens and Hawthorne confirms that both authors were familiar with and enthusiastically appreciative of each other's early, similar works. But when traits between the two differ in tone and motive (Dickens is "social and humanitarian" whereas Hawthorne is "moral and intellectual"), appreciation wanes, particularly on Dickens's part. A letter to John Forster in 1851 discloses Dickens's disappointment with the artificiality of *Letter* and the unrealistic character of Pearl, noting that the novel as a whole "falls off sadly after that fine opening scene" and that "the psychological part of the story is very much overdone" (see EC6). Chaudhry offers a point-by-point refutation of Dickens's objections, chalking them up to the authors' clashing styles. The "intellectual reality" that pervades Hawthorne's romance creates "a dark heaviness, a severe and concentrated poetic style" that was foreign and unappealing to Dickens and his own tendency toward a more fanciful realism.

161   Gibson, William M. "Faulkner's *The Sound and the Fury*." *Explicator* 22.5 (1964): Item 33.

"Faulkner found the germ for the basic motivation of Quentin Compson [. . .] either in Dante's *Inferno* or in Hawthorne's *Letter*." The latter is more likely since Quentin's perverse hope that his incestuous love for his sister will be, in death, "sanctioned by special divine punishment" closely parallels Hester's "dreaming of love after death in the midst of 'endless retribution.'"

162   Granger, Bruce Ingham.   "Arthur Dimmesdale as Tragic Hero."
        Nineteenth-Century Fiction 19 (1964): 197-203.

Contends first that *Letter* is Dimmesdale's story, since "he alone among
the major characters never functions symbolically" (though "he is the
family figure of Every-Christian"), and second that Dimmesdale is a tragic
hero. Granger defines tragedy as that which arises from a tension between
illusion and reality, or the ideal and the actual, and defines heroic action as
that which is "ethically meaningful." What places Dimmesdale above
Hester is that his grand illusion of paradise is spiritual while hers is
physical and at best "heroically pathetic." Dedicated to the "steady
observance" of Calvinist law as he embarks on his seven-year dark
journey, Dimmesdale eventually chooses the responsible course of action
suggested not by Chillingworth (who advises that he keep silent and
suffer) or by Hester (who begs him to flee), but by Pearl (who entreats him
to make full and public confession). The most critical phase of
Dimmesdale's journey takes place in the forest with Hester, whose
tempting, lawless behavior and desire to escape to an illusory Eden make
her "more his enemy than the diabolical Chillingworth." After a
temporary suspension of his will, Dimmesdale becomes supercharged with
spiritual energy, ready at last to bridge the gap between illusion and reality
by revealing his guilt publicly.

163   Tanner, Bernard R. "Tone as an Approach to *The Scarlet Letter.*" *English
        Journal* 53 (1964): 528-530.

To counter "the sheer fatigue many [high-school] students feel in the face
of what seems to them a gray, somber, belabored moral tone," Tanner
dispenses with guide questions, vocabulary checklists, and background
lectures, focusing on Hawthorne's ironic humor and emphasizing the
complexities of Hawthorne's "voice." In identifying and pointing out six
types of statements and tones (all of which happen to appear within the
first six pages of the novel), students are better equipped to understand
how Hawthorne's "stuffy and ponderously worded" prose has a mocking
tone and are more likely to appreciate Hawthorne's masterful wit and
irony.

1965

Books

164   Spector, Robert Donald, ed. *The Scarlet Letter: Special Aids.* New York:
        Bantam, 1965. 279 pp.

Contains sections on why *Letter* is still popular today (pp. 241-248); how the novel took shape and developed from Hawthorne's notebook entries and "Endicott and the Red Cross" (pp. 249-258); an essay entitled "Community Pressures in *The Scarlet Letter, Intruder in the Dust*, and *The Crucible*" by Donald Koneff that illustrates how environmental, community, and moral problems in the texts determine each author's thinking (pp. 259-265); excerpted "Opinions, Reviews, and Comments" (pp. 267-275) on whether *Letter* is "a great novel" by George Ripley (see ER2), Evert A. Duychinck (see ER1), Orestes A. Brownson (see ER9), and Henry F. Chorley (see ER4); and a biographical sketch (pp. 277-279).

Essays and Studies in Books

165   Fussell, Edwin. "Nathaniel Hawthorne." *Frontier: American Literature and the American West*. Princeton: Princeton UP, 1965. 69-132.

In the literature of James Fenimore Cooper, Hawthorne, Edgar Allan Poe, Henry David Thoreau, Herman Melville, and Walt Whitman, the Westward Movement in America involves a journey to rebirth on an imaginative frontier. For Hawthorne, the East signifies the Old World and the past, the West the future and meaning of America—most often symbolized by the forest, which is "a free image, indeterminate and pluralistic, suggesting the widest range of personal and cultural possibilities." In *Letter* (pp. 91-114), which Fussell defines as a Western novel, Hawthorne applies aspects of the western frontier to New England's past. Hester is a frontiers-woman whose actions parallel the New World experience of both transplantation and taking root, Pearl is the "Spirit of the West," and the letter "A" signifies "America" itself.

166   Grant, Douglas. Introduction. *The Scarlet Letter*. By Nathaniel Hawthorne. 1850. London: Oxford UP, 1965. vii-xix.

Provides general biographical information about the author, notes several early tales that take up the symbolic treatment of sin and guilt before *Letter* ("Endicott and the Red Cross," "The Minister's Black Veil," "Rappaccini's Daughter," and "Young Goodman Brown"), and discusses "The Custom-House" as "an excellent contrast to the detachment and economy of the story itself" and as reflecting the influence of Scott's historical novel, *Heart of Midlothian* (1818)—especially the introductory chapter that establishes a vital link between the past and present. Grant also briefly notes parallels between *Letter* and John Gibson Lockhart's *Adam Blair* (1822), and makes reference to Hawthorne's use of several gothic devices.

167   Levin, David. "Nathaniel Hawthorne: *The Scarlet Letter.*" *The American Novel from James Fenimore Cooper to William Faulkner.* Ed. Wallace Stegner. New York: Basic Books, 1965. 13-24.

With *Letter*, Hawthorne gave the American novel "a new intensity of psychological analysis" by skillfully blending allegory and historical romance with a moral emphasis. Levin explains the value of both Hawthorne's method and his presentation of the three main "sinners," noting especially that the added dimension of complex human characters in the novel was something entirely new to the romance genre. "Hawthorne's great achievement in this simple story is [in relating] the allegory of sinners and the conflict between intellect and natural emotion so that we see not only his judgment of a historical community but also his clear perception of human psychology and the human predicament in almost any community."

Journal Essays and Notes

168   Black, Stephen A. "*The Scarlet Letter*: Death by Symbols." *Paunch* 24 (1965): 51-74.

Pursues "the literal line of the story" and considers only those symbols that exist in the perceptions of the characters, since it is most likely that Hawthorne attempts to represent human experience realistically in *Letter*. "The key, throughout the novel, to Hester's and Dimmesdale's attitudes toward life and death is their proclivity—one which they share with the rest of the community—to construct symbolic interpretations of real events, things, and people." As Hester gradually evolves to the point where she reacts to people and events realistically rather than symbolically, to regard Pearl as a real child instead of as an "imp of evil," she experiences a heightened desire to live and an increased willingness to accept herself. Dimmesdale, on the other hand, remains hopelessly estranged from reality, retreating "farther and farther into his public masquerade." The only time his mind clears is when he learns from Hester of Chillingworth's true identity as "a mere man" and not an intangible, symbolic agent of Satan. Finally freed of his own confusion and weakness, Dimmesdale gives himself over completely to his "public idol" in the last scaffold scene.

169   Bridgman, Richard. "As Hester Prynne Lay Dying." *English Language Notes* 2 (1965): 294-296.

Despite William Faulkner's disinclination to admit borrowing from Hawthorne, the "pointed resemblance" between *Letter* and *As I Lay Dying* (1930) indicates "deliberate planning" on his part. Core situations in both novels are, after all, identical: a married woman who despises her hump-backed scholar husband commits adultery in the woods with a hypocritical, spineless minister and has a child "of great price" (Pearl/Jewel) who functions for her as agent of salvation. Yet Faulkner's novel is much darker in plot and character development, making it seem that "*As I Lay Dying* everywhere travesties the constituents of *Letter*."

170   Crews, Frederick. "The Ruined Wall: Unconscious Motivation in *The Scarlet Letter*." *New England Quarterly* 38 (1965): 312-330.

This psychological reading undermines the customary views of *Letter* as "a fictive illustration of the terrible consequences of sin" and finds guilt rather than sin or temptation to be the soul's chief enemy in *Letter*. Dimmesdale, whose real crime is one of symbolic incest in which Chillingworth and Hester stand as father and mother to him as "son," is doomed by his own moral sensitivity "which seems to boil down to squeamishness rather than virtue." His trouble "isn't so much his libidinous nature but its weakness before his tyrannous self-accusations and his persistent wish to be holy." Ultimately Dimmesdale's "horror of sin" leads not to repentance but to a sick, paralyzing vision that can only lead to his suicide. [See Crews's fuller psychological exploration of *Letter* in his influential *Sins of the Fathers* (182).]

171   Ellis, James. "Frost's 'Desert Places' and Hawthorne." *English Record* 15 (1965): 15-17.

Because *Letter* is the probable source of Robert Frost's poem "Desert Places," the desert places referred to do not indicate "a sense of spiritual loneliness" but rather the speaker's "recognition of man's capacity for moral evil." Acknowledging his own desert places, or moral wilderness, frightens Frost's speaker as he watches snow falling at night and explains why the poem's last stanza closes with his somber contemplation "of a world which is barren." [For another essay on the connection between *Letter* and Frost's poem "Desert Places," see 317.]

172   Kearns, Francis E. "Margaret Fuller as a Model for Hester Prynne." *Jahrbuch für Amerikastudien* 10 (1965): 191-197.

Much critical attention has been paid to similarities between Margaret Fuller and Zenobia in *Blithedale Romance*, but few similarities have been noted between Fuller and Hester Prynne. While it remains purely speculative that Fuller was the model for Hester, there are many noteworthy coincidences. Most importantly, both share similar agonizing social predicaments as mothers of children of "questionable legitimacy" trying to face "the problem of survival in a rigidly Puritan society." Other parallels include a concern with social reform and the role of women in society; a desire to counsel and comfort disadvantaged, repressed women; an intellectual development cultivated in an enforced isolation that leads to humanitarian acts; and consideration of similar escape routes from puritanical environments. Connections can even be pointed out between their two illegitimate children, Pearl and Angelo, whose names hint of religious symbolism.

173   Lucke, Jessie Ryon. "Hawthorne's Madonna Image in *The Scarlet Letter*." *New England Quarterly* 38 (1965): 391-392.

Lucke finds in Louise Hall Tharp's *The Peabody Sisters of Salem* (1950) the answer to her inquiry regarding the "perversely elfin" comparison in *Letter* of Hester to the Madonna. The image was "undoubtedly" suggested to Hawthorne by his wife's reminiscences about Cuba, and pertains to a strange Cuban custom whereby a slave mistress and her children are sarcastically referred to as a "holy family."

174   Marks, William S., III. "The Psychology of the Uncanny in Lawrence's 'The Rocking-Horse Winner.'" *Modern Fiction Studies* 11 (1965-66): 381-392.

Lawrence's "notorious" Freudian reading of *Letter* as "an historical allegory of the fall of Puritan New England and the rise of an effeminate neo-Aztec culture in America" (see EC18) is similar to his exploration of the uncanny and demonic in his story, and reveals definite parallels with Hawthorne's novel. The situations of Hester and Pearl parallel those of Hester Cresswell and her son, Paul (particularly each woman's psycho-sexual motivation). Also, the spiritual narcissism of Dimmesdale parallels that of Paul. The major difference between the two works is that "Lawrence has neatly substituted Freud's Oedipal boy for both Hester's lover Dimmesdale and little Pearl in order to strengthen his tragi-comic fable." Conforming to a Freudian analysis of the Faust figure, Lawrence believed that in *Letter* and in "The Rocking-Horse Winner" that "the discrediting of the real father [. . .] precipitates the tragedy."

175   Nolte, William H. "Hawthorne's Dimmesdale: A Small Man Gone Wrong." *New England Quarterly* 38 (1965): 168-186.

Hawthorne was contemptuous of Dimmesdale and the Puritans (whom he treats with "bitterness and hatred"), though his ironic presentation of both has caused some confusion among critics (namely Régis Michaud, Randall Stewart, and Mark Van Doren) who mistakenly elevate Dimmesdale's position above Hester's. Dimmesdale is "the weakest of all Hawthorne's creations," characterized by "self-pity, cowardice, hypocrisy, masochism, egotistic humility, and overbearing Puritanism." He contrasts with Hester and Chillingworth who are *both* superior to him (Pearl not being included because she is "almost pure symbol"). Most noble is Hester, a "nineteenth-century heroine with transcendentalist coloration, placed, ironically, among bigoted seventeenth-century Puritans." She is, like her creator, a romantic, but "one can only regret her bad taste" in selecting a lover so despicable and unworthy of her love. Chillingworth is "not altogether contemptible" for two reasons: his desire for revenge is justifiable and he proves kind to both Hester and Pearl. Nothing good can be said about Dimmesdale, whose religious fanaticism and pathology should not be sympathized with by critics who erroneously equate his masochistic suffering with heroism. His suffering degrades, not ennobles, him, as is witnessed in his last pathetic act in the novel's weak conclusion (which smacks of Hawthorne's rushing to finish the book). Dimmesdale's self-aggrandizing, dying confession costs him nothing, since it is designed exclusively to win immortal life at the last possible moment.

176   Seib, Kenneth. "A Note on Hawthorne's Pearl." *ESQ: A Journal of the American Renaissance* 39 (1965): 20-21.

Because the chapter "The Child at the Brook-Side" shows many similarities between Pearl and the Middle-English poem "Pearl," the anonymous Pearl poet must have been "a major literary influence" on Hawthorne. "Both children have identical names, both stand on the far side of streams, both chastise, both are bathed in rays of sunshine [. . .], and both are attuned to things spiritual" and are "described with imagery of light and flowers." But because the first published edition of "Pearl" did not appear until 1864, such an influence is impossible. It is "merely by chance" that Hawthorne and his predecessor happened upon "the same theme, situation, and imagery." [For another study that detects similarities between Pearl and the Pearl poet's heroine, see Dorena Allen Wright (433).]

177   Steinke, Russell. "The Scarlet Letters of Puritanism." *University Review* 31 (1965): 289-291.

"The main characters of the novel are bruised by two pervasive agents of oppression: the Puritan orthodoxy [manifested in the scaffold, prison, church, market, and crowd] and the human predicament [represented by the forest and ocean]." Because the first agent assumes all importance, it turns the authoritarian, socio-political world of Puritan New England into a perverting sham that sacrifices any true sense of morality on "the altar of absolutes." The brain-washing tyranny that tortures Hester and Dimmesdale is "a living nightmare" akin to a reverse of George Orwell's *1984* in that it speaks chillingly of the warping grasp of any "puritanic strains of ideology and spirit" from the past. The "tragic secret" of *Letter,* which is the source of the novel's power and originality, is that Hawthorne and his characters balance a consideration of "the mysteries, the perplexities, the possibilities of life itself" in the midst of a crippling Puritan theocracy.

178   Warren, Austin. *"The Scarlet Letter*: A Literary Exercise in Moral Theology." *Southern Review* 1 (1965): 22-45.*

Discusses Hawthorne's exhaustive examination of sin and morality, as well as investigates the ambiguous moral center of *Letter* that provides no sure guide by which to interpret the views of the two main protagonists. While Hawthorne concentrates on such facets as "concealment of sin, penance, and penitence; the distinction between the comparatively lighter sins of passion and the graver sins of cold blood—pride, calculated revenge; [and] the legacy of sin in making one detect, or suspect, it in others," his primary focus stems not from an interest in the moral aspects of sin but from his aesthetic and psychological fascination with it. Hester and Dimmesdale are Hawthorne's most introspective and meditative characters, but it is not to them that one may look for Hawthorne's ultimate "moral." Because "truth-finding" has a dialectical nature, absolute truth and ultimate reality are not wholly imparted to Hester, Dimmesdale, the "chorus" of the community, nor even to Hawthorne's narrator. Hawthorne's absolute truth and reality are left undefined, for there is no moral finally contained in the novel, only the implied hope that wisdom, tolerance, and sense of merciful forgiveness will—when given enough time—replace foolish intolerance and harsh judgmentalism. [See Thomas F. Walsh (1966) for a challenge to Warren's assertion that Hawthorne was careless in his handling of Dimmesdale's Election-Day sermon.]

*Reprinted in Warren's *Connections* (East Lansing: Michigan UP, 1970. 45-69).

179   Wellborn, Grace Pleasant. "The Golden Thread in *The Scarlet Letter."* *Southern Folklore Quarterly* 29 (1965): 169-178.

While much has been made of Hawthorne's use of light and shadow in *Letter*, little attention has been paid to the symbolic colors yellow (or gold) and red, both of which appear prominently and sometimes together. Gold, associated with sunshine images, symbolizes joy and divine truth. Such sunshine images—found especially in five scenes (the three scaffold scenes, the meeting at the Governor's mansion, and the forest scene)— work to advance Hawthorne's telling of the Eden story as "his lovers move from sin and darkness to light and transformation." Functioning in a similar way is the color red, which appears 121 times and has the two-fold function of representing sin or evil on the one hand and atonement on the other. Thus, while the scarlet letter first represents Hester's sin (and is contrasted by the "celestial illumination" symbolized by the gold thread that keeps it in place), its meaning is transformed as it becomes associated with the red-hot burning heat of the purgatorial cleansing of guilt. Red is further used to associate evil with Chillingworth, self-torture with Dimmesdale, and punishing purgatorial flames with Pearl.

180 Young, Philip. "Hawthorne and 100 Years: A Report from the Academy." *Kenyon Review* 27 (1965): 215-232.

This playful and nearly irreverent "report" not only questions the significance of the new Centenary Edition of *Letter* that appeared in 1962 (since it contains barely perceptible differences from the 1883 Riverside edition and includes practically meaningless and unappreciable "textual revelations") but also considers the recently published *Hawthorne Centenary Essays* (1964) as unnecessary ("we did not, honest to God, need eighteen"), because Hawthorne has already been "explicated, allegorized, source-hunted, theologized, annotated, romanticized, de-romanticized, decoded, psychoanalyzed, and mythologized" practically to death—with no end in sight. Two surges of interest in recent Hawthorne studies that Young predicts are merely signs of the current times are (1) that interest in Hawthorne's texts is superseding interest in Hawthorne, and (2) that current biographers (with "practically no insight" despite their large collections of information) are intent on establishing the "white myth" of Hawthorne as "a rather normal, ordinary, open, and well-adjusted sort of fellow," just at the time when critics "have been coming up with a full display of radical ambiguity, paradox, irony, and a complexity rich to the point of impenetrability in his works." Young attempts to knock the wind out of the sails of all potential Hawthorne critics when he concludes with, "I am convinced we really understand him now." [For citations and annotations for the three introductions to the Centenary Edition, see 122, 123, and 124. For a technical review of the edition, see 148. For the three essays on *Letter* that appeared in *Hawthorne Centenary Essays*, see 154, 156, and 158.]

1966

Books

181   O'Brien, Frank. *Pennant Key-Indexed Study Guide to The Scarlet Letter*. New York: Bantam Books, 1966. 74 pp.

Contains a plot diagram that breaks down chapters and characters in historical and literary time, a key map of Salem, a "chronolog" (a timeline of selected American and British writers/poets from 1800-1950), biography and chronology of Hawthorne's life, introduction and complete background (with history of Puritanism and early Salem), both capsule and comprehensive (chapter by chapter) summaries, critical and character analyses, a question and answer section, areas for possible research, a bibliography, and a glossary of relevant people, places, and events.

Essays and Studies in Books

182   Crews, Frederick. "The Ruined Wall." *The Sins of the Fathers: Hawthorne's Psychological Themes*. New York: Oxford UP, 1966. 136-153.

This groundbreaking psychoanalytic reading* of *Letter* approaches the novel's famous psychological ambiguities through the character of Dimmesdale (and expands upon 170, Crews's 1965 essay). The source of Dimmesdale's anguish and vulnerability is not Chillingworth but his own remorse and guilt, which Hawthorne describes as a "ruined wall" that cannot be repaired. The irreparable "ruined wall" becomes a metaphor for the inner mechanism of Dimmesdale's psychological torment, implying his "double" torture of combating sin and guilt while trying at the same time to repress his sexual desire ("libidinal impulse") for Hester. Hawthorne's metaphor ultimately "demands that we see Dimmesdale not as a free moral agent but as a victim of feelings he can neither understand nor control" (140). This point can be extended to include Chillingworth and Hester, whose own minds are altered by the consequences of the adulterous act. Finally, the tragedy of *Letter* springs not from Puritan society's imposition of false social ideals on the three main characters but from their own inner worlds of frustrated ideas.

*It has been remarked in numerous places that Crews's analysis serves as an important corrective to previous studies that focus exclusively on moral and religious themes in the novel and fail to explore the conflicting, inner complexities of Hawthorne's imagination.   However, other critics—

including Crews himself—will later fault the book's insistence on divorcing Hawthorne's moral and religious themes from his psychological themes, and even question the relevance of psychoanalytic criticism. See Michael Vannoy Adams's essay (439) for a critique of Crews's later attitude.

183   Edel, Leon. "Hawthorne's Symbolism and Psychoanalysis." *Hidden Patterns*. Eds. L. F. Manheim and E. B. Manheim. New York: Macmillan, 1966. 93-111.

The two disciplines of literary criticism and psychoanalysis are "distinctly complementary" in their use of symbols to illuminate meaning (since the critic studies symbols to enlarge general understanding and the psychoanalyst studies symbols to assist patients in better understanding themselves). The "biographical symbolism" of *Letter* shows that the novel is "a symbol for Hawthorne as well as for the personages of his Puritan story." *Letter* can be seen as a symbol of its creator's consciousness, as an imaginative effort to work through the "profound and painful dilemma" of the alienated, withdrawn individual who struggles to achieve reunion with society.

184   Fiedler, Leslie A. "Achievement and Frustration." *Love and Death in the American Novel*. Revised edition. New York: Stein and Day, 1966. 217-305.

Fiedler asserts the validity of the earlier edition in 1960 (see 89) and thus only "prunes" and "condenses" his original text, hoping that it will be read as something of a "gothic novel (complete with touches of black humor)." His analysis of *Letter* is condensed into a succinct discussion (pp. 227-239) of Hawthorne's "shadowy and sterilized" treatment of passion. Although the novel was considered racy in its own day, it actually advocates the redemptive denial of passion and the necessity of self-restraint. As before, Fiedler concludes that Hawthorne was "unable to break through the limitations of his era or to repress the shame he felt at trifling with them," and was only able to write an "elegiac treatise on the death of love."

185   Gish, Lillian, Mark Van Doren, and Lyman Bryson. "*The Scarlet Letter*." *Invitation to Learning: English and American Novels*. Ed. George D. Crothers. New York: Basic Books, 1966. 211-222.

This three-way conversation was originally broadcast by the CBS Radio Network on the program "Invitation to Learning." The three casually discuss the novel's creation, import, and influence.

186   Kaul, A.N., ed. *Hawthorne: A Collection of Critical Essays*. Englewood
       Cliffs: Prentice-Hall, 1966.

       Included in this collection of twelve essays on Hawthorne's symbolism
       and meaning (along with an introduction, chronology, notes, and selected
       bibliography) are reprints of Yvor Winters's "Maule's Curse" (EC40), Q.
       D. Leavis's "Hawthorne as Poet" (13), Larzer Ziff's "The Ethical
       Dimension of 'The Custom-House'" (76), and Mark Van Doren's "*The
       Scarlet Letter*" (EC36).

187   Kjørven, Johannes.   "Hawthorne, and the Significance of History."
       Americana Norvegica: Norwegian Contributions to American Studies.
       Vol. 1. Eds. Sigmund Skard and Henry H. Wasser. Philadelphia: U of
       Pennsylvania P, 1966. 110-160.

       This lengthy essay investigates Hawthorne's treatment and understanding
       of history, pointing out that the "narrative technique and content in his
       work are based upon an imputation of guilt and eventual resolution
       through history." While several past studies treat both Hawthorne and
       history—such as those by R. W. B. Lewis (37), Hyatt H. Waggoner (38),
       F. O. Matthiessen (EC20), and Roy R. Male (56), none try consistently "to
       interrelate Hawthorne's sense of the past with his deep artistic interest in
       the operation of moral laws." History thus becomes inseparable from
       Hawthorne's concept of the moral identity of his characters, as can be seen
       in "Wakefield," "Young Goodman Brown," and the novels, *Letter*
       included (pp. 140-143), where the characters "grow in moral stature as
       they come to see themselves not only against the background of their own
       life stories, but against the background of the march of ages."

188   Smith, David E. "Bunyan and Hawthorne: *The Scarlet Letter*." *John
       Bunyan in America*. Bloomington: U of Indiana P, 1966. 62-75.

       Traces John Bunyan's pervasive influence on Hawthorne by noting the
       ways in which the allegory of *Letter* clearly models itself after *Pilgrim's
       Progress*—especially in its borrowing of three primary images: the
       disingenuous pilgrim, pathways and byways chosen by individuals in a
       labyrinthine wilderness, and the unsuccessful search for the Celestial city.
       The allegorical setting of the New England colony represents "the
       wilderness of this world, flanked on one side by the City of Destruction
       (Europe), and on the other by the dark chaos of the primeval forest.
       Dimmesdale is a burdened 'Christian' who combines in his character the
       weakness of Pliable and the gullibility of Ignorance, but who, like
       Christian, despite his temptations away from the straight path into the

bypaths of the wilderness, ultimately is relieved of his external and internal burdens."

Journal Essays and Notes

189   Cassill, R. V. "That Blue-Eyed Darling Nathaniel." *Horizon* 8 (1966): 32-39.

This general assessment of Hawthorne's career evaluates the import of D. H. Lawrence's famous remark (in EC18) that Hawthorne "knew disagreeable things in his inner soul," and examines most closely the "lucky design" that culminated in *Letter*, which Cassill describes as the "peak" around which his other novels and short stories are only "foothills." "For all its gloom and whisper of abominations," *Letter* is valuable to our grasp of early American life and even America's "present conscience." The novel "does not yield very gratefully to Freudian analysis or other currently available methodologies," but patiently "waits perhaps to be read as a deeply disguised self-portrait."

190   Hawthorne, Manning. *"The Scarlet Letter."* *Literary Half-Yearly* 2 (1966): 37-39.

This journal could not be located.

191   Houston, Neal B. "Hester Prynne as Eternal Feminine." *Discourse* 9 (1966): 230-244.*

Argues that critics who overscore Hester's intellect and view her as a "Puritan Fausta" (namely W. C. Brownell [EC3], William Bysshe Stein [22], and Leslie Fiedler [89]) fail to see her true role as "eternal feminine," dedicated to her "womanly purpose" of guiding Dimmesdale to salvation. It is more accurate to view her as the counterpart of Gretchen, with Dimmesdale as the Puritan Faust and Chillingworth as Puritan Mephistopheles. Compared by Hawthorne with "Divine Maternity," "Hester exhibits the spiritual qualities of the Eternal Feminine from the beginning of the tale to its end," resisting fatal temptations, controlling perilous thoughts, acting always to perpetuate good and to affirm life, and remaining "true to her purpose in life"—by supporting and spiritually redeeming Dimmesdale. When Dimmesdale, following his Election-Day sermon, at last recognizes Hester as "the earthly embodiment of all that is holy and eternal," he is ready to confess and be saved.

*Reprinted in *Real: The Journal of Liberal Arts* (21 [1996]: 29-39).

192   Hyman, Lawrence W.   "Moral Values and the Literary Experience."
       Journal of Aesthetics and Art Criticism 24 (1966): 538-547.

Rejects recent contextualist or "disinterested" approaches to literature,
advocating "a new concept of creativity" that asserts a certain fluidity in
an artist's conception of his own ideas as he tries them out in a specific
literary form. *Letter* is the prime example (among three others—George
Herbert's "The Flower," Thomas Hardy's "A Drizzling Easter Morning,"
and Leo Tolstoy's *Anna Karenina*) of an imaginative work that "tests" and
"tries" ideas and feelings instead of presenting fixed notions of them. This
theory, which discounts the possibility that a moral scheme can be found
to embrace every action in the novel, explains Hawthorne's moral
ambivalence and why there is no critical agreement "as to whether
Hawthorne wants us to sympathize with Hester or Dimmesdale." Because
Hawthorne is interested in testing—not proving—his convictions, the
moral "to be true" is bound up with the total experience generated by the
novel, not by any comprehensive view that a single human perspective
could produce.

193   Josipovici, Gabriel.   "Hawthorne's Modernity."   *Critical Quarterly* 8
       (1966): 351-360.

Examines two critics who have noted Hawthorne's "ambiguity and
interest in compulsive situations," Yvor Winters in "Maule's Curse"
(EC40) and Frederick Crews in *The Sins of the Fathers* (182), and assesses
their contributions to Hawthorne's status as modern writer. Only in *Letter*
and a handful of stories is Hawthorne at his best, however, and far more
consciously in control of his "logic of compulsion" than Crews allows.

194   Ridout, Albert K.   "*The Scarlet Letter* and Student Verse."   *English
       Journal* 55 (1966): 885-886.

An effective strategy for teaching high school students an appreciation for
Letter is to study the novel in-depth in class through oral presentations on
specific topics and then to assign students to write a sonnet that borrows
the persona of one of the characters in the novel. The end result, three
samples of which Ridout includes, requires close attention to characters'
emotions.

195   Smith, Julian.   "Hawthorne and a Salem Enemy."   *Essex Institute
       Historical Collections* 102 (1966): 299-302.

Building on critic Alfred A. Kern's suggestion that Hawthorne was
exacting revenge on "secret and cunning" Salem enemy Richard S. Rogers

by satirizing him in "Feathertop" (the man had proved instrumental in Hawthorne's removal from the Custom House), Smith proposes that Hawthorne "carried the personal satire of "The Custom-House" into the novel proper, taking a "satiric jibe" at Rogers by "immolating" him in the person of Roger Chillingworth. Evidence to support this theory can be found in the novel itself, where, first of all, Chillingworth is never (save one time) addressed or referred to without his first name (when "in no other novel does Hawthorne use a first and last name together consistently"). Second, the name "Roger" is the only name in the novel that "does not seem to have any easily discernible allegorical, historical, or literary significance." Thus the likelihood that "Hawthorne wanted to keep 'Roger' before he eyes of the Salem readers who knew of his grievance against Rogers."

196   Van Deusen, Marshall. "Narrative Tone in 'The Custom-House' and *The Scarlet Letter.*" *Nineteenth-Century Fiction* 21 (1966): 61-71.

Considers the "maladjustment" of tone between the two parts by considering how the distinctive narrative voice in "The Custom-House" echoes in the novel that follows, bind[ing] the two parts of the book into an indissoluble whole." The "wry, quizzical irony of [Hawthorne's pretense of finding the manuscript of Hester's story in the attic of the Custom House] sets a tonal pattern which introduces, and in large measure defines, the problems of knowledge, historical and relative, real and absolute, which are such an important part of the thematic material of the book." Hawthorne's pretense has been misconstrued by critics as his attempt at literary verisimilitude, but in reality it reflects a symbolic ambiguity—which filters throughout the volume—and implies Hawthorne's awareness of the problem of "the meaning of historical authenticity." Hawthorne's decapitated surveyor/narrator should not be viewed as a kind of comical fool whose viewpoint we should reject because of his questionable and bumbling descriptions of the issues of the novel; instead he should be seen as integrally related to the narrative, illuminating the historical, epistemological, and ethical themes of the whole book. [For a thesis similar to Van Deusen's, see Harry C. West's "Hawthorne's Editorial Pose" (299).]

197   Wagner, Linda Welshimer. "Embryonic Characterization in 'The Custom-House.'" *The English Record* 16 (1966): 32-35.

"The Custom-House" not only provides the "geneses" for the characters of Hester, Dimmesdale, and Chillingworth, but "also contains Hawthorne's theories of characterization." Wagner notes "significant parallels" between the three "type" figures represented in "The Custom-House" and

110

the protagonists of the novel, linking the Inspector's proud sensuality with Hester's, the General's introspective intellectualism with Chillingworth's, and the customs official's duty-oriented integrity with Dimmesdale's. Further proof that Hawthorne intends for readers to make this textual comparison appears in Hawthorne's "hint" in "The Custom-House": the process description of the difficulty he encounters in creating rich, imaginative figures out of the outlines of "ordinary characters." This blending of "the Actual and the Imaginary" provides the "neutral territory" of Hawthorne's romance.

198   Walsh, Thomas F. "Dimmesdale's Election Sermon." *ESQ: A Journal of the American Renaissance* 44 (1966): 64-66.

Challenging Austin Warren's opinion (in 178) that Hawthorne carelessly handled the "subject-matter" of Dimmesdale's Election-Day sermon—in particular Hawthorne's "curiously irrelevant" references to New England's "glorious destiny" that betray his "regional loyalties." The minister's sermon is in keeping with actual seventeenth-century election sermons of New England, and its spiritual connotations serve as a prelude to the genuinely "triumphant ignominy" achieved in Dimmesdale's confession-death.

1967

Books

199   White, Sidney Howard. *Barron's Simplified Approach to The Scarlet Letter.* Woodbury: Barron's Educational Series, 1967. 114 pp.

Included are a chronology that places Hawthorne in historical and literary context; an introduction and overview of the novel; a chapter-by-chapter summary; evaluations of Pearl, Dimmesdale, and Hester; excerpts from selected criticism*; topics for discussion and papers; and suggestions for further reading.

*The brief excerpts are from the reviews and criticism of George B. Loring (ER7), Orestes A. Brownson (ER9), Henry James (EC15), Anthony Trollope (EC33), W. C. Brownell (EC3), D. H. Lawrence (EC18), Herbert Gorman (EC10), Régis Michaud (EC21), F. O. Matthiessen (EC20), Leland Schubert (EC26), Mark Van Doren (EC36), Richard Harter Fogle (15), Frederic I. Carpenter (EC4), Hyatt H. Waggoner (38), Malcolm Cowley (59), Roy R. Male (56), Hubert H. Hoeltje (125), A. N. Kaul (139), and Bruce Ingham Granger (162).

Essays and Studies in Books

200   Franklin, Howard Bruce. Introduction. *The Scarlet Letter and Other Writings by Nathaniel Hawthorne*. Philadelphia: J. B. Lippincott, 1967. 1-18.

Discusses the relation of *Letter* to two of Hawthorne's short stories that feature similar "fiendish showmen": "Main-street," which Hawthorne originally intended to publish in the same volume as *Letter*, and "Ethan Brand," which Hawthorne most likely had also intended to publish together with the above-mentioned texts. "The Custom-House, "Main-street," and "Ethan Brand" actually "combine to form the stage for *Letter*, a book that explores the relations between private and public affairs in terms of guilt and exposure." Here, as in his other historical fiction, Hawthorne uses private guilt to display the public disease known as history." Franklin acknowledges that critics in the past have usefully divided the action of *Letter* into five acts, but he shows—by way of a chart—that "each of these acts can be located historically, not only with reference to events in America but also to events in England." (Note for instance that the novel begins in 1642, the date of the beginning of the English Civil War between King Charles I and the Puritan Parliament, and that the novel ends in 1649, the year the Puritans beheaded King Charles.) This chart shows "precisely what kind of statement [the novel] is making about the relations between private guilt and public affairs, between psychology and history."

201   Levin, David. "Hawthorne's Romances: the Value of Puritan History." *In Defense of Historical Literature*. New York: Hill and Wang, 1967. 98-117.

Hawthorne combines "an extremely skillful re-creation of the Puritan past with a forceful statement on the central issues of nineteenth-century romanticism" in *Letter* (pp. 102-113). The success of the novel largely derives from Hawthorne's thorough knowledge of Puritan history and his ability to retain the moral emphasis of his allegory while also remaining faithful to romantic psychology. Historical genius lies in Hawthorne's "concentration on a self-punishing minister trying unsuccessfully to achieve true penitence; on an adulteress who, though cruelly treated by the community, still seems eligible for regeneration; on a vengeful husband whose self-justification makes a caricature of predestination." Levin discusses each of the three sinners in turn—the partially contrite sinner (Hester), the secret sinner (Dimmesdale), and the Unpardonable Sinner (Chillingworth), and concludes with consideration of the relationships between Hawthorne's knowledge of New England history and the narrative techniques in his historical fiction.

202   Mizener, Arthur. "Nathaniel Hawthorne: *The Scarlet Letter*." *Twelve Great American Novels*. New York: New American Library, 1967. 9-18.

Geared toward the inexperienced reader of classic novels, Mizener's analyses seek only to inspire interest and be "useful." The real interest and excitement of *Letter* do not lie in the plot but in the "deep and subtle perception of the spiritual life" that surrounds the key scaffold scenes. The novel, one of Hawthorne's several self-described "allegories of the heart," is actually about the spiritual drama within Hawthorne's own consciousness, revealing just how "profoundly subjective" his representations of reality were.

203   Tharpe, Jac. "Shades in Niflheim." *Nathaniel Hawthorne: Identity and Knowledge*. Carbondale: Southern Illinois UP, 1967. 95-109.

Reinterprets Hawthorne's work in the context of Western literature because Hawthorne tried to avoid or conceal his influences—and especially because American criticism ("insular if not chauvinistic") has severely limited both his sources and influence, never taking into account that Hawthorne was, for instance, certainly influenced by Goethe and LeSage, and that he most likely influenced the work of Dostoevsky and Robert Musil. In his chapter on *Letter*, Tharpe focuses on Hawthorne's use of the themes of identity and knowledge. Much of the novel involves the characters' failed attempts at truly knowing one another, despite their complicity and their mutual desires to be known. Even the community as a whole—in the long, seven-year span of the novel—never seems to interpret properly the four main characters and thereby violates what little sense of individuality the four possess. In such a hopeless, artificial environment (that anticipates twentieth-century literature), there can be no real awareness or resolution between characters—whose meaningless actions only lead to perpetual suffering and condemnation.

Journal Essays and Notes

204   Baughman, Ernest W. "Public Confession and *The Scarlet Letter*." *New England Quarterly* 40 (1967): 532-550.

Explores Hawthorne's historically accurate use of public confession in *Letter* to confirm that the novel's ending—often complained of by critics for its seeming inauthenticity—is constructed with complete fidelity to Puritan law and theology in Massachusetts Bay Colony, and is thus historically and aesthetically justified. The novel hinges on the inevitability of Dimmesdale's public confession and its subsequent effect on the lives of Hester, Pearl, and Chillingworth—and it is absolutely consistent with Puritan practices and the essential beliefs of the period. Even Hawthorne's refusal to confirm "a happy reunion in heaven for Hester and Dimmesdale" or affirm that the two will be redeemed at all is in perfect accord with Puritan doctrine. Baughman submits several public confession cases from seventeenth-century New England to help explain the psychology of Letter's characters; he also speculates that, following Dimmesdale's death, Hester also publicly confesses and then baptizes Pearl before they go abroad. [For an essay that builds upon Baughman's investigation into the Puritan tradition of public confession to explain Dimmesdale's behavior, see Reiner Smolinski (552).]

205   Bruccoli, Matthew J. "Notes on the Destruction of *The Scarlet Letter* Manuscript." *Studies in Bibliography* 20 (1967): 257-259.

Of the two explanations of how the *Letter* manuscript was destroyed—(1) that Hawthorne burned it himself and (2) that printers in James T. Fields's firm casually discarded it (this theory coming from Hawthorne's less-than-reliable son, Julian)—the former is almost certainly the truth, as evidence attests from a letter dated from 1904 by Fields's widow. In the letter, Annie Fields protests Julian's derogatory treatment of her husband in *Hawthorne and His Circle* (1903), and petitions him to retract his claim, because she had personally heard from Hawthorne himself that he had "put [the manuscript] up the chimney."

206   Canaday, Nicholas, Jr. "'Some Sweet Moral Blossom': A Note on Hawthorne's Rose." *Papers on Language and Literature* 3 (1967): 186-187.

If Canto 29 of Dante's *Purgatorio* is the source of the rose symbolism in the first chapter of *Letter*, then the meaning of the rose extends beyond its usual association as a beautiful and amoral emblem of wild nature (like Pearl)—and Hawthorne's phrase "some sweet moral blossom" adds a further, Christian, dimension to the novel. A procession of elders in Canto 29 is crowned with red roses, "emblematic of the charity of the New Testament." Thus, just as the redemptive charity of the New Testament follows the dark Old Testament, so "from the pigweed of sin springs the immortal soul of Pearl."

207   Coanda, Richard Joseph. "Hawthorne's Scarlet Alphabet." *Renascence* 19 (1967): 161-166.

Inspired in part by Leslie A. Fiedler's comments about American literature's mythic qualities in *Love and Death in the American Novel* (89), Coanda's exegesis of *Letter* considers that Hawthorne followed in the footsteps of Samuel Taylor Coleridge, Percy Bysshe Shelley, and Ralph Waldo Emerson in his employment of the poetic symbol and in his tendency to "idealize actuality and [seek] infinity in the finite." Coanda speculates that Hawthorne particularly followed Coleridge's example by personifying mental states: the New England community (the human body), Hester (heart), Chillingworth (head), Dimmesdale (primary imagination), and Pearl (secondary imagination). Hawthorne "may have hinted through the initials of the names Hester, Arthur, Roger, and Pearl that only their union could form the Aeolian instrument of American harmony [the heavenly "harp"] to herald the new age of psychological awareness."

208   Gottschalk, Jane. "The Continuity of American Letters in *The Scarlet Letter* and 'The Beast in the Jungle.'" *Wisconsin Studies in Literature* 4 (1967): 39-45.

A similar "underlying perception of man" in *Letter* and James's "The Beast in the Jungle" (1903) helps to establish a continuing tradition in American letters. In addition to sharing focuses on psychological tensions, "both works depend on a perception of values that are not material, both subordinate action and dialogue to an analysis of conduct, and both have universal application despite their differences in approach and execution." [For another essay that links *Letter* to "The Beast in the Jungle," see Michael Couson Berthold (441).]

209   Lasser, Michael L. "Mirror Imagery in *The Scarlet Letter.*" *English Journal* 56 (1967): 274-277.

Though not pervasive, mirror imagery functions in *Letter* in several ways: to "blur the line between what the major characters believe and what really is," to call attention to a deeper reality beyond the obvious, and to enable characters to see into themselves or into the secret hearts of others. For example, Pearl's eyes are a mirror for Hester's fears, while her lawless actions similarly "reflect" or mirror Hester's longing to be free. Likewise, Chillingworth's frequent insistence that the eyes mirror the soul proves true for himself both when he reads Dimmesdale's secret and when he recognizes his own evil, while Dimmesdale's private vigils before a mirror reflect his own tormented mind and conscience.

210   Lohmann, Christoph. "The Burden of the Past in Hawthorne's American Romances." *South Atlantic Quarterly* 66 (1967): 92-104.

Builds on several "corrective" re-interpretations of Hawthorne's use of the past (which argue that Hawthorne's work is more than a romantic idealization of his somber past), asserting that it is not the past's picturesque quality that attracted Hawthorne but its symbolic quality. Lohmann considers how the past "assumes a moral, ethical, and theological function, so that its treatment is frequently identical with [Hawthorne's] treatment of sin and guilt." In effect, his insistence on man's connection to the past really expresses Hawthorne's "profound conviction" that man must accept his own sinful state as well as the sins of his predecessors. Hawthorne repeatedly examines this connection between the inescapable past and the problem of sin in his romances (the first three of which are discussed in this essay), but most notably in *Letter*, where he comes to grips with his own family's past and explores "as a first step in the process of expiation, the nature of the sin and guilt he has inherited from his progenitors." To further advance this theme, Hawthorne purposely begins the novel with the adulterous sin already behind his characters to identify their sin with the past—not to mention that Hawthorne also implies the interconnectedness of the past and the present by comparing his own stifling situation in "The Custom-House" with Hester's experience. That Hester returns to Boston at the end also reinforces Hawthorne's theme of the inescapable burden of sin and the past. What's more, Hawthorne denies the myth of America as the New Eden to show that New England is no prelapsarian utopia but merely an extension or continuation of the Old World. Hence Pearl's transference to Europe will not prevent her from "enacting the sins of her forebears" and "handing this burden down to future generations."

211   McCall, Dan. "The Design of Hawthorne's 'Custom-House.'" *Nineteenth-Century Fiction* 21 (1967): 349-358.

"Modern critical formulae devised to explain the connection [between "The Custom-House" and the romance] are vague and misleading" (specifically those of Charles Feidelson, Jr. [21] and Charles O'Donnell [100] for their incompatible linking of the novel's aesthetic and moral problems). The organic connection between the two is best understood as the conflict between Hawthorne's artistic and social responsibilities. "'The Custom-House' is built around two main questions which Hawthorne asks himself: first, What is my relationship to my homeland and, second, What is my life's work?" Put most simply, "The Custom-House" exhibits Hawthorne's struggle to work out the answers to these two questions that deal with his responsibility to his community and his estranged position as an artist committed to his work. After Hawthorne moves progressively throughout the sketch from official and social concerns to more private, imaginative interests (illustrating that "real-life" problems can be solved by turning inward to self-examination), he links his own alienated experience to Hester's and thereby simultaneously sets the reader up to view her sympathetically in the opening scaffold scene, and implies that "the American community fails and frustrates the impulses of creative people by forcing them back too much upon themselves."

212   Powers, Lyall H. "Hawthorne and Faulkner and the Pearl of Great Price." *Papers of the Michigan Academy of Science, Arts, and Letters* 52 (1969): 391-401.

Compares *Letter* with both *The Sound and the Fury* (1929) and *Light in August* (1932) to "illuminate a rather dark corner of Faulkner's work" that has only "scarcely been noted." Concerned in this essay with the problem of assigning Christ-like roles to Benjy Compson and Joe Christmas, Powers briefly compares their roles to that of Pearl in *Letter*, concluding that all three are living reminders of sin who nevertheless urgently seek acceptance and love.

213   Sahs, Viola. "The Myth of America in Hawthorne's *The Scarlet Letter*." *Kwartalnik Neofilologeczny* 14 (1967): 245-267.

Asserts that Edwin Fussell's thesis in *Frontier: American Literature and the American West* (165)—that *Letter* is a novel of the Western frontier and that the scarlet "A" stands for America itself—is only partly right. It is more accurate to say that "the myth of America" includes both its Puritan and Western inheritance. "The Western dream of Paradise on Earth and the vision of the New Canaan merge into the myth of an ideal America." It is this "myth" that lies at the core of the novel and is the "key" to its symbolic meaning, since *Letter* "attempt[s] to recreate in imaginative terms the American experiment and to discover and analyze the basic traits of the national character which account for the shortcomings of the dream." *Letter* is best viewed as the first in a trilogy (*House of the Seven Gables* and *Blithedale Romance* to follow) that addresses the complicated subject of the American character.* "A rather painstaking analysis" of the three main characters in *Letter* reveals that both Dimmesdale and Chillingworth are unfit to begin a New World because of their inability to discard "old values," and, although Hester undergoes a "new birth" in her rebellion against the old order, she is too tainted by her sin to bring about a new order. It is up to the Edenic Pearl to suggest Hawthorne's "answer to how this vision of the New World can be brought about": "by means of deep knowledge of the evil and sinfulness of the world, and man's attempt to break with it, to regenerate the human heart and to endure the suffering it brings."

*A. N. Kaul makes the same observation in his 1963 *The American Vision: Actual and Ideal Society in Nineteenth-Century Fiction* (see 139).

1968

Books

214   Gerber, John C., ed. *Twentieth-Century Interpretations of The Scarlet Letter: A Collection of Critical Essays.* Englewood Cliffs: Prentice-Hall, 1968. 120 pp.

Divided into four parts, this collection of critical essays contains representative selections under the headings of Background, Form, Techniques, and Interpretations, and includes an introduction by Gerber (see 216, below), as well as a chronology of important dates and a brief selected bibliography. Under "Background" appear Hawthorne's own germinal ideas for *Letter* from *The American Notebooks*, "Endicott and the Red Cross," and complete reprinted essays by Charles Ryskamp (85) and Joseph Schwartz (146). Under "Form" are brief excerpts from essays by Gordon Roper (EC25), Leland Schubert (EC26), and Hugh N. MacLean (42). "Techniques" contains selections from pieces by F. O. Matthiessen (EC20), Richard Harter Fogle (15), Hyatt H. Waggoner (38), Donald A. Ringe (6), and William Bysshe Stein (22); and the fourth section on "Interpretations" has complete articles by Charles Child Walcott (28) and Edward H. Davidson (142), and excerpts from the works of Frederick Crews (182), John C. Gerber (EC9), Ernest Sandeen (135), and Leslie A. Fiedler (89).

Essays and Studies in Books

215   Gale, Robert L. *"The Scarlet Letter." Plots and Characters in the Fiction and Sketches of Nathaniel Hawthorne.* Hamden: Archon Books, 1968. 136-144.

This alphabetically-indexed reference book thoroughly summarizes sketches, short stories, and novels that span Hawthorne's earliest to latest literary efforts. The chapter on *Letter* examines precisely what the title of the book suggests.

216   Gerber, John C. Introduction. *Twentieth-Century Interpretations of The Scarlet Letter: A Collection of Critical Essays.* Ed. John C. Gerber. Englewood Cliffs: Prentice-Hall, 1968. 1-15.

Provides necessary historical background; information on the writing of *Letter*; considerations of form, content, and setting; a breakdown of the "architecture" of the book; presentation of the complex literary devices employed throughout (allegory, irony, ambiguity, dichotomy, archetypes); and a discussion of the novel's reception and evolving reputation. According to Gerber, nothing unifies *Letter* so much as its insistent concern with guilt and how that guilt affects the human psyche. Hawthorne's handling of sin in his exploration of human morality is more sophisticated than that attempted by his contemporaries because he alone presents sin as relative instead of absolute, showing the effects of sin to be psychologically ambiguous instead of clearly detrimental to the sinner. If Hawthorne is sympathetic to Hester, however, it is only because she eventually supports a middle ground of temperance and moderation, striking a positive balance between head and heart and thus checking her desire to lead a feminist reform movement.

217   McElroy, John. "The Conventionality of *The Scarlet Letter*." *Melville and Hawthorne in the Berkshires: A Symposium.* Ed. Howard P. Vincent. Kent: Ohio State UP, 1968. 89-97.

Examines *Letter* in the context of the nineteenth-century "Puritan novel" tradition as it developed between the years 1823 and 1850. After outlining both general and specific likenesses between *Letter* and earlier works of its type, McElroy concludes that "Hawthorne knew at least some of the eighteen Puritan novels which preceded his masterpiece," and "they affected his composition of a novel set in seventeenth-century New England." In fact, Hawthorne's novel adopts several fundamental conventions of the native tradition for establishing historical authenticity and authority (such as the "found manuscript" convention, a two-part structure involving a love plot and a historical plot, and an effort to dissipate some of the gloom associated with Puritans and to display instances of the Puritans' popularly-held superstitions), as well as presents main characters who all have counterparts in earlier novels.

218   Nayyar, Sewak. "Sin and Redemption in *The Scarlet Letter*." *Variations on American Literature.* Ed. Darshan Singh Maini. New Delhi: U.S. Education Foundation in India, 1968. 53-57.

The true "sin" in *Letter* is not adultery but Chillingworth's sin of intellectual pride that leads to "estrangement and isolation from humanity." Because Hester and eventually Dimmesdale acknowledge their adultery before the public, they are redeemed of their sin.

219   Noble, David W. "The Jeremiahs: James Fenimore Cooper, Nathaniel Hawthorne, Herman Melville." *The Eternal Adam and the New World Garden: The Central Myth in the American Novel Since 1830*. New York: George Braziller, 1968. 3-47.

Uses American literature to contradict the commonplace assumption among American historical writers that America has escaped the fate of European nations to live in "timeless harmony with nature." This particular chapter focuses on three nineteenth-century authors who, after testing in their fiction the soaring national faith in an innocent American Adam who prevails under Jacksonian democracy, insist that the self-made man cannot transcend the limitations of social institutions and innate human failings. Hawthorne believed that the roots of the American Adam myth extended back to Puritanism in England and that man's innately sinful nature—the human condition itself—prevented the paradisiacal fantasy of a New World Eden from coming true. In *Letter* (pp. 24-34), Hawthorne makes clear that, because the Puritans denied their own sinfulness (their very humanity) and their "historical parents, [or] their lineage to the Eternal Adam," their mission was doomed to failure. Thus what is revealed in the novel "is the human tragedy that must follow any attempt of Americans to live in alienation from the rest of the human race." Chillingworth, "the sterile philosopher-theologian," is "the archetypal Puritan," who sends his wife to the New World Eden to be "isolated from the mortal world of Europe" and to "live contentedly by his abstract principles of lifeless impotency." Dimmesdale, on the other hand, is "the symbolic son upon whom the burden of conflict with the Puritan father has fallen." In the end, Dimmesdale realizes that escape in the forest would be choosing, as does Chillingworth, "to withdraw his name from the roll of mankind." And so he at last comes to accept his own personal responsibility as a father, and to give Hester and Pearl "the law that will make them a part of the community and fulfill their humanity."

220   Waggoner, Hyatt H., and George Monteriro. Introduction. *The Scarlet Letter*. By Nathaniel Hawthorne. 1850. San Francisco: Chandler, 1968. xiii-lii.*

Although Hawthorne "endeavored to take a cheerful view of life's possibilities, images of decline and loss came to him more readily than those of ascent or 'progress.'" Part one of this lengthy introduction relates Hawthorne's personal family history as well as reviews his entire writing career; part two recounts *Letter*'s composition history, immediate popularity, and the 1850 reviews; and part three assesses Hawthorne's and *Letter*'s contemporary relevance in relation to Ralph Waldo Emerson and the latter's more optimistic ideas. Because Hawthorne was such a "conspicuously divided and tortured person," obsessed with secret guilt and thoughts of death, he was unable to transcend experiences of guilt and suffering as Emerson so easily did. Yet Emerson's view was neither realistic nor mature. Hawthorne was correct in sensing that "the tragic view of life [is] the only one an intelligent and sensitive person can honestly hold" and that "suffering and defeat [are] inevitably and always the law of life." For Hawthorne in *Letter* at least, there can be no escape from the tragic conflicts the novel presents and no escape for Hester, despite his obvious sympathy for her.

*Waggoner expands on part three of this introduction in his 1979 book *The Presence of Hawthorne* (see 374).

221   Willett, Maurita. "The Letter A, Gules, and the Black Bubble." *Melville and Hawthorne in the Berkshires: A Symposium.* Ed. Howard P. Vincent. Kent: Kent State UP, 1968. 70-78.

Considers the theme, style, and imagery of *Letter* and *Moby-Dick*, essaying to show how the endings of each—similar in their "concentration on points of light," are "rhythmically and logically" and aesthetically appropriate for their respective stories. The scarlet "A" that shines against a dark background befits the gloomy Puritan tale of hopelessness, stoic courage, and acquiescence, while the saving black bubble of Queequeg's coffin at "the heart of that "murderous circle of sharks and seahawks" provides a quiet salvation from chaos and violence and a temporary, optimistic resolution to the extreme positions explored in *Moby-Dick*.

Journal Essays and Notes

222   Katz, Seymour. "'Character,' 'Nature,' and Allegory in *The Scarlet Letter.*" *Nineteenth-Century Fiction* 23 (1968): 3-17.

Critics who attribute *Letter*'s abstract quality to the characters' allegorical function are mistaken, because "neither the manner of construction nor the characters are accurately interpreted as allegorical." Hawthorne's characterizations are closer to those of realistic fiction than of allegorical personification, as is indicated by his systematic use of the terms "nature" and "character" to describe them. For each of the four main people, Hawthorne posits a "nature" and a "character," nature referring to "the amount and kind of physical, emotion, and intellectual potentialities" that are attributed to each's personality and character referring to "the internalized principles which control and direct the potentialities of nature" as each grows in time and social experience. These concepts become the "intellectual scaffolding upon which Hawthorne attempted to construct realistic characters" and thus to project a realistic action that springs from them. When the role of the narrative voice is examined, an allegorical interpretation of the novel becomes all the more inappropriate, since by deliberately creating an unreliable narrator, Hawthorne enhances our sense of the reality of his fictional persons and also hints at the existence of a supernatural moral order in the novel. [See 277 for Walter Shear's essay on characterization in *Letter* that disagrees with Katz's approach to the novel.]

223   Kaul, A. N. "Character and Motive in *The Scarlet Letter*." *Critical Quarterly* 10 (1968): 373-384.

Rather than the "three-pronged" traditional approaches to *Letter* that typically provide background of Puritan theology, address Hawthorne's concept of sin, and consider the literary techniques of allegory and symbolism, this essay focuses exclusively on "the heart of Hawthorne's tale": specifically three questions involving character and motive. "Why does Hester choose to stay in Boston? Why does she later settle on a plan of flight? Why does the reader seem to know that the plan is "a futile and foredoomed venture?" The expository chapters in the novel (neglected by critics like Malcolm Cowley in 59) point to Hester's inner conflict between her allegiance to Puritan ideology and her commitment to love. As the novel develops—Dimmesdale and Pearl each representing the "cleavage" in Hester's tragic world—and Hester spiritually evolves, this tension between public duty and private loyalty to Dimmesdale is resolved, "leaving her to contend only with the pressure of external hostility." But because Dimmesdale has not evolved in a similar way and is committed solely to his faith, he fails Hester and her plan for freedom and happiness.

224   Maes-Jelinek, Hena. "Roger Chillingworth: An Example of the Creative Process in *The Scarlet Letter*." *English Studies* 49 (1968): 341-348.

Considering that Chillingworth belongs to Hawthorne's "heartless inquisitor" category of character, it is unlikely that Alfred S. Reid's speculation is accurate in *The Yellow Ruff and the Scarlet Letter: A Source of Hawthorne's Novel* (see 35) that Chillingworth's character—and not just his name—was modeled after the seventeenth-century "Anglican divine" William Chillingworth. A far more apt comparison can be drawn between Chillingworth's character and the Puritan Francis Cheynell, who ruthlessly and detrimentally tormented the historical William

Chillingworth on his deathbed by trying to force confession for "so-called" spiritual errors. Cheynell's inhumane nature and vindictive attitude toward his victim make him a much more likely historical counterpart for Chillingworth's character. Further, although Hester's character seems to parallel that of seventeenth-century William Prynne, she has as little in common with the historical Prynne (noted for his intolerance and cruelty) as Chillingworth does with his historical namesake.

225   McCall, Dan. "Hawthorne's 'Familiar Kind of Preface.'" *ELH* 35 (1968): 422-439.

Reads the numerous and "uneasy contradictions" in Hawthorne's prefaces sequentially as evidence of his"growing uncertainty about what he was doing and his gradual loss of power." Hawthorne's complaint in the preface to *Marble Faun*, for instance, that America lacked "the shadow, the antiquity, the mystery, the supremely picturesque and gloomy wrong" is clearly inaccurate since America had each of these characteristics when he constructed his masterpiece, *Letter*.

226   Skey, Miriam. "The Letter A." *Kyushu American Literature* 23 (1968): 1-10.

Considering "the meanings and implications" of the scarlet letter "A," an interpretation will only be "fair and valid" when both its benign and malignant associations are considered. For just as the letter ("presented as beautiful as well as ugly") inspires "love and hate, regard and scorn," so its color is also symbolically associated with both good and bad—with nature, blood, fire, and even the flush of physical health. The letter finally "represents nothing less than human nature—the ambiguity of life—the whole of humanity."

227   Stubbs, John C. "Hawthorne's *The Scarlet Letter*: The Theory of the Romance and the Use of the New England Situation." *PMLA* 83 (1968): 1439-1447.

Letter's subtitle, *A Romance*, indicates that Hawthorne drew on the popular mid-nineteenth-century romance genre (identified by Americans at the time with specifically American situations) "to clarify his medium and to call attention to his delving into a particular American historical experience." The first half of the essay examines "the general theory of the romance and Hawthorne's adoption of its tenets," proposing that the primary goal of romance is to establish an artistic distance by balancing opposites like verisimilitude and ideality, the natural and the marvelous, history and fiction. The second half explores "the aspects of New England history treated by contemporary romances and Hawthorne's mastery and development of their central situation." The development of the New England romance, patterned after the methods and situations in the anonymous *Witch of New England* (1824), evolved into more complicated romances like John Lothrop Motley's *Merry-Mount: A Romance of the Massachusetts Colony* (1849) that perfected the basic conflict of the "fair Puritan" versus the "black Puritan." For Hawthorne, Hester is the "fair Puritan" playing to Chillingworth's "black Puritan," but he "transcends the conventions of the New England romance and enters into structured ambiguity" in creating his "complex hero," Dimmesdale, who internalizes and synthesizes the opposing forces in the romance. [See 251 for a continuation of Stubbs's discussion of the "fair Puritan" vs. the "black Puritan." The latter part of his argument is reproduced nearly identically in an essay by L. S. R. Krishna Sastry (316)].

228   Stubbs, John C. "A Note on the Source of Hawthorne's Heraldic Device in *The Scarlet Letter*." *Notes and Queries* 15 (1968): 175-176.

Despite the importance of the heraldic device ("On a field, sable, the letter A, gules") to "hold poised one last time the conflicting elements of [*Letter*]," its "likely source" has been overlooked in the introductory chapter of Sir Walter Scott's *Waverly* (1814). A passage in the opening section of *Waverly* that resonates with "the augustness of heraldic language" specifically contrasts the colors "sable" and "gules," associating black with "subverted and indirect malignant feelings" and equating red with "open and direct intense emotion."

229   Whelan, Robert Emmet, Jr. "Hester Prynne's Little Pearl: Sacred and Profane Love." *American Literature* 39 (1968): 488-505.

Pearl is the key to understanding *Letter*, for her "sole reality is that of an allegorical mirror which multitudinously reflects the intricate tangle of love and passion uniting Hester and Dimmesdale." She, whose stages of life allegorically mark the different stages of Hester's love for Dimmesdale, is also the sole remedy for their sin—since salvation only comes to Dimmesdale when he finally acknowledges her after the Election-Day sermon and to Hester when her love for Dimmesdale is transformed thereafter (following his heroic example) into religious purity. Their profane love becomes sacred through the years (assuring their placements in heaven) only because of their association with Pearl (who herself becomes a symbol of holy love). The novel can therefore be seen as "a battle of the virtues and vices within the hearts of Hester and Dimmesdale, a war that Love and Truth under the guise of little Pearl wage with Cowardice and Falsehood under the guise of old Roger Chillingworth."

230   Whelan, Robert Emmet, Jr. "Roger Chillingworth's Whole Business Is Reflection." *Research Studies* 37 (1968): 298-312.

Chillingworth is "the legitimate literary descendant of Monsieur du Miroir, the mysterious Frenchman who gives his name to the sketch wherein Hawthorne meditates upon his own reflection in various mirrors." As a "living mirror," Chillingworth personifies Cowardice and ineffectual Remorse and thus serves the purely allegorical duty of reflecting and commenting upon the inner lives of Hester and Dimmesdale—though especially of mirroring Dimmesdale's "introspective descent into his own soul." Hawthorne links "Dimmesdale's reluctance to look straightforward at his cowardice" with his "failure to recognize Chillingworth as his enemy," although at the end, "Love, Truth, and Courage under the guise of little Pearl utterly defeat Cowardice, Falsehood, and Merciless Introspection under the guise of old Roger Chillingworth," leaving him to die "like an uprooted weed that lies wilting in the sun."

231   Whitford, Kathryn. "'On a Field, Sable, the Letter 'A,' Gules.'" *Lock Haven Review* 10 (1968): 33-38.

Although the "apparent incongruity" of Hester's "meek reappearance" in Boston at the end of *Letter* has proven to be considerably troublesome for critics (at least to those willing to admit Hester's dominance in the novel and to consider the problems thus raised by her return), Hester's return is not incomprehensible when viewed within the framework of Puritan theology. Puritan belief in the resurrection of the flesh on Judgment Day inspires Hester's reappearance, offering her the only hope of seeing Dimmesdale once more. "Buried side by side, Hester and Dimmesdale will rise side by side in mutual recognition." Thus Hester remains true to her unpenitent self, returning to Boston only to ensure her burial—and final confrontation—with her lover. Just as the novel opens with the "trial that preceded the sentencing and punishment of Hester," so "it closes appropriately by anticipating the trial of the Judgment Day"—when "both partners in adultery will be present."

1969

Essays and Studies in Books

232   Briggs, Austin. "The Damnation of Theron Ware." *The Novels of Harold Frederic*. Ithaca: Cornell UP, 1969. 97-139.

Pages 132-135 of this chapter address similarities between *The Damnation of Theron Ware* (1896) and *Letter*. Frederic once "declared that his determination to write had been inspired by his 'literary parentage,' Erckmann-Chatrian on one side, Nathaniel Hawthorne on the other." In the forest scene between the lovers Celia and the Reverend Ware, Frederic follows "detail for detail" the climactic forest confrontation of Hester and Dimmesdale—although he invokes Hawthorne "perversely," denying and inverting "what is basic in Hawthorne's fiction, the assumption that all human acts have large and lasting consequences, that the acknowledgment of sin is the prerequisite for redemption."

233   Cady, Edwin Harrison. Introduction. *The Scarlet Letter*. By Nathaniel Hawthorne. 1850. Columbus: Merrill, 1969. v-xiv.

This essay, which aims "to introduce the reader of *Letter* to knowledge about the conditions and circumstances surrounding its creation," is divided into four sections: "The Man and the Moment," "The Creative Ground," "Sources," and "Salem and 'The Custom-House.'"

234   Cohen, B. Bernard. *The Recognition of Nathaniel Hawthorne: Selected Criticism Since 1828*. Ann Arbor: U of Michigan P, 1969.

Covers three periods of Hawthorne criticism (1828-1864, 1865-1910, and 1911 to the Present) and offers a helpful, lengthy preface that summarizes each section of reprinted, excerpted critical reviews and essays, many of which focus on *Letter*. Each excerpt is also prefaced by a biographical description of its author, as well as each author's estimation of Hawthorne. Post-1950 works that address *Letter* are by William Van O'Connor (64), Hyatt H. Waggoner (38), Hubert H. Hoeltje (125), Martin Green (143), Terence Martin (132), and Frederick Crews (182). [Pre-1950 excerpted works that discuss *Letter* are by Henry F. Chorley (ER4), Herman Melville (ER6), George B. Loring (ER7), Arthur Cleveland Coxe (ER10), George Parsons Lathrop (EC17), Anthony Trollope (EC33), Henry James (EC15), William Dean Howells (EC14), and W. C. Brownell (EC3).]

235   Elder, Marjorie J. "Hawthorne's Aesthetic Practices: *The Scarlet Letter* and *The Marble Faun*." *Nathaniel Hawthorne: Transcendental Symbolist*. Athens: Ohio UP, 1969. 121-170.

Seeking to show that Hawthorne gradually became a transcendental symbolist as the result of his associations with the transcendentalists (such as the Peabodys, Bronson Alcott, Margaret Fuller, Ralph Waldo Emerson, and Henry David Thoreau), Elder examines his aesthetic theories and

126

intentions as they developed and became refined. Elder's investigation is prompted by "many recent and extensive criticisms of Hawthorne which show no regard for literary history, ignore Hawthorne's own purposes, and impose upon his works preconceived critical theories which often fail to interpret him satisfactorily."* Explorations of *Letter* and *Marble Faun* in particular show that Hawthorne's "mingling of the Actual and the Imaginative, his presentation of Truth, his use of light, arrangement of scenes, creation of characters, and handling and development of incidents" proves that he used transcendental symbolism.

*Elder does not cite specific examples of these "criticisms."

236   Fogle, Richard Harter. "*The Scarlet Letter.*" *Hawthorne's Imagery: The Proper Light and Shadow in the Major Romances.* Norman: Oklahoma UP, 1969. 22-47.

This book, which supplements Fogle's 1952 study of *Hawthorne's Fiction: The Light and the Dark* (see 15), examines the "light and the dark" theme once again, but this time specifically in terms of image patterns. "Hawthorne's use of light and darkness is central to his art and thought," and close attention to this pattern potentially yields reliable insights into the novel as a whole. Fogle offers no definitive remarks about *Letter*, but rather stays deliberately suggestive in both his general interpretation of the "gloomy book" and his demonstration of "the artistic logic of Pearl's final emergence into light." The light imagery, particularly the use of sunlight, that surrounds Hester, Dimmesdale, Pearl, and Chillingworth in the crucial forest chapters (16-19) is revealing since the sun persistently shines on Pearl while only fleetingly on Hester and Dimmesdale. After emerging from the forest, where he experiences (to a limited degree) the sympathetic "light" of Nature, Dimmesdale comes to accept his own limitations and the dualism of the human condition—and it is this new knowledge that allows him to enter his "plea of guilty at the bar of Eternal Justice" as the sympathetic sun finally streams down on him following the Election-Day Sermon.

237   McPherson, Hugo. "The New England Myth: A Mirror for Puritans: *The Scarlet Letter.*" *Hawthorne as Myth-Maker: A Study in Imagination.* Toronto: U of Toronto P, 1969. 170-190.

While the collection of essays as a whole attempts to define the "myth-making nature" of Hawthorne's "cryptic" imagination, Part III illuminates the "radical coherence" among the four major romances (studying the character types, image patterns, and narrative structure) and relates the novels to Hawthorne's larger vision and personal mythology. The chapter on *Letter*, which begins with an argument against readings of the novel that fail to get beyond its explicit moral/psychological issues to see that *Letter* is a critique of the stifling narrowness of Puritan America, explores the mythic qualities, themes, and imagery of the story by reviewing the action chronologically. *Letter* is viewed in relation to the mythology (of iron men, Dark Ladies, mercurial heroes, and frail princesses) of the tales and romances and is much less about sin than about an "account of the plight of the Dark Lady and the mercurial hero, menaced by a tyrannical old man of reason in a community which reveres law above all else, sees human nature as depraved, and fears passion and imagination equally." The torturous seven-year quest of Hester and Dimmesdale for the meaning of the scarlet "A" and its physical manifestation in Pearl is at the center of the tale. The letter finally becomes "Hawthorne's emblem of the human heart—of its imperfection, and its labyrinthine mixture of good and evil," and as such is best understood as a "talisman" or token of our common nature. As the living letter, the "New World" Pearl, whom Hawthorne will not have inherit the guilt of the Christian tradition, becomes the "luminous prophecy" of a new breed of heroine, anticipating such American embodiments of hope as Hawthorne's Phoebe, Priscilla, and Hilda.

238   Porte, Joel. "The Dark Blossom of Romance." *The Romance in America: Studies in Cooper, Poe, Hawthorne, Melville, and James.* Middleton: Wesleyan UP, 1969. 98-114.

Discusses Hawthorne as one of several nineteenth-century writers of romance whose work is characterized not only by a heavy reliance on archetypal figures, symbols, parable, dream, and fantasy, but also by a self-conscious need to define its own aims so that romance becomes the theme as well as the form of the fiction. Porte associates Hawthorne's craft as an artist with guilt (guilt becoming the necessary avenue that leads to insight about the human condition), and similarly views the guilt, pain, and suffering of the three primary characters in *Letter* in creative, artistic, and even sexual terms. Since "the only true 'flower' that blooms out of human ruin is that provided by the imagination of the artist," romance itself becomes "the dark blossom that flourishes on the tomb of human experience." Hester, Dimmesdale, Chillingworth, and Hawthorne "aspire to the condition of the romancer—a position of spiritual depth and understanding earned through sympathy with or experience of pain." Because Chillingworth is unable to "invest his secret passion in a symbolic art capable of relieving himself and others," however, his artistic insights are dangerous, and his character comes to represent the dark, sinister side of romance. Overall, though, the novel, which grows out of

Hester's search for sexual fulfillment and expression, illustrates the process by which past pain and secret suffering flower into moral truth.

Journal Essays and Notes

239 Abel, Darrel. "Black Glove and Pink Ribbon: Hawthorne's Metonymic Symbols." *New England Quarterly* 42 (1969): 163-180.*

Examines Hawthorne's use of similar equivocal metonymies in *Letter* and "Young Goodman Brown." Both Dimmesdale's black glove (mistakenly left during the midnight scaffold scene and recovered by the sexton) and Faith's pink ribbon (found in the dark woods by Goodman Brown himself) function as central symbols in their respective narratives in that they are tokens of an "unresolved tension between official appearance and essential truth." Both meaning-laden symbols, found at crucial points in the middle of the tales, similarly reveal the clash in historical Puritan society between the godly community and the ungodly wilderness, or between faith and doubt. The glove and the ribbon are thus equivocal as "ocular proofs," because they suggest that there is no intrinsic or absolute truth but only the arbitrary determinations of individual perceptions. Hawthorne's truly "brilliant historical imagination" results from his ability to capture the confusions of the subjective Puritan self's conception of reality and to expose and even exploit that epistemological uncertainty as a way of commenting on the arbitrary nature of recorded history—which itself is only an interpretation of experience, or a "dream of meaning." [See 266 for Abel's supplement to this essay, a further exploration of the meaning behind Dimmesdale's dropped glove. For another essay that compares *Letter* and "Young Goodman Brown," see Allison Ensor (256).]

*Reprinted in Abel's *The Moral Picturesque: Studies in Hawthorne's Fiction* (see 559).

240 Bell, John M. "Hawthorne's *The Scarlet Letter*: An Artist's Intuitive Understanding of Plague, Armor and Health." *Journal of Orgonomy* 3 (1969): 102-115.

Letter is radical in that it "embodies a remarkable understanding of both human armoring and the social origins of that armoring." A "vision of unarmored life and love" challenges "the theology, the philosophical assumptions, and the sexual mores of our patriarchal culture." The tale cannot be read properly without one's being introduced to it through "The Custom-House," where Hawthorne suggests an awareness of a new type of artistic perception at odds with the stultifying, mechanistic, prison of society. This "wholly different logos" takes oppositional principles and juxtaposes them, unifying body and soul, flesh and spirit, in such a way that "neatly anticipates" Hester's involvement with the "mechanistic" Chillingworth and the "mystical" Dimmesdale" and hints at a unified view of the human condition. Yet Hester's role in the novel, "as a consciously wrought type of the Virgin Mary," is to "provide a proper means" for Pearl's incarnation. A fusion of Hester's passion and warmth with Dimmesdale's intelligence, Pearl represents Hawthorne's new logos, the true, unarmored center of the novel, and "the real fulfillment of this tale." Her foreignness from the basic beliefs and attitudes of Puritan culture, especially after she departs from America, hearkens back to the tragic awareness of Hawthorne in "The Custom-House," an awareness "of what could be, within the context of what is."

241 Bergeron, David M. "Arthur Miller's *The Crucible* and Nathaniel Hawthorne: Some Parallels." *English Journal* 58 (1969): 47-55.

Finds "strikingly similar" parallels between *The Crucible* (1953) and *Letter*, particularly in setting, language, characters, and themes. Puritan New England provides the ideal landscape for both Hawthorne and Miller to create their respective dramas that focus on the sins of adultery and hypocrisy, that share the common theme of "the necessity of moral commitment," and that explore the dark depths of the human heart. Similarities can be found between Dimmesdale/John Proctor, Dimmesdale/Rev. Hale, and Chillingworth/Parris/Hale/Danforth/Abigail. Both play and novel also attack "naïve, propositional religious faith" and suggest "with differing degrees of emphasis that one must at times lose his faith to find and save himself."

242 Dillingham, William B. "Arthur Dimmesdale's Confession." *Studies in the Literary Imagination* 2.1 (1969): 21-26.

Protests against interpretations of the novel that support Dimmesdale's salvation and argues in a manner similar to Edward H. Davidson in "Dimmesdale's Fall" (see 142) that Dimmesdale "dies a damned man." "Dimmesdale's weakness as a man and the subtle ambiguity of his confession" reflects his "unalterable isolation from mankind." So removed is the cowardly Dimmesdale from his parishioners and from his own true self, in fact, that his confession becomes "the final irony of his alienated existence." In the last scaffold scene, as in the first two, Dimmesdale "is given the opportunity to remove his mask" but fails. The only difference in this final scene, however, is that Dimmesdale—"not a miraculously changed man" by any means—does not realize that he is still consistently deceiving himself with his vague confession, just as he is deceiving the community. "He was too weak to be true in life and therefore *could* not be true when it was time for him to die."

243   Janssen, James G. "Dimmesdale's 'Lurid Playfulness.'" *American Transcendental Quarterly* 1 (1969): 30-34.

The "process of release from prideful hypocrisy" that leads up to Dimmesdale's moment of truth and revelation can be charted in his two scenes of "lurid playfulness." These two vital scenes—the midnight scaffold scene in chapter twelve and the place in chapter twenty that describes his crazed return from the forest to the village—are Hawthorne's "keys" to understanding Dimmesdale's ascent. In each, Dimmesdale's mind makes "an involuntary effort to relieve itself by a kind of lurid playfulness." The "sanative effect" of Dimmesdale's outbursts of ludicrous laughter enables him not only to find humor in his impossible situation but also to see beyond his prison of hypocrisy and pride to the real, moral world to which he advances in the end.

244   Kraft, Quentin G. "The Central Problem of James's Fictional Thought from *The Scarlet Letter* to *Roderick Hudson*." *ELH* 36 (1969): 416-439.

Letter provides an introductory context for an analysis of *Roderick Hudson* (1876) in that it, like Henry James's novel, comes to a "dialectical stalemate" in its consideration of the opposing forces of life-giving freedom and life-denying morality so central to the American experience. Hawthorne perceives the freedom/morality opposition as "absolute and therefore irresolvable," not because he lacked a preference for one option over the other but because he saw that "genuine human relationships require not only that freedom be qualified by moral concern but also that morality exists within a context of freedom." *Roderick Hudson* shares Hawthorne's thematic concern and is structured by the same "thwarted dialectic" that appears to invite an "either/or" judgment while it actually supports only a "both the one and the other" view. To choose one side over the other weakens interpretations of both novels.

245   Levy, Leo B. "The Landscape Modes of *The Scarlet Letter*." *Nineteenth-Century Fiction* 23 (1969): 377-392.

Analyzes how the traditions of the sublime and the picturesque determine the setting, structure, and meaning of *Letter*, enabling Hawthorne to unite his psychic and pictorial intentions. The wilderness landscape, which makes tangible Hester's spiritual isolation from the Puritan community, provides an index to the shifting emotions—and even to the moral conditions—of the characters (with sunlight corresponding to positive, lawless, and shameful feelings, and gloom corresponding to oppressive, negative, and repressed feelings). The "religious sublime" (defined as an abstract sort of "religious experience free of a narrow or dogmatic base") likewise enabled Hawthorne to dramatize the conflict between religious compliance and moral error, as well as to communicate a profound love of nature and even to impose democratic sentiment upon Puritan society.

246   Okamoto, Katsumi. *"The Scarlet Letter*: Struggle Toward Integrity." *Studies in English Literature* 46 (1969): 45-61.

Relates the "unmitigatedly dark" and "absolutely pessimistic and sinister" ending that appears to be "devoid of love and sympathy" to the novel as a whole. Despite his tragic view of human nature and his unresolvable conflict between Puritan and romantic strains of thought, Hawthorne yet implies that the "old order" will be "superseded by a new order founded upon the intrinsic beauty of a human soul." "Love illuminates the dark pages of *Letter*," and we find solace not in Dimmesdale's selfish confession (which is "made not out of his warm affection for humanity [or for Hester or Pearl], but rather by reason of the very intensity of his [own personal] anguish"), but in Hester's love for both him and Pearl. Her heroic and sacrificial endurance—coupled by the shaking revelation of Dimmesdale's "complete withdrawal" of love—leads her to reject moral independence and rejoin the magnetic chain of humanity, thus to share "in the sins and defects of man."

247   Stephens, Rosemary. "'A' is for 'Art' in *The Scarlet Letter*." *American Transcendental Quarterly* 1 (1969): 23-27.

In the allegory of *Letter*, "A" stands for the sin of "art." Although some critics have argued that Hawthorne equates his own artistic efforts with Dimmesdale's, a much richer reading of the novel can be formulated if Hawthorne's art is associated with Hester's, which is represented by her needlework and Pearl. Stephens covers familiar ground in suggesting the similarities between Hawthorne's and Hester's romantic insights as outcasts from American society, and in equating Hester's return to Boston with Hawthorne's compulsion to stay in Salem following his dismissal from the Custom House. She concludes that "the office" of the scarlet letter—and the novel itself—is to make American society "aware of its responsibility to the artist."

248   Stokes, E[dward]. *"Bleak House* and *The Scarlet Letter*." *Journal of the Australasian Universities Language and Literature Association* 32 (1969): 177-189.

Argues that "Dickens, in the part of *Bleak House* [1852-3] centered round Lady Dedlock, borrowed quite extensively from *Letter*; that several situations and scenes in *Bleak House* are strongly reminiscent of situations and scenes in *Letter*; particularly, that one of Dickens's major characters, Tulkinghorn, is modeled on one of Hawthorne's, Chillingworth." In addition to borrowing Hawthorne's somber brand of romance and the situation of women characters giving birth to illegitimate daughters, Dickens most likely "combine[d] in the person of Lady Dedlock the roles of both Hester and Dimmesdale." More significant is the "striking" connection between Tulkinghorn and Chillingworth, whose similarities include an elderly, dark appearance; a "dim-eyed but acute" perception; a cold, inscrutable demeanor used to hide their roles as "investigator[s] of secret guilt and self-ordained agent[s] of retribution"; an "aura" of death and decay; and a "semi-supernatural power." Dickens's own unfavorable review of Chillingworth's "much overdone" psychological aspect (see EC6) accounts for the major differences between Chillingworth and the less thoroughly developed character of Tulkinghorn.

1970

Books

249   Turner, Arlin. *The Merrill Studies in The Scarlet Letter*. Columbus: Charles E. Merrill, 1970. 153 pp.

Included in this four-part collection of significant writings by major literary critics and scholars are essays regarding *Letter*'s origins and composition (by James T. Fields, Hubert H. Hoeltje [33], and Charles Ryskamp [85]); four famous reviews from 1850 (by Evert A. Duychinck [ER1], E. P. Whipple [ER3], George Ripley [ER2], and Henry F. Chorley [ER4]); three late-nineteenth-century evaluations (by Henry James [EC15], Anthony Trollope [EC33], and W. D. Howells [EC14]); and four divergent twentieth-century reassessments of *Letter* (by John E. Hart [5], Daniel Hoffman [106], Earl H. Rovit [119], and Austin Warren [178]).

Essays and Studies in Books

250   Crowley, J. Donald, ed. *"The Scarlet Letter." Hawthorne: The Critical Heritage*. New York: Barnes and Noble, 1970. 151-184.

This collection of early reviews of *Letter* includes excerpts by Evert A. Duychinck (ER1), George Ripley (ER2), E. P. Whipple (ER3), Henry F. Chorley (ER4), Anne W. Abbott (ER5), George B. Loring (ER7), Orestes A. Brownson (ER9), and Arthur Cleveland Coxe (ER10).

251   Stubbs, John C. *"The Scarlet Letter*: 'A Tale of Human Frailty and Sorrow.'" *The Pursuit of Form: A Study of Hawthorne and the Romance.* Chicago: U of Illinois P, 1970. 81-100.

The essence of Hawthorne's fiction resides in his sense of form. Contrary to critics like Richard Harter Fogle (15), Hyatt H. Wagonner (38), and Roy R. Male (56) who emphasize ambiguity above all else in their discussions of form, "Hawthorne exerts much more control over his material than most critics are willing to admit." He not only orders and structures things with mechanical precision and craftsmanship but also develops and emphasizes the highly-contrived artifice of the romance form. Despite what most critics believe about *Letter*'s numerous levels of symbolic meaning, the novel contains only *one* level of interpretation (aside from the literal). Central to the story is the conflict of the "black Puritan" and the "fair Puritan." This blatantly conventional opposition, of black and white forces pitted against one another to represent the extreme positions of the novel's ethical and moral argument, is purposely designed to call attention to *Letter*'s artifice. Between these conflicting forces stands the romance's "most complex" and "real" character, Dimmesdale, who encompasses in his personality both of the extremes embodied in the characters of Hester (as the "Fair Puritan" of unrestricted human emotions) and Chillingworth (as the "Black Puritan" of severe restrictions on social conduct). Pearl becomes the humanizing force that enables Dimmesdale finally to come to terms with his own capacity for emotions both good and evil, at which time he enters—during the triumphant final scaffold scene—into a heroic and sympathetic understanding of his fellow men. Unlike Dimmesdale, Hester cannot reconcile the opposing forces of passion and restraint, and "to the end she is the fair Puritan restricted by black Puritanism."

Journal Essays and Notes

252   Baym, Nina. "Passion and Authority in *The Scarlet Letter.*" *New England Quarterly* 43 (1970): 209-230.*

Finding fault with critics who argue for Hawthorne's Puritan vision, Baym accounts for discrepancies between true Puritan dogma and the historically inaccurate theology practiced by Hawthorne's "dour Victorian" Puritans. The intentional replacement of Puritan religion with nineteenth-century sentimental piety results from Hawthorne's romantic vision. What ultimately keeps Hester and Dimmesdale apart are not their different religious principles but their very different ties to the community. Having transgressed a social code determined by an authoritarian and conservative society, Hester views the letter as a badge of honor (and finally rejects the judgment of the letter), while Dimmesdale considers it a token of profound shame (and takes the judgment of the letter on himself). As primarily symbolic characters, Pearl and Chillingworth stand for projections of Hester and Dimmesdale's respective perceptions of their sin, Pearl (as Hester's id) the manifestation of an act that is beautiful, "wild, unmanageable, and unpredictable," while Chillingworth (as Dimmesdale's superego) is "the vengeful and embittered husband who has been offended by [the loathsome error]." [Baym explains that the historical Puritans believed God was the "immediate, personal, overwhelmingly present, inescapable Alpha and Omega of Puritan life," but Hawthorne's Puritans view God as "a remote, vague, occasional concept ceremoniously invoked at the last minute and in cases of emergency."]

*Reprinted in Baym's *The Shape of Hawthorne's Career* (see 339).

253   Bergman, Herbert. "'The Interior of a Heart': *The Crucible* and *The Scarlet Letter*." *University College Quarterly* 15 (1970): 27-32.

Arthur Miller's play *The Crucible* (1953) and *Letter* share similar Puritan settings, themes, and characters. "Both deal with the sanctity of the individual soul, both include characters who are frauds, both have sinners escape damnation by refusing to live with a lie, both have worse sinners who violate the sanctity of the soul, both have adulterers." Of the many differences briefly noted, the most crucial dissimilarity between the two works is that Miller "goes beyond the interior psychological question of the effect of fraud" to consider "the exterior question of public hysteria" in Salem.

254   Canaday, Nicholas, Jr. "Hawthorne's *The Scarlet Letter*." *Explicator* 28 (1970): Item 39.

When Hester appears in the opening scaffold scene, Hawthorne introduces a young Puritan wife who pities and sympathizes with Hester because she lacks the iron visage and sensibility of the other Puritan women. Yet this character is dead by the final scaffold scene, destroyed apparently because she "is all tenderness" and is thus ill-equipped to survive in the severe environment of the Puritans. This character not only suggests Hawthorne's "saddest indictment of Puritanism" but also points to the fact that Hester only survives because she is strong enough to deny her feminine tenderness and turn her life from feeling to thought.

255   Clark, C. E. Frazer, Jr. "Posthumous Papers of a Decapitated Surveyor:
       The Scarlet Letter in the Salem Press." *Studies in the Novel* 2 (1970):
       395-419.

Demonstrates the active role that the Salem newspapers—particularly the
Salem Register and the *Salem Gazette*—played in publicizing
Hawthorne's dismissal from the Custom House. When word of the
"political decapitation" spread, both papers capitalized on Hawthorne's
"newsworthiness," the *Register* passionately defending Hawthorne's
removal from office and the *Gazette* advocating his reinstatement. The
press coverage not only bolstered Hawthorne's career, further establishing
him as a "figure of national importance" with the reading public, but also
proved to be "an effective pre-sales campaign for *Letter*." Following
Letter's publication, both newspapers immediately commissioned reviews.
Caleb Foote's review for the *Gazette*—with conspicuously absent mention
of "The Custom-House"—was favorable, while John Chapman's review
for the *Register* expressed outrage over "The Custom-House" for being
"so atrocious, so heartless, so undisguised, so utterly inexcusable" for its
"calumnious caricatures of inoffensive men."

256   Ensor, Allison. "'Whispers of the Bad Angel': A *Scarlet Letter* Passage as
       a Commentary on Hawthorne's 'Young Goodman Brown.'" *Studies in
       Short Fiction* 7 (1970): 467-469.

Finding that a passage from the fifth chapter of *Letter* ("Hester at Her
Needle") serves as revealing commentary upon "Young Goodman
Brown," Ensor sees a parallel between Hester's suspicion that a "bad
angel" mysteriously imparts "knowledge of the hidden sin in other hearts"
and Brown's similar conviction that he is privy to the evil in men's hearts.
Yet, while Brown yields to his corrupt suspicion that all men are
hypocritical sinners, thereby losing faith in mankind, Hester sustains her
faith in mankind because she believes herself guiltier than all other
sinners. Thus Brown exempts himself from the corrupt human condition,
while Hester seeks to prove that she is no different from her fellow
sinners. [For another essay that compares *Letter* and "Young Goodman
Brown," see Darrel Abel (239).]

257   Lease, Benjamin. "Hawthorne and 'A Certain Venerable Personage':
       New Light on 'The Custom-House.'" *Jahrbuch für Amerikastudien* 15
       (1970): 201-207.

Hawthorne's "central target" in "The Custom-House" is not C. W.
Upham—as has been commonly assumed—but prominent Salem citizen
William Lee, who was permanent Inspector at the Custom House and, like

Upham, instrumental in engineering Hawthorne's dismissal. Details in Hawthorne's satiric sketch of the life and employment of the "certain permanent Inspector" would have been "instantly and unmistakably" recognized by Salem readers as a description of Lee, as a "sharply critical" review from the Salem *Register* makes clear. Hawthorne's Preface to the Second Edition, written just nine days after the review was published, directly addresses readers of the *Register*'s review and makes no apologies for publicly humiliating Lee in his original description of the "certain venerable personage." [See 273 for another essay by Lease on the same subject.]

258   Stanton, Robert. *"The Scarlet Letter* as Dialectic of Temperament and Idea." *Studies in the Novel* 2 (1970): 474-486.

Chalking up *Letter*'s dilemma of conformity (Dimmesdale) vs. individualism (Hester) to ambiguity or ambivalence on Hawthorne's part "seems rather a surrender than a solution." It makes more sense to say that Hester and Dimmesdale exemplify "a pair of contrasting temperaments" (with Pearl and Chillingworth functioning as projections of the two main characters' natures). The philosophies of orthodox Puritanism and self-reliant romanticism suit their respective personalities (Dimmesdale's as "introceptive" and Hester's as "emanative"), and the novel thus revolves around "the interplay between their temperaments and the philosophical positions they adopt." Hawthorne concludes the novel "with a synthesis of the two ideological stances," implying his attraction to both, as well as his melancholy realization that they are not compatible.

1971

Essays and Studies in Books

259   Anderson, Quentin. "Hawthorne's Boston." *The Imperial Self: An Essay in American Literary and Cultural History*. New York: Alfred A. Knopf, 1971. 59-87.

Views Hawthorne as "an essential reference point" in the attempt to chart the "American flight from culture" and the "spiritual imperialism" reflected in the work of Ralph Waldo Emerson, Walt Whitman, and Henry James. Unlike his contemporaries, Hawthorne was deeply committed to society and viewed "human selves as fostered in a net of relations, finding their meaning and value only through those relations." In the creation of "his own Boston" in *Letter*, Hawthorne dramatizes his rejection of the "modern" nineteenth-century view that society is "a set of attitudes and powers which exert a coercive power from which the individual seeks to be distinct." The novel is actually more closely akin to English novels than American novels in its embrace of society, especially those of Jane Austin, George Eliot, and Anthony Trollope. The action of the first thirteen chapters emphasizes "their use of reciprocal responses on the part of the town and the principal characters"—which proves that *Letter* focuses not on the "imaginative undoing of communal ties" but on the "character strength of the bonds that unite men, women, and children in a society and how they may and must be used to constrain the imperious inward demands of fantasy and obsession." [Anderson often refers to Frederick Crews's *Sins of the Fathers* (182), which argues that the "demands of fantasy and obsession" in *Letter* are rooted in sexual energies.]

260 Becker, John E. *Hawthorne's Historical Allegory: An Examination of the American Conscience.* Port Washington: Kennikat Press, 1971.

Seeking to define Hawthorne in terms of allegory and to show how Hawthorne reformulates allegory in his fiction, this book contains separate chapters on "The Custom House" (pp. 61-87) and *The Scarlet Letter* (pp. 88-154). Because the nineteenth century experienced the breakdown of the world of shared values, traditional allegory could no longer be written (since author and audience no longer shared a common value system). Hawthorne uses "The Custom-House" to distance the reader, to make him more aware that an original depth of thought and feeling, and not a communal morality, is at work behind the veil of the fiction. Ultimately, *Letter* is an open-ended allegory whose meaning appears gradually as the reader (1) comes to realize that Hawthorne is operating on multiple allegorical levels and (2) finally sees allegorization as a phenomenon of human psychology. This two-part insight transforms Hawthorne's allegory of America's past and present into a kind of superior realism.

261 Bell, Michael Davitt. "A Home in the Wilderness: Hawthorne's Historical Themes." *Hawthorne and the Historical Romance of New England.* Princeton: Princeton UP, 1971. 107-146.*

Seeking to redress critical neglect of the historical dimensions of Hawthorne's fiction, Bell relates works set in seventeenth-century New England with those of his contemporaries—finding that most historical romances waver in their presentations of Puritans as either liberators or oppressors (Hawthorne tending to present first-generation Puritans as the former and decadent second- and third-generation Puritans as the latter). The tension between Old and New World values in "Endicott and the Red Cross," "The Gentle Boy," and "The May-Pole of Merry Mount" extends to *Letter* (pp. 126-146), which "chronicles Hester's movement from a heraldry of the Old World to a heraldry of the New—from a 'token of antique gentility' to a token better suited to symbolize life in New England." This change from Old World passion and idealism to New World starkness and practicality permeates the entire book. Hester's "scarlet" side cannot survive in New England; at best, it can be transmitted to Pearl, who is never at home in Boston and so permanently leaves New England for Europe. Bell also compares several of the historical figures in the tale (John Wilson, Richard Bellingham, and John Winthrop) to Dimmesdale, contrasting the virtue, strength, and noble severity of the first-generation Puritans with the youthful, squeamish, hypocritical Dimmesdale who seeks to rebel against his dominating elders. The burden of history and the notion of democratic progress eventually prove to be too much for Dimmesdale to bear, and so it is Hester alone—whose character provides continuity between past and present—who finds a true home in the wilderness after adapting herself to conditions necessary for survival in New England. [Bell briefly addresses Hester again in his next chapter, "Fathers and Daughters" (pp. 149-190), where he argues that *Letter* (pp. 184-190) repudiates the conventional opposition of the fair and dark heroine. By associating his rich, passionate, dark-haired heroine with the wildness of nature, Hawthorne subverts the symbolic values of the "natural," tame, and fair maiden. Hawthorne also argues (through the character of Hester) against the notion of historical progress and a new, liberating start for America that lies behind the visions of so many of his contemporaries.]

*An excerpt of Bell's essay appears as "The Young Minister and the Puritan Fathers: A Note on History in *The Scarlet Letter*" in the *Nathaniel Hawthorne Journal 1971* (Ed. C. E. Frazer Clark, Jr. Washington: NCR Microcard Editions, 1971. 159-168).

262   Butterfield, R. W. Introduction. *The Scarlet Letter*. By Nathaniel Hawthorne. 1850. New York: Everyman's Library, 1971. vii-xvii.

Compares the vast differences between the intellectual and moral climates of seventeenth- and nineteenth-century New England, placing Hawthorne's sensibilities and leanings somewhere in the middle: "[Letter's] moderation and reasonableness act as a critically ironic foil both to the fanatical Puritanism it directly depicts and to the romantic libertarianism it implicitly examines." Butterfield covers setting, background on the Puritan theocracy, character analysis and motivation, and concludes with a brief discussion of the novel as "moral allegory."

263   Hirsch, David J. "Hawthorne: The Intellectual as Outsider." *Reality and Idea in the Early American Novel*. The Hague: Mouton, 1971. 123-164.

Calls into question the notion that the novel, presumably a faithful representation of "reality," belongs to England, while the exclusive domain of American writers has been, and is, romance, essentially a flight from "reality." Just because Hawthorne called his longer works of fiction "romances" is no reason to assume that he intended them as an advertisement of his "turning away from reality." *Letter* (pp. 124-151) was the New World's first real "fulfillment" of the novel as influenced by both eighteenth-century rationalism and nineteenth-century romanticism, achieving literary success while other novels of his era failed. Adding to F. O. Matthiessen's explanation (in EC20) that *Letter*'s achievement as the first great American novel is largely due to "continual correspondences" between "external events and inner significances," Hirsch argues that its success results from a borrowing and transformation of the most famous literature of adultery in history—the medieval romance of courtly love. Hawthorne transmutes the conventions by "tearing out their specifically Pagan and Catholic origins, and using them to portray a psychological condition growing out of a Protestant ethic." He "recreates the courtly lover's capacity for intense suffering as a psychological state" and minimizes the sexual significance of the tradition. Dimmesdale is the Puritan embodiment of the courtly lover—living in "ecstasy" for guilt instead of love. Like the mystic, Dimmesdale seeks union with God (far above union with his fellow man), but he never experiences illumination and true purification—even though he purges himself of corruption during the final public scaffold scene. [Hirsch also suggests that, because Dimmesdale is divided between his responsibilities to God and man, he actually anticipates the "agony" of modern consciousness.]

264   Josipovici, Gabriel. "Hawthorne: Allegory and Compulsion." *The World and the Book: A Study of Modern Fiction.* Stanford: Stanford UP, 1971. 155-178.

What links modern classics is a common insistence that "what previous generations had taken for *the world* was only *the world seen through the spectacles of habit.*" Hawthorne's *Letter*, particularly his ambiguous presentation of characters and events, shows a close connection between the problems raised by Puritanism and those explored by the English romantics and the French symbolists. Hawthorne exploits the ambiguity within Puritanism itself to suggest that Puritan values offer only one possible way of interpreting reality. He does not simply substitute a natural view of things in favor of a Puritan method, however, as some critics who favor Hester's superior character are wont to believe. Josipovici examines the midnight scaffold scene in which the letter supernaturally appears in the sky, and shows how the community's multiple interpretations of the letter confirm that meaning is determined entirely and arbitrarily by the assumptions and "language" each person brings to it. Hawthorne is primarily interested in neither theology nor psychology but instead in ways of perceiving reality and communicating experience. He warns of making too much sense of experience, of trying to force conventional meaning on our limited understandings of ourselves, the process of which inevitably involves a deadly, Chillingworth-like probing of secrets that become destroyed when finally revealed. Until humans establish a hieroglyphic language that more accurately assigns universal meanings to natural signs, Hawthorne implies, ambiguity is best—especially since limiting/defining anyone or anything is to act like Hester's Puritan accusers.

265   Vance, William L. "Tragedy and 'The Tragic Power of Laughter': *The Scarlet Letter* and *The House of the Seven Gables*." *Nathaniel Hawthorne Journal 1971*. Ed. C. E. Frazer Clark, Jr. Washington: NCR Microcard Editions, 1971. 232-254.

Relates similarities between *Letter*, a true tragedy, and *House of the Seven Gables*, a tragicomedy, suggesting that both rely on humor to add "texture" or variation to the dominant, sober tone of the novels. Satire, irony, and comic characterizations are all employed in *Letter* as modes that augment the experience of the tragic, and they can be seen in the excessively stern characterization of the Puritans, in the eccentric behavior of Pearl, in the demonically humorous character of Chillingworth, and in the diction and point of view of Hawthorne in "The Custom-House." Humor is used far more liberally in *House of the Seven Gables*, since in this later novel Hawthorne intended to lighten the gloom of *Letter* and depict a "more amusing and harmonious representation of life."

Journal Essays and Notes

266   Abel, Darrel. "Hawthorne's *Scarlet Letter*." *Explicator* 29 (1971): Item 62.

Building on the ideas generated in his 1969 essay (see 239), Abel adds that, while Dimmesdale's dropping of his glove in the midnight scaffold scene signifies his impulse "to drop deception and sin," he is still too proud to rescind his status as visible saint in daylight and so accepts the glove back again at the sexton's request. This behavior corresponds curiously to Hester's in the forest scene, where she "throws away and afterwards takes up again her scarlet letter." These two incidents, Abel concludes, are perhaps designed to beg an examination of their contrasts.

267   Baumgartner, Alex M., and Michael J. Hoffman. "Illusion and Role in *The Scarlet Letter*." *Papers on Language and Literature* 7 (1971): 168-184.*

The thesis of this essay is that "Hawthorne attempted to embody his belief that man must escape from the crippling illusions of which all societies' metaphysical and ethical assumptions are comprised, and further that man must escape from the roles forced upon him by his society in order to discover the reality of his 'self.'" Just as in "The Custom-House," where Hawthorne presents himself as an independent, factual, and direct observor who distances himself from both the "dreamy" illusions of transcendentalism and from "negative romantic isolation and alienation," so in the novel he refuses to assert his own interpretation of events—instead establishing as his moral the importance of abandoning illusions and roles while remaining in society. Hester and Chillingworth suffer under transcendental illusions, while Dimmesdale "is both victim and manipulator" of his own social role as minister. Pearl alone is unencumbered by a social role; "she is reality." Hester's role in the novel "recedes steadily in importance" following the forest scene with Dimmesdale, because, with the Election-Day sermon, Dimmesdale asserts himself as the true hero of the novel, "the only character with the strength both to face reality directly and still accept his obligation to the community."

*See 281 for Hoffman's expansion of this essay in *The Subversive Imagination*.

268   Borden, Caroline. "Bourgeois Social Relations in Nathaniel Hawthorne." *Literature and Ideology* 10 (1971): 21-28.

Arguing from a Marxist perspective, Borden attacks *Letter* (as well as Hawthorne's status as a "classic" writer) generally on the grounds that the novel follows the despicable bourgeois tradition of helping to "strengthen a society based on oppression, exploitation, and the private ownership of means of production." In other words, *Letter* operates under the pretense of an investigation of evil and moral responsibility, using the mystifying technique of ambiguity to disguise the fact that what masquerades as a luke-warm encouragement of individualism over social responsibility is actually an absolute refusal to repudiate or criticize bourgeois social relations. What's more, Hawthorne irresponsibly presents a type of subjective, non-social individualism to his readers that does not exist in the real world, since all people are social beings whose identities are formed and forever influenced by their class circumstances.

269   Caruthers, Clifford M. "The 'Povera Picciola' and *The Scarlet Letter.*"
       Papers on Language and Literature 7 (1971): 90-94.

Although the rosebush symbolizes sensual passion at the beginning of the
novel, the fact that its meaning gradually shifts to connote Christian
salvation may indicate Hawthorne's having been influenced by the 1836
popular French novel *Picciola*, by Joseph Xavier Boniface Saintine. In
this earlier novel, a small plant, the "povera Picciola" ("poor little thing")
has a humbling, moral influence upon a vain and prideful prisoner of the
French Revolution. Saintine endows the treasured flower with a "mystical
moral power" and likens the flower—as Hawthorne does—to a beloved
female character. Caruthers attempts to confirm the likelihood that
Hawthorne "had *Picciola* in mind when he conceived his symbolic
rosebush" by speculating that Hawthorne was "in all likelihood" aware of
the 1849 Philadelphia reprint of *Picciola*, especially since he was
conversant in French, was fond of French books, and had checked out a
historical French book, Lamartine's *History of the Girondists*, from the
Salem Athenaeum on September 13, 1849.

270   Eakin, Paul John. "Hawthorne's Imagination and the Structure of 'The
       Custom-House.'" *American Literature* 43 (1971): 346-358.

Claiming to be one of too few critics who recognize the significance of
"the Custom-House" as "a piece in its own right," Eakin argues that its
concern with the function of the imagination was designed structurally by
Hawthorne to illustrate his "dramatization of his own experience of the
creative process," a gradual process that "moves inward as it were through
a series of concentric circles, from setting to character to author, until he
stands at last in the presence of his true subject, himself." The preface
essentially details Hawthorne's theme of the blighted imagination and is
his "meticulous record of the movement of his imagination from its initial
sleep" when he worked in the unhealthy environment of the Custom
House until its "rude rousing" in 1849 when his political "beheading"
provided the aesthetic distance that enabled him to emerge once more as a
literary man and to recognize that his true subject is the living past. As
soon as the life of the Custom House "lay like a dream before him," he
could write.

271   Griffin, Gerald R. "Hawthorne and 'The New England Village': Internal
       Evidence and a New Genesis of *The Scarlet Letter.*" *Essex Institute
       Historical Collections* 107 (1971): 268-279.

Long attributed to Hawthorne, the "apocryphal" short story "The New
England Village" contains in it "the first genesis" of *Letter* (with respect to

later short stories that also contain germs of the novel). In addition to portraying the sin, guilt, isolation, and hypocrisy that thematically define *Letter*, this "relatively undistinguished" and critically neglected story "holds within it the skeletal framework for the Rev. Arthur Dimmesdale." William Forester is "a shadowy prefigure of the anguished Dimmesdale" in several respects. He is "a guilty man possessed of a hyperactive conscience," he has a powerful blackmailer who is aware of his secret transgressions, he wastes away from the psychological ravages of sin, and he dies shortly after a confession to a "merciful" God that renders his persecutor powerless. Such parallels and similarities do not exhaust connections between the short story and Hawthorne's greatest novel, though they certainly support and perhaps help to confirm that "The New England Village" was indeed written by Hawthorne.

272   Kummings, Donald D. "Hawthorne's 'The Custom House' and the Conditions of Fiction in America." *CEA Critic* 33.3 (1971): 15-18.

Hawthorne presents himself in "The Custom-House" as an American artist attempting to create not only fiction but also an indigenous American literature. It is both "the problem and practice" of the sketch to suggest how this public (indeed, national) art relates to Hawthorne's private romantic vision. Kummings summarizes the main points of "The Custom-House," explains Hawthorne's relation to the past and his need to justify writing the romance, examines themes of isolation and alienation, and discusses the theoretical method of achieving the "neutral territory" of romance.

273   Lease, Benjamin. "Salem vs. Hawthorne: An Early Review of *The Scarlet Letter*." *New England Quarterly* 44 (1971): 110-117.*

The "certain venerable personage" vilified in "The Custom-House" is not C. W. Upham—as many "modern critics" mistakenly aver—but William Lee, "the seventy-nine-year-old permanent Inspector of the Salem Custom House." Descriptions of the Inspector in Hawthorne's savage portrait prove without a doubt that William Lee is the man to whom Hawthorne refers in the preface, as a long-forgotten review of *Letter* seems to attest. This review in the Salem *Register* (dated March 21, 1850), which was most likely written by the journal's editor John Chapman (who was also "an active participant in the Whig conspiracy against Hawthorne"), briefly praises the novel before launching into an outraged attack of "The Custom-House" that accuses Hawthorne of being a "a despicable lampooner" of "inoffensive men." Chapman likens Hawthorne's "irreverent" attack on Lee, "so atrocious, so heartless, so undisguised, so utterly inexcusable" to Chillingworth's wreaking of revenge on

Dimmesdale. It is this analogy that incited Hawthorne to write his Preface to the Second Edition nine days later and to address it to the readers of Chapman's review.

*See 257 for Lease's first (and very similar) essay on the subject of Hawthorne's satiric portrait of William Lee in "The Custom-House."

274   Manierre, William R. "The Role of Sympathy in *The Scarlet Letter*." *Texas Studies in Literature and Language* 13 (1971): 497-507.

Hawthorne's use of the term "sympathy" carries important associational references and represents a level of irony that has gone unnoticed. Sympathy has tri-fold meaning: first, as a positive, harmonious and "basically empathetic response"; second, and much more complexly, as a simultaneously negative, antagonistic response that repulses because it involves a kind of psychological familiarity with or a recommitting of sin on the part of the observer; and third, as a manipulation or paradoxical reversal of the Puritan concept of grace. "The negative associations of the repeatedly appearing term are balanced and given new dimensions of meaning by its link with the entirely affirmative associations of the term and concept it redefines." Appearing in the novel "no fewer than 35 times," sympathy is therefore a highly complex notion in *Letter*. Sympathy for evil or sinful things enables Chillingworth to find out Hester's lover, vastly augments Dimmesdale's efficiency as a minister, describes Nature's response to the lovers' forest meeting, and supports Hester blackmailing tactic when appealing to Dimmesdale to prevent the authorities from taking Pearl away from her ("I will not lose the child! Speak thou for me! Thou knowest, for thou hast sympathies which these men lack!"). Thus sympathy in *Letter* serves as a rather special device "on the level both of technique and meaning; it adds connotative and denotative richness to a book already rich in suggestion, symbol, and ambivalence."

275   Manierre, William R. "Some Apparent Confusions in *The Scarlet Letter*." *CEA Critic* 33 (1971): 9-13.

The "richly complex texture of irony, ambiguity, and suggestion" in *Letter* illustrates Hawthorne's vision of "the limitations and unreliability of human perception and judgment," but these devices give way to incoherence in the novel's concluding chapters: "motivation becomes ill-defined and needlessly ambivalent; explicit authorial commentary becomes less reliable than hitherto; apparent inconsistencies become downright contradictions; and meanings become hopelessly blurred." Particularly troubling is that Chillingworth deliberately lets word leak out of his intentions to book passage with the lovers, when this "irrational" disclosure might lead Hester and Dimmesdale to reconsider their plans— and thus foil Chillingworth's goal of achieving Dimmesdale's damnation. The narrator is also "flatly contradictory" in his statement about Chillingworth's success or failure in damning Dimmesdale (since he states that Chillingworth has achieved the "completest triumph and consummation of revenge" over Dimmesdale three pages after acknowledging Dimmesdale's escape from him). Further, "grammatical ambiguities" abound, as do inconsistencies regarding Pearl's own function in the novel as savior of Hester's soul, leading one to wonder why the narrator describes Pearl's "errand as a messenger of anguish" as "all fulfilled" at a point in the novel when Hester's "psychological condition is unalterably at odds." "One can only assume that the contradictions and confusions which have formerly been associated with the perceptual limitations of the characters, have now become a condition of the author's presentation and a reflection of his own loss of control."

276   Martin, Terence. "Dimmesdale's Ultimate Sermon." *Arizona Quarterly* 27 (1971): 230-240.

Because he deliberately chooses to deny the reader access to the "mental or spiritual process by means of which Dimmesdale comes to the scaffold" for his public confession, "Hawthorne's presentation of Dimmesdale functions to set up the third scaffold scene—how, finally, self-delusion, pride, and a capacity for eloquence (energized by passion) evoke the ultimate sermon which not even Dimmesdale can withstand." Martin carefully examines Dimmesdale's strange behavior following his forest meeting with Hester, arguing that Dimmesdale is more inspired than ever to write the "ultimate" Election-Day sermon once he is won over to Hester's plan of escape—since he egotistically views the opportunity to deliver that all-important sermon (often considered the pinnacle of any Puritan reverend's career) as the perfect way to "cap" his ministry and achieve the lofty position of "Puritan hero-saint" before giving himself up to what he knows is "deadly sin." Yet self-deluded till the end, Dimmesdale performs the sermon with such astonishing eloquence that it actually becomes "the instrument for self-conversion," saving himself, in effect, by "preach[ing] his way to public confession."

277   Shear, Walter. "Characterization in *The Scarlet Letter*." *Midwest Quarterly* 12 (1971): 437-454.

Seymour Katz's recent, trendy approach to the characters in *Letter* (that considers them in "a basically realistic context" [see 222]) does an injustice to the novel. *Letter* "can be best understood not merely in relationship to the extremely romantic but to the more popular literature of Hawthorne's day." Hawthorne employs sentimental and melodramatic characterizations and devices—such as the seduction tale, the triangle relationship, and the motif of the beneficent influence of the little child)—to "strike at the core" of the sentimentalist's "easy theology" that confirmed a "virtually inevitable moral order," and to raise questions about the human ability to perceive moral order. Though harsh in its treatment of the "outrageous spiritual righteousness" of the sentimental tradition, *Letter* yet reflects "a concern with an idealism which has some kinship with sentimentalism." Hawthorne's combination of romantic and sentimental elements in the four primary characters creates "a study of organic growth" that ultimately shows how "the self discovers its value in the value it sees in others."

278   Stouck, David. "The Surveyor of 'The Custom-House': A Narrator for *The Scarlet Letter." The Centennial Review* 15 (1971): 309-29.

Explores the enigmatic role of the narrator, suggesting that his "deliberately ambiguous and hypothetical manner" not only accounts for the "astonishing range of responses" to the novel but also establishes a crucial link between "The Custom-House" and *Letter*—since the narrator's voice throughout the novel is an extension of the distinctly dramatized surveyor in the sketch. The "emotional structure" of the narrator's apparently casual reflections in "The Custom-House" is divided into three parts: "the return to Salem," where the narrator confronts the ghosts of his guilt-inspiring Puritan forefathers; "the custom's officers," where the narrator symbolically masters his feelings of inadequacy by asserting power over the aging, insecure custom's officials; and "the writing of the romance" itself, through which Hawthorne releases all feelings of guilt and his dreadful sense of alienation from the ancestral community. Hester, Dimmesdale, and Chillingworth are all "dream-like projections" of the narrator's alienated state of mind, because they too experience the double bind of not being able to leave the scene of their "guilty drama" while simultaneously remaining unable to establish a meaningful relationship with the larger community.

279   Williams, Melvin G. "Hawthorne's Ministers of Spiritual Torment." *Christianity and Literature* 20.4 (1971): 18-23.

Discusses Hawthorne's depiction of sinning or hypocritical Puritan ministers in such tales as "Young Goodman Brown," "The Gentle Boy," "The Minister's Black Veil," and *Letter*, the last two of which are Hawthorne's most complex—with ministers whose hypersensitive consciences and "shadowy encounters with evil" ironically make them more effective pastors. For all of Hawthorne's negative portrayals of the intolerant Puritan mind in these stories, though, the "earnest" Puritans still outrank the "frigid-spirited" religious liberals and transcendentalists of his own day who sought to ignore the evil in man's heart altogether.

1972

Essays and Studies in Books

280 Fossum, Robert H. "Of Time and Identity: *The Scarlet Letter.*" *Hawthorne's Inviolable Circle: The Problem of Time.* Deland: Everett/Edwards, 1972. 105-126.

Letter and a large number of Hawthorne's tales "center on the ways in which time, especially the past, affects a man's psychological state, his sense of identity, [and] his relations with other men." The novel is above all about the significance of the past (despite opinions to the contrary by such critics as Harry Levin [70] and F. O. Matthiessen [EC20]), and the living past is its theme, purpose, and setting. Hawthorne makes his peace with the past in "The Custom-House" and goes on to suggest in the tale proper that it is impossible to achieve identity and fulfillment without recognizing that the past is an integral part of the present and future. Of the three main characters, only Hester refuses to let the past destroy her, redefining her place in time at the end by maintaining the continuity of past and present.

281 Hoffman, Michael J. "The Anti-Transcendental Reaction: Illusion and Role in *The Scarlet Letter.*" *The Subversive Imagination.* Port Washington: Kennikat, 1972. 70-86.*

Charting the gradual shift from romantic to realist fiction in this study of romantic culture and consciousness, Hoffman places Hawthorne's *Letter* and Melville's *Moby-Dick* (1851) squarely in the middle of the transition, because both authors tended toward realism and rejected the antidemocratic and antinomian implications of transcendentalism, the principles of which provided no legitimate safeguard against the violation of one individual by another. The "realist impulse" is particularly strong in *Letter* with its concern about two problems: "the traditional Romantic dilemma of establishing a new relationship between the individual self and its social role; and the belief that men's illusions—their refusal or their inability to see the world as it really is—are the major impediments to their forging this relationship." For Hawthorne, man can achieve salvation only by coming to terms with reality as the majority perceives it. The individual must find a way to participate empathetically in the social order and come to realize that banding together is a must "for reasons of love as well as survival." Although Hester accepts (to a degree) the implications of her label and comes to serve the community that once dismissed her, she ultimately points out the inadequacy of her punishment, rising above it and thus never truly accepting life "as it really is." *Letter* ultimately becomes Dimmesdale's book, since "he is the only character with the strength to face reality directly and still to accept his obligation to the community." Through Dimmesdale, Hawthorne not only rejects romantic isolation and alienation but also reveals the weaknesses of Hester's transcendental vision of love's redemptive value.

*See 267 for an earlier version of this essay.

282 Kaplan, Harold. "Hawthorne: The Need to Become Human." *Democratic Humanism and American Literature*. Chicago: U of Chicago P, 1972. 129-158.

Letter dramatizes Hawthorne's commitment to democracy and deep respect for the "human" protagonist, enacting his theme of "sympathy as a moral communion based on the shared sense of suffering." Hawthorne's mind mediated among terms of contrast, predisposing him to be an allegorist and to explain the roles and actions assigned to his three major "divided" characters. Chillingworth represents "an excess of intellect"; Hester represents an excess of vital, natural force; and Dimmesdale (the most tortured of the three) represents an excess of spirit, "caught between the force of intellect and the force of passion." The narrative focuses on this "arena of division and conflict" between the three main characters in their struggles between public and private selves, and tries to get them to "break out of moral and existential isolation" through sympathy for their fellow men. Indeed, Hawthorne stresses their public roles throughout (Dimmesdale as public teacher and standard bearer of morality, Chillingworth as doctor, healer, and man of wisdom, and Hester as sinner and self-sacrificing server of community). Hawthorne's democratic goal is to transform the community members into humanized beings who transcend their own abusive, self-destructive, and simplistic laws to reach "a luminous consciousness, a moral readiness or sympathy" when engaging in social relations. Only Hester and Dimmesdale appear to unite in the scaffold scene, moving together "in the common shape of the human being" as they reverse and exchange values.

283 Noble, David W. "The Analysis of Alienation by Twentieth-Century Social Scientists and Nineteenth-Century Novelists: The Example of Hawthorne's *The Scarlet Letter*." *Myths and Realities: Conflicting Values*

in America. Eds. Berkley Kalin and Clayton Robinson. Memphis: Memphis State UP, 1972. 5-19.

Scientific ideas from Thomas Kuhn's *The Structure of Scientific Revolutions* (1970) about "the alienation of intellectuals in modern society" apply to *Letter*. Like the physicists of the late nineteenth century, the romantic novelists of the early nineteenth century rejected the modern belief that "the individual [could stand] apart from experience as a neutral observer," living out a concept known as "negative revolution." The individual's resulting experience of alienation comes from denying humanity's function as "cultural creator" of "positive revolutions." Hawthorne, who "was certain that it was the very nature of man to engage in such creativity and that no amount of Puritan repression could contain this instinct of creativity," sets up Hester and Dimmesdale as positive contributors to a truly New World culture who are held back by Chillingworth's medieval "theology of non-creativity."

Journal Essays and Notes

284   Abel, Darrel. "'The Strong Division-Lines of Nature.'" *ATQ* 14 (1972): 23-31.*

Abel considers Hawthorne's ambivalent feelings about Margaret Fuller (evident in his creation of passionate, intellectual female characters like Hester, Zenobia, and Miriam), and compares and contrasts Hawthorne's and Fuller's ideas about the "proper" place of women in society. While both authors basically agree about women's "propriety" (both identify the incompetence of purely masculine men and purely feminine women), Hawthorne clearly disagrees with Fuller about sexual roles and condemns women who intrude into the masculine sphere. Hawthorne's ideal heroine has both "carnal capability and spiritual vitality," although the latter attribute is missing from "dark ladies" like Hester, whom Abel then compares with Anne Hutchinson. Despite being clearly sympathetic with both "strong-minded, passionate women beaten down by [masculine] authority" and their "impulse toward liberation from the bondage of [their] sex," Hawthorne nevertheless condemns their waywardness and, particularly, their departure from "Woman's propriety."

*Reprinted in Abel's *The Moral Picturesque: Studies in Hawthorne's Fiction* (see 559).

285   Andola, John A. "Pearl: Symbolic Link Between Two Worlds." *Ball State University Forum* 13 (1972): 60-67.

Just as the pearl links the world of the sea with the world of human beings, so Hawthorne's symbolic Pearl links two worlds, or rather "several pairs of worlds," in *Letter*: love and sin, the real world and spiritual world, Hester and Dimmesdale. Not intended by Hawthorne to be realistic, Pearl is "imbued with delicately balanced ambiguities and symbolic powers" and functions as a literary tool to unite the novel's various opposing forces.

286   Barker-Benfield, Ben.   "Anne Hutchinson and the Puritan Attitude Toward Women." *Feminist Studies* 1 (1972): 65-96.

Delves into the Puritan mindset that not only excluded women from participation in the "priesthood of all believers" (the idea that all regenerate men were illumined with divine truth and were priests unto themselves), but also restricted them from "the relief afforded men by covenant theology," which in part was self-servingly designed to afford more power to men over women than the initial Protestant dynamic had allowed. Anne Hutchinson's antinomianism, perceived by John Winthrop as a sexual threat that was intensified by her private midwifery connections to women, was in part a response to the need of Puritan women to relate more directly to God and therefore to undo their total dependence on men—whom they were supposed to reverence and obey as the representatives of God. Hawthorne's awareness of this dimension of the Antinomian controversy is evident in his view of Puritan history presented in *Letter* (pp. 87-90). Hawthorne was aware of the "profound sexual bias" involved in the legalisms of covenant theology, a bias responsible for the suppression of women and the banishment ofHutchinson, and so he presents Hester as a similar feminine threat to the masculine social and theological order, sympathetically contrasting her "antique gentility, softness, beauty, complexity, and fallibility" as a maternal woman with the "grim male soldier-magistrates." Hester's banishment not only "represent[s] the exclusion of all of those [feminine] qualities from a place of value in the American character," but also reflects Hawthorne's way of commenting on the continuing separation of the sexes in nineteenth-century America.

287   Benoit, Raymond.   "Theology and Literature: *The Scarlet Letter*." *Bucknell Review* 20 (1972): 83-92.*

In *Letter*, Hawthorne uses literature and theology to "develop a theory and a way of writing to accord with what he believed about Christianity and about the way human nature develops morally." He explores the basic human need "to reconcile disparates into new wholes" first in "The Custom-House" and then in the fiction itself through the character of

Pearl. Thrust into the Puritan world, with its one-sided emphasis on rationality and law (whence comes a passionless approach to reality), is the mystery of the letter "A," which mystery is not meant to be solved but to be enjoyed for its richness of meaning. As the symbolic representation of the letter's artistic and religious possibilities, Pearl connects the material and the spiritual, the coveted union of which is articulated in "The Custom-House" as the "neutral territory" of art.

*For Benoit's slightly revised version of this article, see "A Letter—the Letter A: Nathaniel Hawthorne" in *Single Nature's Double Name: The Collectedness of the Conflicting in British and American Romanticism* (The Hague: Mouton, 1973, 83-94). Benoit selects *Letter* as one of several nineteenth-century British and American romantic works that show "a continuity in the chiastic mode indicative of the Romantic imagination." Like Ralph Waldo Emerson, Walt Whitman, and Henry David Thoreau, Hawthorne "Americanized" the romantic movement in his driving quest to balance and reconcile the simultaneous "pulls" of the finite and the infinite.

288   Browning, Preston M. "Hester Prynne as Secular Saint." *Midwest Quarterly* 13 (1972): 351-362.

In the character of Hester, Hawthorne offers a remarkably modern alternative to Dimmesdale's Puritanism that anticipates the twentieth-century Christian view of redemption. Through the existential concept of "secular sainthood" (the contemporary term first suggested by R. W. B. Lewis in *The Picaresque Saint*), the sacred emerges from a paradoxical combination of "the natural and seemingly profane." Dietrich Bonhoeffer referred to this movement from orthodox Christian thought (supernatural salvation) to secular sanctity (historical salvation) as "religionless Christianity." In asmuch this modern Christian belief entails an individual's sharing in the world's sufferings to experience validation and redemption, Hester appears to demonstrate "an extraordinary conformity" to her faith, no less so than Dimmesdale to his. But whereas Dimmesdale selects death as the means of choosing his supernatural God, Hester chooses life by being faithful to hers. [See 294 for another essay that views Hawthorne as bridging the gap between secularity and theology.]

289   Colacurcio, Michael [J.]. "Footsteps of Anne Hutchinson: The Context of *The Scarlet Letter*." *English Literary History* 39 (1972): 459-494.*

Asking "what *Letter* may mean if it does indeed call up a fairly exclusive set of associations from Puritanism's most crucial theological controversy," Colacurcio explores Hawthorne's use of

Hutchinsonian/antinomian motifs (treating similarities between Hester and Anne Hutchinson that relate to gender, sex, and freedom) and "Cottonesque ramifications" (which suggest parallels between Dimmesdale and John Cotton. Hawthorne's theme of romantic individualism may have been first formulated in the theological context of Puritan heresy, but his rebellious characters are returned in the end to something of a "neonomian norm" whereby all disruptive social excesses are restrained once again by the world's law. [See470 for Nina Baym's suggestion that Hawthorne is less likely to have modeled Hester after Anne Hutchinson than from George Sand's novels.]

*This essay is reprinted with minor revisions in Colacurcio's *Doctrine and Difference: Essays in the Literature of New England* (New York: Routledge, 1997. 177-204). See Colacurcio's 1985 essay "'The Woman's Own Choice" (486) for another discussion that links the Puritan past with Hawthorne's time.

290   Holmes, Edward M. "Requiem for a Scarlet Nun." *Costerus* 5 (1972): 35-49.

Draws "limited" parallels between *Letter* and William Faulkner's play *Requiem for a Nun* (1951), such as "a like use of past and present in an attempt to arrest time," "similar visions of the functions and needs of the community," a comparable delineation of sinful characters who rise morally above their persecutors, "choice of the same moral theme" on the need for openness, "a strongly implied certainty about the necessity of man's forbearance toward man, and an equal yearning [for] and yet uncertainty about God's mercy to man." These elements, Holmes contends, imply more similarities between the two authors than have hitherto been recognized regarding their assertions on "man's position in the universe." Comparisons also extend to the main characters in each work, between the social mandate-breaking Hester Prynne and Nancy Mannigoe (the "nigger dopefiend whore") and between Arthur Dimmesdale and Temple Drake, the latter of whom are unable to escape their respective roles as spiritual leader and "smart young matron."

291   Isani, Mukhtar Ali. "Hawthorne and the Branding of William Prynne." *New England Quarterly* 45 (1972): 182-195.

Investigates accounts of the seventeenth-century English feud between Archbishop Laud and William Prynne as a likely and potential source for Hawthorne's creation of Hester, Chillingworth, and Dimmesdale. Isani provides notable parallels between the life of William Prynne (first as persecuted but defiant man, then as vengeful persecutor) and certain names, characters, and events as they unfold in *Letter*. As one whose deviation from orthodoxy resulted in the unusually harsh punishment of having his cheeks branded by the conformity-enforcing Laud, Prynne can be compared to Hester (and Laud to the Puritans); and as one who methodically and maliciously wreaked revenge against his persecutor and enemy, Prynne can be compared to Chillingworth. Parallels can also be found in the relation of the theologian William Chillingworth (who bore an unusual connection to Laud) to his fictional namesake, as well as in the clerical positions of power held by Laud and Dimmesdale, both of whom, as "injurers" who became the "injured," suffered at the hands of their enemies.

292   Jenkins, R. B. "A New Look at an Old Tombstone." *New England Quarterly* 45 (1972): 417-421.

"A number of Hawthorne scholars [namely Theodore Munger (EC23), Leland Schubert (EC26), Richard H. Fogle (15), Harry Levin (70), John C. Stubbs (227), and Charles Leavitt (153)] have [erroneously] read the final sentence of *Letter*—'On a Field, Sable, the Letter A, Gules'—as if it were an epitaph on Hester Prynne's tombstone" rather than Hawthorne's description of the escutcheon's curious device in the last sentence of the romance. Textual evidence, coupled with knowledge of heraldic terminology, proves that no such motto or inscription appears on the tombstone. On the dark shield appears simply the capital letter "A." In fact, two chapters in *Letter* that anticipate Hester's future headstone ("The Recognition" and "Hester at Her Needle") foreshadow its destined, infamous appearance as a lone "A" on a "simple slab of slate." The "A" is "originally intended for Dimmesdale and only secondarily for Hester Prynne," since Dimmesdale is buried "many, many years" before she, and it "seems unlikely that Dimmesdale's grave would have been unmarked for all those years before Hester's death." Thus "the shield and A must have been meant for Dimmesdale [signifying "Angel"], not Hester, though serving as a fitting symbol for both." [See 313, "Another Look at an Old Tombstone," which disagrees with Jenkins's assertion that the source of the motto comes from Sir Walter Scott's *Waverly*. See also 320 for an essay that disagrees with another of Jenkins's assumptions about the heraldic motto.]

293   Kane, Patricia. "The Fallen Woman as Free-Thinker in *The French Lieutenant's Woman* and *The Scarlet Letter*." *Notes on Contemporary Literature* 2 (1972): 8-10.

Letter and *The French Lieutenant's Woman* (1969) are similar in that Hawthorne and John Fowles both offer "masculine explanation[s]" for their free-thinking, fallen women. Both also connect their heroines' passionate natures and sexual unconventionality with their superior intellectual capacities. Presented by each author as a cause-and-effect scenario, the situations of both stories develop thus: the sexual transgressions of Hester and Sarah lead to social ostracism, which in turn encourages their freedom to speculate on alternative ways of living that were unacceptable to conventional-minded women in Puritan New England and prudish Victorian England.

294   Kushen, Betty. "Love's Martyrs: *The Scarlet Letter* as Secular Cross." *Literature and Psychology* 22 (1972): 108-120.

Letter is "an essay into the psychology of religious experience" that revitalizes or modernizes the "atrophied doctrine[s]" of Catholicism and Puritanism by drawing an analogy between the trinity of Hester, Dimmesdale, and Chillingworth and the archetypal holy family of Mary, Christ, and the Old Testament Jehovah. Offering his readers "a timeless and universal familial template with whom to identify," Hawthorne "moves from divine punishment administered by a wrathful God to internalized punishment meted out at the behest of the individual consciences of his protagonists." Dimmesdale in particular suffers under shame, exhibiting Hawthorne's "modernized" conception of psychic punishment by internally burning with the stigma—and further enhancing his guilt by his own torturing superego's Oedipal conflict (since he has seduced the wife of "an almost omniscient father-confidant" and experiences continual libidinous impulses toward the maternal Hester). The emotional effects of Hester's and Dimmesdale's mutually-shared infamy extend to the state of self-punishing martyrdom which the letter imposes on the two, both of whom indulge in identifications of self-abnegation with religious suffering for common humanity. [For another essay that illustrates how Hawthorne bridges the gap between secularity and theology, see 288.]

295   Lease, Benjamin. "'The Whole is a Prose Poem': An Early Review of *The Scarlet Letter*." *American Literature* 44 (1972): 128-130.

Reproduces a "hitherto unnoticed anonymous review in the Boston *Post* of March 21, 1850 (just five days after the publication of the novel)" that not only strikingly anticipates Q. D. Leavis's influential analysis of *Letter* (13) as "a prose poem" but also antedates Herman Melville's famous pronouncement (in ER6) that Hawthorne "says NO! in thunder." Also noteworthy is the review's complete neglect of "The Custom-House," indicating that the novel's immediate and widespread popularity was not entirely due to its scandalous introduction.

296   Slethaug, Gordon E.   *"Felix Culpa* in Hawthorne's 'Custom-House.'"
        English Review 23.3 (1972): 32-41.

Although recent critics "admit to a certain relationship" between "The
Custom-House" and *Letter*, "they fail to discuss the centrality of the
Fortunate Fall theme in the introduction," which fall is "the guiding
principle" in the book and the sketch. The "old Puritan vitality and strong
socio-spiritual leadership" of the seventeenth century compares with the
"pervasive somnambulance and ennui" that characterizes the "decadent
moderns" in "The Custom-House." Hawthorne actually implies that "the
seeds of nineteenth-century corruption were already sown by the Puritans"
(especially in that the excesses of transcendentalism and "business-
materialism" can be traced to an Edwardsian mystical idealism and the
"so-called" Puritan work ethic).   The Fortunate Fall theme is first
illustrated through the character in "The Custom-House" who "combines
the best characteristics of the Puritans and the Moderns," General Miller,
the Collector, whose violent war experience leads to a genuine
compassion and love of beauty.   In the novel, the character who
corresponds best with the Collector is Dimmesdale, whose experience
with sin results in a dramatically improved ability to preach and counsel.
Of course the *felix culpa* motif applies in "The Custom-House" to
Hawthorne, too, since the ill fortune of his political decapitation "turns out
to be his salvation."

297   Todd, Robert E.   "The Magna Mater Archetype in *The Scarlet Letter.*"
        New England Quarterly 45 (1972): 421-429.

Argues that much of the novel's duality or ambivalence is expressed
through the character of Hester, who can be interpreted paradoxically as
both saint and sinner. Hester corresponds to Jung's archetypal figure of
"The Magna Mater," or Great Mother; and in her fulfillment of the bipolar
and ambivalent role of "good" and "terrible" mother, she has a decisive
influence on the fate of Dimmesdale. As a symbol of creative/destructive
duality or the "womb-tomb" character of the Magna Mater, Hester is "both
a source of destruction and death on the one hand, and a source of love
and rebirth on the other."

298   Wentersdorf, Karl P.   "The Element of Witchcraft in *The Scarlet Letter.*"
        Folklore 83 (1972): 132-153.

Although Hawthorne seems to come closest in *Letter* to achieving an ideal
balance between allegory and historical romance (especially in his
creation of "flesh-and-blood" characters, rather than abstract

personifications of moral types or theological concepts), Wentersdorft wonders whether references to the midnight ceremonies in the forest involving the witch Mistress Hibbins and the mysterious Black Man are meant to function symbolically (as most critics suggest) or at a literal level of meaning. The invitations to Hester and Dimmesdale to join the two in the forest may well be Hawthorne's "expressionistic device for revealing the inner conflicts and temptations of the two lovers," but the characters of Hibbins (as "Temptation") and the Black Man (as "Satan") are nonetheless rooted in history, as was the widespread practice of witchcraft. Wentersdorf traces the existence of witch cults and coven meetings in the seventeenth century and speculates that witchcraft practices took place in New England, since "Hawthorne believed that some kind of cultic witches' meetings had been a historical reality and intended that the references to such meetings in *Letter* were to be interpreted literally." Hawthorne's intentional ambiguity regarding the historicity of such episodes in the novel is, in fact, "part of a carefully planned technique for coping with possible skepticism on the part of his readers regarding the existence of witches," as well as "a way of drawing attention to the difficulty of getting at the truths of history." Since the Puritans attributed fiction to the work of the devil, the element of witchcraft in *Letter*, as it "merges subtly with the other elements of literary allegory," constitutes "an unobtrusive but unmistakable satire on the Puritan aesthetic."

299   West, Harry C. "Hawthorne's Editorial Pose." *American Literature* 44 (1972): 208-221.

Suggesting that Hawthorne's attitude toward his material is closer to that of editor than historian (as David Levin [201] and Michael Davitt Bell [261] argue), West examines the editorial pose that Hawthorne adopts in "The Custom-House" and shows how that pose actually creates the narrative tone in the novel and in other tales and romances (a tone that is "consistently more interested in meaning and significance than in realism or factual accuracy"). Hawthorne locates the starting point or source for his tales "somewhere in the public domain," and he uses his editorial pose not only to promote his readers' trust in him as a practical-minded author whose interests are congenial with those of his audience (which believed that fiction was distasteful "idle fantasy"), but also to provide the imaginative latitude necessary to treat "certain lurid and supernatural subjects," and even to furnish the proper aesthetic distance from material necessary to create an air of ambiguity about the exact nature of events.

1973

Essays and Studies in Books

300   Brodhead, Richard H.   "New and Old Tales: *The Scarlet Letter.*"
       Hawthorne, Melville, and the Novel. Chicago: U of Chicago P, 1973. 43-
       68.

This psycho-social approach argues that Hawthorne gathers the historical,
moral, and psychological themes of past works and fully integrates and
realizes them in *Letter* as "the self-conscious culmination of his artistic
career." What accounts for *Letter*'s singular intensity is its ability to
engage so fully in the reconciliation of opposites, to present so vividly in
his characters the psychic turmoil that results from the conflict between
restrictive Puritan orthodoxy and free expression of the self's desires,
needs, and powers. The social and psychological phenomena are further
complicated by the novel's involvement with the symbolic mode and its
inclusion of two radically incommensurate fictional modes: the romance
and historical realism.

301   Ehrenpreis, Anne Henry.   "Elizabeth Gaskell and Nathaniel Hawthorne."
       Nathaniel Hawthorne Journal 1973. Ed. C. E. Frazer Clark, Jr.
       Englewood: Microcard Edition Books, 1973. 89-119.

Emphasizing similarities between the personal and creative lives of
Gaskell and Hawthorne, Ehrenpreis maintains that *Letter* most likely
influenced Gaskell's *Ruth* (1853) and points out connections between the
two works that indicate "surprising common ground." Both share the bold
theme of an unwed mother's fall and subsequent rehabilitation in her
community through atonement, good works, and, especially, the
instrumental mother-daughter relationship. This essay also discusses
Henry Arthur Bright, a mutual acquaintance of Hawthorne and Gaskell
and a "go-between" for the two authors; speculates that Gaskell indirectly
influenced *Marble Faun*; and suggests that similar treatments of witchcraft
in their stories indicate that both adopted material from the same source,
Charles W. Upham's *Lectures on Witchcraft* (1831).

302   Hays, Peter L.   "Why Seven Years in *The Scarlet Letter*?" *Nathaniel
       Hawthorne Journal 1972.* Ed. C. E. Frazer Clark, Jr. Washington: NCR
       Microcard Edition Books, 1973. 251-253.

Noting that Hawthorne calls attention several times to *Letter*'s duration of
exactly seven years (from June 1642 to late spring 1649), Hays points out
that the time frame is anything but arbitrary, since seven years was the
standard period of apprenticeship and indentured servitude in America.
The extensive series of images throughout the novel that express various
forms of bondage indicate that, for Hawthorne, seven years penance was

the allotted time necessary for his "bound" hero and heroine to achieve through penance and public service "a higher and purer state."

303   Heilbrun, Carolyn G. "The Woman as Hero." *Toward a Recognition of Androgyny.* New York: Alfred A. Knopf, 1973. 49-112.

Groups *Letter* along with *Clarissa, Vanity Fair,* and *Wuthering Heights* as "great androgynous novels before the twentieth century" and compares *Letter* with Samuel Richardson's *Clarissa* (pp. 62-67) for several "noteworthy similarities," such as the two heroines' strong "sense of [themselves];" their deliberate choices of "living with and through the fact" of their sexual indiscretions in "the soil of [their] sin, and nowhere else"; their mythical greatness, martyrdom, and sainthood; and especially that "both turn the apparent waste of their lives into tremendous sources of androgynous energy." Hawthorne never follows the conventional view of woman's limitations in his creation of Hester, despite his own limiting conventional views and anti-feminist opinions. "The greatest miracle of *Letter* is the extent to which the book allows the magnificence of that one act of love to shine as the single living moment in a hard and sterile world."

304   Jacobsen, Eric. "'Stationing' in *Paradise Lost* and *The Scarlet Letter.*" *Americana-Norwegica.* Vol 4. Ed. Brita Seyersted. *Norwegian Contributions to American Studies Dedicated to Sigmund Skard.* Oslo: Oslo University Publishers, 1973. 107-122.

An important feature of Milton's descriptive technique is what Jacobsen calls "stationing," or "the firm placing of his characters in relation to spacial objects." Considering this "working with time, space, and the outward and inward eye for literary and doctrinal purposes, " Jacobsen traces certain similarities of visual technique in *Paradise Lost* (1667) and *Letter,* especially their presentations of the Fortunate Fall. Both authors saw the world "through a glass darkly," but Milton saw more clearly and stably a vision of transgression and atonement. Hawthorne permits the reader to see neither original transgression nor definitive consequence, and he presents his series of tableaux sometimes in Christian terms, sometimes not. Jacobsen questions the nature of such sketchiness and ambiguity (denying the impulse to accuse Hawthorne of "muddled thinking"), and wonders whether Hawthorne's "whole elaborate system of symbols and significances, so skillfully constructed" is not in fact "a mere wilderness of mirrors in a universe of death." The end of the novel may be an enlarged and darker reading of Hawthorne's words in "The Custom-House," that "all these details, so completely seen, are so spiritualized by the unusual light, that they seem to lose their actual substance, and become things of intellect."

305   Levy, Leo B. "The Notebook Source and the Eighteenth-Century Context of Hawthorne's Theory of Romance." *Nathaniel Hawthorne Journal 1973.* Ed. C. E. Frazer Clark, Jr. Englewood: Microcard Edition Books, 1973. 120-129.

Examines the relationship of the "neutral ground" moonlight passage in "The Custom-House" and Hawthorne's 1848 notebook entry that first describes his aesthetic and psychological theories on Romance (the latter of which does not mention the terms "Actual," "Imaginary," or "neutral territory"). Hawthorne's conception of the creative process, and, specifically, his view of the relationship of memory to the imagination, finds its origin in "the associational aesthetics and 'common sense' realism of the Eighteenth century," Levy contends, particularly from Archibald Alison's associationalist ideas in *Essays on the Nature and Principles of Taste* (1812) and realist Lord Kames's "theory of ideal presence" in *Elements of Criticism* (1762).

306   Mann, Charles W. "D. H. Lawrence: Notes on Reading Hawthorne's *The Scarlet Letter.*" *Nathaniel Hawthorne Journal 1973.* Ed. C. E. Frazer Clark, Jr. Englewood: Microcard Edition Books, 1973. 8-25.

Provides a transcription of D. H. Lawrence's eight-and-a-half pages of "long-forgotten" original notes on *Letter* that eventually—after at least three revisions—became his chapter on Hawthorne in *Studies in Classic American Literature* (EC18). The notes are "slight in content," mostly containing quotations from the novel (the Everyman's Library edition published by J. M. Dent in London and E. P. Dutton in New York), but they are interesting in that they record Lawrence's fascination not only with "the demonic and exotic underpinnings of the Puritan tale" but especially with Pearl. Lawrence's notes begin on page 70 of the novel, indicating that he found "The Custom-House" preface to be "superfluous."

307   Mills, Nicolaus. "Nathaniel Hawthorne and George Eliot." *American and English Fiction in the Nineteenth Century: An Antigenre Critique and Comparison.* Bloomington: Indiana UP, 1973. 52-73.

Goes against common critical assumptions and standard generalizations that assume vast differences between nineteenth-century English fiction (which follows a strict novelistic, mannerish tradition) and American fiction (which follows a romantic tradition due to the landscape's "thin" societal texture).* Instead of dividing these works into such exclusive genres, Mills compares eight English and American representative works for their important similarities and unique characteristics. The "seduction theme" in *Letter* and *Adam Bede* (1859) relates to the religious dilemma of the Fall depicted in each. In both novels, the meaning of the two forbidden love affairs is understood in terms of the consequences of each sexual act, with passion as subordinate to the broader social and religious issues. While the social judgments of Hester and Hetty are very similar, the religious transformations of Arthur and Adam lead to different novelistic conclusions—based on the nature of the differences between Hawthorne's and Eliot's religious visions. Eliot's final emphasis is on the communal implications of Adam's religious growth, but Hawthorne's conclusion is more ambiguous, and we are not so certain of how God's will has revealed itself—or if Dimmesdale is saved after all.

*Mills's argument goes most specifically against Richard Chase's in *The American Novel and Its Tradition* (55) and Lionel Trilling's in *The Liberal Imagination* (New York:Viking Press, 1950). For other comparisons between *Letter* and *Adam Bede*, refer to "Comparisons" in the Subject Index.

308   Vogel, Dan. "Hawthorne's Concept of Tragedy in *The Scarlet Letter.*" *Nathaniel Hawthorne Journal 1972.* Ed. C. E. Frazer Clark, Jr. Washington: NCR Microcard Editions, 1973. 183-193.

Stresses that Hawthorne's concept of tragedy originates not so much in Greek tragedy* as in "the pervasive morality and lingering fatalism inherent in Christianity." Hawthorne enacts the tragedy of "triumphant ignominy" in the Christian tradition through Dimmesdale's (Adam's) fall, with the "serpentine" and loathsome Chillingworth ironically serving as Dimmesdale's partner in enacting the tragic hero's ennobling catharsis and redemption after long suffering. No such catharsis awaits the melodramatic Hester, however, because she is "morally dense," unable to imagine a world without Dimmesdale's love. Hester is further incapable—whereas Chillingworth *is* capable—of envisioning herself a part of a divinely predetermined chain of events that necessarily has a tragic end. In his final speech on the scaffold at the end of the novel (a scene suggestive of Christ's crucifixion), Dimmesdale consecrates Hawthorne's tragic vision of the moral purpose in the consequences of sin.

*Vogel disagrees with Malcolm Cowley's "Five Acts of *The Scarlet Letter*" for its emphasis on Greek tragedy (59, 68).

Journal Essays and Notes

309   Axelsson, Arne I. "Isolation and Interdependence as Structure in *The Scarlet Letter*." *Studia Neophilologica* 45 (1973): 392-402.

Argues against "unsatisfactory" interpretations that attempt unconvincingly to prove that the novel is about sin and guilt, stressing that *Letter* is actually "about human isolation and interdependence." The four main characters are "types of human 'isolatoes'": Hester as proud and passionate idealist whose "emotional mistakes" lead to isolation; Dimmesdale as sensitive and passive man whose "indissoluble inner tension" leads to isolation; Chillingworth "whose inhuman occupation leads to his separation from humanity"; and Pearl, the "innocent victim, whose isolation from society and play-mates is the result of the negligence, mistakes, or sins of the people about her." The romance is structured around the four characters' shattered positions in respect to each other and to society (with the three scaffold scenes illustrating stages in their development), and the plot develops toward an increased sense of coherence and integration among them. The most positive result (since Hester and Dimmesdale's integration remains doubtful) is "Pearl's total integration with humanity and a most positive relationship with her mother." Even Chillingworth seems to share in the reunion at the end, since his bond of hate, which is "better than no bond at all," permits him "a kind of post-humous movement in the direction of interdependence."

310   Barnes, Daniel R. "Two Reviews of *The Scarlet Letter* in *Holden's Dollar Magazine*." *American Literature* 44 (1973): 648-652.

Discusses two anonymous reviews of *Letter* published in *Holden's Dollar Magazine* that "have thus far escaped notice." The first, reproduced here and dated May 1850, is almost certainly the work of *Holden*'s editor at the time, Charles F. Briggs. (Although Perry Miller cites Briggs in *The Raven and the Whale* (1956) as having left the editorship in March of 1850, Briggs's own "farewell letter" to readers in June 1850 suggests otherwise.) While the review showers praise on the morally "unobjectionable" novel and finds the introduction to be "a pleasant piece of gossippry" [sic], it urges that "Hawthorne would be doing himself a good turn by omitting ["The Custom-House"] in the next edition," since "it does not prepare the mind for the romance and is therefore an encumbrance." The second review, first published in June 1850 and not included here, was definitely written by the Rev. Henry Giles and "is by far the longest review of *Letter* yet discovered: a 7,500 word essay" that is "one of the most perceptive analyses of the romance written during Hawthorne's lifetime." [For an article that corroborates Barnes's evidence that Rev. Henry Giles wrote a review of *Letter* for *Holden's Dollar Magazine*, see Richard Tuerk (332).]

162

311   Baym, Nina. "The Romantic *Malgré Lui*: Hawthorne in the Custom
        House." *ESQ: A Journal of the American Renaissance* 19 (1973): 14-25.

Conceives of "The Custom-House" as "a narrative in its own right," as an
"autobiographical romance" in which Hawthorne not only chronicles the
steps to his eventual, permanent commitment to writing romances, but also
works through his conflicts—"between social norms and imperatives on
the one hand, private fulfillment and desires on the other"—that ultimately
led to expression in *Letter*. Within this context, the romance itself "figures
both as an autobiographical event and as an example of Hawthorne's art,"
the purpose of which is to express the creative life that is so frequently
stifled by authority and social institutions.   Romance in the novel is
symbolized by the beautiful, passionate Hester, "who speaks to
Dimmesdale and Hawthorne both when she says, 'What hast thou to do
with all these iron men, and their opinions?'"   Hester becomes
Hawthorne's purpose and guide, representing in eroticized form
"everything the Transcendentalists stand for."   Her transformation of the
transcendentalist's spirit that involves a mixture of "sex, passion,
eroticism, flesh, the earth" creates a less pure, less divine, more
ambiguous kind of romanticism (which incidentally explains why the sin
in the novel is sexual). "The Custom-House" is a version of *Letter* where
"the work is shown in its setting in the artist's life."   In the end, "we can
read *Letter* without reference to the preface; but the preface, like the
setting for a gem, is incomplete without *Letter*."

312   Huffman, Clifford Chalmers. "History in Hawthorne's 'Custom-House.'"
        *Clio: An Interdisciplinary Journal of Literature, History, and the
        Philosophy of History* 2 (1973): 161-169.

In "The Custom-House," Hawthorne indirectly establishes his hoped-for
connection between his persona and the reader by connecting the past with
the present.   This narrative strategy unites the reader with Hawthorne's
Puritan ancestors, and in the process associates Hawthorne with those
ancestors. Huffmann also illustrates Hawthorne's awareness of history by
comparing the narrator in "The Custom-House" with Sir Guyon in Book II
of Spenser's *The Faerie Queene* ("a closely parallel allegorical
narrative"), noting that both questing protagonists free themselves from
similar inabilities to embrace humanity and take meaningful action in life
by "exposing" themselves to history and recognizing the role cultural
continuity plays in human life.

313   Osborn, Robert, and Marijane Osborn.   "Another Look at an Old
        Tombstone." *New England Quarterly* 46 (1973): 278-279.

Although "R. B. Jenkins [in 292] rightly corrects the misreading of those who have imagined the actual wording as well as the device of the A to have been carved on the tombstone," he is mistaken in identifying Sir Walter Scott's *Waverly* as the motto's source. Robert Louis Brant (in 73) pointed out that the motto is actually based upon the last line of Marvell's poem, "The Unfortunate Lover" ("In a Field Sable a Lover Gules"). Brant did not go the extra mile, however, to consider Hawthorne's use of the quotation in the context of Marvell's poem, "where the heraldic symbol is an ironic reduction." Just as Marvell's unfortunate lover transcends the ephemeral and historical "To make impression upon Time," so "Hawthorne's letter survives its specific temporal connotations [. . .] to become an ambivalent title, a 'mystic symbol.'"

314   Swann, Charles. "Hawthorne: History Versus Romance." *Journal of American Studies* 7 (1973): 153-170.

Criticism that stresses the non-realistic romance form as dominating nineteenth-century American fiction (such as that by Charles Feidelson, Jr. [21], R. W. B. Lewis [37], Richard Chase [55], Leslie A. Fiedler [89], Daniel Hoffman [106], and Joel Porte [238]) "makes for a false and unbalanced response to much American literature." Swann offers *Letter* as proof that such critics distort and limit literary history, and he scoffs at their assumption that American culture lacks a past and that our Democratic society has no awareness of class. He takes Joel Porte's cue, that "without Hawthorne there could be no firm theory of American romance," and shows how the critical orthodoxy is mistaken—at least in Hawthorne's case. Far from being a symbolist or allegorical novel, *Letter* is a critical examination of "symbolic modes of perception." In fact, "Hawthorne criticizes Romantic claims of a self-assertive love by placing those claims against the idea of a whole society"; Hester returns to New England in the end because she, too, "chooses reality over symbol" and gives "primacy to the historical and social life of man." Though he employs elements of the Romance form, the novel is political, deriving its meaning and structures from the world of history, being most concerned with "the problems of man in society and his existence in history." "The Custom-House" is direct proof of Hawthorne's stress on this interconnectedness, since it does not permit the novel to "float free" and so roots it firmly in concrete social, historical, and psychological contexts. Swann offers the additional view that it is wrong to try to identify whom the novel "belongs" to, Hester or Dimmesdale, since its central meaning "can only be embodied in a group." [For more on Hawthorne's rejection of symbolic modes of perception, see Swann's later essay (651).]

315   Warren, Robert Penn.   "Hawthorne Revisited: Some Remarks on Hellfiredness." *Sewanee Review* 81 (1973): 95-111.

The "thematic tension" in *Letter* is derived from Hawthorne's insistence on intellectualizing emotion in order both to reveal and conceal. As a way of broaching a discussion of the ironic contrasts that abound in the novel, Warren pays close attention to form and structure, both of which may be seen to function as an "expression of emotion and meaning" revealing that Hawthorne's true concern in this work—and in his fiction at large—lies in "the tension between the demands of spirit and those of nature." The perpetual tension between flesh and spirit, "the essence of life," necessitates "the pitiful instances of waste, the irremediable askewness of life which the story, taken as a whole, delineates."

1974

Essays and Studies in Books

316   Sastry, L. S. R. Krishna. "The Dark is Light Enough: Hawthorne's *The Scarlet Letter*." *Indian Studies in American Fiction*. Eds. M. K. Naik, S. K. Desai, and S. Mokashi-Punekar. Delhi: Macmillan India, 1974. 1-15.

The majority of the essay reprises old ideas (considering the oft-discussed pre-1850 works by Hawthorne that contained the germinal ideas for *Letter*, the nineteenth-century romance mode of writing, and the novel's structure), but Sastry also suggests that although Hester (the fair Puritan) and Chillingworth (the black Puritan) both conform to established conventions of New England romance, "it is in the conception of the hero, Arthur Dimmesdale, that Hawthorne [introduces] the element of 'structured ambiguity.'" Dimmesdale is actually a curious blend of Hester and Chillingworth, and the fact that his "moral striving" and "spiritual grandeur" lead to a tragic death of "triumphant transcendence" lends some light to the dark tale. [See John C. Stubbs (227 and 251) for a very similar argument.]

317   Stone, Edward. "Other 'Desert Places': Frost and Hawthorne." *Frost: Centennial Essays*. Eds. Jac L. Tharpe and Peggy Prenshaw. Jackson: U of Mississippi P, 1974. 275-287.

Robert Frost appropriated the title of his poem "Desert Places" from a passage in *Letter* that describes Hester's dangerous state of mind after suffering under "society-inflicted ostracism" and "self-inflicted seclusion." Frost's situation in the poem actually bears a striking similarity to Hester Prynne's, because both figures are "spiritual outcasts nursing in private a view that separates them from society." The forest in both novel and poem serves to create and hide an inner rebellion of mind and heart against orthodoxy, creating a "heresy" that is the natural outgrowth of loneliness. [See 171 for another essay on *Letter* and Frost's "Desert Places."]

Journal Essays and Notes

318   Doherty, Joseph F. "Hawthorne's Communal Paradigm: The American Novel Reconsidered." *Genre* 7 (1974): 30-53.

Argues that discussions of American fiction tend to underscore the importance of those novels that refuse the "apocalyptic-antinomian" impulse, examining *Letter* as one such work that defies the typical archetypal American hero's refusal of social responsibility, compromise, and confinement. Committed instead to the interests of "community building" (insisting from the outset that "individual identities are possible only within the boundaried conditions of social relationships necessarily requiring curtailment of the self and an at least provisional commitment to the social realm"), the novel in fact serves as "the exemplum of an entire constellation of later works" that follow his example in this sympathetic study of "the costs, compromises, necessities, and consolations attached to the *agon* of *communitas*." As a paradigmatic American work that encouraged an entire literary moment geared toward sociality, *Letter* was groundbreaking. For Hawthorne, truly human identities are only possible to the extent that "Hester, Dimmesdale, Pearl, and even Chillingworth confront the inescapability of Boston and embrace the necessity of interdependent relationships"—converting by novel's end "a hostile and alienated Puritan crowd" into "a community built on genuine solidarity."

319   Estrin, Mark W. "'Triumphant Ignominy': *The Scarlet Letter* on Screen." *Literature/Film Quarterly* 2 (1974): 110-122.*

Since *Letter* practically begs for cinematic representation—with so many scenes resembling tableaux or static pictures—it comes as no surprise that the 1926 silent film version of *Letter* by Victor Sjöström presents a powerful recreation of Hawthorne's story through its satisfying series of "static moments photographed out of time, without dialogue." Despite several "hauntingly beautiful" scenes and an "odd" faithfulness to Hawthorne's "exquisite visual sense," the screen version unfortunately allows Hollywood melodrama to replace Hawthorne's emphasis on the concealment of emotion as well as his idea of the Romance. Most noticeable is the fact that the relationship of Hester and Dimmesdale often gets reduced to conventional "boy-meets-girl" status. Several other aspects of the film are shaped by "similar exigencies of formula." Each of the main characters, for instance, is flattened into a one-dimensional, melodramatic figure (Hester into a cream puff, Dimmesdale into a viril but rejected hero, and Chillingworth into a vengeance-seeking demon), while the Puritans themselves are reduced, in their supporting roles, to caricature. Overall, the film marks a significant event in our cinematic past, but it "misses the mark" since Hester's and Dimmesdale's actions, which are intended to be seen as "growing out of Puritan culture and its moral outlook," are "romanticized as the antithesis of a vicious and silly society."

*An abridged and slightly revised version of this article appears under the title "'Triumphant Ignominy' on the Screen" in *The Classic American Novel and the Movies* (Ed. Gerald Peary and Roger Shatzkin. New York: Frederick Ungar Publishing, 1977. 20-29.)

320   Greenwood, Douglas. "The Heraldic Device in *The Scarlet Letter*: Hawthorne's Symbolic Use of the Past." *American Literature* 46 (1974): 207-210.

Agreeing with R. B. Jenkins's interpretation (in 292) that the final sentence of the novel, "On a Field, Sable, the Letter A, Gules," is only the narrator's description of the heraldic device itself and not an epitaph (yet faulting Jenkins for erroneously and "simply careless[ly]" citing Richard Harter Fogle as one of several critics who have made such a mistake in interpreting Hawthorne's last sentence of the novel), Greeenwood nonetheless takes issue with one of Jenkins's assumptions about the heraldic device's ability to render its own appropriate motto—since it is only a hypothetical, learned "herald's *wording*" that might serve as a motto. Like Jenkins, many other critics have "baffling[ly]" misinterpreted Hawthorne's "clear" prose. From a purely heraldic standpoint, there is no ambiguity: "'field' [is] the heraldic term for 'shield,' 'sable' the graphic representation for black, and 'gules' the term for red." On the tombstone is engraved a shield upon which the letter "A" sets. Hester and Dimmesdale's own bitterly-earned coat of arms, as well as the adult Pearl's new coat of arms that appear on seals in letters to her mother, speak to "pride, vanity, and atonement," and "seem to point to the 'moral' of *Letter*: we are all tainted by sin, but redemption is possible."

321   Irwin, John T. "The Symbol of the Hieroglyphics in the American Renaissance." *American Quarterly* 26 (1974): 103-126.*

Popular and academic interest in Egyptian antiquities in the nineteenth century naturally filtered into the writing of American Renaissance authors, especially after famous reports that Jean François Champollion single-handedly deciphered Egyptian hieroglyphic writing. Champollion's triumph provided Ralph Waldo Emerson, Henry David Thoreau, Hawthorne, and Herman Melville "with a metaphor which they could use to examine the symbolic process from a variety of viewpoints." But whereas Emerson and Thoreau had no trouble claiming the transparency of natural signs to reveal the divine and mysterious, Hawthorne (in *Letter*) and Melville (in *Moby-Dick*) maintained the essentially undecipherable character of the hieroglyph. To their way of thinking, "the enigmatic, ambiguous character of the hieroglyph was its very significance," and man—in any historical moment—could project any number of possible interpretations and values to the emblem. Thus in *Letter* (in which the importance of hieroglyphics cannot be overestimated), the very point is *not* to assign one true meaning to Hester's insignia, but rather to present "a host of possible meanings from which to choose." Hawthorne also shrouds the details of Pearl's ultimate fate from the reader because she, as the "living hieroglyphic," must remain ambiguous. Further, the fact that Hawthorne (1) sets the novel in the seventeenth century, (2) ostensibly maintains that it is written in the eighteenth century, and (3) "edits" it in the nineteenth century implies his belief in the relativity of truth to one person's historical perspective (and may even be Hawthorne's way of scoffing at the sensational news accounts surrounding Champollion's exclusive cracking of the elusive code, since they deny hundreds of years of prior interpretations of the Rosetta stone that Champollion certainly would have researched and relied upon prior to making his discovery). [See Viola's Sachs in 404 for another essay that addresses America's cultural obsession with Egyptology and hieroglyphics.]

*Irwin expands his treatment of Hawthorne and Melville in his book-length study, *American Hieroglyphics: The Symbol of the Egyptian Hieroglyphics in the American Renaissance* (389).

322 Lefcowitz, Allan. "Apologia Pro Roger Prynne: A Psychological Study." *Literature and Psychology* 24 (1974): 34-44.

In part an elaboration of Frederick Crews's observation (in 182) that Chillingworth cannot, in all fairness, be reduced to the personification of evil when his motive for revenge hinges upon naturalistic and psychological impulses, Lefcowitz argues two specific points in this Freudian analysis: first, allegorical readings of Chillingworth deny his complex and realistic character, and second, Chillingworth's pathological jealousy stems from an unresolved Oedipal conflict. Chillingworth is not so much caught up in a romantic tragedy as in a "complex domestic tragedy," the logical outgrowth of submerged childhood insecurities about his physical impairment. That Hester's and Dimmesdale's judgments about his diabolical nature are actually projected from their own self-serving, guilty consciences lend credence to this reading, as do the narrator's hyperbolic and ambivalent estimates of the "fiendish" Chillingworth. The story adds further doubt to Chillingworth's evil nature in both the narrator's suggestion that the character is a victim of his own "uncontrollable compulsion[s]" and in Chillingworth's curious decision to leave Pearl heiress to his considerable fortune. Lefcowitz concludes that the "raw psychological" idea for Chillingworth's character had its roots in Hawthorne's own past, since, like Hawthorne—who suffered a serious debilitating foot injury in his childhood—Chillingworth "developed intellectual potency as a sublimation for his lack of physical potency."

323   Lesser, M. X. "Dimmesdale's Wordless Sermon." *American Notes and Queries* 12 (1974): 93-94.

Suggests a "historically authentic" basis for Dimmesdale's indistinguishable or "wordless" Election-Day sermon. The reason Hester only hears its sounds and cannot make out its meaning—and, more relevant, the reason that Hawthorne does not offer any text of the sermon to his readers—may be because no Election-Day sermon dating around the period of the novel's setting (1642-1649) exists, having never been printed. The earliest Election-Day sermon extant was delivered by John Norton in 1661 and published at Cambridge in 1664.

324   May, Charles E. "Pearl as Christ and Antichrist." *American Transcendental Quarterly* 24 Supplement 1 (1974): 8-11.

Although Hawthorne explores the Christ/Anti-Christ conflict in "Young Goodman Brown" and "The May-Pole of Merry Mount," he examines it in more detail in *Letter*, where the "initial image of the Madonna and Child establishes a motif central to the 'power of blackness' which pervades the novel. For although Pearl is never again referred to as the Son of God, the constant reference as the Daughter of Satan picks up the image and inverts it." Pearl is seen by the Puritans as the Antichrist, the child of Satan, but she actually "functions as a Christ child who promises, yet is ultimately prevented from fulfilling, the hope of a 'startling redemption' from the Puritan milieu; she challenges conventional Puritan moral and social values until stifled by Dimmesdale's reassertion of those values at the end." Hawthorne only hints at Pearl's foiled potential as a prophetess in the novel's conclusion, implying that "such a prophet of freedom must be crucified," or in her case, "be humanized into the controlled world of Church and State."

325   Smith, Julian. "Hester, Sweet Hester Prynne—*The Scarlet Letter* in the
        Movie Market Place." *Literature/Film Quarterly* 2 (1974): 99-109.

Victor Sjöström's 1926 film version of *Letter* sterilized and sweetened
Hawthorne's bitter vision so that "it should in no way give offense to any
group strong enough to affect its commercial success." Thus Hawthorne's
story becomes a "commercially exploitable property" and cultural artifact
of the 1920s that reflects the likes and dislikes of the "wholesome" movie-
going masses—making the first half of the picture "cheerful and sunny to
hold off the inevitable darkness" and the second, darker half "crammed
with gratuitous comic relief." But one should keep in mind that, although
the Hollywood adaptation barely resembles Hawthorne's original and the
film's historically inaccurate set design is "ridiculous," the film is
nonetheless "a work of no small genius." It was, after all, designed to turn
a profit for MGM. Hawthorne himself was just as concerned with
economic considerations when he shaped the novel, perhaps setting the
opening scene in the market place as "a covert reminder that all important
ideas, attitudes, and even personal relationships in America must stand the
test of the market."

326   Ward, J. A. "Self-Revelation in *The Scarlet Letter*." *Rice University
        Studies* 61.1 (1974): 141-150.

Considers *Letter* an extension of the "various public-private antitheses
dealt with in the preface," and argues that Dimmesdale's struggle to
confess his part in the adultery "provides the essential structure of the self-
revelation process" that defines the volume as a whole. His character
demonstrates the psychological necessity of openness on three planes of
being: "to the self, so that one has full self-awareness; to one's most
intimate relations; and to the community as a whole." Hawthorne
alternates these three planes of being throughout the novel, consistenly
illustrating acts in which intimacy and openness are frustrated. Of the
three primary characters, Dimmesdale has the fullest interior world,
although he achieves "honest relations" on all three levels of his personal
existence during his public confession. That he dies immediately after
reaching this height might be Hawthorne's way of suggesting that such an
ideal relation between private and public worlds is not truly possible on
earth.

1975

Essays and Studies in Books

327   Clark, C. E. Frazer, Jr. *"The Scarlet Letter*: A 'Fourteen-Mile-Long Story.'" *Nathaniel Hawthorne Journal 1975.* Ed. C. E. Frazer Clark, Jr. Englewood: Microcard Editions, 1975. 3-4.

Reproduces an unpublished letter from Hawthorne to an admiring autograph collector that shows how accommodating and generous Hawthorne's replies to his fans were, especially since they often contained allusions to whatever piece of fiction he was working on at the time. This one, dated February 4, 1850, to a "Miss L. Jewett of Boston," refers to the composition and publication of *Letter*: "I have been very much engaged in finishing a book—one end of which was already in press in Boston, while the other was still in my brain, here in Salem; whence it appears that the story (horrible to think) is no less than fourteen miles long!"

328   Crowley, J. Donald, ed. *Hawthorne: A Collection of Criticism.* New York: McGraw-Hill, 1975.

In this compilation of reprinted criticism which represents "recent critical efforts to define exactly the character of Hawthorne's achievement, the nature and causes of his failures, the basic assumptions of his art, and the conditions of his development" are two pieces on *Letter*: Marshall Van Deusen's "Narrative Tone in 'The Custom-House' and *The Scarlet Letter*" (196) and Richard Harter Fogle's "*The Scarlet Letter*" (15).

329   Janssen, James G. "Pride and Prophecy: The Final Irony of *The Scarlet Letter.*" *Nathaniel Hawthorne Journal 1975.* Ed. C. E. Frazer Clark, Jr. Englewood: Microcard Editions, 1975. 241-247.

Hawthorne employs "one final and crucial bit of irony" at the end of *Letter* in describing Hester as a self-effacing counselor of repressed women. Despite the appearance of her submission to Puritan authority and her protestations of unworthiness to pioneer a change that would "establish the whole relation between man and woman on a surer ground of mutual happiness," Hester "has indeed become the prophetess she denies she can be." What's more, "hers becomes the image of greatness in the act of denying the possibility for such stature." This self-renunciation can be read ironically when one explores earlier chapters for "the psychological dimension of Hester's penance and 'sisterhood,'" most notably her ambiguous reaction to her sin and lack of true penitence.

330   Owens, Louis. "Paulding's 'The Dumb Girl': A Source of *The Scarlet Letter.*" *Nathaniel Hawthorne Journal 1974.* Ed. C. E. Frazer Clark, Jr. Englewood: Microcard Editions, 1975. 240-249.

James K. Paulding's "The Dumb Girl," from an 1830 collection of tales entitled *The Chronicles of the City of Gotham*, may have been a significant source for *Letter*. Although similarities between the two have been briefly noted in the past (by Amos L. Herold in 1926 and Ralph M. Aderman in 1956), no critic has as yet pursued a real comparison—which should certainly be justified, since Hawthorne professed admiration for Paulding and specifically included the tale's plot summary in the *American Notebooks*. Of the numerous parallels between the two, the most noteworthy are similarities in setting, character (Hester and Phoebe Angevine are both dark beauties who are seduced and do not/cannot speak out to name their seducers, while the guilt-tortured Dimmesdale and Walter Avery are both accomplished, admired men in their respective communities), and climactic scenes (in which both pairs of lovers are united before the eyes of God with their illegitimate children). Even "The Custom-House" shows resemblance to Paulding's introduction to "The Dumb Girl," called "Memoir of the Unknown Author," in which the author denies having written the tales and insists that he purchased them in a public auction. In summary, "Paulding's investigation into the psychology of his time, the phenomenon of guilt and penance (or crime and punishment), and the function of society as a tool for social punishment, all predate and prefigure Hawthorne's major work."

331   Scheuermann, Mona. "Outside the Human Circle: Views from Hawthorne and Godwin." *Nathaniel Hawthorne Journal 1975*. Ed. C. E. Frazer Clark, Jr. Englewood: Microcard Editions, 1975. 182-191.

Notes "similarities of psychological structuring" in *Letter* and William Godwin's *Caleb Williams* (1793). Both authors shared dark visions that included a concern with the "psychology of alienation" that can best be revealed by comparing the parallel relationships of Falkland/Caleb and Dimmesdale/Chillingworth. "Both Godwin and Hawthorne focus on the situation which arises when an individual with [. . .] a secret is preyed upon by someone who senses his vulnerability and his need to communicate." It is "Hawthorne's treatment of that secret, and of the vulnerability it forces on the bearer of the secret" that "owes so much to Godwin's treatment of the same theme in *Caleb Williams*.

332   Tuerk, Richard. "'An Exceedingly Pleasant Mention': *The Scarlet Letter* and *Holden's Dollar Magazine*." *Nathaniel Hawthorne Journal 1974*. Ed. C. E. Frazer Clark, Jr. Englewood: Microcard Editions, 1975. 209-230.

Hawthorne's grateful reference to Cornelius Matthews (in a letter that Hawthorne wrote to Evert A. Duychinck) as the author of an anonymous, "exceedingly pleasant mention" of *Letter* in *Holden's Dollar Magazine* is inaccurate. "Irrefutable evidence" suggests that the author of the anonymous, favorable review that appears in the June 5, 1850, issue of *Dollar Magazine* is in fact the Rev. Henry Giles. A slightly revised version of the unsigned essay later appeared in a book by Giles entitled *Illustrations of Genius Magazine* (although Giles makes no mention of the earlier printing). Tuerk offers as further proof a collation table between the two texts, as well as a reprint of the entire review. "The reviewer's recognition that [*Letter*] is a tightly unified whole and that the characters must be judged in the context of that whole anticipates many of the tenets of New Criticism." The nineteenth-century review further anticipates modern studies in its refusal to judge the sins of Hester and Dimmesdale (since we all have the potential to sin but not always the temptation) and in its emphasis on *Letter*'s profound social implications. [For another essay on the reviews of *Letter* that appeared in *Holden's Dollar Magazine*, see Daniel Barnes (310).]

Journal Essays and Notes

333   Arora, V. N. "The Archetypal Pattern of Individuation in Hawthorne's *The Scarlet Letter*." *Panjab University Research Bulletin* 6 (1975): 19-23.*

Traces "the perennial struggle between two Jungian archetypes, the persona and the shadow, for the domination of the ego" in *Letter*. Hawthorne dramatizes this conflict between persona (the "socially accepted and socially imposed mask behind which dwells the true ego") and shadow (the "rejected and usually imprisoned set of desires, emotions, and attitudes") for the possession of the ego in all three of his main characters, showing that excessive or exclusive association with the persona at the expense of the shadow poses a risk of "disintegration of the personality." Because Dimmesdale identifies too closely with his public persona, denying his shadow until the very end when the persona becomes weak enough to let the ego recognize the shadow, his reconciliation of the two costs him his life. Chillingworth also has difficulty reconciling his persona and shadow, but his shadow wins out as he is steadily transformed into a fiend. Hester is remarkable for her sustained and "delicate balance" between persona and shadow, but she eventually subdues her shadow, domesticating it.

*This essay was reprinted under the new title "Archetypal Approach to Literature: An Analysis of Hawthorne's *The Scarlet Letter*" in *Twentieth-Century American Criticism: Interdisciplinary Approaches* (Ed. Rajnath. New Delhi: Arnold-Heinemann Publishers, 1977. 256-262).

334   Autrey, Max L. "A Source for Roger Chillingworth." *American Transcendental Quarterly* 26 (1975): 24-26.

The immensely popular "penny-dreadful" attributed to James Malcolm Rymer, *Varney the Vampire: or, The Feast of Blood* (1847), most likely furnished Hawthorne with one of his sources for Chillingworth's character. In addition to providing the specific surname of "Chillingworth," Rymer's novel also contains specific personality traits (an intellectualism developed late in life that turns into an diabolical interest in the black arts), plot development (in that Dr. Chillingworth observes and secretly persecutes his patient Sir Francis Varney), and themes (involving the dangers of over-intellectualism and the resulting imbalance that comes from rejecting the spiritual side of humanity) that supplied Hawthorne with ideas for creating Roger Chillingworth.

335   Brumm, Ursula. "Hawthorne's 'The Custom-House' and the Problem of Point of View in Historical Fiction." *Anglica* 93 (1975): 391-412.

Adds to recent symbolist, structuralist, and contextualist assessments by such critics as Charles Feidelson, Jr., (21), Charles R. O'Donnell (100), Sam Baskett (111), Dan McCall (211), and Marshall Van Deusen (196) who—in the minority—attempt to establish a connection between "The Custom-House" and the novel. Their approaches all mistakenly assume an "organic unity" linking the two that a "historicist" approach does not. "The Custom-House" exists within a literary tradition that draws upon and blends four models: the widespread tradition of prefaces and autobiographical sketches, the framing techniques and strong national impulse of Scott's historical novels, the tradition of the English essay (and more specifically the mode of characterization in the essays of Charles Lamb), and the "acute and troubled sense of American history" that stemmed from profound, defining hardships in the late seventeenth century and created a distinct American consciousness. Taken all together, these blended forms initiate a new kind of genre—preface, frame, essay, sketch, tale, and discourse—all rolled into one. "The Custom-House" and the romance are not bound by organic unity but by "a calculated disparity" in the narrator's disjunctive roles as fictive romancer on the one hand and historian on the other. "The Custom-House" therefore becomes a vehicle for Hawthorne's "historical concern," establishing "a perspective on history which he may have found impossible to integrate into the novel's narrative point of view."

336   Cox, James M. "*The Scarlet Letter*: Through the Old Manse and the Custom House." *Virginia Quarterly Review* 51 (1975): 432-447.

Approaches *Letter* by way of examining the prefaces "The Old Manse" and "The Custom-House," both of which address Hawthorne's life as "a man whose art caused his life—whose art, in other words, was the primary cause of the world he invented." Hawthorne "puts himself before his fiction" in these two prefaces by first distinguishing between Hawthorne's sketches (lighthearted and whimsical "portraits of the artist") and the more mature tales (haunting, gloomy, and obscure actions overseen by a sensitive, speculative narrator). In defining the nature of his artistic accomplishment and establishing an intimate but non-confessional tone in "The Old Manse," Hawthorne anticipates "The Custom-House," which is "in large measure a sequel to 'The Old Manse'" since it at last blends Hawthorne's competing creative forces and puts together his greatest sketch and his greatest tale. "The Custom-House" becomes, in a sense, the "original sin" of the novel that necessarily displaces the sin committed by Hester and Dimmesdale, because it discloses Hawthorne's own "original sin: the sin of art itself."

337   Hansen, Elaine Tuttle. "Ambiguity and the Narrator in *The Scarlet Letter*." *Journal of Narrative Technique* 5 (1975): 147-163.

Following in the footsteps of such critics as Hyatt H. Waggoner (38) and Roy Harvey Pearce (158) who consider the narrator's primary role in establishing an aura of ambiguity, Hansen stresses that he is a character in his own right, whose distinctive language of uncertainty is actually Hawthorne's "primary method of characterizing the narrator as artist, his struggles with his art, and their correspondence to the moral values supported by the novel." Hawthorne's consistent techniques of narrative equivocation illuminate the aesthetic and moral meaning of the romance and encourage the reader, who is wary of the narrator's "inconsistency of consciousness," to a "moral flexibility" and sympathetic perception of Hester that is otherwise denied her by the Puritan community.

338   Sanderlin, Reed. "Hawthorne's *Scarlet Letter*: A Study of the Meaning of Meaning." *Southern Humanities Review* 9 (1975): 145-157.

Concurring with the insights of Charles Feidelson, Jr., (in 21) that our contemporary concern with epistemology stems from the nineteenth century, Sanderlin nonetheless takes issue with Feidelson's assessment that the symbolic mode was the only way for several authors to perceive absolute reality. *Letter* is, in fact, "Hawthorne's exploration of the problems inherent in symbolism," or, more specifically, that *Letter* is an examination of "the processes at work within a culture when the traditionally defined and accepted symbols get challenged"—the "A," of course, being the novel's key symbol that traces out the ways symbols erode and change. Hawthorne's heavy reliance upon the techniques of ambiguity, combined with a similarly equivocal narrative point of view, works together with his characterizations of Hester, Dimmesdale, and Pearl to illustrate his point about the inevitability of the "breakdown of symbols chosen by society to embody the complex clustering of social, moral, and theological absolutes it believe[s] in." Hester "represents the redefinition of the letter itself," while Dimmesdale illustrates the fate of one stuck between belief and disbelief in symbols to shape his world, and Pearl "the physical manifestation of the symbol-destroying tendecies of both Hester and Dimmesdale."

1976

Essays and Studies in Books

339   Baym, Nina. "The Major Phase I, 1850." *The Shape of Hawthorne's Career*. Ithaca: Cornell UP, 1976. 123-151.*

Examines Hawthorne's literary development, finding that "in the movement from common sense to romanticism to—potentially—realism, Hawthorne epitomized the history of fiction in nineteenth-century America." Baym also takes issue with critics from the 1950s (such as Richard Harter Fogle [15], Roy R. Male [56], and Hyatt H. Waggoner [38]) who viewed Hawthorne—despite his obvious secular bent and distrust of doctrine—"anachronistically as a neo-orthodox writer controlled by a vision at once Christian and tragic." The apologetic, self-deprecating stance Hawthorne takes in early works disappears with *Letter*, marking his aggressive entrance into the romantic phase of his writing. The novel also marks the first time that Hawthorne portrays society as deliberately repressive and unresponsive to personal, private needs. He still argues the necessity of the individual to be integrated with society, but now he acknowledges that assimilation in a society that does not allow for individual expression comes only at great cost to the individual. Essentially, Hawthorne defines in this novel what will be "the focus of all four of his completed long romances: the conflict between passionate, self-assertive, and self-expressive inner drives and the repressing counterforces that exist in society and are also internalized within the self." This analysis of *Letter* focuses on the expressive and passionate nature of Hester and Dimmesdale's act (as opposed to the resulting punishment of it), since the novel itself originated as an imaginative expression of Hawthorne's own feelings of social defiance and discontent in an environment that suppressed passion and any subversions of authority.

*See 406 for a similar essay by Baym that examines Hawthorne's romanticism and critiques New Criticism.

340   Fryer, Judith. "Hester Prynne: The Dark Lady as 'Deviant.'" *The Faces of Eve: Women in the Nineteenth-Century American Novel.* New York: Oxford UP, 1976. 72-84.

Approaching the myth of America as the "New World Garden of Eden," Fryer complains that the "American Adam" has become a stock figure of "authentic" cultural interpretations of America, while the American Eve has been completely ignored—despite her being "a figure of primary importance to nineteenth-century thinkers, and especially to novelists." Hester is Hawthorne's most perfect Eve, combining sensuality with an "ethereal essence"—as well as suggesting "deviant" androgynous characteristics such as self-reliance, sturdy force, and courage that threaten the patriarchal community at large. Hawthorne's ambivalence and ambiguity about Hester actually reflect his attempt to work out his own ambiguous feelings about himself as artist, man, and member of the human community. While he needed the security of community, he simultaneously felt estranged—as alienated artist—from that community which defined "masculinity" in terms of success in the commercial world. Yet when Hawthorne is ultimately confronted with making a choice between alienated individualism and communal repression, his final sympathies are still ambiguous.

341   Stout, Janis P. "Hawthorne's Moral Geography." *Sodoms in Eden: The City in American Fiction Before 1860.* Westport: Greenwood, 1976. 91-119.

Pages 96-101 discuss the "multi-level tension between town and forest" in *Letter.* Despite the fact that there is no actual urban setting in the novel, there is a perceived tension between the Puritan village (which Hawthorne associated with the head) and the still alien forest wilderness (which he associated with the heart) that operates structurally in a pattern of flight and return.

Journal Essays and Notes

342   Geraldi, Robert. "Biblical and Religious Sources and Parallels in *The Scarlet Letter.*" *USF Language Quarterly* 15 (1976): 31-34.

Attributes Hawthorne's famous ambiguity and frequent "lack of determination" in *Letter* to his refusal to guess at the inscrutable ways of "divine will." Hawthorne was very interested in the Bible, having modeled *Letter* on four specific books: the Psalms, Proverbs, Ecclesiastes, and the Song of Songs. Geraldi bases his thesis on six points: the first "on the criticism that Hawthorne makes of the judgment of the Puritans," the second "on the importance of sin as a source of grace," the third "on the application of the 32nd Psalm" to create the characters of Hester and Dimmesdale, the fourth "on the admonishments against adultery which appear in the Book of Proverbs" (6:27-33), the fifth "on the transitory presentation of a pantheistic sensuality" in the forest chapter "A Flood of Sunshine" that is reminiscent of "some verses from the Song of Songs," and, the sixth "on the parodistic presentation of the passion of Christ" on Election Day and pervasive use of red and black symbolism in the novel. [Geraldi qualifies his argument near the end by saying, "Perhaps it may be said that these comparisons are not completely clear."]

1977

Essays and Studies in Books

343   Dauber, Kenneth. "A Typical Illusion." *Rediscovering Hawthorne.* Princeton: Princeton UP, 1977. 87-117.

Letter establishes "the psyche itself as a subjectivity bound to history." Because the psyche is historically determined, Hawthorne is unable to break free in *Letter* from the constrained, sterile world of "The Custom-House." Even though he writes the sketch to declare his independence from Salem and its oppressive, guilt-inspiring Puritan past, Hawthorne is yet inextricably bound to his culture and is unable to escape it even in the imaginative effort of his fictional tale. As a result, the novel—which is "remarkably unhinged" in its fragmented, dislocated presentation—becomes more Hawthorne's heritage than his creation, and his efforts to celebrate freedom and love become doomed by the coercive power of allegory, a genre which Dauber defines as a "typical illusion." Each main character's destiny is dictated by the coercive power of allegory as it enforces itself upon Hawthorne, and in his re-enactment of the Fortunate Fall, all attempts to realize the grand potentialities of his characters and to escape or reshape the allegory of sin and regeneration prove futile. Hawthorne ends up fully entrenched in the Puritan schema, finally reinforcing the alienation, isolation, and death of "The Custom-House" atmosphere.

344   Gilmore, Michael T. "Nathaniel Hawthorne: *The Scarlet Letter.*" *The Middle Way: Puritanism and Ideology in American Romantic Fiction.* New Brunswick: Rutgers UP, 1977. 70-114.

In his book, which focuses mainly on Hawthorne and Herman Melville but also offers brief treatment of Henry James, Gilmore "seeks to trace some of the connections between the Puritan mind of the colonial era and the great flowering of American literature of the nineteenth century," arguing that "the Puritan ideal of inner-worldly sainthood—the ideal of the middle way—decisively influenced the formal and thematic concerns of the prose romance." In addition to being romantic fiction writers, these authors were also social and political critics "who carried on the Puritan spirit and called attention to the gap between the promise of America and its actual achievement." Although Hawthorne was attracted to radical extremes, he was a firm advocate of moderation and the metaphysical "middle way," staking out an analogous position as romancer (with the concept of "neutral territory") that cherished "the spirit as well as the world and tempered justice with mercy and love." In the confessional "Custom-House" preface, Hawthorne presents himself not only as overcome with guilt and fear of punishment for sin but also as mired in an inability to write anything that would preserve him from extinction. Divinity intervenes to rescue him from damnation as a "tolerably good Surveyor of the Customs," and he achieves something of a spiritual rebirth when he is "terminated" from his position and can work on a worthwhile spiritual project that brings saving grace as it "seeks to exhume a buried world and to revive an allegiance that his countrymen have lost sight of in their pursuit of more worldly goals." In fact, Hawthorne's deepest commitment as an artist was to the ideal of inner-worldly sainthood, and so he measured the heroes of his romance against the Puritan standard of "living in the world without being of it." It is only "by publicly owning membership in the brotherhood of sin that the believing Christian can hope to attain the state of visible sainthood that Dimmesdale—and Hawthorne—achieve at the last." Even Hester finally exchanges the covenant of works for the covenant of grace, finding, again, like Hawthorne, a secular equivalent to the theological stance of the American Puritans.

345   Staal, Arie. *"The Scarlet Letter*: An Integration of Narrative Modes." *Hawthorne's Narrative Art*. New York: Revisionist Press, 1977. 78-96.

Claims to study two neglected areas in the field of literary criticism: the multi-faceted nature of foreshadowing and Hawthorne's skillful "rhetorical heightening and guiding of reader expectations." What gives *Letter* its celebrated "density and concentration" is Hawthorne's "incorporation and blending of a number of modes of foreshadowing." The short length of the novel "precluded too frequent a repetition of incidents to heighten anticipation, requiring instead a greater reliance upon characterization and philosophical necessity to guide reader expectations." "Anticipative techniques" such as plot patterning, conjecture, prediction, art objects, natural phenomena, and linguistic subtleties are employed throughout to foreshadow the outcome of the novel and to hint at the circumscribed options available to protagonists who are hopelessly bound "within a sphere of necessity."

Journal Essays and Notes

346   Gitenstein, Barbara. "The Seventh Commandment: Adultery as Barometer of Communal Disintegration: A Comparison of Nathaniel Hawthorne's *The Scarlet Letter* and Isaac Bashevis Singer's *The Destruction of Kreshev*." *Comparatist: Journal of the Southern Comparative Literature Association* 1 (1977): 16-22.

Establishes four superficial points of comparison between *Letter* and twentieth-century Yiddish novel *The Destruction of Kreshev* that involve similar points of view, settings (in towns that are both refuges from a moral wilderness), characters (parallels between both Hester/Lise as beautiful, exotic, outcast, and intellectually-minded adulteresses who tend "to speculate beyond the realms of propriety and safety" and their husbands Chillingworth/Shloimele, who are both "perverted by the over-intelletualization of life"), and structures. The two stories "share a great deal" in that they are both "tales of adultery which stress adultery as the barometer of communal decay"—with egotism and isolation having enhanced or allowed for sin in the first place.

347   Marks, Patricia. "'Red Letters' and 'Showers of Blood': Hawthorne's Debt to Increase Mather." *American Notes and Queries* 15 (1977): 100-105.

Postulates that Hawthorne got the idea for "the atmospheric phenomenon" that appears during Dimmesdale's midnight vigil (in chapter 12) from Increase Mather's *Kometographia: Or a Discourse Concerning Comets* (1683). This discourse, along with two other essays written by Mather ("Heaven's Alarm to the World" and "The Latter Sign"), was designed to protect the Puritan religious phenomenology surrounding meteors from naturalistic interpretations by the likes of Edmund Halley and Sir Isaac Newton. Although Charles Ryskamp has already shown (in 85) that Hawthorne used Caleb Snow's *The History of Boston* to verify "red and fiery" comets in the seventeenth-century New Engand night sky, Mather's works are much more specific in their description and discussion of comets as "prognosticks," as both causal factors and as indicators (the latter of which Dimmesdale's meteor classifies). While no proof exists that Hawthorne was familiar with *Kometographia*, the dedication to Mather's book states that comets have occasionally appeared as "*Red Letters*, Asterisms, or pointing Hands, to awaken unto a more heedful attention and serious consideration, the dead hearted sleeping and secure World of Mankind." At the very least, these parallels suggest that Hawthorne was quite familiar with Puritan superstitions surrounding comets—enough so that he was able to capture with remarkable accuracy the Puritan world view.

348   Newberry, Frederick. "Tradition and Disinheritance in *The Scarlet Letter*." *ESQ: A Journal of the American Renaissance* 23 (1977): 1-26.*

Asserting that *Letter* is "above all else [. . .] about history," Newberry shows that the novel contrasts the dominant forces of Puritanism ("severity, rigidity, intolerance, iconoclasm, militancy, and persecution") with the recessive, gentler forces of Puritanism associated with English ancestry ("sympathy, charity, gaiety, respect for tradition, and appreciation of art"). Hawthorne presents "the dominant and recessive dualism as an historical principle" in the novel and uses this tension between the mother country and its colony as a structuring device (which makes *Letter* "the only major American novel that concentrates directly on the seventeenth-century historical transition between the Old and New Worlds"). Further, Hawthorne takes up in *Letter* where he leaves off in "The Custom-House," "allying himself with an English ancestry whose aesthetic and spiritual traditions are antithetical to those of his [oppressively self-righteous] Puritan forebears and his [smug, materialistic] contemporaries." Hawthorne focuses specifically in the novel on a period of American and English history (1642-1649) when the dominant forces of Puritanism were in danger of "totally disinheriting themselves from the richest traditions of their past"—traditions symbolically represented in the characters of Hester, Pearl, and Dimmesdale (all of whom are surrounded with Old-World motifs, are embued with the recessive traits of Puritanism, and dramatize "the mitigating alternative to the Puritans' militancy, persecution, and iconoclasm which becomes their major legacies to New England"). It is no mistake that these figures "recede from American history—Hester with her gorgeous Renaissance-style artistry; Pearl, the symbol of that art; and Dimmesdale with his influential power of sympathy"—to make way for the harsher historic forces represented by Governor Bellingham and Endicott.

*See 539 for Newberry's slightly revised verison of this essay and a chapter on "The Custom-House."

349   Rackham, Jeff. "Hawthorne's Method in Moonlight Madness."
Publication of the Arkansas Philological Association 3.2 (1977): 47-52.

Troubled by critical readings of *House of the Seven Gables* that use a
convenient *Deus ex Machina* to explain away the "seemingly contrived"
happy ending, Rackham argues that attention to the structural and
symbolic importance of chapters 13 and 14—both of which clearly relate
to Hawthorne's aesthetic theory of Romance as described in "The Custom-
House"—easily resolves the novel's key difficulties. These scenes from
House of the Seven Gables (in the first of which Holgrave acts as a
"symbolic mirror" in his retelling of the Pyncheon family legend and in
the second of which the rising moon has a mesmerizing effect on both
Holgrave and Phoebe) are "the fulcrum of the novel" because they mimic
Hawthorne's description of the moonlit atmosphere needed for the
imagination to transcend the limits of surface reality, thus creating the
romantic ambiance that allows for the "possible" happy ending rather than
the "probable" tragic ending.

350   Stone, Edward. "Chillingworth and His 'Dark Necessity.'" *College
Literature* 4 (1977): 136-143.

Reasserts Austin Warren's assessment of *Letter* as "a literary exercise in
moral theology" (178) by way of refuting Martin Green's assertion (in
143) that Chillingworth's character does not dramatically develop in the
novel but emerges from the start as darkly fiendish. Chillingworth
changes a great deal (and can even be described as two people), since he
initially takes responsibility for his own mistakes and failures—when he
blames himself for Hester's fate in the prison—and later guiltlessly
defends his devilish actions to Hester as decreed by fate. Although the
narrator does not qualify Chillingworth's latter remark, the reader must
not mistakenly project Chillingworth's dogmatic fatalism onto Hawthorne,
who asserts everywhere in his fiction the primacy of the will to alter
events. The discrepancy in Chillingworth's thinking serves a purely
dramatic (not theological) purpose in the novel: "to show [Chillingworth]
as being both dishonest to his beliefs and to himself."

351   Thomas, Lloyd Spencer. "Scarlet Sundays: Updike vs. Hawthorne." *CEA
Critic* 39 (1977): 16-17.

In his "running travesty" of *Letter*, Updike's "clever burlesque" *A Month
of Sundays* (1975) "transforms the grave world of puritan Boston into a
contemporary vaudeville" that comments on contemporary morality. The
effect is a ludicrous diminution of Hawthorne's theme, as well as a very

subtle insight into the work of an American master: "Updike sees more comedy in Hawthorne than most literary critics usually allow him."

352   Wallace, Robert K. "A Probable Source for Dorothea and Casaubon: Hester and Chillingworth." *English Studies* 58 (1977): 23-25.

George Eliot possibly modeled two of her main characters in *Middlemarch* (1871-72) from *Letter*'s Hester and Chillingworth. "The striking parallels between Hester's and Dorothea's marriages, combined with George Eliot's admiration of Hawthorne and her re-reading of *Letter* in the year she began to write fiction [1857] [. . .], all point to Hester and her mis-shapen scholar as one of the ingredients which led George Eliot to create Dorothea and hers." Whereas Hawthorne only hints at the Prynne's unnatural marriage, however, Eliot fully develops the "folly" of Dorothea and Casaubon's.

1978

Books

353   Bradley, Sculley, Richmond Croom Beatty, E. Hudson Long, and Seymour [L.] Gross, eds. *The Scarlet Letter by Nathaniel Hawthorne: An Annotated Text, Backgrounds and Sources, Essays in Criticism.* 2nd edition. New York: W. W. Norton, 1978.* 439 pp.

Several changes have been made in this new edition (besides a few emendations to the text and some minor adjustments to the informational footnotes to the novel—deleting all of those that offer interpretation). To "The Scholar and the Sources" section are added excerpts from Ernest W. Baughman's "Public Confession and *The Scarlet Letter*" (204) and Michael J. Colacurcio's "Footsteps of Anne Hutchinson: The Context of *The Scarlet Letter*" (289). Instead of beginning the "Criticism" section with Henry James (as in the previous edition), Gross introduces it with earlier excerpts from five contemporary reviews by Evert A. Duychinck (ER1), E. P. Whipple (ER3), Henry F. Chorley (ER4), George B. Loring (ER7), and Arthur Cleveland Coxe (ER10). Also new to "Criticism" is a section on "The Custom-House" that includes four essays: Sam S. Baskett's "*The* (Complete) *Scarlet Letter*" (111), Marshall Van Deusen's "Narrative Tone in 'The Custom-House' and *The Scarlet Letter*" (196), David Stouck's "The Surveyor of 'The Custom-House': A Narrator for *The Scarlet Letter*" (278), and Nina Baym's "The Romantic *Malgré Lui*: Hawthorne in 'The Custom-House'" (311). Of the 20 remaining essays in criticism, ten of the original nineteen have been retained: Henry James's *Hawthorne* (EC15), W. C. Brownell's *American Prose Masters* (EC3), F.

O. Matthiessen's *American Renaissance* (EC20), Frederic I. Carpenter's "Scarlet A Minus" (EC4), Richard Harter Fogle's *Hawthorne's Fiction: The Light and the Dark* (15), Hyatt H. Waggoner's *Hawthorne: A Critical Study* (38), R. W. B. Lewis's *The American Adam* (37), Roy R. Male's *Hawthorne's Tragic Vision* (56), Seymour L. Gross's "'Solitude, and Love, and Anguish': The Tragic Design of *The Scarlet Letter*" (95), and Daniel Hoffman's *Form and Fable in American Fiction* (106). The following essays have been added: John C. Gerber's "Form and Content in *The Scarlet Letter*" (EC9), Darrel Abel's "Hawthorne's Hester" (16), Ernest Sandeen's "*The Scarlet Letter* as a Love Story" (135), Frederick Crews's *The Sins of the Fathers* (182), Charles Feidelson, Jr.,'s "*The Scarlet Letter*" (154), Leo B. Levy's "The Landscape Modes of *The Scarlet Letter*" (245), Joel Porte's *The Romance in America* (238), John C. Stubbs's *The Pursuit of Form* (251), Gabriel Josipovici's *The World and the Book* (264), and John E. Becker's *Hawthorne's Historical Allegory* (260). A selected bibliography (pp. 436-439) concludes the volume.

*For the first edition, see 102. For the third edition, see 557.

Essays and Studies in Books

354 McPherson, Hugo. "How Hot is *The Scarlet Letter?*" *Essays in Honor of Russel B. Nye.* Ed. Joseph Waldmeir. East Lansing: Michigan State UP, 1978. 141-150.

Critics have been "too long deceived [. . .] about this book," which is far more than an "account of sin, expiation, and forgiveness in the traditional Christian pattern" or a working out of the conflict between the head and the heart. *Letter* was very "hot," or racy, in its own time, and was actually Hawthorne's "major analysis of the problems of the American past, and his roles of sexy ladies and artistic men—problems which had a historic continuity from Hester and Arthur/Author in the seventeenth century to the "Custom House" world of the mid-nineteenth century, and on into the perverse era of twentieth-century America." Hawthorne apparently felt that his rebellious hero and heroine were out of place in their seventeenth-century New England and would have been outcasts in his time, as well. The scarlet "A" is not as hot as it used to be, McPherson concludes, noting from a sociological standpoint that, in modern times, blond women exert the most influential power in society, while men have generally "lost the sway they enjoyed in Puritan New England," allowing themselves to be manipulated.

184

355   Sims, Diana Mae. "Chillingworth's Clue in *The Scarlet Letter*."
        Nathaniel Hawthorne Journal 1976. Ed. C. E. Frazer Clark, Jr.
        Englewood: Information Handling Services, 1978. 292-293.

        Suggests that Chillingworth, upon his arrival in Boston, immediately and
        "astonishing[ly]" detects Dimmesdale as Hester's secret partner because
        Dimmesdale gives himself away when he, with hand on his heart,
        expresses gratitude and relief for Hester's "lone martyrdom"—an
        expression inconsistent with his position as minister to a Puritan
        community.

356   Smith, Henry Nash. "Hawthorne: The Politics of Romance." *Democracy
        and the Novel: Popular Resistance to Classic American Writers*. New
        York: Oxford UP, 1978. 16-34.

        Hawthorne was one of several nineteenth-century novelists who "collided"
        with the "solidity, the durability, the imperviousness of the secular faith or
        ideology lying at the base of American popular culture." Despite his
        desire to accommodate his readers, Hawthorne resisted the demand to
        represent the "cheerful surface of prosperity and contentment that was
        supposed to prevail in American society," and instead consistently
        challenged social institutions and the prevailing common-sense
        philosophy of the day by exploring the dark underside of the psyche and
        revealing "the truth of the human heart." Especially in *Letter*, Hawthorne
        investigates the concept of "perspectivism" by privileging the
        "truthfulness" of the inner world of private experience over the illusive
        outer world of institutions and observed behavior, suggesting that "the
        very idea of a solid, orderly universe existing independently of
        consciousness" is doubtful. To prove his point that the human mind can
        never truly discover the absolute truth about external reality but only hold
        an infinite series of partial views, Hawthorne frequently hinges the plot on
        both ontological and epistemological uncertainties and has his narrator
        often adopt different points of view throughout the novel. [For an essay
        that argues the opposite point—that Hawthorne was quite entrenched in
        the institutions of his day and had no interest whatever in challenging
        them—see Jonathan Arac (508).]

357   Stone, Edward. "Of Lambence and Hawthorne's Hell Fire." *Nathaniel
        Hawthorne Journal 1976*. Ed. C. E. Frazer Clark, Jr. Englewood:
        Information Handling Services, 1978. 196-204.

        Despite Hawthorne's insistence that *Letter* lacked any sunshiny light or
        levity (which too many critics have accepted at face value), the fact
        remains, as Anthony Trollope first suggested in the nineteenth century (in

EC33), that "warmth, whimsy—even wit makes its appearance" in the supposedly "hell-fired" novel that never departs from its "stern and somber aspect." Stone finds curious the absence of winter (to establish gloomy setting) in the novel, since, indeed, it is almost perpetually summer, and cites other instances where "lambent" fires light up the dark story with "testiness, amusement, acidity, [and] sarcasm," such as humorous intrusions from the imp-like Pearl and a specific reference in chapter ten ("The Leech and His Patient") where Dimmesdale has fallen asleep reading a book "of vast ability in the somniferous school of literature."

Journal Essays and Notes

358   Balakian, Anna. "' . . . and the pursuit of happiness': *The Scarlet Letter* and *A Spy in the House of Love*." *Mosaic* 11 (1978): 163-170.

Compares Anaïs Nin's *A Spy in the House of Love* (1959) with *Letter* not because both novels focus on the subject of adultery but because both address "the repercussions [that adultery] has or the questions its raises with respect to such issues as the nature of love, the nature of marriage, and most of all the problem of individual integrity." If the comparison between Hester and Sabina is made exclusively on the basis of sex and sin, "the gap between these two tales of adultery seems like millions of light years." But both heroines seek freedom and some sort of redemption—though the types of redemption differ, since each author subscribes to a different philosophy, Hawthorne to "essentialism" (which makes Hester's character static and sure of itself) and Nin to "existentialism" (which makes Sabina ever on a quest for self-discovery). Both female characters are cognizant of a "need for a fundamental revision of premises underlying the relationship between humans."

359   Bush, Clive. "The Circle and the Labyrinth: Vision and Speech in the 'hardly accomplished revolution' of Hawthorne's *The Scarlet Letter*." *Acta Literaria Academiae Scientiarum Hungaricae* 20 (1978): 29-51.

Not available for review.

360   Dunne, Michael. "Hawthorne, the Reader, and Hester Prynne." *Interpretations: Studies in Language and Literature* 10 (1978): 34-40.

Despite his sympathy for Hester, Hawthorne could not, in good conscience, allow her to run away with Dimmesdale and "get what she wants," because such a triumph would have gone againt his "conservative social [and moral] philosophy." Hawthorne initially sets up the reader to sympathize with Hester when she is compared favorably with the severe, morally inflexible Puritans; but as the novel goes on, and Hester's supposedly "positive" values are compared with the "negative" values of the Puritan society, the scales get tipped in the direction of the Puritans—because it is with them that Hawthorne shares an allegiance to moral and social order. Thus it is in the interest of securing the welfare of society that Hawthorne dooms Hester to return to Boston in the end—though out of his "old affection" for Hester, and for the affection he imagines his sympathetic readers will feel for her, he leaves her fate ambiguous.

361   Franzosa, John. "'The Custom-House,' *The Scarlet Letter*, and Hawthorne's Separation from Salem." *ESQ: A Journal of the American Renaissance* 24 (1978): 57-71.

A highly-perceptive, early review of *Letter* written by John Chapman in the Salem *Register* (March 21, 1850) "not only demonstrated the unity of ["The Custom-House"] and the narrative it introduces, but unwittingly identified the important psychological themes operating in *Letter*"— especially those themes that pertain to "dependence—nourishment, loss, and rejection" and that take priority, developmentally-speaking, over "more mature relationships between self and other" that thematically define the novel. Applying contemporary psychoanalytic theory to Hawthorne's themes of dependence and finding the source of those themes in Hawthorne's childhood and adult life, Franzosa argues that "the figure of maternity seems to provide the ground on which the drama is played out," a "particular type of maternal figure which embodies both masculine and feminine characteristics." Hawthorne's "fantasy of a 'man-like' or phallic mother" dominates *Letter*, stemming from Hawthorne's insecurities over and desire to reunite with his own absent father. Just as the phallic mother represents Hawthorne's denial of other losses— "whether mother, Salem, Custom House, or Elizabethan gaiety"—so "The Custom-House" and the romance itself (which is riddled with the linked themes of "possession and intrusion") represent Hawthorne's futile attempt to come to terms with those losses and the feelings of dependency that those lost relationships had fostered.

362   Moldenhauer, Joseph J. "'Bartleby' and 'The Custom House.'" *Delta English Studies* 7 (1978): 21-62.

In addition to modeling his characterization of Bartleby on the "craftily subversive Hawthorne, whose moody soul was attuned to universal blackness and bleakness," Melville adapted such elements from "The Custom-House" as "narrative manner, characterization, symbolism, and theme." Both works "confront the issue of authority and its paradoxes;

both dramatize the opposition between the lure of security and the risks of self-trust; both treat the conflict between public and private values; [and] both record the abeyance or loss of vital energies. The influence of place upon a sensitive spirit, the impediments to meaningful intercourse, and the vicissitudes of political appointment are other common thematic features in the two texts." Moldenhauer does not intend to prove that Hawthorne's sketch was necessarily Melville's source; the comparison is rather to show how both tales "mutually illuminate one another" and highlight interesting differences between the two authors, since "Hawthorne's tendency toward artistic closure and at least provisional faith contrasts vividly with Melville's open-ended literary structures and fascination with ambiguity."

363   Nissenbaum, Stephen. "The Firing of Nathaniel Hawthorne." *Essex Institute Historical Collections* 114 (1978): 57-86.

Presents a detailed study of the traumatic series of events and political circumstances that led to Hawthorne's embarrassing dismissal from his position at the Salem Custom House in 1849, concluding that "*Letter* itself, rather than "The Custom-House," is Hawthorne's autobiographical testament." Whereas Hawthorne clearly downplays his humiliation in "The Custom-House" by adopting the pose of the detached and nonchalant litterateur, he projects his anger and humiliation onto his protagonists in the novel—drawing several distinct parallels: (1) between his public dismissal and Hester's agonizing, ignominious ordeal in the opening scaffold scene (despite her "veil of composure"); (2) between his and her "fantastically embroidered flourishes" of artistry; (3) and between his own undisclosed complicity in the events surrounding his removal from office and Dimmesdale's cover up of guilt through the appearance of sanctity and the apparent sincerity of his powerful rhetoric. Nissenbaum even suggests a possible connection between Salem Whig Leader Charles Upham and Chillingworth, the latter of whom makes it his life's purpose in the novel "to bring about the destruction of a sensitive young man."

364   Pinsker, Sanford. "The Scaffold as Hinge: A Note on the Structure of *The Scarlet Letter*." *College Literature* 5 (1978): 144-145.

Hoping "to expand the implications" of Hawthorne's strategic placement of the scaffold scenes to lend symmetry to the novel's structure (as suggested most forcefully in the past by John C. Gerber [EC9] and G. Thomas Tanselle [138]), Pinsker argues that chapter 12 is not only *Letter*'s middle chapter but also "its structural hinge." As such, this chapter on Dimmesdale's midnight vigil divides the novel in such a way that chapters 13 through 24 "are roughly mirror images" of chapters one through 12. The schema is not perfect—and hence the word "roughly" to describe the parallelism—but it does afford "a deeper appreciation of the way the novel's structure folds back upon itself."

365   Stein, William Bysshe. "The Rhetoric of 'P. P.' in *The Scarlet Letter*." *ATQ* 39 (1978): 281-299.

Asserts that what links "The Custom-House" and the novel is "flippant, nonsensical, and irreverent" verbal trickery that dramatizes—somewhere between "jest and earnest"—the discrepancy between illusion and reality, especially in terms of the arbitrary nature of language. This "entwined focus supplies the answer to [Hawthorne's] multiple interpretation of events, a strategy of nonsense devised to ridicule complacent formulas of logic, theological, philosophical, scientific, or commonsensical. So considered, the language of his fiction interprets only itself, obedient to the wayward laws of the imagination." Hawthorne borrows the persona of Alexander Pope's "famous P. P. Clerk of this Parish" in order to enact his self-parody in the person of surveyor Jonathan Pue, and "to write a burlesque on the naïve conception of the creative act." The irony of Hawthorne's parody on "hack craftsmanship" in both "The Custom-House" and *Letter* is that Hawthorne himself anticipated that his contemporaries would be too gullible and stupid to recognize the volume's reliance upon "rhetorical masquerade"—that its very "syntax, reference, and idiom idiotically unite to produce a miscarriage of meaning even more idiotic than the maudlin gesture of didacticism on the surface level."

366   Weldon, Roberta. "From 'The Old Manse' to 'The Custom-House': The Growth of the Artist's Mind." *Texas Studies in Literature and Language* 20 (1978): 36-47.

"The Old Manse" and "The Custom-House" frame significant years for Hawthorne that "provide touchstones for measuring the growth of the artist's mind." Parallels in the narrative voice, tone, motifs, and themes suggest that Hawthorne wanted in "The Custom-House" to give his readers "a broader perspective to his more distant past—his days at the Old Manse—and to respond to the [more naïve, unsophisticated, yet happier] point of view expressed in the earlier essay."

1979

Books

367   Roth, Margaret Ann, ed. *A Teacher's Guide to The Scarlet Letter: A Four-Part Television Drama Produced by WGBH Boston.* Boston: WGBH Educational Foundation, 1979. 62 pp.

Intended for teachers whose students will be reading *Letter* in conjunction with watching the supplemental four-hour television version produced by WGBH Boston in 1979, this professionally prepared guide (with ample photographs and illustrations) has several helpful features divided into sections: "The Novel and the Program," "How to Use This Guide," "The Errand of the Early Puritans," "Life in Puritan New England," "Nathaniel Hawthorne," "The Making of *Letter*," and comments by Producer-Director Rick Hauser. Each of the episodes has a corresponding critical synopsis of the organization, emphasis, techniques, and central issues of that segment, and "following each synopsis are discussion questions and a sample exercise involving a comparison of the novel and the television dramatization." Also included is the entire shooting script for the television adaptation.

Essays and Studies in Books

368   Berryman, Charles. "Puritan Romance: Nathaniel Hawthorne." *From Wilderness to Wasteland: The Trial of the Puritan God in the American Imagination.* Port Washington: Kennikat Press, 1979. 121-145.

Provides a general discussion of Hawthorne's "tragic literature" as a critique of Puritan theology, and focuses a good deal on *Letter* (pp. 121-123, 126-129, 139-145), which alone among Hawthorne's works represents the "religious crossroads" of the American Renaissance. "Hawthorne brought to American literature a critical and psychological fascination with the very roots of religious behavior. He provided a skeptical and tragic analysis of the forbidden impulses, the secret guilts, the tormented pleasures of both the Puritan and Transcendental faiths." *Letter* is truly tragic when one sees that it represents two points of view simultaneously, the Puritan and transcendental, which are not only religious opposites but also tragically inseparable. (Berryman notes incidentally that "Puritan-minded" critics tend to side with Dimmesdale and praise his ultimate rejection of Hester, while "transcendental-minded" critics sympathize with Hester and blame her intolerant Puritan society for persecuting a heroine of nature.) Hester, whose conflicted feelings represent "in dramatic form the crossroads of the [nineteenth-century] religious imagination," is truly divided between these two sensibilities and therefore the only character to achieve full tragic stature in the novel.

369   Gollin, Rita K. "The Mirror and the Labyrinth: *The Scarlet Letter*." *Nathaniel Hawthorne and the Truth of Dreams.* Baton Rouge: Louisiana State UP, 1979. 140-151.

This sub-chapter from Gollin's discussion of the narrative function of "dreams and reverie" in Hawthorne's novels ("The Romances," pp. 140-213) contends that Hester's and Dimmesdale's introspective and "psychologically necessary" daydreams are "integral" to an understanding of their characters, as well as to the novel's exploration of the causes and consequences of sin. Hester's daydream occurs during the initial scaffold scene where "she takes inner refuge from her public shame" within the "mirror" of her imagination and discovers her private resources of strength, while Dimmesdale's more abstract, tormented reverie takes place in the privacy of his study and reveals his "inner mortification" just before he wanders into the "midnight travesty of public shame on the scaffold." Dimmesdale is paralyzed, "too cowardly to move forward into an inner forest like Hester's," and unable to distinguish between reality and fantasy until he wakes from his "dreamlike confusion" at the end to achieve "spiritual exaltation." Hester, on the other hand, whose inner life is more absorbing than her outer experience, finally "put[s] away" her escapist "mirror of self" after Dimmesdale's death and lives to serve others.

370   Porte, Joel. Introduction. "Viewing *The Scarlet Letter*." *The Scarlet Letter*. By Nathaniel Hawthorne. 1850. New York: Dell, 1979. 7-20.

Included in this paperback edition, as the introduction discusses, is an eight-page black-and-white photographic insert from the WGBH Boston television production of *Letter* that aired in April of1979. This particular edition (which I was unable to acquire) attests to the popular and media attention given the novel following the PBS telecast.

371   Pryse, Marjorie. "*The Scarlet Letter*: Social Stigma and Art." *The Mark and the Knowledge: Social Stigma and Art*. Columbus: Ohio State UP, 1979. 15-48.

Characterizing American literature as "the fiction of social and metaphysical isolation," Pryse focuses in this book on several pieces (Hawthorne's *Letter*, Herman Melville's *Moby-Dick*, William Faulkner's *Light in August*, and Ralph Ellison's *Invisible Man*) that share a common concern with social stigma. In Hawthorne's portrayal of the conflict between the individual and community in *Letter*, his "marked" character, Hester Prynne, transcends the social and metaphysical isolation imposed upon her by the Puritan community. Her external conflict compares throughout the novel with Dimmesdale's internal conflict, which stems from his spiritual uneasiness and feelings of "social discreditability." Hawthorne's comparison of the suffering endured by both characters calls attention to the pervasive metaphysical insecurity among the Puritans that inspired an intolerance of difference, paradox, or ambiguity—and so led to their impulse to "mark" or label individuals in the face of uncertainty. Although the stigma of the scarlet letter is originally intended to show God's will by making the "nonmanifest manifest" and to strengthen the community's social identity by excluding the "offender" (Hester), it eventually and ironically reveals the dangers of relying on the revealed meaning of marks and signs, as well as shows the Puritans' "absolute mortal inability to know what has been preordained." In the end, to see the difference between viewing the novel as a study of "marking" rather than as a study of isolation from society (the more traditional approach) is to see Hawthorne's art not simply as historical romance but as an epistemological process in and of itself.

372   Quilligan, Maureen. "The Text: Allegorical Action as Commentary on a Threshold Text." *The Language of Allegory: Defining the Genre.* Ithaca: Cornell UP, 1979. 51-64.

Questions the textual nature of allegorical narrative in three works, *Piers Plowman, Letter* (pp. 51-58), and *The Fairie Queene*, to argue that the "classic" allegorical form is "both threshold text and commentary." To recognize, for instance, that allegory is not just narrative but critical commentary as well is "to see at once the overall structure of *The Scarlet Letter.*" When the novel is read as a self-consciously metaphorical and allegorical narrative that continually refers back to the meaning of the "moral blossom" in the opening "threshold" scene (in which Hester emerges from the prison and stands next to the wild rosebush), it can be seen to offer Hawthorne's critical comment on the problem of interpretation itself, the real subject of his story. When Pearl remarks that her life began when she was plucked from the rosebush, she is associated with the "moral blossom" of the rosebush as well as with the letter and thus "the letter itself becomes the moral blossom, and all the various interpretations of it offered throughout the book (of which Pearl is only one) become the real 'moral' of the story."

373   Ryken, Leland. "Hawthorne's *Scarlet Letter.*" *Triumphs of the Imagination: Literature in Christian Perspective.* Downers Grove: InterVarsity Press, 1979. 114-120.

Argues that Hawthorne's novel embodies three distinct world views—the Puritan, the romantic, and the Christian—and then sets out to measure them against a Christian standard. The story "ultimately affirms the Christian world view and contains within itself the antidote to the Puritan and Romantic world views."

374   Waggoner, Hyatt H. "Dark Light on the Letter." *The Presence of Hawthorne*. Baton Rouge: Louisiana State UP, 1979. 67-75.*

Compares Hawthorne's "modern," tragic vision with Ralph Waldo Emerson's more old-fashioned, positive, and hopeful vision of life, arguing that "Hawthorne's predominant concern in his fiction is with just those experiences of guilt and limitation that Emerson thought it possible to transcend." Since sin cannot be "outgrown" and life must be presented "as it is" instead of how it should be, there is no hope for lightening *Letter* (as the sympathetic Hawthorne felt compelled to do) so that the hero and heroine might escape from the tragic conflicts in the novel, such as society vs. the individual, law vs. natural impulse, and duty vs. desire.

*Waggoner's chapter on *Letter* here is very similar to part three of his introduction to Letter in 1968 (see 220).

Journal Essays and Notes

375   Berner, Robert L. "A Key to 'The Custom-House.'" *ATQ* 41 (1979): 33-43.

"'The Custom-House' has not been adequately understood in terms of its structure, in terms of the relationship of that structure to that of the romance, or in terms of its significance for an understanding of Hawthorne's basic concerns in all four of his longer fictions." Hawthorne arranges his experience in the Salem Custom house in four, roughly-equivalent stages (the first describes the Custom-house setting, the second characterizes the custom-house "inmates," the third covers Surveyor Pue and his manuscript, and the fourth describes Hawthorne's "escape as 'a citizen of somewhere else' to the world of the artist"), all of which correspond to the movement in four stages of Hester's development in the romance. Further linking the sketch to the romance are parallels between the "permanent Inspector" and Chillingworth, the Collector and Dimmesdale, the "man of business" and Hester, and the narrator/artist/representative of spirit from "The Custom-House" and the Boston crowd that populates the novel. These four types in the sketch also correspond to characters in *House of the Seven Gables*, *Blithedale Romance*, and *Marble Faun*, not only indicating that Hawthorne formulated his mature artistic vision while writing "The Custom-House," but also suggesting, since they reappear over and over, that the combination of these types comprise Hawthorne's vision of the human condition.

376   Canaday, Nicholas, Jr. "Another Look at Arthur Dimmesdale." *CEA Critic* 41 (1979): 13-16.

Although it is tempting to "slight" the cowardly Dimmesdale for other primary characters—the more engaging Hester, the fascinatingly diabolical Chillingworth, and the enigmatic Pearl—Hawthorne's characterization of the minister belies a hasty dismissal.   The same strengths that originally made Dimmesdale "a great man"—his natural charisma and sexual magnetism, his justifiable pride, and his "deliberate refusal to indulge in self-examination"—betray him, as examination of his inner life suggests.   Ironically, one of these damning strengths saves Dimmesdale in the end, since it is his pride that motivates his over-blown ego to write and deliver a "splendid" and redeeming farewell Election-Day sermon.   [For a similar reading that argues more strenuously that Dimmesdale's Election-Day sermon converts and saves him, see Terence Martin's "Dimmesdale's Ultimate Sermon" (276).]

377   Darnell, Donald.   *"The Scarlet Letter*: Hawthorne's Emblem Book." *Studies in American Fiction* 7 (1979): 153-162.

This illustrated essay (drawings by Betty Watson) shows how Hawthorne employed the Renaissance emblem "pictorial-moral" tradition "to structure his treatment of man's sin, fall, and moral growth" in *Letter*. "A series of emblems develops the narrative and provides *explicit* interpretation of the novel's themes." Hawthorne's emblematic method— his habit of arresting action and explaining the moral significance of tableaux that practically "demand explication"—is most apparent in the three scaffold scenes and in the presentation of Pearl.

378   Gervais, Ronald J. "'A Papist among the Puritans': Icon and Logos in *The Scarlet Letter*." *ESQ: A Journal of the American Renaissance* 25 (1979): 11-16.

Expanding on Frederick Newberry's demonstration (in 348) of the conflict between the Puritans' "dominant iconoclasm and a recessive Catholic-Renaissance iconography," Gervais points out that the struggle may be more accurately depicted as between the iconographic and the "logological," or between "an older Anglo-Catholic pictorial symbolism that encourages mutability and ambiguity, and the newer Puritan linguistic logic that attempts to fix definite meanings." *Letter* is "organized structurally and thematically around this unnatural split between icon and logos," with Hester representing the spiritual icon in material, sensuous form and Dimmesdale representing the Puritan "primacy of the word." Both characters also represent two different and incomplete ways of thinking, Hester of unrestricted, unconscious thinking and Dimmesdale of logic-governed, conscious thinking. The burden of the novel is to restore to the Puritan world "a qualified and tenuous connection between icon and logos"—a task that is completed during Dimmesdale's Election-Day sermon when he not only "reveals the icon that joins him to Hester" but also dies in her arms in the tableaux of "an iconic pietà," an image first named by Newberry.

379   Gollin, Rita K. "Hawthorne on Film." *Nathaniel Hawthorne Society Newsletter* 5 (1979): 6-7.

Included in this list of films on Hawthorne's works are the brief descriptions of five film versions of *Letter* that appeared between 1917 and 1979. [For more specific information about these five film versions of *Letter*, see especially Michael Dunne (807) and Bruce Daniels (846), but also refer to "Movie Versions" in the Subject Index.]

380   Hilgers, Thomas L. "The Psychology of Conflict Resolution in *The Scarlet Letter*: A Non-Freudian Approach." *ATQ* 43 (1979): 211-224.

Since Hawthorne's psychological insights clearly reflect an interest in "the interplay among elements of public and private stimuli, understanding, and action," it is rather limiting for Freudian critics—such as Régis Michaud (EC21), Frederick Crews (182), and Allan Lefcowitz (322)—to over-emphasize as they do the "*intra*psychic' conflicts in the novel (those relating to personal or private guilt) and completely neglect the "*inter*psychic" conflicts (those sustained by and resolved within social settings). With reference to Leon Festinger's post-Freudian theory of "cognitive dissonance," Dimmesdale can be seen as "a case study" in conflict resolution. His public/private conflicts are illustrated most pointedly when he bitterly acknowledges "the contrast between what I seem and what I am." The novel is structured around his three efforts to reduce tension-producing dissonance and eliminate the contrasts. Only when he works through this series of changing cognitions (the first involving assimilation or conformity with others, the second requiring a forced change in the environment, and the third involving the formulation of new cognitive insights) does Dimmesdale resolve incongruence and achieve both theological and psychological consonance.

381   Idol, John L., Jr., and Sterling K. Eisiminger. "A Preliminary List of Operas Based on Hawthorne's Fiction." *Nathaniel Hawthorne Society Newsletter* 5 (1979): 5-6.

Contains a list of all the operas that draw directly or indirectly from Hawthorne's fiction, including three by the title of *Hester Prynne* and ten entitled *The Scarlet Letter*.

382   Jones, Buford.   "*The Scarlet Letter*: WGBH Television Drama." *Nathaniel Hawthorne Society Newsletter* 5 (1979): 10-11.

This section of Jones's annual "Current Hawthorne Bibliography" includes bibliographic information on fourteen reviews of the WGBH television production of *Letter* as they appeared in *TV World*, *Americana Magazine*, *Durham Morning Herald*, Baltimore *Sun*, *North Caroline Leader*, *Newsweek*, *New York*, *MS.*, *Smithsonian*, *Tobacco Road*, *New York Times*, *TV Guide*, *The Lamp*, and *Chronicle of Higher Education*. Also included is the citation for a teacher's guide to the television production (see 367 for its complete annotation).

383   Kesterson, David B.   "Updike and Hawthorne: Not So Strange Bedfellows." *Notes on Modern American Literature* 19 (1979): Item 11.

John Updike's *A Month of Sundays* (1975) shows tremendous indebtedness to *Letter* in characterization, structure, and theme. It tells the tale of the reverend Thomas Marshfield, who, like Dimmesdale, is "caught in a quagmire of quasi-belief and hampered by an inability to overcome his obsession with sex." Unhappy in his marriage to the prudish Jane Chillingworth and guilty of several adulterous affairs, Marshfield is sentenced by his parish to a month of Sundays in a desert sanitarium that is run by none other than the ample and sexual Ms. Prynne, about whom Marshfield feels erotic thoughts until they finally make love on his last day of confinement.   Just as Hawthorne's novel structurally revolves around the three scaffold scenes, so Updike's revolves around Marshfield's four Sunday sermons.   Both hypocritical ministers eventually overcome their dishonesty with themselves and others, and both come to "see themselves as part of fallen man and accept that condition." Hawthorne and Updike specifically concern themselves with the fears of isolation and alienation, stressing the importance of "experiencing meaningful human relationships."

384   Lewis, Paul.   "Mournful Mysteries: Gothic Speculation in *The Scarlet Letter*." *ATQ* 44 (1979): 279-293.

Since revaluation of the Gothic in recent years focuses on ambiguity, mystery, and "the intense observation and speculation mystery stimulates in the minds of both characters and readers," Lewis finds that Hawthorne's use of American Gothic conventions in *Letter* extends far beyond creating a hackneyed "Walpolesque atmosphere" complete with conventional supernatural images (such as the "A" in the night sky) and spooky character types (Mistress Hibbins and Roger Chillingworth). "Hawthorne's adaptation of Gothic mystery and stereotypes contributes to both the thematic richness and the complex characterization of the work"—especially in his employing the Gothic to plumb the profound depths of "the uncertainty and confusion of human life." In Hester's character especially, Hawthorne redefines "the three conventional roles for leading female characters in the classic English Gothic novel of Radcliffe and Lewis: the heroine, the temptress, and the fallen woman." She deviates from these types most strikingly in her ability to survive "as a thinking woman." Simply "too human, too rounded, in short too interesting to be a Gothic character," Hester embraces "the potential for growth inherent in mystery." Unlike Chillingworth who denies the reality of mystery, and unlike Dimmesdale who transforms mysterious questions into debilitating guilt, and especially "unlike the traditional Gothic heroine who survives only to return to the predictable world she remembers, Hester forges a new world for herself by discovering that the highest function of mystery is that it challenges orthodoxies that distort and limit our access to the truth."

385   Person, Leland S., Jr. *"The Scarlet Letter* and the Myth of the Divine Child." *ATQ* 44 (1979): 295-309.

Hawthorne employed "a universal myth of the Divine Child in *Letter,* whose implications clarify not only Pearl's role in the novel but also Hawthorne's conception of his art, his attitude toward the interplay of the past and the present, and his perception of the role of myth in history." Pearl's multiple symbolic functions can be understood by drawing from the archetype/myth studies of Carl Jung and C. Kerényi that assign such characteristics to the Divine Child as royalty (often symbolized by jewels or flowers), solitariness, a connection to nature moreso than to society, and antagonism toward the father. Pearl's outcast status as an elusive and wild child of nature "not only links her to the Divine Child archetype, but establishes her most important role in the novel: to embody the future of Puritan society, the accommodation of society and the wilderness, history and myth." As a redemptive figure, Pearl is ultimately "the harbinger of a potentially new society," used by Hawthorne to expiate the shame associated with ancestral sins. Her "very uprootedness" from provincial American society embodies Hawthorne's hope to redeem the world, as well as his hope that his own children will remain free from and uncorrupted by a haunted, malignant past. Ultimately, however, Pearl's dissociation from the Puritan world signals a failure on Hawthorne's part to reconcile her (and his) conflicting forces, and suggests that his "character of flame" was finally "too hot to handle."

1980

Essays and Studies in Books

386 Bell, Michael Davitt. "The Death of the Spirit: Nathaniel Hawthorne." *The Development of American Romance: The Sacrifice of Relation.* Chicago: U of Chicago P, 1980. 169-193.

Briefly demonstrates (pp. 176-181) that Hawthorne's project of "recovering his imagination, which constitutes the main action of 'The Custom-House' as Hester's rebellion constitutes that of *Letter*, is not easily accomplished." Because Hawthorne "does not confuse what the imagination can momentarily achieve in romance with what individual or social rebellion can accomplish in history," the imaginative freedom achieved in "The Custom-House" is never incorporated in the re-enactment of Puritan history in *Letter*.

387 Eberwein, Jane Donahue. "'The Scribbler of Bygone Days': Perceptions of Time in Hawthorne's 'Custom-House.'" *Nathaniel Hawthorne Journal 1977*. Ed. C. E. Frazer Clark, Jr. Detroit: Bruccoli Clark Publishers, 1980. 239-247.

Besides "capitalizing on the publicity which attended his dismissal from the Salem appointment," providing a link to several of his other short stories, and generally providing an introduction to Hester's story, "The Custom-House" serves to highlight Hawthorne's "curiously elongated sense of time." The temporal sequence of the sketch, in which time is neither "linear nor even cyclic" but "eschatological, like that of the early Puritans," reveals Hawthorne's "idiosyncratic grasp of time." What's more, "this inherently Puritan perspective on time which sees eternity in an instant of apparently minor experience and sees values in events in proportion to the spiritual enlightenment they offer helps to clarify Hawthorne's anomalous use of time in *Letter* itself." That Hawthorne evokes a sense of history while simultaneously addressing contemporary events not only suggests his status as an artist of "mythic, timeless imagination" but also brings colonial values back to life and blurs the gap between past and present.

388 Gollin, Rita K. "Hester, Hetty, and the Two Arthurs." *Nathaniel Hawthorne Journal 1977*. Ed. C. E. Frazer Clark, Jr. Detroit: Bruccoli Clark Publishers, 1980. 319-322.

Compares the "unhappy lovers" in *Letter* and George Eliot's *Adam Bede* (1859) to establish Hawthorne's possible (and likely) influence on Eliot—especially in terms of moral vision and sympathetic understanding of human limitations. Not only do Hester/Hetty and Arthur Dimmesdale/Arthur Donnithorne share "provocative similarities," but so do the novels' plots and settings. In each novel, for instance, "a forest meeting leads to the birth of an illegitimate child and the heroine's imprisonment." And for both sets of lovers, "the woods are a place of passion, confusion, and moral error."

389   Irwin, John T. "Hawthorne and Melville." *American Hieroglyphics: The Symbol of the Egyptian Hieroglyphics in the American Renaissance*. New Haven: Yale UP, 1980. 239-349.

Expanding his earlier essay on the same subject (see 321), Irwin examines the "impact of the decipherment of the Egyptian hieroglyphics on nineteenth-century American literature" and "relates the image of the hieroglyphics to the larger reciprocal questions of the origin and limits of symbolization." For Hawthorne (pp. 239-284), as for Herman Melville, the "ambiguous character of the hieroglyphics was [his] prime significance" because he found in the hieroglyph the "linguistic analogue of an enigmatic world" where there is no objective truth but only limitless individual perspectives projected upon "indeterminate ground." In *Letter* (pp. 239-254, 274-284), Hester's insignia is a hieroglyphic emblem that ambiguously implies not merely one true meaning but a host of possible meanings. The multiple perspectives created from this hieroglyphic sign extend to include a sense of "hieroglyphic doubleness" experienced by Hester, Dimmesdale, Chillingworth, and Pearl when they encounter situations that make them continually confront the interplay of "self and image." Even Hawthorne (or his narrator) seems to have difficulty maintaining "continuity of identity" as the "masked" author of his text.

390   Lane, Gary. "Structural Dynamics and the Unknowable in *The Scarlet Letter*." *Nathaniel Hawthorne Journal 1977*. Ed. C. E. Frazer Clark, Jr. Detroit: Bruccoli Clark Publishers, 1980. 323-330.

Considers the "structural importance" of Pearl to the novel, emphasizing that consideration of her character is often erroneously neglected in most critical assessments of the "major" characters in the novel. Pearl's "co-equality with Hester, Dimmesdale, and Chillingworth" best expresses Hawthorne's keen feeling about the "essential ambiguity of the human condition." This "thematic unknowability" is actually a structural principle of the book that consistently blurs "the distinctions between illusion and reality," and ambivalently blurs the differences and similarities between the four main characters.

391   Mayhook, J. Jeffrey. "'Bearings Unknown to English Heraldry' in *The Scarlet Letter*." *Nathaniel Hawthorne Journal 1977*. Ed. C. E. Frazer Clark, Jr. Detroit: Bruccoli Clark Publishers, 1980. 173-214.

Establishes Hawthorne's interest in heraldry and points out passages in *Letter* in which heraldry functions as one the central themes of the novel. After reviewing the history of the science of heraldry and examining "image clusters" associated with the tradition (such as swords, breastplates, banners, and escutcheons), Mayhook shows how Hawthorne employs devices of heraldry first in several short stories ("Earth's Holocaust," "Endicott and the Red Cross," "Howe's Masquerade," and "The May-Pole of Merry Mount") and then in *Letter*—where Hawthorne questions the relationship of human nobility and the objects of heraldry, and displays most prominently through a comparison of the Puritans and Hester the movement from armorial to moral heraldry. Heraldic language and imagery also permeate (with irony) "The Custom-House," setting the stage for what is to come in the novel: Hawthorne's fashioning of "a new heraldry unknown in the Old World" that is marked by a "shift from a heraldry encumbered by ostentation, vanity and pride, to a heraldry upheld by moral gentility."

392   Mellow, James R. *Nathaniel Hawthorne in His Times*. Boston: Houghton Mifflin, 1980.

This award-winning biography provides (pp. 292-316) the events in Hawthorne's life directly before, during, and after composition of *Letter*. Out of the "emotional upheaval of that dismal summer of political recriminations and private grief" (losing both his position in the Custom House and his mother), the novel developed as something of a powerful "gathering-in" of the obsessive themes that had haunted him for a decade. Hawthorne clearly identified with all three of his "guilty" primary characters—with Hester's public humiliations, Dimmesdale's sense of himself as a victimized sinner, and Chillingworth's hidden identity as both wronged man and secret avenger. His professional and personal experiences thus "afforded him an understanding of the secret psychological springs of guilt" and enabled him to work cathartically through the dramatic action of the novel.

393   Sachs, Viola. "*The Scarlet Letter*: An Initiatory Reading." *Linguistique, Civilisation, Littérature*. Ed. André Bordeaux. Paris: Didier, 1980. 105-115.

The scarlet letter itself constitutes the organizing principle of the book. An examination of the letter's associations with colors, numbers, and graphic forms, as well as an analysis of the novel's countless allusions to the Puritans, to the Bible, to different alphabets, and to ancient pagan cultures, indicate that "Hawthorne conceived of the scarlet letter as being the sign of a New World, of America encompassing all myths and cultures."

394   Spengemann, William C. "Poetic Autobiography: *The Scarlet Letter*." *The Forms of Autobiography: Episodes in the History of a Literary Genre.* New Haven: Yale UP, 1980. 132-165.

Traces "the evolution of autobiographical forms" from the Middle Ages to the nineteenth century, citing St. Augustine's *Confessions* as a work that meets "the strictest formal prescriptions for the genre" and Hawthorne's *Letter* as a work that "retains no vestige of the self-biographical mode." Spengemann considers *Letter* a "prime example of poetic autobiography," meaning that Hawthorne transfers his innermost concerns and divided self (as both public and private) to the complex natures and roles of his fictional characters. Although Hawthorne only "half knew it," he did find "his true being, his true society, and his immortality in *Letter*" by "poetically healing" his conflicted self in a fictional "complete being" that he could never quite manage to become in real life.

395   Stone, Edward. "The 'Many Morals' of *The Scarlet Letter*." *Nathaniel Hawthorne Journal 1977.* Ed. C. E. Frazer Clark, Jr. Detroit: Bruccoli Clark Publishers, 1980. 215-238.

Places Hawthorne in the context of the nineteenth-century American artist to assess whether *Letter* has one moral, several morals, or no moral at all. As Hawthorne was well aware, reader expectations demanded an artist's attention to morality, and thus he most likely pretended compliance in order to satisfy private, personal demands on his art. His fiction clearly shows Hawthorne's own uncomfortable or ambivalent relation to his body of work as he "oscillated, now priest, now heretic" in his attitude toward the moralistic tradition of art. His deliberate vagueness about the moral of *Letter* is best interpreted as his own attempt to satisfy both himself as artist in his "scientific investigation of sick souls" and his reading public as seekers of "edification through entertainment"—although he surely anticipated the criticism he would receive in his own day for the "amoralized detachment of his relationship to his sinning literary creations."

201

396   Turner, Arlin. *"The Scarlet Letter." Nathaniel Hawthorne: A Biography.*
       Oxford: Oxford UP, 1980. 188-207.

       Although the biography does not offer a critical evaluation of *Letter*, it
       does place the novel in the context of Hawthorne's life at the time of its
       composition. Turner also briefly inspects the romance for Hawthorne's
       literary methods, shows how *Letter* interweaves the major themes from
       several earlier tales, and examines the impact of the early reviews on
       Hawthorne. [For another biography that also appeared in 1980 and *does*
       include critical commentary on Hawthorne's novel, see James R. Mellow
       (392).]

Journal Essays and Notes

397   Bayer, John G. "Narrative Techniques and the Oral Tradition in *The
       Scarlet Letter." American Literature* 52 (1980): 250-263.

       All disagreement among critics over the relation of "The Custom-House"
       to the novel is cleared up once the sketch is seen as an "exordium"
       designed by the audience-loathing Hawthorne "to enlist reader
       cooperation" or to win the reader over to a sympathetic appreciation of his
       way of thinking in *Letter*.   Anxiously anticipating a hostile and
       contemptuous audience (characterized by "skepticism, discrimination, and
       Yankee practicality"), Hawthorne employs the "persuasive tactics" of
       rhetorical oratory that he picked up in college (largely from Blair's
       Rhetoric) to manipulate overtly and covertly the author-reader relationship
       and to encourage "compassion, understanding, [and] imagination." Such
       tactics include "outright flattery," a professed commonality of experience
       with the reader, self-depreciation, and an editorial pose to legitimize the
       fictional story for a realism-loving audience.   Hawthorne's "oratorical
       display" filters into the novel itself, too, energizing the dynamics of the
       plot and even informing the episodic, highly scenic structure of the novel.
       These devices not only were "aimed at enlisting reader sympathy," but
       also were "conscious efforts to build toward closure in the narrative."
       Taken together, the oral dimensions that link the introduction to the novel
       "confirm the judgment that *Letter* is a fictional exemplar of a residually
       oral age."

398   Ellis, James. "Human Sexuality, the Sacrament of Matrimony, and the
       Paradox of the Fortunate Fall in *The Scarlet Letter." Christianity and
       Literature* 29.4 (1980): 53-60.

       From a Christian point of view, Dimmesdale is the novel's protagonist,
       and the novel illustrates how pride and sexuality function in the working

out of Dimmesdale's "Fortunate Fall." Man's struggle to reconcile his sexual nature (represented by Hester) with his spiritual aspiration after God (represented by Dimmesdale) can only be won through the "blending" sacrament of matrimony, and thus his adultery is, in effect, the starting point of Dimmesdale's journey to renounce his pre-adulterous sin of pride and to regain Paradise—whereby Pearl becomes the means to achieve it. This Christian reading does not exclude Hester from redemption. She functions in her new role at novel's end as "a kind of female John the Baptist, speaking to the women of Boston in anticipation of 'the destined prophetess to come.'"

399   Green, Carlanda. "'The Custom-House': Hawthorne's Dark Wood of Error." *New England Quarterly* 53 (1980): 184-195.

Reads "The Custom-House" as "the emblematic journey of an artist who lost his way," or, more specifically, as Hawthorne's "classical dramatization of his struggle to redefine himself." Using a mock-serious tone, Hawthorne casts his Custom-House experience in Salem (his "city of error") in symbolic terms reminiscent of classical descents into hell by Homer, Virgil, and Dante, choosing such motifs as "the descent into the world of the dead, the talisman of the visitor, portraits of the dead, and the return to the living." Most important about the classical descent to the underworld is what lesson it imparts to the traveler upon his return to the human community. Hawthorne learns the importance of balance and harmony in one's life—of the need for "the spiritual, the ideal, and the aesthetic" to match "the rational, the pragmatic, and the physical." Green cites several clever parallels, such as the eagle that "threatens intruders with thunderbolts, barbed arrows, and wicked claws" to replace the guard-dog Cerberus (who guards the entrance to Hades) and the gluttonous Inspector to substitute for Dante's Hog, Ciacco. Just as "Dante has his Beatrice, Odysseus his Athena, and Aeneas his Deiphoebe to rescue them from error," so Hawthorne "is providentially led to Hester Prynne." Through the assistance of Surveyor Pue, "Hester becomes Hawthorne's way out of the depravity of [the] decayed world" into the brightly-lit world of the living.

400   Hutchison, Earl R., Sr. "Antiquity and Mythology in *The Scarlet Letter*: The Primary Sources." *Arizona Quarterly* 36 (1980): 99-110.

Argues that "the English and American sources [for the novel] are relegated to secondary importance" when one considers the primary sources for the characters and plot in Greek antiquity and mythology (the information on which Hutchison finds exclusively in the *Encyclopedia Britannica*). Hawthorne modeled Hester, Dimmesdale, and Chillingworth partly on the beautiful and impious Hetaira Phryne (a courtesan), her lover Hypereides (the great orator who defends her), and her rejected suitor Euthias (known as an informer and blackmailer). Hester is also modeled on Aphrodite (her scarlet "A" standing for Aphrodite in this case), since the triangular affair between Aphrodite, Hephaestus (her lame artist husband), and Ares (her lover) that produces the illicit offspring Harmonia "correlates exactly with Hester, Roger, Arthur, and Pearl" and "adds a breathtaking third dimension to the novel." Hutchison concludes that "the failure to note the allusions to Aphrodite and Hetaira Phryne in the novel results in a concomitant failure to note a major Hawthorne theme in it— paganism and an earthy, healthy love of life."

401 Oggel, L. Terry. "Twin Tongues of Flame: Hawthorne's Pearl and Barth's Jeannine as the Morally Redemptive Child." *Naussau Review* 4 (1980): 41-49.

Views Pearl as the prototype of a distinctly American (though minor) child-type who "rescues adults from deficiencies of thought and errors of perception," and whose "type" lives on in contemporary literature in the child character of Jeannine in John Barth's *The Floating Opera* (1956). Oggel examines the morally redemptive functions of Pearl and Jeannine within their "singularly similar narratives" in an attempt to shed light on the pre-Hawthorne origin of their specific type of character. The type was likely modeled from Ralph Waldo Emerson's phrase "child of fire" (implying the "power and brilliance of inspired vision"), a phrase which Emerson adapted from Jonathan Edwards's reference to children as "heirs of hell." These non-sentimental, illegitimately-sired "characters of flame" repesent truth, provide "constant visible evidence of the[ir] parents' bond, a bond denied by both fathers," and ultimately function as forces for redemptive love.

402 Reilly, Charlie. "A Conversation with John Updike." *Canto* 3 (1980): 148-178.

This interview includes Updike's comments (pp. 153-155) on the connection and similarities between *A Month of Sundays* and *Letter*, and contains Updike's open acknowledgment that he had *Letter* in mind when writing his novel, as well as his statement that *A Month of Sundays* is a kind of retelling of *Letter* from Dimmesdale's point of view.

403 Rowe, John Carlos. "The Internal Conflict of Romantic Narrative: Hegel's *Phenomenology* and Hawthorne's *The Scarlet Letter*." *Modern Language Notes* 95 (1980): 1203-1231.

Rowe relates *Letter* to Hegel's *Phenomenology of Spirit* (1807) and argues that both texts are governed by a far-reaching social and historical vision. Since both express the "phenomenology of self-consciousness," Hawthorne's "ambivalence concerning the orthodoxy of Puritanism and Hester's passionate yearning for freedom is the equivalent to the internal contradictions that mobilize the forces of Hegelian dialectics." Hester's process of self-consciousness occurs in stages that constitute Hegel's *dramatis personae* in *Phenomenology*, a process associated with Hawthorne's central problems of "social transvaluation" and imaginative self-realization through art.

404   Sachs, Viola. "The Gnosis of Hawthorne and Melville: An Interpretation of *The Scarlet Letter* and *Moby-Dick*." *American Quarterly* 32 (1980): 123-143.

Incessant references in *Letter* and *Moby-Dick* (1851) to mysteries and hidden meanings reveal that the organizing principle of both novels is the desire to manifest the divine, the cosmic origins of life. Reacting against all institutions in their day that recognize only one truth or creed, Hawthorne and Herman Melville counter the external level of their texts (that corresponds to the profane world) with a hidden, mythic dimension (replete with "cyclical and spiral images, the interplay of darkness and light, colors, numbers, and the evocation of geometrical and graphical forms") that "evokes the sacred world, marked by wholeness." The "revelation of the spirit" is reserved only for those acute "initiate" readers "who are willing to work their way through a labyrinth of symbols, key words, signs to the hidden center" of each novel where "the transmission of this gnosis, of the original Word, leads to the spiritual salvation of America." Hawthorne's and Melville's interest in creating their own sacred scripts coincides not only with national interest in developing a uniquely American language to suit the New World, but also with the cultural obsession with Egyptology and hieroglyphics. Their respective hieroglyphs (the "A" and the whale) "symbolize the matter that has to be dissolved so that the Spirit of America, conceived as a new cosmic order, can become manifest." *Letter* becomes the "the manifestation of a cosmic order which effects the fusion of myths from different cultures and above all stands for the *coincidentia oppositorum* of the fundamental dichotomies of American culture: civilization/wilderness, Christian/heathan, the White Man/the Red Man/the Black Man." But unlike Melville, who "comes to terms with himself and realizes the full implications of what he is writing," Hawthorne "is not in full command of his text," since he is ambivalent "towards his own thoughts and self." [For two other essays that examine the nineteenth-century fascination with Egyptology and hieroglyphics, see John T. Irwin in 321 and 389.]

405 Small, Michel. "Hawthorne's *The Scarlet Letter*: Arthur Dimmesdale's Manipulation of Language." *American Imago* 37 (1980): 113-123.

Defines Dimmesdale's eloquent use of language in psychoanalytic terms, as a manipulative disguise of his aggressive and libidinal urges (the latter of which Small often terms sadistic and anal). Rather than helping Dimmesdale to master the conflict between his ideal and libidinal selves, language actually serves to perpetuate the conflict through his sermons— on the one hand by consciously maintaining his "nearly angelic ego-ideal" and thereby stroking his damaged self-esteem, and on the other by unconsciously releasing and gratifying his sexual impulses. Dimmesdale's manipulative language "also provides him a way of attempting to purge himself of guilt and shame without really exposing himself publicly," and becomes the instrument by which he acts out his sexual impulses in "conscious verbal fantasy." Eventually, Dimmesdale's juggling of language begins to master him, and his "triumphant" last sermon becomes, unbeknownst to him, "yet another magical denial of his 'animal nature,' another manipulation." Dimmesdale's duplicitous use of language parallels Hawthorne's own self-protective ambivalent stance in his fiction: both result from a fear of exposing the inner self. Hawthorne is, however, "finally too honest to misuse his art" and is thus more successful than his fictional counterpart in his desire to reveal his true character—albeit a veiled version—to his readers through language. [For a similar essay on Dimmesdale's manipulation of language, see Kenneth D. Pimple (715).]

1981

Essays and Studies in Books

406 Baym, Nina. "The Significance of Plot in Hawthorne's Romances." *Ruined Eden of the Present: Hawthorne, Melville, and Poe: Critical Essays in Honor of Darrel Abel.* Ed. G. R. Thompson and Virgil L. Lokke. West Lafayette: Purdue UP, 1981. 49-70.*

Argues that New Criticism tended to deny Hawthorne's radical and romantic tendencies, reducing his fictions "as though they were poems, eloquent but plotless expressions of feeling and attitude." While Darrel Abel participated in the revisionary work that followed New Criticism, his readings of Hawthorne's novels yet reflect a New Critical bias that essentially ignores Hawthorne's plots "because of the constraints of [New Criticism's] implicit male-oriented ideology and its explicit anti-romanticism." Two of Abel's best-remembered articles on *Letter*, for example (pp. 49-58), "Hawthorne's Hester" (see 16) and "Hawthorne's Dimmesdale" (see 46), argue that Hawthorne portrays Hester as "woefully inadequate" and that Dimmesdale is the novel's true protagonist. But such attempts to diminish Hester's significance are untenable because they deny close attention to plot; for structurally, the majority of the novel—and even "The Custom-House"—is given over to consideration of Hester alone, the true protagonist of the novel.

*See 339 for an earlier essay by Baym that examines Hawthorne's romanticism and the limitations of New Critical analyses of the novel.

407   Johnson, Claudia D[urst]. "'To Step Aside Out of the Narrow Circle': "The Custom-House" and *The Scarlet Letter." The Productive Tension of Hawthorne's Art.* U of Alabama P, 1981. 46-66.

Contrary to critics who view Hawthorne's art in terms of competing organic/mechanical philosophies, Johnson argues that it was torn between his own conception of "moral" and artistic organicism. Hawthorne dramatizes this conflict between creativity and morality in "The Custom-House" and *Letter*, first discarding the view that the vocation of artist necessarily requires an "infernal inwardness" that separates him from humanity, and then altruistically discovering that true creative greatness requires the artist's active participation in the business of life and action. This discovery comes with a price to the artist, however, because it involves a "moral-psychological journey" and a "regenerative descent into an inner hell." Dimmesdale's fall, unlike Hester's, is never regenerative since he remains incurably self-deceived and hypocritical until the end. However, just as Dimmesdale deludes himself with "half-measures like scourging himself in secret" in the hope of cleansing his soul and attaining glory without the messy process of involving the public with the truth of his relation to Hester and Pearl, so Hester is mistaken in her belief that "charitable acts will dispel her guilt and isolation, that they will wipe her slate clean and even change her fallen, sin-inclined nature." In acting out disingenuous parts, in becoming "good Puritans" instead of honestly affirming their forbidden creativity, Dimmesdale and Hester are scarcely part of the world, "Puritanically" denying the beauty of what the scarlet "A" really encompasses: *everything* in human nature, both the light and the dark.

408   Male, Roy R. "Hawthorne's Literal Figures." *Ruined Eden of the Present: Hawthorne, Melville, and Poe: Critical Essays in Honor of Darrel Abel.* Ed. G. R. Thompson and Virgil L. Lokke. West Lafayette: Purdue UP, 1981. 71-92.

Applies a diagram created by M. H. Abrams (intended to simplify the multiple and interrelated aspects of language) to chart Hawthorne's "verbal performance" in relation to that of his leading contemporaries. Of all of Hawthorne's tales, *Letter* (pp. 86-90) most clearly shows Hawthorne's "oscillation between the literal and the figurative," revealing that his attitude toward language was basically expressive, with heavy emphasis on its graphic dimension, and that he especially enjoyed exploiting the arbitrary nature of language—with its referential and self-reflexive qualities. *Letter* is "the only fictive work that perfectly fuses the expressive, representational, and objective aspects of language, transforming even its fragments into capital."

409 Marx, Leo. "The Puzzle of Anti-Urbanism in Classic American Literature." *Literature and the Urban Experience.* Ed. Michael C. Jaye and Ann Chalmers Watts. New Brunswick: Rutgers UP, 1981. 63-80.*

Reconsidering "the bias against the city that allegedly makes itself felt in our classic American literature," Marx argues that the attitude mistaken for anti-urbanism and pro-pastoralism is actually an expression of something else, a "continuous replaying or testing of the Emersonian doctrine of self-reliance as the epitome of 'the natural.'" The "seeming anti-urbanism" in *Letter* (pp. 67-73) suggested by Hester's identification with the untrammeled forest and the freedom found there is not a repudiation of Boston's "cityness" but of the Puritan society whose power is concentrated there. Thus Hawthorne makes no attempt to recreate realistically the character of daily life in seventeenth-century Boston, but instead uses the prison, the cemetery, and the scaffold to represent "the hard, reality-oriented, authoritarian spirit of the Calvinists." Such a focus on the grim and repressive qualities of Boston has nothing to do with what is intrinsic to urban life, but instead reveals Hawthorne's judgment of the Puritan way of life.

*Reprinted in Marx's *The Pilot and the Passenger: Essays on Literature, Technology, and the Culture of the United States* (New York: Oxford UP, 1988. 208-227.) See 416 for an earlier version of Marx's article under the title "Two Tales of the City: Anti-Urbanism in American Literature."

410 Mellow, James R. "Hawthorne's Divided Genius." Introduction. *The Scarlet Letter and The House of the Seven Gables.* Signet Classic edition. New York: Penguin Books, 1981. v-xvi.

Letter and *House of the Seven Gables* "represent the opposing poles of [Hawthorne's] divided genius," the first a "stark allegorical drama" characteristic of his brooding imagination and the second a highly detailed critique of American materialism geared more to the tastes of his genteel readers. Mellow addresses *Letter*'s contemporary reception and Hawthorne's fears that the novel's gloominess would repel his readers, reviews Hawthorne's political and professional career, and provides biographical information that cautions against accepting the traditional portrait of the author as a gloomy hermit. "The real significance of Hawthorne's classic novel is its psychological force," or the connections between physical suffering and repressed guilt that Hawthorne discovers, and the "premature Freudian" exploration, through Chillingworth's character, of "the manipulative techniques of psychoanalysis." What makes all of his writing so great, however, is Hawthorne's method of ambivalence, his ability to balance contradictory assumptions and to sustain those tensions through opposing symbols.

411   Ringe, Donald A. "Romantic Iconology in *The Scarlet Letter* and *The Blithedale Romance*." *Ruined Eden of the Present: Hawthorne, Melville, and Poe: Critical Essays in Honor of Darrel Abel*. Ed. G. R. Thompson and Virgil L. Lokke. West Lafayette: Purdue UP, 1981. 93-107.

Relates the content and imagery of *Letter* and *Blithedale Romance*, finding that the latter complements the former. "That Coverdale thinks of the Blithedale experience in terms of his Pilgrim forebears is highly suggestive and directs our attention back to *Letter*, where a similar community of devoted reformers is presented through much the same spatial metaphor"—of an "island" utopia that isolates itself from surrounding chaotic and lawless wastes of space. Both utopian societies necessarily founder because of "the incurable weakness and fallibility of human nature," but Blithedale's failure actually serves to show the complete decadent collapse in the nineteenth century of "those millennial ideas that had haunted the New England mind for a full two hundred years." "The smallness and thinness of the contemporary characters is [sic] obvious when they are compared with those in the earlier book. Coverdale and Hollingsworth lack the moral agony of Dimmesdale, Zenobia lacks the strength of Hester Prynne, and the magician, Westervelt, seems almost trivial beside the satanic Chillingworth. Blithedale is only a game for some rather ineffectual nineteenth-century intellectuals and reformers, who lack the purpose and passion of their ancestors."

412   Torgovnick, Marianna. "Communal Themes and the Outer Frame of *The Scarlet Letter*." *Closure in the Novel*. Princeton: Princeton UP, 1981. 80-100, 216-217.

Letter's "inner frame" makes up the many chapters of one-to-one confrontations between characters. The "outer frame," composed of "The

Custom-House" and the "Conclusion," not only intensifies the reader's sense of the novel's circularity but also and more importantly provides a crucial thematic statement regarding the individual's relationship to society. Just as "The Custom-House" evaluates Hawthorne's communal ties to Puritanism and Salem, so the final chapter of *Letter* considers his characters' unavoidable ties to the Puritan community despite their individual desires. Thus the inner and outer frames together provide the form Hawthorne needs to construct his position on the problematic relationship between the individual and his larger community by the alternation of conflicting perspectives. "The 'Conclusion' allows a self-aware Hawthorne to make a final juxtaposition of criticism and endorsement of the established social order. His compromise resolution is essentially the tough-minded statement that both viewpoints do and must coexist."

Journal Essays and Notes

413   Bergmann, Harriet. "Henry Adams's *Esther*: No Faith in the Patriarchy." *Markham Review* 10 (1981): 63 67.

Offers brief parallels between Adams's title character and Hawthorne's Hester, noting that both authors emphasize gender and sex roles. Circumstances direct both similarly-named characters to assume a freedom of intellectual speculation that leads to plans of escape that are condemned by their clergyman lovers who in turn reject them. Whereas Hester is eventually redeemed by a life of good works, Esther Dudley is "socialized into triviality" after losing her love, rejecting religion and continuing her intellectual wanderings.

414   Jordan, Gretchen Graf. "Adultery and Its Fruit in *The Scarlet Letter* and *The Power and the Glory*: The Relation of Meaning and Form." *Yale Review* 71 (1981): 72-87.

Cites parallels between *Letter* and Graham Green's *The Power and the Glory* (1940) that stem from both authors' preoccupations with the same moral theme of spiritual rebirth that is illustrated metaphorically by "a priest, an illicit sexual act, and a bastard daughter." In addition to sharing the same Fortunate Fall subject and similar names of the illegitimate daughters (Pearl/Coral), both novels share structural correspondences (the motif of the night journey that leads to spiritual regeneration, love for another over love for oneself, and finally a sacrificial death that leaves the question of salvation ambiguously open), the pervasive tone of ambiguity and irony, and real-world settings in a particular place and time that function as the stage for richly symbolic action. Through the priest

210

figures, both novels also function as cultural registers or historical studies
of threatening psychological changes during their respective time periods
(Dimmesdale representing New England Calvinism and the Whiskey
Priest typifying Mexican Catholicism—both illustrating how the religious
institutions falter as a result of having become "overintellectualized,
repressive, and incapable of responding to basic human needs"). The most
interesting difference between the two novels is Green's "uglification" and
sterilization of "much that he found beautiful in Hawthorne" (including
the death of Coral), reflecting an increasing emphasis on ugliness and
sterility in twentieth-century fiction in which there seems to be no place
for a "child as a symbol of hope and rebirth."

415   Manheim, Leonard F. "Outside Looking In: Evidences of Primal-Scene
       Fantasy in Hawthorne's Fiction." *Literature and Psychology* 31.1 (1981):
       4-15.

Traces "the progress, in a psychological fashion, of increasing
sophistication in [Hawthorne's] process of depicting viewer-and-viewed"
in his fiction, touching on "The Minister's Black Veil," "Wakefield,"
"Young Goodman Brown" and *Letter*. *Letter* is Hawthorne's most
complicated depiction of the primal-scene fantasy in "its basic aspect of
observer and observed" (probably because it was written under traumatic
circumstances), placing Hester on display for observation and creating an
"example of unusual voyeurism" in the relationship between Dimmesdale
and Chillingworth. By giving life to Chillingworth's probing, peeping-
Tom character, who gives "evidence of the ambivalence which led
[Hawthorne] to resist the analytic drive at the same time as he felt the need
for it," Hawthorne reaches "the point of zenith in his heroic [and lifelong]
attempt at self-analysis and purgation" of guilt.

416   Marx, Leo. "Two Tales of the City: Anti-Urbanism in American
       Literature." *New Boston Review* 6 (1981): 12-13, 14, 16.

See 409 for Marx's revised version of this essay. *Letter* and *The Great
Gatsby* (1925) represent classic American writers' susceptibility to and a
"continuous replaying or testing" of an Emersonian transcendental
pastoralism. Any "anti-urbanism" detected in American writing is not due
to any animosity for city life per se (a concept "grossly reductive and
misleading"), but rather to an adverse reaction to "the kind of society
whose power is concentrated [in a city.]" Thus Hawthorne's judgment of
Puritan culuture, "not his personal feelings about cities as places to live, is
what governs the way he writes about Boston in *Letter*." Likewise, F.
Scott Fitzgerald represents New York "not chiefly for what it is, but for
what it means." Gatsby's "green vision of America," like Hester's own

pastoral dream, is illusory and ends in "manifest failure," exposing "the glorious impracticality of the pastoral alternative each has posed to urban reality."

417   Merrill, Robert. "Another Look at the American Romance." *Modern Philology* 78 (1981): 379-392.

Arguing that the theory of the American romance advanced by Richard Chase (in 55) and Joel Porte (in 238) misleads readers to misread our classics, Merrill reconsiders the implications of reading a novel like *Letter* as a "romance." First of all, the term "romance" means something very different to today's modern critics than it did in Hawthorne's day, when it more or less signified fiction (and corresponds to our modern conception of the novel today). Second, the commonplace tendency among critics to label *Letter* as an allegorical romance not only "reduces" the novel but also distorts and overlooks several of its novelistic qualities, the most important of which involves a concern with the effects of social experience on individuals. Merrill argues against the three exaggerated features most commonly cited as evidence of *Letter*'s genre as allegorical romance—"the supposed 'thinness' of its social context, its reliance on 'marvelous' or supernatural materials, and its use of 'flat' or emblematic characters"—and concludes that Hawthorne's novelistic treatment of his characters' tragic actions points to the centrality of that dramatic action rather than to the book's archetypal meaning.

418   Price, Barbara. "Substance and Shadow: Mirror Imagery in *The Scarlet Letter*." *Publications of the Missouri Philological Association* 6 (1981): 35-38.

Although the contrast in *Letter* between light and dark has been discussed at length (most notably by Richard Harter Fogle in 15 and 236), there has been no significant discussion of mirror imagery in the novel—that Hawthorne uses to advance his theme of the difference between appearance and reality. The distorted image created by a reflection is most often "a more accurate representation of reality than is the object being reflected," as when Hester views herself in Governor Bellingham's armor and sees the scarlet letter magnified to overwhelming proportions: "an accurate representation of the impression the letter makes upon its beholders." Other notable examples include Pearl gazing into the armor to produce the distorted image of a devilish imp, the scene in which Hester imagines Dimmesdale's reflected image when she looks into Pearl's eyes, and the instance in chapter 11, "The Interior of a Heart," when Dimmesdale stares into a mirror and beholds, among other specters displayed there, Hester and Pearl.

1982

Essays and Studies in Books

419   Baym, Nina. "Thwarted Nature: Nathaniel Hawthorne as Feminist."
       American Novelists Revisted: Essays in Feminist Criticism. Ed. Fritz
       Fleischmann. Boston: Hall, 1982. 58-77.

Rejects the "grossly reductive" work of most "pre-feminist" and feminist
critics who depict Hawthorne as "conservative in his view of women's
place, patronizing in his estimate of their capacities, while all the while
secretly fearful of their sexual power," and argues that Hawthorne's
extensive portrayals of women actually reveal feminist tendencies. In fact,
his female protagonists consistently "represent desirable and valuable
qualities lacking in the male protagonist." These qualities have the
potential of transferring to the male through "erotic alliance or marriage"
with the female, but when the male fails to make the alliance and rejects
the female, he is judged harshly by the narrator. "Ultimately, [Hawthorne]
holds men and the society that men have created responsible for mistaking
neurosis for truth, and elevating error into law, custom, and morality."
Hawthorne's compelling tales about mistreated women therefore "depict
what he condemns." In *Letter*, for example (pp. 73-76), the narrator
clearly allies himself with Hester, and "despite occasional adverse
judgments, devotes himself to her cause." Unlike her wimpy, self-
absorbed male counterparts, Hester maintains both "inner integrity" and
"outer responsiveness"; and her heroic, self-sacrificing actions in the face
of adversity help the reader to "read" her letter as a "badge of honor," not
a "mark of negation." Most important about Hawthorne's characterization
of Hester is that Hester's marriage to Chillingworth and erotic relationship
with Dimmesdale are downplayed so that her essential nature is not
defined by her relation to either man. Instead, "she is portrayed primarily
in relation to the difficulties in her social situation, in relation to herself,
and in relation to Pearl."

420   Kinkead-Weekes, Mark.   "The Letter, the Picture, and the Mirror:
       Hawthorne's Framing of *The Scarlet Letter.*" *Nathaniel Hawthorne: New
       Critical Essays.* Ed. A. Robert Lee. London and Totowa: Vision Press
       and Barnes and Noble, 1982. 68-87.

Most critiques of *Letter* that focus on Hawthorne's dark or tragic vision
fail to come to terms with the impersonal, remote nature—the obtrusive
artfulness—of the tale. This persistent impression that the characters are
"statuesque" and the scenes are "not drama but tableau" points to

Hawthorne's framing technique in creating the suggestive, overall "picture" of the novel. The "clues" that point to this curious and "strenuously simple" technique are introduced in "The Custom-House" and realized in *Letter*—where it becomes clear that Hawthorne's conception of Romance is "the picturing of the actual and the reflection of that picture in a mirror." The romance is then worked out in a flux of contrasting, "circling rhythms" and "shifting angles and lightings." When *Letter* is viewed in this way, Hawthorne's prose (which contains such qualities of a mirror as surface polish, impermeability, objectivity, imperturbability, and distance) seems less personal, confessional, or romantic than it does public, "artful," and Augustan. Ultimately "his art is not a symbolism drawing all referents into itself but a hieroglyph, a sacred writing (letter *and* picture *and* mirror), a verge to a wholeness that can only be hauntingly reflected, beyond, within." [For something of a companion piece to this essay, see A. Robert Lee directly below (421).]

421   Lee, A Robert. "'Like a Dream Behind Me': Hawthorne's 'The Custom-House' and *The Scarlet Letter.*" *Nathaniel Hawthorne: New Critical Essays.* Ed. A Robert Lee. London and Totowa: Vision Press and Barnes and Noble, 1982. 48-67.

Intended to complement Mark Kinkead-Weekes's essay (see 420), this piece establishes "The Custom-House" as a "narrative in its own imaginative right," which "cannily discloses [Hawthorne's] working procedures as a romancer and constitutes an indispensable pathway into *Letter* itself." Despite the vast attention bestowed on *Letter*, comparatively few critical eyes have focused on "The Custom-House." Such neglect of the "utter organic importance" of reading the two pieces together renders a profound critical disservice to the novel, especially because the suffocating, paralytic Salem described in the sketch is undeniably akin to the Boston depicted in *Letter*. The preface "serves to define the Romance; to convey Hawthorne's sense of what for an American writer constitutes a usable past; to allegorize the deeply inward creative process whereby energies seemingly at ebb recover and are re-deployed; and to set up intimate writerly and readerly terms of reference whereby the ensuing fiction might most profitably be understood." In short, *Letter* "acts to fulfill all the promptings of 'The Custom-House.'"

422   Peach, Linden. "Imaginative Sympathy: Hawthorne's British Soul-Mate." *British Influence on the Birth of American Literature.* New York: St. Martin's Press, 1982. 91-137, 204-206.

Discusses the general tendency of early nineteenth-century American writers to "submit" to British influences despite their intention to create a distinct literature that would be a radical departure from that of the Old World. Sir Walter Scott's *Heart of Midlothian* (1818) had a particularly strong influence on Hawthorne's *Letter*. In addition to having striking similarities in plot and character (unmarried mothers forced to declare their sexual indiscretions and lawlessness before their outraged Puritan communities), both novels share parallel approaches to history, display similar uses of the supernatural, and present scathing critiques of persecuting, intolerant forefathers (for Scott the Presbyterian Calvinists and for Hawthorne the Puritans). Both Scott and Hawthorne ultimately set forth a "thesis of imaginative sympathy" in these novels, calling attention to a need for "a sympathetic understanding of others that is rooted in recognizing the dark aspect of one's own psyche." In general, Hawthorne saw in Scott's novel "a means through which he could explore the limitations of those who would deny sexual passion as an amoral force in human nature [and] interpret human behavior according to a rigid, inflexible, moral code." Hawthorne's adaptation also suggests fundamental differences between himself and Scott, since Hawthorne is much more drawn toward lawlessness and "the anarchic, amoral aspects of human nature" that Scott never pursued.

Journal Essays and Notes

423   Baker, Sheridan. "Hawthorne's Evidence." *Philological Quarterly* 61 (1982): 481-483.

Forcefully argues that critic Robert E. Abrams is mistaken—and is entirely missing Hawthorne's point—in "My Kinsman, Major Molineux" (*Philological Quarterly* 58 [1979]: 336-347) where he cites both the story's "climactic experience" and the ending of *Letter* when Dimmesdale bares his chest as examples of Hawthorne's deliberate authorial ambiguity. Both Robin's nightmarish midnight procession and Dimmesdale's scarlet letter are not open to interpretation as to their reality. Of the scarlet letter on Dimmesdale's chest, it is its *origin*, not its *actuality* that produces the several theories from which the Puritan community and the reader may choose. Hawthorne's "whole point" of the chapter "The Revelation of the Scarlet Letter," is, after all, to show "how witnesses will rationalize, and even rationalize away, the evidence before their eyes." The chapter title alone indicates the unmistakable reality of the letter, which is not "*a* Scarlet Letter" or "*Another* Scarlet Letter" but "*the* Scarlet Letter"—"the real one the book has been about, that of the hidden hypocritical guilt rather than the one emblazoned on Hester." To allow, as Abrams does, the possibility that the letter is not really there is "to ignore Hawthorne evidence and to blunt the force of his authorship."

424   Baym, Nina. "Nathaniel Hawthorne and His Mother: A Biographical Speculation." *American Literature* 54 (1982): 1-27.

Speculating that it was the death of Hawthorne's mother that inspired the writing of *Letter* rather than his dismissal from the Custom House (which merely freed him to write the novel), Baym suggests that Hester—a woman and a mother—is a "complex memorial" to his mother. Baym offers a biographical account of Hawthorne's relationship with his mother that goes against accounts of early biographers who misrepresent Elizabeth Hawthorne as overly domineering, reclusive, and cold, as well as underestimate her influence on her son. In fact, Hawthorne (despite his own efforts to put forth the same "legend" of his mother) was deeply attached to his mother and created his novel to "rescue its heroine from the oblivion of death and to rectify the injustices that were done to her in life." Baym further suggests that Hawthorne's working out of Hester's character—creating his mother fictionally just as his mother had created him in life—implies a repudiation of the father figure and also his wish "to be free of lifelong dependency on maternal power, the wish to have one's mother all to oneself."

425   Bell, Millicent. "The Obliquity of Signs: *The Scarlet Letter*." *Massachusetts Review* 23 (1982): 9-26.

Cites the frequently used synonymous words "type," "emblem," "token," and "hieroglyph" in the novel that all contain suggestive (and vague) symbolic value to argue that *Letter* is "an essay in semiology" whose theme is "the obliquity or indeterminacy of signs." Hawthorne's profound concern with his own inability to discern higher truth or a definitive sense of spiritual reality accounts for the novel's insistent ambiguity and methodical indeterminacy (and places him on the threshold of the modern condition—as a pre-deconstructionist aware of the subjective nature of signs). He gives play throughout to all of his divided attitudes about the nature of meaning and reality, thus explaining why the narrator consistently offers alternative readings of particular symbols but refuses to interpret events for the reader.

426   Branch, Watson. "From Allegory to Romance: Hawthorne's Transformation of *The Scarlet Letter*." *Modern Philology* 80 (1982): 145-160.

Proposes that the romance's many imperfections—its "unnecessary repetitions," inconsistencies in characterization and motivation, and problems with narrative development—result from Hawthorne's rushed and incomplete revision of the manuscript. Branch has particular trouble with Chillingworth's lack of interest to punish Hester's infidelity and Hester's failure to reveal Chillingworth's true identity to Dimmesdale, and he claims that a simple explanation accounts for all the novel's flaws. In the original "germinal" version of *Letter*, Hester and Chillingworth were not married, and the story was strictly an allegorical tale of the conflict between the Satanic Chillingworth and the sinning minister. In the final romantic version, which Hawthorne was too hurried by his publisher to revise adequately, Chillingworth's status as "wronged husband" conflicts with his earlier characterization as Satanic investigator. Similarly, Hester's character shows Hawthorne's conflicting characterization because, in the latter version, he portrays her in a softer, more sympathetic light than in the former. Also inconsistent in the final version is Dimmesdale's insensitive behavior, particularly his inability to acknowledge that he has wronged Chillingworth. [See Hershel Parker (502) for a refutation of Branch's theory on the incomplete manuscript.]

427   Cottom, Daniel. "Hawthorne Versus Hester: The Ghostly Dialectic of Romance in *The Scarlet Letter*." *Texas Studies in Literature and Language* 24 (1982): 47-67.

Placing himself beyond the realm of judgment, Hawthorne's diffident narrator in both "The Custom-House" and *Letter* associates himself with the "safe" symbolic realm of romance while he is careful to dissociate himself from Hester's "demonic realm of nature." Hawthorne's equivocal style, linked to a ghostly and otherworldly transcendence (in the sense that it creates for him "an otherworldly style of being in which even the most profound differences that arise in the world—including the most severe conflicts over supernatural beliefs—can coexist without needing to be brought to a resolution"), contrasts with the prison-like physicality that Hester cannot escape, largely because she is a woman (women can't transcend physicality or social judgment unless they become witches) and because the tangible physical presence of Pearl cannot be debated—since her actuality "cannot coexist peacefully with the imaginary." Although both Hawthorne and Hester are lawless ghosts of disembodied spheres, he is of the free Imaginary realm and she of the fetter-bound Actual realm trapped by her "unequivocable transgression," and so only Hawthorne can escape through the realm of romance—superior over someone like Hester who ventures to "mar" symbolic action with real action. "In effect, Hester and the others are the scapegoats of his stylistic sensibility as much as they are the victims of Puritan law, and the work of romance is thus made an argument for its narrator's deliverance from their fate."

428   Hudgins, Andrew. "Landscape and Movement in *The Scarlet Letter*." *South Dakota Review* 19.4 (1982): 5-17.

Examines the "literary geography" of *Letter* to reveal "an even deeper structuring of the romance than has previously been brought to light." The punishing scaffold is the center of the novel's world, out of which radiate "in concentric circles" the town itself, the forest, and "an outermost uncircumscribed realm which includes Indian territory and Europe." Hester moves in and out of this literal, emotional, and spiritual landscape, and she "returns repeatedly to the scaffold, only to find the strength [each time] to move farther and farther into the distant circles of her potential movement." Yet, after experiencing "all the world available to her," Hester realizes that she is most comfortable living on the periphery—to "balance off her centrifugal and centripetal drives and live in equipose of the outskirts of town, between the restraints of town and the license of the wilderness."

429   Marston, Jane. "Howells' *A Modern Instance*." *Explicator* 40 (1982): 41.

Argues that "full understanding of a passage near the end of William Dean Howells' *A Modern Instance* (1882) depends upon awareness of the parallelism between Flavia, the child described in the passage, and Hawthorne's Pearl." As products of " a broken home and of parents who have lost their religious certitude," both "demonic" characters serve as potential warnings of future degenerative social institutions.

430   Newberry, Frederick. "*The Red Badge of Courage* and *The Scarlet Letter*." *Arizona Quarterly* 38 (1982): 101-115.

Invites a comparison of the two novels, inasmuch as it appears Stephen Crane's *Red Badge of Courage* [1895] owes a fairly substantial debt to *Letter* that extends beyond the obvious surface parallels of the scarlet emblems in both titles, the consistent exploitation throughout both of the colors red, black, and gold, as well as symmetrically-structured narratives that are both arranged in twenty-four chapters. Detecting a "kinship in language and style," Newberry notes that "Hawthorne's 'tale of human frailty and sorrow' and Crane's treatment of Henry Fleming's initiation into a world of pain and struggle present the question of guilt and remorse in nearly identical psychological fashion." Newberry compares Henry's guilty plight with that of Dimmesdale's (equating the imagined "letters of guilt" that burn into the "nervous and highly sensitive" boy's forehead and the badge he hypocritically accepts with the shame-inspired burning letter that Dimmesdale bears on his breast), even suggesting a similar religious sensibility between the two characters. Henry and Hester also resemble one another, to the extent that both wear badges that bear different private and public meanings, suggesting their authors' mutually "flexible connotations of symbols."

431   Ragussis, Michael. "Family Discourse and Fiction in *The Scarlet Letter*." *ELH* 49 (1982): 863-888.*

The dangerous "ban of silence" that appears to be imposed on everyone in the novel originates not with the Puritan censors but with the four family members, whose refusal/failure to know or name one another constitutes the chief crime in *Letter*: the "crime of silence." Throughout, Hawthorne shows the family—through linguistic acts of secrecy and deception—"as the creator of its own system of suppression, torture, and violation." Family discourse continually undercuts itself as the necessary result of the "linguistic deadlock," painfully delaying not only the recognition of enemy and kindred but also the denouement of the tale. What's more, Dimmesdale's eventual confession "turns [the reader] back to the prefatory essay, where we find Hawthorne's [Dimmesdale-like] desire to confess the truth and the complex desires and laws that possess the author himself in the contest between speech and silence."

*See 516 for Ragussis's updated version of this essay. Another minor revision of this essay appears in 637 under a slightly different title from the original version: "Silence, Family Discourse, and Fiction in *The Scarlet Letter*."

432   White, Paula K. "'Original Signification': Post Structuralism and *The Scarlet Letter*." *Kentucky Philological Association Bulletin* (No volume number given) (1982): 41-54.

Post-structuralism advances criticism of Hawthorne (and other American Renaissance writers) past the dead end of New Criticism because it moves beyond consideration of the symbol and facilitates "an awareness of the symbolic function of language itself." In "The Custom-House," which emphasizes the activity of reading, Hawthorne suggestively primes the reader for accepting the burden of responsibility to interpret the text for himself. The narrative proper, which "teaches us about subjectivity and change," develops in such a way that the reader becomes less and less sure of what he knows to be true, creating a "profoundly unsetting effect" until the reader realizes that interpretation itself is the subject of the romance. *Letter* thus "destroys belief in the objective, eternal value of signs and renders interpretation increasingly problematical"—so that the only truly "original signification" in the novel is Hawthorne's, when he created the "fictive web" around a "rag of scarlet cloth."

433   Wright, Dorena Allen. "The Meeting at the Brook-Side: Beatrice, the Pearl-Maiden, and Pearl Prynne." *ESQ: A Journal of the American Renaissance* 28 (1982): 112-120.

Wright builds upon Anne Marie McNamara's biblical reading of the novel (see 50) (which asserts Pearl's narrative function in the novel as the "Tongues of Fire" agent of Dimmesdale's redemption) by suggesting that Hawthorne's religious inspiration for Pearl's part in Dimmesdale's enlightenment comes actually from two other sources: the anonymous Middle-English poem *Pearl* and Dante's *Divine Comedy*. Parallels among Hawthorne's Pearl, the *Pearl*-poet's Pearl-maiden, and Dante's Beatrice include ornate dress, radiant appearance, and unusually acute wisdom as a moral guide. The influence of these medieval precursors is not only apparent in the forest scene in which characters meet across a glittering stream, but can also be seen to "inform Hawthorne's conception of Pearl throughout the novel." Hawthorne is ultimately more concerned with man's relation to man than with man's relation to God; and thus Pearl is "human rather than divine." Her enactment of Dimmesdale's *secular* salvation unites him at last with humanity, not his heavenly father.

1983

Essays and Studies in Books

434   Baym, Nina. Introduction. *The Scarlet Letter: A Romance.* By Nathaniel Hawthorne. 1850. New York: Penguin Books, 1983. 1-24.

Explains Hawthorne's historical situation as a nineteenth-century American writer in a developing market economy; shows how "The Custom-House" and *Letter* are "intricately tied" to his private life experiences and feelings of rejection, previous writings, and "intense inner defiance" of social regulations; and argues that Hester is the "first and arguably still the greatest heroine in American literature." *Letter* works through three main conflicts of individual and social restraint: private versus public life, "spirit versus the letter," and the matriarchal versus the patriarchal ideal.

435   Bryson, Norman. "Hawthorne's Illegible Letter." *Teaching the Text.* Ed. Susanne Kappeler and Norman Bryson. London: Routeledge and Kegan Paul, 1983. 92-108.

Argues that *Letter*'s designated status as a "classic" (with a fixed "holism of meaning") does the novel a disservice to students coming to it for the first time with fresh insights—especially because Hawthorne's aim was to

220

"tear," "slash," and "destroy continuous meaning" for the reader. In presenting contradictory views of both his characters and Puritanism, Hawthorne by no means writes "ambiguously"; instead, he creates a narrative strategy of duplicity that refuses to present stabilized characters, thematic centrality, or even a clear climax. Perhaps this strategy was the only way that Hawthorne could "expiate his sense of complicity in the cruelty of his inherited culture, by rendering impossible precisely that kind of judgmental activity which was its most conspicuous [. . .] characteristic."

436   Herzog, Kristin. "The Scarlet A: Aboriginal and Awesome." *Women, Ethnics, and Exotics: Images of Power in Mid-Nineteenth-Century American Fiction.* Knoxville: U of Tennessee Press, 1983. 7-16.

Hester's lawless passion and wild nature are identified with the American Indian in *Letter.* This "aboriginal" aspect ("inwardly passionate, outwardly composed"), coupled with her exotic, voluptuous appearance, separates her completely from the Puritan community. However, Hester is also associated with the redemptive image of Divine Maternity, possessing an angel-like mercy. She is fully described, then, as both an "aboriginal" and an "awesome" figure (suggesting yet more meanings for the "A"), one who tempers "the primitive strength of these two types" with suffering and faith in the hope that a life of dedicated service will give her existence new meaning. Whereas Dimmesdale exemplifies "mere" spirituality, Hester represents a lively, creative Puritanism that seeks God's grace in a powerful commitment to human action and selfless living. This idea of "Romantic primitivism tempered by suffering and faith" structures the novel, especially since "Hester's Indian-like qualities of strength, passion, endurance, dignity, and independence are deemed admirable and are contrasted [throughout] with the narrow-mindedness of the Puritan system and the weakness of Dimmesdale."

437   Martin, Terence. "*The Scarlet Letter.*" *Nathaniel Hawthorne.* Rev. ed. Boston: G. K. Hall, 1983. 105-127.

This chapter on *Letter* in the revised edition of Martin's 1965 book (see asterisk under 132) shows virtually no revision except for the addition of two supporting references to critics Frederick Crews (from *Sins of the Fathers* [182]) and Nina Baym (from *The Shape of Hawthorne's Career* [339]) that enhance his discussion of the characters' multiple natures.

438   Simonson, Harold P.   "Puritan Faith, Romantic Imagination, and Hawthorne's Dilemma." *Radical Discontinuities: American Romanticism*

and Christian Consciousness. East Brunswick: Fairleigh Dickinson UP, 1983. 44-78.

Addresses Hawthorne's "two colliding realities," Calvinist and romantic, that "penetrated and permeated his deepest consciousness." These conflicting interpretations of God, nature, and self are explored in *Letter* (pp. 62-78) in the characters of Dimmesdale and Hester—in whom Hawthorne confronts the consequences of commitment to one "reality" or the other. The paradoxes inherent in the Christian vision make Dimmesdale's moral dilemma (which climaxes dramatically in the forest scene with Hester) far more complicated and torturous than Hester's personal romantic vision, although twentieth-century readers tend to sympathize more with Hester's plight and view her as the heroine of the novel. To view Hester as the heroine, however, is to "lessen the tug between Romantic imagination and Puritan faith" and to "diminish the significance of Dimmesdale's internal conflict between these polarities, a conflict that serves as the novel's dramatic locus and projects not only Hawthorne's dilemma but that of his time." For, while Hester can simply unclasp her letter to be free of its burden (since the letter's punishing symbolism does not touch her deeper nature), Dimmesdale, who feels the weight of his sin burning within him, cannot. As for Dimmesdale's conflict, "Notwithstanding his complex psychological condition, which includes guilt, hypocrisy, libidinous fantasies, and archetypal wanderings, his life is necessarily a crisis of Christian paradoxes that culminate when submission is his freedom, weakness his strength, ignominy his triumph, and death his life."

Journal Essays and Notes

439   Adams, Michael Vannoy. "Pathography, Hawthorne, and the History of Psychological Ideas." *ESQ: A Journal of the American Renaissance* 29 (1983): 113-126.

Taking issue with Frederick Crews's recent and "misguided" rejection of psychoanalysis as a viable approach to literature* (for throwing "Freud out with the couch")—when Crews should have simply recognized the particular deficiencies of his pathographical method in his famous *Sins of the Fathers* (see 182) (that being the conventional psychoanalytic assumption that an author's characters reflect psychological symptoms of his own neurosis), Adams insists that *Letter can* be significantly and validly treated by psychoanalytic criticism, especially in light of the fact that Hawthorne was not neurotic (nor obsessed with incest) but was a "great psychologist" in his own right, clearly a precursor of Freud. After all, many of the psychological themes in the novel are not symptoms of unconscious conflict but evidence of "quite conscious" psychological knowledge on Hawthorne's part. Adams provides ten psychoanalytic propositions implicit in the novel: "insights [that] anticipate Freud's views on demonic possession and neurotic obsession; the psychosomatic etiology of symptoms; the denial of sexual desire; the method of free association and the ethical responsibility of the psychoanalyst; the perversity of masochism; dreams and hysterical symptoms as a return of the repressed; paranoia and projection; slips of the tongue as examples of the psychopathology of everyday life; the discontents of civilization; the conflict between the life instinct and the death instinct; and, in his notion of a 'profounder self' whose influence is involuntary but intentional, the very idea of depth psychology and unconscious motivation."

*Adams specifically cites Crews's two studies "Analysis Terminable" (in *Commentary* 70 [1980]: 25) and *Out of My System: Psychoanalysis, Ideology, and Critical Method* (New York: Oxford UP, 1975), in the latter of which Crews acknowledges that forcing adultery to be a symbol for incest in *Letter* is to force "a peculiarly silly kind of allegory" in which "the work in its singularity is sacrificed to the interpretive scheme instead of being illuminated by it."

440   Barnett, Louise K. "Speech and Society in *The Scarlet Letter*." *ESQ: A Journal of the American Renaissance* 29 (1983): 16-24.*

Though Barnett makes no specific reference to critics whose viewpoints she opposes, she argues persuasively against post-structuralist readings that insist on "the faulty instrumentality of language" to communicate meaning or truth in the novel. *Letter* actually "demonstrates a [distinctly unmodern] confidence in the resources of language to communicate meaning."   "That truthful speech occurs so seldom" amongst the characters can be attributed to the "accusatory, judgmental, commanding, and threatening" nature of the Puritan society—which language reflects. Tensions between the individual and society inhibit or deform honest speech in public, especially for a character like Dimmesdale who gives his full allegiance to public language, "the speech of belongingness" (although to a lesser extent for Hester and Chillingworth, whose deceptive silences are a "form of verbal rebellion that asserts the primacy of self-expression over the collective vision"). The poles of speech and silence can actually be seen to define public and private worlds and create the dynamic of *Letter*. The forest scene is a prime example of Hawthorne's "linking of truthful speech with the private world and silence or deceptive utterance with the public," since this scene calls attention to the sad truth in the novel (when the plan for escape falls through) that private speech cannot be sustained in a public context where language only reinforces communally-shared values and negates all socially unacceptable impulses.

*For Barnett's revised and updated version of this essay, see 690.

441   Berthold, Michael Couson. "The Idea of 'Too Late' in James's 'The Beast in the Jungle.'" *Henry James Review* 4 (1983): 128-139.

The "too late" idea that stimulated Henry James's imagination in "The Beast in the Jungle" derives in part from Hawthorne's *American Notebooks* and less directly from *Letter*—where the characters of Hester and Dimmesdale "can be regarded as counterparts of May Bartram and John Marcher," especially in the sense that the quietly devoted Hester and May offer themselves to their self-obsessed, tormented loves, even though both women sense that it is too late for the men to exchange their false lives for truer ones. [For another essay that links *Letter* to "The Beast in the Jungle," see Jane Gottschalk (208).]

442   Buell, Lawrence. "Rival Romantic Interpretations of New England Puritanism: Hawthorne Versus Stowe." *Texas Studies in Literature and Language* 25 (1983): 77-99.*

Compares Hawthorne's *Letter* and Harriet Beecher Stowe's *The Minister's Wooing* (1859), noting many similarities and differences in the two fictional presentations of New England's past. "The central device in both books is to take an undogmatic, intuitively perceptive, liberal female sensibility and set it against a more traditional, dated, culture-bound, male sensibility." Indeed, the central characters in each are a neurotic Puritan minister (Arthur Dimmsdale/Samuel Hopkins) and an unconventional, more emotionally-developed heroine (Hester Prynne/Mary Scudder) who rebels against the Puritan repressiveness that drives her lover to "extremes of morbidity and despair." The difference between Hawthorne's and Stowe's presentations of Puritan life is actually "much in keeping with the split between [liberal] and orthodox intellectuals over the meaning of the Puritan legacy." Stowe belonged to the conservative orthodox camp that conceived of "old-time New England as the 'seed-bed' of all that is best in modern America," and so she enthusiastically presents New England's past as an idyllic pastoral state that developed the model for piety and conduct that would be followed in the 1800s. Hawthorne, on the other hand, like other liberal intellectuals of his day (in the "Unitarian-Transcendental mainstream"), found fault with the old Puritan tradition, and so presented it in his fiction as "grim, melancholy, and austere." Stowe was also more interested than was Hawthorne in presenting "family romance" and detailing the social structures and external lives of the

Puritans, while Hawthorne was more devoted to a psychological portrayal of "the inner stresses and self-deceptions caused by hypocrisy, by the inability to accept grace, and by the uncertainty as to whether one is to be saved."

*For a minor revision of Buell's essay, see "Hawthorne and Stowe as Rival Interpreters of New England Puritanism" in his *New England Literary Culture: From Revolution Through Renaissance* (Cambridge: Cambridge UP, 1986. 261-280).

443   Foster, Dennis. "The Embroidered Sin: Confessional Evasion in *The Scarlet Letter.*" *Criticism* 25 (1983): 141-163.

Ironically achieving "his greatest spiritual success by using the forms of Puritan orthodoxy to express a secular, sexual passion," Dimmesdale gains power as he sins anew with each eloquently-delivered, "confessional" sermon that deceptively and thus necessarily fails to deliver either secular or divine truth. Foster (who refers to Michel Foucault, Jacques Derrida, and René Girard) suggests that Dimmesdale's attraction to sin—and to Hester in particular—stems from his very desire to transgress, since, for him, "the attraction of the forbidden lies in its inverse relation to the unattainable divine." In other words, Dimmesdale wants to sin so that he can continually "re-create the limits of the law that he can violate." The effect of his "confessional evasions" and his lack of penitence is an increased desire for more indulgent, arduous confessions spoken in evasive double language (a type of language that Chillingworth appropriates from Dimmesdale in his relentless pursuit to possess the minister). What Dimmesdale discovers in this process are "the pleasures of a will to power, the narcissistic gratification of finding reflected in his listeners not the 'solemn music' of the divine but the idolatry that constitutes his own fascination with his speech and his sin." Dimmesdale's duplicitous use of language compares with Hawthorne's similar rhetorical strategies in "The Custom-House." The narrator's devious use of rhetorical artifice, like Dimmesdale's, is employed to couch his "infatuation with his own desire."

444   Griffith, Clark. "Pearl's Green A: *The Scarlet Letter* and American History." *Australasian Journal of American Studies* 2 (1983): 21-33.

Asserts that *Letter* is ultimately about the failure in American history, despite the desire to make a fresh start as the "Citty on the hill," to "put down roots of affection" and to "nurture and celebrate life." Pearl assumes the deeply allegorical function of "Young America" itself, misunderstood, neglected, and even despised by each community member (including Hester and Dimmesdale*) who is reminded by her presence "of how poison has infected the New World." When Pearl dons the seaweed green "A" while playing on the peninsula coast, she enacts a dream of escape and fantasizes about freedom, companionship, and the gift of a new self-image. Throughout the novel, her character brings to light all that is meanest and most rigid in the adults around her, and even when she is redeemed at the end by Dimmesdale's confession, she is still in the hands of the neglectful and self-serving, but at least she is now free to seek her green "A" elsewhere.

*Griffith claims that Hester cherishes Pearl only because the child is her father's daughter and that Hester exploits Pearl to taunt Dimmesdale and remind him of their union. Likewise, Griffith proposes that Dimmesdale sees Pearl as a "succubus," a "little red distraction" whom he dreads and wishes would vanish.

445   Hutner, Gordon. "Secrets and Sympathy in *The Scarlet Letter*." *Mosaic* 16 (1983): 113-124.*

Explores "the nature and implications of Hawthorne's strategies for simultaneously concealing and revealing secrets" in "The Custom-House" and *Letter*. Hawthorne's confessional procedure of eliciting the "kind" reader's sympathetic apprehension of truths that he will not or cannot reveal is at work both in his lighthearted and witty sidestepping around his experience of painful public exposure after losing his position in the Custom House and in his description of Hester's own humiliation (which is, of course, a subtle analogue to his own). Hawthorne's evasive concealment of his "secret" (which perhaps hides the truth of his own criminal activities in the Custom House) equates with Dimmesdale's defensive rhetorical strategies of conveying and withholding the truth of his relationship to Hester and Pearl. Just as Hawthorne interjects humor as a strategy for contending with his disgrace in "The Custom-House" (by making "jokes about decapitation or by poking fun at his cohorts"), so he has Dimmesdale employ the same defensive, Freudian kind of "exaltation of the ego" in making self-mocking, vague confessions and by inflicting self-punishments. Hawthorne even makes Dimmesdale's final revelation into a riddle—since "naming the secret" would "run counter to the narrative logic of both the romance and the preface."

*For Hutner's own development of this subject, see his *Secrets and Sympathy: Forms of Disclosure in Hawthorne's Novels* (566).

226

446   Ketterer, David. "'Circle of Acquaintance': Mistress Hibbins and the
       Hermetic Design of *The Scarlet Letter.*" *English Studies in Canada* 9
       (1983): 294-311.

Mistress Hibbins "looms so large in the overall design of the romance"
because her character provides Hawthorne with a way of working out his
"double bind" as both an artist and the descendant of a witch-killing
ancestor. Refusing to vindicate "the persecuting spirit of John Hathorne"
by portraying Hibbins as the embodiment of evil, Hawthorne instead
presents her as a "victim of misjustice," building up her melodramatic
presence so that she becomes essential in terms of her contribution to the
"hermetic circle" of fluid relationships formed by her and the four major
characters in the book (she was created by Hawthorne to close the circle or
to "heal the breach" between Chillingworth and Pearl, who themselves
"do not make a very natural pair or "dissolve" well into one another).
Ketterer examines the "characterological geometry" that creates out of the
five characters a pentangle "composed of five letter A's" (he includes a
diagram), concluding that the circle of character relationships is intended
as an analogue for unified relatedness. Thus Mistress Hibbins's role in the
novel is more subtle and positive than has heretofore been considered,
since she exhibits Hawthorne's good/evil ambivalence and even provides
a bridge between the community and the wilderness. As an ambiguous
embodiment of alienation and hypocrisy on the one hand and the artistic
truth of communal unity on the other, Mistress Hibbins—as a witch—is
also a metaphor for Hawthorne's own artistic "wizardry," which is
described in the novel (as is Pearl's "witchery") as "an imaginative or
artistic force for empathy."

447   Leverenz, David. "Mrs. Hawthorne's Headache: Reading *The Scarlet
       Letter.*" *Nineteenth-Century Fiction* 37 (1983): 552-575.*

Leverenz finds it curious that "what starts as a feminist revolt against
punitive patriarchal authority ends in a muddle of sympathetic pity for
ambiguous victims," and looks to the profoundly contradictory, elusive
narrator for clues to Hawthorne's allegiance with and condemnation of his
characters. Leverenz treats Hawthorne's narrative stance as a subversion
of communal values, focusing on "Hawthorne's profoundly contradictory
affinities with a rebellious, autonomous female psyche and an intrusive
male accuser." It is actually Hawthorne's "unresolved conflicts about
anger, authority, male rivalry, and female autonomy" that make the story
so powerful to modern readers and so accessible to critical inquiry. A
formalist examination of these conflicts opens the novel up to questions of
social history and reveal "the text's intimate, ambivalent relationship to
the author's own life and to the contemporary interpretive community."

*For a slightly modified version of this essay (under the same title), see Leverenz's *Manhood and the American Renaissance* (Ithaca: Cornell UP, 1989. 259-278). New to the piece is an extension of the thesis, which "explores the text as an expression of conflicts both in [Hawthorne's] feelings and in contemporary gender conventions," but now also "argues that the narrator's attempt to transcend his narrative's conflicts not only stifles [Hester's] subjectivity, but implicates him in an exceptionally narcissistic resolution of male rivalry." Thus what starts out in the novel as a feminist argument in favor of Hester's rebellion and strength in comparison to the weak Dimmesdale turns into the story of the spiritual triumph of Dimmesdale and the subjection of Hester and Pearl into "softened" domestics. For another, more substantial revision of Leverenz's essay, see 641.

448   Parsons, Melinda B., and William M. Ramsey. "*The Scarlet Letter* and Herbal Tradition." *ESQ: A Journal of the American Renaissance* 29 (1983): 197-207.

Documents the complicated European folklore history in art and literature of the burdock plant,* which is one of the three poisonous plants mentioned in *Letter*'s opening scene to contrast with the wild rosebush. Parsons and Ramsey speculate about the likelihood of Hawthorne's knowledge of the plant's double symbolic meaning as both the positive "caritas" (charity, salvation) and the negative "cupiditas" (associated with lust and the serpent). The combined symbolic meaning of virtue and vice, of "the symbolic juxtapositions of earthly corruption with divine salvation," was applied to the plant in the late Renaissance and extended into the nineteenth century through botanical handbooks, and thus Hawthorne may well have been familiar with the plant's complex history when he introduces the burdock in three scenes in the novel—the opening scene, the scene where Pearl decorates Hester's scarlet letter with burdock burs, and the scene in which Chillingworth tells Dimmesdale that he gathered for one of his potions the "dark, flabby leaf" of the burdock from the unmarked grave of a secret sinner.

*Article includes several Baroque paintings and illustrations of burdock plants. For more on Chillingworth's poisons, see 475 and 503.

449   Ruderman, Judith. "The New Adam and Eve." *Southern Humanities Review* 17 (1983): 225-236.

Stressing Hawthorne's influence on D. H. Lawrence, Ruderman cites several instances in which Lawrence interprets *Letter* in his 1923 *Studies in Classic American Literature* (EC18) as a re-enactment and inversion of the Adam and Eve story—especially in an early version of the essay in which he writes, "In this myth of the second Fall, it is the serpent who marries Eve, it is the spiritual Adam who is brought down to prostitution." Hawthorne's adaptation of the biblical story was so entrenched in Lawrence's mind that he replayed it many times in his own fiction, though especially in *The Fox* (1922), which similarly "recounts the consequences of repressing one's desires" and replaces the sensual, serpentine Hester with Ellen March, the ethereal Dimmesdale with Jill Banford, and the "sensual serpent" Chillingworth with Henry Grenfel.

450   Sarracino, Carmine. *"The Scarlet Letter* and a New Ethic." *College Literature* 10 (1983): 50-59.

Applies Eric Neumann's exploration of "old ethic" vs. "new ethic" in *Depth Psychology and a New Ethic* (1973) to *Letter*, equating Dimmesdale's unhealthy attachment to Puritanism with "old ethic" (involving the suppression and repression of all negative tendencies that stem from the individual's need to obey the "collective" and construct a "façade personality") and Hester's dedication to a free-spirited, pre-transcendental code of conduct with "new ethic." The "root malaise" of Dimmesdale and his very vulnerability to a parasitic leech like Chillingworth (a "shadow figure" who represents Dimmesdale's forbidden desires and tendencies) is the result of following "an ethical structure which by its very nature breeds a schizoid division of personality." Because Hester is representative of the new ethic personality and does not construct a façade personality to hide her dark side, she does not create a shadow figure and thus is invulnerable to Chillingworth's insidious diabolism. Hawthorne's insight here, like Neumann's, is that no person can be victimized by another but only by his own weakness and incompleteness. "Conquer that weakness," Hawthorne implies, "and the victimizer melts away like a shadow before light." Hawthorne does not imply that the "new ethic" should completely replace the old ethic, athough the novel does address the ethical "shift"—most prominently through the character of Pearl, who at the end represents "the evolution of ethical consciousness Hawthorne envisions [. . .] that proceeds in slow, generational steps" to an ideal, healthy balance between old and new.

451   Weldon, Roberta. *"The Rose Tattoo*: A Modern Version of *The Scarlet Letter." Interpretations* 15 (1983): 70-77.

The Rose Tattoo (1950), an early comedy by Tennessee Williams, is "strongly indebted to Hawthorne's *Letter*" in that "it bears a decided similarity to Hawthorne's novel in both its central symbol and its main theme." Both works focus on the conflicts experienced by strong, passionate seamstresses who become outcasts in their communities because of excessive attachments to their lovers—the intense and futile commitments to whom are reflected in the ambiguous symbols they bear. As the heroines grapple to escape the constraints of their religions and to retain "their ideals in a world that denies their value," they also—like their authors—come to terms with "the universal human question of isolation and failure to communicate." Parallels extend to the daughters, Pearl and Rosa, who are both symbols incarnate, the scarlet letter and the rose tattoo "endowed with life." What makes the play characteristically modern, however, are its parodic elements that convert Hawthorne's tragedy into a comedy, that insist upon the triumph of life over death and for love to be permitted "the full flowering of its power."

1984

Books

452 Sheldon, Sara. *Nathaniel Hawthorne's The Scarlet Letter*. Woodbury: Barron's, 1984. 121 pp.

Part of the "Barron's Book Notes" series, this text contains introductory material about "the author and his times," plot, characters, setting, themes, symbolism, and structure, as well as scene-by-scene discussion and analysis. Also included is a section entitled "A Step Beyond," which includes sample tests and answers, term paper ideas, suggestions for further reading, a glossary, and a few excerpted words (a paragraph devoted to each) by critics on several subjects: theme (by Leslie A. Fiedler [89]), Puritanism (by Henry James [EC15]), symbolism (by Charles Feidelson, Jr., [21]), and characters (by Mark Van Doren [EC36]).

Essays and Studies in Books

453 Baker, Larry. "The PBS *Scarlet Letter*: Showing Versus Telling." *Nathaniel Hawthorne Journal 1978*. Ed. C. E. Frazer Clark, Jr. Detroit: Bruccoli Clark Publishers, 1984. 219-229.

Examines the script of the PBS adaptation of *Letter*, arguing that the main weakness is its three-part "insensitivity to context": "diminution of language" (such as the script's slashing of 80% of Dimmesdale's dying oration), "magnification of language" (which does away with intentional ambiguity), and "omission of language" (which edits out vital content). To put it most plainly, the novel is just "not good material for a television adaptation." In the novel form, "the pattern of reification, condensation of image and action, is coupled with Hawthorne's conscious efforts to create ambiguity by his use of 'it seemed' and 'it might have been' language, his multiple perspectives, his double negatives, his optional interpretations." These two critical and complicated characteristics, "actualized metaphor" and "ambiguous meaning," which involve condensed and expanded language, simply do not translate well from "written word" to "visual image," no matter how closely screen adaptors adhere to the original dialogue and script.

454   Bales, Kent. "Pictures, Signs, and Stereotypes in Hawthorne's Meditations on the Origins of American Culture." *The Origins and Originality of American Culture.* Ed. Tibor Frank. Budapest: Akadémiai Kiadó, 1984. 35-44.

Exhibiting the "conflict between two world views, between two spheres of meaning," *Letter* is Hawthorne's "most deliberate and sustained study of the transformation of the old into the new," of the cultural shift from "Puritan to democrat." In the process of trying, with limited success, to change the "signs" (literary stereotypes and cultural conventions) of both Hester's and his own times, Hawthorne shows—especially in the three scaffold scenes—just how interconnected the past really is with the present, and how arbitrary and vulnerable systems of belief are. In the first scaffold scene, Hester is presented as a "negative exemplum," but she is transformed by Hawthorne's evocation of the visual stereotype of the Virgin Mary into a positive sign. In the second scaffold scene, when the ambiguous "A" appears in the night sky and is interpreted differently by its witnesses, Hawthorne demonstrates most deliberately of all just how arbitrary systems of belief and signs are. And in the last scene, although Dimmesdale is accepted by the Puritans as a "sainted apostle and Modern Christ," Hawthorne encourages readers to reject both of those stereotypes and arrive at their own conclusions regarding the two competing interpretive systems.

455   Baris, Sharon Deykin. "The American Daniel as Seen in Hawthorne's *The Scarlet Letter.*" *Biblical Patterns in Modern Literature.* Eds. David H. Hirsch and Nehama Aschkenasy. Chico: Scholars Press, 1984. 173-185.

"Owing to the prominence of the Puritan tradition in American culture, the literature of the United States has, from its origins, been strongly motivated by biblical thinking and imagery." The biblical figure of Daniel, whose prophetic dream of a glorious destiny "is the source for the assumption that America is a privileged world," is adapted by Hawthorne in *Letter* and split into "two putative, contending American Daniels." Both Chillingworth and Dimmesdale are submitted as potential Daniels who come to the marketplace to "judge and save," having envisioned a "high and glorious destiny" for New England. Conceivably, the novel should be recognized as having been divided by Hawthorne into two main sections, each dominated by its own very different, imperfect Daniel who "struggles to impose his view" upon both Hester and the world while at the same time denying "the humanizing factors of life."

456   Clark, Robert. "Nathaniel Hawthorne: *The Scarlet Letter*: The Adulterous Allegory of American Art." *History and Myth in American Fiction, 1823-1852.* New York: St. Martin's Press, 1984. 110-124.

When James Fenimore Cooper and Hawthorne denied that their romances were reality-based or politically motivated, they were not being honest, because they felt pressured to "conced[e] to critical demands that their works be mere entertainments." Actually, their works were "acutely addressed to the political life of the nation," articulating the dominant ideological contradictions of their historical moments. Hawthorne's art in particular is formed by "the contradiction between a desire for regeneration and a knowledge that history has proved regeneration to be a mythological project." *Letter* represents the disparity between the ideal and the actual in New England's Puritan past, revealing doubts about "regeneration" being possible in America. "In showing that the Puritans failed to build a New World because they had not abandoned the Old World need for hierarchy and repressive order, Hawthorne evidences his agreement with contemporary Democratic ideology."

457   Dolis, John. "Hawthorne's Letter." *Notebooks in Cultural Analysis: An Annual Review.* Ed. Norman F. Catnor. Durham: Duke UP, 1984. 103-123.*

In this post-structuralist essay that builds on ideas developed by Sigmund Freud, Jacques Lacan, and Jacques Derrida, Dolis focuses on Hawthorne's struggle to assert "authorship" over his text. He contemplates the way meaning is generated and assigned in *Letter*—beginning with an explanation of the way in which Hawthorne ascertains the significance of the letter found in the attic (by opposing the "authority of the logos" and seeking meaning in the heart, where "a multiplicity of versions" may figure forth). Just as the letter "multiplies its meaning across the otherness of itself, so too with the subject: the signifier acquires its meaning from the other signifiers, resisting a transcendental signified." In other words, Hawthorne, the letter, and the characters themselves acquire identity by their relation to others. "Hawthorne's pre-text ["The Custom-House"], Pearl's correspondence, Dimmesdale's confession, Hester's embroidery—

each inscribes the story of the self in the context of the other to which it corresponds; each discourse makes the other its own."

*See 692 for Dolis's expansion of this essay.

458   Edwards, Lee R. "Lilies That Fester: The Divine Compromise in *Clarissa* and *The Scarlet Letter.*" *Psyche as Hero: Female Heroism and Fictional Form.* Middletown: Wesleyan UP, 1984. 29-61.

In Samuel Richardson's *Clarissa* (1748-49) and Hawthorne's *Letter*, the heroism of Clarissa and Hester "threatens primary social structures and challenges the moral and ethical imperatives animating domestic and communal life." Both heroines are very much alike in their appraisals of their "psychologically invasive" and "physically enclosing" environments and in their isolation-induced experiences of material and spiritual freedom. Yet despite the fact that Richardson and Hawthorne use their heroines to "expose the rapacity and inhumanity" of dominant men, Clarissa's and Hester's efforts to subvert patriarchal structures are ultimately rejected. Their heroic possibilities remain undeveloped and unfulfilled because neither author is "comfortable" with incarnating a vision—no matter how hopeful—that proves "antithetical to social stability."

459   Erlich, Gloria. "The Access of Power." *Family Themes and Hawthorne's Fiction: The Tenacious Web.* New Brunswick: Rutgers UP, 1984. 1-34.

This "thematic study of the continuities between Hawthorne's life and his art" examines "the psychological and experiential sources of his fiction." Erlich draws from Hawthorne's childhood—the loss of his biological father—to argue that "maternal presence and paternal absence are the positive and negative poles that generate" *Letter* (pp. 26-30). The action of the novel is initiated, therefore, by Pearl's search among several father-figures (Chillingworth, Dimmesdale, and the Puritan elders) for her "true" father and his parental recognition, and the grand finale involves the restoration of the true biological family. Like Pearl, whose biological father is Dimmesdale and whose surrogate father (at least in terms of financial support) becomes Chillingworth, Hawthorne at a young age experienced the death of his father and the subsequent support of his surrogate father, his uncle Robert Manning.

460   Friedman, Donald Flanell. Foreword. *The Scarlet Letter.* By Nathaniel Hawthorne. 1850. New York: Chatham River Press, 1984. vii-ix.

Letter, which is timeless because it deals with "issues of individual freedom and the right to determine one's own moral code," was groundbreaking for its "penetrating psychological insight" at a time when delving into mental states and hidden motives was most uncommon in fiction. Overall, the foreword offers a very general summary of *Letter*, briefly addressing "The Custom-House," feminism, fatalism, and the novel's imagistic language.

461   Hodgens, Lisa. "Hawthorne's Last Period or Death Rattle in a Moonlit Room." *Nathaniel Hawthorne Journal 1978.* Ed. C. E. Frazer Clark, Jr. Detroit: Bruccoli Clark Publishers, 1984. 231-238.

Hawthorne anticipated his own eventual collapse as a creative artist in "The Custom-House." The sketch describes a period in his career when his creative powers were ebbing—as when, years later, he was working on his late, fragmented fiction (*The Ancestral Footstep, Doctor Grimshawe's Secret, Septimius Felton,* and *The Dolliver Romance*). While at work on these last pieces, however, when Hawthorne again found himself in "a moonlit room with only dead images and unrealized themes," he could not find that "neutral territory" that enabled him in "The Custom-House" to become a literary man again.

462   Lloyd-Smith, Allen Gardner. "The Elaborated Sign of the Scarlet Letter." *Eve Tempted: Writing and Sexuality in Hawthorne's Fiction.* London: Croom Helm, 1984. 9-30.*

Because the scarlet letter serves as an elaborated "double sign"—as both a precise, "historically determined signifier" (of adultery) and the initial alphabetic sign that calls attention to language and the act of writing—its meaning is both fixed and open. Although Hester's punishment requires that "she should be written on and be unable to efface the inscription," she "writes on the community in 'manifold emblematic devices,'" and the message that she writes is the message of her own exegesis of the letter, a luxuriant exfoliation as subversive of the colony's official statues as it is of the bare outline of the typographic sign 'A.'" Jacques Derrida's analysis of Rousseau's *Essay on the Origin of Language* provides suggestive commentary on the "language vs. voice" typology issues involved in *Letter*. Just as Rousseau situates the written word as removed from the actual spoken word, so Hawthorne does the same in the novel. By being written on, Hester becomes inextricably associated with written language—so that when she comes to identify with the letter that speaks for her, she suffers a two-fold displacement from her true self.

234

*For an updated version of this essay, see 551—under a slightly different name: Allen Lloyd Smith.

463   McWilliams, John P.   "Narrower Souls: the Character of Doom." *Hawthorne, Melville, and the American Character: A Looking-Glass Business*. Cambridge: Cambridge UP, 1984. 64-70.

Discusses the gradual degeneration of the moral and religious Puritan character that coincided with the development of New England from colony to progressive republic.   Hawthorne attributes the inevitable Puritan "generational decline" to a slackening of faith, a resentment of saintly forefathers, and, above all, a perpetual chafing through time under the heavy burden of guilt.   The resulting decline in inner strength and integrity is portrayed in *Letter* in the youthful Arthur Dimmesdale, whose hypocritical and prideful character develops a crippling combination of traits: "veneration for the elders, a suppressed desire to deface their saintliness, outward conformity to sanctified behavior, and an unwillingness to test one's inner feelings in the world."   In a view of Hester that is contrary to "modern-day" interpretations of her character, McWilliams argues that critics focus far too exclusively on the few passages in the novel that detail Hester's subversive nature at the expense of the majority of the novel which consistently represents her as torn between her guilt-inspiring theological heritage and the fulfillment she still feels from her shameless experience of human passion.   When Hester is viewed in this way, her return to Boston at the end is neither uncharacteristic nor demeaning of her character, but rather a triumphant and proud tribute to her strength and honesty.

464   Nissenbaum, Stephen.   Introduction.   *The Scarlet Letter and Selected Writings*. By Nathaniel Hawthorne.   New York: Modern Library, 1984. vii-xlii.

Considers the connection between *Letter* and Hawthorne's life, concentrating on Hawthorne's "strategy" in "The Custom-House" of denying any connection between himself and his tale of torturous guilt and sin.   As "the tail that wagged the dog," "The Custom-House" sketch sold the novel in the first place, but its relevance to twentieth-century readers has unfortunately been questioned.   In it, in coded, "breezy" language, Hawthorne not only confesses his doubts about the integrity of his own art, but also "superbly disguise[s]" his humiliation and shame over being ousted from his position as surveyor—just as Dimmesdale attempts to "keep up a public image of innocence and sanctity" by manipulating his listeners with a confession "not intended to be deciphered" and presenting himself in a flattering light with no "peril of discovery."   Unlike

Hawthorne and Dimmesdale, however, the earnest Hester does not seek renown or approval, making no effort to win recognition. Because she does not share their ambition, only her art is pure. Nissenbaum further finds that "The Great Stone Face" was written as a "rehearsal" for *Letter*, because it also engages the topic of what ambition can do to "adulterate" the integrity of one's art. [See Hershel Parker (502) for a "corrective" reading of Nissenbaum's points about "The "Custom-House."]

465   Scheuermann, Mona.   "The American Novel of Seduction: An Explanation of the Omission of the Sex Act in *The Scarlet Letter.*" *Nathaniel Hawthorne Journal 1978.* Ed. C. E. Frazer Clark, Jr. Detroit: Bruccoli Clark Publishers, 1984. 105-118.

"The shape of the American novel of seduction is traceable to distinct elements in American culture that come to their fullest literary fruition in *Letter.*" Scheuermann places the novel within the American tradition of the eighteenth-century novel of seduction, which focuses not on the events that lead up to seduction but on the psychological consequences of the act itself. The sex act takes place "off stage" in *Letter* not because—as Leslic A. Fiedler has suggested (in 89)—Hawthorne is afraid of sex and its implications, but because he is "simply writing out of an American tradition which sees the illicit sex act as a psychological catalyst rather than as a social counter." Hawthorne is thus "more interested in the ways Hester deals with herself psychologically than in the particular stimulus (in this case adultery) which precipitates her social-psychological crises."

466   Trócsányi, Miklos. "Two Views of American Puritanism: Hawthorne's *The Scarlet Letter* and Miller's *The Crucible.*" *The Origins and Originality of American Culture.* Ed. Tibor Frank. Budapest: Akadémiai Kiadó, 1984. 63-71.

Discusses Hawthorne's and Arthur Miller's presentations of Puritanism. "Hawthorne's *Letter* provides an imaginative description of mid-seventeenth century Puritanism in the Boston region, while Miller's *The Crucible* (1953) presents an internalized drama of the witchcraft trials [. . .] in 1692." Both seem to present New England Puritanism indirectly through its negative effects on the individual, but *Letter* is more a "study of personal-national past as responsible for the present" while *The Crucible* is primarily concerned with keeping the past in the past and showing "the nature and origins of Puritanism in America."

467   Warren, Joyce W. "The Claims of the Other: Nathaniel Hawthorne." *The American Narcissus: Individualism and Women in Nineteenth-Century American Fiction.* New Brunswick: Rutgers UP, 1984. 189-230.

Unlike most nineteenth-century American writers, Hawthorne created "fully drawn women characters" that went beyond the "stereotyped image of American femininity," particularly "the independent, rebellious, [and] strong-willed" Hester, Zenobia, and Miriam. While these "flesh-and-blood" women are not down-staged by their male counterparts, they are also not permitted to become "heroic leaders or independent public figures," because Hawthorne "did not subscribe to the individualism [for either sex] that characterized nineteenth-century America." That Hester rejects individual self-assertion at the end of *Letter* is not evidence of Hawthorne's "cruel, misogynistic hamstringing" (as many critics typically assume), but is instead expressive of his belief that close association with humanity is far more important than self-centered devotion to ideals and ambition to change the world. Hawthorne clearly agrees with Hester about a need for more equitable treatment of women and for more opportunities for their self-fulfillment (especially since she is clearly the most admirable character in the novel, even after having been limited and abused in different ways by both Chillingworth and Dimmesdale). Warren complicates her reading of Hawthorne's attitude toward his powerful heroines by examining his relationships with his mother, sisters, and wife, concluding that, while Hawthorne knew that the conventional heroine in literature did not reflect a true picture of the "duality" of womanhood, he still preferred to split the "true" image and to privilege the gentler feminine type over the independent-minded, rebellious type.

468   Young, Philip. "Fathers and Sons and Lovers." *Hawthorne's Secret : An Untold Tale*. Boston: David R. Godine Press, 1984. 89-147.

Argues that Hawthorne did in fact harbor a "dark secret" that explains his fictional obsession with experiences of sin and guilt, this secret involving the ancestral family incest of the first American Mannings in the seventeenth century (Nicholas Manning and his two sisters, Anstice and Margaret). Young connects this shameful and publicly-known sexual transgression to a possibly incestuous relationship between Hawthorne and his sister Elizabeth, who serves as the model for Hawthorne's "dark ladies" in his fiction. Hawthorne comes closest to dealing with the weight of his secret in the "buried story" of the sexual sin of Hester and Dimmesdale (discussed on pp. 137-147). Yet—and this is what Young finds is the "weakness at the heart" of the novel—Hawthorne unwittingly reveals the truly "hell-fired" nature of the novel by awkwardly and unrealistically portraying the relatively common sexual sin of adultery as an "unreal horror" that inspires absolute repulsion in onlookers who view Hester's "A." Clearly, Hawthorne is thinking about something else, and that is that "in Hawthorne's mind Hester's A is an I." Like Dimmesdale,

Hawthorne imagines that the truth has remained under cover, that he has gotten away with confessing his secret and keeping it, too.

Journal Essays and Notes

469   Allen, William Rodney.   "Mr. Head and Hawthorne: Allusion and Controversy in Flannery O'Connor's 'The Artificial Nigger.'" *Studies in Short Fiction* 21 (1984): 17-23.

Notes "persistent echoes" of "The Custom-House" in the opening paragraph of O'Connor's story "The Artificial Nigger." Hawthorne's own "Fortunate Fall" from bored surveyor into inspired artist parallels Head's religious conversion: both reach "a point of seeming disaster that paradoxically proves to be the route to [their] salvation." Yet O'Connor's mock-heroic treatment of the moonlit scene (comically using Hawthorne's "lofty formal rhetoric" to describe a scene of "backwoods actuality") shows that, while she is indebted to Hawthorne and his concept of the transformative power of the imagination, she "forces her protagonists into a more well-lit, public, tangible environment—into a fictional space more realistic than Hawthorne's 'neutral territory.'"

470   Baym, Nina.   "George Sand in American Reviews: A Context for Hester." *Nathaniel Hawthorne Society Newsletter* 10.2 (1984): 12-15.

Letter shows signs of influence by the French novelists, George Sand in particular.   In fact, "the terms in which Hester gives up her [reformist aspirations and] claim to speak for women are much more clearly derived from the George Sand [novel craze of the 1840s] than from any revisionary study of Anne Hutchinson" (as suggested by Michael J. Colacurcio in 289).   Hawthorne uses Sand's example late in his novel to appease the public (by having Hester dissociate herself from radical feminist movements) at the same time that he attempts to entice it (by associating his Puritan heroine with the racy Sand).

471   Bush, Sargent, Jr.   "Hawthorne's Prison Rose: An English Antecedent in the Salem *Gazette*." *New England Quarterly* 57 (1984): 255-263.

"It seems more than a little likely" that Hawthorne's idea for contrasting the wild rosebush with the prison door came from an anonymous story that appeared in the Salem *Gazette* in 1843 entitled "Prison Roses."   Like *Letter*, the story is about a wronged "virtuous matron, victimized by circumstances and conflicting duties," who is visited by "an innocent [and fatherless] young girl who is associated with rose blossoms."   In both, also, the "steel-encased prison door is directly contrasted with the roses blooming in the sunshine, and in each case the flowers offer consolation to the condemned criminal on the way 'from prison to judgment.'" Some evidence supports the likelihood that Hawthorne read the *Gazette* at that time, and three of Hawthorne's *American Notebook* entries from 1843-44 "make use of [prison/flower] imagery directly recalling that story."

472   Davis, Sarah I. "Another View of Hester and the Antinomians." *Studies in American Fiction* 12 (1984): 189-198.

Contends that the "germ" of *Letter*'s form and subject lies in Hawthorne's biographical sketch of "Mrs. [Anne] Hutchinson" (1830), although Hawthorne's harsh treatment of Hutchinson is softened in his reinterpretation of her in *Grandfather's Chair* (1940) before it evolves into its almost reverential sanctification in *Letter*, "where the sainted Anne Hutchinson is the prototype of the ideal feminist reformer whose coming Hester anticipates." Davis traces other Puritan sources for the novel (by John Winthrop, John Cotton, Cotton Mather, and Edward Johnson) and traces the characters back to historical figures—indicating similarities not only between Hester and Hutchinson but also between Dimmesdale and John Cotton, and Chillingworth and Henry Vane. The Antinomian controversy gave Hawthorne "images, characters, and motives" that strategically "enabled him to study guilt and atonement in a composite seventeenth-century Puritan setting," and suggested to him, above all, that abandoning community "risk[s] the loss of meaning."

473   Downing, David B. "The Swelling Waves: Visuality, Metaphor, and Bodily Reality in *The Scarlet Letter*." *Studies in American Fiction* 12 (1984): 13-28.

Focuses on Hawthorne's engagement with both "visual and non-visual dimensions" as they concern the dichotomous head/heart or mind/body relationship in *Letter*, especially with reference to Dimmesdale's own conflicting words and emotions. Arguing that the metaphorical "Tongue of Flame" "provides a visual image of the non-visual energy that charges [Dimmesdale's] language," Downing finds that the "ultimate tragedy" of the novel arises from Dimmesdale's inability to reconcile conventional religious language with the underlying suppressed emotions he so powerfully expresses. Because of his "duplicitous" nature, Dimmesdale is never able to achieve the kind of "aesthetic synthesis" between visible words and invisible feelings in the way that Hester can and does. The "Tongue of Flame" metaphor for flowing language and bodily energy parallels Hawthorne's own ability to join the "energies of the physical world" with the abstractions of language.

474   Hunt, Lester H. *"The Scarlet Letter*: Hawthorne's Theory of Moral Sentiments." *Philosophy and Literature* 8 (1984): 75-88.

Proposes that Hawthorne contradicts the ideas set forth in Adam Smith's *The Theory of Moral Sentiments* (1759) on the compatible relationship between morality and sympathy. Hawthorne found morality and sympathy, though both important, to be incompatible notions (since "one does not sympathize when one morally disapproves")—especially in a moralistic utopian community like Puritan Boston, where punishments for immoral behavior that are designed to regulate conduct actually "rupture relations of sympathy" and thus have the unintended effect of expelling the law-breaker from human kinship. (Hawthorne in fact indirectly speaks to the failure of any utopian community based on artificial moral codes, since virtue and natural happiness would always necessarily be at odds.) "Hester's eventual fate calls into question the efficacy of the moral method of regulation of conduct." In a similar manner, morality—or dependence on a socially-sanctioned moral code—fails Dimmesdale, too, acting as the "prime mover" that sets him apart from healthy relationships and personally devastates him. Entering a sympathetic relationship *is* possible, according to Hawthorne (as well as Smith), but it comes "only at the price of self-revelation, or 'truth,'" as in the brief exchange between Dimmesdale and Pearl at the end of the novel.

475   Khan, Jemshed A. "Atropine Poisoning in Hawthorne's *The Scarlet Letter*." *New England Journal of Medicine* 311 (9 August 1984): 414-416.*

Dr. Khan attributes Dimmesdale's "bizarre behavior and ultimate demise" to atropine poisoning, which Chillingworth administers in small doses to the minister over many years. Khan cites evidence from the text to establish the likelihood of his intriguing thesis (such as Chillingworth's familiarity with the deadly plants nightshade, henbane, and poison dogwood, as well as Chillingworth's motive for wanting Dimmesdale to suffer a lingering and painful death), and then reviews Dimmesdale's symptoms and behavior over the course of the novel—suggesting that the supernatural "A" in the heavens is a visual hallucination and that the burning letter on Dimmesdale's breast can be attributed to an atropine-induced "diffuse nonpunctate erythematous rash."

*See Thomas Pribek (503) for an extension of Khan's thesis, and see also Melinda B. Parsons and William M. Ramsey (448) for more information on the deadly herbs and plants that Chillingworth had at his disposal.

476   Lindborg, Henry J. "Hawthorne's Chillingworth: Alchemist and Physiognomist." *Transactions of the Wisconsin Academy of Sciences, Arts, and Letters* 72 (1984): 8-16.

Explores Chillingworth's transformation "from a high-minded philosopher to a fiend" and links that metamorphosis to the novel's patterns of change, especially the pattern of death and rebirth that affects each of the main characters (including Hawthorne after his "decapitation" in "The Custom-House"). Chillingworth adopts a fiendish nature after his figurative death as Prynne, at which time his efforts to discover Dimmesdale's secret transform him into a malicious demon. "To enhance the psychological revelations of the book and to provide ironic counterpoint to the limitations of the Puritan perspective," Hawthorne assigns to Chillingworth the double roles of physiognomist and alchemist. By thus expanding the novel's "symbolic frames of reference," Hawthorne enables Chillingworth to "propel the minister toward a rebirth which fits patterns of both alchemical and Christian symbolism."

477   Moers, Ellen. "*The Scarlet Letter*: A Political Reading." *Prospects* 9 (1984): 49-70.

Just as Hawthorne's attack on Salem dominates "The Custom-House," so the prison-like seventeenth-century town of Boston—the "hated smalltown" American locale "of stifling provincialism and moralizing hypocrisy"—is the center of the novel, its "true ending" being Pearl's fortunate escape to Europe. Reversing the popular nineteenth-century formula of the seduction novel by socializing the moral issues and investing Dimmesdale rather than Hester with pathos, Hawthorne uses the Puritan community—whose power is political moreso than social—as a "countervailing force against his individual lovers," so emphasizing its pervasive might over them that the central issue of the novel is publicity itself. The very moral of *Letter* "centers not on the [adulterous] deed but on its 'cover-up,' placing the sinner in relationship not to his God but to his public." With such an emphasis on publicity, the novel is neither "moral nor Christian, nor historical, but in a broad sense political"—reflecting Hawthorne's often-overlooked "gusto for American politics," his "bias toward Jacksonian democracy," and his "'locofoco' radicalism." Dimmesdale's "only moral standard is the public one," meaning that his conflict is not between himself and God but between himself and his Puritan community, with his Election-Day "speech" his "final political apotheosis." Moers expresses voicing annoyance with Hawthorne for sympathizing with Dimmesdale's guilty suffering rather than Hester's, and speculates that such sympathy stemmed from masculine guilt over his own possible premarital sex life.

478   Quirk, T[homas]. "Hawthorne's Last Tales and 'The Custom-House.'"
       ESQ: A Journal of the American Renaissance 30 (1984): 220-231.

Four of Hawthorne's stories that appeared after the 1846 publication of
Mosses from an Old Manse deal "more directly and in sharper focus" with
his theories of artistic and literary composition than do the earlier tales
"The Artist of the Beautiful" and "Drowne's Wooden Image." "'Main-
street' dramatizes the writer's concern with narrative [specifically
"incompetent artistic invention" in popular fiction], 'Feathertop' and 'The
Snow-Image' with the creation of believable characters [while also
addressing "indiscriminate public reception" to artistic contrivance], and
'The Great Stone Face' with aesthetic response [representing through the
character of Ernest "the noblest expression of human capability," which is
the embodiment of both creativity and receptivity]. This last [story] is the
most interesting and significant because it was apparently written only
shortly before *Letter* and is clearly paralleled by 'The Custom-House" in
its reiteration of the same aesthetic ideas. Furthermore, "'The Great Stone
Face' and 'The Custom-House' may be considered companion pieces,
expressing the author's most mature and firmly held aesthetic principles,
the latter work giving Hawthorne's critical estimate of his own place in the
hierarchy of ethical and aesthetic sensibility which he potrayed in 'The
Great Stone Face.'"

479   Shulman, Robert. "The Artist in the Slammer: Hawthorne, Melville, Poe,
       and the Prison of Their Times." *Studies in English Literature* 14 (1984):
       79-88.*

Using *Letter* as his chief illustration, Shulman shows how symbolism
offered Hawthorne, Herman Melville, and Edgar Allan Poe possibilities
for indirection and subversion—the techniques of the inmate—to survive
in the repressive marketplace society that held the artist prisoner.
Hawthorne tried to disguise his concerns that America was a prison for the
artist by creating a story set in the seventeenth century that was "really"
about nineteenth-century social punitive rigidity and heartlessness.
Hester's letter provides an alternative to the official symbols of the
scaffold and prison, embodying "both the rebellious energies of the artist
and the official attitudes of the society the artist both accepts and
subverts." While the narrator represents the more public side of
Hawthorne's identity, Hester and Dimmesdale represent two versions of
the private "romantic creator" who "take[s] us closer to the 'inmost Me'
that Hawthorne was so careful to conceal." Hester embodies "a
compelling individualism" that closely represents Hawthorne's "deepest
feelings about his own creativity and identity." Through Dimmesdale

Hawthorne "explores another version of the romantic creator, a gifted artist whose inner dynamics necessitate the obverse of Hester's individualism." Threatened by what he most fears, loves, and needs, Dimmesdale is a "classic conservative" who requires the "iron framework" of Puritan orthodoxy to support and confine him. "Much of the power of *Letter* comes from Hawthorne's willingness to give full, complex expression to his ambivalent feelings about these divided segments of his nature."

*An expanded version of this article (which does not offer anything new in its discussion of *Letter*) appears in Shulman's *Social Criticism and Nineteenth-Century American Fictions* (Columbia: U of Missouri P, 1987. 176-196).

480   Vivan, Itala. "The Scar in the Letter: An Eye on the Occult in Hawthorne's Text." *Social Science Information* 23 (1984): 155-179.

Hawthorne drew widely from the traditional repertoire of the occult—witchcraft, magic, alchemy, heraldry, and gnosis—and linked these arcana, which are deployed in the novel through themes, symbols, and allusions, with the unifying, esoteric emblem of the scarlet letter. His use of the occult is designed to "enchant, seduce, and hold in the circle of this enchantment" the "eye/I" of the reader, both to puzzle and to entice him with scattered "pieces and fragments traced from and referring to various esoteric worlds and levels, each of which is reversed and contradicted by the incident of the letter, which baffles them all." In other words, Hawthorne strategically arranged *Letter* with enigmatic and labyrinthine occult allusions that were designed with reader participation in mind in that the reader's eye "imposes order on the various pieces of the puzzle/design which does not seem to exist without such an eye, without the mystic union the eye creates in the text."

1985

Books

481   Colacurcio, Michael J., ed. *New Essays on The Scarlet Letter*. New York: Cambridge UP, 1985. 164 pp.

Part of the "American Novel Series," this volume contains an introduction by Colacurcio, four "fresh" and original historical approaches to *Letter* that attempt to enter into "the spirit in which Hawthorne once constructed his romance of sin and of signs" (by Michael Davitt Bell, David Van Leer,

Michael J. Colacurcio, and Carol Bensick), and a "judiciously selected" bibliography of criticism. See annotations below.

Essays and Studies in Books

482   Bell, Michael Davitt. "Arts of Deception: Hawthorne, 'Romance,' and *The Scarlet Letter.*" *New Essays on The Scarlet Letter.* Ed. Michael J. Colacurcio. New York: Cambridge UP, 1985. 29-56.*

Examines the highly deceptive quality of Hawthorne's writing that is overlooked by the "superficial skimmer of pages" by comparing the "slippery evasiveness" of Hawthorne's description of romance and related comments on his fiction (in the prefaces to *Letter* and *House of the Seven Gables*) with the action of *Letter*. Hawthorne never actually defines romance in these prefaces, although several critics (such as Lionel Trilling and Richard Chase [55]) have used his highly suggestive language to their advantage in supporting their own definitions of American romance. The careful reader will also find that Hawthorne deflates his own pretense of factual authenticity regarding the Surveyor Pue manuscript story in "The Custom-House." Hawthorne's deceptiveness issues from the nineteenth-century "reputation" of romance, which was considered a dangerous moral poison associated with antisocial and abnormal behavior. Hawthorne "adopts a series of masks and poses in order to [. . .] obscure—and yet still hint at—the true authority behind his fiction," which is himself and his projected subversive imagination. In *Letter*, Hawthorne continues to hide and reveal his "essential traits by projecting them into his characters." Hester and Dimmesdale both "mediate between their own subversive impulses and the orthodox expectations of the society in which they live their public lives." While Dimmesdale is a failed romancer, however, deceiving himself above all, Hester masterfully expresses and conceals her impulses and individuality, rebelling through indirection and ironic subversion.

*Reprinted in *Culture Genre, and Literary Vocation: Selected Essays on American Literature* (Chicago: U of Chicago P, 2000. 32-53).

483   Bensick, Carol [M.] "His Folly, Her Weakness: Demystified Adultery in *The Scarlet Letter.*" *New Essays on The Scarlet Letter.* Ed. Michael J. Colacurcio. New York: Cambridge UP, 1985. 137-159.

A comparison of Hawthorne's and Tolstoy's "novels of adultery" (*Letter* and *Anna Karenina* [1873]) reveals Hawthorne's refusal on moral grounds to perpetuate the fictional genre's classic tradition (which usually assumes that the pitiable adulteress in question necessarily suffers a miserable fate because of conventional religio-moral prescriptions dictated by society). Over the course of *Letter*, the issue of a mismatched couple's marital infidelity becomes less a "fateful tragedy" than a practical social problem that does not necessarily have to have debilitating effects. According to Hawthorne in *Letter*, the true crime of adultery lies not in the act itself but in Hester's and Chillingworth's inability to forgive each other for an injurious marriage in which both had developed "two mutually exclusive and equally impossible sets of expectations [. . .] that their own cultures had long since set up." When adultery is considered as a fact of social experience rather than one of transcendent morality or political symbolism, it "ceases to be an occasion of judgment and becomes an opportunity for charity." Yet, while Hawthorne allows Hester to survive and Pearl to find happiness, insisting that the grim fate of the classic adulteress is not sealed, Tolstoy appears to reestablish by intent the somber tradition.

484   Carton, Evan. "The Prison Door." *The Rhetoric of American Romance: Dialectic and Identity in Emerson, Dickinson, Poe, and Hawthorne.* Baltimore: Johns Hopkins UP, 1985. 191-227.

Deals primarily with Hawthorne's formation of a personal and social identity in *Letter* (pp. 191-216), although similar, briefer, attention is paid to *House of the Seven Gables*, as well, which is Hawthorne's failed attempt to create a "healthier" work than *Letter*. In *Letter*, Hawthorne addresses the issue of "representation" as opposed to "deviation," meaning that he deals with the tension between what appears to be represented and what is actually perceived. Essentially, Hawthorne "withholds or unsettles all the bases for absolute moral, social, or ontological judgments," and even ambiguously toys with the reader's perception of romance itself, since its own "imputation of insularity and triviality" has little to do with "the dangerous and dynamic engagement with community, time, and physical experience that 'The Custom-House' and *Letter* exemplify."

485   Colacurcio, Michael J. "The Spirit and the Sign." Introduction. *New Essays on The Scarlet Letter.* Ed. Michael J. Colacurcio. New York: Cambridge UP, 1985. 1-28.

This introduction to a collection of essays "presents details of the novel's composition, publication history, and contemporary reception, as well as a survey of the major critical trends and readings from first publication to the present." Before launching into an admittedly "quite selective and self-consciously partial" survey of the early and modern criticism, Colacurcio stresses the "openness" of Hawthorne's literary situation in 1849, as well as implies that the relation between "The Custom-House" and *Letter* may be more dubious than most contemporary critics allow. Colacurcio concludes his thorough survey with the assessment that *Letter*'s power resides not only in "its power to prove, over and over again, that it means more than it (or we) can prove," but also in its "power to say more than one person could ever quite *mean*."

486   Colacurcio, Michael J. "'The Woman's Own Choice': Sex, Metaphor, and the Puritan 'Sources' of *The Scarlet Letter*." *New Essays on The Scarlet Letter*. Ed. Michael J. Colacurcio. New York: Cambridge UP, 1985. 101-135.*

Building on source studies that emphasize Hawthorne's borrowing of Caleb Snow's *History of Boston* for *Letter*'s historical setting and plot (Charles Ryskamp's being the most notable [see 85]), Colacurcio turns to an earlier, perhaps even more critically important prime source, which conveys the extreme political strife and sexual confusion at the heart of the Puritan theocracy. John Winthrop's *History of New England* may even be Hawthorne's *subject* in *Letter*, not just one of its vital sources, because the novel may be seen to "strategically epitomize an entire context of Puritan thought." As a historical novel based on a community whose self-projected image was of a "Utopia of human virtue and happiness," *Letter* appears "not as a moralistic reflection on the consequences of 'sin' in the Puritan sense, or even as a psychological analysis of 'guilt' in either the Freudian or the supposedly universal sense, but rather as a speculative probing of the power of sexual figures to structure religious ideology and confuse natural experience." That Hester rightly challenges her judgmental community and the whole range of inappropriate, hypocritical attitudes taken by the ministers (Dimmesdale included), magistrates, and populace alike is part of Hawthorne's method of showing that the "splendid intellectual edifice" of Puritanism has been "reared on a foundation of murk."

*This essay is reprinted with only minor changes in Colacurcio's *Doctrine and Difference: Essays in the Literature of New England* (New York: Routledge, 1997. 205-227).

487   Donohue, Agnes McNeill. "*The Scarlet Letter*: 'A' is for Apple." *Hawthorne: Calvin's Ironic Stepchild*. Kent: Kent State UP, 1985. 35-67, 343-345.

Despite Hawthorne's ambivalence toward the Puritan dogmas of total depravity and predestination, his "artistic imagination, creative consciousness, and conscience" were conditioned by the damnatory theology of Calvinism. Over and over, the "black flower" of Calvin's doctrine of total depravity stimulated Hawthorne's imagination to "dramatize pitiful sinners' attempts 'to spit from the mouth the withered apple seed' of the lost Eden. That these attempts are futile, that the corrupt seed grows rankly and with malignant haste and finally chokes the doomed sinners—this vision is Hawthorne's personal tragic-ironic apocalypse." *Letter* entails a "mutation" of the Fall, with "the disobedience taking the form of sexuality." Chillingworth ("the Calvinist Jehovah-devil-God") sends the passionate Hester (Eve) to the Eden of the New World, but she seduces Dimmesdale (Adam), causing the outraged Chillingworth to take vengeance on them. That Pearl escapes the damnation is of little consequence, since she often suffers humiliation and trauma prior to becoming a true "human being" (not to mention that "three souls are lost so that the Pearl may become a fragile human child"). Donohue provides an extensive reading of *Letter* divided into six-parts, addressing theme and intention (the Fall, Hawthorne's tragic view, isolation, and alienation), voice (aesthetic distance, point of view, setting, tone, and diction), symbolism, structure, character, and judgment/final interpretation.

488   Gilmore, Michael T. "To Speak in the Marketplace: *The Scarlet Letter*." *American Romanticism and the Marketplace*. Chicago: U of Chicago P, 1985. 71-95.

Exploring how "the commercialization of society and culture profoundly affected the American romantics and had a shaping influence on the themes and form of their art," Gilmore focuses in his overall project on the work of Ralph Waldo Emerson, Henry David Thoreau, Hawthorne, and Walt Whitman to show how each "objected to the reduction of literature to the status of a commodity" for the general public. Hawthorne in particular expressed resentment and ambivalent feelings about the changes transforming his role from "esteemed artist for a select few" to "writer-for-the-masses." Since *Letter* was the product of Hawthorne's urgent need to compose a best seller, it contains "at its heart" his dilemma "as someone both eager for and fearful of popular success." His attempt to come to terms with "hav[ing] to sell but want[ing] to speak the truth" can be discerned everywhere in the novel. The characters of Hester and Dimmesdale suffer the effects of "being scrutinized" for who they really are, and the novel is consistently preoccupied with communication difficulties, acts of ambiguous speaking and writing, and "linguistic inhibition." Like Dimmesdale, Hawthorne ultimately "rejects clarity in favor of obfuscation" as his method for both dealing with the public and resolving his conflicted feelings. At the end of the novel, Hawthorne "links his readers to the spectators in the Boston marketplace and leaves them as much in the dark as the most befuddled Puritan."

489   Greenwald, Elissa "The Symbol as Symptom: Romance and Repression in Hawthorne's *The Scarlet Letter*." *The Psychoanalytic Study of Literature*. Ed. Joseph Reppen and Maurice Charney. Hillsdale: Analytic Press, 1985. 149-166.

Shows that "The Custom-House" is "not only thematically appropriate but psychically necessary to the story it introduces" because "it not only establishes Hawthorne's literary method—the way of writing and reading 'romance'—but makes that method the necessary condition for the writer's and reader's entry into the world of *Letter*." Hawthorne's description of the realm of romance in the sketch is similar to Freud's definition of "the protected realm" of the "transference" (the cite of creative activity) in psychoanalysis. Romance thus becomes a cure for Hawthorne's creative difficulties and his psychological conflicts. Hawthorne also induces his readers to consider reading romance as self-cures for their "ailments."

490   Greiner, Donald J. *Adultery in the American Novel: Updike, James, and Hawthorne*. Columbia: U of South Carolina P, 1985.

Greiner provides readings of *Letter* (pp. 60-62, 115-119, 125-128), *Marble Faun*, and Henry James's *The Golden Bowl* (1904) before turning to John Updike's "marriage novels" in chapter four "(Adultery and Updike's Marriage Novels," pp. 97-121) and showing how Hawthorne and James served as a frame of reference for Updike in his treatment of adultery. Whereas Hawthorne perceives adultery primarily as a moral issue and as a religious transgression (and was careful to establish a narrative distance from his racy material by setting *Letter* in the distant past—thereby neither violating Puritan morality nor "the contemporary standard of strict silence in all matters physical"), and James perceives adultery as a social problem that can undermine social and economic stability, Updike perceives it as an individual matter that incorporates both moral and social considerations. For all three authors, guilt inspired from sexual knowledge prompts the artist to creativity.

491   Horton, Tonia L. "The Born Outcast: Nathaniel Hawthorne's Pearl and Symbolic Action in *The Scarlet Letter*." *Ritual in the United States: Acts and Representations*. Ed. Don Harness. Tampa: American Studies Press, 1985. 10-14.

Hawthorne devised Pearl as an outlaw, a "born outcast of the infantile world," to work through his primary theme of individual freedom vs. social order. She functions as an "inverted symbol" (she "turns the world upside down" and creates disorder from her lawless behavior) throughout the tale and represents not only "the pre-social period prior to a defined order of society" but also the "fledgling new democracy" in America as Hawthorne confronted it.

492   Kamuf, Peggy. "Hawthorne's Genres: The Letter of the Law *Appliquée*." *After Strange Texts: The Role of Theory in the Study of Literature.* Ed. Gregory S. Jay and David L. Miller. Tuscaloosa: U of Alabama P, 1985. 69-84.

This combined deconstructionist and feminist approach to *Letter* delves into the novel's underlying participation in the machinations of patriarchal power and authority. In the first place, Hawthorne's insistence on the narrative category of "romance" illustrates his desire to distinguish between the novel form (as "a scribbling of feminine design") and his more serious masculine "art." The text of the letter—the literary text—connects with the letter of the law (a connection "between the written work and its interpretation according to the laws of genre"). In the first two scaffold scenes, gender differences are apparent because "the letter and the law of its interpretation are displayed with contrasting effect." The letter is an instance of "display" in both scenes, a display that the "law condemns as ostentatious spectacle" in Hester's case (as both legal punishment and manifestation of the "duplicity within the law itself") but that "the law invokes as the instrument of righteous truth" in Dimmesdale's case (where interpretation of the minister's revelation of the meteor's meaning divides the community).

493   Matthews, John T. "Intertextuality and Originality: Hawthorne, Faulkner, Updike." *Intertextuality in Faulkner.* Ed. Michel Gresset and Noel Polk. Jackson: UP of Mississippi, 1985. 144-157.

"Assesses the conditions for originality" in the responses to adultery in the Gospel of Jesus, *Letter*, William Faulkner's *As I Lay Dying* (1930), and John Updike's *A Month of Sundays* (1975) to show first how "the Law of others' discourse manifests itself as literary contexts for each work," and second that each "ponders how the urge to construct an original utterance and identity is a transgression of law and convention that nevertheless depends upon [that urge] for its fulfillment." All three novels "inquire into the conventions, the customs, of writing, and in doing so, they cast and recast the recognition that the originality of a work is constituted in the movement that displaces its origin, that textuality is always intertextuality, and that, in the master image of all three novels, adultery represents the constitution of authenticity through a proscribed act." Adultery is implicated in art, for there can be no true originality because any "new" text is necessarily adulterated by its relation to previous works). Just as Hawthorne affiliates adultery with writing in *Letter*, so Faulkner and Updike affliliate their novels with Hawthorne's by "rewriting" *Letter*.

494   Stokes, Edward. *Hawthorne's Influence on Dickens and George Eliot*. St. Lucia: U of Queensland P, 1985.

This two-part study illustrates Charles Dickens's and George Eliot's indebtedness to Hawthorne. Both parts are broken into several sections that (1) provide evidence of each author's knowledge of Hawthorne's work, (2) offer previous critical comparisons of each author with Hawthorne, and then (3) present Stokes's own findings. Striking similarities exist between the "somber romances" of *Letter* and *Bleak House* (1852-53), with Lady Dedlock combining traits of Hester and Dimmesdale and with Tulkinghorm resembling Chillingworth, indicating that Dickens borrowed "quite extensively" from Hawthorne (pp. 30-49). Hawthorne had even more pervasive influence on Eliot's *Adam Bede* (1859)· Hetty Sorrel/Hester Prynne are dark-haired adulteresses with illegitimate children and Arthur Donnithorne/Arthur Dimmesdale are hypocrites (pp. 122-146). Beyond the parallels in structure, characterization, and style between *Adam Bede* and *Letter* appears further evidence (pp. 114-117, 162-173) to support *Letter*'s influence on *Scenes of Clerical Life* (1857) and *Silas Marner*(1861).

495   Tompkins, Jane. "Masterpiece Theater: The Politics of Hawthorne's Literary Reputation." *Sensational Designs: The Cultural Work of American Fiction 1790-1860*. New York: Oxford UP, 1985. 1-39.

This book questions the processes through which canonical texts achieve their classic status and uses Hawthorne's reputation as a case in point—arguing that his reputation arose not from the "intrinsic merit" of his work but rather from "the complex of circumstances that make texts visible initially and then maintain them in their preeminent position." Hawthorne was, in fact, admired in his own day for reasons very different from the ones for which he is admired today (originally, for the simplicity of his wording, for his presentations of democratic life and of humbler aspects of the American scene, for his infusion of spirituality into his works, and for his sympathetic power). Thus, with respect to *Letter* (pp. 20-23, 24-25), "Because modern commentators have tended to ignore the context within which nineteenth-century authors and critics worked, their view of the criticism that was written on *Letter* in the nineteenth century has failed to take account of the cultural circumstances that shaped Hawthorne's novel for his contemporaries." George B. Loring's 1850 review of *Letter* (see

ER7), for example, is largely praised by modern critics for its impassioned defense of Hawthorne from narrowly-based doctrinal attacks of the novel, but what modern critics fail to see is that Loring's review is actually "part of a political and ideological struggle taking place between liberal and conservative branches of Protestant Christianity." Since the grounds for critical approval are always shifting, it is fallacious to argue that a "classic" work transcends the limitations of its age and appeals to critics and readers across the centuries. The true test of greatness lies in a work's ability to appeal for different reasons to different readers and critics throughout time.

496   Van Leer, David. "Hester's Labyrinth: Transcendental Rhetoric in Puritan Boston." *New Essays on The Scarlet Letter.* Ed. Michael J. Colacurcio. New York: Cambridge UP, 1985. 57-100.*

With special attention paid to the method of the narrative, Van Leer examines inconsistencies in Hawthorne's mixing of seventeenth-century Puritan and nineteenth-century transcendental ideas and vocabularies in *Letter.* The conflation of seventeenth- and nineteenth-century rhetoric contributes to the narrative unreliability, moral uncertainty, linguistic imprecision, and tonal peculiarities in both the preface and the novel. Such contradictions suggest first that the narrator's pronouncements of meaning should not be trusted, and second (and more radically) that Hawthorne is addressing an overall concern with the subjectivity of all determined meanings, coming to terms with how meaning and language function similarly in life and society at any given time. Most simply, Hawthorne does not see the interpretive shift from Puritan typology to transcendentalist symbolism as an improvement, or even a change, since both are committed to "a dangerously mechanistic model of the continuity between world and mind, body and soul" in which the spiritual is believed to be reflected in the material.

*For Van Leer's revision of this essay that reshifts the focus to the scientific language employed in *Letter*, see 592.

497   Von Frank, Albert J. "Hawthorne's Provincial Imagination." *The Sacred Game: Provincialism and Frontier Consciousness in American Literature, 1630-1860.* New York: Cambridge UP, 1985. 79-96.

A brief examination (pp. 91-96) of "The Hollow of the Three Hills" and "The Snow-Image" helps in estimating "the extent to which Hawthorne's masterpiece, *Letter*, owes its great strengths to an imagination richly provoked and sternly disciplined by a lifetime's experience with a provincial environment." When taken together, the stories present—as does the novel—the dangers of subscribing too exclusively to the competing and incompatible world views of allegory (which Hawthorne associated with "the death-in-life stiffness of intolerance and bigotry") and symbolism (which Hawthorne associated with ultimate freedom, warmth, and vitality). Hawthorne sought a middle ground that tempered the two modes and provided "preservation" for his fictional children in "a satisfactory home." The central dramatic issue of *Letter*, therefore, is Pearl's legitimacy and the creation for her of a proper home. Because "the Puritan establishment naturally adopts the allegorical mode" and Hester "occupies a symbolic realm of mysteriously shifting, fluid meanings," it remains up to Dimmesdale to discover a "neutral territory" between these fatal opposites and make it prevail for Pearl's well-being and development. Once he recognizes and rejects "the inherent selfishness in the Puritan allegorical mode, with its reliance on force and its fundamental lack of reverence for the human soul" and "the selfishness of the symbolic mode with its commitment to individual salvation through escape," Dimmesdale is able to reach out to others and be transformed from an ineffectual boy into "a man, a husband, and a father," thus serving to resolve the "grand conflict" of the novel.

Journal Essays and Notes

498   Burt, John. "Romance, Character, and the Bounds of Sense." *Raritan* 5 (1985): 74-89.

Though his essay grapples with the dilemma of the American romancer in general, Burt uses Hawthorne and, particularly, Hawthorne's theory of romance in "The Custom-House," as the prime illustration of the connections between realism and romance, romance and politics. Hawthorne "seeks an imaginative freedom within the constraints of an esthetic tradition, and he conceives of that freedom in a way which bears certain clear analogies to the operation of private conscience within the constraints of public equity and law." The result of so many conflicts is, logically, both liberating and limiting, creating "excruciatingly undecidable" interpretations and excesses of meanings—for Hawthorne, for his characters, and for his readers.

499   Freed, Richard C. "Hawthorne's Reflexive Imagination: *The Scarlet Letter* as Compositional Allegory." *ATQ* 56 (1985): 31-54.

Examines the relationship among Hester, Dimmesdale, Chillingworth, and Pearl to provide insight into Hawthorne's composition process. *Letter* is "an allegory of composition," or, more simply, is about the compositional process itself—with Pearl as "the work in progress" who demands to be written truthfully, with Hester, Dimmesdale, and Chillingworth as Pearl's "authors" whose "relations to each other and to Pearl constitute an allegory of the compositional process." Whereas Pearl's development parallels the process by which Hawthorne develops his germinating idea in "The Custom-House," Hester's relationship with Pearl parallels Hawthorne's own relationship to his text. Chillingworth represents the "cold and relentless search for fact and meaning" in the past, and Dimmesdale adds the elements of warmth, imagination, and passion to the story. "In the figure of Dimmesdale," especially through his sermons that disguise his contradictions and desires, "we find the conflict in Hawthorne between the man who writes and the being who lives in the world." The novel's movement from deception to revelation, enacted not only by Dimmesdale and Chillingworth but by the narrator who throughout the story gradually alters his attitude from meddling and merciless to sympathetic and understanding, ends when Pearl is humanized by Dimmesdale's kiss. The "spell" of composition is broken at this point, and the search for fact, meaning, and "truth" is at last over.

500   John, Richard. "Hawthorne's Boston Custom House." *Nathaniel Hawthorne Society Newsletter* 11.1 (1985): 15-17.

Clears up the long-assumed notion that the Boston Custom House, where Hawthorne worked as a very well-paid measurer between 1839 and 1841 (before he voluntarily relinquished the position to pursue his literary ambitions), was a nondescript five-story brick building. This Custom House was actually a two-story, magnificent structure with 20-foot ceilings—a fact which helps to clarify Hawthorne's scattered references to it. While he worked in this Custom House, hundreds of disordered records stored in the attic of the building were organized for preservation, and these records might very well have provided Hawthorne's inspiration for his "searching exploration of Boston's long-vanished past" in *Letter*.

501   Martin, Luther H. "Hawthorne's *The Scarlet Letter*: A is for Alchemy?" *ATQ* 58 (1985): 31-42.

Advocates an "alchemical" reading of the novel over a "gnostic" interpretation because the former embraces opposites and assumes a continuity between spirit and matter, whereas the latter supposes a strict dualism and alienation of body from soul, matter from spirit. Hawthorne clearly links physical and spiritual transformations in the novel, and he seems to exhibit knowledge of alchemy through color symbolism (the opposition of red and black especially) and through the four main characters, all of whom embody an internal/external continuity. "Chillingworth is the black alchemist and the scarlet letter itself is the red-gold philosopher's stone, the transformed and transforming emblem which is central to every chapter in the novel." While Chillingworth makes up the black, so Hester constitutes the red and Dimmesdale the white to create the "chromatic trichotomy of alchemical transformation." The union of Hester and Dimmesdale is an "alchemical wedding" of the red and white that produces a "mercurial child of gold" who is the "catalytic agent" for the spiritual union of her parents. "Just as the scarlet letter is the philosopher's stone for alchemical transformations within the novel itself, so it fires the fancy of the alchemist-artist" in "The Custom-House" as well, serving as a metaphor for art and presenting in an alchemical framework Hawthorne's rationale for uniting passion and intellect.

502   Parker, Hershel. "The Germ Theory of *The Scarlet Letter*." *Nathaniel Hawthorne Society Newsletter* 11.1 (1985): 11-13.

Disputes the "germ" theory of *Letter* (the theory that James T. Fields persuaded Hawthorne to enlarge his work in progress to novel length and to publish it by itself in a volume), which originated with Fields himself. Parker questions Fields's account—finding in it many inconsistencies, and wonders why it has been *so* readily and wholeheartedly received as truth that no Hawthorne critic has ever challenged it (Parker claims to be a Melvillean).* Without a doubt, Fields persuaded Hawthorne to publish the work separately (without other tales and sketches), but it is highly unlikely that there was ever a shorter "germ" version of *Letter* that Fields read in its entirety (as he claimed) during his twenty-minute train ride from Salem to Boston. It is almost certain that the version Fields initially read was the final version we know today, minus the last three chapters. Fields is thus misleading in his claim that "persuading Hawthorne to enlarge the story was a consequence of his persuading Hawthorne to publish it separately," because Fields clearly had nothing at all to do with the tale reaching its final length.

*See Stephen Nissenbaum (in 464), who wholeheartedly accepts Fields's original account. According to Parker, Nissenbaum also incorrectly accepts the legend that the decision to add "The Custom-House" was made at the last minute after the book was already set in type. Parker's thesis also claims to "correct" Watson Branch's theory (in 426) that imperfections in the novel can be attributed to Hawthorne's "hurried efforts" to provide a completed manuscript for Fields.

503   Pribek, Thomas. "A Note on Chillingworth's Poisons." *Nathaniel Hawthorne Society Newsletter* 11.2 (1985): 11-12.

In "illustrating the complexity of Chillingworth's revenge upon the minister," Pribek borrows the findings of Jemshed A. Khan, M.D. (see 475) and Melinda B. Parsons and William M. Ramsey (see 448) to speculate that Chillingworth did, in fact, poison Dimmesdale with both atropine and scopolamine—related alkaloids that are "truth-stimulating" drugs known to cause cases of "muttering delirium."

504   Reynolds, Larry J. *"The Scarlet Letter* and Revolutions Abroad." *American Literature* 57 (1985): 44-67.*

Analyzing the impact of the failed European Revolutions of 1848-1849 on the "masterpieces" of the American Renaissance, Reynolds focuses on *Letter*'s influence by three major forces: the violent and bloody revolutions abroad, the historical accounts of those revolutions by Francois Guizot and Alphonse de Lamartine, and Margaret Fuller's revolutionary activities in Italy. These forces give structural and thematic shape to the novel's scaffold scenes and Hawthorne's presentation of himself as a "decapitated" surveyor in "The Custom-House." What's more, Hawthorne chose the 1642-1649 time frame (the dates of the English Civil War) for events in the novel to further enhance his treatment of revolutionary themes. "The book that he wrote in the wake of the revolutions indicates that they reaffirmed his skepticism about revolution and reform and inspired a strong reactionary spirit, which underlies the work." Knowledge of Hawthorne's skepticism and fear of revolutionary activities helps to explain inconsistencies in his treatment of Hester and Dimmesdale, especially in terms of the sympathy he affords them until they attempt to overthrow the established order.

*Reprinted in Reynolds's *European Revolutions and the American Literary Renaissance* (New Haven: Yale UP, 1988. 79-96).

505   Stineback, David. "Gender, Hawthorne, and Literary Criticism." *Mosaic* 18 (1985): 91-100.

Challenges critics who fault Hawthorne's ambivalent and inconsistent portrayals of women—Hester Prynne, especially, though also Zenobia in *Blithedale Romance* and Martha in "The Shaker Bridal"—and argues that Hawthorne's "flawed" portrayals of women are consistent with the complicated politics of sexual relations in nineteenth-century America. Hawthorne's ambivalence toward the liberation of women, so frequently documented by his critics, is actually the result of his struggle "in the context of his Judeo-Christian, Jacksonian culture with an issue that he cannot be expected to resolve," meaning that his lack of resolution is *not* "a flaw in his work." Given the cultural pressures on him to secure women in their proper sphere in the "cult of true womanhood," Hawthorne's inconsistent though sensitive, sympathetic treatment of what he acknowledges to be women's inadequate, intolerable place in society is nothing short of courageous and liberated.

1986

Books

506   Baym, Nina. *The Scarlet Letter: A Reading.* Boston: Twayne, 1986. 116 pp.

As the first in the Twayne series on "masterworks" of literature, this guidebook is designed for student use as a critical introduction to *Letter* that "explains the impact and lasting appeal" of the novel. Following a chronology of Hawthorne's life, a brief overview of the novel's historical context and relevance, and a review of its critical reception is a six-part comprehensive examination of the novel that includes analysis of plot and structure, setting, and characters, an essay on the character role of the scarlet letter in *The Scarlet Letter*, treatment of themes, and an explanation of the connection between *The Scarlet Letter* and "The Custom-House." The study concludes with a briefly annotated bibliography of selected primary and secondary sources, as well as an index.

507   Bloom, Harold, ed. *Nathaniel Hawthorne's The Scarlet Letter.* New York: Chelsea House, 1986. 144 pp.

As part of the *Modern Critical Interpretations* series, Bloom's volume includes an "Editor's Note," an introduction (see 510), a collection of seven modern critical essays* that Bloom boasts make up "the best criticism yet published on Hawthorne's finest long fiction," a "chronolog" of Hawthorne's life and works, and a bibliography.

*Six of the chronologically-arranged essays are reprinted from articles and books and are, respectively, A. N. Kaul's "Nathaniel Hawthorne: Heir and Critic of the Puritan Tradition" (139), Michael J. Colacurcio's "Footsteps of Anne Hutchinson: The Context of *The Scarlet Letter*" (289), Richard H. Brodhead's "New and Old Tales: *The Scarlet Letter*" (300), Michael Ragussis's "Family Discourse and Fiction in *The Scarlet Letter*" (431), Norman Bryson's "Hawthorne's Illegible Letter" (435), and Evan Carton's "The Prison Door" (484). The seventh essay, by Scott Derrick, is published here for the first time: "Prometheus Ashamed: *The Scarlet Letter* and the Masculinity of Art" (512). See individual entries below for Bloom's introduction and Derrick's piece.

Essays and Studies in Books

508   Arac, Jonathan. "The Politics of *The Scarlet Letter*." *Ideology and Classic American Literature*. Ed. Sacvan Bercovitch and Myra Jehlen. New York: Cambridge UP, 1986. 247-266.

In working out the concept of a definable American ideology, Arac studies the "A-politics" of *Letter* to find in it a distinctly historical American process of mystification ("indeterminacy") and a great dislike for extremes. After negotiating the "conflicting realities of past and present, the overlays of Puritan, agrarian, commercial, and industrial ways of life that [Hawthorne] encountered in New England, as well as the tension between American politics as a continuing revolution and as patronage, mere 'rotation,'" Arac juxtaposes *Letter* and Hawthorne's campaign biography *The Life of Franklin Pierce* (1852) to find that "the organization of (in)action in both books works through a structure of conflicting values related to the political impasse of the 1850s." He next relates *Letter* to the major issues of its time and to cultural patterns that reach back to the country's founding texts (the *Declaration of Independence*, the *Federalist Papers*, and the *Constitution*), and in all cases finds a defended logic of "inaction" and gradualism* which helps to explain the historical politics involved with Hester's change at the end of the novel from rebel outcast to agent of socialization. [For an essay that builds on Arac's New Historicist approach to *Letter*, see Jennifer Fleischner (660).]

*Arac takes issue with Arlin Turner's insistence on Hawthorne's extensive involvement in politics (see 396), as well as with Henry Nash Smith's claim that Hawthorne challenges all institutions in his novel (356).

509   Barbour, James, and Thomas Quirk, eds. *Romanticism: Critical Essays in American Literature*. New York: Garland, 1986.

The section on *Letter* (pp. 203-251) contains three reprinted essays: John C. Gerber's "Form and Content in *The Scarlet Letter* (EC9), James M. Cox's "*The Scarlet Letter*: Through the Old Manse and the Custom House" (336), and Frederick Crew's "The Ruined Wall" (182).

510   Bloom, Harold. Introduction. *Nathaniel Hawthorne's The Scarlet Letter*. Ed. Harold Bloom. New York: Chelsea House, 1986. 1-8.

Bloom isolates an antithetical strain—both Gnostic and Emersonian—in the romance, first by identifying elements of Gnostic symbolism in the supernatural depiction of the all-knowing Pearl and second by speculating that Hester and Pearl are actually "intense representations of two very different aspects of Emersonianism": spunky self-reliance (Hester) and anarchic antinomianism (Pearl). Bloom asserts that the novel "marks the true beginning of American prose fiction, the absolute point of origin from which we can trace the sequence that goes from Herman Melville and Henry James to William Faulkner and Thomas Pynchon and that domesticates great narrative art in America."

511   Brodhead, Richard [H.]. "Late James: The Lost Art of the Late Style." *The School of Hawthorne*. New York: Oxford UP, 1986. 166-200.

Examining the fiction of Herman Melville, William Dean Howells, Henry James, and William Faulkner, this book traces the artistic legacy of Hawthorne "to establish the centrality of Hawthorne to a line of writers virtually unbroken from his time into modernity." Hawthorne's impact, though striking, figures differently for each author. *Letter* and James's *The Golden Bowl* (1904) belong to a tradition of romance. James recovers not only Hawthorne's stylistic mannerisms but also his display of artifice—reconstructing and then going beyond "Hawthornesque romance."

512   Derrick, Scott [S.]. "Prometheus Ashamed: *The Scarlet Letter* and the Masculinity of Art." *Nathaniel Hawthorne's The Scarlet Letter*. Ed. Harold Bloom. New York: Chelsea House, 1986. 121-127.

Argues that *Letter* is a "powerful Promethean account of the gender struggles of the American male artist." A "double" anxiety appears in the novel: a "desire that writing should be masculine" but also "a fear that it somehow is irreducibly feminine and comes from feminine sources." Hawthorne's uneasiness with his profession is revealed both in "The Custom-House"—where Hawthorne voices his distress over the lack of appreciation by his ancestors and his contemporaries in the masculine world of custom-house commerce—and in the novel proper, where, throughout, "the generative power of imagination is feminine." Derrick views Hester's artistic sewing in the context of Hawthorne's sketch, "Mrs. Hutchinson" (1830), as "a strategy of containment" on Hawthorne's part that moves her away from the "masculine" field of art. Once safely removed from an arena that would inspire Hawthorne's envy or desire, Hester is then "repressed, silent, and co-opted," made to play her part in the nineteenth-century cult of true womanhood, though "in Puritan garb." Dimmesdale also seems to be a feminized figure, "more the product of Hawthorne's own sentimental age than of the seventeenth century." Yet Hawthorne confers on Dimmesdale (whose feminization is equated with sin, shame, secrecy, and guilt) a "Pentecostal gift of passion" that imbues his speech with such eloquence that it "re-masculinizes" him when he gives the triumphant Election-Day sermon. In that sermon, Dimmesdale establishes "the political centrality of art, gathering the faithful in a victory which is at once masculine and socially transforming, and healing the split between private selves and public roles." Dimmesdale also implies in his dying words that he has out-suffered Hester, that hers has been "but the shadow of what he bears on his own breast" and thus that "his A is bigger than hers."

513   Elliott, Emory. "Art, Religion, and the Problem of Authority in *Pierre*." *Ideology and Classic American Literature*. Ed. Sacvan Bercovitch and Myra Jehlen. New York: Cambridge UP, 1986. 337-351.

In connection with "the role of the artist" in Herman Melville's *Pierre* (1852), Elliot explores Hawthorne's anxiety-ridden appraisal of that same role in *Letter*. Both authors keenly felt the isolation associated with the "weak and peripheral" profession of authorship in mid-nineteenth-century America, and both recognized that the pervasive American ideology insisted on economic productivity while it inhibited the production of serious literature. Hawthorne links Hester and Dimmesdale, as types of artists, to the narrator of "The Custom-House" "to illuminate a historical continuity that ties his own situation to theirs." The three artists suffer guilt, self-doubt, and isolation as a result of living in similar ages of "sexual and artistic anxiety." Both Hawthorne and Melville explore the tension between the individual and his cultural heritage, depicting characters who destroy themselves when they deny their own originality, imagination, love, and art, and become obsessed with proving their commitment to "popular," accepted beliefs of the established ideology. "In both Pierre and Dimmesdale, pride and ambition are combined with an incapacity to define themselves apart from the values of their culture, and these inner forces set them on a disastrous course that can only end in self-annihilation." And Isabel and Hester, though "bold antinomian women" who stand by their men and " possess radical new visions of what may still be humanly possible," are unable to effect any real change alone.

514   Forrer, Richard. "Nathaniel Hawthorne's *The Scarlet Letter*: Another Hybrid Theodicy." *Theodicies in Conflict: A Dilemma in Puritan Ethics and Nineteenth-Century American Literature*. Westport: Greenwood, 1986. 137-161, 253-258.

Hawthorne reformulates the Puritan legacy in *Letter*, exploring the human potential for corruptibility and self-destruction, concluding with something of a new theodicy that is a "precarious synthesis of rationalistic and Puritan beliefs." Hawthorne questions the adequacy of the Puritan

religion to account for human suffering and tragedy on three distinct levels
("the narrator's psychological analysis of both the inner lives of the main
characters and their tragic relationships, Dimmesdale's use of the Puritan
theodicy to make sense of his own suffering, and the narrator's own
critical evaluation of the Puritan theodicy in terms of both its
psychological consequences and its interpretation of psychological
processes"), all of which Forrer explores in detail through a careful
examination of three characters: Hester (who displays an almost
"masochistic pleasure in suffering" the punishment prescribed by her
Puritan community), Dimmesdale (whose acts suggest the futility of trying
to redeem past misdeeds through self-punishment), and the narrator (who
serves to raise doubts in the reader's mind about the dangers involved in
subscribing fully to the Puritan way of perceiving the world).

515   Jehlen, Myra. "Plain and Fancy Fictions." *American Incarnation: The
Individual, the Nation, and the Continent.* Cambridge: Harvard UP, 1986.
123-152.

In this study of the "culminating evolution of individualism," Jehlen
briefly discusses *Letter* (pp. 135-142) as Hawthorne's "blasphemous"
attempt at re-inventing or re-imagining America's material landscape.
Although Hester sets out to build herself a new world in America, she
ends up acquiescing to the social conventions that represent the country.
Just as the rebellious spirit of the letter dies with her in the last chapter
when she becomes "definitively contained by the grave," so does
Hawthorne's radical attempt in "adulterously" conceiving of a fictional
"other" America fail when he concludes the novel with an affirmation of
the existing values of America.

516   Ragussis, Michael. *"The Scarlet Letter." Acts of Naming: The Family
Plot in Fiction.* New York: Oxford UP, 1986. 65-86.*

In *Letter*, the act of naming "the child within the domain of the family"
lays bare the novel's deepest levels of plot. "While the text derives much
of its intensity of focus from the community's interest in [the hidden name
of Hester's partner in crime], *Letter* shows us a family that is tragically
splintered because all four of its members are unnamed or misnamed."
The paralyzing silence—which originates with Hester's refusal to name
Pearl's father, Dimmesdale's refusal to name himself as Hester's lover,
Chillingworth's command that Hester not speak his true name, and
Hester's refusal to explain to Pearl the name whose abbreviation she wears
on her bosom—becomes empowered to "obscure, to erase, to violate, and
to orphan." If there is any crime in the novel, then, it is not the crime of
sexual transgression but the crime of silence—which is rectified only

when the literal act of naming the family is replaced by Dimmesdale's "safe," third-person confession that humanizes yet protects him from the merciless blaming of the Puritan community.

*See 431 for Ragussis's original version of this essay under the title "Family Discourse and Fiction in *The Scarlet Letter*."

517   Wolford, Chester. "Intimations of Epic in *The Scarlet Letter*." *Forms of the Fantastic*. Ed. Jan Hokenson and Howard Pearce. Westport: Greenwood, 1986. 61-68.

Epic conventions run pervasively throughout *Letter* (i.e., the novel is politically motivated, is based upon a single action, merges the actual with the imaginary, shows concern with time and history, begins in *medias res*, makes constant use of *dei ex machina*, includes outward manifestations of inward conditions, and ends tragically). Hawthorne imitates traditional epic even in the opening scaffold scene where there occurs a debate among "divines" and common folk to determine the fate of an "unruly mortal." Wolford points out several allusions to *The Iliad*, *The Aeneid*, *The Odyssey*, and *The Inferno*, noting similarities in structure (*The Iliad*, *The Odyssey*, and *Letter* all have twenty-four sections), characterization (Hester's excessive pride, noble lineage, and isolation from society are similar to Achilles'), and plot (Dimmesdale's journey through hell imitates Dante's epic). Most important and fundamental to formal epic is the replacement of former world views with new ones, and, thus *Letter* repudiates the Puritan view and hints at a more democratic, free, and sympathetic way of life for America that is eventually achieved only in the mind of Pearl.

Journal Essays and Notes

518   Banting, Pamela. "Miss A and Mrs. B: The Letter of Pleasure in *The Scarlet Letter* and *As For Me and My House*." *North Dakota Quarterly* 54 (1986): 30-40.

Makes connections between Sinclair Ross's *As For Me and My House* and *Letter*, observing that both male-authored texts, which "attempt to appropriate the feminine text" of their heroines, "play out the dialectic between male and female" in "an erotics of space" (with *Letter* telling "the tale of the abuse of Eve by the New World Adam within the context of American Adamic mythology" and *As For Me and My House* narrating a "mistrust of the Garden"). Hester and Mrs. Bentley are "intimately connected with a preacher," and both characters connect sexuality and language in their constructions of "texts," Hester expressing her desire with the elaborately embellished letter and Mrs. Bentley with her endless diary entries. Both texts of desire also stem from "thwarted attempt[s] to find a direct erotic relation to the man"—with Hester's attempt distinguished by its insufficiency and Mrs. Bentley's by its excess. Art for these women is not then "therapy, religious or personal," but "desire in language" or "an erotics of writing."

519   Brumm, Ursula. "The Motif of the Pastor as an Unsuitable Suitor: The Religious Crisis in American Novels of the Nineteenth Century." *Amerikastudien* 31 (1986): 61-70.

Hawthorne's theme of religious doubt that was fictionalized in *Letter* as "a conflict within a love plot which involves a pastor and his female parishioner, a conflict that renders the pastor unable to fulfill his role as lover," appears later in the nineteenth century in such works as Harriet Beecher Stowe's *The Minister's Wooing* (1859), Henry Adams's *Esther* (1884), Margaret Deland's *John Ward, Preacher* (1888), and Harold Frederic's *The Damnation of Theron Ware* (1896). Also borrowed from Hawthorne's novel by these authors who similarly address the nineteenth-century conflict "between belief and doubt, between orthodox and liberal faith," are plot, structure, and characters. "Hester and Dimmesdale in various respects served as models for the lovers of these later novels, which took up motifs attached to these figures in order to discuss not only tensions between faith and doubt, but, more generally, failures of established religion in its service to humanity. The figure of Hester, furthermore, prefigures the later heroines' rebellion against a religion and church in which the female element is insufficiently represented." Although none of Hester's literary descendents—Mary, Esther, or Helen—reaches Hester's stature, they "make claims for what was already recognized by Hawthorne in *Letter* and was with increasing urgency felt as a basic deficiency in American or indeed Protestant religious life."

520   Cuddy, Lois A. "Mother-Daughter Identity in *The Scarlet Letter*." *Mosaic* 19 (1986): 101-115.

"When viewed from a psychoanalytic and feminist perspective, *Letter* becomes a case study of mother-daughter identification and bonding. Pearl functions not only as an illustration of mother-daughter symbiosis and of the stages in child development, but also as Hawthorne's unique strategy for clarifying the complexity of his heroine." Hawthorne's paradoxical presentation of Pearl as both "sprite" and "demon offspring" anticipates modern psychological perceptions of "normal" children in "abnormal" situations, and is intended to contrast sharply with the distorted Puritan point of view of children as small versions of adults.

Because Pearl further serves to reflect or provide confrontation with conflicting forces within Hester's and Dimmesdale's consciences or unconsciouses, she is thus the avenue to the personal salvation and psychological redemption of both.

521   Daniel, Clay.   *"The Scarlet Letter*: Hawthorne, Freud, and the Transcendentalists." *ATQ* 61 (1986): 23-36.

Arguing from a Freudian perspective, Daniel claims that *Letter* can be read both as Hawthorne's rejection of Concord transcendentalism and as the product of his attempt to resolve his Oedipal complex. Hawthorne's first struggle with and temporary triumph over his inhibiting complex occurred during his stay at Brook Farm when he came to associate his "fellow farmers' claims for the sanctity of natural urges" with his own Oedipal complex, and denied them both so that he could pursue a moral and sexually healthy relationship with his wife-to-be, Sophia Peabody. But Hawthorne's Oedipal instincts were exacerbated once again following the death of his mother and are incorporated into *Letter*, where Hawthorne once again examines those instincts and ultimately rejects them through the Oedipal drama of his primary characters, with Chillingworth playing the part of his father returned from the dead, Hester playing Hawthorne's mother, and Dimmesdale playing Hawthorne as guilty son/lover. While Daniel admits that his reading is "necessarily reductive" (the novel's composition was triggered exclusively by Hawthorne's mother's death), he considers it valuable in that, through the lens of a psychological reading, *Letter*'s ending seems to exhibit evidence of Hawthorne's psychological maturation, of his hard-won belief that "men must learn to overcome nature, not succumb to it." "As we see in the final pages of the story," Daniel clarifies, "Hawthorne comes to terms with his Oedipal feelings sufficiently to reject his Oedipal love for his mother to the extent that he forfeits the hope that he and his dead mother could ever meet 'hereafter, in an everlasting and pure reunion.'"

522   Dawson, Hugh J. "Hester Prynne, William Hathorne, and the Bay Colony Adultery Laws of 1641-42." *ESQ: A Journal of the American Renaissance* 32 (1986): 225-231.

Finds a historical basis for Hester's light sentencing for adultery that not only points to Hawthorne's careful attention to the Bay Colony adultery laws of 1641-1642, but also negatively alludes to his ancestor William Hathorne's involvement in the writing of the harsh reform laws. By June of 1642, the time of Hester's sentencing, Puritan legal history explicitly dictates (in Article 94 of the Bay Colony's "Body of Liberties") that execution was the punishment for adultery (to which the stern and ugly

Puritan woman in the crowd—associated with William Hathorne—refers in the novel's opening scene when she insists that both the Bible and "the statute-book" call for capital punishment for Hester's shameful offense). But Hawthorne takes into account that Hester's crime had been committed *before* the new laws had gone into effect, and thus attributes Hester's lenient sentencing to the merciful court officials who came before Hathorne and who were more like the compassionate and "angelic" Governor Winthrop who historically opposed Hathorne for the latter's zealotry in fixing inflexible punishments.

523   Dawson, Hugh J. "Hugues Merle's *Hester et Perle* and Nathaniel Hawthorne's *The Scarlet Letter.*" *Journal of the Walters Art Gallery* 44 (1986): 123-127.

Investigates the veracity of the claim that a work of art by nineteenth-century painter Hugues Merle in the Walters Art Gallery entitled "Hester et Perle. (*La Lettre Rouge*)" was praised by Hawthorne with "hearty approval" for having "fulfilled perfectly his ideal" of the opening scaffold scene. In the first place, Hawthorne could never have seen the painting, since it remained in Paris until after Hawthorne's death, and second, some of the details describing the opening scene are an inaccurate reflection of the novel: in the painting Hester is seated, the background is completely barren save the distant appearance of two male figures, and Pearl appears to be approximately two years old. Not entirely discounting the possibility that Hawthorne saw some form of this painting, Dawson suggests that Hawthorne may have viewed and admired the mood (if not the accuracy) of the painting through a photograph that was sent to him by William Walters in 1861, the record for which is catalogued in the diary of George Lucas, a nineteenth-century American art agent in Paris. Two photographs accompany the essay.

524   Dawson, Hugh J. "*The Scarlet Letter*'s Angry Eagle and the Salem Custom House." *Essex Institute Historical Collections* 122.1 (1986): 30-34.

Compares the actual wooden American eagle that still resides above the portico of the Salem Custom House with the "angry eagle" described in Hawthorne's satiric prefatory sketch to *Letter*. "Inexplicable" discrepancies between the carving (created in 1826 by local woodcarver Joseph True) and Hawthorne's inaccurate description of it suggest either faulty recollection on Hawthorne's part or, more likely, that his "resentful mischaracterization" of the emblematic bird was intended. Article contains two photographs of the eagle.

525   Kearns, Edward A. "Projection and Mirror: The Psychology of *The Scarlet Letter*." *Journal of Evolutionary Psychology* 7 (1986): 57-68.

Asserts that *Letter* is "a tale of projection, with Hester serving as "a mirror for the fears, passions, guilts, and desires of all who gaze upon her," and proposes that the similar projections of Hester and Dimmesdale "form the basis of Hester's tragedy and Dimmesdale's villainous, suicidal vanity." In Jungian terms, both characters lack "the wholeness of being" that comes with emotional and spiritual maturity, the lack of which makes them "a perfect couple, a matched pair whose twisted and stunted identities reflect one another in tragic, dusky grief." Afraid of her own sexuality, distrustful of her intellect, and suffering under the dominance of the father image (which makes Chillingworth an ideal mate since he would "complement her 'logos' while aiding her in the suppression of her sexuality"), Hester fails to grow. Yet she is still attracted to intellectuals "because they mirror latent powers in herself," and she is particularly drawn to Dimmesdale "because he represents the *potential* for the unity of *both* elements [passion and reason] in *herself*." Dimmesdale is, unfortunately, just as unconsciously unbalanced as Hester is, suffering from the smothering and restrictive image of the mother (leading him instinctively to the maternal, self-sacrificing Hester). Although Pearl provides the clue to a satisfactory resolution of her parents' dilemmas—impying throughout that a conscious recognition of their repressed/suppressed feelings would free them from their obsessive behaviors, both characters fail, Dimmesdale betraying Hester and dying an "ego-maniacal fool" after making "a mockery of confession," and Hester psychologically confined to the label forced upon her by the Puritan community and by herself.

526   Lindborg, Henry J. "Hawthorne's Enoch: Prophetic Irony in *The Scarlet Letter*." *Transactions of the Wisconsin Academy of Sciences, Arts, and Letters* 74 (1986): 122-125.

The frequent identification of Dimmesdale's character with angels in *Letter* reflects the popular belief—both in Puritan times and in Hawthorne's day—of the blurred distinction between men and angels. Since his "apostolic" gifts are linked to his passion for Hester and his guilt in hiding his parentage of Pearl, Lindborg likens Dimmesdale to the prophet Enoch, who was associated with fallen angels. Lindborg also parallels Pearl's role in the novel to Noah, who in the *Book of Enoch* also possesses otherworldly qualities. Further, Dimmesdale's identification with angels "is given greater ironic force by his prophetic office for the community," that of publicly admitting Pearl to be his daughter and thus resolving the novel's tension between passion and law.

527   Miller, Edwin Haviland. "Hawthorne at the Salem Custom House."
       Nathaniel Hawthorne Review 12.1 (1986): 15-16.

Unearths the self-published memoir of Salemite Henry B. Hill entitled
"Jottings from Memory, From 1823 to 1901," noteworthy for its "modest
and gentle" reminiscences until its description of Hawthorne at the
Custom House in the late 1840s.   Hill paints Hawthorne as a
condescending, "hard-looking customer" who "seemed ashamed to look at
anyone," and stresses that Hawthorne's introduction to *Letter*, in which
"he berates the old men he found there," is shameful and unfounded in its
criticisms, since Hill claims to have been "personally acquainted with
most of these men and knew how faithfully and conscientiously they
performed their duties." That Hawthorne points out their shortcomings,
Hill concludes, is evidence not of their deficiencies (of which they had
none), but of his own "meanness of character" and lack of "true
manhood."

528   Oehlschlaeger, Fritz. "Passion, Authority, and Faith in *The Damnation of
       Theron Ware.*" *American Literature* 58 (1986): 238-255.

Suggests that the "romantic revisionist reading[s]" of *Letter* by Nina Baym
(in 252) and Michael J. Colacurcio (in 289) can just as easily be applied to
Harold Frederic's *The Damnation of Theron Ware* (1896), since Frederic's
novel—similar in many ways to *Letter* in its tale of powerful female
sexuality and a minister's adultery—is not so much "an innocent's fall
into corrupt sexuality but a critique of the way corrupt authority poisons
sexuality." Frederic does not focus solely on the conflict between female
sexuality and male authority, however. He also condemns religious and
secular authority in general (admiring only the religious value of
repentance). Yet, although Frederic undercuts all the authority figures in
his novel, he simultaneously explores through his egotistic, godless main
character the problem of a lack of clear authority in nineteenth-century
Protestant America to confirm identity or to help establish one's place in
society.

529   Pribek, Thomas. "Hawthorne's Blackstone." *American Notes and
       Queries* 34 (1986): 142-144.

Speculates that the source for the passage on the Reverend William
Blackstone in *Letter*—which has yet to be discovered by critics—derives
from Francis Baylies's *An Historical Memoir of the Colony of New
Plymouth* (1830), in which Blackstone is described as having "planted the
first [apple-tree] orchard in New England" and having tamed a bull on

which he occasionally rode. [See Frederick Newberry (602) for a refutation of Pribek's thesis.]

530 Rozakis, Laurie N. "Another Possible Source for Hawthorne's Hester Prynne." *ATQ* 59 (1986): 63-71.

Having personally searched King's Chapel Burial Grounds in Boston for some clue to a historically "real" Hester Prynne, Rozakis claims to have found the "A" emblazoned tombstone of Elizabeth Pain, wife of Samuel Pain, who was tried and acquitted for the murder of her child. What's more, a barely-decipherable, weathered plaque lies next to Pain's gravemarker and identifies the woman buried there as the model for Hawthorne's fictional Hester Prynne—although, to Rozakis's knowledge, no scholar has ever acknowledged this plaque or the stone to which it refers (and it remains a mystery as to who was responsible for the explanatory tablet). It is likely that Hawthorne knew of Pain's grave marker (which bears a great similarity to Hester's), since the cemetery was located right next to the Boston Athenaeum. It is not known, however, whether Hawthorne had access to the historical records that detail Pain's case—which use the archaic terms "spinster," "illegitimate," and "fornication" to describe the married woman's crime.

531 Walter, James. "The Letter and the Spirit in Hawthorne's Allegory of American Experience." *ESQ: A Journal of the American Renaissance* 32 (1986): 36-54.

Even though the often-emphasized multiplicity of conflicting meanings and devices of ambiguity in *Letter* seem to point to a pervasive despondency and a grim conclusion (particularly with the appearance of the gloomy grave marker), there are indications in the novel that actually confirm a hopeful and positive "determinacy of meaning in all the signs constituting the novel's world." Just as Hawthorne deliberately undercuts "grounds for certainty in [the novel's] moral universe," so he also meticulously "prepares the reader against any final death of hope and imagination" with other faith-building and imagination-shaping devices that hint at a truth beyond the literal surface of the temporal world of Puritan signs—such as the restricted point of view of the narrator, several allegorically significant scenes that exaggerate allegory's arbitrariness, the obsessive use of the radiating qualities of light, and frequent hints at miraculous and supernatural power. By combining "The Custom-House" with *Letter*, Hawthorne also implies "a consistency of national character" between reductive seventeenth-century literalism in America and nineteenth-century materialism, offering vision, imagination, and intuition as an alternative, creative form of perception. The contrast between the two centuries is meant by Hawthorne to signify hope for America, to offer hints of a historical "redeeming presence" in order to help his contemporaries and future readers "shed the literalist film from their natural eyes and to remember what they have known in faith, hope, and love."

1987

Essays and Studies in Books

532   Chai, Leon. *"The Scarlet Letter." The Romantic Foundations of the American Renaissance.* Ithaca: Cornell UP, 1987. 49-55.

Hawthorne's writing has more affinities with French romanticism than with German or English romanticism in its tendency to "psychologize" symbolism and view nature not as a manifestation of divine essence but as "a symbolic image of the thoughts that fill individual consciousness." When *Letter* is viewed with this tendency in mind, the scarlet letter itself, moral law, and even grace become symbolic projections of states of mind in which their meanings are continually obscured at the same time that they are suggested.

533   Cox, James M. "Reflections on Hawthorne's Nature." *American Letters and the Historical Consciousness: Essays in Honor of Lewis P. Simpson.* Baton Rouge: Louisiana State UP, 1987. 137-157.

Discusses Hawthorne's body of work in relation to his voyeuristic life, suggesting that Hawthorne's infamous twelve years of solitude following his graduation from college determined a creative life of private reflection over one of lived experience. Cox also addresses the political dimensions of Hawthorne's art, as well as his conflicted feelings of pride and shame regarding the profession of authorship and his related obsession with "sin, shame, sympathy, and judgment." Hawthorne's "capacity to feel both the seduction and the sin of art in a single instant is at the heart of his imaginative power," as in *Letter*, wherein Hawthorne "distributes the motives of the artist and democratizes the guilt among the characters."

534   Dekker, George. *The American Historical Romance.* New York: Cambridge UP, 1987.

In chapter five, "Hawthorne and the Ironies of New England History" (pp. 129-185), Dekker considers *Letter* (pp. 159-172) and several of the tales in the context of Sir Walter Scott's Waverly legacy in American fiction, offering an ironic reading of Dimmesdale's Election-Day sermon and focusing specifically on "Hawthorne's ambivalent view of the forces of progress as represented by the seventeenth-century Puritan colonists of New England and the eighteenth-century patriots who wrested independence from Britain." Chapter seven, "The Hero and Heroine of Historical Romance" (pp. 220-271), discusses the close relation between *Letter* and Scott's *The Heart of Midlothian* (1818) and assesses the influence of the Waverly-model on Hawthorne's own historical romance. Just as Scott subverts traditional gender-role stereotypes to explore "the nature of dependence in human relationships" but eventually conforms to the expectations of "a society which rejects revolution but accepts gradual change," so Hawthorne (like Edith Wharton and Willa Cather after him) expresses a strikingly similar awareness with his own heroes and heroines of how gender roles are slowly and historically conditioned.

535   DeSalvo, Louise. *"The Scarlet Letter, A Romance."* *Nathaniel Hawthorne.* Atlantic Highlands: Humanities Press International, 1987. 57-76.

Finds that *Letter*, as well as Hawthorne's other romances, is an "uneasy masculine exploration of, and reaction to, the radical, revolutionary claims that the feminists of his time were making about the nature of women, and the solutions to the reality of their abject outsider economic, political, and legal status within the American system." Hawthorne uses the novel to control and rewrite his own past "into a version that would provide him with less virulent male ancestors and that would present them to the world as less sadistic than they in fact were." In doing so, Hawthorne misrepresents historical reality by presenting Puritan men as more fair-minded than their vengeful women counterparts (especially in terms of the initial reaction of the men and the women to Hester's punishment when she first appears on the scaffold). DeSalvo offers new insights to account for Hawthorne's ambivalent feelings about women, namely that "Hawthorne irrationally blamed his mother for having abandoned him through her death," and that "he also blamed her for losing his position at the Custom-House." She notes further instances of Hawthorne's possible misogyny in his depiction of Pearl's salvation, which comes not from her mother's tireless efforts, but from the single moment in which Dimmesdale acknowledges her before he dies.

536   Lang, Amy Schrager. "An American Jezebel: Hawthorne and *The Scarlet Letter.*" *Prophetic Woman: Anne Hutchinson and the Problem of Dissent in the Literature of New England.* Berkeley: U of California P, 1987. 161-192.

Nineteenth-century New England writers had a tendency to model their powerful female dissenters and lawless women figures in their fiction from Anne Hutchinson. Hawthorne's "Mrs. Hutchinson" sketch (1830), which ultimately condemns the seventeenth-century "heretic" for stepping out of the feminine role prescribed for her, compares Hutchinson to the "damned mob of scribbling women" sentimental novelists of the 1830s—whose "irregular status" as women is similarly linked by "feminine ambition." Hawthorne views their assertions of autonomy and their challenges to patriarchal authority to be as dramatic as Hutchinson's antinomianism, and he transfers their threatening power to the character of Hester in *Letter*. Hester's own "domestic failings," which lead to the sin of adultery, radical individualism, and dangerous intellectual antinomianism, are restored in the end when she repents her sinful past and resumes the "part" or role of a "true" woman and inspires a "glorious vision of the future." In a sense, "Hawthorne returns Hester to Hutchinson's original error and corrects it."

537   Levy, Laurie. Forward. *The Scarlet Letter*. By Nathaniel Hawthorne. 1850. New York: Portland House Illustrated Classics, 1987. ix-xi.

Before citing Hawthorne as "one of the first Americans to use fiction as a vehicle for psychological insight," Levy very briefly summarizes the action of the novel and estimates *Letter*'s ability to transform Hester's set of circumstances into a tale "of universality." She also calls attention to the illustrations (several in color) by English watercolorist Hugh Thompson, whose drawings throughout the large-print text "combine the diverse elements of fantasy and realism that work to complement Hawthorne's vision."

538   Morse, David. "Nathaniel Hawthorne: Excessive Interpretation." *American Romanticism*. Vol. 1. Totowa: Barnes and Noble, 1987. 169-220.

Hawthorne depicts himself as incapable of "rising to the levels of excessiveness" that his "exaggerated, lurid, and fanciful" characters do in much of his fiction, and he often claims that a consistent failure of imagination has led him to cultivate his own Hilda-like talents in humbly recording historical events. Yet images of excess abound, especially in *Letter* (pp. 192-206), where "images of the romanticized past are depicted with such extraordinary vividness that they seem to reproach the blurred and inauthentic present." Morse focuses on "the excess of the letter" in the opening marketplace scene, noting how crisply Puritan moralism is distinguished from Hester's rebellious spirit—and how "Hester demonstrates by her striking example that our sense of human possibility can be enlarged." She converts the condemning letter into a symbol of extravagance, freedom, and independence that eventually "shatters the torpor of the everyday with unimpeachable signs of authenticity and truth." Morse's analysis also indicates the influence on *Letter* by Sir Walter Scott's *Peveril of the Peak* (in terms of the representation of history and the affinity between Pearl and Fennela), and William Godwin's *Caleb Williams* (in its call for sincerity and openness).

539   Newberry, Frederick. *Hawthorne's Divided Loyalties: England and America in His Works*. Rutherford: Fairleigh Dickinson UP, 1987.*

Newberry not only explores the ways in which seventeenth-century Puritanism detrimentally severed the rich cultural and artistic traditions of Old World England from the New World, but also shows how Hawthorne recovers an English aesthetic tradition in his re-evaluation of colonial history. Hawthorne's works set in the seventeenth century lament the impoverished culture that the narrow-minded, intolerant, and self-righteous Puritans passed on to later generations. These works introduce curiously anachronistic mediating figures to serve as bright alternatives to Puritan gloom and severity—as positive "adaptation[s] of the best of Old World culture [brought] to New World experience." Chapter four, "The Recovery of English Traditions in 'The Old Manse' and 'The Custom-House' (pp. 134-166), establishes a foundation for Newberry's reading of *Letter* as "a probing analysis of the early loss of [English cultural] virtues in seventeenth-century Boston." In it he shows how the success of the American artists in "Drowne's Wooden Image" and "The Artist of the Beautiful" depends upon defying the Puritan iconoclastic tradition. In "The Old Manse" and "The Custom-House," the fictional artists defy that negative tradition and embrace the cultural and aesthetic traditions of England. In chapter five, "Disinheritance and Recovery of English Traditions in *The Scarlet Letter*" (pp. 167-193), Newberry "explores the historical roots of the barren aesthetic condition in which [Hawthorne] finds himself" in the nineteenth century, explaining that Hawthorne's attempt to recover the broken ties between Old and New Worlds is through a fictional artistic predecessor (Hester) who represents a mixture of both Worlds.

*For Newberry's earlier essay on the tension between the Old and New Worlds in *Letter*, see 348.

540   Pease, Donald. *Visionary Compacts: American Renaissance Writings in Cultural Context*. Madison: U of Wisconsin P, 1987.

Chapters two and three, "Hawthorne's Discovery of a Pre-Revolutionary Past" (pp. 49-80) and "A Romance with the Public Will" (pp. 81-107), deal exclusively with "The Custom-House" and *Letter*, addressing Hawthorne's concern with the debilitating lack of shared cultural responsibility in America and the need for each individual to replace self-interest with concern for the well-being of the overall community in order for the nation to prosper. Unlike many of his contemporaries who viewed the past as an abstract ideal exempt from continued development, Hawthorne viewed it as continuous, as something Americans inherit and keep alive in the present to understand themselves communally and culturally. His historical romance becomes a social means of reactivating a collective memory and restoring vitality to public life, just as "The Custom-House" itself—with its pre-Revolutionary "ghosts"—removes Hawthorne from his self-enclosed sphere of self-interest and returns him to a world of communal purposes. In investing the present with a cultural memory, Hawthorne performs a necessary cultural task with his romance, as well as comes to terms with his own tendency to alienate himself from the public world through the "private" characters of Hester and Dimmesdale—who, like he, discover the crucial reciprocity between public and private worlds required to create a healthy sense of communal intimacy.

541   Schriber, Mary Suzanne. "Nathaniel Hawthorne: A Pilgrimage to a Dovecote." *Gender and the Writer's Imagination: From Cooper to Wharton.* Lexington: UP of Kentucky, 1987. 45-85, 192-197.

Uses the concepts of "woman's nature" and "woman's sphere" as a frame of reference for assessing the "constricting" sexual politics represented in nineteenth-century novels by James Fenimore Cooper, Hawthorne, William Dean Howells, Henry James, and Edith Wharton. Despite his efforts to challenge cultural assumptions and expectations, Hawthorne, like the other four writers, was caught up in the "insidiousness of the culture's ideology of woman," and ended up losing his nerve and actually reinforcing his culture's predispositions about women. In *Letter* (pp. 46-60), "the most dramatic example in our literature of the culture's horizon of expectations," Hawthorne's "radically imaginative characterization" of his bold heroine is "foiled by the restrictions that a priori ideas of woman lead him to place on Hester." He "invest[s] his narrator with a series of speculations that serve to undermine the meaning of Hester's character and the unity of the romance," thus making his "cultural challenge" little more than "a gentleman's pilgrimage to a fair-haired heroine in a dovecote." What's more, Hawthorne's remaining novels suggest an awareness of his failed effort with *Letter* and reveal the imaginative

272

"shackles" that prevented him from ever again venturing too far beyond gender stereotypes of women in romance.

Journal Essays and Notes

542   Bronstein, Zelda. "The Parabolic Ploys of *The Scarlet Letter*." *American Quarterly* 39 (1987): 193-210.

To exact revenge on his political enemies and to cast aspersions on the local community of Salem, Hawthorne deviously and ingeniously set up *Letter* as a modern-day parable to match the biblical parable of the Old Testament prophet Nathan (referred to in chapter nine of *Letter*, and in which King David finally acknowledges how despicable his act of killing Bathsheba's husband was when Nathan cleverly tells the King a parable that turns out to be about him and his murderous act). In like fashion, Hawthorne "beguiles his public into self-condemnation by getting them to denounce in [the Puritans] what they would never acknowledge, much less condemn, in themselves." Hawthorne uses sexual intolerance in the novel as a metaphor for the political intolerance of nineteenth-century America—even aligning sexual transgression with the artistic process, inasmuch as he specifically defies in both "The Custom-House" and *Letter* the prevailing nineteenth-century ban on fiction that is expressly political. By forcing his readers to recognize their bigoted likeness to the Puritans, Hawthorne thwarted his contemporary public's desire to find only flattering images of itself in American fiction. This parabolic strategy not only enabled Hawthorne to oppose the prevailing ideology, but also simultaneously allowed him to escape detection for challenging its hypocrisy.

543   Brooke-Rose, Christine. "A for But: 'The Custom-House' in Hawthorne's *The Scarlet Letter*." *Word and Image: A Journal of Verbal Visual Inquiry* 3 (1987): 143-155.

Hoping to persuade the reader (whom she directly addresses throughout) of the "poetic truth" of *Letter*, Brooke-Rose is emboldened enough by recent work on "iconicity" and "spatio-temporal representation in fiction" to offer a reading of the novel that intends to link "The Custom-House" with the novel proper—by showing that the introduction is, in fact, the "threshold" of the antithesis-ridden narrative. Insisting that the introductory sketch has been understood by critics as only "purely autobiographical" and also assuming the reader's familiarity with the argot of several psychoanalytic, structuralist, and deconstructive theorists, Brooke-Rose suggests that Hawthorne employs a parodic, "forking antithetical style" in "The Custom-House" that clearly belongs to what

Roland Barthes calls "the Symbolic Code." This obsessive exploitation of oppositions—youth and age, past and present, good and evil, knowledge and innocence—stems from Hawthorne's split public/private personality and is projected into the story itself, giving it its peculiar intensity. The complex forking style, which Brooke-Rose exemplifies with several charts and graphs, also "mimes the very hieroglyph that symbolizes that ambiguity," or, in other words, symbolizes "If-But-And-Though," and can actually be charted to form the chief symbol of the novel, the letter "A."

544   Clark, Michael. "Another Look at the Scaffold Scenes in Hawthorne's *The Scarlet Letter.*" *ATQ* New Series 1 (1987): 135-144.

Although the scaffold scenes have often been noted for their structural and thematic importance, they have never been considered in relation to fundamental romantic principles, as "Hawthorne's examination of the central problem of literary transcendentalism: the interrelationship of man, nature, and the ideal." More specifically, the three scaffold scenes are studies of heathen nature, higher law, and human community (in that order), which together reflect that Hawthorne did not share Ralph Waldo Emerson's and Henry David Thoreau's optimism about the individual's divine right to disregard human law in order to discover intuitively a higher truth in Nature. On the contrary, Hawthorne cautions the individual against privileging either nature or divine truth over human law. Of paramount importance is "the human community's interpretation of nature and divine truth." Intuition must not be trusted, Dimmesdale stresses to Hester during his voluntary confession in the final scaffold scene, and "the human community's laws must be the final authority that man can know." That Hester resumes wearing the scarlet letter years later implies that she, too, finally subsumes her "romantic values" to the Puritan community's long-established laws.

545   Dawson, Hugh J. "The Triptych Design of *The Scarlet Letter.*" *Nathaniel Hawthorne Review* 13.1 (1987): 12-14.

The three scaffold scenes do not simply serve to structure the novel or to illuminate the severity of Puritan moralism. The unity achieved by the three scaffold scenes "resides in their allusiveness; it derives not from their implying a near-mathematical symmetry of structure but from the strikingly visual address of the triad of scaffold tableaux." In the three scenes appear visual analogues of Christian art, namely the three panels of a triptych, which for centuries has served "to celebrate and teach the relation of central figures and events in the drama of Christian history."

546   Flores, Ralph. "Ungrounding Allegory: The Dead-Living Letter in Hawthorne's *The Scarlet Letter.*" *Criticism* 29 (1987): 313-340.

Through a deconstructionist approach, Flores argues that most critics overlook the deeply "allegorical texture" of *Letter* because the novel fails to offer firmly didactic statements about its allegorical personifications. This seeming lack of allegorical technique, Flores cautions, stems from the fact that *Letter* concerns itself with the very process of constructing meaning—so that the process itself is "allegorized, theatricalized, and even occasionally mocked." Thus the allegory of *Letter* is "groundless" in its estimate of the impossibility of arriving at truth, but it also "ungrounds" the usual assumptions of traditional life-affirming allegory through its characters (all of whom are "uncanny" and "flat" allegorical personifications) "whose assertions of life are problematically entangled with death, dying, and deadness."

547   Greiner, Donald J. "Updike on Hawthorne." *Nathaniel Hawthorne Review* 13.1 (1987): 1-4.

Reproduces Greiner's interview with John Updike on his two novels, *A Month of Sundays* (1975) and *Roger's Version* (1986), both of which refer directly to *Letter*. The former is something of an update of Dimmesdale, while the latter is the update of Chillingworth. In the interview, Updike acknowledges having completed a third novel, this one an update of Hester's character.

548   Jones, Grace. "Literary Kinship: Nathaniel Hawthorne, John Fowles, and Their Scarlet Women." *South Atlantic Quarterly* 86 (1987): 69-78.

While some of the connections between *Letter* and *The French Lieutenant's Woman* (1969) are obvious, such as the similarities between the two heroine adulteresses, Hester and Sarah, and their female offspring, Pearl and Lalage (as well as Sarah's gratuitous pricking of her finger on a hawthorn tree), no one has addressed the fact that "some of the very traits that have led critics to call Fowles experimental in [his novel] are those for which he is most indebted to Hawthorne." Such traits include "his thematic use of ambiguity; his obsession with and use of the past; and his deliberate confusion of narrator and character. Finally one wonders if Fowles does not purposefully hold out to us the Hester/Sarah comparison to draw attention away from the pervasiveness of Hawthorne's influence—acknowledgment of which might lead to a reassessment of the novelty of *The French Lieutenant's Woman.*" The kinship of Hester and Sarah might also be Fowles's way of universalizing, "both through time and nationality, the plight of the human spirit trapped in an unsympathetic age."

549   McMaster-Harrison, June. "'What Hast Thou Done with Her?': Anagogical Clues to the Lost Feminine." *Canadian Woman Studies* 8 (1987): 49-53.

Referring to Gnostic interpretations of scripture, this essay uses Jungian "Depth Psychology" to investigate the deliberate suppression of allusions to the feminine principle in the godhead and how this sense of loss echoes throughout Western literature and consciousness. McMaster-Harrison finds several instances in nineteenth-century American literature of a deep "longing for a feminine principle wholly lacking in the Puritanical image of God," citing Herman Melville, Hawthorne, and Walt Whitman as authors whose work reflects visionary, "anagogical" (dealing with the redemption of the soul) clues to the lost feminine, as if they instinctively felt that something was amiss in their culture's Calvinist understanding of the nature of the divine. In *Letter*, Hawthorne creates an anagogical symbol of the lost principle in Hester, who foresees a Second Coming that will recover the lost feminine.

550   Newberry, Frederick. "A Red-Hot A and a Lusting Divine: Sources for *The Scarlet Letter*." *New England Quarterly* 60 (1987): 256-264.

Finds "tantalizing" historical evidence for real-life Puritan sources for Hester, Dimmesdale, and Chillingworth in the 1651 case trial in Maine of George Rogers and Mrs. Mary Batchellor, wife of former minister Stephen Batchellor. That Mary was actually branded with the letter "A" six weeks after the delivery of her illegitimate child may have provided Hawthorne with a few crucial details surrounding his heroine's plight in *Letter*, and may also account for the references in both "The Custom-House" and the novel to the letter's figurative scorching heat. Other likely historical borrowings include the Reverend Stephen Batchellor's Dimmesdale-like guilt and fear of detection over his *own* attempted adulterous behavior, as well as the same man's very advanced age of ninety when he married Mary and she committed her adulterous affair, a situation that likens him to Chillingworth.

551   Smith, Allen Lloyd. "The Elaborated Sign of *The Scarlet Letter*." *ATQ* New Series 1 (1987): 69-82.*

The scarlet letter represents not only the first letter of the alphabet (standing for language and especially writing) but also an "historically determined signifier" of adultery and a "token of the truth" of Surveyor

Pue's story that also links the past with the present. Hawthorne "embroiders" the letter with further meanings, considering it as an "elaborated sign" that indicates three areas of interrelated concern: "the question of writing (especially as the shadow of the spoken or unspoken); the issue of allegory and typology; and the aesthetics of preordained response." Hawthorne intends the sign to have so many antagonistic meanings that assignment of any particular symbol becomes impossible— thus indicating his mistrust of any supposedly certain knowledge (whether delivered in speech or writing), while also calling attention to his desire for the letter to be read as "an exceptional object carrying a significant message which must be interpreted to the community (for which it may be prophetic at least in the sense that it explains the community to itself, or in the sense that typology offers the possibility of a reapprehension of the past in view of its prefigurative aspect)." Smith reduces the conflict between natural and institutional law in the novel to the "whole matter of voice versus writing," concluding that the engraved tombstone at the end signals a "victory for the written."

*For Smith's earlier version of this essay (under the name Allen Gardner Lloyd-Smith), see 462.

552   Smolinski, Reiner.   "Covenant Theology and Arthur Dimmesdale's Pelagianism." *ATQ* New Series 1 (1987): 211-231.

Attending to the common critical debate over whether Dimmesdale is damned or saved at the end of the novel, Smolinski suggests that Puritan theology—and Hawthorne's in-depth knowledge of Puritan divinity—is key in ending the controversy. He builds on Ernest W. Baughman's investigation (in 204) into the Puritan tradition of public confession to explain Dimmesdale's behavior, adding several other historically accurate and theologically sound precepts that Hawthorne employed to further inform the character's psychological motivation and final act of confession. Dimmesdale's dilemma in the novel grows out of his interior dilemma over the covenants of Grace and Works. His heretical application of the Covenant of Works, or his "Pelagian belief of redemption through works," tortures him practically to a psychotic state of mind throughout the novel as he suffers despairingly through the long process of conversion. At the end, during the final scaffold scene when he publicly confesses, Dimmesdale finally "acknowledges God's grace as the only means of his redemption" and rejects Chillingworth's (Satan's) last attempt at getting him to privilege his earthly achievements over grace itself. At this point Dimmesdale also denies his enemy's insistence that the infamy of the public confession would be far more detrimental than the minister's soul-cleansing revelation of his sin. As a truly penitent sinner now, according to Puritan dogma, Dimmesdale is saved on the scaffold of public ignominy, as is hinted through Hawthorne's emphasis on the New Testament qualities of "mercy, forgiveness, and long-suffering."

553   Stout, Janis P.   "The Fallen Woman and the Conflicted Author: Hawthorne and Hardy." *ATQ* New Series 1 (1987): 233-246.

Examines three literary works from the Victorian era that question through their heroines the "stereotyped assumptions regarding the social role and moral nature of women," namely *Letter*, *Blithedale Romance*, and Thomas Hardy's *Tess of the D'Urbervilles* (1891). Hester, Zenobia, and Tess are all fallen women whose authors are so sympathetic with their plights that Hawthorne and Hardy question not only "the correctness of society's moral judgments of [them], but the judgmental mentality itself." In the end, however, neither Hawthorne nor Hardy can resolve his conflicted ambivalence toward the fallen woman, and both are likewise unable to shake the nagging belief in the importance of female chastity.

554   Swann, Charles.   "Hester and the Second Coming: A Note on the Conclusion to *The Scarlet Letter*." *Journal of American Studies* 21 (1987): 264-268.

Attempting to come to terms with Hester's decision to return to Boston at the end, Swann argues against "inadequate" readings of the novel (mentioned are Austin Warren [178], Michael J. Colacurcio [289], and Nina Baym [339]) that underestimate or downplay Hester's radical, feminist nature. "She is more subversive than is usually recognized in that she desires and prophesies a radical subversion of the patriarchal structures of her society—and, most importantly, of the religion that legitimates that patriarchy." Hester's prophecy that Christ will return to earth in the Second Coming as a woman is a more radical perspective than that held by Anne Hutchinson, Margaret Fuller, or Shaker foundress Mother Lee Ann. Swann compares Hester's prophecy with Dimmesdale's own prophecy during his Election-Day sermon when he anticipates the glorious future of New England, and Swann notes that "it is a nice irony that the clergyman makes a secular prophecy while the laywoman makes a religious one." While Swann does not wish his extreme reading to appear to "outfeminize the feminists," he suggests that a close reading of the passages in question prohibits any other conclusion.

555   Yin, Xiao-Huang. "*The Scarlet Letter* in China." *American Quarterly* 39 (1987): 551-562.

Examines the three Chinese translations of *Letter* that have appeared in the twentieth century to illustrate not only the novel's immense popularity among Chinese readers, but also the varied approaches to literary criticism that China has undergone in three historical stages as its politics has shifted. The 1934 translation reflects Western-style criticism (structurally resembling a Norton critical edition and containing many "grand gestures" geared to impress elite readers) and emphasizes the importance of Christianity and education. The second translation, a Soviet-style edition published in 1954 and titled "The Song of the Rustic Poor," was designed for the general Chinese reader as mass education of the dogma of the Stalin era and has a distinctly anti-religious and anti-feminist flavor. The third translation, appearing in 1981 and reflecting the more sophisticated historical-sociological method of criticism that blossomed when the Soviet Union split from China, is more independently analytical and more carefully researched. None of the three translations, Yin notes in conclusion, contains "The Custom-House," an oversight that he speculates may be reconsidered in a future translation.

556   Young, Virginia Hudson.   "D. H. Lawrence and Hester Prynne." *Publications of the Arkansas Philological Association* 13 (1987): 67-78.

Although Lawrence knew his *Studies in Classic American Literature* (see EC18) was "really very good," he also understood that the volume would give his readers "fits and convulsions." Young agrees with Lawrence's assessment of his own eccentric text, especially since Lawrence "so egregiously misread[s]" Hester's character. Troubled by Lawrence's vehemently negative reading of Hester, Young sets about to judge it by Lawrence's own set of criteria for the critic; he "must be emotionally alive in every fiber, intellectually capable and skillful in essential logic, and then morally very honest." In view of these three determinants—emotion, logic, and morality—Young concludes that Lawrence was too caught up in his overly-heightened emotional response to be fair and reasonable, too eager to dismiss the "sophisticated ranges of Hester's emotion" and "the diverse attitudes through which Hester evolves" because of his own intruding and bitter personal memories of insidious lovers and a beloved mother who died too early.

1988

Books

557   Gross, Seymour [L.], Sculley Bradley, Richmond Croom Beatty, and E. Hudson Long, eds. *The Scarlet Letter: An Authoritative Text, Essays in*

Criticism and Scholarship. Third edition. New York: W. W. Norton, 1988. 443 pp.

This third edition (see 102 and 353 for the first and second) omits the section entitled "Records Based on Primary Sources," as well as deletes seven essays that appeared in the second edition. (Gross is also now listed as primary editor) Seven recent essays are added: Frederick Newberry's "Tradition and Disinheritance in *The Scarlet Letter*" (348), Robert L. Berner's "A Key to 'The Custom-House" (375), Richard II. Brodhead's "New and Old Tales: *The Scarlet Letter*" (300), Nina Baym's "The Significance of Plot in Hawthorne's Romances" (406), Daniel Cottom's "Hawthorne Versus Hester: The Ghostly Dialectic of Romance in *The Scarlet Letter*" (427), David Leverenz's "Mrs. Hawthorne's Headache: Reading *The Scarlet Letter*" (447), and Dennis Fosters's "The Embroidered Sin: Confessional Evasion in *The Scarlet Letter*" (443). The bibliography, which is now divided into readings on "The Custom-House" and *The Scarlet Letter*, has been expanded to include a total of 171 items, and a chronology of Hawthorne's life has been added.

558   Kesterson, David B., ed. *Critical Essays on Hawthorne's The Scarlet Letter.* Boston: G. K. Hall, 1988. 222 pp.

Part of the "Critical Essays on American Literature" Series, this volume contains an introduction by Kesterson, twenty reprinted reviews and articles that trace *Letter*'s critical reputation, as well as four original essays and an index. Reviewers include C. E. Frazer Clark, Jr., (255), Evert A. Duychinck (ER1), George Ripley (ER2), E. P. Whipple (ER3), Henry F. Chorley (ER4), Anne W. Abbott (ER5), Orestes A. Brownson (ER9), and Arthur Cleveland Coxe (ER10). Pre-1950 criticism includes excerpts from Henry James's *Nathaniel Hawthorne* (EC15), William Dean Howells's *Heroines in Fiction* (EC14), W. C. Brownell's *American Prose Masters* (EC3), Frederick I. Carpenter's "Scarlet A Minus" (EC4), and John C. Gerber's "Form and Content in *The Scarlet Letter*" (EC9). Post-1950 criticism includes excerpts from Roy Male's *Hawthorne's Tragic Vision* (56), Frederick Crews's *The Sins of the Fathers* (182), Terence Martin's "Dimmesdale's Ultimate Sermon" (276), Arne I. Axelsson's "Isolation and Interdependence as Structure in *The Scarlet Letter* (309), Nina Baym's *The Shape of Hawthorne's Career* (339), Hyatt H. Waggoner's *The Presence of Hawthorne* (374), and Millicent Bell's "The Obliquity of Signs: *The Scarlet Letter*" (425). Separate entries for Kesterson's introduction and the four original essays by Rita K. Gollin, Thomas Woodson, James Mellard, and Richard Rust are below.

Essays and Studies in Books

559   Abel, Darrel. *The Moral Picturesque: Studies in Hawthorne's Fiction.*
       West Lafayette: Purdue UP, 1988.

Part three of this four-part volume of reprinted essays on Hawthorne's
preoccupation with "how the ideal appears in the real world, and the
distinction and relation of the sexes," focuses specifically on *Letter* and
includes (some under altered titles): "The Strong Division-Lines of
Nature" (284), "Hester: In the Dark Labyrinth of the Mind" (16), "Pearl:
The Scarlet Letter Endowed with Life" (10), "Chillingworth: The Devil in
Boston" (24), and "Dimmesdale: Fugitive From Wrath" (46). (Part Two,
on Hawthorne's "Materials and Techniques," contains the reprinted essay,
"Metonymic Symbols: Black Glove and Pink Ribbon" [239].)

560   Bercovitch, Sacvan. "Representing Revolution: The Example of Hester
       Prynne." *The Early Republic: The Making of a Nation—The Making of a
       Culture.* Ed. Steve Ickringill. Amsterdam: Free UP, 1988. 29-51.

This New Historicist approach argues that *Letter* illustrates the "absence"
or "ambiguity" at the heart of American representations of revolution.
Bercovitch explicates the famous one-line paragraph, "the scarlet letter
had not done its office," to show the relationship between rhetoric and
culture, as well as to examine the relation between process and closure.
On political, moral, aesthetic, and historical levels, the scarlet letter
functions as a "do-it-yourself" guide to the process (or telos) of
Americanization. The symbolic scarlet letter actually joins the novel's
two turbulent historical time frames, the fictional frame (from 1642-1649)
and the authorial frame (from 1848-1852), in order for Hawthorne to
"acknowledge the threat of cultural fragmentation and to evade the
conflict." As such, the letter acts as an agent of reconciliation of
conflicting forces. Just as Hawthorne can reverse the disruptive effects of
his removal from political office "by reaching back to the text that relates
him to the growth of the country," so Hester at the end of her tale reverses
the disruptive effects of her symbol by looking forward to a vision of a
"brighter period" that relates her most intimate hopes to the progress of
history." In this manner, Hawthorne links past and present, shaping the
course of progress from theocracy to democracy. [For more on this
subject of the "office" of the scarlet letter, see Bercovitch's "The A-
Politics of Ambiguity in *The Scarlet Letter* (575) and his greatly
influential book-length study *The Office of The Scarlet Letter* (635).]

561 Carlson, Rae. "Exemplary Lives: The Uses of Psychobiography for Theory Development." *Psychobiography and Life Narratives*. Ed. Dan P. McAdams and Richard L. Ochberg. Durham: Duke UP, 1988. 105-138.

Borrowing psychologist S. S. Tomkins's "script theory" (which argues that people are like playwrights, constructing dramatic narratives to make sense of their lives), Carlson reinterprets aspects of the lives of Hawthorne and Eleanor Marx (Karl Marx's daughter). The section on Hawthorne (pp. 112-123) employs Gloria Erlich's 1984 study of Hawthorne, *Family Themes and Hawthorne's Fiction: The Tenacious Web* (459) to explore Tomkins's theory of a "nuclear script," a script "marked by ambivalence or confusion about one's most cherished goals." Hawthorne's two major losses in 1849—his job and his mother—sufficiently energized the "dilatory and inhibited author" to produce *Letter* "in a frenzy of creativity" at an "astonishing speed." The novel, which contains a great many autobiographical features, illustrates over and over how "good things turn bad."

562 Dawson, Hugh J. "Discovered in Paris: An Earlier First Illustrated Edition of *The Scarlet Letter*." *Studies in the American Renaissance*. Ed. Joel Myerson. Charlottesville: UP of Virginia, 1988. 271-280.

The first illustrated edition of *Letter* to appear in any language is *La Lettre Rouge A* (1853), translated by Paul Émile Daurand Forgues (under the pseudonym "Old Nick"). It is notable not only for its status as the first illustrated edition (preceding the London illustrated edition by four years), but for its radical alteration of Hawthorne's text. Forgues's translation, which Dawson calls a "sharply abbreviated and corrupt version" of the original, is "a wholesale transmutation of what Hawthorne had written and published in America three years earlier. The richer dimensions of the romance are scrapped in reducing the masterpiece to a sentimental tale." Dawson suspects that the Paris publishing firm of Gonet that commissioned Forgues's translation had intended the piece for a popular illustrated magazine. Dreadful sketches by Jules Jacques Veyrassat that are "utterly alien to the milieu of Puritan Boston" accompany the edition (five illustrations of which are included here). [For more of Veyrassat's shoddy illustrations, see Hugh J. Dawson's "The Original Illustrations of *The Scarlet Letter*" (657).]

563 Gollin, Rita K. "'Again a Literary Man': Vocation and *The Scarlet Letter*." *Critical Essays on Hawthorne's The Scarlet Letter*. Ed. David B. Kesterson. Boston: G. K. Hall, 1988. 171-183.

This biographical study addresses Hawthorne's anguished and "impractical" decision to become a professional writer instead of choosing a "more worthy and useful" career. The entire novel draws on Hawthorne's problem of deciding what to do with his life, and through the characters of Bellingham, Dimmesdale, and Chillingworth, Hawthorne explains why he refused to become—respectively—a lawyer, a minister, or a doctor (although he nonetheless identifies with each of them). He most resembles his "proud, intelligent, passionate, and creative" heroine, whose private and independent existence is condemned "by the self-righteous multitude." Returning to his more natural intellectual, imaginative life after the mind-numbing position of Custom House surveyor, Hawthorne turns his shameful firing into vindication in both "The Custom-House" and *Letter*. Like Hester, Hawthorne discovers the true power of his artistry only when he is left to his own resources.

564   Hanson, Elizabeth. "Hawthorne and the Indian." *The American Indian in American Literature: A Study in Metaphor.* Lewiston: Edwin Mellen Press, 1988. 26-33.

"The keynote of Hawthorne's employment of the Indian is neither longing for the mobility or spirituality of Indian experience, nor a denial of the Indian's savagery, but uneasiness." In *Letter*, Hawthorne connects the symbolic Indian—free, unrestrained, and potentially destructive—with Hester's estranged experience within the Puritan community in order to suggest the tension between wildness and order in her quest for identity.

565   Harris, Kenneth Marc. *Hypocrisy and Self-Deception in Hawthorne's Fiction.* Charlottesville: UP of Virginia, 1988.

Explores Hawthorne's obsession with hypocrisy and self-deception in his romances, proposing that his fascination relates to an interest with early American hypocrites and self-deceivers among Puritan clergy and their congregations in their joint efforts to detect "imposter saints." Harris demonstrates "a gradual building up of Hawthorne's interest in hypocrisy and self-deception in the period before *Letter* and the slow winding down or at least leveling off of it afterwards as he begins to turn in new directions." Harris devotes two chapters to *Letter*: "*The Scarlet Letter*: A World of Hypocrites" (pp. 46-67) and "Arthur Dimmesdale: The Hypocrite Saint" (pp. 68-88). In the first, he argues that, because Hester's inner reality is concealed by her "outward appearance of charitable affection to all mankind," she is "dangerously close to becoming as bad a hypocrite as any of her hypocritical persecutors." Only when she draws from Dimmesdale's example to overcome hypocrisy and reaffirm her true identity does she become "a sort of colonial Dear Abby." In the second chapter, Harris continues his discussion of Hawthorne's conception of hypocrisy and self-deception, arguing that Hawthorne was sympathetic to Dimmesdale because he himself regarded self-delusion as a common human failing. In the "Everyman" character's frustrated search for authentic selfhood, "the guilt he unquestionably acquires is mitigated and perhaps entirely overcome because the moral and ontological aspects of his self-deception so closely coincide." The pressing moral message of Dimmesdale's experience may well be that " a frail mortal who sets himself up as a martyr to truth will instead [necessarily] become a paragon of hypocrisy."

566   Hutner, Gordon. "Secrets and Sympathy in *The Scarlet Letter*." *Secrets and Sympathy: Forms of Disclosure in Hawthorne's Novels*. Athens: U of Georgia P, 1988. 17-63.*

The narrative method of "simultaneously concealing and revealing" secrets is "fundamental to Hawthorne's view of the mind, the life of society, and the life of the text." Hutner finds (in this expansion of his earlier essay, 445) that a dynamic relation exists between "The Custom-House" and *Letter* because the sketch and the novel share a "rhetoric of secrecy" that intimately relates Hester and Dimmesdale's ordeal to the traumatic and embarrassing Custom-House experience that stimulated Hawthorne to write the romance. Both sketch and novel also adopt "narrative strategies that elicit the reader's sympathetic response to a secret destined to remain indeterminate." Through the use of undisclosed secrets, Hawthorne tries to stimulate the reader to develop a "kind and apprehensive" sympathy that is essential to an understanding of the narrative and even to the ambiguous, indeterminate, nature of their own experiences.

*For Hutner's earlier study on "Secrets and Sympathy," see 445.

567   Kesterson, David B. Introduction. *Critical Essays on Hawthorne's The Scarlet Letter*. Ed. David B. Kesterson. Boston: G. K. Hall, 1988. 1-18.

As a means of prefacing the large collection of reviews and essays in the volume, Kesterson catalogs and occasionally evaluates the vast criticism of *Letter* as it has appeared since the novel's publication, focusing mostly on pre-1960s criticism. He concludes—after exploring trends in scholarship and addressing the debate over whether Hester or Dimmesdale is the leading character in the novel—that *Letter*'s very ambiguity and elusiveness are what have made it such a critical playground for all types of scholars over the years.

568   Mellard, James M. "Pearl and Hester: A Lacanian Reading." *Critical Essays on Hawthorne's The Scarlet Letter*. Ed. David B. Kesterson. Boston: G. K. Hall, 1988. 193-211.

Letter illustrates Lacanian psychoanalytic principles "because it focuses on four major characters whose experiences exemplify the major psychoanalytic issues as Jacques Lacan conceives them." Promoting Lacanian theory over "limited" Freudian theory because it is more conducive to literary analysis, Mellard chooses to focus on two out of these four main characters (Pearl and Hester instead of Dimmesdale and Chillingworth) because they exhibit "normal" as opposed to "neurotic" or "psychotic" behavior as "subjects of consciousness." Pearl best illustrates the normal developmental processes of a child passing through the "mirror stage" (in which a child recognizes her own identity as separate from mother and comes to identify with or "imprint" on the mother), and Hester (whose "psychic split" is prompted by the "power of the cultural gaze") exemplifies "the dynamics of the registers of the Imaginary and the Symbolic in the adult subject." Hester's crime, in other words, reveals her "psychic involvement with the Imaginary," while her punishment illustrates the "dominating authority of the cultural Symbolic."

569   Person, Leland, S., Jr. "*The Scarlet Letter* and *The House of the Seven Gables*: Resisting the Seductive Power of Art." *Aesthetic Headaches: Women and a Masculine Poetics in Poe, Melville, and Hawthorne*. Athens :U of Georgia P, 1988. 122-145.

Person's overall book examines the fiction of Edgar Allan Poe, Herman Melville, and Hawthorne for their representations of female characters as artists or sources of artistic vision, and argues that current views of these authors' "male writing" have not done justice to the complexity of their "masculine poetics." Person takes issue not only with typological criticism (such as that by Leslie Fiedler [89], Joel Porte [238], and Judith Fryer [340]) that seriously limits discussions of the role of women with its phallocentric treatment of characters, but also with critics like Nina Baym who argue that Hawthorne was a feminist or protofeminist writer [419]). These male writers clearly showed a marked ambivalence toward many of their female characters, and—more importantly—they resisted the objectification of women and used vital, creative female characters in order to challenge or even subvert conventional notions of masculinity. In *Letter* (pp. 122-138), Hawthorne "measures his artistic powers between Hester and Dimmesdale, and thus between a strong femininity and a weak masculinity." Despite Dimmesdale's "surrender of power" to Hester, she is unfortunately unable to transcend the original meaning of the letter for her Puritan community that "concentrates her identity in an art object" and "eclipses her efforts to define herself." Her objectification at the end then becomes less an assertion of Hawthorne's masculine power than of his demonstrated fear of a lack of sympathetic response of audiences for true artists.

570   Reynolds, David S. *Beneath the American Renaissance: The Subversive Imagination in the Age of Emerson and Melville*. New York: Alfred A Knopf, 1988.

In "delving beneath the American Renaissance," Reynolds draws from hitherto neglected popular modes and stereotypes that he claims were imported into classic literary texts. Chapter four, "Hawthorne and the Reform Impulse" (pp. 113-134), discusses the influence of Hawthorne's contemporary reform culture in creating the "quintessential, sophisticated benign-subversive text" of *Letter*, and explains that the novel is not as original in its conception of ideas as has been previously thought. Hawthorne's debt is not only to his reform culture—from which Hawthorne drew "searing ironies" and images of "hidden corruption," "veiled rottonness," and "inward venom"—but also to popular reform literature of the day, from which Hawthorne borrowed and transformed "key images and themes." In a section of chapter nine entitled "*Letter* and Popular Sensationalism" (pp. 259-268), Reynolds also describes how Hawthorne similarly "reshaped" popular sensational themes (such as the "oxymoronic oppressor, the "likable criminal," and the "clergyman sex scandal") and violent themes (of burning, poison, nightmare visions, and distorted perspectives) to fit *Letter*. *Letter* and George Lippard's sensational best-seller *The Quaker City* (1845) have many similarities (indicating that Hawthorne was trying to "tap the popular market" created by Lippard's novel), but Reynolds is careful to qualify the comparison by asserting the superiority of Hawthorne's novel because its dealings with the introspective earnestness and seriousness of Puritanism does not allow the narrative to get carried away with gratuitous and amoral sensationalism. In fact, Hawthorne fuses Puritanism with his contemporary reform culture, managing to "invest the Puritan past with modern ambiguity and to invest nineteenth-century reform themes with a new symbolic resonance."

571   Rowe, Joyce A. "Bleak Dreams: Restriction and Aspiration in *The Scarlet Letter*." *Equivocal Endings in Classic American Novels*. New York: Cambridge UP, 1988. 27-45.

A "culturally consistent pattern" of deliberate and contradictory evasiveness appears in the endings of four classic American novels: *Letter*, *Huckleberry Finn*, *The Ambassadors*, and *The Great Gatsby*. Such equivocal conclusions (that involve a curious reversal of "truths" that are carefully established and developed in each novel) actually suggest a specifically American literary tendency for idealistic, visionary characters to refuse letting their dreams die to accommodate mainstream society. Although the protagonists' visionary ambitions are not realized but instead cause them great personal suffering in isolation, each novel's ending still seems to redeem or rehabilitate the ideal in some way as the protagonist refuses to abandon hope. Hester Prynne is one such "spiritual orphan" who is "trapped by realities of self and circumstance which inevitably confound visionary goals"—but who nonetheless insists "on the redemptive power of [her] dream" for a future equitable relation between the sexes. Her seemingly submissive remaining years in Boston reflect Hawthorne's way of avoiding "the dangers of both the repressed and the revolutionary self" while yet representing "an exchange of energies between these two extremes within the public sphere."

572   Rust, Richard D. "'Take Shame" and "Be True": Hawthorne and His Characters in *The Scarlet Letter.*" *Critical Essays on Hawthorne's The Scarlet Letter.* Ed. David B. Kesterson. Boston: G. K. Hall, 1988. 211-218.

Hawthorne expiates ancestral guilt (involving William Hathorne's persecution of Quakers and John Hathorne's persecution of "witches") and contemporary disgraces by "writing a novel in which being put to shame is the greatest form of humiliation and taking shame the crux of personal redemption." Rust establishes a link between Hawthorne's "confessional" purposes for writing *Letter* and the climactic actions of Dimmesdale and Hester that involve a sincere though painful acceptance of shame which is simultaneously a proud and purifying "act of being true." The tension throughout the novel between concealing and revealing shame is resolved in the end, at which time the appalling hypocrisy, self-righteousness, and condemning nature of the Puritans is ironically highlighted.

573   Thickstun, Margaret Olofson. "Adultery Versus Idolatry: The Hierarchy of Sin in *The Scarlet Letter.*" *Fictions of the Feminine: Puritan Doctrine and the Representation of Women.* Ithaca: Cornell UP, 1988. 132-156.

Throughout Puritan fiction there exists a "recurrent pattern in which male protagonists displace female characters from their traditional roles as Brides of Christ and representatives of chastity" in order to "deflect their ambivalence about human frailty onto women." Hawthorne's *Letter,* however, addresses the "conflation of female sexuality and spiritual inadequacy" inherent in Puritan texts by authors such as Edmund Spenser, John Milton, and John Bunyan. Hawthorne "reconstructs the Puritan world [. . .] to expose its biases" and "presents Hester's situation as a radical critique of Puritan sexual stereotyping." Yet he is unable to distance himself from the Puritan perspective on Hester's affair because his own century's culture tended to restate the "Puritan problem" with sexuality, but in different terms. (This "problem" refers to "the tension between love of this world and devotion to God," and its salient locus in the female sexual body.) As Thickstun argues, "the action chronicled throughout the romance is idolatry, not adultery." *Letter* reaffirms a hierarchy of sin that elevates the crime of the spirit over the crime of the flesh by appropriating sexuality as a metaphor for spiritual truth." The sin that intrigues Hawthorne in *Letter* is thus not the offstage sin of passion but Chillingworth's attempts to seduce Dimmesdale to despair. As the "bride of Christ" figure whose spiritual chastity is threatened, "Dimmesdale becomes the 'heroine' of *Letter,* structurally reenacting the artistic displacement of the feminine in Puritan allegory."

574   Woodson, Thomas.   "Hawthorne, Upham, and *The Scarlet Letter.*"
       Critical Essays on Hawthorne's The Scarlet Letter.   Ed. David B.
       Kesterson. Boston: G. K. Hall, 1988. 183 193.

Drawing from Hawthorne's published *Letters,* Woodson reconstructs "the invisible motive, the transition that took place in Hawthorne's imagination from the facts of his own humiliating dismissal to the plot and characters of *Letter.*" What he discovers is that the novel's characterization and plot reveal Hawthorne's desire to "'immolate' a political victim" after having been dismissed from the Custom House office, namely Hawthorne's principal adversary, Charles Wentworth Upham. Woodson provides the full history of Hawthorne's relationship with Upham, beginning with the influential minister's arrival in Salem in 1824 and his befriending of Hawthorne, and concluding with Upham's signing of the detailed letter to Washington, D.C., that prevented Hawthorne's reinstatement. "It is in the context of Upham's treachery and his own irreverent ideas about the relation of history to literature that Hawthorne conceived the character of Dimmesdale." *Letter* not only challenges the Whig view of American progress, but also becomes the first fictional work to make a Puritan minister's weakness of character (modeled after Upham's) the tragic center of the action.

Journal Essays and Notes

575   Bercovitch, Sacvan. "The A-Politics of Ambiguity in *The Scarlet Letter.*"
       New Literary History 19 (1988): 629-654.

Paying exclusive attention to the meaning behind Hester's return to Boston at the end of the novel, Bercovitch describes the letter's true four-fold "office" (political, moral, aesthetic, and historical) and highlights its "overarching ideological design." Instead of arguing for Hawthorne's celebrated evasiveness and ambiguity, contending as so many critics do that the letter is "an arbitrary sign of transient social structure," Bercovitch insists that the letter's meaning is, quite to the contrary, not open-ended at all. It reflects a strategic plurality of meaning—one that symbolically combines and reconciles "process" and "closure"—and in fact reflects the turbulent historical time frame in which *Letter* was written (during the pre-Civil War Compromise Resolutions of 1850). The novel thus transforms Hawthorne's own fears of social fragmentation into "a story of socialization" that calls for Hester's consent (more courageous than rebellion, Bercovitch argues) and not merely her conformity. This consent is the true office of the letter, implying a slow and gradual reform through the moral imperative of compromise in continuity. The "threat of diversity is converted" through the symbol of the letter into "the pleasure of multiple-choice pluralism, where the implied answer ('all of the above') guarantees consensus." [For Bercovitch's earlier essay that similarly treats the "office" of the scarlet letter, see 560. See also his essay directly below (576). For his book-length study of the subject, where this essay (575) is reprinted, see *The Office of The Scarlet Letter* (635).]

576   Bercovitch, Sacvan.   "Hawthorne's A-Morality of Compromise." *Representations* 24 (1988): 1-27.

Developing ideas advanced by New Historicists Jonathan Arac (in 508), Larry J. Reynolds (in 504), and Donald Pease (in 540), and elaborating on the historical issues examined in his essay directly above (575), "The A-Politics of Ambiguity in *The Scarlet Letter*," Bercovitch argues not only that *Letter*'s pre-Revolutionary American setting provided an ideal political background with which Hawthorne could craft his tale subtly around propaganda aimed against nineteenth-century radical abolitionists, but also that the novel is a "cultural artifact" which contains among its subtexts a warning against the fruitless dangers of European-style radicalism. Hawthorne found growing evidence of such threatening revolutionary activity spreading into the U.S. in the Whig victory over the Democrats and in the women's rights movement. Hester's curious return to Boston at novel's end—which proves that the problematic "office" of the "A" is actually socialization—signals Hawthorne's belief that radical resistance leads to a dead end and that greater value lies in (1) compromise, (2) gradualist accommodation with progressive ideology, and (3) working within the system. [This same essay is also reprinted in 637. For two other essays by Bercovitch that also treat the "office" of the scarlet letter, see 560 and 575. For his book-length study of the subject, where this essay is reprinted, see *The Office of The Scarlet Letter* (635).]

577   Dalke, Anne French.   "The Sensational Fiction of Hawthorne and Melville." *Studies in American Fiction* 16 (1988): 195-207.

By putting the motifs of male-dominated sensational novels in their own fiction (which include, in a nut shell, melodramatic accounts of crime and poverty that are distinguished by sexually-aggressive, strong, and independent female seducers who destroy their innocent male victims), Hawthorne and Herman Melville "executed an attack on the female sentimental mode and clearly identified themselves with the practitioners of a genre of a different gender." Both authors "subtly developed" the subgenre for their own purposes—Hawthorne to lend "multiple levels of meaning" to *Letter* and Melville to create "the strange permutations" of *Pierre* (1852)—but both were similarly attracted to sensational fiction's reversal of "all sentimental clichés regarding sexual roles and their economic implications." The man-like Hester and the effeminate Dimmesdale perfectly illustrate the reversal of traditional sex roles that is characteristic of sensational fiction, just as the "fratricidal rivalry" between Chillingworth and Dimmesdale fits the category of "brother seducers" who also appear regularly in the fiction. However, although Hawthorne's novel follows the formula of sensational novels (that would have appealed mostly to men), "The Custom-House" introduction, with its "pleasant mood" and "domestic aura," aims at capturing female sentimental readers.

578   Diehl, Joanne Feit. "Re-Reading the Letter: Hawthorne, the Fetish, and the (Family) Romance." *New Literary History* 19 (1988): 655-673.*

This psychoanalytic reading, which builds upon the ideas of Clay Daniel (521), Allan Lefcowitz (322), and Nina Baym (424), concentrates on the scarlet letter as a "fetishistic object" that represents the conflict between a guilt-inspiring desire for the mother and its necessary repression. The "A," which functions for Dimmesdale as the forbidden Oedipal desire, serves to empower (and imprison) Hester, because the experience of mothering affords her the capacity to transmute the stigma of shame into a badge of commitment and charity.

*This essay is reprinted in 637.

579   Emerick, Ronald. "Baby Chillingworth: Hawthorne's Use of Heredity in *The Scarlet Letter*." *Bucknell Review* 31.2 (1988): 45-59.

Despite the fact that several characters (the narrator included) suggest Pearl's inheritance from both mother and father, Hawthorne offers little or no proof of influence from Dimmsdale's traits—contending that any moral function Pearl performs in the novel comes not from a moral awareness inherited from her father but from her own unusually acute ability to discern truth. In fact, Pearl has more in common with Chillingworth (her "surrogate father"), since both share "an intuitive, almost uncanny perception of truth, and both are described as perverse, diabolic tormentors." Both Pearl and Chillingworth serve as "pricks of conscience" to Hester and Dimmesdale, but here the similarities end, since Chillingworth's purpose is evil, while Pearl's is "to achieve the repentance of her parents"—a purpose that actually earns Pearl her own salvation at the end when Dimmesdale's acknowledgment of his paternity humanizes her from her "natural, amoral state."

580   Hennelly, Mark M., Jr. *"The Scarlet Letter*: A Play-Day for the Whole World?" *New England Quarterly* 61 (1988): 530-554.

Examines the metaphors and acts of play that recur throughout the novel and reflect Hawthorne's own ambivalent attitudes on "the sterility of secular life, the repressive nature of Puritanism, the un-self-conscious innocence of childhood, the relationships between nature and nurture, the value of imaginative activity, the impediments to satisfying interpersonal relationships, especially those of the heart, and finally the possibility of creating some brave new world where play will neither be prohibited nor perverted but practiced both freely and responsibly." Three specific constituents reveal Hawthorne's divided attitudes toward play: depictions of his career in "The Custom-House," the major characters (with Hester as playful but conflicted, Dimmesdale as perverting play, Chillingworth as spoiling play, and Pearl as a "pure personification of a playful imp of the polymorphous perverse" whose function is to mock the scarlet letter and gleefully "cure by wholesome play"), and the Election-Day "Holiday" at the end of the novel that seems to advance an apocalyptic, utopian vision of a new society. Ultimately, it is apparent that Hawthorne's attempt "to reinstill this 'elect' community with 'mirthful recreation' is doomed," and he bewails the loss of "the forgotten art of gaiety" amongst the "sternly repressed" Puritans.

581   Herbert, T. Walter. "Nathaniel Hawthorne, Una Hawthorne, and *The Scarlet Letter*: Interactive Selfhoods and the Cultural Construction of Gender." *PMLA* 103 (1988): 285-297.

Relating *Letter* to the cultural construction of gender in the nineteenth century, Herbert argues that the novel not only addresses Hawthorne's anxieties about his own masculinity (often through the "womanly" Dimmesdale), but also manifests through the characterization of Pearl Hawthorne's concerns about his daughter Una's femininity. Having named Una after Edmund Spenser's fairy "maiden of holiness," the Hawthornes felt terribly conflicted when she blossomed into anything but her passive and angelic namesake. "Little Pearl is made to enact the qualities that most troubled Hawthorne in his daughter, and she is eventually delivered from them." In other words, Hawthorne "surrounds little Pearl with "a therapeutic program, which includes a diagnosis of her difficulty and a prescription for cure, grounded on the gender categories that he considered natural and that defined a femininity he hoped his daughter would grow into." During the "naturalization" process whereby Hester and Dimmesdale swap and "repair" their aberrant sexual identities (which are fully repaired at the novel's end when Hester helps Dimmesdale mount the scaffold and submits to his will), Pearl's "unearthly contradictions" are conveniently resolved. Yet, for all Hawthorne's insistence on the proper spheres for men and women, he still resists conventional definitions of both manhood and womanhood, most likely "because he recognized that his own character was in some respects deeply at odds with these definitions of normality."

582   Rovit, Earl. "Purloined, Scarlet, and Dead Letters in Classic American Fiction." *Sewanee Review* 96 (1988): 418-432.

Musing speculatively on connections between Edgar Allan Poe's "The Purloined Letter," Hawthorne's *Letter*, and Herman Melville's "Bartleby, the Scrivener," Rovit detects in the three authors an intense sensitivity to "letters." Similar personal circumstances (all three lost their fathers in childhood and all made alphabetical adjustments to their names) and powerful cultural changes "made the question of identity especially compelling and problematic" for Poe, Hawthorne, and Melville, who were already highly attune to "ambiguities of reading and writing and reality, the problems of forgery and misinterpretation, the inherent antagonism between the letter that killeth and the spirit that giveth life, the incompatibilities between self and society, between the Word and the Flesh, and the problem of meaning and meaninglessness." Rovit resists offering a conclusion to these paralells, largely because, he says, to suggest any "potential significances" would be "arrogant and irresponsible."

583   Scheiber, Andrew J. "Public Force, Private Sentiment: Hawthorne and the Gender of Politics." *ATQ* New Series 2 (1988): 285-299.

Perceives that *Letter* "is less concerned with the politics of gender than with the gender of politics, observed in the domination of human institutions by a masculine ethos of intellect and power, to the exclusion of the 'moderating' tendencies [. . .] of woman's tenderness and moral sense." Thus, in depicting "an American society deformed by its subjugation and pejoration of the 'feminine' values he wishes Hester to embrace," Hawthorne does not betray Hester at the end by forcing her to abandon her powerful "masculine" traits and to resume her oppressive gender role (as many feminist critics argue). Rather, Hawthorne simply does not valorize her rejection of tender passion, feeling, and sympathy that go along with her adoption of a life of thought. In fact, he despairs that her "'feminine' gifts are accorded no place in the social and political structure unless they are allied with an attitude of subservience which in effect neutralizes their power." Abandoning "the private, inner core of 'passion and feeling' for the more public arena of 'intellectual speculation'" is not solely damaging to Hester. For, just as Dimmesdale is at odds with the masculine ethos of his seventeenth-century society and suffers for being forced to suppress the burdens of his heart, so Hawthorne is privately tormented in the nineteenth century by feelings of inadequacy over his own publicly-devalued "feminine impulse, that of the creative imagination." [For another essay that also views Hawthorne as illustrating in *Letter* the redemptive potential of feminine values, see Cynthia S. Jordan (588). See also James J. Waite (585) for the argument that Hawthorne endorses men and women's androgynous nature.]

584   Swann, Charles. "Three Textual Problems in Hawthorne's Fiction." *Notes and Queries* 35 (1988): 322-324.

Two of the three textual problems that Swann emends from the Centenary Editions are in *Letter*. Both occur in chapter nineteen, the first from a passage in which Hester is described incorrectly as having "hopefully, . . . a sense of inevitable doom upon her," when Hawthorne intended a comparison (one minute she is hopeful, and the next she feels doomed). The second error is from a passage in which the word "wrath" is clumsily and inaccurately repeated. The "shadowy wrath of Pearl's image" in the water should probably read "wraith," which means "water spirit," according to one definition in the *Oxford English Dictionary*.

585   Waite, James J. "Nathaniel Hawthorne and the Feminine Ethos." *Journal of American Culture* 11.4 (1988): 23-33.

Raised and surrounded by women during his formative years, Hawthorne developed an androgynous nature that made him sympathetic to the plight of both men and women, whose socially-prescribed gender roles limit and disable both genders. He used his fiction as a platform from which to appeal to men, especially about the naturally androgynous character of the sexes—although his fictional men most often reject their feminine traits and fail to see that their masculinity would be enhanced and completed by embracing those traits. Waite examines six of Hawthorne's women as examples of the author's androgynous vision in which humanity could potentially "rise above petty differences in order to become unified and complete": Zenobia and Priscilla of *Blithedale Romance*, Beatrice of "Rappaccini's Daughter," Georgianna of "The Birth-mark," and Hester and Pearl of *Letter*. Most of the essay considers the androgynous Hester and Pearl, who challenge man's ability to know the female. Men in the story fail miserably and are destroyed, while Hester and Pearl both survive. The other women in the story also learn to accept new definitions of femininity, eventually "mov[ing] from distant critics to Hester's ardent disciples."

1989

Essays and Studies in Books

586   Ellis, William. "The Case of Hawthorne: History, Manners, and the Idea of Community." *The Theory of the American Romance: An Ideology in American Intellectual History*. Ann Arbor: UMI Research Press, 1989. 105-113.

Examines in detail the "demerits" of the theory of American "exceptionalism" in explaining the "alleged" differences between nineteenth-century American "romances" and English "novels." Ellis argues that American and European novels evolved out of the same literary tradition and that the novelists shared identical interests and concerns, and even suggests that American novels are overrated when compared to English novels—since they are "short-winded, insubstantial affair[s]" that neglect the "significance of social portraiture." *Letter*—influenced by Sir Walter Scott—is one of the exceptions, however, because of its interests in society and history. *Letter*, in fact, develops just as A. N. Kaul suggests that American novels do in *The American Vision* (see 139), beginning as a novel of manners but eventually turning its attention from the "actual" society it examines to a more "ideal" society that, in this case, "combine[s] the creativity, color, and richness of aristocratic Elizabethan culture with the speculative freedom and egalitarianism of the democratic enlightenment."

587   Greenwald, Elissa. "From Picture to Portrait: *The Scarlet Letter* and *The Portrait of a Lady*." *Realism and the Romance: Nathaniel Hawthorne,*

Henry James, and American Fiction. Ann Arbor: UMI Research Press, 1989. 57-77.

Demonstrates the relation of romance and realism in the novels of Hawthorne and James to challenge the commonplace assertion that romance is an American genre and realism is a European genre. Although most critics claim that James "perfects" or "completes" Hawthorne's static romances by realistically fleshing out the latter's themes, characters, and plots, Greenwald finds that careful assessment of Hawthorne's influence "rather shows the interpenetration of romance and realism in James's Anglo-American art." James fuses the subjective consciousness and objective details in *Letter* to "revolutionize" the form of the novel in *The Portrait of a Lady* (1881), "transform[ing] [. . .] Hawthorne's static pictorialism into a more dramatic narrative, changing picture into portrait."

588   Jordan, Cynthia S. "Inhabiting the Second Story: Hawthorne's Houses." *Second Stories: The Politics of Language, Form, and Gender in Early American Fictions.* Chapel Hill: U of North Carolina P, 1989. 152-179.

James Fenimore Cooper, Edgar Allan Poe, Hawthorne, and Herman Melville experimented with narrative form to recover the "lost second stories" of such marginal figures as women, Indians, and artists; in so doing, they criticize the "patriarchal linguistic politics" of their elitist forefathers (Franklin, Brackenridge, and Brockden Brown) who sought to silence opposing views and "otherness" in American culture. As a "second-story artist," Hawthorne develops "complex and detailed characterizations" in *Letter* and *House of the Seven Gables* "that show the harmful effects of patriarchal culture on individuals and language," and he "uses feminine sympathy as a metaphor for the only corrective to patriarchal legalism." His "task" in *Letter* is to call attention to the "long hereditary habit" of patriarchal domination and oppression and to "erase its deep print" from our minds by creating an unconventional heroine who challenges and threatens the dominant culture's ideology—and who speaks for "the redemptive potential of feminine and maternal values in American culture." Yet Hawthorne cannot erase the fact that all of his characters have been socially and culturally programmed to think in patriarchal terms—and so "the dangerous psychological effects of living in a seriously polarized culture" must be experienced by Hester. She is, despite Hawthorne's sympathy and regret for her plight, damaged and thus as impotent to effect change as her male counterpart because of their lifelong acculturation. [See Andrew J. Sceiber (583) for an essay that similarly argues for the redemptive potential of feminine values in *Letter*.

See also James J. Waite (585) for a discussion of Hawthorne's vision of the "naturally androgynous character of the sexes."]

589   Luedtke, Luther S.   "Hawthorne's Oriental Women: The First Dark Ladies." *Nathaniel Hawthorne and the Romance of the Orient.* Bloomington: Indiana UP, 1989. 165-193.

Convinced that foreign and Eastern sources for Hawthorne's writing have not been sufficiently explored, Luedtke posits cultural and biographical readings of Beatrice Rappaccini, Hester Prynne, Zenobia, and Miriam Schaefer. The relationships between these passionate "Oriental beauties" and their male admirers who both desire and fear them "were grounded in the many first-hand accounts Hawthorne had read of purdah, seraglios, and their captives in the East." In the section entitled *"The Scarlet Letter*: "Doth the universe lie within the compass of yonder town?" (pp. 181-187), Luedtke explores Hawthorne's method of luridly intermixing light and dark "to a dramatic conclusion for both the Eastern maid and her male visitor." Hester's luxuriant, exotic characteristics (making her the "Oriental Other") attract Dimmesdale, (the archetypal somber Puritan), and their brief union produces a "hybrid flower" in Pearl. [For another essay that explores an Eastern connection to *Letter*, see Judie Newman (840).]

590   Sarbu, Aladár. "The Topicality of *The Scarlet Letter*." *Americana and Hungarica.* Ed. Charlotte Kretzoi. Budapest: L. Eotvos UP, 1989. 35-55.*

Covers familiar ground in arguing how the "carefully manipulated parallel" between seventeenth-century Puritan New England and mid-nineteenth-century "romantic" America illuminates Hawthorne's concept of historical progress and his belief that all values are man-made "typical illusions" that have only a temporary validity in history. The narrator's (and Hawthorne's) seeming fidelity to Puritan theology and morality is all an illusion, which makes unsatisfactory all criticism that seeks to align Hawthorne's cast of mind with that of his seventeenth-century forebears. His vision is undoubtedly romantic, as the extreme subjectivism of perception throughout *Letter* exemplifies a "romantic realization of the expressive theory of art." Hester's real problem in *Letter* is that she is too advanced for her Puritan society's time. "The injustice suffered by Hester only exemplifies the injustice suffered by women in Hawthorne's own age, and both injustices are subsumed in an even more universal theme, that of the conflict, inevitable as it is, between individual freedom and social restriction."

*Reprinted in *The Reality of Appearances: Vision and Representation in Emerson, Hawthorne, and Melville* (Budapest: Akadémiai Kiadó, 1996. 80-98).

591   Schwab, Gabriele. "Seduced by Witches: Nathaniel Hawthorne's *The Scarlet Letter* in the Context of New England Witchcraft Fictions." *Seduction and Theory: Readings of Gender, Representation, and Rhetoric.* Ed. Dianne Hunter. Urbana: U of Illinois P, 1989. 170-191.*

Schwab's "psycho-historical cultural critique" of *Letter* analyzes the novel with reference to Hawthorne's fictional adaptations of the 1692 witchcraft trials in Salem. The "witchcraft pattern" (of women labeled as "other" who are seduced by the devil) in the novel does not fictionalize historical witches but instead "reveal[s] the witch stereotype as a cultural pattern of interpretation used by the New England Puritans against deviant women in general." The cultural perception of deviant women as witches lingered well into the nineteenth century, witnessed in many popular New England witchcraft narratives, and the image of the witch is replaced in Hawthorne's novel with the image of woman as adulteress or heretic. Just as Hester "seduces" the parishioners into re-evaluating her social role by inverting the cultural meaning of the letter, so she (or Hawthorne) seduces the reader into resisting the values of the Puritan-minded narrator and encourages reading her tale against the grain. Hester's decision at the end not to flee the community, however, makes her victimization "fall back all the more vehemently on the violence and destructiveness inherent in the Puritan norms of 'femininity' and 'female deviancy.'"

*This essay appears in a slightly updated form in *The Mirror and the Killer-Queen: Otherness in Literary Language* (Bloomington: Indiana UP, 1996. 103-123).

592   Van Leer, David. "Hawthorne's Alchemy: The Language of Science in *The Scarlet Letter*." *Nature Transfigured: Science and Literature, 1700-1900*. Ed. John Christie and Sally Shuttleworth. Manchester: Manchester UP, 1989. 102-120.

This extract from an essay first published in *New Essays on The Scarlet Letter* (see 496) contains a new title and new introduction (the summary of which follows). Hawthorne was, at best, skeptical about scientific advancements, viewing "the deleterious psychological effects of scientific experimentation" as an outrage against humanity. Not only do Hawthorne's scientist characters consistently and inhumanely exploit others in their murderously insensitive quests for knowledge, but his fiction in general shows a marked concern with the "disastrous influence" scientific language has on modern discourse. Chillingworth, for example, embodies all the worst characteristics of scientists in Hawthorne's short stories, but "the novel's real case against science is directed less against the scientific practices of this alchemist than against the scientific theories, even scientific vocabularies, that underwrite the thoughts of all the characters"—especially those of Hester.

593   Wagenknecht, Edward. "*The Scarlet Letter.*" *Nathaniel Hawthorne: The Man, His Tales and Romances.* New York: Continuum, 1989. 78-95.

Discusses the circumstances under which *Letter* was produced and provides a brief synopsis of the story's events, addresses Hawthorne's "omnipresent" symbolism and ambiguity; reflects upon the numerous biblical, classical, English, and American sources (including Hawthorne's own earlier writings); considers with many references to the novel and to past criticism the four leading characters; and speculates about the gigantic critical commentary that exists for a novel of such "classical simplicity"—concluding that the attention paid has been well justified. Wagenknecht pays only brief attention to "The Custom-House," however, finding it "hopelessly out of tune with the story itself."

594   Yellin, Jean Fagan. "Nathaniel Hawthorne's *The Scarlet Letter.*" *Women and Sisters: The Anti-Slavery Feminists in American Culture.* New Haven: Yale UP, 1989. 125-150.

After explaining how the "Woman and Sister emblem" of the "exposed and enchained" female slave was adopted in the "powerful discourse" of such nineteenth-century American antislavery feminists as Lydia Maria Child, Angelina Grimké, Sarah Grimké, and Margaret Fuller, Yellin explores the political subtext of several nineteenth-century literary classics that adopted the feminists' motifs and mottoes "but emptied them of their antislavery feminist content and filled them instead with a contradictory content." The chapter on Hawthorne shows how *Letter* uses the antislavery women's iconographic motifs to reject the ideology upon which they are based. "Repeatedly addressing the concerns of the antislavery women, the book explores Hester's ideas [. . .] in relation to her identity (her womanhood) and her membership in the community (her sisterhood)." Hester initially appears like a slave on the scaffold before her community, utterly dehumanized and isolated. Hawthorne seems to sympathize wholeheartedly with her oppression, making *Letter* on one level appear to be a critique of patriarchal ideologies and structures. As the novel develops, however, Hawthorne clearly rejects the new feminist definitions of womanhood and endorses traditional patriarchal notions after all by having Hester learn to "accept her lot" in life and conform to patriarchal definitions of womanhood. [Two photographs of nineteenth-century sculptures containing antislavery iconography, Harriet Hosmer's *Zenobia in Chains* (1859) and Howard Roberts's *Hester Prynne* (1872), accompany the essay.]

Journal Essays and Notes

595   Cody, David C. "'The Dead Live Again': Hawthorne's Palingenic Art." *ESQ: A Journal of the American Renaissance* 35 (1989): 23-41.

Ever fascinated with reviving the past, Hawthorne shows in his fiction an interest in and familiarity with the popular nineteenth-century pseudoscience of "Palingenesis," the "partly chemical, partly magical, and wholly imaginary" process by which the ghostly image of a dead object could be revived from its ashes. In "The Custom-House" especially, where Hawthorne employs palingenic imagery by "recreating" the ghostly image of Surveyor Pue, the palingenic process also functions as a metaphor for the creative process. Out of "old newspapers, aged books, and yellowed manuscripts," Hawthorne reconstructs the past and recalls the ghosts of his ancestors to life. [For a very different essay that also examines Hawthorne's resurrection of the dead in "The Custom-House," see Eric Savoy (716).]

596   Davis, Sarah I. "Self in the Market Place, or A for Alienation." *South Atlantic Review* 54.2 (1989): 75-92.

Steeped in twentieth-century romantic theory (which Davis believes Hawthorne anticipates), this essay submits that the central thematic conflict in *Letter*, illustrated dynamically in Hester and Dimmesdale's secret romantic attachment, is between "self" and Puritan social role. (Davis views as counterparts of the romantic poles of "self" and "role" the gothic figures of the witch and black man on the one hand and the "bathetic" Puritan authorities on the other.) Although this tension is unremitting, it can be instructive—as in Hester's case. But whereas Hester is "a striking example of the self's discovery of value through alienation," Dimmesdale's overemphasis on his social role does him irreparable damage. And like Dimmesdale, Chillingworth also destroys the "self" by denying Hester and his true identity.

597   Elbert, Monika M. "Hester on the Scaffold, Dimmesdale in the Closet: Hawthorne's Seven-Year Itch." *Essays in Literature* 16 (1989): 234-255.

This biographical and historical analysis of the novel investigates Hawthorne's preoccupation with the institution of marriage—particularly the Puritan and nineteenth-century civil laws favoring divorce after seven years of desertion. Hawthorne's personal view of the split between rational and idealized responses to "matters of the heart" (suggested by his own dueling conceptions of Sophia's love for him before they were legally married) becomes the basis of characterization in the novel—Chillingworth and Dimmesdale taking the rational view, while Hester and Hawthorne take the idealized view that marriage is a private, passionate affair that transcends the law. The true crime in the novel is not adultery, but the seven-year interval between which neither Dimmesdale nor Chillingworth comes into contact with Hester. Likewise, the real adulterer in the novel is Dimmesdale, who denies Hester and their self-consecrated marriage, and who instead becomes involved in an almost erotic, obsessive relationship with Chillingworth. The scaffold scenes in the novel are "tantamount to a divorce proceeding," the first of which divorces the guiltless Hester from the "untrue" husband Chillingworth and starts her "on the path to independence"; the second divorces Dimmesdale from Chillingworth, and the third frees Hester from Dimmesdale, liberating her at last from the bonds of marriage in the eyes of both Church and State. Elbert concludes with two speculations, that Chillingworth may actually lie buried beside Dimmesdale instead of Hester (since Hawthorne indicates that love and hate are, after all, the same thing at bottom), and that *Letter*, because it was written in the seventh year of his own marriage to Sophia, is perhaps "the personal manifestation of [Hawthorne's] own seven-year itch."

598   Elbert, Monika M. "No (Wo)man's Land: Hawthorne's 'Neutral Territory' and Hester's 'Magic Circle' as Home." *Mid-Hudson Language Studies* 12.2 (1989): 27-39.

Just as Hawthorne's reconstruction of history and his concept of "home" are subjective and mythologized in "The Custom-House" (and elsewhere), so Hester's sense of home is likewise fabricated and based on myth, "not bounded by geographical or historical constructs" and "beyond the constraints of the patriarchal notions of the Old and the New Worlds." When Hawthorne removes himself from history by declaring that he is "a citizen of somewhere else" in the introductory sketch, he acknowledges—though New Historicists would disagree—that it is not a social or popular mythology that he employs to find his real home, but is instead the individual, subjective vision created by his own psyche. Whereas Dimmesdale and Chillingworth "both respond to traditional categorizing and historicizing of the meaning of home" in *Letter*, Hester, like Hawthorne, subversively personalizes her sense of home and history, thus separating her from historical time (or from a "patriarchal notion of linear time") in her isolated cottage by the sea, locked "in a [timeless] sphere unto herself," so that she deals only with "the present, the moment of her realities." Elbert wonders what the reader is to make of the "more mythic than historically real" ending when Hester returns to her "extraordinarily unusual" life in New England. Is the "patriarchal voice of the [moralizing] narrator" forcing Hester into a male, historical notion of home, or is he remaining consistent with his "feminization" of history (and Elbert's "feminine reading") by having Hester return "to be herself, to do what she knows best, to nurture and to live on her own neutral territory, a place which she has carved out for herself"?

599   Greiner, Donald J. "Body and Soul: John Updike and *The Scarlet Letter.*" *Journal of Modern Literature* 15 (1989): 475-495.

Updike's Hawthornian trilogy (*A Month of Sundays* [1975], *Roger's Version* [1986], and *S.* [1988]) is "not a direct reflection but a transformation of [*Letter*]." Greiner discusses three other documents published by Updike—an essay on Hawthorne's religious belief, an introduction to *Roger's Version*, and a short interview about Hawthorne—to argue within the context of Updike's understanding of modern theology (especially as it is influenced by Karl Barth) that these documents frame an analysis of the trilogy "that points to Updike's rejection of Hawthorne's separation of body and soul." Updike rejects Hawthorne's distinction between "the corrupt material and the pure spiritual" because it "warps consideration of the erotic." He struggles instead in his novels "toward a unity of the extremes" so that "his characters unify faith and fornication," without having to wear the guilty "A."

600   Hull, Richard. "'I Have No Heavenly Father': Foucauldian Epistemes in *The Scarlet Letter.*" *ATQ* 3 (1989): 309-323.

The "historical disparity" that exists between characters and the narrator in terms of their interpretations of reality closely parallels Michel Foucault's description of three historically-specific conditions of meaning, or "epistemes," making Hawthorne something of a "harbinger" of Foucault. Dimmesdale, Hester, and Pearl appear to be "caught in these shifts of meaning," Dimmesdale to the "Renaissance" or Puritan episteme (in which language and signs were invested with divine meaning); Hester to the "Classical" seventeenth-century episteme (which rebelled against the orthodoxy of the Renaissance episteme), and Pearl—as well as the narrator and Chillingworth—to the "Modern" or late-eighteenth-century episteme (in which interpretations of reality break off all kinship with the divine and signs are in themselves meaningless). While Dimmesdale never wavers from the outmoded world view of the Renaissance, Hester seems to operate out of all three configurations, oscillating between

Dimmesdale's ("reading" Pearl at times as a sign from heaven) and Pearl's to finally cross the threshold of modernity completely. However, as Hawthorne straddles the shift from the classical to the modern episteme where signs are no longer interpretable but are left as enigmas, it becomes apparent that he, like Pearl, "stands for the modern, but longs for 'classical clarity.'" [For a later, similar reading by Hull that considers how signs are interpreted differently in *Letter*, see 865.]

601   Kain, Geoffrey. "*The Scarlet Letter* and the Red Star: Hawthorne's Appeal to China's Students of American Literature." *Nathaniel Hawthorne Review* 15.2 (1989): 9-10.

Contemplating the fact that his Chinese university students continually and unanimously recognize *Letter* as their "number one" favorite work of American literature, Kain surmises that the novel "embodies a reality that more closely parallels their experience than it does the experience of most any contemporary American reader"—because its cry for a freer expression of love represents to them similar "obstacles to romance posed by [their] domineering Chinese educational/political machinery." In essence, there is "a striking parallel between the unbending fundamentalist dogma of seventeenth-century New England Puritanism and the atheistic dogma of twentieth-century Chinese communism."

602   Newberry, Frederick. "Hawthorne's Knowledge of William Blackstone: A Rebuttal." *Nathaniel Hawthorne Review* 15.2 (1989): 11.

Refutes Thomas Pribek's suggestion (in 529) that Hawthorne's reference to the Reverend William Blackstone in *Letter* derives from Francis Baylies' 1830 *An Historical Memoir of the Colony of New Plymouth*. Newberry argues instead that Caleb Snow's *History of Boston* (1825), which Hawthorne read, is the most likely source for Hawthorne's knowledge of Blackstone.

603   Newfield, Christopher. "The Politics of Male Suffering: Masochism and Hegemony in the American Renaissance." *Differences: A Journal of Feminist Cultural Studies* 1 (1989): 55-87.

Relying heavily on Freudian and deconstructive theory—and building on Sacvan Bercovitch's "consensual" reading of the novel (see 575) that is based on the "higher laws of both/and"—Newfield places the novel within a nineteenth-century social context in which "ideal American manhood" is divided between two types: "the domineering economic and spiritual pioneer" and "the submissive bachelor or husband." Hawthorne is particularly interested in the difference between "dominant and submissive heterosexual men," and casts Dimmesdale as the latter in order to show that "masculine anxiety, self-doubt, self-effacement, and masochism" actually have a great deal to do with masculine authority. Dimmesdale dominates Hester by cunningly feminizing himself with long-suffering male weakness—by "affirming [his] marginality in a way that aligns [him] socially with women." Thus his marginal status (making him "a missing link between men and women") separates him from patriarchy "only to more subtly empower it." In this way, by miming femininity, Dimmesdale gains Hester's support and sympathy—fully controlling her, in other words, when she mistakenly thinks she is consenting. Dimmesdale publicly maintains his powerful "feminine" weakness through passive "doubleness" or ambivalence—and through the belief that his dominating Puritan influence is liberally hegemonic and dialectic (rather than tyrannical and authoritarian). But privately Dimmesdale's gender ambivalence (which finally destroys him) becomes overtly contradictory, and he turns to "reflexive" masochism and its accompanying desire for weakness, submission, and a "pre-Oedipal reunion with his mother."

604   Person, Leland S., Jr. "Hester's Revenge: The Power of Silence in *The Scarlet Letter*." *Nineteenth-Century Literature* 43 (1989): 465-483.

Argues that Hester's silence in *Letter* derives from her strategic plot to exact revenge on Dimmesdale for betraying her. Far from indicating repression or evasion (as several other critics have suggested), Hester's silence—which "forms the plot and determines the fate of the other characters"—demonstrates the "active, political power of passive resistance" that is associated with Hawthorne's "own desire to enact revenge upon his political enemies, the Salem Whigs (especially the Reverend Charles Upham) who had forced his removal from his job as Custom-House surveyor." By refusing to name Dimmesdale as her lover at the novel's outset, Hester knowingly punishes him, compelling him to add hypocrisy to sin and "to suffer *in* silence *for* his silence." This punishment, like a form of blackmail, serves her interests, since she can then pressure Dimmesdale to exert his considerable political influence on her behalf when she needs it (as when the Puritans threaten to take Pearl away from her). When Chillingworth makes Hester swear to keep his identity a secret, her complicit silence serves her own purposes yet again, since to keep Chillingworth's secret from Dimmesdale encourages the two men to develop the love/hate relationship that will inevitably climax in both their deaths—and leave her Chillingworth's money. Person admits that his evidence is largely circumstantial (Would Hester really want Dimmesdale to suffer? Is she really after Chillingworth's fortune?), but he maintains that Hester has several opportunities to break her vow of silence to end her lover's intense suffering but chooses not to.

605   Poindexter, Mark. *"Fatal Attraction* and the Grammar of Kinship." *Journal of Evolutionary Psychology* 9 (1989): 65-72.

As fictional, cautionary tales of adultery, the 1987 film *Fatal Attraction*, Sloan Wilson's popular 1950s novel and film *The Man in the Gray Flannel Suit*, and *Letter* all share elements in common. However, the "grammar" of the extramarital affair in *Fatal Attraction* is radically different from those in the other two stories because it lacks what the other two share: "a sense of bonds created by sexual intimacy and procreation so strong that even the legitimate spouse (who, according to social norms, has been wronged by the infidelity) is drawn into a pseudo-kinship that involves at least some positive effect."

606   Schamberger, J. Edward.   "The Failure of 'a citty upon a hill': Architectural Images in *The Scarlet Letter.*" *Essex Institute Historical Collections* 125.1 (1989): 9-24.

Although actually dealing very little with *Letter* itself and devoting the bulk of his essay to the history of Salem's maritime industry and a description of the construction of the Custom House, Schamberger relates how Hawthorne, in both "The Custom-House" and the novel proper, associates Salem's "inevitable" decay and decline (and his own lost post as surveyor) with Puritanic righteousness and the federal government's own insensitive, autocratic power.   In *Letter*, Hawthorne makes sure to imply that "the failure of the Puritan venture lay in its leaders' persecution of their people," and especially to condemn the ironic and cruel Puritan practice of denying others' civil liberties.   Article includes three illustrations and two photographs.

607   Scharnhorst, Gary. "'Now You Can Write Your Book': Two Myths in Hawthorne Biography." *Nathaniel Hawthorne Review* 15.2 (1989): 6-9.*

Concerns the origin and accuracy of the controversial passage in Julian Hawthorne's biography *Nathaniel Hawthorne and His Wife* (1884) that describes Nathaniel's decision to begin *Letter* on the very day he was dismissed from the Salem Custom House (June 8, 1849). Scharnhorst investigates various publications of the legend, several of which were in print before Julian cited it in his biography, and concludes that Julian—whose reputation as an editor and biographer "is roughly equivalent to that of a paid police informant"—might in fact have been accurate. It is most likely that Sophia relayed the entire incident to her lifetime friend William Henry Channing, who revealed the story first to the *Boston Transcript* following her death in 1871.

*Reprinted in Scharhorst's 1992 collection of criticism (see 670).

608   Wilson, Raymond J., III. *"Roger's Version:* Updike's Negative-Solid Model of *The Scarlet Letter." Modern Fiction Studies* 35 (1989): 241-250.

The "deeply encoded" key to John Updike's *Roger's Version* is its central image of a "negative solid." Updike hides the Hawthorne framework behind his novel so that the reader will not apprehend too quickly or too apparently that his novel is a reversal of *Letter.* "The Hawthorne allusions, if seen after a delay in which the reader ponders the book on its own, adds thematic cohesion to *Roger's Version,* along with the structural coherence derived from Hawthorne." Eventually, "the reader's mind twines *Letter* with its negative image, *Roger's Version,* to create the helix of meaning." Updike reverses the "polarity" of Hawthorne's story so that it will speak to a modern, God-forsaken, hedonist culture, and thus he transforms the tragedy into a comedy and "demonstrates that human beings can introduce some decency into their lives even without believing in a punishing, or materially proven, or intervening God."

1990

Books

609   Bloom, Harold, ed. *Hester Prynne.* New York: Chelsea House, 1990. 200 pp.

Belonging to the "Major Literary Characters" series, this volume claims to gather together "a representative selection of the best literary criticism that has been devoted to analyzing the character of Hester Prynne," and is divided into two sections of collected essays, the first containing twelve brief critical extracts about Hester and the second presenting eleven full-length, reprinted essays on the heroine. Other features include an introduction by Bloom (see 611) that emphasizes "Hester's centrality as the inaugural heroine of the Protestant will in American prose fiction," a bibliography, and index. Section one contains critical abstracts by the following: Anthony Trollope (EC33), Francis Hovey Stoddard (EC32), William Dean Howells (EC14), Newton Arvin (EC1), Mark Van Doren (EC36), R. W. B. Lewis (37), Harry Levin (70), Frederick Crews (182), Carolyn G. Heilbrun (303), Richard H. Brodhead (300), Sacvan Bercovitch,* and Nina Baym (506). Section two contains full-length essays by the following: D. H. Lawrence (EC18), Leslie A. Fiedler (184), Austin Warren (178), Michael Davitt Bell (261), Robert Penn Warren

(315), Judith Fryer (340), Kristin Herzog (436), Evan Carton (484), Carol M. Bensick (483), James M. Mellard (568), and David S. Reynolds (570).

*Sacvan Bercovitch's 1975 book *The Puritan Origins of the American Self* (New Haven: Yale UP) is not recognized in this bibliography because *Letter* is not given significant treatment in it.

Essays and Studies in Books

610   Anderson, Douglas. "Hawthorne's Marriages." *A House Divided: Domesticity and Community in American Literature.* Ed. Douglas Anderson. New York: Cambridge UP, 1990. 97-120.

Arguing that "an unusually complex treatment of marriage" is the central subject in Hawthorne's fiction, Anderson explores images of gender, marriage, and family that appear in several short stories (such as "The May-Pole of Merry Mount," "Ethan Brand," and "The Birth-mark") and in *Letter* (pp. 112-120). John Winthrop's "A Modell of Christian Charity" may well have contributed to Hawthorne's depiction of troubled marriages—as a literal model for all sorts of relationships that are desperate for Winthrop's brand of sympathetic charity. Winthrop's presence in *Letter* appears in "Hawthorne's systematic application of the binding imagery of the family throughout the text" and not just in the scene when his death is mentioned on the evening of the prophetic meteor. The many despairing and lonely figures in failed marriages in *Letter*, "so numerous as to defy description," beg for Winthrop's view of "human life that embraces children as well as guilty lovers and wronged husbands."

611   Bloom, Harold. Introduction. *Hester Prynne.* Ed. Harold Bloom. New York: Chelsea House, 1990. 1-4.

Hester is "at once the ideal object of Hawthorne's desire and a troubled projection of Hawthorne's authorial subjectivity, cast out from him but never definitively." In this general introduction that covers a variety of subjects relating to the heroine, Bloom examines Hester's "charisma" as "implicit sexual power," her religion as a combination of Calvinism and Emersonian self-reliance, and her "miraculous" survival of an "outrageously dreadful societal and erotic context." Of her "compromised condition" at the book's close, Hawthorne "defrauds her, for the sake of his art."

612   Cady, Edwin H[arrison], and Louis J. Budd, eds. *On Hawthorne: The Best from American Literature.* Durham: Duke UP, 1990.

This volume compiles what the editors believe are some of the best critical pieces ever published on Hawthorne in the periodical *American Literature*, including the following pieces on *Letter*: Hugh N. MacLean's "Hawthorne's *Scarlet Letter*: 'The Dark Problem on This Life'" (42), Anne Marie McNamara's "The Character of Flame: The Function of Pearl in *The Scarlet Letter*" (50), Robert E. Whelan's "Hester Prynne's Little Pearl: Sacred and Profane Love" (229), Nina Baym's "Nathaniel Hawthorne and His Mother: A Biographical Speculation" (424), and Larry J. Reynolds's *"The Scarlet Letter and Revolutions Abroad"* (504).

613   Dziedzic, Piotr. "Anguish and Exhaustion: Fowles's and Hawthorne's Studies in Scarlet." *Discourse and Character*. Ed. Wojciech Kalaga and Tadeusz Slawek. Katowice: Uniwersytet Slaski, 1990. 76-84.

While the narrative strategies in John Fowles's *The French Lieutenant's Woman* (1969) and *Letter* differ considerably, both novelistic ventures into the past contain stories in which "the future [each author's present] invades the past." In the tension between restraint and liberation, and between conformity and defiance, specific shifts occur in the social and ideological milieus at the center of each text. Ahead of their respective times, heroines Hester Prynne and Sarah Woodruff (the "scarlet woman of Lyme") signal that their worlds are eroding and in transition, imposing their own designs on both repressive communities by giving the assigned punishments entirely new meanings.

614   Elbert, Monika [M.]. "A is for Authority (but whose is it?): *The Scarlet Letter*." *Encoding the Letter "A": Gender and Authority in Hawthorne's Early Fiction*. Frankfurt am Main: Haag and Herchen, 1990. 188-244.

This historicist-feminist approach examines six early stories ("My Kinsman, Major Molineux," "Roger Malvin's Burial," "The Birth-mark," "Rappaccini's Daughter," "The Artist of the Beautiful," and "Ethan Brand") that lead up to and anticipate *Letter* to show how Hawthorne challenges patriarchal traditions of organized religion and empirical science and to illustrate Hawthorne's modernist belief that "no objective truth can exist" since "reality lies in the individual consciousness." Elbert views *Letter* as "a direct offshoot of Hawthorne's tales of initiation and tales of science, in which the protagonists are simultaneously trying to negate and validate the authority of the[ir] father figures" and who themselves fail because they rely on phallocentric thought and exclude women. Hawthorne both acknowledges and rejects theological and scientific truths (personified in the emotionally and intellectually deficient characters of Dimmesdale and Chillingworth)—and implies that "his stance on authority is ultimately ambivalent, and feminine." Of all the characters in the novel, it is only the maternal Hester whose nurturing, imaginative qualities contribute to her espousal of individualism and allow various representations of truth to coexist.

615   Friesner, Scott. "The Fantastic Through 'The Custom House': Hawthorne's American Romance." *The Shape of the Fantastic.* Ed. Olena H. Saciuk. New York: Greenwood, 1990. 33-42.

After establishing that "The Custom-House" authorizes "the fantastic border zone" between the actual and the imaginary, author and audience, and past and present, Friesner compares Hawthorne's appropriation of Romance in *Letter* with that of Washington Irving's. Unlike Irving, whose tales offer a "reasonable" explanation of fantastic elements, Hawthorne refuses "to discredit or disavow the eruption of the fantastic." Hawthorne pays tribute to Irving in his introduction (referring to Irving's Headless Horseman when he describes himself as being politically "decapitated" and possibly even establishing a kinship with Irving's Geoffrey Crayon), but he sets his version of Romance apart from Irving's because he saw in it uses far grander than mere entertainment or escape from reality. He aligns the fantastic with what he believes is the greater wisdom of the heart (which corresponds to a deeper reality than reason), and merges history with functionality in a "fantastic continuum," an "unfinished and open-ended process" that offers a renewed historical perception of America that he believed is necessarily open to the possibility of the supernatural.

616   Gabler-Hover, Janet. "'I Take the Shame Upon Myself': Ethical Veracity in *The Scarlet Letter.*" *Truth in American Fiction: The Legacy of Rhetorical Idealism.* Athens: U of Georgia P, 1990. 85-120.

Challenges deconstructionists by arguing for ethical readings of eighteenth- and nineteenth-century American novels that offer closure and a distinctive moral program, that even affirm the "truth-telling power" of language while simultaneously warning of the dangerous potential of emotionally charged public rhetoric to mystify audiences. Hawthorne was disgusted with the predominant lack of moral awareness in his own time, and he expresses in "The Custom-House" a sense of personal responsibility by linking himself to a historical tradition of guilt ("taking shame upon himself"). This theme extends to the novel itself, implying throughout that ethics should unite men in a common bond of sympathy and a shared impulse for self-regulation. Whereas deconstuctionists equate "stable" language in *Letter* with patriarchally-determined law and view desire as the force that "healthily" erodes the stability of the sign (basically figuring that law/authority and desire/passion exist in dialectical opposition and that language and meaning are indeterminate), Gabler-Hover suggests instead that law and desire function together in the novel as excuses for characters to avoid personal responsibility and a sense of accountability for their actions. For example, Hester's red letter functions as an authoritative punishment that allows her to harbor her passion secretly and indulge herself in the belief that fate is to blame instead of herself; and Dimmesdale's compelling eloquence aligns itself with the authority of religious law and so allows him to repress his sin and perpetuate his hypocrisy. Hester and Dimmesdale's relationship parallels that of Dante's doomed lovers in the *Inferno*, although the former couple save themselves at the end by denying their self-indulgent behavior and taking full responsibility for their actions in place of the substitutive external authority of the law.

617   Girgus, Sam B. "The Law of the Fathers: Hawthorne." *Desire and the Political Unconscious in American Literature*. New York: St. Martin's Press, 1990. 49-78.

Insisting that readers are mistaken who equate Hawthorne with Puritanism, Girgus contends that Hawthorne was instead very much a man of his own time, responding in his works to a pervasive nineteenth-century quest for psychic unity and community. While "Young Goodman Brown" and "My Kinsman, Major Molineux" concentrate on the theme of the search for a father figure (anticipating the Freudian Oedipal conflict), *Letter* (pp. 66-75) "constitutes an extended elaboration of [the] tenuous connection between the signifier and the signified" whereby the community's search for Pearl's father becomes "a dramatization of the linguistic tension of the Oedipal complex." By focusing on Hester as heroine, Hawthorne "takes his narratives [prior to *Letter*] of the Oedipal pattern of desire and consensus to a new dimension of structuration." Ultimately, however, the individual search for stability, social harmony, and fulfillment of personal desire ends in failure because of the "impurity of the human psyche," and thus Hawthorne's search for psychic unity and community remains frustrated.

618   Harding, Brian. Introduction. *The Scarlet Letter*. By Nathaniel Hawthorne. 1850. Ed. Brian Harding. Oxford: Oxford UP, 1990. vii-xlii.

This lengthy introduction to the "Oxford World's Classics edition" touches on several critical issues. It provides historical background relating to the Puritans; suggests how gender issues come into play in the novel (considering the Antinomian controversy surrounding Anne Hutchinson and explaining the impact of Margaret Fuller's *Woman in the*

Nineteenth Century [1845]); addresses the difficulty of determining meaning in the novel and provides a survey of critical opinion on the subject; considers the function of the narrator and his relation to the characters (Dimmesdale especially); and explores the relation of "The Custom-House" sketch to the novel. Harding contends that "the originality of Hawthorne's narrative lies in its association between authority and signification" because signifiers and signifieds never remain fixed in *Letter*. Not only is the system of signification problematized, but with it the whole system of moral certainty that produced it. This strategy of Hawthorne's "undermines the stability of the system by which the values of the Puritan theocracy are maintained."

619   Hurst, Mary Jane. "Parent-Child Discourse." *The Voice of the Child in American Literature: Linguistic Approaches to Fictional Child Language.* Lexington: UP of Kentucky, 1990. 64-94.

In chapter four of this linguistic and stylistic analysis of children's speech in American fiction, Hurst discusses "Hawthorne's Pearl" (pp. 66-75), arguing first that Hawthorne creates a believable child portrait in Pearl and second that the "security and restriction of the culture surrounding Hester and Pearl create the characters' conflicts." The parent-child discourse in the novel reveals the ways that language "connects or fails to connect." Language connects Hester and Pearl but fails to connect Dimmesdale and Pearl. Hurst concludes that "the success or failure of parent-child communication is vital for *Letter* in both its literal and symbolic contexts."

620   Martin, Robert K. "Hester Prynne, C'est Moi: Nathaniel Hawthorne and the Anxieties of Gender." *Engendering Men: The Question of Male Feminist Criticism.* Eds. Joseph Boone and Michael Cadden. New York: Routledge, 1990. 122-139.

Hawthorne's anxieties about the feminizing effects of his vocation as an artist surface in his ambivalent representation of female artists in *Letter* and *Blithedale Romance* and explain "the multiple voices and refusals of certainty" in much of his fiction. Possibly Hawthorne's threatened sense of self emerged in response to his own and his culture's gender and class anxieties (i.e. the newly independent woman and the "new gay man"). Martin begins with an examination of the gendered language of "The Custom-House," arguing that the sketch is "above all an essay in sexual politics" that reveals—along with the novel itself—Hawthorne's desire to abandon the sterile world of men and speak both to and through creative, powerful women. He is figuratively resurrected in Hester, wearing her clothes (donning the "A" makes him guilty of "transvestism") and assuming her crime of art that refuses gender boundaries. *Blithedale*

Romance further complicates Hawthorne's construction of male heterosexual identity and his view of the woman artist found in *Letter* by exploring different stereotypes of femininity and masculinity through the contrasted characters of Zenobia/Priscilla and Coverdale/Hollingsworth.

621   Scheer, Steven C. "Errors of Truth: Deconstruction in *The Scarlet Letter*." *Pious Impostures and Unproven Words: The Romance of Deconstruction in Nineteenth-Century America*. Lanham: UP of America, 1990. 32-49.

Argues that Hawthorne deconstructs the Puritan system in *Letter*. Using the oft-debated chapters involving Dimmesdale's public confession (whether he is saved or damned) and the "Conclusion" (whether the scarlet "A" burns on Dimmesdale's chest or is merely imagined) to prove his point, Scheer calls attention to the fact that Hawthorne purposely suggests more than one way to interpret several key scenes. Most important is not that readers and critics come away with disparate opinions but that the Puritans themselves do—despite their arrogant assumption "that they are absolutely right when it comes to passing judgment on the sins of their fellow human beings." These contradictory assertions made by the Puritans show that Hawthorne is actually deconstructing the Puritan community in *Letter*. He shows that the Puritan construction of reality is an artifice and thus rejects Puritanism's "morbidly absolutist totalization." In fact, the novel implies the revisionary nature of all reading and writing, and in the process it oscillates between accepting or rejecting the interconnection of sin, art, and artifice. [See Catherine H. Zuckert's essay directly below (622) for an argument that reaches a similar conclusion: that Hawthorne "deconstructs" Puritan beliefs by pointing out the contradictions inherent in them.]

622   Zuckert, Catherine H. "Hawthorne's Politics of Passion." *Natural Right and the American Imagination: Political Philosophy in Novel Form*. Ed. Catherine H. Zuckert. Savage: Rowan and Littlefield, 1990. 63-98.

Comments on the "generally neglected political thrust" in Hawthorne's romances that explores the question: "How can [human beings] best organize civil society to overcome their natural faults [of selfishness and contentiousness]?" Zuckert examines *Letter*, *Blithedale Romance*, and *House of the Seven Gables* for the answer to the question that involves a critical balance between freedom and self-restraint. In *Letter* (pp. 66-71), as in the other novels, Hawthorne leaves "the lesson implicit by letting the plot serve as his commentary on the political setting." The stringent moral legislation of the Puritans clearly does not work, since human passions— especially sexual desire—cannot (and should not) always remain repressed. To force "sinners" like Hester and Dimmesdale to confess their weaknesses in public "is to lose sight of both the origin and the rationale for human association in the first place." Such confessions suggest that human beings can avoid all error, thus revealing the contradictions in the Puritans' own fundamental doctrine of Original Sin.

Journal Essays and Notes

623   Doherty, Gerald. "Uncovering Plots: Secret Agents in *The Scarlet Letter*." *Arizona Quarterly* 46 (1990): 13-32.

First approaching "The Custom-House" to demystify its "devious and circumambulatory" nature and to establish its crucial link to the text (which is more complicated than most critics realize), Doherty then finds evidence of a "deep structural design" in the novel, "a link between 'knot' [the symbol] and plot, figure and story, trope and narrative. In other words, "the novel may be read as an allegory of the intimate co-implication of the 'knot' of the letter and the plot of the narrative, one which displays the method by which the original threads of the 'knot' [. . .] are unraveled and rewoven into the complex plot of the story." After setting up a theoretical framework based on the ideas of Jacques Derrida, Paul Ricoeur, and other linguistic theorists, Doherty focuses on three major plot structures that revolve around a larger tropological plot that "at once inaugurates, motivates, and concludes [the characters'] destinies," demonstrating how *Letter* "epitomizes the deep-level transactions between metaphorical process and narrative plot and design."

624   Elbert, Monika M. "Hester's Maternity: Stigma or Weapon?" *ESQ: A Journal of the American Renaissance* 36 (1990): 174-207.

Analyzes "the politics of mothering" in *Letter* to determine whether Hester's maternity is ultimately a "stigma" or a "weapon." Hester's unique "brand" of maternity empowers her and directly contradicts patriarchal definitions of female sexuality and maternity Even more threatened by Hester than the control-obsessed Puritan patriarchs, though, are the "matriphobic," menopausal women in the community who, in the opening scaffold scene, venomously attack Hester's free-spirited, self-reliant, sexually vibrant character and in the process betray their own senses of woman's powerlessness in patriarchy (especially since "maternity is seen as a commodity," and these women are deemed "worthless" because they are past their fertile years). More than just a biological mother, Hester is an emotional mother—nurturing Pearl, Dimmesdale (and even Chillingworth in the past), Hawthorne (who, like Dimmesdale, longs for a surrogate mother), and the entire community of women by the end of the novel. She thrives in her Puritan community "by living as a [single] mother on her own terms" and refusing male definitions of either sexuality or maternity. Hester "chooses to emphasize her (m)otherness," and even flaunts it, using her silence not as revenge, as Leland S. Person would have it (in 604), but "as her refusal to participate in male discourse and thus as a sign of triumph over the male reality." In other words, Hester accentuates or celebrates what French feminist theorists refer to as "la différence," ultimately finding liberation, creative energy, and the ability to speak several "sublanguages" within the community through the experience of raising an "unruly" daughter. Elbert closes her discussion by offering yet another meaning to the letter "A," that being "Amazon," since Hester is "a woman larger than life."

625   Fleischner, Jennifer. "Female Eroticism, Confession, and Interpretation in Nathaniel Hawthorne." *Nineteenth-Century Literature* 44 (1990): 514-533.

"Hawthorne locates female eroticism as the origin of meaning" in his fiction, as "the enabling force of his imagination." Although Faith Brown, Hester, Zenobia, and Miriam "are the focus of the interpreter's stare at the center of Hawthorne's narratives," their male admirers/lovers fearfully reject their erotic power and manage to reject it climactically through the "central trope" of a duplicitously evasive confession that shuts down or cuts off the process of interpretation between "writer and reader, narrator and listener." Thus the "betrayals of eroticism coincide with the endings of all four works," since Brown, Dimmesdale, Coverdale, and Kenyon embrace idealized, virginal versions of the female that signal the death to experience, the end of interpretation, and "thus "the end of the male artist's capacity for production."

626   Gatta, John. "The Apocalyptic End of *The Scarlet Letter*." *Texas Studies in Language and Literature* 32 (1990): 506-521.

Finding that the narrative of *Letter* "moves within the stark framework of Christian revelation concerning death, judgment, and the soul's search for earthly and eternal salvation," Gatta argues for a religious reading of the novel that places Hawthorne's interests less in the psychology of sin and more in "the struggle to apprehend saving truth." He reads Hawthorne's deliberately incomplete climax of revelation in chapter 23 ("The Revelation of the Scarlet Letter") as "apocalyptic" in the biblical sense, suggesting that The Book of Revelation supplied the inevitable pretext for the "tragically numinous close" of the novel where only Dimmesdale experiences a sense of relieved triumph and closure. Gatta similarly views the scarlet "A" itself as "a numinous icon" that reveals "the unknowability of sacred truth on earth while pointing toward a definitive resolution beyond unbounded ambiguity" and away from "a wholly unresolved chaos of secular indeterminacy." Hawthorne's interest in maintaining religious and epistemological mystery is further apparent in the way that Hester and Dimmesdale's "consecrated" love for one another resonates with an "intuitive Catholic proclivity toward mythic naturalism, iconism, and sacramentalism." [For another essay that considers the relation of *Letter* to The Book of Revelation, see Evans Lansing Smith (634).]

627   Gatta, John. "*The Scarlet Letter* as Pre-Text for Flannery O'Connor's 'Good Country People.'" *Nathaniel Hawthorne Review* 16.2 (1990): 6-9.*

Finds striking temperamental and spiritual affinities between Hawthorne and O'Connor, citing an "incarnational demonism" as passed down from *Letter* to "Good Country People." Gatta considers the way in which *Letter* "offers a kind of Satanic pre-text for the spiritual confrontation O'Connor presents in her comically devastating tale." Chillingworth's dual role as Dimmesdale's demon and savior is recast in the character of Manley Pointer, who similarly preys on the unsuspecting Mrs. Hopewell. Both tales also revolve around a central symbol (scarlet letter/wooden leg). Further, the vacuous, self-deceived character of Joy-Hulga resembles Dimmesdale with her "disposition toward intellectual self-deception" and with her "weak heart"; and both characters reflect each author's fears of their own self-insulating, artistic tendencies.

*Gatta's article is reprinted in *Hawthorne and Women: Engendering and Expanding the Hawthorne Tradition* (Eds. John L. Idol, Jr., and Melinda M. Ponder. Amherst: U of Massachusetts P, 1999. 271-277).

628   Hoffman, Elizabeth Aycock. "Political Power in *The Scarlet Letter*." *ATQ* New Series 4 (1990): 12-39.

Drawing from Michel Foucault's observations in *Discipline and Punish* and placing *Letter* within the historical context of modern penology, Hoffman argues that the novel is Hawthorne's examination of the social methods of discipline by which self-reliant individuals (himself included) are made to conform to the utilitarian principles of the larger community. Hawthorne compares the effectiveness of two models of discipline, the first being the punitive political power that enforces Hester's punishment and calls for the public spectacle on the scaffold for "instructive purposes," and the second being Hester's more personal, private punishment by Pearl, whose torments and lawless behavior make Hester "recognize a higher than human law that authenticates the necessity of discipline." This latter, more effective punishment (which changes

Hester's private image of herself, transforming the "original political-legal meaning of the letter's semiotic into the personal, transcendent 'truth' for Hester") compares with the one enacted insidiously by Chillingworth on Dimmesdale. Although Hawthorne is clearly a champion of the second method of discipline, he seems to undermine his own critical view "about the expediencies of political mechanisms of social control" by ultimately using Pearl's character to justify the necessity of disciplinary "interventions and domination." [For more on the subject of private and public punishment (as influenced by Foucault), see Nancy Roberts (798).]

629　Jones, Buford. "What the Permanent Inspector Thought of His Portrait." *Nathaniel Hawthorne Review* 16.1 (1990): 16-17.

Provides a long-forgotten account of the venerable inspector William Lee's "later reaction" to Hawthorne's satiric portrayal of him in "The Custom-House." Not only Lee but a great many other Salemites expressed contempt for and outrage over Hawthorne's "unworthy" and "vicious" motives—and spoke of Hawthorne with such bitter hatred as to account for Hawthorne's expeditious move from Salem following the publication of *Letter*.

630　Powers, Douglas. "Pearl's Discovery of Herself in *The Scarlet Letter*." *Nathaniel Hawthorne Review* 16.1 (1990): 12-15.

Most criticism fails to acknowledge that Pearl is, in addition to being a symbol, also "a child trying to discover herself." Powers approaches the character of Pearl from a developmental point of view, observing that the energetic behavior and inquisitive expressions of this realistically portrayed figure indicate "a puzzled, confused child growing up in an eccentric, isolated environment." In the final scaffold scene, the experience of Dimmesdale acknowledging her creates a "clearing pattern" in Pearl's mind, and she is able to become a complete girl whose energy can then be redirected to growing up.

631　Rao, P. G. Rama. "Woman Undefeated: Sakuntala and Hester Prynne." *Journal of Literary Studies* 14.1 (1990): 1-18.

Hester "may profitably be compared" with the heroine of Kalidasa's ancient Sanskrit play *Abhi jnana-Sakuntala*, since "both are beautiful and passionate and exemplify great patience, perseverance, and a passive courage which would not admit defeat and despair." Rao bases the comparison exclusively on loose plot similarities, discussing how both tales involve separated lovers who—after the women are rejected, bear illegitimate children, raise them on their own, and grow penitent—are reunited years later, their love having shifted from a physical to a moral and spiritual plane. [For a more thorough examination of the parallels between the two, see Gupta's 1993 essay "Kalidasa's *Sakuntala*and Hawthorne's *The Scarlet Letter*" (709).]

632   Reed, Jon B. "'A Letter,—the Letter A': A Portrait of the Artist as Hester Prynne." *ESQ: A Journal of the American Renaissance* 36 (1990): 78-107.

The ambiguity of the scarlet letter is "the major empowering force of the novel" through which Hawthorne identifies himself with Hester and the "mystical sanctity that gives her a special authority to make art." The novel strategically allegorizes the "authorial self" so that Hawthorne can justify and validate his vocation while also critiquing the socio-political and moral climate of nineteenth-century America. Hawthorne's "preoccupation with his status as an artist and the place of the artist in his society" permeates both "The Custom-House" and *Letter*, where Hawthorne associates his art with a "particularly feminine sensibility" (that is naturally tied with economic and political powerlessness) before going on to show that Hester's artistry makes her extremely valuable to her community—turning her weakness, sin, and shame into an almost sacred, redemptive, and authoritative power. Dimmesdale represents "the theocratic father" who dominates American society and denies his responsibility to Hester's "liberating art" (Pearl). His death after acknowledging his fatherhood strongly implies that "the true American work of art is so subversive that its recognition and acceptance in America has the power to destroy the old order; hence the necessity for Pearl, the finished work, to go to Europe to find its appreciation." In the novel's conclusion, Hester is empowered in her decision to return to Boston, "remaining liminal by choice (or artistic necessity)." If Hester is read in "her role as the representation of the artist, then fulfillment lies not in the happy completion of her own narrative, but in the happy completion of the finished product of her art," Pearl, who will be "loved, admired, and rewarded" for her "unique American beauty." Since Hester cannot live in a foreign environment if she is truly to remain an artist, she is compelled to return to the edge of society, "to the soil that nurtured the art" in the first place.

633   Shindo, Suzuko. "The Black Man in *The Scarlet Letter*." *Studies in American Literature* 27 (1990): 1-16.

Explores the figure of the Black Man in *Letter*, who appears as Chillingworth, that "Faustian scholar" who is (considering his European background as something of a magician) "a physician, alchemist,

316

occultist—an authentic wizard." Once he arrives in Boston, however, "he has been well contaminated by the devil's art," and he puts Hester under his magic spell again, turning her into a witch to do his bidding (the first time he mesmerized her was in offering marriage, a spell that continued until she crossed the ocean). Chillingworth's metamorphosis quickens "as he burns with jealousy and vengeful thoughts towards Dimmesdale," and his character is increasingly described in terms of damning red fire and blackness. Dimmesdale is almost damned himself by Hester's offer to escape in the forest scene, although he comes to suspect that she—as the wife of the Black Man—is one of Satan's emissaries, as well, and so he rises above them both to achieve spiritual rebirth, convinced that they were both sent to afflict him and test his fidelity to God.

634   Smith, Evans Lansing. "Re-Figuring Revelations: Nathaniel Hawthorne's *The Scarlet Letter*." *ATQ* New Series 4 (1990): 91-104.

"Allusions to the Book of Revelation determine the basis of the novel's theme and structure to an extent not fully recognized by most critics of the novel." It is likely that Hawthorne (who attempts "a comprehensive refiguration of the Biblical apocalypse" in the novel) defines "apocalypse" from its root meaning as an uncovering of hidden or buried secrets, and uses it to raise hermeneutical and epistemological questions relevant to the debates during his time about Emersonian transcendentalism and the materialist secularism of Jacksonian democracy (about both of which he was skeptical). Hawthorne's employment of the apocalyptic typology of the Bible extends beyond the image of the end of the old world and the creation of the new to include "four other Biblical themes derived from Revelation which play crucial roles in the novel: the notion of unveiling, prophecy, the last battle, resurrection and judgment. These five aspects of Revelation, often mixed together, form the basis of the novel's structure and theme, as is most clearly evident in the famous scaffold scenes, which are the skeleton of the plot." Smith's conclusion that the novel retains the "veil" of the world (or the hidden meaning of life) without destroying it draws from Douglas Robinson's *American Apocalypses: The Image of the End of the World in American Literature* (Baltimore: Johns Hopkins UP, 1985). The uncovering of the scarlet letter itself "is tantalizingly partial," Smith suggests, "exactly that revelation within history which transforms its witnesses but does not finally, ultimately annihilate or illuminate them." [See John Gatta (626) for another reading of the novel that argues for Hawthorne's use of the Book of Revelation.]

1991

Books

635   Bercovitch, Sacvan. *The Office of The Scarlet Letter.* Baltimore: Johns
       Hopkins UP, 1991. 175 pp.

This influential study examines the purpose and goal of the letter's
mystifying "office," the eventual fulfillment of which can be seen to
encapsulate the novel's symbolic method of combined "process" and
"closure" and bring into view the enormous imaginative resources of mid-
nineteenth-century American liberalism. Hester's return to Boston at the
end not only reconciles the various antinomies that surround her
throughout the novel but also anticipates Hawthorne's recovery of Puritan
New England in writing *Letter.* This study is in part a commentary on the
process of interpreting the complex social practices and cultural ideals of
mid-nineteenth century America, while it is also an integration of
ideological and aesthetic criticism.   Chapters one and two provide a
historical reading of the novel, while chapters three and four present a
rhetorical analysis of certain key mid-nineteenth-century issues. Two of
these four chapters in the book appeared previously: "The A-Politics of
Ambiguity in *The Scarlet Letter* (575) and "Hawthorne's A-Morality of
Compromise" (576). [See 691 for Bercovitch's continuation of this topic,
this time focusing exclusively on Hester Prynne's return to New England.
Several critics either take issue with or build upon Bercovitch's stance of
ideological consent in this study.   Refer to the Subject Index under
"Bercovitch, Sacvan" for individual entries.]

636   Berlant, Lauren. *The Anatomy of National Fantasy: Hawthorne, Utopia,
       and Everyday Life.* Chicago: U of Chicago P, 1991. 269 pp.

Traces the ways in which national identity and citizenship function in
Hawthorne, focusing primarily on the representation of America in *Letter.*
The three main chapters on *Letter* that form the core of this study ("The
Paradise of Law in *Letter*" [pp. 57-95], "The State of Madness:
Conscience, Popular Memory, and Narrative in *Letter*" [pp. 97-159], and
"The Nationalist Preface" [161-189]) analyze the official, popular, and
subjective modes and effects of collective/national identity that
characterize both the narrator's representation of Puritan culture and his
allusive construction of the national-political present tense. Hawthorne's
method of critiquing official nationalist discourse involves
experimentation with citizenship and popular national/utopian fantasy,
whereby he writes a new kind of early American history that allows for a
return to subjectivity, to material experience, and to everyday life in order
to reconfigure what it means to be an American citizen.

637   Murfin, Ross C., ed. *Case Studies in Contemporary Criticism: Nathaniel Hawthorne: The Scarlet Letter.* Boston: Bedford Books of St. Martin's Press, 1991. 371 pp.

Includes the complete authoritative text (the Centenary Edition) with introductory biographical and historical background; a survey of the major critical responses to the novel from 1850-1990; plus five essays (one original and four "newly revised"* essays) from different contemporary critical perspectives—by Joanne Feit Diehl (psychoanalytic [578]), David Leverenz (reader-response [641], Shari Benstock (feminist [639]), Michael Ragussis (deconstructive [431]), and Sacvan Bercovitch (New Historicist [576]). A clear and helpful introduction prefaces each critical approach, as does a bibliography and glossary of critical and theoretical terms for each critical perspective (359-368).

*Only one of the four revised essays is different enough from its original to warrant a new citation and annotation (see David Leverenz below [641]).

638   Poe, Elizabeth Ann, ed. *Teacher's Guide to the Signet Classic Edition of Nathaniel Hawthorne's The Scarlet Letter.* New York: Penguin USA, 1991. 24 pp.

This teaching approach to the novel "encourages student involvement" and "emphasizes the significance this classic literary work holds for the lives of its readers." Divided into three sections, this brief guide first offers an overview of the novel that includes a synopsis of plot, commentary on the novel, introduction to Hawthorne's life, description of the literary scene during Hawthorne's time, and historical commentary on Puritan New England. The second section, which contains suggestions and activities for teaching the novel before, during, and after specific chapters are read ("The Custom-House" not included), is geared to different ability levels of students; and the third section provides ideas for extending students' learning to include current events, literary criticism, and other literary works.

Essays and Studies in Books

639   Benstock, Shari. "The Scarlet Letter (a)dorée, or the Female Body Embroidered." *Case Studies in Contemporary Criticism: Nathaniel Hawthorne: The Scarlet Letter.* Ed. Ross C. Murfin. Boston: Bedford Books of St. Martin's Press, 1991. 288-303.

This reading, largely informed by French feminist theory, views Hester as the victim of male fantasies ranging from those that concern "the female body" to the controlling "fantasy of absolute sexual difference that lies at the very heart of women's repression and exploitation." Hester subverts her patriarchal Puritan society's attempt to reduce her to the simple identity of adulteress by artfully altering and embellishing the meaning behind the symbolic letter. The novel teaches us—as Hester does—to distrust traditional, specifically-masculine modes of interpretation, as well as occasionally to dissociate meaning from gender and challenge the logic of binary oppositions.

640   Hutchinson, Stuart. "Hawthorne: *The Scarlet Letter*." *The American Scene: Essays on Nineteenth-Century American Literature*. New York: St. Martin's Press, 1991. 37-56.

This overview of *Letter*, which shows virtually no reference to or knowledge of contemporary criticism on the novel, considers how questions of personal and national identity are linked to Hawthorne's sense of history. Above all, the novel is the expression of Hawthorne's double nature, his desire to construct meaning and truth in a world where all meanings are elusive and always shifting.

641   Leverenz, David. "Mrs. Hawthorne's Headache: Reading *The Scarlet Letter*." *Case Studies in Contemporary Criticism: Nathaniel Hawthorne: The Scarlet Letter*. Ed. Ross C. Murfin. Boston: Bedford Books of St. Martin's Press, 1991. 263-274.*

Building upon reader-response approaches to *Letter* advanced by Richard Brodhead (in 300) and Kenneth Dauber (343), Leverenz provides in this newly-revised essay* a history of readers' responses to the novel, discussing the contrary reactions of contemporary readers against the background of *Letter*'s early reception. The novel's several levels of meaning both "induce" and "undermine" the interpretive expectations of its readers, making the relation between text and community ambivalent at best. Hawthorne's self-conscious relation to his readers further "abets, displaces, and conceals his story's unresolved tensions," making the text even more resistant to single interpretations.

*For Leverenz's original essay that appeared in 1983, see 447.

642   Maddox, Lucy. "Saving the Family: Hawthorne, Child, and Sedgwick." *Removals: Nineteenth-Century American Literature and the Politics of Indian Affairs*. New York: Oxford UP, 1991. 89-130.

320

Examines three novels that focus on Puritan history, Lydia Maria Child's *Hobomok* (1824), Catherine Maria Sedgwick's *Hope Leslie* (1827), and Hawthorne's *Letter*, finding that the writers' treatment of seventeenth-century America is determined by their "concerns for the present and future of nineteenth-century America," specifically by their responses to "the Indian question" and "the woman question." *Letter* (pp. 118-126) is considered particularly for Hawthorne's association of Hester, a female wanderer and outsider, with both the Indians and the famous Puritan captives Anne Hutchinson, Hannah Duston, and Mary Rowlandson. Hawthorne brings together several key themes in the novel: "the uselessness of reform movements, the moral dangers to which reformers expose themselves, and the disappearance of the Indians." Hester is "saved" from wandering the moral wilderness "like the wild Indian in the woods" by her maternal attachment to Pearl. Further, she assimilates herself into the "captivity" of Puritan patriarchy in order to save future women from the fate of the female wanderer.

643   Mellard, James M. "Inscriptions of the Subject: *The Scarlet Letter*." *Using Lacan, Reading Fiction*. Urbana: U of Illinois P, 1991. 69-106.

This psychoanalytic approach applies the language theories of Jacques Lacan to *Letter*, "not only provid[ing] an opening into important analytic concepts," but also "adduc[ing] important new insights into the interrelations of the work's major figures." Hawthorne's romance is valuably approached through Lacanian principles, "not only because it represents important functions (the mirror stage and the Oedipal complex), but also because it focuses on four major characters whose experiences exemplify versions of subjectivity Lacan determines through psychoanalysis": "normal" (Pearl and Hester) and "pathological" (Dimmesdale and Chillingworth). For instance, in Pearl, "Hawthorne's language richly reveals the emergence of the mirror stage and the Oedipus encounter and resolution. Likewise, Hawthorne's language reveals [. . .] in the creation of Hester Prynne some of the problems any subject encounters in the interrelations of the registers of the Imaginary and the Symbolic, particularly in connection with that concept Lacan has popularized called 'the gaze.' Lacanian theory also yields much in relation to the two other major characters in the tale. In Arthur Dimmesdale we see Hawthorne limning a character caught in a neurosis, but moving in the end toward a problematic cure. Finally, around Roger Chillingworth one may see the distortion of the subject associated with psychosis, but ironically, at the same time the function Lacan associates with the analyst and the great Other."

644   Miller, Edwin Haviland. "Intercourse with the World: *The Scarlet Letter*." *Salem Is My Dwelling Place: A Life of Nathaniel Hawthorne*. Iowa City: U of Iowa P, 1991. 278-298.

Above all, *Letter* is a "family romance" that emphasizes each of the four main characters' searches for roots, love, and a society in which the patriarchal code is humanized by matriarchal values. The story is a "veiled résumé" of Hawthorne's life that signifes his method of handling his grief following the death of his mother in 1849. When *Letter* is read in this autobiographical fashion, the "A" on Hester's breast chiefly signifies "Absence," and the four main characters collectively constitute Hawthorne's own complex self-portrait. "The story is concentrated on the 'A' on Hester's breast [which symbolizes fertility, nurturing, and creativity], and the sea imagery evokes the cradle endlessly rocking, birth and death, Aphrodite and the Eternal Mother, and a gentle boy's loss of his father at sea in his youth and of a mother in age."

645   Murfin, Ross C. "Introduction: The Biographical and Historical Background." *Case Studies in Contemporary Criticism Nathaniel Hawthorne: The Scarlet Letter*. Ed. Ross C. Murfin. Boston: Bedford Books of St. Martin's Press, 1991. 3-19.

The title speaks accurately to the content of the introduction. Murfin presents the novel as "a complicated mix of biography and history, of seventeenth- and nineteenth-century history, and, most important, of history and the imagination that brings it to life."

646   Person, Leland S., Jr. "Inscribing Paternity: Nathaniel Hawthorne as a Nineteenth-Century Father." *Studies in the American Renaissance*. Ed. Joel Myerson. Charlottesville: U of Virginia Press, 1991. 225-244.

Examines *Letter* and Hawthorne's evolving attitude about fatherhood (biologically and literarily speaking) in the context of conflicting attitudes toward childrearing in the nineteenth-century, especially in light of Henry Clarke Wright's 1854 discourse on *Marriage and Parentage*. Hawthorne's initial anxieties about parenting, coupled with his heavy financial burdens, are reflected not only in the character of Una (who exhibits through her behavior the popular nineteenth-century belief in parental determinism),* but also in his "exaggerated portrait" of Dimmesdale as absent father. Dimmesdale's fears that Pearl reflects his own physical and psychological aspects mirror Hawthorne's similar worries that Una inherited characteristics from his own dark nature. As "a compelling case study of the psychology and ethos of nineteenth-century American fatherhood," Hawthorne's "devastating portrait of fatherhood" in *Letter* illuminates not only the author's "low point in his feelings about fatherhood" but also "an ongoing nineteenth-century dialogue about parentage and, especially, about a father's biological, psychological, and moral responsibilities to his children." [For another essay that addresses the nineteenth-century belief in parental determinism as it is illustrated in domestic advice literature, see Franny Nudelman (813).]

647   Pfister, Joel. "Sowing Dragons' Teeth: Personal Life and Revolution in *The Scarlet Letter*." *The Production of Personal Life: Class, Gender, and the Psychological in Hawthorne's Fiction.* Stanford: Stanford UP, 1991. 122-143.

Examines Hawthorne's celebrated preoccupation with the "psychological" in his fiction within the historical context of a distinctly middle-class personal life that made certain assumptions about family, gender, emotional relations, the body, and sexuality. Pfister departs from the assumptions of critics who apply psychoanalysis to Hawthorne's fictions, arguing instead that a great many writers in the mid-nineteenth century (such as Margaret Fuller, Sarah Grimké, Fanny Fern, Lydia Maria Child, and Harriet Beecher Stowe) expressed the same historically-specific cultural and ideological concerns regarding the "production of the category of the 'psychological.'" With respect to *Letter*, "Hawthorne's anxiety about the cultural revolution that might result from the emancipation of women from middle-class angelhood underlies his revealingly awkward narrative endeavors to feminize Pearl and her scarlet mother." His determination to uphold the mythic impression of social order despite the threatening pressures of "armed to the teeth" dragon women is "the key" to this reading the novel. Pearl, who serves as a feminist conscience for Hester, rejects middle-class Puritan "normality" until Hawthorne humanizes and domesticates her in the final theatrical scaffold scene. The ambitious revolutionary efforts of Hester and Dimmesdale are likewise checked at novel's end, and Hawthorne's real "pearl" of wisdom seems to reinforce the middle-class ideology that calls for the humanizing effects of domesticity.

648   Railton, Stephen. "'To Open an Intercourse with the World': Hawthorne's *Scarlet Letter*." *Authorship and Audience: Literary Performance in the American Renaissance.* Princeton: Princeton UP, 1991. 107-131.*

Hawthorne's attention to "rhetorical exigencies" is more exemplary than that of the other four nineteenth-century American authors of "undisputed masterpieces of the American Renaissance"—Ralph Waldo Emerson, Herman Melville, Henry David Thoreau, and Walt Whitman—because he sought a heartfelt, sympathetic union within a social milieu instead of seeking an isolated, transcendent relationship with nature. Despite his own fits of impatience with an intellectually inferior audience, Hawthorne felt strongly about opening an "intercourse with the [middle-class] world" and relating to as large a contemporary audience as he possibly could. Like "Ethan Brand" before it, *Letter*'s main preoccupation involves showing how "one's relation to the universe is inescapably qualified by the existence of history and other people." Hawthorne anxiously anticipated "the grotesque failure of American society as a potential audience," and so he cast the intolerant, unsympathetic Puritan spectators in the role of audience in the novel to cue his own readers to such moral shortcomings and to show them how to respond properly to his characters and to his art.

*For an updated version of this essay (under a different title), see 699.

649   Rogers, Franklin R. "Lost in a Moral Wilderness: Hawthorne, *The Scarlet Letter." Occidental Ideographs: Image, Sequence, and Literary History.* Lewisburg: Bucknell UP, 1991. 76-99.

Chapter three of this "study of the complex interplay between the verbal and visual" examines the artistic principles governing *Letter*. Rogers explores the dialectic between the literal and the figurative—or "the ideographic aspect" of the novel as he calls it—to reveal the overall structure of the novel. Tracing the consistent visual "metaphoric pattern" of closures and interior spaces throughout, "the open versus the hidden, the transparent versus the opaque, the straight path versus the labyrinthine way," reveals the architectural structure divided into balanced halves. Essentially, because the novel opens with a prison door and closes with a tombstone image, Hester can be seen to progress sadly—without hope of escape—from one interior space to another through the "magnificent edifice" of Hawthorne's story, of which "The Custom-House" is the "entrance hall."

650   Ruland, Richard, and Malcolm Bradbury. "Yea-Saying and Nay-Saying." *From Puritanism to Postmodernism: A History of American Literature.* New York: Viking Press, 1991. 139-177.

Section two (pp. 144-164) of this chapter that discusses Ralph Waldo Emerson, Hawthorne, Herman Melville, and Emily Dickinson surveys Hawthorne's major works, especially *Letter* (pp. 144-149), which "is a careful measuring of the historical, religious, literary, and emotional distance that separated the Puritan New England of the past from the transcendentalist New England of the present, of the change from the old 'iron world' to the world of 'freedom of speculation' which Hester [. . .]

embodies." Insisting on the necessity of social existence as well as on the importance of an Emersonian-like self-reliance, Hawthorne's novel is "a tragedy of the divided claims made by the natural and the social self."

651   Swann, Charles. *"The Scarlet Letter* and the Language of History: Past Imperfect, Present Imperfect, Future Perfect?" *Nathaniel Hawthorne: Tradition and Revolution.* Cambridge: Cambridge UP, 1991. 75-95.

Disagreeing with New Historicists who see Hawthorne as a "quietist neo-conservative in the sheep's clothing of a (Jacksonian) democrat" (and building on an earlier essay with a similar subject—314), Swann argues that Hawthorne is much more subversive and ironic than such critics acknowledge. His reading of *Letter* focuses on the role of society in the novel and finds no endorsement of passivity or a liberal gradualist view.* Hawthorne sees history as "a struggle between the authoritative claims of tradition on the one hand and the conflicting but equally valid claims of the desires for revolutionary transformation on the other." The very existence of *Letter* is just such a product of history—Hawthorne's contemporary political and personal history intersecting with a wider public history; and while the novel is profoundly concerned with the functions and powers of the letter "A," it is really a criticism of symbolic modes of perception and definition. Indeed, the main narrative argues that symbols are merely the product of history, and therefore the progress of time and history will vanquish for Hester and Dimmesdale the Puritan community's dehumanizing attempt to freeze time and meaning with the punishment of the scarlet letter. Even "The Custom-House" suggests that symbols contain no innate meaning in themselves, since the physical scarlet "A" only derives its meaning when its historical context is known. And despite what critics such as Michael J. Colacurcio (in 289), Austin Warren (in 178), and Nina Baym (in 419) believe about Hester's ambiguous return to New England at novel's end, Hester *is* genuinely subversive in her radical prophecy that calls for a complete restructuring of society and the religion that legitimates that patriarchy, and so the ending—as well as Hawthorne's own judgment of Hester—remains deliberately open to the future. Just like the readers of the novel itself, Hawthorne and Hester are not trapped in the conservative positions of the past or even the present.

*Swann reacts here explicitly to New Historicists Sacvan Bercovitch (see 560, 575, 576, and 635) and Jonathan Arac (see 508).

Journal Essays and Notes

652   Anderson, Douglas. "Jefferson, Hawthorne, and 'The Custom-House.'"
       Nineteenth-Century Literature 46 (1991): 309-326.

Examining the relationship of *Letter* to Hawthorne's political
circumstances in which it was written, Anderson adds to the twenty years
of differing accounts by Michael Davitt Bell (in 261), Stephen
Nissenbaum (in 363), Henry Nash Smith (in 356), and Jonathan Arac (in
508) to argue that Hawthorne's knowledge of the public amendations
made to Thomas Jefferson's "Declaration of Independence" by Congress
not only played a decisive role in the artistic and political design of "The
Custom-House" but also influenced his decision in the preface to the
second edition of *Letter* not to change one word to appease those who had
taken offense at its "excesses." In addition to pointing out rhetorical and
textual similarities between the Declaration and Hawthorne's novel,
Anderson contrasts Jefferson's "heavily edited language" with
Hawthorne's resolution to let his own words stand. Instances in the novel
express Hawthorne's concern with the "mixed nature" or adulteration of
"ceremonial texts," such as in descriptions of Hester's punitive letter and
Dimmesdale's public speeches.

653   Bartley, William. "'The Synthesis of Love and Fear': Nathaniel
       Hawthorne and the Virtue of Reverence." *Modern Philology* 88 (1991):
       382-397.

Examines the climactic passage, troubling for critics, in which Hawthorne
denies the reader's curiosity about the details of Dimmesdale's revelation
when he bares his chest ("It was revealed! But it were irreverent to
describe that revelation."), and argues that the passage is only problematic
for twentieth-century readers (and "inaccurate" critics) who are unfamiliar
with Hawthorne's use of the morally descriptive word "irreverent."
Although Bartley did not find the exact meaning that he was looking for in
the *Oxford English Dictionary* or Webster's *Dictionary*, he clarifies the
terms employed in the latter source that describe reverence as a synthesis
of love and fear (a "profoundly moral sensitivity to the irreducibility of
phenomena"), and then meticulously traces that definition's identical use
of such nineteenth-century authors as Harriet Beecher Stowe, Herman
Melville, Ralph Waldo Emerson, Samuel Taylor Coleridge, Henry James,
and Jeremy Taylor. The term "irreverent" also implies the separation of
the probing, curious intellect from the sympathetic heart. In frustrating
our curiosity, therefore, Hawthorne anticipates the reader's irreverent
desire to gawk at the scandalous and pathetic figure of the minister; and
therefore, after having "judge[d] the propriety of satisfying our curiosity,"
Hawthorne protectively suppresses the details of the revelation from the

"lust of the eyes," thereby reducing the risk of our loss of sympathy for Dimmesdale.

654   Budick, Emily Miller. "Hester's Skepticism, Hawthorne's Faith; or, What Does a Woman Doubt? Instituting the American Romance Tradition." *New Literary History* 22 (1991): 199-211.*

Letter opposes tendencies in Puritan society (those relating to federal theology and the principle of visible sanctity) to resolve any and all doubts concerning itself and the reality of its embodiment of the divine. Like other American historical novels written in the romance tradition, *Letter* both acknowledges that "doubt is the condition of our lives in this world" and encourages a reconciliation of uncertainties and the social commitment to think and act determinately. With an impulse toward liberal democracy, Hawthorne exposes false assumptions of Puritan patriarchy (specifically involving the issues of matrilineal genealogy and "patriarchy's abuse of history" in its efforts to control female sexuality) and "promotes a system of community and history predicated upon the preservation rather than the settling of radical doubt." More interested in "facilitating the processes of historical inheritance" than with "reconstructing the idea of history," Hawthorne explores the need to deal with doubts by entertaining throughout the novel the question of Pearl's paternity—even suggesting his own personal parallel to Hester's illegitimate daughter, since Pearl's desire to know her father is similar to his own creative need to inherit Surveyor Pue and perhaps even recover a female "predecessor" or mother in Hester.

*For a similar, later study by Budick, see 768.

655   Brown, Gillian. "Hawthorne, Inheritance, and Women's Property." *Studies in the Novel* 23 (1991):107-118.

Viewing *House of the Seven Gables* in the context of nineteenth-century property right reforms for women (which served to increase women's autonomy and to secure their own personal wealth), Brown suggests that such reforms account for Hawthorne's presentation of domestic womanhood as a solution to the horrific moral and economic problems of inheritance—illustrated through Phoebe's domestic ministrations. Hawthorne examines woman in the context of mid-nineteenth-century property reforms even "more spectacularly" in *Letter*, where his "liberalization of [. . .] American moral and economic conventions of property and family" translates radically into "a virtual legitimation of adultery" as Pearl succeeds to Chillingworth's estate. The novel ends up redeeming the inheritance of adultery, "entitling Pearl to the estate for which her illegitimacy, according to American laws of inheritance, ordinarily would disqualify her." In doing so, "Hawthorne rescinds adultery's power of nullification and restores the safe passage of inheritance" from mother to daughter.

656 Budick, Emily Miller. "James's Portrait of Female Skepticism." *Henry James Review* 12 (1991): 154-158.*

Argues that James's *Portrait of a Lady* (1881) inherits Hawthorne's insights in *Letter* about the implications of traditional patriarchal control over women, but also perpetuates Hawthorne's "error" of casting female skepticism in "decidedly male terms." In other words, James's novel achieves its "most compelling interrelationship" with *Letter* in its depiction of the mother/daughter relationship—most especially with Isabel Archer's questioning of Pansy's paternity (just as Hester occasionally doubts her parental connection to her daughter). Both Hawthorne and James expose the sexism of patriarchy and indicate one of the ways that men have traditionally gained control over women—by knowing with certainty who their children are. In keeping the biological relation of children to maternal parent mysterious, both authors—through their female heroines—comment on "the mystery of love itself" (since both Hester and Isabel ultimately define themselves in relation to their beloved illegitimate daughters, Pearl and Pansy) and "the mystery of [their] own sexual being." But James goes further than Hawthorne does in his critique of patriarchy, "graphically realiz[ing] what is only suggestively implied in Hawthorne's novel: that a primary goal of patriarchal society is self-replication [of the father], perpetuated infinitely into the future, and that women and children are the vehicles of this desire for the unadulterated reproduction of the self."

*For Budick's later essay on the novel as a "family romance," see 720.

657 Dawson, Hugh J. "The Original Illustrations of *The Scarlet Letter*." *Nathaniel Hawthorne Review* 17.2 (1991): 9-13.

Reproduces the fifteen woodcut sketches (by Jules Jacques Veyrassat) that accompanied the dreadfully abridged French translation, *La Lettre rouge A*, that appeared in 1855 by "Old Nick" (the pseudonym for Paul Emile Daurand Forgues.) What surprises Dawson most about the popular French artist's inaccurate renderings is not so much the "manifest neglect of even elementary history research into the architecture and dress of Massachusetts Bay Colony," but Veyrassat's outright "deficiency of draughtsmanship" in rendering Hester and Dimmesdale—both of whom are supposed to be strikingly attractive but here are unrecognizable in their grotesqueness. [For Dawson's earlier essay on this French translation, see 562.]

658   Dreyer, Eileen. "'Confession' in *The Scarlet Letter*." *Journal of American Studies* 25 (1991): 78-81.

Toeing the middle line in her argument that Hawthorne was neither too careless a reader to adapt his sources with any degree of accuracy nor "painstakingly exact" in his historical borrowings (as Michael Colacucio asserts in his 1984 study, *The Province of Piety: Moral History in Hawthorne's Early Tales*), Dreyer suggests that a compromise between the two views is most likely the accurate one. Two historical sources most likely helped Hawthorne in mentally drafting ideas for *Letter*, Thomas Fuller's *The Worthies of England* and Thomas Broughton's *An Historical Dictionary of All Religions*. The latter text connects William Chillingworth to a controversy involving the distinction in Catholic dogma between attrition and contrition—terms that Hawthorne perhaps translates into "penance" and "penitence" and illustrates through the characters of Dimmesdale (penance) and Hester (penitence). This imperfect adaptation indicates that Hawthorne's readings "gave him ideas which he worked into his stories loosely, without undue concern for historical accuracy, so long as the effect [that] his borrowing achieved was satisfactory."

659   Duvall, John N. "The Pleasure of Textual/Sexual Wrestling: Pornography and Heresy in *Roger's Version*." *Modern Fiction Studies* 37 (1991): 81-95.

Duvall inquires into the ways that John Updike engages with "the erotics of reading and writing" in *Roger's Version* (1986) after having been influenced by Roland Barthes' concept of "the pleasures of the text." Recognizing Updike's debt to Barthes "enables a clearer articulation of the nature of Roger's homoerotic desire for Dale, a desire only hinted at in the Dimmesdale-Chillingworth relationship of *Letter*."

660   Fleischner, Jennifer. "Hawthorne and the Politics of Slavery." *Studies in the Novel* 23 (1991): 96-106.

In "the relationship between Hawthorne's own political situation in 1850 and *Letter* is a prototype of the displaced connections among the nation's political situation with regard to slavery in 1850, Hawthorne's own political allegiances, the politics of *Letter*, and the politics of his 'political' writings." Fleischner builds on Jonathan Arac's essay on the "politics of indeterminacy" in *Letter* (see 508) and identifies a series of strategic "interlocking displacements" enacted by Hawthorne to evade the issue of slavery that actually correspond to a pervasive mid-nineteenth-century cultural response to slavery. These oppositions between politics vs. art, public vs. private, and political activist vs. domestic pacifist not only appear in the novel but also lie embedded in Hawthorne's more overt political writings—*Life of Franklin Pierce*, "Chiefly About War Matters," and "The Custom-House"—all of which imply his pro-Union ties and the Northern belief in compromise toward the slavery debate (that no political action is necessary since slavery will die out on its own). To deflect the reader's perception of his stance on slavery (since slavery was such a delicate subject), Hawthorne evades the connection between his art and his politics—even going so far in the prefaces to his romances to insist on "the apolitical nature of art and the distance of the artist from concurrent events." With its emphasis on the split between public and private identity, *Letter* enacts the cultural rift between public and private that was experienced "between federal rights and states rights in the debates over slavery." The novel works out its own political problem regarding the conflict between public and private ties, which proves to be too agonizing for Dimmesdale and which "hushes" Hester's political activism by making her a "Victorian angel of the house."

661   Gollin, Rita K. *"The Scarlet Letter." From Cover to Cover: The Presentation of Hawthorne's Major Romances.* Ed. Richard C. Fyffe. *Essex Institute Historical Collections* 127.1 (1991): 12-30.*

Analyzing the "literary commodity" that *Letter* has bcome since its first edition appeared in 1850, Gollin traces numerous significant editions throughout the past century-and-a-half for their unique characteristics—whether they be patriotic editions, expensive illustrated editions, cheap texts designed for schoolchildren, lurid paperback editions, book club editions, scholarly critical editions, or the Centenary Edition. Paying attention throughout her survey to the marketing strategies employed by publishers, Gollin notes that these editions not only attest to *Letter*'s importance and staying power among successive generations of readers but also illuminate, through countless and varied introductions to the texts, how "each edition embodies the concerns of its period (whether in the time of gilded-age prosperity or the poverty of the Depression years), as when an introduction disseminated in the 1930s discusses Hawthorne's need to support his family, a fifties introduction talks about witchhunts, or an eighties introduction presents an author and a heroine who are victimized by society and yet triumph over it." Ultimately, these texts "amply demonstrate" that *Letter* "remains an intellectual challenge, and that no intelligent reader can be its passive recipient." Essay includes four illustrations.

*The bibliographic citation for this essay appears to contain both journal and book elements, indicating a special issue of *Essex Institute Historical Collections*. See 679 for Peter Hartigan's query about one of the editions Gollin mentions.

662   Gollin, Rita K. "Wim Wenders' *Scarlet Letter*." *Nathaniel Hawthorne Review* 17.2 (1991): 21-22.

Wim Wenders's unusual and yet admirable 1972 film adaptation of *Letter* omits and changes an "astounding" number of crucial scenes and details from the original story (all of which Gollin briefly notes). Among the omissions, for instance, Gollin cites "no scaffold scenes, no midnight meteor, no forest meeting, no removal of Hester's cap or her A, and no claim that 'What we did had a consecration of its own.' Chillingworth does not die, Hester does not return to America, there is no gravestone, no probing of psychological motives, no entry in Hester's mind or Dimmesdale's." In the end, Wenders's version of *Letter* "turns out to be an unusual way of appreciating Hawthorne's larger achievement."

663   Hardy, Donald E. "The Monomythic Fortunate Fall in *The Scarlet Letter*." *Panjab University Research Bulletin* 22 (1991): 3-11.

Within the mythic structure of *Letter*, the progress of Dimmesdale's "Fortunate Fall" parallels the structure of Joseph Campbell's "monomythic journey" in *The Hero with a Thousand Faces*. Hardy outlines Campbell's myth (which consists of a call to adventure, a threshold crossing, and a descent into the underworld, where dark adventures culminate in a supreme ordeal) and traces the stages of the journey in *Letter*, finding that Dimmesdale successfully completes the journey from innocence to experience through the combined help of Hester and Pearl and in spite of Chillingworth's interference.

664   Madsen, Deborah L. "'A for Abolition': Hawthorne's Bond-Servant and the Shadow of Slavery." *Journal of American Studies* 25 (1991): 255-259.

Finds affinities between Hawthorne's "Chiefly About War-Matters" and *Letter* in terms of Hawthorne's indictment of slavery (commodifying both blacks and whites) and his attitude about the problematic, one-sided way that our Founding Fathers unanimously defined a modern, democratic America. Madsen parallels Hawthorne's historical outlook on black slavery in "War-Matters" with white bondage in *Letter* (the latter illustrated through the character of Governor Bellingham's white, seven-year bond-servant), and finds that both are informed by an awareness of the "doubleness of the American myth" in their complex interpretations of colonial history—which signify "freedom for some and the denial of natural rights for others." Denying or suppressing the "semantic potential" of America was "the rhetorical equivalent of slavery" for Hawthorne, who offers in *Letter* "a critique of the whole issue of 'Fathers' and their right to determine identity." Dimmesdale makes Pearl into a "commodity," literally attributing to her an "exchange value" that is assessed in terms of the reputation he must surrender if he is to acknowledge her. Once Pearl is "defined," however, she experiences, as does her mother, personal "freedom within social constraints." Unlike Dimmesdale, Pearl and Hester become comfortable determining their own identities, a determination that translates into Hawthorne's hope on a national scale: that "the opportunity for self-determination" "may liberate America into genuine democracy."

665   Marks, Alfred H.   "*The Scarlet Letter* and Tieck's 'The Elves.'" *Nathaniel Hawthorne Review* 17.2 (1991): 1, 3-5.

The similarities in plot and imagery between Tieck's "The Elves" and Hawthorne's *Letter* are "pronounced." "The Elves" actually lent "a subdued tinge of the wild and wonderful" to other Hawthorne writings that were composed between 1843 and 1851 (such as *The American Notebooks*, "The Snow-Image," and "Feathertop"), but nowhere is the combined hellish/angelic elfin behavior more apparent than in *Letter*. Marks compares Tieck's Elfrida, who is "associated with roses, the color red, and fire," with the elf-like character of Pearl, and further notes parallels between the stories that involve secret forest meetings, secret symbols, hidden identities, and magical brooks.

666   Parulis, Cheryl.   "Hawthorne's Genre of Romance: The Seduction of Betrayal in *The Scarlet Letter*." *Collages and Bricolages: The Journal of International Writing* 5 (1991): 108-116.

Wonders whether Hawthorne has "transcended the stereotypes" of women or "merely reinforced them." Hester embraces her "otherness" in order to be excluded from "the whole system of ancient prejudice," "refusing to be defined by sterotypical inclusiveness." Yet, despite the fact that she is the "forerunner of the new woman"—and that "her story and struggle are an early development in the evolution of a truly feminine consciousness not completely overshadowed by patriarchy"—Hawthorne is unfortunately too "bound by his 'maleness'" to let Hester "be all she could be." Thus the answer to the question of whether Hawthorne transcends the stereotypes or reinforces them is "in some ways [that Hawthorne] has done neither" and "in other ways he has done both."

667   Stich, Klaus P. "Hawthorne's Intimations of Alchemy." *ATQ* New Series 5 (1991): 15-30.

Examines references to alchemy—usually not taken seriously by critics because they are brief—in Hawthorne's fiction, focusing particularly on those found in "The Great Carbuncle," *Letter*, and *Marble Faun*. When such references are viewed in light of explorations by nineteenth-century alchemy scholars Ethan Allen Hitchcock and Mary Ann Atwood, as well as by Carl Jung in the twentieth century, all of whom thought of alchemy as "hermetic philosophy" (with its focus on the ancient dictum "know thyself"), Hawthorne's multiple and ambiguous meanings can be seen to have their basis, at least partly, in alchemy. In *Letter*, "alchemy not only accommodates the other important meanings of the letter A," but also helps to explain the principle characters: Chillingworth and Dimmesdale represent "the scientific and religious extremes of alchemy" (healing and controlling others with their respective knowledge of science and philosophy), Hester represents the union of their "powers" (and is symbolically associated with the strength of Isis), and Pearl is the "healing agent, without whom Hester could not have fused her powers of intellect and feeling."

668   Stryz, Jan. "The Other Ghost in *Beloved*: The Spectre of *The Scarlet Letter*." *Genre* 24 (1991): 417-434.

In its attempt to articulate an African-American aesthetic, *Beloved* (1988) falls into the tradition of American Romance—which dismantles and reconstructs social definitions, and redefines space and time. *Beloved* employs images and elements from *Letter* partially to create "both culturally authorized and unauthorized forms of expression" and to wage "a battle against white patriarchal authority." So *Beloved* is "haunted" by a "literary father" (Hawthorne) after all, including several images that generate from *Letter* (such as Sethe's wanting to murder her little girl to save the child from her mother's fate, a similar use of flashbacks, and a red-velvet obsessed Hester/Pearl character-type named Amy ["A-me"] who quests after her dead mother's former home in Boston). But *Beloved* dissociates those images from its source and ultimately displaces the image of the father for the body of the mother.

669   Winnington, G. Peter. "Peake's Thing and Hawthorne's Pearl." *Peake Studies* (2.3 (1991): 15-33.

Tracing several character similarities between Mervyn Peake's *Titus* books and *Letter* (and noting that the "darkness of passion and smoldering revolt" underlies both texts), Winnington parallels Hester and Keda, Pearl and the Thing, and Chillingworth and Steerpike. "After their passionless first marriage to an elderly man, both Hester and Keda express their sensuous natures by behavior that causes them to be ostracized. After the birth of their respective illegitimate daughters [who are mischievous, wild, and associated with witchcraft and bird-like behavior], Keda commits suicide, and Hester is tempted to as well." Similarities also abound between Chillingworth and Steerpike, since in addition to being dark alter egos for other characters (Dimmesdale and Titus), they are both physically deformed, pale-faced scholars and druggists who "act diabolically when their victims are helpless within their power," until their parasitic function is exhausted. So many remarkable parallels do not lead Winnington to conclude that Hawthorne influenced Peake, however, since they both worked within the genre of Romance and "[drew] on the same source in the human heart" and "on the [archetypal] figures that inhabit our unconscious."

1992

Books

670   Scharnhorst, Gary. *The Critical Response to Nathaniel Hawthorne's The Scarlet Letter*. New York: Greenwood Press, 1992. 268 pp.

This valuable collection, number two in a series of "Critical Responses in Arts and Letters," details "the politics of Hawthorne's literary reputation" and provides a chronological record of excerpted highlights (too numerous to mention individually) in the critical response to *Letter*. The volume contains a helpful introduction to the history of the novel's reception and critical commentary over the years; a brief recapitulation of *Letter*'s background and composition history, early critical reception in America and Britain; a reprinting of excerpts from the major critical reviews and essays that have collectively worked to create the novel's classic reputation from 1869-1990;* reviews of stage and film adaptations from 1876 to 1934; a selected bibliography that lists "the most frequently cited and accessible modern scholarship on *Letter*," and an index. Scharnhorst concludes that the remarkable durability of the novel is largely due to the fact that "it has permitted such a wide diversity of readings." Over the years it has been seen as "both a naughty novel and a moral allegory of sin and suffering, both a burlesque and a covertly sympathetic treatment of nineteenth-century feminism and transcendentalism, both a satire of Puritanism and a reliable history of it."

*One essay, "Paradigm and Paramour: Role Reversal in *The Scarlet Letter*," by Marilyn Mueller Wilton, is original to the volume and presented in its entirety in Scharnhorst's collection. See the individual entry below (676).

671   Schiff, James A.   *Updike's Version: Rewriting The Scarlet Letter*. Columbia: U of Missouri P, 1992.

Examines John Updike's "Scarlet Letter" trilogy, composed of *A Month of Sundays* (1975), *Roger's Version* (1986), and *S* (1988), in order to explore the "intertextual dialogue" between the two authors. Each novel is told from the perspective of a contemporary version of one of Hawthorne's protagonists from *Letter* (respectively, Dimmesdale, Chillingworth, and Hester), and sets out to expand, update, satirize, and re-write Hawthorne's text. Schiff detects that Updike expresses "a mixture of devotion [. . .] and aggression" toward his predecessor, both paying homage to Hawthorne and parodying/questioning his authority and moral stance at the same time. In the trilogy, Updike not only rejects "the warfare between body and spirit" that was so central to Hawthorne, but satirizes the former's protagonists for their fragility, prudishness, and self-deception.   He transforms *Letter* "by affirming the corporeal impulse and thus reconciling body and soul," recasting Hawthorne's three "divided" protagonists and demonstrating how the "mythic" American situation persists: "that of individuals struggling within themselves and against their communities in an effort to shake off the past and reinvent the world."   [Schiff recommends two other book-length studies that also examine the relationship of Updike and Hawthorne: Samuel Chase Coale's *In Hawthorne's Shadow: American Romance from Melville to Mailer* (Lexington: UP of Kentucky, 1985) and Donald J. Greiner's *Adultery in the American Novel: Updike, James, and Hawthorne* (see 490).]

Essays and Studies in Books

672   Barszcz, James. "Hawthorne, Emerson, and the Forms of the Frontier." *Desert, Garden, Margin, Range: Literature on the American Frontier*. New York: Twayne, 1992. 44-54.

Argues that there is no real dichotomy between wilderness and civilzation for both Hawthorne and Ralph Waldo Emerson, who assert in their works that the frontier is "less a matter of woods than words; it exists at the borders of the perspectives created by language." Both authors, in fact, saw a "radical continuity" between town and forest. For Hawthorne in *Letter*, the real frontier lies on the edge of human consciousness. In the forest scene, Hester and Dimmesdale's plan to escape the moral and legal codes of the Puritans necessarily fails because the frontier does not actually differ from civilization. They "cannot escape urges of the will and imagination that have shaped the civilzation they would flee," and thus the frontier is unattainable as a "site for social life that is "new, natural, or free." Hawthorne's wilderness, therefore, like Emerson's to a large extent, "serves only as a stage for expressions of human desire."

673   Kramer, Michael P. "Beyond Symbolism: Philosophy of Language in *The Scarlet Letter.*" *Imagining Language in America: From the Revolution to the Civil War.* Princeton: Princeton UP, 1992. 162-197.

While many critics (beginning with Charles Feidelson, Jr., in 1953 [see 21]) have suggested the importance of language to *Letter*, no one has explained clearly how or why language is important to the novel. John T. Irwin (389), Millicent Bell (425), and David Van Leer (496) are misguided in their mutual assumption that the novel "thematicizes language by foregrounding and problematizing the relation between signs and their referents" and that "Hawthorne's political aim is to free Hester, as it were, from the prison house of Puritan language." That Hawthorne "encourages, frustrates, and generally complicates attempts to uncover and generate meanings argues for a broader view of the novel's linguisticity." Building an empiricist argument to suggest the ways that language constitutes political and social life, Kramer uses the filtered-out language of Dimmesdale's emotionally-charged Election-Day sermon to illustrate how words often impede rather than facilitate communication. Dimmesdale's true meaning is translated unambiguously by his non-verbal communication, revealing his "profoundly ambivalent feelings about the Puritans he serves and the woman he loves." The sermon thus answers Hawthorne's own challenge in "The Custom-House"—that public discourse can communicate the "inmost Me." Kramer then contrasts the languages of "The Custom-House" and *Letter* in terms of the "discontinuous" aspects of American experience, arguing that the novel "takes us back to the very origins of American society" and to a world of potential linguistic intimacy in which public and private languages, like natural and civil liberty, were not so separate. In the end, just like "The Devil in Manuscript," "The Minister's Black Veil," and Hawthorne's *Love Letters*, the novel attempts "to discover and communicate meanings—to explore the possibilities of language as a human activity" rather than to champion a particular mode of representation. [For an essay that provides a historical reason to explain Dimmesdale's "filtered out" language, see M. X. Lesser's "Dimmesdale's Wordless Sermon" (323).]

674 Millington, Richard H. "Romance as Revision: *The Scarlet Letter*." *Practicing Romance: Narrative Form and Cultural Engagement in Hawthorne's Fiction.* Princeton: Princeton UP, 1992. 59-104.

Paying close attention to Hawthorne's narrative tactics and synthesizing Freudian psychoanalysis, New Historicism, reader-response theory, and other critical methodologies, Millington views Hawthorne's strategies in his romances as an attempt to find in authorship a valid form of cultural authority, and sees Hawthorne's "narrative practice" of romance as a type of cultural engagement that examines and revises "our affiliation to our culture." Millington identifies a "pattern of return and a series of recurrences" in *Letter* that "make manifest [this] drama of cultural affiliation." The novel attempts to locate the "meaning of living within a community," or how the self functions within a culture and learns to distinguish between "constraint" and "choice" through a series of achieved and failed acts of revision. Whereas Dimmesdale is too inscribed by the conscience-ridden narrative of his culture to make such a distinction, Hester, by her return at novel's end, revises her life by forging a new commonality in the "romance-space" at the margins of culture and becomes Hawthorne's " representative of a revisionary act of mind" (a freedom of mind that avoids solipsism). "By returning to the community and resuming the letter 'of her own free will,' Hester joins an understanding of limitation to an act of choice; she remains faithful to her acts of rebellion by choosing again the cultural context that gave those acts their meaning."

675 Segal, Naomi. "Matrilinear Mothers." *The Adulteress's Child: Authorship and Desire in the Nineteenth-Century Novel.* Cambridge: Polity, 1992. 115-189.

Studying "mothers and their children in the nineteenth-century novel of adultery," Segal groups together *Madame Bovary* (1857), *Anna Karenina* (1873), *Letter*, and *Effi Briest* (1895) as four male-authored texts in which "bad women have daughters." The mother-daughter pair in *Letter* (pp. 146-166) represents punishment as well as potential knowledge. As a marginalized and "uncanny" couple united by the scarlet letter that "declares their femininity against the seething background of their Puritan world," Hester and Pearl (not Hester and Dimmesdale) are at the very center of the novel. When Dimmesdale dies after claiming Pearl as his own, however, so does the "impossible idyll of family" die, along with "the unity of mother and daughter." Pearl hereafter transforms into her father's child, finding and losing him in an instant, becoming "cleansed at last of the bloody birthright which made her a mother's child." Hester is thus "marked out," and "motherhood, at the end, is loneliness."

676 Wilton, Marilyn Mueller. "Paradigm and Paramour: Role Reversal in *The Scarlet Letter*." *The Critical Response to Nathaniel Hawthorne's The Scarlet Letter*. Ed. Gary Scharnhorst. New York: Greenwood Press, 1992. 220-232.

Prepared specifically for Scharnhorst's volume (see 670), this essay "recogniz[es] Hester Prynne as the 'hero' and Arthur Dimmesdale as the 'heroine,'" asserting "Hester's dominance in the plot and accord[ing] Dimmesdale an important but less essential role." Wilton acknowledges that her view of Hester as the paradigmatic "hero" and Dimmesdale as the passive "paramour" and "heroine" is not original (citing Nina Baym [in 506] and Margaret Olofson Thickstun [in 573] for previously recognizing this role reversal), but she contends that she *is* the first to examine that role reversal of conventional male/female literary roles in depth and in parallel comparison. "Because [Hester] embodies the quintessential attributes of the traditional hero and is central to the plot, [she] can be legitimately referred to as the hero of *Letter*, while Dimmesdale's anti-heroic qualities and secondary function subordinate his status to hers."

Journal Essays and Notes

677 Budick, Emily Miller. "Sacvan Bercovitch, Stanley Cavell, and the Romance Theory of American Fiction." *PMLA* 107 (1992): 78-91.

Challenging the "once dominant" romance theory of American fiction (and specifically its disengagement from sociopolitical issues, as theorized by Richard Chase [in 55] and others), Budick employs Americanist philosopher Stanley Cavell's theories on speech and applies them to *Letter* as a way of testing Sacvan Bercovitch's "New Americanist" conception of American ideology in the romance (see 635), particularly on the question of reading the ending as an illustration of textual "dissent" or "consent." Cavell's theory of "aversion" assists in reopening "what Bercovitch sees as the closed ending of a text like *Letter*," showing that Hester's return actually expresses her simultaneous protest *and* consent, and that Hawthorne had similarly established "a richly aversive relation to America."

678 Coale, Samuel [Chase]. "*The Scarlet Letter* as Icon." *ATQ* 6 (1992): 251-262.

Analyzes the "psychology of idolatry" that is not only central to Hawthorne's quasireligious vision and technique as an American romance writer but also symptomatic of the mid-nineteenth-century rage for "tablerappings, mesmerism, and spiritualism" (with the scarlet letter reading "like a self-induced hypnotic trance" that possesses its observers in almost demonic fashion). Hawthorne believed that certain irreducible images (like the letter "A") are not just powerful and enigmatic, but easily take on iconic status, "becoming objects of an almost uncritical devotion" that speak to the human psyche's need to create "sacred" objects. Hawthorne enacts the mode of romance, in fact, to explore this sometimes dangerous process, this "re-enactment of turning images or objects into icon." Creating mystic symbols was Hawthorne's way of "trying to re-create the very enigmatic nature that lies within all perception," his literary method "of making the enigma of perception more visible and palpable." Hawthorne extends the meaning of the icon, fetish, or idol when he illustrates through the Puritans the self-destructive danger of shifting the idolized icon to the individual self (since the Puritans described themselves as "living icons" of the faith). [For more on Mesmerism, see Coale's later studies, 722 and 817.]

679   Hartigan, Peter. *"The Scarlet Letter* and the *Riverside Literature Series."* *Nathaniel Hawthorne Review* 18.1 (1992): 22.

Offers a "query" as to whether Rita K. Gollin's information is accurate in her 1991 cultural study of numerous editions of *Letter* (see 661) when she refers to an 1883 edition in the popular *Riverside Literature Series* that is accompanied "not only [by] a brief introduction but [by] explanatory notes and study questions." In his own studies, Hartigan found no such volume—but he did find an 1899 text of *The Custom House and Main Street* in the *Riverside Literature Series* that is accompanied with an introduction and notes. [While working on this entry, I contacted Dr. Gollin and learned that she has been unable to answer Hartigan's query because she could not locate the original document that she believes listed an 1883 Riverside edition of *Letter*. In my own research, I have located only two 1883 editions of *Letter*: *The Scarlet Letter, A Romance* (Edinburgh: William Paterson, 1883) and *Hawthorne's Scarlet Letter* (Boston: Houghton, Mifflin, 1883. Illustrated by F. O. C. Darley, and with an "Introductory Note" by George Parsons). Whether this latter edition *is* the "School text" belonging to the Riverside series that was designed for school children is unclear.]

680   Kazin, Alfred. "The Opera of *The Scarlet Letter." New York Review of Books* 39 (October 8, 1992): 16, 53-55.

Kazin asks in his opening sentence, "Why is there no opera of *The Scarlet Letter?"* Unaware that there *have* been operas based on *Letter* (see 84, 381, 710, and 825), Kazin emphasizes the operatic characteristics of the novel, which include an "elaborately stylized and formal performance," incessant theatrical images and overwhelming images and symbols, and the near "violent" contrast between the drab Puritans and the electric, elegantly gorgeous Hester. Even the narrator's presence could be easily translated into opera, Kazin observes. The "dark and solemn music of [Hawthorne's] unrelenting commentary on the story [. . .] intervenes in the way an orchestra does at the opera—setting the emotional background and reinforcing it at crucial points."

681   Lease, Benjamin. "Alfred Weber on 'The Custom-House' Sketch: A Supplementary Comment." *Nathaniel Hawthorne Review* 18.2 (1992): 27.

Validates his brief assertion that "Hawthorne had a very shrewd conception of one segment of the public he wanted to reach" with "The Custom-House" by citing Alfred Weber's essay (see 689) on the framing functions of the introductory sketch (in which Weber confirms that Hawthorne's playful blending of "factuality with fancy" was designed to attract the reading public). Hawthorne was tickled that his "vengeful sketch" outraged his political enemies—to whom it was clearly addressed, a fact made unmistakable given the content of the "Preface to the Second Edition, where Hawthorne "makes clear how much he relished the palpable hit he had scored."

682   Li, Haipeng. "Hester Prynne and the Folk Art of Embroidery." *University of Mississippi Studies in English* 10 (1992): 80-85.

Hawthorne was influenced by the folk art of embroidery that was popular in his day, and he associates the symbolic art with his heroine in *Letter* to help illustrate the nature of her character (publicly submissive, privately rebellious). As a highly skilled and important folk artist in her Puritan community, Hester becomes "a form of art in herself," challenging the restrictive Puritan society with her luxurious "personal art and the poetry of her needle."

683   Moore, Thomas R. "Seized by the Button: Rhetorical Positioning at 'The Custom-House' Door." *Nathaniel Hawthorne Review* 18.1 (1992): 1-5.

Examines Hawthorne's "opaque" prose style (as opposed to a "transparent" prose style that is plain and direct) in "The Custom-House," suggesting that Hawthorne's self-conscious rhetorical technique makes for a text that is "marked by veils, shadows, and shifting symbolic imagery and mediated by a capricious sense of the truth." Blurring the boundaries between fiction and non-fiction, Hawthorne calls attention to his elusive and playful style even in his initial two paragraphs, as if to warn the reader that he will be misled and misinformed. Reader-response theory, according to Moore, best explains the tension between author and reader as it is presented in "The Custom-House," because the reader is "forced into the transaction" of deciphering the truth from fiction and is "conducted to the deeper truth of the romance."

684   O'Keefe, Richard R. "An Echo of Emerson in Hawthorne's 'The Custom-House'?" *Nathaniel Hawthorne Review* 18.1 (1992): 9-11.

Compares a list of last names in the next-to-last paragraph of "The Custom-House" (Pingree, Phillips, Shepard, Upton, Kimball, Bertram, and Hunt) to a similar listing of names in Ralph Waldo Emerson's poem "Hamatreya" and deduces—after citing Emerson's likely poetic influence on Hawthorne and exploring phonetic and thematic parallels between the lists—that Hawthorne's "rhythmic prose" in this case mimics Emerson's "prosey verse."

685   Schiff, James A. "Updike's *Roger's Version*: Re-Visualizing *The Scarlet Letter*." *South Atlantic Review* 57.4 (1992): 59-76.

"One of the primary features of *Roger's Version* [1986] that has gone largely unnoticed is Updike's appropriation of the metaphor of visualization from *Letter*." Visualization is not only the central metaphor in *Roger's Version*, however; it also figures largely in Hawthorne's text, which similarly "highlight[s] the ambiguity of vision and the difficulty of seeing clearly." In retelling *Letter* through the eyes of a modern-day Chillingworth (Roger Lambert), John Updike expands upon Hawthorne's tale, liberating "vision" from Victorian ethics and permitting the reader to gratify his voyeuristic urge to see the sex act to which Hawthorne only alludes. Updike also undoes the traditional body/soul division stressed by Hawthorne, emphasizing rather the importance of corporeality, and argues in his novel "that modern technology and knowledge have increased the human possibilities for vision."

686   Schiff, James A. "Updike's *Scarlet Letter* Trilogy: Recasting an American Myth." *Studies in American Fiction* 20 (1992): 17-31.

Regarding the *Scarlet Letter* trilogy, Schiff wonders first why John Updike chose to rewrite Hawthorne's classic and, second, why Updike chose Hawthorne. Updike was attracted to the mythic mode (to which he believes *Letter* belongs) and felt akin to his predecessor, who not only lived in roughly the same geographical location near Boston but whose themes and conflicts Updike shares. Updike also chose Hawthorne as a model so that he might align himself with a tradition of American "masters" and give a "metaphysical darkening" to his own art, "a more sustained reflection upon death and solitude, and a growing interest in voyeurism and vicariously experienced life." In an experimental and postmodern fashion, Updike expands, updates, and satirizes *Letter*, not only calling into question its authority and moral stance but also rejecting the warfare between body and soul that Hawthorne emphasizes— parodying Hawthorne's three major characters for their fragility, prudishness, and self-deception. His revision also appropriates and builds upon two concepts stressed in D. H. Lawrence's treatment of the novel (in *Studies in Classic American Literature* [EC18]): Hawthorne's duplicity and the American quest for renewal. *A Month of Sundays* (1974), *Roger's Version* (1986), and *S.* (1988) thus recast Hawthorne's three protagonists and demonstrate how the "mythic" American situation persists: "individuals struggling within themselves and against their communities in an effort to shake off the past and reinvent the world."

687 Sterling, Laurie A. "Paternal Gold: Translating Inheritance in *The Scarlet Letter*." *ATQ* 6 (1992). 15-30.

Observing that "The Custom-House" and *Letter* both center on "the [economic] issues of valuation and naming," Sterling argues that Hawthorne rejects the authority of the paternal in both, contemptible of the fact that paternal authority in seventeenth- and nineteenth-century America falsely claims "natural," transcendent power to control value assessment and "to name, to define and confine value through lineage and inheritance." Hawthorne recognized that such paternal power reduced complexity into the conventional, artificial, superficial, and debilitating terms of accepted, authorized structures. In "The Custom-House" and the novel proper, Hawthorne addresses the inability of paternal inheritance to fix or name value, blurs the ideas of legitimate heritage and authority (calling attention to the fact that patriarchal authority is not transcendent but man-made, socially and politically inscribed), and finally works to establish a new lineage. Like Hawthorne in the introductory sketch, Pearl is intent on establishing a new heritage for herself as "a citizen of somewhere else," accepting her mother's broad and speculative notion of her value and thus rejecting the authority of the paternal to limit her value, legitimize her by naming her, and then determine her destiny.

688 Swann, Charles. "A Hardy Debt to Hawthorne?" *Notes and Queries* 39 (1992): 188-189.

Although there is no evidence that Thomas Hardy read *Letter*, a scene from *Tess of the d'Urbervilles* (1891) in which Angel Clare's misery

342

throws him into a demoniacal mood is reminiscent of chapter 20 of *Letter* when Dimmesdale entertains fiendish thoughts on his way home from his forest meeting with Hester. Another similarity occurs when Hester and Tess ask their lovers if they think a reunion in the afterlife is likely— although the responses are slightly different (Dimmesdale gives a negative answer to Hester while Angel kisses Tess to avoid a negative reply).

689   Weber, Alfred. "The Framing Functions of Hawthorne's 'The Custom-House' Sketch." *Nathaniel Hawthorne Review* 18.1 (1992): 5-8.

Proposing to answer the question of the relationship of "The Custom-House" to the historical romance it prefaces, Weber asserts that *Letter* is a "framed romance" consisting of two parts: the framing story of "The Custom-House" (involving the manuscript discovery, Surveyor Pue, and Pue's relationship to the narrator) and the "Conclusion," the last chapter of the romance. In addition to discussing Hawthorne's five different purposes for employing the "frame" device, Weber also discusses how the function of "The Custom-House" was changed (despite remaining essentially the same) when Hawthorne learned that it would only preface *Letter* and not "Old-Time Legends" too, as originally planned. Weber further addresses how Hawthorne's "theoretical reflections on the workings of the imaginary and the nature of the romance" in "The Custom-House" "are at the same time a commentary on the double nature of the introductory sketch"—not only as an idealized, imaginative autobiography, but also as an "artist tale" or "Kunstlererzählung"—in which "the position of the artist in his society and the problems of his craft are the central themes." [See 681 for Benjamin Lease's "Supplementary Comment" to Weber's essay.]

1993

Essays and Studies in Books

690   Barnett, Louise K. "Private and Public Speech in *The Scarlet Letter*." *Authority and Speech: Language, Society, and the Self in the American Novel*. Athens: U of Georgia P, 1993. 43-58.

Revised and updated version of her seminal 1983 article on "Speech and Society in *The Scarlet Letter*" (see 440). In this book on "the changing relationship of personal and social expression in the direct discourse of fictive speakers in the American novel," Barnett examines *Letter* for its demonstration of "confidence in the resources of language to communicate meaning"—or its articulation of "a world outside itself" and achievement of "congruity between intention and utterance in fictive speech." She takes issue with Millicent Bell (425) and Evan Carton (484) for their interpretations of the referentiality and "indeterminacy" of Hawthorne's language, arguing that the scarlet letter has one real, stable meaning that is not forgotten throughout the novel—its original one (adultery). If Hawthorne has lost linguistic confidence in anything, it is not in the "sacred grounding of signs" but in "society's interpretation of this 'sacred grounding,' its reification of signs in ways that stifle the human spirit and thus force individuals into deceptive postures and untruthful speech."

691   Bercovitch, Sacvan. "The Return of Hester Prynne." *The Rites of Assent: Transformations in the Symbolic Construction of America.* New York: Routledge, 1993. 194-245.

Building on ideas from his previous essays "The A-Politics of Ambiguity in *The Scarlet Letter*" (575) and "Hawthorne's A-Morality of Compromise" (576), Bercovitch takes on the novel once more to discuss its "fusion of process and telos" that "transmutes opposition into complementarity" and represents the "American liberal symbology." While Hawthorne's meanings may be endless, the scarlet letter itself has a very definitive meaning, purpose, and goal—or else Hawthorne would not be able to emphasize as he does, in the famous one-sentence paragraph, that "the scarlet letter had not done its office." The very coherence of the symbol lies in its capacity to combine both process on one hand, purpose and closure on the other. Hester's return enacts this same sort of fusion in that it "effectually reconciles the various antinomies that surround her throughout the novel: nature and culture, sacred and profane, light and shadow, memory and hope, repression and desire, angel and adulteress, her dream of love and the demands of history and community." The dissenter becomes agent of socialization, reversing the alienating effects of her letter and looking "forward to a brighter period that relates her most intimate hopes to moral and social progress." Her return also anticipates Hawthorne's recovery of Puritan New England, his ability to reverse the disruptive effects of political office by reaching back through the "A" to national origins.

692   Dolis, John. "Being(-)in(-)the-world." *The Style of Hawthorne's Gaze: Regarding Subjectivity.* Tuscaloosa: U of Alabama P, 1993. 138-211.

This subchapter (pp. 170-195), which focuses on Hawthorne's visual style, or the visually deconstructive aspect of Hawthorne's imagination, expands on Dolis's 1984 essay "Hawthorne's Letter" (see 457). Theoretically indebted to Freud, Lacan, Heidegger, Derrida, and Merleau-Ponty, Dolis argues that Hester and, especially, Pearl search for and succeed in finding an origin of meaning (Being), and this origin ultimately resides in language, the starting point for the imaginative, fictive, construction of self in relation to the world (the Other). Thus, for both characters, this origin is implicated in the letter 'A' (for Author-ity), which Hester constructs at the outset and which is concealed in the middle of Pearl's name, waiting to be disclosed in the concluding scaffold scene when Dimmesdale (Arthur/Authority) gives Pearl his name as father, thus overcoming his repression and impotence, twin constituents of the Puritan heritage traced from "The Custom-House" through the scarlet letter tale. Within the Custom House of dead letters, Hawthorne "is provoked to build, to dwell, to construct 'A' text (of) itSelf—the meaning of its being. The office of (the) 'custom' (house) but serves to distinguish Hawthorne from both the Other (readers) and himSelf, to inaugurate the repetition of *The Letter* as it goes its various rounds within the symbolic structure of discourse. Hawthorne's writing *is* this house, the House of Fiction, which constructs a passage(way/*weg*) between self and other: intercourse with the world . . . . Hawthorne's House of Fiction is nothing less than Language, what Heidegger refers to as the house or temple of being."

693 Gilmore, Michael T. "Hawthorne and the Making of the Middle Class." *Discovering Difference: Contemporary Essays in American Culture.* Ed. Christoph K. Lohmann. Bloomington: Indiana UP, 1993. 88-104.*

Taking issue with the critical consensus that class is not an issue in canonical antebellum American literature, as well as with the popular view that Hawthorne contributed to a stabilized and conservative view of the middle class, Gilmore turns to *Letter* to show how Hawthorne "maps the emergence of middle-class identity and simultaneously reveals the self-contradictory and unsettled nature of the new configuration." Far from being a coherent transcript of class sympathies, the novel "undoes its own synchronizations of gender roles, private and public spheres, and socioeconomic categories." In other words, *Letter* illustrates in particular how gender threatens to disrupt nineteenth-century middle-class formation by refusing fixed gender roles in his characterization of Hester and Dimmesdale: "the middle-class mother [Hester] assumes a relation to the social like that of a free-market individualist, while the middle-class father [Dimmesdale] embraces feminized sentiment." This rejection of fixed gender roles not only advertises a problem in Hawthorne's attitude toward middle-class identity and his uncertainty about his own class status, but also reveals tensions endemic to nineteenth-century capitalism and, further, suggests that Hawthorne had "an equivocal sexual identity that inclined toward the female."

*This essay is reprinted in *Rethinking Class: Literary Studies and Social Formations* (Eds. Wai-Chee Dimock and Michael T. Gilmore. New York: Columbia UP, 1994. 215-238).

694   Gupta, R. K. "Point of View in *The Scarlet Letter.*" *Mark Twain and Nineteenth-Century American Literature.* Ed. E. Nageswara Rao. Hyderabad: American Studies Research Centre, 1993. 79-90.

Attempts to locate the specific "literary-textual-source" of the novel's ambiguities (especially Hawthorne's ambivalence towards Hester) in terms of narrative technique. The narrative voice in the novel is not that of Hawthorne, as most critics erroneously assume, but of a "created figure" whose trustworthiness Hawthorne consistently undercuts to reveal the narrator's unreliable nature. The resulting conflict between the romantic, dramatic presentation of the tale and the narrator's conventional, moralistic commentary is the prime source of the "nagging" ambiguities in the depiction of Hester and an all-important feature of the narrative technique in the novel. [For other treatments of narrative voice that Gupta claims have problems of interpretation, see Ernest Sandeen (135), Marshall Van Deusen (196), Seymour Katz (222), David Stouck (278), Elaine Tuttle Hansen (337), John G. Bayer (397), John Carlos Rowe (403), Claudia D. Johnson (407), Daniel Cottom (427), James Walter (531), Zelda Bronstein (542), and Monika Elbert (598 and 614).]

695   Herbert, T. Walter. *Dearest Beloved: The Hawthornes and the Making of the Middle-Class Family.* Berkeley: U of California P, 1993.

This "mutual reading of Hawthorne's biography and art" combines a psycho-cultural family biography and a New Historicist exposé of the "torments intrinsic to the domestic ideal" that dominated nineteenth-century middle-class marriage. Part three describes the Hawthornes' "Marital Politics" as typical of nineteenth-century American couples and then goes on in chapters eleven and twelve, "Double Marriage, Double Adultery" (pp. 184-198) and "Domesticity as Redemption" (pp. 199-211), to show how Hawthorne's own joyful/torturous domestic situation influenced *Letter*. Herbert suggests that the torments and "interlocking emotional contradictions" suffered by Hester, Dimmesdale, Chillingworth, and Pearl in the novel are actually quite "characteristic of nineteenth-century family life" in which the domestic ideal was sought and families attempted to reconcile the conflict between worldly requirements and the claims of the heart. Chapter 11 discusses ways in which faithfulness and adultery are interfused in Hester's marriages to Chillingworth (legal marriage) and Dimmesdale (spiritual marriage), as well as explores the character dynamics of Chillingworth and Dimmesdale, who both function as inseparable opposites, as figures of "split manhood" that further dramatize "a torment endemic to the sexual intimacy of middle-class marriage." Chapter 12, which continues the discussion of *Letter*'s dilemmas of split manhood and true womanhood, finds Hester's commitment to her spiritual marriage to be a "parable of redemptive spiritual intercourse." Her love for Dimmesdale not only rescues the enfeebled minister from his own delibilitated effeminacy, but enables her to transcend her own "manlike" qualities and recover her "true" womanhood—and even paves the way to the final redemptive bonus of delivering Pearl from her own unreal existence.

696   Loving, Jerome. "Hawthorne's Awakening in the Customhouse." *Lost in the Customhouse.* Iowa City: U of Iowa P, 1993. 19-34.

Of the twelve canonized writers examined (from Washington Irving to Theodore Dreiser), each undergoes a spiritual/psychological awakening that proceeds a period in which the "nothingness of existence" is experienced. For Hawthorne, the proper "frame of experience" that allowed him to pass through the "customhouse" of his imagination* to create the free-spirited, complex character of Hester involved his grief following the customhouse firing and the death of his mother. Ironically, although Hawthorne had "lost his head" in the metaphorical customhouse—treading dangerous moral ground in permitting Hester and Dimmesdale to explore freely the "Dark Wood of his imagination" in the forest scenes—he unfortunately found it again when he paused in completing the novel's last three chapters to write the "Custom-House" sketch. As a result of his taking a break to write the conservative, socially-minded introduction, Hester, Dimmesdale, and Hawthorne emerge "safely" from the "Dark Wood"—without "affrighting" readers—as (respectively) priest, nun, and "masked" author.

*Loving uses the customhouse metaphor throughout his book to refer to the antinomian, "baggage-free" spirit of all the American authors discussed.

697   Oleksy, Elżbieta H. "Existential Pathos: *The Scarlet Letter.*" *Plight in Common: Hawthorne and Percy.* New York: Peter Lang, 1993. 37-71.

This comparative study cites "strong psychological and spiritual affinities" between the major novels of Hawthorne and twentieth-century writer Walker Percy, setting up in chapter one a comparison between *Letter* and *The Moviegoer* (1961). (In other chapters Olesky notes parallels between *House of the Seven Gables* and *Lancelot, Marble Faun* and *The Second Coming.*) Olesky views Hawthorne as a precursor of literary existentialism and imposes a Kierkegaardian "structure" onto Hester's experience, suggesting its progressive movement toward an "existential pathos" or a "vanishing telos" (an unattainable goal) that advances in stages: resignation, suffering, guilt, repentance, and faith. The affinities between *Letter* and *The Moviegoer* entail presentations of lonely protagonists on a search that follows Kierkegaard's "stages of existence." The novels share other similarities: both function as open-ended but "negative commentaries on the dangers of excessive introspection," both address "a possibility of more rewarding personal relationships between men and women," and both contain children who function as "the theological-philosophical foci."

698   Poe, Elizabeth Ann. "Alienation from Society in *The Scarlet Letter* and *The Chocolate War*." *Adolescent Literature as a Complement to the Classics.* Ed. Joan F. Kaywell. Norwood: Christopher-Gordon, 1993. 185-194.

Poe's chapter, one of fourteen in this teacher's guide to approaching young adult novels and more difficult canonical works, presents a strategy for pairing Hawthorne's novel (minus "The Custom-House") with one to which teens more readily relate. *Letter* and Robert Cormier's *The Chocolate War* both deal in similar ways with the effects of alienation from society.

699   Railton, Stephen. "The Address of *The Scarlet Letter*." *Readers in History: Nineteenth-Century American Literature and the Contexts of Response.* Ed. James L. Machor. Baltimore: Johns Hopkins UP, 1993. 138-163.

Railton historicizes this reader-response approach by addressing Hawthorne's preoccupation with audience response in *Letter*.* Hawthorne guided his mid-nineteenth-century readers into becoming an "ideal" audience by having them learn from the mistakes of the text's intolerant "audience," the Puritan community—while at the same time demonstrating that "the law must be obeyed." By teaching his contemporary readers how *not* to interpret the scarlet letter, Hawthorne was creating a "fellowship of seekers for the truth of the heart, united by a knowledge of their mutual human frailties." Railton concludes by considering the way in which the novel seems to speak to readers about sympathy and self-knowledge even at the end of the twentieth century.

*For Railton's book on the subject of audience response, in which a chapter appears that is entitled "'To Open an Intercourse with the World': Hawthorne's *Scarlet Letter*," see 648.

700   Rao, P. G. Rama. "The Spiritual Matrix of *The Scarlet Letter.*" *Mark Twain and Nineteenth-Century American Literature.* Ed. E. Nageswara Rao. Hyderabad: American Studies Research Centre, 1993. 91-96.

Arguing that the spiritual aspect of *Letter* has been neglected, Rao briefly suggests parallels between the novel and The Sermon on the Mount from *The New Testament* and some verses from *The Bhagavadgita.* He distinguishes between religion (based on fear) and spirituality (fearless state that involves the highest purity of mind and heart), and equates Hester's spiritual experience of bearing the "double cross" (the scarlet letter and its living embodiment, Pearl) with Christ's, whereby the "cross transforms its bearer and provides insight into God's justice as contrasted with man's." Dimmesdale achieves true spirituality only at the end—and only for a brief moment before he dies. Hester's stoical, unselfish manner of accepting her plight and going through her ordeal like a saint is similar to that described in *The Bhagavadgita.*

701   Wershoven, Carol. "Hester as First Rebel." *Child Brides and Intruders.* Bowling Green: Bowling Green State U Popular P, 1993. 161-176.

The literary line of "intruder" heroines in American literature, those female outsiders who possess a threatening capacity to "see and question" mainstream society, starts with Hawthorne's Hester. The rebellious heroine, along with her daughter, posits an egalitarian community within the existing community that can subvert existing hierarchies. Unlike the weak Dimmesdale who needs the approval that being an "insider" brings, Hester remains committed to living within Puritan society—although not "of it"—as a true minister, so that she can continue to propose an ethics of compassion and generosity to fellow human sinners.

Journal Essays and Notes

702   Bensick, Carol M. "Dimmesdale and His Bachelorhood: 'Priestly Celibacy' in *The Scarlet Letter.*" *Studies in American Fiction* 21 (1993): 103-110.

Seeking a historical source to explain why Dimmesdale, possessed of such a "strong animal nature," remained celibate *before* Hester came along, Bensick finds the answer in Cotton Mather's *Magnalia Christi Americana* (1702), which presents the unmarried New England minister Thomas Parker of Newbury, whose bachelorhood was a constant source of aggravation for John Wilson (who is Dimmesdale's closest associate in the novel), since it was considered a minister's responsibility to have a son to follow in his ministerial footsteps. According to his nephew, Parker did not marry because he feared that marriage would be a rival to his religious faith. In the novel, however, Dimmesdale's "priestly celibacy" seems the result of his own sexual hypocrisy and the perverse gratification he feels in encouraging the sexual attraction of his "idolizing" female parishioners while simultaneously professing celibacy. That he indulged in constant sexual fantasies most likely paved the way to his adulterous union with Hester.

703   Bernstein, Cynthia. "Reading *The Scarlet Letter* Against Hawthorne's Fictional Interpretive Community." *Language and Literature* 18 (1993): 1-20.

Applying Stanley Fish's use of the term "interpretive community" (a social group sharing strategies for interpreting literature that "exist prior to the act of reading and therefore determine the shape of what is read"), Bernstein asserts that Hawthorne creates a "misguided fictional community" in the novel (one that can be compared to Job's in the Bible) to reflect his own harsh and "colorless" persecutors in his Salem community. "Just as Hester is alienated from the community that condemns her, so Hawthorne faces the alienation of his society. "The two parts of *Letter*—"The Custom-House" and [the novel]—establish the connection between Hester and Hawthorne as the scapegoats of their respective interpretive communities" (just as Job is in his community). By confronting the reader with an interpretive community of persecutors in both the novel and the introductory sketch, Hawthorne hoped to establish a new interpretive community—one in his own time and in the future whose sympathies he hoped to win. For "if he has found sympathetic interpretive communities, it is fair to conclude that for Hawthorne, as much as for Hester, *Letter* has done its office." [The essay includes a diagram that summarizes the "interpretive layers of the text": the villagers, the narrator, Hawthorne's ancestors, his Salem residents, contemporary readers of the novel, and future readers.]

704   Browner, Stephanie P. "Authorizing the Body: Scientific Medicine and *The Scarlet Letter*." *Literature and Medicine* 12 (1993): 139-160.

Acknowledging the competing authorities of religion, law, medicine, and literature in the nineteenth-century, *Letter* is anxious to affirm and legitimize the supremacy of literature's social authority as "a more humane and knowing authority" than the others are because it "scrutinizes lives with sympathy and empathy." The romance genre itself suggests Hawthorne's "persistent and self-conscious commitment" to "participate in the nineteenth-century battle for cultural authority by claiming a peculiar power and knowledge for literature"—in romance's ability to "see beyond the surface, investigate moral ambiguities, and attend to psychological complexities." Hawthorne especially condemns contemporary medical practices in America that had been popularized by Paris doctors—the clinical gaze (as analyzed by Michel Foucault), epistemology, and statistical reductions—and represents medicine in the novel as a potentially evil power that Chillingworth demonically and invasively misuses. "Indeed, in *Letter* Hawthorne offers scathing condemnation of the physician's gaze and a tenacious resistance to the medicalization of the body." Hester escapes Chillingworth's limited power, and even the sickly Dimmesdale proves his physician to be ineffectual. In addition to personifying the evils of medicine, Hawthorne rejects specificity and literalness to condemn Puritan and medical epistemologies. Yet even as Hawthorne refuses to fix meaning and asserts that literature "can best see, know, and control the body," he ambivalently reveals "a tension between a desire to celebrate the body and a need to contain it" just as the medical community does. For just as he "gives voice to the untamed body" of Hester, so he "insists upon harnessing the radical implications of his tale."

705   Clasby, Nancy Tenfelde. "Being True: Logos in *The Scarlet Letter*." *Renascence* 45 (1993): 247-256.

Contends that Hawthorne struggled with the logos of Puritan culture and sought to convert the word into deed and flesh. Dimmesdale represents logos and Hester mythos, but together they climactically unite the dualism of head and heart, word and flesh, and achieve full revelation. Clasby implies that the novel focuses specifically on Dimmesdale's struggles, not "finally whether he will prevail against [Chillingworth], but whether he will have the courage to step outside the field of play of the mind to seek his salvation in the heart." While Chillingworth signifies "the demonic potential of rational thought," Hester represents Dimmesdale's "unacknowledged ties to mythos, to heart, to the devalued, feminine mode of awareness." Dimmesdale's union with Hester transforms his consciousness and enables him "to synthesize the divergent capacities of logos and mythos" and to create a "harmonic order" out of opposing forces before he dies a Christ-like sacrificial death.

706   Daniel, Janice B. "'Apples of the Thoughts and Fancies': Nature as Narrator in *The Scarlet Letter*." *ATQ* 7 (1993): 307-319.

Perceives that Hawthorne personifies nature in *Lette* and uses that personification as a second narrative voice that "provides disembodied, personal attitudes" without having to make direct authorial comments to imply sympathy, approval, or criticism. The personification of nature also reveals Hawthorne's underlying theme of the close proximity and interconnectedness of the communities of mankind and nature, best illustrated in Pearl, who more than the other characters, is "receptive to nature's efforts to achieve some level of rapport with humans."

707 Fretz, Eric. "Stylized Processions and the Carnivalesque in Nathaniel Hawthorne's Fiction: A Selected Sampling." *Nathaniel Hawthorne Review* 19.1 (1993): 11-17.

Three of Hawthorne's works, "The May-Pole of Merry Mount," *Letter*, and *Marble Faun*, illustrate the gradual shift of the carnivalesque in nineteenth-century fiction "from a folk expression to a discourse of isolation." More specifically, Hawthorne uses carnivals and stylized public processions as narrative devices that not only "surround his characters while they are engaged in some of life's most crucial decisions" but that also "heighten the contrasts between the serious and the comic." Although the "temporary lapse of social order" that accompanies the processions seems to provide an opportunity for characters to change, Hawthorne invests the festive events with a gloomy irony—"teasing the characters with the possibility of transformation" but denying them access a new life, leading them instead into "ambiguity, frustration, and even death." In *Letter*, the liberating carnival atmosphere of the Election-Day processional only highlights Dimmesdale's guilt and misery: "The contrast between the inner struggles of Dimmesdale and Hester, and the external mirth of the public procession serves to heighten the direful effect of Dimmesdale's confession."

708 Grossman, Jay. "'A' is for Abolition?: Race, Authorship, *The Scarlet Letter*." *Textual Practice* 7 (1993): 13-30.

Attempting to account for the specific recurring image in *Letter* of the black man and the pervasive presence of blackness, Grossman argues that the novel is very much implicated in "antebellum discourses of miscegenation." More specifically, "the representation (or lack of representation) of adulterous sexual relations at the novel's center draws specifically on antebellum fears about miscegenational sexual union by figuring sexual misconduct in distinctly racial terms." In this scenario (which reverses gender roles), Hester is the victimized female slave, Dimmesdale is the empowered black man (obsessively figured by Hawthorne as black and as wearing black clothes and gloves), and Pearl is their illegitimate mulatto offspring—who, as a mixed-breed, must leave racist America for the more liberal Old World in order to enjoy her inheritance at the end. Grossman goes on to account for the black man's invisibility in two recent works of historical criticism that engage the issue of slavery in *Letter* without accounting for the black man in the text. These articles, by Jonathan Arac (508) and Jean Fagan Yellin (594), produce inaccurate "quasi-allegorical" interpretations that can be blamed on their authors' acceptance and internalization of F. O. Matthiessen's famous assertion, taken as gospel truth by generations of readers, that American Renaissance authors either consciously engage with or consciously escape from history—and that Hawthorne purposely "escapes" contemporary events in *Letter*. Grossman wishes to shift future critics' focus "away from an author-centered interpretive paradigm and toward a neo-Marxist assumption about the embeddedness of artistic production wtihin socially constituted networks of meaning." [For another recent study that addresses the issue of slavery in the novel, see Deborah L. Madsen's "'A' for Abolition: Hawthorne's Bond-Servant and the Shadow of Slavery" (664). See also "Slavery" in the Subject Index.]

709 Gupta, R. K. "Kalidasa's *Sakuntala*and Hawthorne's *The Scarlet Letter*." *International Fiction Review* 20 (1993): 58-64.

Finds striking similarities and parallels between *Letter* and Kalidasa's fifth-century Hindu play *Abhi jnana-Sakuntala*. Although there are substantial differences, "similarities of situation, character, and form between the two are so numerous and significant as to merit study in depth and detail." Both Hester and Sakuntala, for instance, marked by impulsive and passionate natures, are "women of great beauty" who make overpowering impacts on their lovers. As the central figures in both works of literature, these women "bear adversity and public disgrace with remarkable courage, showing grace under pressure." Their children, Pearl and Bharat, also invite a comparison, since they are both "volatile, somewhat wayward, and difficult to control or discipline." Both works are also dramatically structured, contain supernatural elements, and pivot around central symbols (the scarlet "A" and a royal ring) that "materially affect the course of events." And on a thematic level, both privilege moral law over the happiness of the individual, and likewise show how suffering refines characters by bringing them wisdom and maturity. [For an earlier essay by Gupta on this same subject, see 631.]

710 Idol, John L., Jr., and Sterling [K.] Eisiminger. "*The Scarlet Letter* as Opera: The First Settings." *Nathaniel Hawthorne Review* 19 (1993): 11-16.

Written for readers (like Alfred Kazin, in 680) who may not be aware that *Letter* has already been made into an opera "at least ten" times, this article describes two such operatic adaptations of the novel. The very first opera was put on in Boston, 1855, by Lucien Southard and F. H. Underwood, and presented selected scenes in which Hester's name had been changed to "Anna" and Chillingworth's to "Albert." The second operatic performance, created by George Parsons Lathrop and Walter Damrosch in 1896, offered a complete setting that nevertheless took great liberties with the novel—omitting Pearl and having Hester commit suicide right after Dimmesdale dies.

711   Johnson, Claudia Durst. "Impotence and Omnipotence in *The Scarlet Letter*." *New England Quarterly* 66 (1993): 594-612.

Demonstrates that "the subject of impotence is much more profoundly intrinsic to *Letter* than has previously been argued and that it amplifies and enriches the subjects of literary dysfunction and ontological disappointment in 'The Custom-House.'" Johnson relates the early American history of attitudes toward impotence (especially the Puritan insistence that sex was a marital duty) to Hawthorne's allusions in the novel that Chillingworth's herbs and roots were used to restore his own "manly exercises," and deduces that—given the cultural stereotype of "the impotent man and his adulterous wife" that is embodied in the novel—Chillingworth's sexual impotence initiates the plot of *Letter*. "The Custom-House," which marks the triumphant end to Hawthorne's literary dysfunction (through the sexual metaphor at the end of the gushing, phallic town pump), links sexual and literary impotence—making the novel "play out a convoluted drama of his own literary dysfunction through the sexuality of his fictional characters." Hester, Chillingworth, and Dimmesdale can thus "be regarded as stages in the narrator's experience with literary creativity and incapacity," Hester representing the fruitful period of his life when he produced stories and children, Chillingworth indicating the middle period in which Hawthorne suffered "over his literary deadness in the customhouse" and had a "tendency to blame others for his deficiencies," and Dimmesdale—whose vocation as a "master of verbal arts" most nearly matches that of the narrator—representing the independent reclaiming of both sexual and literary identity ("self-potency") when he "delivers the greatest of his sermons and acknowledges his fathering of Pearl, his union with Hester."

712   Kalfopoulou, Adrianne. "Hester's Ungathered Hair: Hawthorne and Nineteenth-Century Women's Fiction." *Gramma: Journal of Theory and Criticism* 1 (1993): 40-61.*

Applying Jacques Derrida's definition of "differance" to Hester, Kalfopoulou argues that Hester demonstrates an early literary example of how "difference threatens to take symbolic and cultural fixity apart" and

354

how a dissenting self can only be reinstated into the social fabric by consenting to dominant social values. Hester's "gendered singularity," or creative, sexual potential, is not relinquished until the end of the novel, when she no longer challenges the Puritan social order and "is turned into Hawthorne's mouthpiece for the dissemination of ideals of 'lofty, pure, and beautiful' womanhood"—largely because Hawthorne could not deal fully with the contradictions in Hester's complex nature and so fell back upon the current rhetoric of nineteenth-century True Womanhood. Hester's singularity, therefore, along with her radical potential, is neutralized by her maternal sense and increasingly symbolic status as a model of self-sacrificing, silent Victorian womanhood.

*Reprinted in *A Discussion of the Ideology of the American Dream in the Culture's Female Discourses: The Untidy House* (Lewiston: Edwin Mellen Press, 2000. 19-42).

713   Kimball, Samuel. "Countersigning Aristotle: The Amimetic Challenge of *The Scarlet Letter*." *ATQ* 7 (1993): 141-158.

Although Hawthorne's moral in the novel is to "Be true!" by candidly showing "your worst" or at least some self-disclosing "trait whereby the worst may be inferred," Kimball detects in this deconstructionist reading that the novel's most conspicuous "trait," the scarlet letter, ironically "disrupts the disclosure of the truth which the 'showing freely' of the trait is supposed to guarantee." The "a-mimetic" character of the letter "becomes an ironic and contradictory sign of identification," a sign and the countersign of the Puritan community, both of which Hester accepts and destabilizes through her lavish embellishments of it ("showing freely" a "trait" of herself that "subverts the intended function of such a free showing"). Supporting multiple interpretations (and discussed by Kimball with reference to Derrida's three "modalities of signature"), the letter can thus never be "anchored in a determinable referent," just as Pearl cannot— since Hester suspends her daughter's signification, too. Kimball clarifies such suspension in Derridean terms as placement in an "ex-appropriating mimetic abyss." The a-mimetic light given off by the "A" on the tombstone at the end is an "abyssal illumination" that contradicts Aristotle's declaration in the *Poetics* that the source of all light, even that of "metaphorizing mimesis," is the sun.

714   Natarajan, N. "Semiotic Fission in Hawthorne's A and Pyncheon's V." *Indian Journal of American Studies* 23 (1993): 85-91.

Applies deconstructive semiotics to a comparison of the "signs" in Hawthorne's *Letter* and Thomas Pyncheon's *V* (1963), and argues that

Hawthorne's Custom-House Surveyor (who finds the letter "A") and Pyncheon's Herbert Stencil (who gets the letter "V" from his father's journals) initiate the novels' developing semiotic/semantic concerns with how to regard "signs." These characters represent what Natarajan calls a "devolution from the Saussurian to the Derridean position," as the quests to unify "signs" by connecting "signifieds" to their "objects" end in failure. Hester's is a lifelong struggle to de-link the Puritan signified (adultery) from the signifier ("A"). But whereas Hawthorne's narrator allows Hester to create a rift between the signifier and its original signified in the Puritan milieu, thereby taking the novel to new fields of meaning as a semiotic allegory, the narrator of *V* achieves no such semantic resolution, and Pyncheon's novel ends caught in its own semiotic entropy.

715   Pimple, Kenneth D. "'Subtle, but remorseful hypocrite': Dimmesdale's Moral Character." *Studies in the Novel* 25 (1993): 257-271.

Argues that it is not Hester who seduces the feeble Dimmesdale in the forest scene, but the opposite. It is Dimmesdale who talks Hester into fleeing, and so "Dimmesdale's gravest sin cannot be laid at Hester's feet at all." His "profoundly manipulative doubletalk"—the same that he shrewdly and eloquently employs to his congregation through his speeches and sermons—is composed of both semantic and pragmatic aspects, the former covering the literal meaning of language and the latter covering "the meanings added to utterances by tone of voice, context, and other non-linguistic considerations." Dimmesdale has skillfully mastered both types of language to subtly serve his own interests, often playing them against each other for more powerful linguistic effects. In the forest encounter, Dimmesdale guides the direction of the conversation so that he can first unburden his ongoing misery on Hester and then prompt her to convince him to flee. In manipulating her, he manages to maintain his identity as "a man seduced, taken advantage of by a strong, passionate woman is spite of his better self." Although Dimmesdale does decide in this scene to make a more public acceptance of his status as sinner, his final sermon and confession do not mark any profound change in him (as many critics have argued), but are only "slight variations on the same morally deficient theme he has played these seven years." His desire to "go out with a flourish, to be remembered," is what motivates the dying man to perpetuate the social fiction, through doublespeak, that he is better than he really is. Ultimately, Dimmesdale is dedicated to the two things he cares about most, his social face and his immortal soul, that "split his speaking in twain and slowly tear him asunder." [For a similar study on Dimmesdale's manipulative use of language, see Michel Small (405).]

716   Savoy, Eric. "'Filial Duty': Reading the Patriarchal Body in 'The Custom-House.'" *Studies in the Novel* 25 (1993): 397-417.

Examines the tropes of exhumation referred to as "prosopopoeia" in "The Custom-House" to illustrate that, in presenting himself as a "decapitated Surveyor" who "writes from beyond the grave," Hawthorne was revealing his "filial anxieties" and desire to align himself with his dead, powerful, patriarchal ancestors. In seeking approval from and affiliation with his seventeenth-century Puritan fathers (linking the seventeenth and nineteenth centuries with the eighteenth-century "father" of *Letter*, Surveyor Pue), Hawthorne also writes "his participation in the transhistorical project of surveying and containing women's resistant energies." His historical representation of Hester's punishment and his subversion of Hester's "anticipation of a feminist utopia" show that he inherited the persecuting spirit and "mitigates, or underwrites, the misogynistic atrocities of Puritan New England." Thus "The Custom-House" is "a protracted and rhetorically complex mediation on the gendered, historically determined subjectivity of the male author in postcolonial America." [For another essay that deals with Hawthorne's concept of raising the dead in "The Custom-House," see David C. Cody (595).]

717   Stephenson, Will, and Mimosa Stephenson. "*Adam Blair* and *The Scarlet Letter*." *Nathaniel Hawthorne Review* 19.2 (1993): 1-10.

Presents evidence to support the claim that John Gibson Lockhart's 1822 novel *Adam Blair* influenced Hawthorne when he was writing *Letter*. Confirming Hawthorne's familiarity with Lockhart, the Stephensons compare the two novels and conclude that "it seems likely Hawthorne wrote in active dialogue with it." In these tales of adultery, both Adam Blair and Dimmesdale share similar nervous temperaments and the same mannerism of placing their hands over their hearts; both heroines are darkly beautiful and experience heterodox relations with their Calvinistic communities; and both novels tell of single parents raising "strikingly beautiful little girl[s]." The major characters in *Letter* "are deliberate counterpoints to those in *Adam Blair*," however, "illustrating the consequences if different decisions were made at crucial points in the action." A more radical difference between the two novels involves each author's respective treatment of "the dyads humility/pride, confession/concealment, and forgiveness/vengeance. In each case, Lockhart portrays the positive side and Hawthorne the negative."

718   Tomc, Sandra. "'The Sanctity of the Priesthood': Hawthorne's 'Custom-House.'" *ESQ: A Journal of the American Renaissance* 39 (1993): 161-184.

Hawthorne's dismissal from the Custom House, which severed his connection to public life and forced him into a new reliance on the detestable commercial market, "was strikingly analogous to the more general cultural relocation of authorship from the public to the private sphere." This drastic shift, caused by "emergent entrepreneurial models of authorship with their emphasis on market success over patriotic obligation," can be detected when one compares "The Old Manse" (1846) with "The Custom-House." In the latter, Hawthorne's assured belief in the organic and inviolable bond between civil life and the life of letters is clearly shattered. Further, Hawthorne's description of the author and his relation to his audience in the latter piece stands in sharp relief against that offered in "The Old Manse," where his persona clearly enjoys the system of state patronage and the safety of his remoteness from private competition. "The Custom-House" thus expresses "the unease and dread with which he faced the American artist's modern role as a social outcast." That *Letter* is divided in two (preface and novel) is fitting considering that it is "an unstable, conflicted production divided between two voices, the one public, external, 'diffused among us all,' the other resembling nothing if not the privatized murmurs of the commercial producer" struggling reluctantly to adapt to mid-nineteenth-century private enterprise.

1994

Essays and Studies in Books

719   Auchincloss, Louis. "Three Perfect Novels and What They Have in Common." *The Style's the Man: Reflections on Proust, Fitzgerald, Wharton, Vidal, and Others.* New York: Charles Scribner's Sons, 1994. 167-177.

This reprint of a 1981 address by Auchincloss superficially classifies *Letter, Wuthering Heights* (1848), and *The Great Gatsby* (1925) as "perfect" novels because they are exotic and surreal yet "totally satisfying" "jewels." In *Letter* (pp. 168-172), which Auchincloss deems the most powerful statement in all of literature of the "agony of guilt," Hawthorne employs the stern Puritan New England background as the "perfect laboratory" in which to study his theme.

720   Budick, Emily Miller. "The Romance of the Family: Hawthorne." *Engendering Romance: Women Writers and the Hawthorne Tradition, 1850-1990.* New Haven: Yale UP, 1994. 13-39.

Four twentieth-century women writers, Carson McCullers, Flannery O'Connor, Toni Morrison, and Grace Paley, inherit the American romance tradition (or "Hawthorne" tradition) and actually "write into an originally male, not female, tradition." Although this "skepticist" tradition "largely consists of a resistance to particular ideologies (such as racism, classism, and patriarchy), it in no way suggests the possibility of escaping from society, history, and tradition." This romance fiction, which in *Letter* takes the form of "family romance," actually "discovers ways of recommitting oneself to the world and to other people without yielding to mindless consensus and conformity." Building on Sacvan Bercovitch's idea (in 635) that *Letter* promotes "socialization," and also borrowing Freud's theory of the family romance, Budick examines the relationship between the Western patriarchal tradition and women in connection with the question of Pearl's paternity, arguing that patriarchy developed in the first place as a strategy to control female reproduction and to limit the effects of mothering on culture. Just like "The Custom-House," the novel abounds with confrontations of illegitimacy and doubt," as well as with fears regarding the sterility of the patriarchal tradition—and even the extremes of the matriarchal tradition. Only an acknowledgement of both the male and female traditions can create healthy parent-child relationships that "provide access to the past and facilitate emergence into the future." [For other essays that address Hawthorne's acknowledgment of the value of both male and female traditions and characteristics, see 361, 585, and 588. For another treatment of *Letter* as a "family romance," see 644. For Budick's earlier study on the topic of the parent/child relationship, see 656.]

721   Burbick, Joan. "Complaints of the Heart." *Healing the Republic: The Language of Health and the Culture of Nationalism in Nineteenth-Century America.* New York: Cambridge UP, 1994. 210-222.

Interpreting "nineteenth-century narratives of health written by physicians, social reformers, lay healers, and literary artists in order to expose the conflicts underlying the creation of a national culture in America," Burbick concentrates in chapter ten primarily on *Letter* after an opening section on how Harriet Beecher Stowe's *Uncle Tom's Cabin* (1852) evokes "the cultural discourse of Protestant Christianity" to "heal" the divisions within the country. Like Stowe, Hawthorne was acutely aware that "the republic was in danger of dissolution because its citizens had forgotten the healing words of its ancestors and turned from the religious and cultural messages of the heart." Hawthorne argues that the country's citizens are united not by the sympathetic "language of the heart" (as they should be), but rather by patriarchal, religious law and contracts. While Hawthorne recognized that the printed word could connect an author to a limited group of readers, he shuddered in anticipation of the general public's lack of sympathy and so found it necessary to create boundaries to prevent readers from detecting the "heart's history." Just like his narrator in "The Custom-House" who fears revealing too much and insists on guarding the "inmost Me," so the characters in the novel itself "continually exist at the anxious edge between private knowledge and public revelation." They learn by the end that there is "no possibility of forming a healthy nation out of a group of unsympathetic listeners" because "the sanction of law and the presence of the patriarchs who administer punishment remain as the stern representatives of the emerging nation."

722   Coale, Samuel [Chase]. "The Romance of Mesmerism: Hawthorne's Medium of Romance." *Studies in the American Renaissance*. Ed. Joel Myerson. Charlottesville: UP of Virginia, 1994. 271-288

Troubled over Sacvan Bercovitch's politically liberal and near cheerful reduction of Hawthorne's dark power and mystery (not to mention the acute and very real suffering of his characters) into an "ultimate and consensual reconciliation" in the distant future (see 635), Coale posits a more complicated and grim view—one that insists on Hawthorne's firm belief in irreconcilability and that keeps the dark "values" intact. Coale examines the cultural phenomenon of Mesmerism (specifically the spell-like "gaze" and the hypnotic, magnetic "trance") in the mid-nineteenth century, which influenced Hawthorne's fictional techniques, his gloomy vision, and his theory of the American romance. Hawthorne transformed his knowledge of Mesmerism into "a way of seeing and apprehending the mysteries of the human psyche and its elusive motives." The mesmeric process provided Hawthorne with his pervasive and persuasive powers, with the ability to create the "neutral territory" necessary to write romance—although he was only truly successful in achieving the "delicate balancing act" in *Letter*. [For more on Mesmerism by Coale, see 678 and 817.]

723   Elbert, Monika M. Introduction. *The Scarlet Letter*. By Nathaniel Hawthorne. 1850. New York: Washington Square, 1994. vii-xxxii.

What gives *Letter* its universal appeal is Hawthorne's tremendous knowledge of human psychology, especially his exploration of the "maddening split between a private and a public self." He uses Puritan symbols and landscapes to describe the personal dilemma of the individual caught between natural feelings and man-made laws, something which he felt acutely in his own life. The book cannot be said to privilege one character's vision over another's; instead, the three main characters themselves "are a compendium of the autobiographical persona Hawthorne introduces in "The Custom House": Dimmesdale is Hawthorne the idealist, caught in a marketplace world where he needs to write and work to support a family; Chillingworth is the all-knowing, objective, and at times distant writer who needs space to create and be creative; and Hester, in her unlimited freedom and honesty, represents the artistic truth Hawthorne aspires to achieve."

724   Franchot, Jenny. "The Hawthornian Confessional." *Roads to Rome: The Antebellum Protestant Encounter with Catholicism.* Berkeley: U of California P, 1994. 260-269.

Examining in her book the anti-Catholic "literary engagement" with "meditation, confession, self-mortification, and the attractions of the image" that proliferated in the fiction of mainstream Protestant American writers in the mid-nineteenth century, Franchot devotes a chapter to Hawthorne's perception of the "foreign faith" in *Letter*. Throughout the novel, Hawthorne compares the "banished Anglo-Catholic past of iconographic richness" to the "Puritan past (and, by implication, a nineteenth-century Protestant present) of cold intellection and self-inhibition." Hawthorne connects the Catholic past and the sterile present especially through his characters: "Roger Prynne's emergence from the 'study and the cloister' and his adoption of the pseudonym Chillingworth (the name of a seventeenth-century apologist), Dimmesdale's various identifications with monkish excess and his seclusion of himself within his 'dim interior,' Hester's embodiment of Mother Church in her dual aspect as the Whore of Babylon [. . .] and as the 'image of Divine Maternity,' and finally the scarlet letter's persistent reminder of a recently repudiated Anglo-Catholic ceremonialism all invoke the religious tension between Old and New World cultures." As such characterizations suggest, Hawthorne was acutely critical of the "old, corrupted faith of Rome," and yet the self-created image of himself as a "veiled yet autobiographical speaker [in "The Custom-House"] invokes Catholicism's alleged violations of the Protestant American's political, sexual, and spiritual 'rights' to assure his readers that his will be a properly managed confessional." Ultimately, Hawthorne appears to be confirming his culture's "anti-Catholic values while provocatively commemorating the loss of that despised popish world." [For other studies that detect the tension between Old and New World cultures, see "Old World vs. New World" in the Subject Index, particularly essays by Frederick Newberry

(348 and 539) and John Gatta (795). For more on the subject of Catholicism, see the Subject Index.]

725   Idol, John L., Jr., and Buford Jones, eds. *"The Scarlet Letter." Nathaniel Hawthorne: The Contemporary Reviews.* New York: Cambridge UP, 1994. 117-155.

Part of the "American Critical Archives" series, this volume includes a "proportionate sense of the critical response" to *Letter* and contains partial reviews by Caleb Foote (*Salem Gazette*), Evert A. Duychinck (*Literary World*, ER1), Charles Creighton Hazewell (*Boston Daily Times*), E. P. Whipple (*Graham's Magazine*, ER3), Lewis Gaylord Clark (*Knickerbocker*), Henry F. Chorley (*Athenaeum*, ER4), Anne W. Abbott (*North American Review*, ER5), George B. Loring (*Massachusetts Quarterly Review*, ER7), Orestes A. Brownson (*Brownson's Quarterly Review*, ER9), and Arthur Cleveland Coxe (*Church Review*, ER10). A checklist of 19 additional reviews follows, most of them previously unknown.

726   Portelli, Alessandro. *"The Scarlet Letter* and the Voices of the Heart." *The Text and the Voice: Writing, Speaking, and Democracy in American Literature.* New York: Columbia UP, 1994. 72-77.

Within a larger discussion of the influence of language and culture on one another, this subchapter addresses the conflict between control and passion in *Letter*, equating "voice" with freedom and "writing" with authority, the former associated with the romance form and Dimmesdale, the latter with the novel form and Chillingworth. The scarlet letter itself functions as both written and oral communication, as both fixed sign of punishing control and organic symbol of intense feeling, since it both silences voice and passion and yet expresses passion and the power of feeling at the same time.

727   Shaw, Peter. *"The Scarlet Letter*: The Heretical Temptation." *Recovering American Literature.* Chicago: Ivan R. Dee, 1994. 23-47.

Seeks to recover classic American literature from the post-1960s critics whose "new, radical-academic orthodoxy" stifles free discussions of literature by imposing their own distorted and distorting political agendas. Shaw traces critical opinions and assessments of *Letter* since its publication, focusing particularly on critics' reactions to Hawthorne's "double evocation of both sympathy for and censure of Hester." "Orthodox" critics of the 50s and 60s recognized Hawthorne's divided sympathies in his treatment of Hester, but they resisted the temptation to read the novel "heretically"—or even too conservatively, for that matter, since either strict reading would deny Hawthorne's powerful, ambiguous effect in the novel that is designed to leave unreconciled the conflicting needs of society and the individual. Since the 1970s, however, critics have been inclined to reject the view that the "world's law" has any claim on the individual, and thus Hawthorne's divided sense has become a mockery: a "tortured ambivalence" caused by his own "sublimated sexual anxieties" and "repressed authorial anxieties." In effect, these "narrowly-conceived" and patronizing judgments have dismissed the real "art" of the novel with their arrogant claims about having solved or explained away the ambiguity inherent in it. When critics no longer interpret *Letter* but instead ideologically interrogate it, they reduce "to the single dimension of ideology a book whose central concern is precisely with the warping effects of ideology." [See Robert E. Abrams directly below (728) for a similar approach to the novel that also faults recent critics for their reductive or limiting ideological approaches to the novel. For other readings of the novel that fault modern criticism, see "Modern Criticism, flaws in" in the Subject Index.]

Journal Essays and Notes

728   Abrams, Robert E.   "Critiquing Colonial American Geography: Hawthorne's Landscape of Bewilderment." *Texas Studies in Literature and Language* 36 (1994): 357-379.

Challenges critics like Savcan Bercovitch (635), Donald Pease (540), and Lauren Berlant (636) for inadequately accounting for the way "Hawthorne probes troublesome situations in the New England past" or, more specifically, for attempting to contain or reduce Hawthorne's shifting perspectives, competing frames of reference, enigmatic characters, multiple meanings, and "elusive and ambiguous atmosphere" into a positivistic and stable political vision that mirrors "the very logic of political stability" in the United States. Abrams argues that Hawthorne's volatile and unsettled texts actually register "an underlying lack of coherence in the agitated colonial culture out of which the national republic has issued"—and actually "challenge more integrative models of national formation and development." Abrams substantiates his claim by examining the ways "figures and objects, forms and situations, emerge in contradictory and incongruous ways" in "Young Goodman Brown," *Letter*, and My Kinsman, Major Molineux." In each, Hawthorne "lays bare a far more frail and uncertain historical reality" than that posited by the critics named above. All of the texts paint a picture of the colonial New England landscape in which there is—whether it be the wilderness or the settlement—"a free-floating sense of the unsettled" that "disturbs the settled visibility of forms in space as well as unity of scenic focus." The atmosphere is too volatile and multidimensional to be envisioned as any homogeneous, harmonious cultural space, an observation that leads to theconclusion that none of the stories can be characterized by anything truly "collective," since they are rather emphatically marked by "enigma, dissonance, mutability, and bewilderment." [See Peter Bellis (746) for a similar critique of Sacvan Bercovitch's assumption in 635 that *Letter* participates in nineteenth-century liberal ideology. For other reactions to Bercovitch, refer to his name in the Subject Index.]

729   Ben-Bassat, Hedda. "Marginal Existence and Communal Consensus in *The Scarlet Letter* and *A Fringe of Leaves.*" *Comparatist* 18 (1994): 52-70.

Detecting similarities in theme, structure, and narrative strategy between *Letter* and Patrick White's *A Fringe of Leaves* (1976), Ben-Bassat shows how Hawthorne and White defer to a "similar model of cultural deviance" in dealing with the issue of individual freedom vs. social control. This model involves a three-fold process (borrowed from anthropologist Victor Turner's cultural work on "rites of passage") that is applied to Hester and Ellen Roxburgh after they commit adultery, and involves (1) separation from society, (2) a transitional period of liminality characterized by "a sense of a potentially subversive freedom," and (3) an ultimate return to and "acceptance of (though not total submission to) the order of social structures." While both authors proffer a transgression of social rituals, neither works to subvert those rituals, situating themselves rather "in a marginal sociocultural space—betwixt and between structural classifications." Thus both Hawthorne and White imply the incompatibility of artistic creativity and social containment, and, like their heroines, "define the nature of [their] work from the vantage point of liminal existence"—a position both in and out of accepted norms.

730   Bowers, Edgar. "Hawthorne and the Extremes of Character." *Sewanee Review* 102 (1994): 570-587.

Suggests an affinity between Hawthorne, Emily Dickinson, and Wallace Stevens that typifies the New England temper, namely a belief in "the existence of spiritual extremes, or divisions of character" that Bowers identifies as "torpor" on the one hand and "exuberance" on the other. Though Bowers's discussion of Hawthorne focuses primarily on *Marble Faun*, it briefly addresses *Letter*—showing that the scene directly after the forest meeting with Hester perfectly illustrates how torpor, in this case caused by Dimmesdale's guilty conscience and debilitating acceptance of Puritan codes, is "suddenly released into exuberance."

731   Calinescu, Matei. "Secrecy in Fiction: Textual and Intertextual Secrets in Hawthorne and Updike." *Poetics Today* 15 (1994): 443-465.

Drawing from earlier studies of narrative secrets by Frank Kermode and from Umberto Eco's theory of the "triple intentionality" that shapes acts of literary interpretation (the intention of the author, the intention of the text, and the intention of the reader), Calinescu proposes a reader-based approach to the question of secrecy in fiction (one rooted in the act of re-reading a text for its "secrets" that are missed the first time around), as exemplified by Hawthorne's *Letter* (intratextual secrets) and by Updike's oblique rewriting of Hawthorne's classic in *A Month of Sundays, Roger's Version*, and *S.* (intertextual secrets). Put more simply, Calinescu finds that having read Updike's trilogy as an "ironic transposition" of Hawthorne's novel, he has been made privy (through Updike's "quasi-secret rewriting and the aggressive erotic candor of his narrative voices) to textual and intertextual secrets that he had not recognized when first reading *Letter*. The chattily confessional style of all three reincarnations (Marshfield, Roger Lambert, and Sarah) of *Letter*'s three protagonists (Dimmesdale, Chillingworth, and Hester) illuminates Hawthorne's novel in a new way, revealing in it a prevalent "refusal or postponement of confession" that indicates Hawthorne's extensive use of the rhetoric of secrecy. In fact, *Letter* seems to illustrate "the various roles played by secrecy in human relations. These include the moral and psychological consequences of the need to hide information, the ways by which secrets are concealed and penetrated, and the self-reflexiveness of secrecy (as allegory or ambiguity) in the writing of fiction as conceived by Hawthorne." Ultimately, re-reading fiction over and over alerts one to "the logic of secrecy" and the "art of reading," thus enabling the reader "to discern hidden patterns, verbal or structural, textual or intertextual."

732   Cheyfitz, Eric. "The Irresistibleness of Great Literature: Reconstructing Hawthorne's Politics." *American Literary History* 6 (1994): 539-558.

Cites and indicts three works of *Letter* criticism—F. O. Matthiessen's *American Renaissance* (EC20), Sacvan Bercovitch's *The Office of The Scarlet Letter* (635), and Lauren Berlant's *The Anatomy of National Fantasy* (636)—as examples of "the triumphal procession" of the American literary canon. As all of them make their cases for Hawthorne as "a canonical figure suitable for a progressive ideology," they skirt Hawthorne's "simply reprehensible stand on the slavery issue," pretending to complicate it and often using his biography of Franklin Pierce or his essay "Chiefly About War Matters" to defend their positions—all of which employ the same "rhetoric of American exceptionalism" as

Hawthorne did. Hawthorne's overtly "political" pieces are just as condescendingly equivocal and "ethically empty" on the matter of slavery as *Letter* is, and all of them remarkable for their "rationalization of an immoral political passivity." *Letter* cannot, therefore, be the "central text in a multicultural 'America'" that the above-named authors pretend it to be. Cheyfitz offers as a corrective to these views the notion of giving up canonicity altogether—of dissenting from it, or resisting "inclusion in a liberal consensus" in the name of "pluralism." [For another essay that faults Hawthorne's political passivity, see Christopher Diffee (779).]

733   Harshbarger, Scott. "A 'H—ll-Fired Story': Hawthorne's Rhetoric of Rumor." *College English* 56 (1994): 30-45.

Interprets Hawthorne's strategic and rhetorical use of ambiguity as an effort to establish an intimate connection with his audience. Recognizing how powerful and influential the "rhetoric of rumor" could be with its personal quality combined with anonymous authority (and viewing it as "a displaced or subliminal collective confession, a 'propensity of human nature to tell the very worst of itself'"), Hawthorne "harnessed " its "vital social force" in *Letter*, having drawn on rumors, gossip, and scandalous incidents chronicled in Puritan histories and New England witchcraft literature to create the characters and rhetorical background of his story. Conflicting reports and characterizations, as well as frequent failures of communication and the "distrust of many people," create a "fertile medium for rumor" in the novel, leading to "ascending levels of poetic or humanity-laden truth." After all, Harshbarger shows, "it is through the process of legend making, begun in rumor, that the scarlet letter gathers its symbolic resonance." Thus rumor becomes the "communicative lifeblood of the community" that reflects the social imagination and enacts "a double-edged dynamic symbolic of society itself."

734   Kurjiaka, Susan K. H. "Rage Turned Inward: Woman Against Herself in Hawthorne's Fiction." *Mount Olive Review* 7 (1993-94): 33-40.

"Very aware of the unfair limitations of Victorian women" (especially those who were "over-educated, over-sensitive, and oversexed" for socially-prescribed roles), Hawthorne "condemns these often crippling mythic ideals" in his creation of several "anti-heroines" whose "disallowed sexual passion is perverted into rage turned inward against the self." Three works illustrate "a progression of images of increasingly articulate and tragic women: an unnamed young woman in 'The Hollow of the Three Hills,' Hester Prynne in *Letter*, and Zenobia in *Blithedale Romance*." "Together, these voices seem a cry of pain which Hawthorne creates to rail imaginatively [since he was not one to "publicly espouse causes"] against societal myths about women."

735   Mathé, Sylvie. "The Reader May Not Choose: Oxymoron as Central Figure in Hawthorne's Strategy of Immunity from Choice in *The Scarlet Letter.*" *Style* 26 (1994): 604-633.

Investigates "how and why choice is denied to the reader" in *Letter*, arguing that Hawthorne's "latent stance of multiple meaning" is rooted in "an oxymoronic aesthetics of integration through which opposites and contradictories are ultimately harmonized." Hawthorne's "deceptive" tactics in the novel are designed "to make choice impossible"—obliquity, inconsistency, indirection, misdirection, contradictions, and evasion of disclosure—and relate to "the seminal role played by oxymoron in Hawthorne's strategy of immunity from choice." His use of oxymoron reveals not only his resistance to normative readings but also "his undermining of evaluative judgments, and his politics of integration of exclusion." Like an epiphany, oxymoron further "brings revelation of the whole where the parts cannot suffice, allowing vision and meaning where language fails." Mathé admits that her reading is similar to Sacvan Bercovitch's (in 635) in its reconciliation of opposites, but she contends that her "stylistic reading" differs from his political reading in that it discerns "a poetic resolution of conflict" in Hawthorne's denial of choice and finds "an ideal stylistic congruence" for the symbolic polarities in the novel "in the figure of the oxymoron."

736   Mitchell, Domhnall. "Marginal Notes: Native Americans in *The Scarlet Letter.*" *European Studies Review of Native America* 8 (1994): 47-51.

Although "Native Americans are confined to the outer edges of the narrative and are only occasionally mentioned," "their presence exists as a contributing and unsettling factor on the margins of the text" of *Letter*. Allusions to the Indian function "as a sort of code with which to activate certain culturally inherited preconceptions about Native Americans." These allusions—particularly to the Indians' violence and sexual promiscuity—were intended to influence the reader's response to Chillingworth and Hester, since Hester's act of adultery "links her tangentially with the sexual license of tribal peoples as they are generalized by early Puritans, while Chillingworth, too, is partly driven by a thirst for revenge which is identified as demonic, and by extension conventionally Indian, in its motivation." Thus Hester's self-regulatory morality and sexuality are presented as something "outside, and in opposition to that of the English society in the settlements," and Chillingworth's association with Indians turns him into a "spiritual half-breed" who is bent on the barbaric torture of his victim (much like the Indians depicted in captivity narratives). Mitchell even suggests that, in the forest scene, when Hester suggests a plan of escape into the woods, "Hester plays Pocahontas to Dimmesdale's Smith, with Chillingworth as the Indian villain." But because Dimmesdale's Puritan vision "excludes Indians on any other terms except those of conversion or assimilation," he eventually rejects Hester as someone "whose ethnic identity is both unsettled and unsettling" (idealized Indian though she may be), and in doing so "typifies his community's closure to other modes of seeing." The marginal presence of the Native American in *Letter* also contributes to the thematic debate between patriarchal and matriarchal structures in the book, because Hester and Pearl's wild and "natural" behavior aligns them with Indian tribes, many of which in the Massachusetts area were matrilineal.

737   Phillips, Rod. "Purloined Letters: *The Scarlet Letter* in Kathy Acker's *Blood and Guts in High School.*" *Critique: Studies in Contemporary Fiction* 35 (1994): 173-180.

Defends Kathy Acker's plagiarism in her fiction, in this case her 1978 novel *Blood and Guts in High School* (New York: Grove Weidenfeld), which borrows liberally from *Letter* and takes that "literary 'borrowing' to its most bizarre extreme." Known for her "experimental, fragmented, and disorienting fiction," Acker's "postmodern, punk" novel seems to deny that literature can be property (thus justifying her use of plagiarism), just as it rejects traditional forms of writing. In the book, a ten-year-old character named Janey, held captive by a Persian slave trader and forced to become a whore, writes an autobiography that she describes as a "Book Report" (pp. 65-100) on *Letter*. Janey then uses *Letter* to describe her life, expressing an affinity with Hester who is likewise subject to male oppression, is also a violator of societal rules, and is similarly imprisoned. Thus the "Book Report is "a radical feminist reworking" of Hester's story, "a kind of 'taking back' of a woman's story from a male author." The only problem (and this is where Phillips sails in to rescue Acker from dismissive critics) is that Acker's writing is composed exclusively—sans the plagiarized parts—of vulgar and incoherent collections of profanity (as when Janey "assimilates" Hester Prynne's voice and thoughts when thinking of Dimmesdale and says, "I want to fuck you, Dimwit [. . .]. The only image in my mind is your cock in my cunt"). Phillips, however, is convinced that Acker's post-modern American work is hip, powerful, and "clearly" engaging in social criticism "by using the borrowed text as a touchstone for Janey's present reality" and giving Acker "a device with which to discuss the powers and limitations of literature."

738   Sorrells, David J. "Hawthorne's *The Scarlet Letter*." *Explicator* 53 (1994): 23-25.

The "grim and grisly" town beadle represents "in his aspect the whole dismal severity of the Puritanic code of law" in *Letter*, but he also embodies the duality of the Puritan ethic (the blending of civil and religious authority) in carrying with him both sword and staff of office as he escorts Hester to the scaffold.

739   Tew, Arnold G. "Hawthorne's P. P.: Behind the Comic Mask." *Nathaniel Hawthorne Review* 20.1 (1994): 18-23.

When Hawthorne good naturedly masks himself as "P. P." in "The Custom-House," he is alluding to Alexander Pope and John Gay's "Memoirs of P. P., Clerk of this Parish" (1727)—using their burlesque of a "pompish" and obtuse parish clerk for "comic inspiration" because it "offered situations and characters relevant both to his novel" (thematic "resonances of seduction and ministerial lust") and "to the particularly difficult time of his life during which he wrote *Letter*." Borrowing this humorous narrative persona enabled Hawthorne not only to distance himself from "the pain of his dismissal" from the Custom House but also to "disclaim in advance the attacks of the essay against his enemies," as well as to offset the gloom of *Letter*.

740   Valero-Garcés, Carmen. "Translations of *The Scarlet Letter* into Spanish." *Nathaniel Hawthorne Review* 20.1 (1994): 21-30.

Briefly reviews the early attention Hawthorne received in Europe, especially in Spain, and establishes 20 Spanish or South American translations of *Letter* that were published between the years 1894 and 1985, many of which are evaluated here for quality by comparing them to the original and other Spanish translations.

1995

Books

741   Johnson, Claudia Durst. *Understanding The Scarlet Letter: A Student Casebook to Issues, Sources, and Historical Documents.* Westport: Greenwood Press, 1995. 228 pp.

This interdisciplinary study demonstrates the controversial nature of *Letter* both at the time of its reception and in the late twentieth century, as well as places the novel in its Puritan historical context and Hawthorne's own time through the use of historical, theological, biographical, literary, and sociological documents. The first chapter contains a literary analysis of *Letter* that focuses on the many symbolic meanings of the letter. Chapters two through six focus on the novel's historical context and issues: "the seventeenth-century Puritan background; the place of the wilderness and nature; the Puritans' code of crime and punishment, their basic beliefs and habits of mind; the Antinomian controversy involving Anne Hutchinson; and the witchcraft trials of 1692." Chapters seven and eight make essential links between "The Custom-House" and *Letter*, and chapter nine examines twentieth-century issues pertinent to *Letter* (such as single parenthood, adultery, corporal punishment, separation of church and state, and child custody)—with special emphasis on the unwed mother and the immoral clergyman. Each of the major topics and each document or set of documents are introduced by an essay linking it to *Letter*. Also included are topics for research papers and class discussions, suggestions for further reading, bibliographies, a glossary of terms, and an index.

Essays and Studies in Books

742 Martin, John Stephen. Introduction. *The Scarlet Letter*. By Nathaniel Hawthorne. 1850. Peterborough, Ontario: Broadview Press, 1995. 11-64.

Divided into four sections, this substantial introduction (along with twelve appendices composed of literary/historical documents to which Martin often refers) "navigate[s] between providing a background for Hawthorne's text and giving some critical pointing of issues and problems" for "first-time university readers and to the general reader." It discusses "Hawthorne's Career Before the Writing of *Letter*," "Hawthorne and the Writing of *Letter* as a Romance," "Hawthorne's Romance and the 'Effects' of Narrative Irony," and "Hawthorne's Narrative Art of the Romance: A Reading Response."

743 Nichols, Nina da Vinci. "Hawthorne, the Romancer." *Ariadne's Lives*. Madison: Fairleigh Dickinson UP, 1995. 39-58.

While the overall book explores the function and development of the Ariadne myth in nineteenth-century literature, this chapter treats Hawthorne's revolutionary heroines (Hester, Zenobia, and Miriam—who symbolize "his hopes for the American experiment and his wish to construct a poetics of culture based on love")—in relation to his larger American romance mythology. Hawthorne employs a "supramythic Ariadne" as a "moralized aesthetic" and a "liberator from the joyless Puritan ethos" in Hester (pp. 43-51), whose character splits into three parts (Hester, Mistress Hibbins, and Pearl) to suggest her status as "triadic

370

goddess" in a "labyrinth of desire." The archetypal pattern is further played out in the characters of Chillingworth (Hester's "worldly Theseus") and Dimmesdale (Hester's "tormented Dionysos"), both of whom are "bound by reciprocal ties of tormentor and victim."

744   Sanford, John. "Pearl Prynne in *The Scarlet Letter*: Ad Libs by a Fictitious Character." *A Book of American Women*. Urbana: U of Illinois P, 1995. 17-19.

The self-proclaimed purpose of this book is a "panoramic raising of the national consciousness with respect to women in American life." Interspersed among historical portraits are "imaginative glosses on fictional characters," Pearl being one of them. Sanford reflects (in Pearl's voice) sympathetically on Hester and bitterly on Dimmesdale, referring to the latter as a "snake in the public grass" and as "that one-cent wick!" "My God," Pearl says as she contemplates whether Hester's ordeal was worth it for so slight a man: "To be lit but once and then so dimly!"

745   Walker, Nancy. "Of Hester and Offred." *The Disobedient Writer: Women and Narrative Tradition*. Austin: U of Texas P, 1995. 144-170.

Assessing the relationship between revisionist women writers and the formation of literary tradition, Walker focuses on texts that appropriate and revise earlier, traditional texts in a deliberate, "disobedient" reconstitution that accords with women's experience and vision. Margaret Atwood's *The Handmaid's Tale* (1985), discussed in chapter five, is "by far the most complex revision of Hawthorne's [*Letter*]." Although the two show striking cultural similarities in "the use of fundamentalist religious doctrine as a justification for political repression, the distance between official rhetoric and the 'truth' of actual life, and the use of women as cultural symbols," Atwood's text offers "narrative centrality" to the character of Offred, whereas Hawthorne's holds Hester back from achieving "a freedom of consciousness." Atwood revises, inverts, and extends *Letter*, not only incorporating elements of Hawthorne's story to create her own, but also interrogating "the relationship of the past to the present" in a way that Hawthorne does not—by questioning our ability to know the past or even our own personal histories. "Thus, while on one level Atwood retells Hawthorne's story, granting to Offred/Hester the agency of storyteller, she simultaneously casts doubt on the possibility of any telling of a 'true' story; as her tale is a 'reconstruction' of *Letter*, Offred's/Hester's autobiographical text is both a *self*-construction and a *re*-construction that questions the very concept of the self."

Journal Essays and Notes

746   Bellis, Peter. "Representing Dissent: Hawthorne and the Drama of Revolt." *ESQ: A Journal of the American Renaissance* 41 (1995): 97-119.

Critiquing Sacvan Bercovitch's "powerful and influential reading of the limits of American intellectual and political dissent" in *The Office of The Scarlet Letter* (see 635) for its problematic insistence that literary texts "must always remain confined within the dominant discourse of liberal pluralism," Bellis argues that *Letter* is *not* an "example of ideological containment at work." Hawthorne's romances, by their very nature, create "a hybrid, mediating space where opposites are brought together and authority destabilized." Thus they "work to undermine liberal ideology, countering its narrative of American exceptionalism and national progress with tales of violent disjunction and ideological struggle." Bellis examines two tales that he believes offer Hawthorne's criticism of American ideology "from within": "My Kinsman, Major Molineux" and "Howe's Masquerade." "Where the first story challenges the progressive historiography that Bercovitch identifies with nineteenth-century liberalism, the second focuses even more directly on the problematic relation between aesthetic representation and revolutionary action."

747   Derrick, Scott S. "'A Curious Subject of Observation and Inquiry': Homoeroticism, the Body, and Authorship in Hawthorne's *The Scarlet Letter*." *Novel* 28 (1995): 308-326.

Contends that *Letter* is typical of several homophobic works of nineteenth-century American fiction by men, in the sense that it explores the contemporary cultural and medical debate over the relation of the mind and the body (or, more specifically, the ability of the rational mind to control erotic desire) through a conventional heterosexual plot that is temporarily undermined by a "moment of homoerotic exploration or temptation" that threatens "stable and knowable social experience." Derrick divides his "analysis of the staging of homosexual identity" into three sections: the first discusses the homoerotic dynamics of the text (chapters nine through thirteen detail Chillingworth and Dimmesdale's "sexually diseased," intimate relationship and "foreground the body as an epistemological problem"); the second provides a cultural context to "rigorously" examine the threat of eroticism to the rational mind, to Dimmesdale's "psychic economy," and to the larger "narrative economy" of the novel; and the third demonstrates that Hawthorne links the textual "problems" of homosexuality and "bodily epistemology" to his "master-narrative," which redirects his brief attention to homosexuality back to his "troubled marriage plot" and "produces both the possibilities and limitations for understanding the many bodily 'mysteries' represented in the novel."

748   Dukats, Mara L. "The Hybrid Terrain of Literary Imagination: Maryse Condé's Black Witch of Salem, Nathaniel Hawthorne's Hester Prynne, and Aimé Césaire's Heroic Poetic Voice." *College Literature* 22 (1995): 51-61.*

Maryse Condé exposes the historical marginalization and "voicelessness" of Tituba, rewriting her story and confession to give her a new "hearing" in *I, Tituba, Black Witch of Salem*. Condé sees Tituba's silenced presence as a shaping force in the creation of both the Carribbean hero in Aimé Césaire's "Notebook of a Return to the Native Land" and Hester in *Letter*. Tituba's presence becomes a mediating force in *Letter* that allows Hester to think about her own marginal status and refute her subjugation. By creating a parallel between Tituba and Hester, and showing how Hester functions as a point of reference for Tituba, Condé allows the silenced heroine to intervene in the canon by proposing a revision of the way that we read texts. [For another essay that makes connections between Tituba and Hester (with reference to Maryse Condé's book), see Carolyn Duffey (780).]

*This essay is reprinted in *Race-ing Representation: Voice, History, and Sexuality* (Ed. Kostas Myrsiades and Linda Myrsiades. Lanham: Rowman and Littlefield, 1998. 141-154).

749   Egan, Ken, Jr. "The Adulteress in the Market-Place: Hawthorne and *The Scarlet Letter*." *Studies in the Novel* 27 (1995): 26-41.

Both Hawthorne and his "artistic rebel," Hester, can be seen as "subversive artists who must enter 'the market-place' with a scarlet letter, signifier of pride and shame, achievement and alienation." Hawthorne identifies with Hester beyond her "devilish" artistry, however, equating the empowerment and liberation of artistic reproduction with the act of adultery—and even viewing himself as an "adulteress" of sorts, since his desired career of writing (authorially adulterating "the truth" for the purposes of financial gain) and artistic temperament feminized him and forced him out of the paternalistic 'house of custom.' In other words, "the figure of the adulteress serves as a nexus for complex issues of vocation and gender Hawthorne had to confront at the moment of composing his novel and sketch." Further, Egan suggests that Hawthorne prostituted his own high themes in *Letter* by accompanying them with such popular sensational themes as "sex, adultery, and ministerial misdeeds."

Hawthorne just as shamelessly exploited the humiliation of his scandalous political "decapitation" for financial benefit in "The Custom-House." In this way, Hawthorne can be likened to Hester once she returns to Boston. Both know that "to survive in the marketplace, the author/adulteress must compromise, must balance internal vision against external form, subversive drives against communally sanctioned genres."

750   Gartner, Matthew. *"The Scarlet Letter* and the Book of Esther: Scriptural Letter and Narrative Life." *Studies in American Fiction* 23 (1995): 131-151.

Taking his cue from the fact that "The Custom-House" and the novel participate deeply in Puritan biblicism (and thus indicate Hawthorne's sophisticated grasp of scripture and divinity), Gartner investigates connections between *Letter* and the Book of Esther, suggesting that the novel may be written out of "a sympathetic and imaginative reading" of the biblical text—and even that the Book "serves as a sort of sunken groundwork of hidden scaffolding for Hawthorne's tale." Some of the more striking correspondences include analogies between principal characters (Hester/Queen Esther, Dimmesdale/Mordechai, and Chillingworth/Haman), the sharing of a central plot episode, and thematic congruencies that relate to issues of nationhood, the acts of reading and writing, and the difficulties in controlling textual interpretations of signs. Examination of the novel's hidden scriptural underpinnings leads to the conclusion that Hawthorne may actually have intended it to be read as an updated and revolutionary reading of the biblical text. Support for this conclusion lies in Hawthorne's having hinted at his interest in translating portions of the Bible into an American context in *Blithedale Romance* by naming his narrator, Miles Coverdale, after the character's historical namesake, the first man to translate the entire Bible into English in 1535.

751   Gussman, Deborah. "Inalienable Rights: Fictions of Political Identity in *Hobomok* and *The Scarlet Letter.*" *College Literature* 22 (1995): 58-80.

Setting up her argument by providing background in nineteenth-century laws regarding similar American citizenship rights for Native Americans and women (that "protected" the two groups by legally imposing characteristics of domesticity, dependence, and weakness), Gussman proposes that the literature of the era not only "embodied, reflected, and constructed" these discourses of Republican identity but also addressed the inferior political status of Indians and women by appealing to conceptions of liberty and equality that were "handed down" from Puritans and their revolutionary descendents. "Lydia Maria Child's *Hobomok* (1824) and Hawthorne's *Letter* contribute to these antebellum debates concerning the legal status of women and Native Americans." Authorial persona in each novel similarly fashions a "bid for authenticity and authority" (Hawthorne seemingly rejects an exclusively American political identity for a "literary" one, whereas Child's less privileged social and gendered position makes it impossible "to eschew the political for the literary"). Contrasts mark the constructions of political identities for Hester and Mary Conant. Whereas Hawthorne denies Hester a viable political identity and defeats her hoped-for role as a possible agent of change by internalizing in her a conventional political identity through motherhood and self-abnegation, Child optimistically offers Mary "more rights, more choices, and more substantive political agency" in "a more benevolent, egalitarian republic." Native Americans in both novels stay marginalized and excluded from society, evoking "the discourses that explored the character and fate of Native Americans in the 1850s." Pearl, like Hobomok and his half-white son, is "ultimately unassimilable as an American citizen."

752   Herbert, T. Walter. "Mozart, Hawthorne, and Mario Savio: Aesthetic Power and Political Complicity." *College English* 57 (1995): 397-409.

Urges that the "battle" waged between "traditionalists" (who emphasize aesthetics) and "revisionists" (who emphasize politics) over the value of *Letter* is faulty since the novel, like all great literature, is aesthetically powerful because of—and not in spite of—its social and political context. To prove this point, Herbert employs "Paleopsychology," or "the unearthing of psychic realties that were active in former eras," to explain Sophia Hawthorne's complicated relation to her husband. *Letter* was so powerful for her not because of its self-contained aesthetic unity but because "it spoke to painful dilemmas about gender and sexuality" that plagued both her and Hawthorne in their marriage. In other words, her aesthetic pleasure of his novel actually grew out of sexual politics and her conflicted experience of oppression as a woman/wife/mother of the nineteenth century. Herbert further cites two personal examples of cases in which aesthetic power combined with political complicity to achieve their effect (the playing of a Mozart piece in a Berkeley restaurant and a speech given by Mario Savio during a mid-1960s Civil Rights Demonstration)—which was to overwhelm him with the same type of "magical energy" that exudes from *Letter* and to make him "aware of the moral turbulence by which great literary art persistently lives afresh."

753   Kamaludin, Sabiha. "Basic Instinct and American Culture." *Indian Journal of American Studies* 25 (1995): 113-116.

Finds *Letter* to be one of the first fictions to acknowledge the undeniable sexual instinct, and compares Hester's sexuality to film heroines in *Gone With the Wind* (1932) and *Basic Instinct* (1992), arguing that when females assert strong sexual power, their male counterparts are either doomed to vulnerability and weakness or disappear altogether.

754   Kopley, Richard. "Hawthorne's Transplanting and Transforming of 'The Tell-Tale Heart.'" *Studies in American Fiction* 23 (1995): 231-241.

After searching for a correspondence between Hawthorne and Edgar Allan Poe that extends beyond the long-recognized affinity between *House of the Seven Gables* and "The Fall of the House of Usher" (and encouraged by George Ripley's 1850 observation that several similarities exist between the two writers), Kopley finds convincing evidence that Hawthorne "transplanted and transformed" "The Tell-Tale Heart" into *Letter*. Many parallels can be detected in chapter ten, "The Leech and His Patient," where Hawthorne's language and plot mimics Poe's in his description of a man violating another man (using such words as "old man," "evil eye," "chamber," "creak," "shadow," "cautious," and "stealthily"). The tale and novel also share symmetrical phrasing and structuring, as well as "the crucial theme of man's sinfulness, guilt, and need for confession." But whereas Poe's story concerns damnation, Hawthorne's involves the spiritual salvation brought about by Dimmesdale's own—literally—"tell-tale" heart.

755   Lewis, Charles. "The Ironic Romance of New Historicism: *The Scarlet Letter* and *Beloved* Standing in Side by Side." *Arizona Quarterly* 51 (1995): 33-60.

Examines the "peculiar and rather problematic" correspondences between *Letter* and Toni Morrison's *Beloved* (1988), and argues that Morrison's novel, like Hawthorne's, is a historical romance, but that hers uniquely calls attention to the fact that historical romance fiction and New Historicist criticism are "similar discursive modes" (since both forms of discourse are concerned with the relationship between history, imagination, and textuality). What's more, *Beloved* actually "problematizes" certain new historicist readings of *Letter* that "link Hawthorne's literary aesthetics with liberal ideology and social compromise and consensus regarding slavery"—namely those by "New Americanists" Sacvan Bercovitch (635) and Jonathan Arac (508). Morrison critiques both traditional and New Historicist readings of historical romance in *Beloved*, appropriating the conventions of American historical romance and managing to "retain race and gender as a *presence* in her fiction [not as an "absence," as Bercovitch and Arac claim that

Hawthorne does through various narrative techniques], and deploy that presence as a site of resistance." *Beloved* suggests that "Hawthorne's romantic techniques are not inherently constituted upon the absence of social conflict and the identities of difference, nor do they necessarily signify a repressed presence of that conflict (and the correlative components of social compromise and containment) available to us only by way of a reading that 'restores' that presence to its position as 'absent cause.'"

756   Martin, Terence. "The Power of Generalizations in *The Scarlet Letter*." *Nathaniel Hawthorne Review* 21.2 (1995): 1-6.

General truths (especially historical generalizations) abound in *Letter* but are presented in a manner that is "sophisticated, assured, [and] articulated with a pensive authority." Such powerful generalizations allow Hawthorne to demonstrate the limits of the dangerously inflexible Ramist (binary) logic of the Puritans (which involves seeing the world in terms of binary oppositions and moral absolutes), and also to explode that logic by invoking a vision of complexity.

757   Milliman, Craig. "Hester Prynne as the Artist of the Beautiful." *Publications of the Mississippi Philological Association* n.v. (1995): 82-87.

Owen Warland's dilemma in "The Artist of the Beautiful" (his vacillation between devotion to art and obeisance to conformity), which can be interpreted as an allegorical expression of the artist's struggle, surfaces in *Letter* through the three main characters. Dimmesdale and Chillingworth represent the "seemingly incompatible emotional poles between which the ideal artist vibrates," delicacy of feeling on one end and force of character on the other, while Hester combines the two, synthesizing them in her art. Illustrating Hawthorne's belief that art is "sometimes a blessing and sometimes a curse," Pearl is the key to the allegory since she grows up paralleling the evolution of the letter and true art itself—vilified at first, later co-opted and provisionally accepted by society, and finally institutionalized and revered.

758   Milliman, Craig. "Hawthorne's *The Scarlet Letter*." *Explicator* 53 (1995): 83-85.

Although critics have often remarked on Dimmesdale's rhetorical skills,* very few, it seems, notice that "Hester Prynne is also a master rhetorician." The opening scaffold scene and the scene in the Governor's mansion prove that Hester's skill in using "doublespeak" (borrowing the term from Michael Davitt Bell in 482) is just as effective as Dimmesdale's when communicating a coded message in a public setting. The latter scene especially speaks to Hester's rhetorical ability when she publicly entreats Dimmesdale to speak on her behalf and simultaneously, privately, threatens him three times with a reminder of his role in begetting Pearl (by implying to him alone the carnal use of the verb "to know").

*See "Dimmesdale, as manipulative, master rhetorician" under "Characters" in the Subject Index.

759   Nagy, Phyllis. "*The Scarlet Letter.*" *American Theatre* 12 (1995): 21-38.

Reproduces the playscript for Phyllis Nagy's play *The Scarlet Letter* (1994), which was adapted from Hawthorne's novel. In an interview with the playwright by Douglas Langworthy that precedes the script, Nagy explains what drew her to *Letter* in the first place, and discusses some of the dramatic license she took in writing her play: how and why, for instance, she jazzed up Hawthorne's "lush, descriptive prose" for the stage, added a character named "Brackett" (the town jailer), made Mistress Hibbins "maddeningly sexy," and had Pearl played by an adult actress who would be the same age as Hester's character and who would narrate the story.

760   Newbury, Michael. "Healthful Employment: Hawthorne, Thoreau, and Middle-Class Fitness." *American Quarterly* 47 (1995): 681-714.*

Situates Hawthorne and Henry David Thoreau in the middle of the antebellum middle-class physical fitness movement and the pervasive "cultural anxiety about the expansion of nonmanual work and material nonproductivity," since both authors indicate through their writing an idealization of manual labor and production. Whereas Hawthorne rejects the actual performance of manual labor at Brook Farm but invokes idealized forms of it in correspondence and in "The Custom-House" to figuratively represent his authorial work (elevating artisanal work above base commercial value and reconfiguring it as a healthy form of exercise), Thoreau associates the actual performance of his labors by the pond in *Walden* (1854) with the type of aesthetic work "in which contingencies of material production and economic values vanished." Both authors thus attempt in rhetorical terms, through "labors of the hand," to "reclaim for authorship the virtues and physical health" traditionally associated with manual work, attempting this reclamation "by mediating their representations of authorship through modes of idealized and residual manual work."

*See 797 for Newbury's book-length treatment of this subject.

761   Rajec, Elizabeth Molnar. "Onomastics in *The Scarlet Letter*." *University of Mississippi Studies in English* 11-12 (1993-1995): 455-459.

Proposing that the title of the novel "serves as the master key" to "decipher the connection between the title and the names of the main charactonyms," Rajec traces the etymology (and occasionally historical and literary roots) of the words "scarlet," "Prynne," "Hester," "Arthur Dimmesdale," "Roger Chillingworth," and "Pearl," concluding that "Hawthorne's nomenclature in *Letter* reflects an artistic as well as an authentic picture of the colonial history of the 1640s."

762   Reiss, John. "Hawthorne's *The Scarlet Letter*." *Explicator* 53 (1995): 200-201.

Finds it "surprising that so little critical attention has been given to the allegorical representations of free will and predestination in the main characters of *Letter*," Hester being "clearly associated" with the Papist conception of free will, Chillingworth with predestination, Dimmesdale with a middle ground—a wavering "between a desperate practice of Papist penance and a more dominant belief in Calvinistic predestination," and Pearl with Nature.

763   Sweeney, Susan Elizabeth. "The Madonna, the Women's Room, and *The Scarlet Letter*." *College English* 57 (1995): 410-425.

In this feminist reading that begins with its author-professor's account and interpretation of a pre-tenure dream in which the Madonna appeared to her in the women's room of the conservative Jesuit college where she teaches English, Sweeney discusses the ways her successive readings of (and thus teaching approaches to) *Letter* have changed through the years as a result of her experiences as a woman. Approaching the novel as a reader-response critic and reception theorist, Sweeney cites "accounts of the psychological process by which readers [she and her students] make sense" of *Letter*, and, in particular, explores the image of the Virgin Mary and other Papist imagery (in conflict with Puritan hermeneutics in the novel) that she never recognized before her Catholic students pointed them out to her. Sweeney comes full circle in the article by relating her dream (which seems to highlight her outsider status as a woman, a feminist, and a non-Catholic in her teaching institution) to *Letter*, which similarly concerns complications created by minority gender, politics, and religious identity—as well as addresses analagous conflicts between private self and public persona and questions of "community, identity, and belonging."

764   Tassi, Nina. "Hawthorne's Hester: Female History in Fiction." *CEA Magazine: A Journal of the College English Association* 8 (1995): 5-14.

Taking Anne Hutchinson as his inspiration for creating Hester Prynne, Hawthorne could "freely swim in the turbulent sea of nineteenth-century debates about female freedom while staying at a safe remove from both the hot public exchanges he disliked and his own deep conflicts over female powers." Hawthorne's "Mrs. Hutchinson" sketch (1830) sheds light on *Letter*'s portrayal of the "manly" Hester and the "feminine" Dimmesdale, as Hawthorne rearranges traditional gender traits in his lovers to explore sexually related issues of the advancing women's movement. Beneath his sympathy for Hester (and Hutchinson) lies his "bedrock commitment" to patriarchy, however—and although he does not break Hester's spirit in the end, he denies her true emancipation. [See 827 for Tassi's expanded treatment of this topic.]

765   Welsh, Jim. "Classic Folly: *The Scarlet Letter*." *Literature/Film Quarterly* 23 (1995): 299-300.

Roland Joffé's "foolishly updated though beautifully photographed [movie] version" of the novel offers "an insult to literature of the highest order." *Letter* is "corrupted beyond endurance" in this 1995 presentation of attacking Indians (who were added most likely since the movie version of *Last of the Mohicans* [1992] raked in a good bit of money at the box office) and smug Puritans who need to "lighten up" on the free-spirited, feminist, and "babish" Hester and the Indian-defending, "hunky" Dimmesdale. Welsh is further outraged at the ludicrous characterization of the "absolutely whacked out" Chillingworth (only called Roger Prynne in the movie, surely so as not to confuse non-readers), who is reduced to a "cartoon lunatic." Overall, the film is a "vulgar spectacle" and an "abomination," its only redeeming feature being the glorious Nova Scotia scenery that passes for colonial Massachusetts.

766   Wilson, Raymond J., III. "The Possibility of Realism: 'The Figure in the Carpet' and Hawthorne's Intertext." *Henry James Review* 16 (1995): 142-152.

Unlike critics (such as J. Hillis Miller) who view Henry James's story "The Figure in the Carpet" as a paradigm for the "unreadability" of all texts, Wilson argues that when the story is viewed intertextually with Hawthorne's "The Custom-House" (particularly with the latter's reference to moonlit figures in the carpet), it becomes something quite different. That is, James's story bespeaks the ability of fiction to reveal the truth about reality if—and only if—it is approached with the intellect, the imagination, and the heart. The passage in "The Custom-House" that describes the necessary combination of muted firelight (the heart) and full moonlight (the imagination) for writing romance is most likely the source for James's story, which is a self-conscious dialogue with Hawthorne about the superiority of realism writing over romance writing, as well as his criticism of Hawthorne's choice of genre since "the true and indestructible" can only be extracted from realism's "petty and wearisome incidents and ordinary characters."

1996

Essays and Studies in Books

767   Bona, Damien. "Demi Moore in *The Scarlet Letter* (1995): 'Naked in New England.'" *Hollywood's All-Time Worst Casting Blunders.* Secaucus: Carol Publishers, 1996. 91-94.

Classifying actress Demi Moore's performance in the 1995 film version of *The Scarlet Letter* under the "Error in Eras" section of his book where performers' "personas and modern sensibilities were completely out of place when they traveled to the past," Bona contends that the film's director, Roland Joffé, wanted to "free" Hester and "let her fly" even more badly than he imagines Hawthorne did. In other words, Joffé wanted a liberated woman of the 1990s, and so he ridiculously cast an actress who "would probably be incapable of conveying a sexually repressed [Puritan] character even if she were fitted with a chastity belt." What's worse, Joffé permits a happy ending to the tale of grief and guilt that involves the liberated Hester and Dimmesdale driving off together to the Carolinas.

768   Budick, Emily Miller. "The Romance of History: Nathaniel Hawthorne's *Scarlet Letter." Nineteenth-Century American Romance: Genre and the Construction of Democratic Culture.* New York: Twayne, 1996. 78-99.*

Charting in her book the development of pluralism and democracy in the fiction of James Fenimore Cooper, Edgar Allan Poe, Hawthorne, Herman Melville, and Henry James, Budick begins chapter four by distinguishing Hawthorne's brand of romance fiction from Poe's, noting that while Hawthorne shares Poe's self-consciousness, self-reflexivity, and tendency to focus on the inner workings of the human psyche, he nonetheless discovers a unique and "aversive mode of writing that has direct implications for the continuity of the romance tradition" in the nineteenth and twentieth centuries. Hawthorne's fiction "participates in the skeptical inquiry of Poe's writing" (which insists that there is no real meaning in life except that which is manufactured by self-conscious humans), but it denies that the world is therefore unknowable or meaningless. By creating a connection between the historical past and the "fictionalizing imagination" in *Letter*, Hawthorne renders the historical world allegorical and subverts the Puritans' symbolic way of perceiving reality. When Hawthorne shows how the Puritans' absolute and definitive labeling of Hester falls apart under the multitude of meanings the scarlet letter generates, he is commenting on the rigidity and authoritarianism exemplified in the human tendency to settle and resolve all doubts, as well as providing a critique of patriarchal culture.

*See 654 for a similar, earlier essay by Budick.

769   Easton, Alison. "The Best Harvest of His Mind: *The Scarlet Letter.*" *The Making of the Hawthorne Subject.* Columbia: U of Missouri P, 1996. 189-247, 284-291.

Argues that Hawthorne found the theories on human subjectivity that were his cultural inheritance to be inadequate (Scottish Common-Sense psychology and the romantic ideas of the individual), and so he developed his own theory on the conflicted human subject over the first twenty-five years of his career—with that theory reaching its fullest conceptualization and fictional realization in *Letter*. In a survey of Hawthorne's early writing, Easton contends that critics have neglected to view Hawthorne's body of work as a developing and patterned intellectual and artistic process* that gradually comes to terms with all the contradictions inherent in being "a subject and existing in social relations." Such tensions include "radicalism and conservativism, speculation and orthodoxy, relativism and absolutism, subjectivity and the social order, sympathy and judgment, the 'Imaginary' and the 'Actual.'" Most of Easton's chapter on *Letter* considers how the novel "explores matters of interrogation, interpretation, value judgments, narrative focalization, and closure," largely considering the "complex interaction of individual subjectivity and the social order that creates a divided self-portrayal of subjectivity in the three adult protagonists" (with emphasis on Hawthorne's mirror motif in the novel, which represents "the gap between the various positions the subject is assigned in the social order and those aspects of the self neither accepted nor represented there"). The remaining part "examines resolutions sought and outcomes reached," finding that Hawthorne at last accepts the "complexity and contradiction" that come from a representation of self that is neither totally free to express its individuality and desire nor completely determined by social institutions and circumstance.

770   Haroian-Guerin, Gil. "Hester Prynne: The American Transformation."
       *The Fatal Hero: Diana, Deity of the Moon, as an Archetype of the Modern
       Hero in English Literature.* New York: Peter Lang, 1996. 49-92.

       Like other nineteenth-century novelists who undertook the radical act of
       re-evaluating traditional, one-sided representations of women in American
       and English culture, Hawthorne produced a multi-faceted "hero of
       regeneration" in Hester. Hee creates Hester to herald the destruction of
       stale Puritan ideologies and to usher in fresh modes of thought and action.
       Haroian-Guerin examines the novel's symbolic use of colors and its
       romantic, medieval, and alchemic framework, linking Hester (and Pearl)
       to several configurations of the moon goddess. As a "heterogeneous-
       natured Diana hybrid," Hester transforms herself into a redemptive and
       artistic hero, accepting her earth-bound role as exiled angel and ultimately
       setting in motion a process of feminine rebirth for herself, Pearl, and her
       fellow Bostonian women.

771   Hodges, Elizabeth Perry. "The Letter of the Law: Reading Hawthorne and
       the Law of Adultery." *Law and Literature Perspectives.* Ed. Bruce L.
       Rockwood. New York: Peter Lang, 1996. 133-168.

       Hawthorne's method in "building" *Letter* is "not unlike a lawyer's when
       he builds a case—juxtaposing past and present, precedent and context."
       While Hawthorne recognized the necessity of legal institutions to preserve
       the structures of society against the pressures of autonomy and change, he
       also found just as necessary the need to encourage freedom, passion,
       paradox, and ambiguity (as seen throughout the text in his apparent
       concern with reducing Hester's complex humanity to the fixed meaning
       associated with her scarlet letter). Exposing the limitations of such
       seemingly definable categories as history, religion, and myth in his
       dramatization of the struggle between form and experience, Hawthorne
       questions whether the law is able to bring about structure and
       homogeneity at all. Hodges reviews the complex legal history of adultery
       that helped to inform Puritan law (which involves Christian morality,
       Mosaic law, and early English law) and shows that *Letter* "stands on a
       precarious line between primitive law, where private wrongs are righted
       by an individual act of revenge, and modern state law, where the state
       takes over the job of punishing the wrong." Of all the characters, only
       Hester and Pearl "offer imaginative alternatives to both Puritan formalism
       and the excesses of personal vindictiveness."

772   Ingebretsen, Edward J. "'Entertaining Satan': The American Rite of
       Deviancy." *Maps of Heaven, Maps of Hell: Religious Terror as Memory
       from the Puritans to Stephen King.* Armonk: M. E. Sharpe, 1996. 39-76.

Focuses on the rite of witch-hunting in seventeenth-century New England and its fictional representation as perennial American myth and unifying rite of deviancy, tracing several discourses generated by Salem's shameful practice—from those by Cotton Mather to those by Stephen King—to get at their dual perception of witchcraft as both threat to the social order and as diversion or entertainment. The sub-chapter entitled "Interlude: The House That Hawthorne Haunted" (50-57) argues that Hawthorne's awareness of this dual perception of witchcraft inspired him to rewrite Salem's original theological account of witchcraft and to transform it into romance. In the realm of imaginative fiction, Salem's dark history becomes ambiguous, and the witch-like Hester is converted from a threat to a cultural icon or "an approved focus for community energy."

773   Kalfopoulou, Adrianne. "Gendered Silences and the Problem of Desire in Nathaniel Hawthorne's *The Scarlet Letter*, Gertrude Stein's 'Melanctha,' and Gail Jones's *Corregidora*." *Nationalism and Sexuality: Crises of Identity*. Ed. Yiorgos Kalogeras and Domna Pastourmatzi. Thessaloniki, Greece: Hellenic Association of American Studies, 1996. 115-123.

Hester's subversive identity is entirely subsumed by the symbolic self defined for her by the Puritan social order. Like the heroines of Stein's "Melanctha" and Jones's *Corregidora*, Hester secretly contests the requirements of her gendered social role but is ultimately silenced by Hawthorne when she is made to accept the conventional "rhetoric of nineteenth-century True Womanhood, which required women's piety and subservience to patriarchal authority." Since Hester is domesticated by her maternal role, her unconventional identity is erased altogether in death by a tombstone that acknowledges only the public symbolism of the letter "A."

774   McFarlane, Brian. "*The Scarlet Letter* (1926)." *Novel to Film: An Introduction to the Theory of Adaptation*. Oxford: Clarendon Press, 1996. 39-68.

Hawthorne's "symbolic romance" was transformed into "romantic melodrama" with the commercially successful 1926 silent film adaptation (starring Lillian Gish) that skillfully manipulated the conservative moral climate of Hollywood in the mid-1920s by presenting Hester as a victimized innocent and Dimmesdale as charmingly virile and guiltless in falling for Hester's "innocently beguiling qualities." McFarlane details the process by which the novel's narrative structure was adapted to suit classic Hollywood style, explaining that the film dispenses with "The Custom-House" and "any need for a first-person narrator," lightens the tone of the beginning and treats the plot events of the novel in a linear manner to enhance the story's emotional power (allowing the love affair of Hester and Dimmesdale to develop gradually on-screen and dominate the first third of the movie). The movie further invents a comic sub-plot involving a blundering character named Giles, whose light-hearted "naturalness" and compassion align him with Hester in being ill-suited for the grim, morally rigid Puritan community to which he belongs. McFarlane also explains how the effects of lighting, figure arrangement and posture, and camera distance/angle illustrate the historical perspective on the "phenomenon of adaptation" by producing "visual equivalents for novelistic effects intransigently dependent upon the linguistic medium." An appendix to the chapter (pp. 203-238) presents a shot analysis of each segment of the film.

775   Swisher, Clarice, ed. *Readings on Nathaniel Hawthorne*. San Diego: Greenhaven Press, 1996.

In addition to providing a forward, biography, chronology of events in American history from 1800-1865, a list of Hawthorne's works, and a brief bibliography, this anthology (part of the Greenhaven Literary Companion Series) presents edited and excerpted essays on a variety of topics in a format designed to be accessible to young adult readers. The seven reprinted essays on *Letter* (introduced by a concise summation of its main themes and insights) include excerpts from Stanley T. Williams's "Nathaniel Hawthorne" (23), Charles Feidelson, Jr.,'s *Symbolism and American Literature* (21), Randall Stewart's Introduction to *The American Notebooks* (EC31), Richard Chase's *The American Novel and Its Tradition* (55), Michael Davitt Bell's *Hawthorne and the Historical Romance of New England* (261), Hyatt H. Waggoner's *Hawthorne: A Critical Study* (38), and Randall Stewart and Dorothy Bethurum's *Living Masterpieces of American Literature* (30).

776   Wamser, Garry. "The Scarlet Contract: Puritan Resurgence, the Unwed Mother, and Her Child." *Law and Literature Perspectives*. Ed. Bruce L. Rockwood. New York: Peter Lang, 1996. 381-406.

Drawing from his experiences as a legal services attorney that familiarized him with social and legal attitudes toward adultery, Wamser sees *Letter* as a cautionary tale with extraordinary parallels to the 1994 Republican "Contract With America" and its impact on welfare, mothers, and children. Adultery in the Puritan era was viewed as a problem of immorality best addressed through condemnation and punitive sanctions. With failure to assist unwed mothers in our own time, we "have come full circle to Puritan Boston, punishing the immoral mother and inevitably the innocent child."

Journal Essays and Notes

777   Baym, Nina. "Hawthorne's *Scarlet Letter*: Producing and Maintaining an American Literary Classic." *Journal of Aesthetic Education* 30 (1996): 61-75.

In a manner nearly identical to Jane Tompkins's in her groundbreaking 1985 essay on "The Politics of Hawthorne's Literary Reputation" (495), Baym discusses "how and why [*Letter*] was made *into* a classic"—with none of those reasons having anything to do with Hawthorne's intrinsic greatness or genius. Before tracing "the particulars of its production, reception, and transmission all along the temporal line," Baym presents four historical conditions making it particularly ripe for a "classic" novel to emerge from New England in the mid-nineteenth century (the most pertinent being that literature by New Englanders was strongly encouraged, "with New England subjects and themes presented in a national context" that would secure the reputation of New England as "the historical fountainhead of the nation"). She next surveys Hawthorne's unpromising beginning as a writer and his mediocre writing success until strong literary and political connections were made to "guarantee that future work would be noticed." Having then attracted the attention of a shrewd and important publisher (James T. Fields), Hawthorne and his novel were an instant success, "perhaps less on account of the power of the novel than the political interest of 'The Custom-House.'" A cooperative effort of Hawthorne himself, his publisher (first Ticknor and Fields and then later Houghton, Mifflin), New England reviewers, Hawthorne's friends and family, and then "sociopolitical, critical, publishing, and educational forces in New England" saw to it that *Letter* and Hawthorne's reputation were ever secure. Baym concludes with a final point: "Classics depend on the activities of those who celebrate, criticize, and transmit them," and "these activities are inevitably distorted by self-interest, and by differences in values."

778   Bercovitch, Sacvan. "*The Scarlet Letter*: A Twice-Told Tale." *Nathaniel Hawthorne Review* 22.2 (1996): 1-20.

Sex and violence serve to recontextualize *Letter* in the "freely adapted" 1995 film version by Roland Joffé that stars Demi Moore (Hester), Gary Oldman (Dimmesdale), and Robert Duvall (Chillingworth). This box-office disaster's attempt at pleasing modern audiences with an action-packed story of sexual liberation and the flight to freedom altogether lacks the tragic dimension of the novel and is little more than "a collage of contemporary clichés"—but the film is actually quite similar to *Letter* when one considers that both novel and movie are strategically geared to the concerns of their own times. Bercovitch is interested in the cultural legacy of New England Puritanism here, and he studies how Puritanism was adapted first by Hawthorne in 1850 and then by filmmakers in 1995— curiously finding that both versions represent the volatile historical condition that includes perpetual cultural conflict in interpreting "the American way." The movie places all hope on the free individual (and his own personal fulfillment for self and family), or "individual democracy," while Hawthorne endorses society itself, or "civic democracy," which he hopes will gradually evolve into a state of liberal freedom. Our culture has consistently honored both extremes at once, making the latest movie version of *Letter* a testament to "the continuing resonance of the American Puritan ritual, and to its malleability."

779   Diffee, Christopher. "Postponing Politics in Hawthorne's *Scarlet Letter*." *MLN* 111 (1996): 835-871.

Takes issue with critics like Jonathan Arac (in 508), Sacvan Bercovitch (in 691), and F. O. Matthiessen before them (in EC20) for using Hawthorne's nineteenth-century historical context to excuse his political passivity (by suggesting that Hawthorne's method of "multiple-choice" symbolism, which "form[ed] the aesthetic vehicle through which opposition is transmuted into complementarity," mimicked the nation's experience of social cohesion). Diffee instead faults Hawthorne for his sterile and "equivocal pluralist politics," noting that even Herman Melville and Henry James recognized and sought to make excuses for Hawthorne's passionless, "detached-observer" stance in his allegorical fiction. Hawthorne's love of allegorical representations in fact stemmed from the fact that allegory "communicates something that is only *like* expression," "literally stealing human warmth away until only 'expressive gestures' remain." Diffee proceeds to examine the "mechanism" by which the scarlet letter operates in the novel, noting that the letter "becomes an allegory for the law itself"—reduced to meaninglessness because it is "strangely lacking reference"in its empty and endless referentiality. [For another essay that similarly faults Hawthorne's political passivity, see Eric Cheyfitz (732).]

780   Duffey, Carolyn. "Tituba and Hester in the Intertextual Jail Cell: New World Feminisms in Maryse Condé's *Moi, Tituba, Sorcière Noire de Salem*." *Women in French Studies* 4 (1996): 100-110.

In her 1986 novel, Guadeloupean author Maryse Condé provides an "intertextual, interracial, and intercultural" seventeenth-century Salem meeting in a jail cell between the "muted" black slave Tituba (who was "erased" from history and literature after being accused of witchcraft) and Hawthorne's "still pregnant and quite defiant" Hester Prynne. Condé creates a dialogue between them as a way of addressing the over-emphasized split between women of the first and third worlds—and to call attention to the inaccurate portrait (by Western feminists) of third-world women as victims who suffer under a universalized patriarchal oppression and who lack "control over their own bodies and sexualities." In "artfully staging the politics of this complicated encounter between first and third world feminisms as the accused witch and the alleged adulterous wife" (and parodying modern feminist discourse in the process), Condé grants Tituba the main narrative role and has Hester commit suicide, having "refuse[d] Hawthorne's position for her as the sorrowing mother, punished for her adultery by maternity." It is thus Tituba who survives to resist denying "the female body or the effacement of feminine desire," while "with tragic irony, Hester kills herself, a [feminist] whose body is the place of her despair." [For another essay that discusses the relation between Tituba and Hester in Maryse Condé's book, see Mara L. Dukats (748).]

781   Erlich, Gloria. "Subjectivity and Speculation in Thematic Biography: Nathaniel Hawthorne and Edith Wharton." *Biography and Source Studies* 2 (1996): 79-96.

Making no apologies for her subjective and speculative method in creating "thematic" biography, Erlich defends her distinctive genre (not much respected in academia, she acknowledges) and explains how she came to see the "identity theme" as central to the lives and creative works of Hawthorne and Wharton (fully explored in *Family Themes and Hawthorne's Fiction* [see 459] and *The Sexual Education of Edith Wharton* [1992], which examine the effects of "doubled paternal figures" on Hawthorne's and Wharton's imaginations ("split parenting" affected both, Hawthorne having a father-surrogate after his own father died and Wharton having both a mother and a beloved nanny). Erlich explains that she loosely followed Hawthorne's method in "The Custom-House" in writing these biographies, taking facts and "dead" historical records and then interpreting and vitalizing them "through an imagination awakened by sympathetic heat on the interpreter's own heart." Just as Hawthorne could only write creatively once he had been politically "decapitated," so Erlich could only as an independent scholar (severed from academic ties) cultivate her speculative tendencies (reading Hawthorne's experience of midlife creativity through her own midlife vocational crisis, for instance)

388

and "illuminat[e] the role of subjectivity in research and of transference and identification."

782   Johnston, Paul K. "Killing the Spirit: Anne Hutchinson and the Office of the Scarlet Letter." *Nathaniel Hawthorne Review* 22.1 (1996): 26-35.

Critiquing the New Historical approach to literature—of which Bercovitch's *The Office of The Scarlet Letter* (see 635) is an example—for its limiting "collaborative view" of imaginative literature, Johnston posits a less popular and (a hoped for) ideology-free perspective that celebrates an "oppositional view," and considers the possibility that Hawthorne was operating "more in opposition to the dominant ideology of American culture than Bercovitch suggests." Johnston contends that *Letter* may not be a critique of radicalism at all, but perhaps was intended to advocate Anne Hutchinson's radically antinomian claim during her 1637 Puritan trial that "the letter [Puritan law and authority] killeth, but the spirit giveth life" (a biblical reference from Saint Paul's Second Letter to the Corinthians). If such a reading is accepted, then the scarlet letter actually fulfills its "office" not through Hester's penitent return to America at the end but through Dimmesdale's death on the scaffold. The scarlet letter's killing force claims Dimmesdale but not Hester, although it can also be seen to kill her spirit. Allying himself with Hutchinson's antinomian terms (the killing letter vs. the lifegiving spirit) "to forge the oppositions of the novel," then, Hawthorne does not promote liberal patience as Bercovitch suggests, but instead "provoke[s] a radical impatience." [Johnston's essay is one of three to appear in this issue of the *Nathaniel Hawthorne Review* that responds to Sacvan Bercovitch's *The Office of The Scarlet Letter* (635). See also Robert Milder (787) and Richard Millington (788).]

783   Kearns, Michael. "Narrative Voices in *The Scarlet Letter*." *Nathaniel Hawthorne Review* 22.1 (1996): 36-52.

Applying Mikhail Bakhtin's theory of "heteroglossia" in novelistic discourse to his own analysis of the inconsistencies in the narrative voice in *Letter*, Kearns proposes that the novel is actually "dialogic" or narrated by numerous voices that create "a rhetorical effect consistent with the complex combination of moral and historical circumstances dramatized in the novel." This approach, which makes sense of the frequent anachronisms, historical "leaps" in diction, and inconsistent levels of scientific and historical knowledge associated with a single narrator in the novel, identifies four distinct narrative voices that appear to address distinct audiences: a nineteenth-century psychologist (most likely Hawthorne), a seventeenth-century superstitious Puritan, a romancer/historian who "ventriloquizes" historically inaccurate Puritan beliefs about the soul's salvation, and a sympathetic, philosophical voice that is "heard near the end of the novel." In dialogue, these voices add a richness and complexity to the novel that suggest they were created intentionally so that Hawthorne could both dramatize dissonant voices/perspectives and avoid establishing one single authority (the latter permitting an escape from "the quandary of intentionality").

784   Kilcup, Karen L.   "'Ourselves behind Ourself, Concealed': The Homoerotics of Reading in *The Scarlet Letter*." *ESQ: A Journal of the American Renaissance* 42 (1996): 1-28.

Examines the homoerotic component of the Dimmesdale/Chillingworth relationship (both of whom Hawthorne feminizes and presents with "insecure" gender identities), and also addresses a parallel "teasing" relationship of "hide-and-seek," of concealing and revealing, that exists for Hawthorne in the author/reader dynamic. Kilcup applies gay theorist Diana Fuss's conception of "inside" (heterosexual) and "outside" (homosexual) to her account of the "erotic dialogues" of the novel, which, again, are encapsulated in the homosexual desires of the two male protagonists and include Hawthorne's erotically charged relationship with the reader, to and by whom he is both attracted and repulsed. Hawthorne's teasing ambiguity, his incessant oscillation between "yes" and "no" (of rhetorically soliciting interpretive "penetration, climax, and withdrawal"), mirrors the story's "hidden substantive sexual excess," revealing, more importantly, "the fluidity and interconnectedness of sexual, gender, and racial boundaries." Kilcup also applies Lee Edelman's work in gay theory to her discussions of the dynamics of revelation and concealment, and of the intimate relation between sexual and textual selfhood in *Letter*. She hints suggestively that the "surer ground of mutual happiness" Hawthorne refers to at the end may be the "'golden' homoerotic love" between Chillingworth and Dimmesdale and Hester and her lesbian community of women—and that Hester's return at the end (which teasingly extends the meaning of her "bodily textuality") provides a masterbatory type of lingering self-pleasuring for both Hawthorne and the reader.

785   Lepore, Jill.   "*The Scarlet Letter/Pocahontas*." *American Historical Review* 101.4 (1996): 1166-1168.

Compares two 1995 movies of "New World Encounters"—Roland Joffé's *Letter* and Disney's *Pocahontas*—and cites a "creepy familiarity" between the two "badly written, dull, and not very clever" films. In addition to sharing gross historical inaccuracies, both films also explore "issues central to a sizable chunk of recent historical scholarship: cross-cultural encounters, race, gender, and nature." In fact, both movies "tinker" with historical chronology so that the final action of both films is the brink of war, where the heroes and heroines—Hester and Dimmesdale, Pocahontas and John Smith (who are so "uniquely suited to forging successful cross-cultural relations" in the space of the films)—transcend their violent, racist, patriarchal, prudish historical legacies by showing their twentieth-century, enlightened status and rising above the conflict, the latter two by averting the war and the former by skipping town altogether.

786   Matchie, Thomas. "Louise Erdrich's 'Scarlet Letter': Literary Continuity in *Tales of Burning Love*." *North Dakota Quarterly* 63 (1996): 113-123.

Claims that Native American author Louise Erdrich's *Tales of Burning Love* (1996) is "her contemporary answer—or parallel—to the classic American romantic love novel, *Letter*"—since both share themes such as "the mystery of love between the sexes, the inner and outer worlds through which it is manifested, the dubious connection of sexuality to religion, and how various types of personalities enter into and affect a marriage or lovers' union." Matchie's suggests that the five wives of construction engineer Jack Mauser represent the five faces or postures of Hester and that a "healing" sexual encounter between two of the wives in the back seat of a Ford Explorer is a foil for the destructive relationship of Chillingworth and Dimmesdale. In the eventual sexual reunion of Jack with his favorite—and must elusive—wife Eleanor (who is the husband's "real Hester Prynne") at the novel's end, Erdrich parts ways with Hawthorne to make "sexuality, religion, and nature work together."

787   Milder, Robert. "*The Scarlet Letter* and Its Discontents." *Nathaniel Hawthorne Review* 22.1 (1996): 9-25.

Finds Bercovitch guilty in *The Office of The Scarlet Letter* (635) of applying his own vision of "pluralistic communitarianism" to *Letter* (despite his professed claim of working "within the boundaries of Hawthorne's interpretive framework"). As Milder sees it, Hawthorne's "editorial chastisement" of Hester in the one-sentence paragraph that forms the basis of Bercovitch's study, "The scarlet letter had not done its office," is actually "Hawthorne's about-face on female liberation," and that the root of Hester's dissenting, freethinking ways—which are based on Margaret Fuller's—is sexual frustration. What makes the novel so interesting is that Hawthorne seems both attracted to and repelled by Hester's sexuality. On the one hand, Hawthorne anticipates Freud's "fear of women's sexuality as disruptive and potentially anarchic," and on the other he holds an "anti-Freudian" view of sexuality as "an impulse toward the liberation of human instinct"—which Hawthorne represents through the eroticism of his dark, rebellious heroine. "The question Hawthorne asks through this figure [. . .] is whether the rebellious woman demanding free expression of her nature is the prototype for a new human personality (and ultimately a new social organization) or a splendid atavism whose unduplicated physicality is at war with moral and spiritual progress." In grappling with the proper relationship between "Eros and Civilization" within the community, however, Hawthorne "could envision no social or moral space between the repressiveness of Puritan Boston and the wildness of the forest—in psychic terms, between the superego and the libido," and thus he anxiously opts to suppress and contain Hester's hopes for sexual and psychological liberation. Her final submission to her fate is not "dissent into the gradualism of progress," as Bercovitch suggests, but "seems rather a vehicle on Hawthorne's part for acknowledging and indefinitely postponing the claims both of women for social equality and of sexuality for inclusion in a balanced ideal of human development." [Milder's essay is one of three to appear in this issue of the *Nathaniel Hawthorne Review* that responds to Sacvan Bercovitch's *The Office of The Scarlet Letter* (635). See also Paul K. Johnston (782) and Richard Millington (788).]

788   Millington, Richard [H.]. "*The Office of The Scarlet Letter*: An 'Inside Narrative'?" *Nathaniel Hawthorne Review* 22.1 (1996): 1-8.

This essay, like Milder's (787) and Johnston's (782) above, also addresses Sacvan Bercovitch's *The Office of The Scarlet Letter*. Millington praises Bercovitch's book for its outstanding explanation of *Letter* as an analysis of antebellum American cultural history, as "an allegory of ideology," but criticizes the fact that reading it "is curiously *like* the experience of participating in 'the American ideology' Bercovitch has so brilliantly described." Bercovitch's interpretation not only "flattens" the emotional experience of reading *Letter* by its own obsessive participation in current ideological trends in Americanist literary criticism but also imagines itself exempt from the reality of its own participation in that present middle-class ideological enterprise. Millington demonstrates that Bercovitch's too exclusive focus on freedom and consensus "produces a striking erasure of conflicts within Hawthorne's text" by examining two specific points from Bercovitch's text. He does not view Hester's radicalism, as Bercovitch does, as stemming from her "affiliation to European political history" but rather as distinguished from it, stemming instead from her own emotional commitment and obligations as "generated by her own emotional history [. . .] in the context of the book's own action." And of Hester's return to Boston, Millington takes issue with Bercovitch's interpretation—that her real freedom lies in her consent to ideological containment, her compromise with the liberal consensus—and argues that Hester's return is instead tied to a "sense of fidelity to her emotional [and intellectual] history." Finally dismissing a narrow reading that erases the book's emotional investments, Millington concludes that "Hester's deepest yearning [. . .] is not for freedom but for a reimagined social life [. . .], for a lover and for a community able to accommodate the forms of connection she envisions for them.

789   Smith, Lisa Herb. "'Some Perilous Stuff': What the Religious Reviewers Really Said about *The Scarlet Letter*." *American Periodicals: Journal of History, Criticism, and Bibliography* 6 (1996): 135-143.

Critics have not sufficiently examined the difference in emphasis between the secular and religious reviews of *Letter* in 1850. "While reviewers from secular periodicals tended to gear their discussions toward aesthetic issues, reviewers from religious periodicals consistently concentrated on the doctrinal issues raised by the text." Smith examines the six religious periodicals that reviewed *Letter* (the *Independent, Christian Inquirer, Christian Register, Christian Examiner, Church Review*, and *Brownson's Quarterly Review*), finding that five of them applied theological tenets to their analyses. While most recognized Hawthorne's genius, they all condemned his ethical choices and the lack of morality in *Letter*, and faulted the novel for a variety of specific reasons: choice of illicitly sexual subject matter, false presentation of the New England Puritans, apparent sympathy for its errant characters, and faulty depiction of Christianity. These criticisms were extended to fearful expressions of growing liberalism in nineteenth-century America, which, when exemplified in such novels as *Letter*, encouraged the corruption of their readers' moral sense.

790   Tucker, Edward L. "Darley's Model for Roger Chillingworth." *Nathaniel Hawthorne Review* 22.1 (1996): 53-55.

Briefly discusses the trip taken by New York artist Felix Darley to the Massachusetts Historical Society rooms to study old portraits of Puritans that would serve as models for his series of illustrations for *Letter*. According to an 1859 diary entry by Henry W. Longfellow (to whom Darley's series was dedicated), one in particular served as the model for Chillingworth, although whether the portrait is of Dr. John Clark, co-founder of Rhode Island, or physician John Clarke of Newbury, is debatable.

1997

Essays and Studies in Books

791   Alkana, Joseph. "'But the Past Was Not Dead': Aesthetics, History, and Community in *Grandfather's Chair* and *The Scarlet Letter*." *The Social Self: Hawthorne, Howells, William James, and Nineteenth-Century Psychology*. Lexington: UP of Kentucky, 1997. 56-81.

Juxtaposes Hawthorne's "most radical social critique," *Letter*, against his "highly moralistic children's history," *Grandfather's Chair*, in an attempt to reconcile his apparently simultaneous desire for social cohesion and individual consciousness. When *Letter* is examined in historical reference to early nineteenth-century thinking about aesthetics, which were based on a Common-Sense moral philosophy, Hawthorne's narrative solution to the problem of the self's confrontation with its social and material milieus becomes clear—through the social power of language. The novel is no defense of individualism, after all. When "transgressions" threaten to cut the three main characters off from their social relationships, their individual insights are invalidated. What *is* validated in the novel is social connectedness and sympathy, both of which supply a more constructive basis for social cohesion than did the legalistic Puritan demand for justice. Hester's return to Boston at the end is no mystery, then, as so many critics contend in their efforts to justify Hester's radical individualism. It is merely her sympathetic reaction to the intolerance and legalism of Puritan rule and Hawthorne's way of dramatizing "the possibility of a community in which social authority works to mediate between, rather than isolate, individuals who themselves have successfully internalized regulatory functions."

792   Cocalis, Jane.   "The 'Dark and Abiding Presence' in Nathaniel Hawthorne's *The Scarlet Letter* and Toni Morrison's *Beloved*." *The Calvinist Roots of the Modern Era*.   Ed. Aliki Barnstone, Michael Tomasek Manson, and Carol J. Singley.   Hanover: UP of New England, 1997. 250-262.

A comparison of *Letter* and *Beloved* (1988) shows how Morrison "deliberately retraces and corrects a line of inquiry inaugurated by Hawthorne. Seeing a symbiotic relationship between Puritanism and slavery, Hawthorne inadvertently creates in Hester the possibility of a remarkable heroine who can denounce the societal codes that bind a minority to its confused self-image. While Hawthorne is ambivalent toward this figure, believing that redemption cannot come from 'dusky grief,' Morrison insists that a dark presence is an essential part of mortal being and that, through the agency of such women as Baby Suggs, Sethe, and Denver, redemption will come, not from some outside power, but from within the community itself." Focusing on the racial and sexual tensions only hinted at in Hawthorne's novel, Morison thus revises *Letter* to assert that Hester—as both saint and sinner—is most remarkable because of, and not despite, her fallen state.

793   Derrick, Scott S. "Gender and the Scene of Writing: Homophobia, the Feminine, and Narrative in Nathaniel Hawthorne's *The Scarlet Letter*." *Monumental Anxieties: Homoerotic Desire and Feminine Influence in Nineteenth-Century U.S. Literature*. New Brunswick: Rutgers UP, 1997. 35-65.

As in 512 and 747, Derrick once again considers the troublesome relationship between authorship and masculinity for Hawthorne, arguing that the narrative of "authorial self-making" dominates *Letter*. Because the novel is "essentially a drama of the writing of narrative as the writing of masculine identity," three scenes of writing shadow the text's three scaffold scenes: first, the idealized scene of romance writing in "The Custom-House" that Hawthorne juxtaposes to the creative sterility of masculine relations; second, the midnarrative scene of Dimmesdale's decomposition in his study; and third, Dimmesdale's triumphant writing of his Election-Day sermon. Hawthorne anxiously works out definitions of masculinity and femininity, associating decay and disintegration with the masculine, and energy and power with the feminine.

794   Ford, Karen Jackson. "The Poetics of Excess: Fantastic Flourishes of Gold Thread." *Gender and the Poetics of Excess: Moments of Brocade*. Jackson: UP of Mississippi, 1997. 1-24.

Defined by her Puritan culture in a limiting way, Hester resists silence through a feminine poetics of excess: her flamboyant needlework challenges the cultural significance of the letter "A" and allows her to take symbolic possession of the forces that seek to define her. Hester "rewrites" the letter, whereupon it becomes an inherently plural text available for continuing reinterpretation and excesses of meaning. Ford likens Hester to such women poets as Emily Dickinson, Gertrude Stein, and Sylvia Plath, whose own excessive creative expressions also occurred within boundaries determined by a male tradition.

795   Gatta, John. "The Sacred Woman: The Problem of Hawthorne's Madonnas." *American Madonna: Images of the Divine Woman in Literary Culture*. New York: Oxford UP, 1997. 10-32.

Argues that the "romantic spirituality" of Hawthorne's fictive imagination runs counter to the demythologizing rationalism of both Puritan and liberal

Protestant influences. His imaginative interest in Marian mythology and its goddess affiliations can be found in *Letter* and *Blithedale Romance*, but figures most prominently in *Marble Faun*. Viewed together, these three works ambivalently portray the ideal of sacred womanhood under the dual aspect of Virgin and Mother. Hawthorne transcends Hester's image as adulteress to Divine Mother, associates Zenobia with the divinizing title of "Queen" or fecundity goddess, and links Miriam's engagement with afflicted humanity with divine womanhood.

796 Kazin, Alfred. "Hawthorne and His Puritans." *God and the American Writer*. New York: Alfred A. Knopf, 1997. 24-39.

In his book, Kazin explores the private religious imaginations of writers from Hawthorne to William Faulkner, focusing especially on "the imagination [each author] brings to his tale of religion in human affairs." Chapter one examines Hawthorne's method in writing *Letter* as influenced both by an obsession with his Puritan ancestors and his own religious doubts. While he held an ambiguous contempt for Calvinist theology and for his ancestors, he was fascinated with the perversity in human affairs central to hereditary Calvinism.

797 Newbury, Michael. *Figuring Authorship in Antebellum America*. Stanford: Stanford UP, 1997.*

In this study that shows how "antebellum authors rhetorically reconstructed their work by mediating it through other forms of labor," Newbury twice presents Hawthorne as "an example of the simultaneous pursuit and refusal of commercial success as the measure of artistic success." A subsection of chapter two entitled "Arthur Dimmesdale" (pp. 98-105) discusses Hawthorne's anxieties and defensiveness about professional authorship as they are linked to Dimmesdale's need for exposure and intimacy. Dimmesdale's self-inflicted corporal punishments stem from the realization that his celebrated public status entitles the community to enslave and sacrifice him for consumption—both physically and spiritually. A subsection of chapter three called "Hawthorne's Residual Writing" (pp. 141-149) discusses Hawthorne's efforts in "The Custom-House" and the novel itself (through his writing and Hester Prynne's sewing) to separate "the work of authorship from modes of monetarily motivated, materially non-productive headwork by emphasizing writing's intimate connection to idealized modes of bodily work." Like Henry David Thoreau, Hawthorne viewed authorship as a figurative embodiment of manual labor, setting it outside both the realm of middle-class professional writing and vulgar manual work.*

*For more on Hawthorne's idealization of manual labor, see Newbury's earlier essay, "Healthful Employment: Hawthorne, Thoreau, and Middle-Class Fitness" (760).

798   Roberts, Nancy. "*The Scarlet Letter* and 'The Spectacle of the Scaffold.'" *Schools of Sympathy: Gender and Identification Through the Novel.* Montreal: McGill-Queen's UP, 1997. 46-69.

In her discussion of sympathy and gender, Roberts rereads Hawthorne through the lens of Michel Foucault to isolate some of the crucial issues in the novel about punishment and display. Examining differences in punishment in the seventeenth and the nineteenth century (the seventeenth being an age of public spectacle and the nineteenth, in Foucault's words, an "age of sobriety in punishment"), she demonstrates how *Letter* becomes Hawthorne's creation of a new nineteenth-century spectacle where punishment of both body and soul is played out privately. Dimmesdale's desire to appear as a spectacle of punishment like the self-sacrificing Hester involves something of "cross-gender identification," since such self-sacrificing victimization was associated with woman's "highest calling and deepest desire" in the nineteenth century. Further, Roberts considers multiple definitions of "sympathy" that Hawthorne was working with in the novel—but most notably two kinds: the utilitarian type of eighteenth-century sympathy practiced by Chillingworth that objectifies and separates, and the nineteenth-century romantic concept of sympathy that involves a kind of "moral glue which binds a society of isolated individuals together." This latter type, which draws people together and unites them, is what Hawthorne seeks throughout the novel, beginning in "The Custom-House" where he expresses a desire to form a bond of perfect sympathy with his readers, although he does not expect or anticipate an understanding response. Ultimately, the novel glorifies a position of shame, penance, and humiliation (glorifying Dimmesdale's desire for it), and teaches a self-imposed, internalized discipline and punishment. The lesson in sympathy thus becomes one of restraint, control, and denial. [For more on the subject of private and public punishment (as influenced by Foucault), see Elizabeth Aycock Hoffman (628).]

799   Romero, Lora. "Homosocial Romance: Nathaniel Hawthorne." *Home Fronts: Domesticity and Its Critics in the Antebellum United States.* Durham: Duke UP, 1997. 89-105.

Considers domesticity in relation to the self-reflexive text, examining the sexual and gender politics of *Letter*. The erotic ambiguity or sexual anxiety between Dimmesdale and Chillingworth parallels a section of the

American Notebooks that details Hawthorne's "male homosocial idyll" with Horatio Bridge and a Mr. Schaeffer in Augusta, Maine. The freedom from institutions and conventions that Hawthorne enjoyed in the *Notebooks'* idyll translates in *Letter* into the scarlet letter "A" itself and acts as an agent of defamiliarization that temporarily allows Hester to distance herself from the domestic norm. Thus *Letter*, like Hawthorne's other romances, represents an attempt to dissociate himself from the domestic. In fact, one of the reasons that Hawthorne chose the genre of romance is that he wanted to avoid the "feminine," overly domestic language of realism.

800   Sheriff, John K. "Literary Art/Artistic Women: Linking Subjectivity to Social Significance." *Semiotics*. Eds. C. W. Spinks and John Deely. New York: Peter Lang, 1997. 206-216.

Condemns the "monsters" of the literary establishment whose teaching, critical approaches, and literary theories oppress art instead of valuing and illuminating it from an artistic context. Such poor treatment/interpretation corresponds to the kind Hester receives in *Letter*, the Puritans being incapable of responding to her art "feelingly." After establishing the different ways the main characters interpret or read Hester's symbolic "sign" (Hester as sympathetic artist, Chillingworth as skeptical rationalist, and Dimmesdale as believing theorist), Sheriff then aligns his understanding of the novel's "sign[s] of possibility" with the semiotics of Charles Peirce to evaluate several critical approaches to the novel, almost all of which suppress Hester and deny the importance of her way of seeing. Providing the Peircean theory as a context for meaning shows that *Letter* is partly about heartless responses to signs and offers a hopeful alternative to contemporary responses to the novel. [For a later essay by Sheriff on a nearly identical topic, see 851.]

801   Sutherland, John. "What Are the Prynne's Doing in Boston?" *Can Jane Eyre Be Happy?: More Puzzles in Classic Fiction*. New York: Oxford UP, 1997. 96-101.

Sutherland's playful book "tenderly" investigates the "seeming errors, anomalies, illogicalities, and contradictions" in 32 famous works of fiction, and questions in this chapter "what series of events brought Hester Prynne to Massachusetts." He speculates about Hester and Chillingworth's marriage, which Hester agreed to in order to relieve her parents' financial difficulties, and considers a number of "puzzles" such as (1) what Englishman Roger Prynne was doing in Amsterdam, (2) why—as a known alchemist and ambitious scholar—he would set his sights on a superstitious and primitive colony in America, and (3) why he would send

398

his beautiful young wife ahead of him with so little money that she would have to earn her living through needlework. Sutherland concludes that Roger Prynne imagined that he could satisfy his wife in their marriage if he could pursue his alchemical studies and discover the fabled "elixir" of life, which would not only restore him bodily but also be an aphrodisiac to stimulate Hester's desire. It may be, Sutherland continues (knowing full well that his line of inquiry goes "deeper into hypothesis than most readers will find it useful to go"), that the "impotent" Prynne sent his wife—who may well have still been a virgin—"to an excessively puritanical community as one might send a daughter to a convent," to protect her "virtue" until he was ready to make claim to it.

802   Telgen, Diane. *"The Scarlet Letter." Novels for Students: Presenting Analysis, Context, and Criticism on Commonly Studied Poetry.* Ed. Diane Telgen. Detroit: Gale Research, 1997. 306-328.

Contains an overview of the novel; a bibliography; plot summary; description of characters, themes, and style; and topics for additional study. It further offers historical context, a critical overview, and titles of selected criticism on *Letter*. Telgen also considers the novel's adaptations in movies, sound recordings, and audio study guides.

803   Woidat, Caroline.   "Talking Back to Schoolteacher: Morrison's Confrontation with Hawthorne in *Beloved*." *Toni Morrison: Critical and Theoretical Approaches.* Ed. Nancy J. Peterson. Baltimore: Johns Hopkins UP, 1997. 181-200.

Toni Morrison deconstructs the canonized "white text" of *Letter* in *Beloved* (1988) in an effort to "talk back" or redefine the monolithic, homogenous American canon.   While Hawthorne condemned the institution of slavery, he feared the dissolution of the Union even more, and so he paradoxically defended the Union by minimizing or disguising the issue of slavery in both *Grandfather's Chair* and *Letter*. The narrative of *Letter*, "characterized by its own repression of slavery's evils in order to achieve social consensus," is rewritten in *Beloved* as the story of a black slave. The character of Sethe is "something of a black Hester Prynne," but one who subverts Hawthorne's text; for, while Hester serves as an allegorical figure of patient submission to tyrannical authority, Sethe violently rebels, enacting the revolution that Hester entrusts to the course of "progress."

Journal Essays and Notes

804   Barlowe, Jamie. "Rereading Women: Hester Prynne-ism and the Scarlet Mob of Scribblers." *American Literary History* 9 (1997): 197-225.*

Charging contemporary male literary critics of *Letter* as guilty of "Hester Prynne-ism," or of trying to stifle not only Hester Prynne's unique voice but those of women scholars who write about the novel, Barlowe critiques conservative practices in mainstream Hawthorne scholarship (from the 1950s to the 1990s) that perpetuate the same type of "limiting, sexist cultural practice of Othering" as the Puritans exhibit in *Letter*—including those recent male critics who offer "radical" interpretations of Hawthorne and Hester even as they ironically remain conservative in their relation to women. Barlowe cites dozens of recognized studies on *Letter* by men to illustrate "examples of marginalization and adversarial relationships to women's scholarship," and claims that the few examples of women's feminist criticism on the novel that *are* actually addressed by male critics are "appropriated, disputed, marginalized, reviled, trivialized, sexualized, and/or generally ignored." She concludes by emphasizing the vast importance of women's scholarship, stating that it "must destabilize and disrupt the body of scholarship so that it presses us all to examine academic and cultural assumptions and practices that objectify, exclude, and/or nominalize the Other." Following the article is a ten-page bibliography of women's scholarship on *Letter*, the sheer numbers of which (216 entries) ostensibly attest to how much criticism by women on the subject has been neglected. [Three scholars immediately commented on Barlowe's essay, and then Barlowe responded to them—the citations and annotations for which all appear below. See Jamie Barlowe (805), Emily Miller Budick (806), T. Walter Herbert (809), and Leland S. Person, Jr., (814).]

*See 853 for Barlowe's book-length study of this subject.

805   Barlowe, Jamie. "Response to the Responses." *American Literary History* 9 (1997): 238-243.

Replying to the three critics who responded to her essay (see 806, 809, and 814), but mostly using the space of her reply to address and rebut Budick's objections, Barlowe uses the mostly complimentary reviews of T. Walter Herbert and Leland S. Person to protectively align herself with them (citing "shared contexts") against Budick, who stands "on different contextual ground." Barlowe reasserts her critical position that women's scholarship is ignored in "malestream" criticism and justifies her empirical examination of all the scholarship, but refuses to provide "a point-by-point refutation of the more than twenty errors" that Budick cites in attempting "to falsify both [her] factual and theorized claims." Barlowe concludes by suggesting something of a metaphorical burying of the hatchet, entreating Budick to realize that they are both on the same feminist side and to engage the "problem [. . .] for what it is and work together to solve it."

806   Budick, Emily Miller. "We Damned-If-You-Do, Damned-If-You-Don't Mob of Scribbling Scholars." *American Literary History* 9 (1997): 233-237.

"For all its opposition to Othering," Barlowe's essay (see 804) "indulges in an extraordinary amount of it, preventing differences from emerging by decontextualizing and marginalizing other scholars and scholarship." The essay not only oversimplifies multiple and competing critical approaches, but "also reduces to two groups—male and female—the many critics of differing generations, genders, sexual orientations, races, religions, immigrant status, nationalities, and so on, who have employed various critical systems in different and unique ways over a 140-year period of changing sociopolitical orientations to literature." In a nut shell, Barlowe needs "to more precisely contextualize her conclusions." In addition, Budick faults Barlowe for blurring the "distinctions between biological gender and gendered argumentation," as well as questions the legitimacy of the lengthy bibliography of "women's scholarship" on the novel at the end of Barlowe's essay. In the end, Budick finds Barlowe's "sweeping" condemnation of the American literary establishment sophomoric, especially since it seems to reduce most criticism into two types: "male" (bad) criticism and "female" (good) criticism.

807   Dunne, Michael. *"The Scarlet Letter* on Film: Ninety Years of Revisioning." *Literature/Film Quarterly* 25 (1997): 30-40.

Although *Letter*'s cinematic potential makes it seem destined and well suited for film, there has still been no film adaptation to do the novel justice, because "successive generations have revisioned Hawthorne's work in accord with the values and prejudices of their own times." Dunne reviews the five major adaptations (the 1926 version starring Lillian Gish and directed by Victor Sjöström, the 1934 talkie directed by Richard Vignola and starring Colleen Moore, the 1972 German version by Wim Wenders, the 1979 PBS release by Rich Hauser, and Roland Joffé's 1995 debacle)—all of which were "too rooted in the time in which [they were] produced to do justice to a nineteenth-century tale about seventeenth-century characters."

808   Elbert, Monika M. "Hawthorne's Reconceptualization of Transcendentalist Charity." *ATQ* 11 (1997): 213-232.

Fostering liberal individualism over communal values, transcendentalist thinkers like Ralph Waldo Emerson and Henry David Thoreau disavowed any connection to organized or institutionalized charity and offered inhumane judgments of those subjected to poverty. Hawthorne, however, was extremely sympathetic to the plight of the poor (most likely because of the charity he and his mother were forced to accept from the Mannings), and encourages self-reliance in his New England novels only after communal or family help is provided to the poverty-stricken individual. Elbert considers such "charity cases" as Hester in *Letter*, Hepzibah and Uncle Venner in *House of the Seven Gables*, and Priscilla in *Blithedale Romance*, who all learn dignified self-sufficiency through distant support from family or community members. Maintaining a sense of dignity through partial independence is what Hawthorne argues for in these novels, as it transforms or redeems these charity cases into independent members of communities who then possess charitable impulses of their own.

809   Herbert, T. Walter. "Response to Jamie Barlowe, 'Rereading Women . . . .'" *American Literary History* 9 (1997): 230-232.

Agrees with Barlowe's "important" assessment of the male-dominated tradition of Hawthorne scholarship (in 804), but finds her argument outdated (retaining "the atmosphere of yesterday's bandwagon") since feminist scholarship has transformed Hawthorne's criticism and mainstream criticism, both of which now include several "distinguished female exemplars." Walter defends Hawthorne's novel from Barlowe's assault of its conservative and sexist male politics, and he vindicates recent male critics from Barlowe's charge that they belittle women's feminist scholarship on *Letter*, demuring over her assumption that "[a critical dialogue amongst fellow scholars] is limited to persons who agree with each other."

810   Khan, Jalal-Uddin. "Patterns of Isolation and Interconnectedness in Hawthorne's *The Scarlet Letter*." *Indian Journal of American Studies* 27 (1997): 1-11.

Letter continues to appeal to modern audiences because of "the way it interweaves the moments of isolation and interconnectedness among its principle characters." Such moments of interconnectedness serve to "heighten their suspenseful estrangement and intensify their passionate need to stay connected not only with their loved ones but with the rest of the society as well by all means available to them." Urgent efforts are in vain, however, and, since the novel's tensions are never resolved and the principle characters remain "supremely isolated" from each other, the novel continues to speak to modern readers.

811   Korobkin, Laura Hanft. "*The Scarlet Letter* of the Law: Hawthorne and Criminal Justice." *Novel* 30 (1997): 193-217.

Like several critics before her (namely Sacvan Bercovitch [in 635] and Jonathan Arac [in 508]) who read *Letter* as a response to the political anxieties of 1850, Korobkin approaches the novel specifically from the larger cultural debate following the 1850 Fugitive Slave Law about personal decisions to obey or resist the strictures of law. The novel's "historical manipulations" of the law illuminate the political and racial climate of 1850 and the problems among Northerners with the Compromise of 1850. Never one to advocate abolition, Hawthorne used his novel as the subtle platform from which to condemn both independent judgment of laws and violent resistance to their enforcement (positioning Chillingworth as the loathsome and fear-inspiring vigilante). Hawthorne wished for Hester to represent the situation of the ordinary reader (and not the artist, as so many critics have argued in the past)—hoping that white Northern readers would learn from her example: that dissociating oneself from public political action is "truly heroic and intellectually liberating." He is also sure to erase any reference to the issue of slavery itself, exchanging Hester's likely punishment at the whipping post for the more lenient punishment she receives, since had she been whipped (as her crime historically warranted), the novel would have "irrevocably positioned her as a slave surrogate, an object of pity and a spur to activism." Despite his best efforts, however, Hawthorne cannot entirely eradicate what Toni Morrison calls the "Africanist presence" in the "shadowy margins" of his novel. But he does his best in applying "the literary qualities of evocativeness, complexity, and imaginative richness" to a hotly debated law-related issue.

812   Last, Suzan. "Hawthorne's Feminine Voices: Reading *The Scarlet Letter* as a Woman." *Journal of Narrative Technique* 27 (1997): 349-376.

Letter's lack of consistency and coherence in voice and vision reveal Hawthorne's departure from "masculine" forms of discourse and his entrance into the "feminine" world of romance in telling Hester's story. Last examines "The Custom-House" and *Letter* for places where Hawthorne appears to be distancing himself from the masculine world, and traces both nineteenth- and twentieth-century critical interpretations of the novel's conflicted authorial voice—arguing that Hawthorne's conflicted stance is best revealed in his critical/sympathetic presentation of the marginalized perspectives of Hester, Pearl, and Mistress Hibbins.

Narrative equivocation throughout the novel, more common in nineteenth-century feminine writing than masculine writing, implies that Hawthorne perhaps aligned himself with fellow female "scribblers" whose works allow for multiple and even contradictory interpretations. Such juggling of multiple narrative voices, perspectives, and ideologies also hints at Hawthorne's profound sympathy for oppressed women.

813   Nudelman, Franny. "'Emblem and Product of Sin': The Poisoned Child in *The Scarlet Letter* and Domestic Advice Literature." *Yale Journal of Criticism* 10 (1997): 193-213.

Discusses the symbolic relation between Pearl and the letter "A," arguing that critics have underemphasized Pearl's disciplinary powers over her mother. Whereas the isolating effects of the letter actually permit Hester to conceal her rebellious nature, Pearl's expressive behavior reveals and punishes her deviance, thus fulfilling the letter's office. Hester relates to the figure of the "poisonous mother" in nineteenth-century domestic advice literature, whose secret character is "maternally transmitted" to and made manifest in her offspring.* Pearl, as an "animated version of her mother's transgression," ultimately functions as the agent of communal discipline, offering the Puritan community access to Hester's hidden interior.

*For more on the nineteenth-century belief in parental determinism as it is reflected in the literature of the age, see Leland S. Person, Jr., (646).

814   Person, Leland S., Jr. "*A* for Affirmative Action?" *American Literary History* 9 (1997): 226-229.

After having reacted "with astonishment" to Barlowe's evidence (see 804) for the absence of women in male-authored criticism on *Letter* (and sighing with relief that he is listed by her as one of the few "good guys" who does "engage with and/or cite women's scholarship"), Person praises Barlowe with an "A+" for inaugurating a new stage of feminist metacriticism, and agrees wholeheartedly with her that literary criticism demands affirmative action "in the best sense—equality not just under the sign of the superscript number but equality in the text and in the critical discourse."

815   Polette, Keith. "Text and Textile: Sacred and Profane Fashion Statements in Flannery O'Connor's 'A Good Man is Hard to Find.'" *JAISA: Journal for the Interdisciplinary Study of the Arts* 2 (1997): 63-80.

O'Connor modernizes Hawthorne's pattern of "outfitting" a text with ideas of clothing that communicate multiple and symbolic ideas extending beyond the realm of conventional sign systems. Polette compares the "symbolic fabric" in O'Connor's story to Hawthorne's *Letter* and "Minister's Black Veil," considering how the Misfit's stolen shirt, Hester's stitched letter, and the minister's veil become internalized symbolic images capable of producing positive interior transformations to both the wearers and their viewers. Such transformations are enacted when "allegorical signs that signify an occluded and one-sided vision of character are converted into symbols that express the wholeness of the human being."

1998

Books

816   Morey, Eileen. *Readings on The Scarlet Letter*. San Diego: Greenhaven Press, 1998. 154 pp.

Part of the Greenhaven Press Literary Companion Series, this guide contains fourteen critical essays (edited for brevity and comprehension levels of young adults) that relate to structure and style, characters, and major themes. Additional features include an annotated table of contents, a brief introduction, summations of each essay, a biography of Hawthorne, a chronology of Hawthorne's life and career, bibliographical references, and an index. Under the heading of "Structure and Style" are brief excerpts from the following: Mark Van Doren's *Nathaniel Hawthorne* (EC36), Henry James's *Hawthorne* (EC15), Richard Harter Fogle's *Hawthorne's Fiction: The Light and the Dark* (15), Roy R. Male's *Hawthorne's Tragic Vision* (56), Gordon Roper's Introduction to *The Scarlet Letter and Selected Prose Works* (EC25), and David Levin's "Nathaniel Hawthorne: *The Scarlet Letter*" (167). The second chapter on "Characters" contains excerpts from these four works: Edward Wagenknecht's *Nathaniel Hawthorne: The Man, His Tales and Romances* (593), Hyatt H. Waggoner's *Hawthorne: A Critical Study* (38), Anne Marie McNamara's "The Character of Flame: The Function of Pearl in *The Scarlet Letter*" (50) and Nina Baym's *The Shape of Hawthorne's Career* (339). The last chapter on "Major Themes" contains excerpts from the following four sources: Frederick Newberry's *Hawthorne's Divided Loyalties: England and America in His Works* (539), Alison Easton's *The Making of the Hawthorne Subject* (769), Claudia Durst Johnson's *Understanding the Scarlet Letter: A Student Casebook to Issues, Sources, and Historical Documents* (741), and John E. Becker's *Hawthorne's Historical Allegory: An Examination of the American Conscience* (260).

Essays and Studies in Books

817   Coale, Samuel Chase. "The Spell of the Scarlet Letter: A Mesmeric Mystery." *Mesmerism and Hawthorne: Mediums of American Romance.* Tuscaloosa: U of Alabama P, 1998. 69-90, 175-178.

Though Hawthorne dismissed the pseudo-science of mesmerism as a "humbug," Coale detects similarities between mesmerists' trances/performances and Hawthorne's process of writing romances. Hawthorne actually used the very mesmeric forces he morally opposed to describe and produce the techniques and strategies of his art. Ultimately, the mystery of the interaction between observer and icon, spectator and object, underlies Hawthorne's vision of romance. Nowhere is this vision more fully manifested than in *Letter*. "The discovery of the scarlet letter in 'The Custom-House,' at the beginning of the romance, and the interpretive description within chapters 16 through 19, from 'A Forest Walk' to 'The Child at the Brookside,' exactly parallel the mesmeric structure of transition and trance as does the overall structure of the book itself." In fact, Hawthorne structures the dark novel as if he is "casting a spell," whereby the letter "spellbinds" all of the characters with its ambiguous power so that all human activity and interpretation become "contradictory, predatory, paradoxical, and morally confused." [For Coale's earlier essays on the topic of mesmerism, see 678 and 722.]

818   Gable, Harvey L. *"The Scarlet Letter." Liquid Fire: Transcendental Mysticism in the Romances of Nathaniel Hawthorne.* New York: Peter Lang, 1998. 71-108.

Prioritizing spiritual over physical reality in the romances reveals not only Hawthorne's transcendental sympathies but also his interest in the science of animal magnetism. His ideas developed from three important influences: nineteenth-century language theory as represented by the biblical hermeneutics of Horace Bushnell, Ralph Waldo Emerson's transcendentalism, and J. P. F. Deleuze's theories on animal magnetism. These influences enabled Hawthorne to experiment with a "new" kind of discourse that would allow him to express the truth of human nature. *Letter* is Hawthorne's first full-scale implementation of this new kind of fiction, and each subsequent romance becomes more deeply invested in it, *Marble Faun* being the most perfected. Ultimately, all the romances hinge on a fundamental vision of the unity of being, the conception of reality comprised of an interlocking web or tapestry of natural (and not man-made) forces of which the self is a part and from which it derives meaning. *Letter* "makes this point negatively: it is the story of a woman who becomes a free symbol, a letter without context or meaning, by virtue of having been ripped from the fabric of her culture." Although Hester struggles against this very "fabric of reality" and is unable to break through the frozen barrier of reserve to "transform the mute letter A into voluble speech," Hawthorne is able, through the redemptive power of his fiction, to return Hester "posthumously to the electric chain of human sympathy from which she had been detached."

819   Harding, Brian. *Nathaniel Hawthorne: Critical Assessments*. Robertsbridge: Helm Information, 1998.

Massive, four-volume set of critical responses to Hawthorne's work. Volume 1 assesses works from the 1840s to 1860; Volume 2 contains reviews, obituaries, biographical pieces, and criticism from 1860 to 1900; Volume 3, which includes post-1900 critical responses to the short stories, the *English Notebooks*, and the four romances, contains the following essays (in their entirety) on *Letter*: D. H. Lawrence's "Nathaniel Hawthorne and *The Scarlet Letter*" (EC18), Frederic I. Carpenter's "Scarlet A Minus" (EC4), Leslie A. Fiedler's "Achievement and Frustration" (184), Terence Martin's "Dimmesdale's Ultimate Sermon" (276), David Leverenz's "Mrs. Hawthorne's Headache: Reading *The Scarlet Letter*" (447), Larry J. Reynolds's "*The Scarlet Letter* and Revolutions Abroad" (504), Jonathan Arac's "The Politics of *The Scarlet Letter*" (508), Brian Harding's Introduction to *The Scarlet Letter* (618), and Sacvan Bercovitch's "The A-Politics of Ambiguity in *The Scarlet Letter*" (575). Volume 4 covers such topics as Hawthorne's reputation, the writing of romance, his relation to Henry James, as well as issues of feminism, symbolism, and allegory.

820   Mitchell, Thomas R. "'Speak Thou for Me': The 'Strange Earnestness' of *The Scarlet Letter*." *Hawthorne's Fuller Mystery*. Amherst: U of Massachusetts Press, 1998. 125-158.

Contends that Hawthorne wrote some of his most powerful fiction in a private, controlled attempt to work out his intellectual stance toward Fuller's ideas and his personal feelings for her, examining Hawthorne's expressed ambivalence about the "riddle" of Margaret Fuller's almost mythic character, even years after her death. In *Letter*, a rewrite of "Rappaccini's Daughter," Hawthorne embodies Fuller as "the Hester who inspires Hawthorne's sympathetic admiration and respect as well as his fears and guilt." Mitchell begins his chapter by locating the creative origins of the novel in Hawthorne's relationship with Fuller (arguing that little else can be found in source studies to explain the novel's preoccupation with passion and adultery).* He then argues that "Fuller figured much more deeply in Hawthorne's imagination before and during the writing of *Letter* than anyone has suspected" (citing interesting facts about their friendship, as well as their shared ideas on marriage, divorce, women's place in society, and the "fluidity" of gender). The romance itself is like Dimmesdale's "strange[ly] earnest" Election-Day sermon in that it is written for two audiences: the general reader/congregation as well as the second, secret audience of "one mind and heart of perfect sympathy" (Fuller/Hester). In other words, Hawthorne not only works out his guilty feelings toward Fuller in the novel but also writes "to, for, and about her." That readers do not realize that Hawthorne speaks for and about Fuller at the close of the romance (imagining the possibility that Fuller/Hester would return to New England "to subvert the patriarchal culture that had condemned her and made wretched other women") accounts for the fact that the ironic ending has gone by "largely unappreciated." [For more on the relation of Hawthorne and Fuller, see Frances E. Kearns—the first to argue for Fuller as a model for Hester (172). See also Larry J. Reynolds (504) and Sacvan Bercovitch (635) for other arguments that support Fuller as a model for the "socially and sexually threatening Hester "]

*See 465, 477, 483, and 849 for source studies that speculate that Hawthorne was writing in the tradition of adultery/seduction novels. Similar conventions might also have been borrowed from nineteenth-century sensational fiction (570, 577, and 749).

821 Reid, Margaret. "From Revolutionary Legends to *The Scarlet Letter*: Casting Characters for Early American Romanticism." *Comparative Romances: Power, Gender, Subjectivity.* Ed. Larry H. Peer. Columbia: Camden House, 1998. 59-80.

Tries to pinpoint the beginnings of romanticism, linking popular eighteenth-century legends of the revolutionary era with Hawthorne's text, since all are "self-defining narratives" that challenge cultural definitions of "lived history" and share symbolic strategies in the presentation of the exile's attraction to community. In *Letter*, Hawthorne directly addresses the foundations of American symbolic language, finding danger in both the "theoretical" nature of Puritan rhetoric and nineteenth-century American symbology. Making a progressive argument for "a new infusion of history into theory," he "locates the cultural and epistemological origins of national identity within a fusion of language and symbolism" and demonstrates through the shifting meaning of the elusive scarlet letter that the language of romantic symbolism is an ever-changing process.

408

822   Richard, Claude. "Nathaniel Hawthorne: The Attic of the Letter."
       American Letters. Trans. Carol Mastrangelo Bové. Philadelphia: U of
       Pennsylvania P, 1998. 44-57.

       Female sexuality in *Letter* functions in the narrative's displacement of
       patriarchal structures. In "The Custom-House," which frames Hester's
       tale of persecution and critiques nineteenth-century Massachusetts,
       Hawthorne parallels Hester and his own oppositional position. Thus he
       sets the stage for the pornographic spectacle of Hester's scarlet "A," which
       is associated with the literary imagination and becomes an artistic means
       of liberation.

823   Simms, Donna D. "Be True: Moral Dilemma in *The Scarlet Letter*."
       *Analyzing the Different Voice: Feminist Psychological Theory and
       Literary Texts*. Eds. Jerilyn Fisher and Ellen S. Silber. Lanham: Rowman
       and Littlefield, 1998. 239-253.

       Adapts   Nona   Lyons's   elaborations   of   Carol   Gilligan's
       psychological/feminist theory on "gender-related" moral perspectives in
       order "to better understand the irreconcilable difference" between Hester's
       and Dimmesdale's moral decision-making in *Letter*. Most simply, "they
       do not live by the same truth." While Dimmesdale exemplifies a morality
       based on justice, truth, and law, Hester exemplifies one based on
       connection with others, care, personal responsibility, and loyalty. "While
       Arthur's life is lived upon the rack of solitary moralizing, Hester's is
       shaped by her need to maintain relationships. These two ways of defining
       the self correspond to the extreme positions these characters take on the
       moral spectrum, and [. . .] both pay a heavy price for their limited points
       of view." Hawthorne finally argues for the validity of both perspectives
       (although Dimmesdale's voice dominates Hester's within the setting of the
       novel), with his protagonists triumphing in their own separate ways.
       Chillingworth and Pearl act as "complex amalgams of the perspectives of
       justice and care," although Chillingworth perverts morality and loyalty
       while Pearl synthesizes the two moral orientations and "points toward the
       future and new possibilities for women."

Journal Essays and Notes

824   Dolis, John. "Hawthorne's Circe: Turning Water to (S)wine." *Nathaniel
       Hawthorne Review* 24.1 (1998): 36-45.

       Playfully connects the "gourmandizing discourse" in "Circe's Palace"
       with that in "The Custom-House," both serving as an "hors-d'oeuvre" to
       Letter and prefiguring the novel's "dirty work" by expressing

Hawthorne's disgust over the stultifying environment of "bureaucratic scribbling" in his work place. Circe's spell over Ulysses's men (which turns them into mindless "swine") compares with the lethargic spell that is seemingly imposed on the "headless," unproductive Custom House employees. Yielding a Circe-like power, Hawthorne magically transforms the useless reality of the Custom House into living romance with *Letter*. The implications of this analysis extend to a general discussion of Hawthorne's writing as it was influenced by nineteenth-century domestic ideology. Dolis concludes that Hawthorne avoids the lethargic "spell" of domesticity because home, like "The Custom-House," is the empty space that waits for the real discourse to begin.

825   Koegel, John. "Walter Damrosch, *The Scarlet Letter*." *Notes* 55 (1998): 189-195.

Favorably reviews the Nineteenth-Century American Musical Theater's sixteen-part series (launched in 1994, and of which Walter Damrosch's 1896 opera of *Letter* is the sixteenth) that makes available "a significant and large sampling of musical-theater pieces composed and performed in the United States. Koegel's article discusses Damrosch's entire musical career in language that only those educated in Music history could fully appreciate. Of the performance of *Letter* (pp. 193-194), for instance, Koegel writes that "Walter Damrosch's opera *Letter* of 1896, set to a libretto by George Parsons Lathrop from Nathaniel Hawthorne's novel, is significant for many reasons [. . .]. *Letter* was the most ambitious American grand opera of the nineteenth century after William Henry Fry's much earlier *Leonora* of 1845. Whereas Fry relied on the Italian bel canto tradition for inspiration, Damrosch looked towards the German school, especially the works of Richard Wagner, for his model."

826   Minton, Shira Pavis. "Hawthorne and the Handmaid: An Examination of the Law's Use as a Tool of Oppression." *Wisconsin Women's Law Journal* 13 (1998): 45-73.

As a lawyer addressing other lawyers, Minton uses *Letter* and Margaret Atwood's *The Handmaid's Tale* (1985) "to question the moral rightness of the laws that perpetuate unequal treatment based on gender" (qualifying her use of the novels by stating that "a great author can sum up [. . .] in one paragraph what a hundred legal scholars struggle to explain in as many treatises). More specifically, the novels illustrate two of the ways that law is used as a "social tool" for oppressing women: to harness a woman's autonomy and to control female sexuality/power. The two texts examine the same general themes, "the theme of male domination of female sexuality, and the use of law to set up rigid prescriptions of

410

conduct for women as regards their sexual selves." *Letter* is especially "relevant to an historical inquiry into the origins of misogynist law—specifically, the law against female adultery." In these novels, and today (where society places control on women's bodies in several ways: "the encroachment on the right to abortion; the forced use of Depo Provera for drug users; the growing rights of the fetus movement; rape law; incest"), law controls women's sexuality because that sexuality is "a power that awes and frightens male society."

827   Tassi, Nina. "Hester's Prisons: Sex, Intellect, and Gender in *The Scarlet Letter*." *CEA Critic* 60 (1998): 23-36.

Letter does not so much exhibit Hawthorne's feminism or anti-feminism so much as his "passionate conflicts about the masculine and feminine genders." Hawthorne hides his ambivalent authorial voice behind other voices (Surveyor Pue, Surveyor "Hawthorne," the ambiguous narrator, and several characters) to create "a cover for himself, behind which he freely experiments with questions of gender, even reversing traditional ideas of feminine and masculine traits." Just as Hawthorne characterized Anne Hutchinson (one of his models for Hester) in his 1830 sketch, so he similarly presents Hester in contradictory terms that disclose a complicated attitute "of praise/blame, desire/fear, and sympathy/censure." Drawn to her confident sexuality and superior intellect, he yet fears these same "masculine" traits in her—especially because of insecurities surrounding his own effeminate nature (which he represents in Dimmesdale). Ultimately unshakable in his commitment to patriarchy and true to his Puritan inheritance, Hawthorne sides with the minister and contains Hester (more out of fear of her threatening "wildness of mind" than of her errant sexuality)—re-establishing in the final scaffold scene the "correct" social roles. [See 764 for an earlier essay by Tassi on the same topic.]

1999

Books

828   Cowley, Julian. *The Scarlet Letter, Nathaniel Hawthorne: Notes.* Harlow: Longman, 1999.

This book is not available for review. There are currently two holders—neither of whom was willing to give it up.

829   Kennedy-Andrews, Elmer, ed. *Nathaniel Hawthorne: The Scarlet Letter.* New York: Columbia UP, 1999. 208 pp.

This "Columbia Critical Guide" offers an account and sampling of secondary sources relating to *Letter* and contains an introduction and six chapters broken into the following categories: "Contemporary Responses and Early Studies," which includes excerpts from several early reviews and from studies by Henry James (EC15), George Woodberry (EC41), and D. H. Lawrence (EC18); "Formalist and Postformalist Approaches," which contains New Critical studies by F. O Matthiessen (EC20), Leland Schubert (EC26), Yvor Winters (EC40), and Hyatt H. Waggoner (38), as well as more "eclectic" New Criticism by Darrel Abel (46), Roy R. Male (56), R. W. B. Lewis (37), Richard Chase (55), Harry Levin (70), William Bysshe Stein (22), Leslie A. Fiedler (89), and Hugo McPherson (237); "Historical Approaches," which "consider the evolution of 'Historicist' criticism into 'New Historicist' criticism" and contain fragments by Michael J. Colacurcio (486), Larry J. Reynolds (504), Jonathan Arac (508), and Michael Davitt Bell (482); "Psychoanalytical Approaches" by Joseph Levi (26), Frederick Crews (182), Richard Brodhead (300), Clay Daniel (521), and Joanne Feit Diehl (578); "Feminist Criticism" by Nina Baym (339, 406, and 419), Judith Fryer (340), Mary Suzanne Schriber (541), and Leland S. Person, Jr., (569), and "Reader-Response, Phenomenological, and Post-Structuralist Approaches" by Richard H. Brodhead (300) and Kenneth Dauber (343) in the first category, John Carlos Rowe (403) representing the Phenomenological approach, and, finally, Evan Carton (484), John Dolis (457), and Peggy Kamuf (492) representing a post-structuralist approach to the novel. Also accompanying the text are notes, a bibliography, and an index.

Essays and Studies in Books

830   Assmann, Aleida. "Space, Place, Land: Changing Concepts of Territory in English and American Fiction." *Borderlands: Negotiating Boundaries in Post-Colonial Writing.* Ed. Monika Reif-Hülser. Amsterdam, Netherlands: Rodopi, 1999. 57-68.

Charts changing concepts of territory ("space, place, and land") as cultural perspectives change in three post-colonial fictions from three different centuries: Daniel Defoe's *Robinson Crusoe* (1719), *Letter*, and Leslie Marmon Silko's *Ceremony* (1977). While Crusoe's tradition-bound father forbids his son to leave home, the more modern Hawthorne in "The Custom-House" feels no intrinsic ties to his native Salem and intends that his children "shall strike their roots into unaccustomed earth." Yet Defoe and Hawthorne (both Puritans) similarly relate guilt and place. "Mobility is associated with guilt" in *Robinson Crusoe*, while in *Letter*, Hester's "lack of mobility, being bound to a place, is a symptom of guilt." In

Silko's Native-American novel (not related in this essay to the first two), the idea of land takes on cosmic and mystic value.

831   Bensick, Carol M. "Mary Ward, *The Scarlet Letter*, and Hawthorne: 'Partly Sympathy and Partly Rebellion.'" *Hawthorne and Women: Engendering and Expanding the Hawthorne Tradition*. Eds. John L. Idol, Jr., and Melinda M. Ponder. Amherst: U of Massachusetts P, 1999. 159-167.

Concerned with how gender inflects a letter written by nineteenth-century English novelist Mary Ward to commemorate the hundredth anniversary of Hawthorne's birth, Bensick senses an indignant and conflicted response to Hester Prynne's unrequited love story, one which is carefully masked because Ward's letter is intended to be a tribute to Hawthorne rather than an attack on his shabby treatment of women characters by their male counterparts.

832   Berryman, Charles. "Faith or Fiction: Updike and the American Renaissance." *John Updike and Religion: The Sense of the Sacred and the Motions of Grace*. Ed. James Yerkes. Grand Rapids: Eerdmans, 1999. 195-207.

Updike's revision of *Letter* in *S* (1988) lacks the powerful tragic vision associated with Hawthorne (and more broadly with the American Renaissance) largely because of religious differences in the time periods of both authors. Hawthorne felt compelled to disguise his religious doubts and "dark sentiments" from an audience that shared a common faith, whereas Updike could openly question religious dogma for his more secular audience. Likewise, while Hawthorne took his subject matter quite seriously (viewing adultery as the "tragic conflict of body and soul"), Updike comically flaunts graphic details of sexual encounters and adulterous acts in several of his novels. Because Updike's fiction typically lacks the tensions and conflicts inherent in Hawthorne's text, he "may be limited to a realistic tour of the human comedy because so many of his readers are beyond any tragic concern or need to aim another harpoon at the image of a hidden God."

833   Bromley, Roger. "Imagining the Puritan Body: The 1995 Cinematic Version of Nathaniel Hawthorne's *The Scarlet Letter*." *Adaptations: From Text to Screen, Screen to Text*. Eds. Deborah Cartmell and Imelda Whelehan. London: Routledge, 1999. 63-80.

The 1995 "liberal" film version of the novel "reverses the characteristic privileging hierarchy of Puritanism, but in making space for women as agents it succeeds only in inverting its organizing principles in the form of contemporary hedonism. In the process, the central dynamic of the text's conflict is reduced to the level of an individual struggle in which [. . .] the sovereign self triumphs over the oppressive constraints of society." Rather than presenting the "complex individual/community dialectic" that is the source of *Letter*'s conflict, this film version merely depicts society as a "medium through which the individual seeks expression." The Puritan context of an authoritarian theocracy is downplayed into non-existence, Hester becomes a "caricature feminist" who "wears the scarlet letter like the 'S' of Superwoman," Dimmesdale is depicted as a "heroic action figure," and Pearl is reduced to a "static toddler." The film's greatest flaw, however (far more important than the fact that "it tries to pack in too many contradictory features, verges on the melodramatic and the absurd at times, lacks focus and direction, and is not helped by weak central performances"), is that it "gives credence to the ideology of the 'imperial self'" and thereby completely abandons the message of Hawthorne's text.

834   Elbert, Monika M. "Bourgeois Sexuality and the Gothic Plot in Wharton and Hawthorne." *Hawthorne and Women: Engendering and Expanding the Hawthorne Tradition.* Eds. John L. Idol, Jr., and Melinda M. Ponder. Amherst: U of Massachusetts P, 1999. 258-270.

Traces the Hawthornian influence on Wharton's depiction of gender, class, and genealogy by comparing *Letter* with *Summer* (1917). Both use Gothic conventions to describe class fluctuations and tensions that accompany a burgeoning capitalist society, and both express this central Gothic issue through the image of woman's body as sexual commodity. In their focus on the deterioration and regeneration of the Gothic family and of society at large, Hawthorne and Wharton expose the sexual obsessiveness and potential anarchy of the bourgeois family.

835   Friedman, Robert S. "The Sphere of Thought and Feeling." *Hawthorne's Romances: Social Drama and the Metaphor of Geometry.* Amsterdam: Harwood Academic, 1999. 53-82.

Critiques the major romances through the theories of ritual, symbology, and social drama of cultural anthropologist Victor Turner, arguing that geometric symbols function as "catalytic metaphors that shape our responses to fictional characters and narrators to the contexts that influenced their author." The presence of the circle in *Letter* (particularly the gold-embroidered border that encloses Hester's scarlet letter), along with other references to spheres, orbs, and circles, is interpreted as a geometric form that performs a specific two-fold "office" in the text, demonstrating "the importance of the ideas of borders and boundaries to the characters within the text" and reflecting "the geometrically circular form of the narrative itself." Hester's continual redefinition of her liminality in relation to her community "demands that we question all the specific boundaries that the circle marks out in the novel, including those in which Hester, Pearl, Dimmesdale and Chillingworth are contained and those they transgress, but also the parameters of the novelist, his acquisition and retelling of 'Pue's tale,' and the limitations and freedoms in the very act of retelling." [For other readings that consider Hawthorne's or Hester's relation to concentric circles (or boundaries), see Paul John Eakin (270) and Andrew Hudgins (428).]

836 Goodenough, Elizabeth N. "'Demons of Wickedness, Angels of Delight': Hawthorne, Woolf, and the Child." *Hawthorne and Women: Engendering and Expanding the Hawthorne Tradition.* Eds. John L. Idol, Jr., and Melinda M. Ponder. Amherst: U of Massachusetts P, 1999. 226-236.

The fiction of both Hawthorne and Virginia Woolf contains elfish/demonic representations of children that symbolize the creative power and freedom of the unfettered imagination to live in a world of its own making. Their work also exposes similar concerns with origins and the past, early emotional deprivations, authorial self-doubts, and a protracted sense of their creators as literary outsiders. The essay includes a brief comparison of Hawthorne's Pearl and Woolf's James Ramsay from *To the Lighthouse* (1927). Through the characaterizations of Pearl and James, both authors express "antipatriarchal rage in the idealization of a childlike inwardness and creative potential." Both novels were inspired by children and written in response to "the death of the mother" in order to "exorcise the past."

837 Johnson, Claudia Durst. "National Politics and Literary Neighbors: Discord in Concord." *Hawthorne and Women: Engendering and Expanding the Hawthorne Tradition.* Eds. John L. Idol, Jr., and Melinda M. Ponder. Amherst: U of Massachusetts P, 1999. 104-120.

Despite the discordant personal, literary, and political activity that strained relations between the neighboring Hawthorne and Alcott families during the Civil War era, Hawthorne's fiction still positively influenced Louisa May Alcott, who borrowed *Letter*'s themes of gender and the family in *Work* (1873) and "Transcendental Wild Oats" (1876). More specifically, these themes—which were adapted by Alcott as her method of dealing with her own dysfunctional family—include "the power of and disjunction between woman's labor and man's vocation, the turmoil suffered by the powerful mother, and the disruption in the traditional family."

838   McCall, Dan. *Citizens of Somewhere Else: Nathaniel Hawthorne and Henry James.* Ithaca: Cornell UP, 1999.

Expanding in this book on his previous articles, McCall includes two chapters that focus on *Letter*: "The Design of 'The Custom-House" (pp. 36-44) and "The Tongue of Flame" (pp. 45-70). The first (see 211 for an earlier version) argues that the "modern critical formulae devised to explain the connection" between the sketch and the novel are "vague and misleading." He especially takes issue with critics who "obscure the moral force of the essay" with "esthetic theory" and who argue that Hawthorne works out his aesthetic problems through the moral dilemmas experienced by his own characters. If it does anything, "The Custom-House" connects Hawthorne's intimately related concerns regarding his relationship to America and his life's work as an author. As his emphasis shifts from the actual to the imaginary, Hawthorne links his own experience to Hester's, implying that America "fails and frustrates impulses of creative people by forcing them back too much upon themselves." Its aptness as an introduction to the novel lies in its sense that "the validations of the community have given way and that the individual by himself cannot adequately make meaning out of experience." The second essay concerns itself with a variety of matters pertaining to *Letter*, on Hester's symbolic letter as enforcing a world of anti-allegory, since its meaning is continually interpreted inconsistently by the Puritans; on how her story contradicts the prevailing optimism and celebration of individualism of the day by exploring the causes and consequences of the rigid mind; and, finally, on the tension between natural impulse and repressive social force. The novel (the point of which is "to subvert the resonance of public speech") seems to build toward the forest scene (privileging natural impulse) in which Hester and Dimmesdale accomplish in silence the true "tongue of flame"—resonant silence; yet the ending of the novel seems sadly formulaic and a "pious retraction" as personal desire gives way to community solidarity. By the narrator's own admission, Dimmesdale achieves the tongue of flame (relating to power and humanity) during his Election-Day sermon. There is a partial recovery of Hawthorne's bold statement of rebellion at the end, however. Hester returns to the only place she is "not allowed to belong," her badge of shame converted into "a coat of arms."

839   Newman, Judie. "Guru Industries, Ltd.: Red Letter Religion in Updike's *S.*" *John Updike and Religion: The Sense of the Sacred and the Motions of Grace.* Ed. James Yerkes. Grand Rapids: Eerdmans, 1999. 228-241.

Whereas Hawthorne chose to emphasize Puritan religious history and gloss over the emergent mercantile and imperialist enterprise in his contemporary Salem, Updike clearly establishes in *S* (1988) a satire of Eastern religion and American materialism. While Updike's novel engages with issues concerning women and patriarchal power as so many critics have argued, it is yet "the economic revenge of the previously exploited that occupies center stage." His heroine, Sarah (who should be viewed more as "Indian-as-Other" rather than as "Sarah-as-Hester"), a far cry from Hawthorne's Hester Prynne, depicts "the commercial uses to which the 'Other' can be put and the advantages of exotic identity for religious marketing purposes." Hester's story is an untold story (she is most marked by her silence), undercutting its society by its secret content, and Sarah's story is a "read" story (in epistolary form), an elaborate retelling of a story with which we are already familiar—but with emphasis on crass, exploitative economics.

840   Newman, Judie. "Spaces In-Between: Hester Prynne as the Salem Bibi in Bharati Mukherjee's *The Holder of the World.*" *Borderlands: Negotiating Boundaries in Post-Colonial Writing.* Ed. Monika Reif-Hülser. Amsterdam, Netherlands: Rodopi, 1999. 69-87.

Notes significant parallels between Hawthorne's Hester Prynne and Mukherjee's Hannah Easton, the "Salem bibi" (the white mistress from Salem) who travels between seventeenth-century Massachusetts and pre-colonial India and has an affair with an Indian lover and then a child out of wedlock, Pearl Singh. Mukherjee rewrites *Letter* in *The Holder of the World* (1993) not only to "get out of the ghetto of minority writing" and to fill in the gaps between the foreign and the domestic that Hawthorne purposely leaves open in his novel (these gaps relating to "the space of imperial expansion and Eastern plunder which was the foundation of New England's fortunes," as well as the "conspicuous space between the Puritan 'beginnings' in mid-seventeenth century and the era of decline in the nineteenth"), but also to challenge New Historicist critics who have traditionally neglected the topic of Hawthorne and the East and have all but ignored the true Indian connection. [See Luther S. Luedtke (589) for an essay that considers an Oriental source for *Letter*.]

841   Nudelman, Franny. "Toward a Reader's History: 'Ghosts Might Enter Here.'" *Hawthorne and Women: Engendering and Expanding the Hawthorne Tradition.* Eds. John L. Idol, Jr., and Melinda M. Ponder. Amherst: U of Massachusetts P, 1999. 278-285.

Links Gothic conventions in Toni Morrison's *Beloved* (1988) to Hawthorne's *Letter*, focusing on each author's preoccupation with the the dead returning to life, the sins of the mothers (respectively infanticide and adultery), and the mothers' relations to unruly, otherworldly daughters. Hawthorne and Morrison are both interested in "tak[ing] up our relation to our collective past," and especially the possibility of reconciling violently fragmented families. Both novels are haunted by daughters who bring the past, specifically their mothers' sins, back to life, in an effort to learn their origins and ultimately reconstitute the family by reconciling with both mother and father.

842   Pennell, Melissa McFarland. *"The Scarlet Letter." Student Companion to Nathaniel Hawthorne*. Westport· Greenwood Press, 1999. 67-87.

This critical introduction to *Letter* in the latest volume of the "Student Companions to Classic Writers" series "offers the student and the general reader background that will assist in understanding and interpreting" the romance. It provides background on the "multiple purposes" of "The Custom-House" (such as to vent Hawthorne's frustrations over the termination of his job, to voice his position on politics as well as the nature of authorship and authority, and to create an introduction to the symbols and themes that appear in the novel); explains Hawthorne's choices in establishing setting, plot, and structure; clarifies the development of the primary characters and the role of minor characaters, themes (including the relationship between individual and state, the difference between private and public self, the consequences of passion and repression, and the tension between nature and culture), and symbols; and provides historical context and a brief account of how the novel clearly invites a feminist reading.

843   Plath, James. "Giving the Devil His Due: Leeching and Edification of Spirit in *The Scarlet Letter* and *The Witches of Eastwick*." *John Updike and Religion: The Sense of the Sacred and the Motions of Grace*. Ed. James Yerkes. Grand Rapids: Eerdmans, 1999. 208-227.

Finds several parallels between *The Witches of Eastwick* (1984) and *Letter*, and asserts that this particular John Updike novel is actually more Hawthornesque than his *Scarlet Letter* trilogy because it "gives voice to characters relegated to the background in Hawthorne's novel—the witches, the townspeople, and the 'black man' himself.'" Updike forces readers to confront the enormous gap between the spiritual and secular spheres of the two novels by abandoning the "hyper-religious" moral society of *Letter* where adultery is considered an aberration and instead "giving the devil his due" by presenting adultery as endemic. Updike not only banishes guilt in the secular state of Eastwick but also suggests that "natural" evil is actually edifying to the three witches as Van Horne "leeches" the boredom out of their lives.

844   Wineapple, Brenda. Introduction. *The Scarlet Letter.* By Nathaniel Hawthorne. 1850. New York: New American Library, 1999. vii-xv.

Explains how Hester "saved her creator from despair and certain penury." Hawthorne had long been interested in the fate of strong women who suffered under Puritan scrutiny, and he identified with his heroine's quiet rebellious nature and marginalized status in the community. Both decide to work within the social order to change America's future in this story "of characters physically and sexually alienated from themselves, each other, and the body politic."

Journal Essays and Notes

845   Daniels, Bruce. "Bad Movie/Worse History: The 1995 Unmaking of *The Scarlet Letter.*" *Journal of Popular Culture* 32 (1999): 1-11.

Why did both the movie-going public and critical reviewers of Joffé's 1995 version of *Letter* hate the film "with a vehemence usually reserved for child molesters"? Daniels counts the ways, citing numerous reasons for the $60 million movie to fail so "spectacularly." Its "heavy-handed political correctness" takes first prize for interjecting Hester's "absurdly ahistorical," "wisecracking, confrontational" feminism at every opportunity (just as the movie takes advantage of every opportunity to showcase Hester's [Demi Moore's] nudity: "she bathes more than anyone else in the seventeenth century"). The movie's "silly" and patronizing treatment of Native Americans comes in second, complete with what appear to be obvious "out-takes" from a variety of recent popular films that feature either Puritans or Indians. Historically inaccurate background and bad period-piece costuming tie for third place in their contribution to the film's absurdity, as does the unfortunate and tragic slashing of the novel's "ambiguities and multiple layers of meaning" that reduce it to nothing more than a "cheap melodrama." The most serious offense, however, that which presents "the greatest affront to history," is how inaccurately and unfairly the movie depicts the Puritan world, "pillor[ying] an entire people and feed[ing] a long-standing animosity towards Puritanism that scholars have been trying to overcome for most of the twentieth century."

846   Daniels, Bruce. "Hollywood's Hester Prynne: *The Scarlet Letter* and Puritanism in the Movies." *Canadian Review of American Studies* 29 (1999): 27-60.

Extensively examines the five feature-length film versions of *Letter* that have been made between the years 1910 and 1995: the "cliché-bound" 1926 MGM silent film by Victor Sjöström starring Lillian Gish; the 1934 independent release of a "slapstick talkie" by Robert Vignola that starred Colleen Moore; a "high-minded" German-language version in 1973 directed by Wim Wenders; the "meticulous but labored" four-hour PBS film serialized on television in 1970, and the "preposterous 1995 extravaganza" made by Roland Joffé and starring Demi Moore. Daniels is baffled by all of the films because, while they "reflect the changing technologies and tastes of the movie industry," none of them reflects advances in twentieth-century historical writing and professional scholarship on Puritanism, and thus they all present the inaccurate image of Puritans as "repressive, censorious bigots." Of all the movies, Wim Wenders's version best "captures the essence of Hawthorne's classic," largely because it is more concerned with artistry and meaning ("with essence, with mystery, with humanity, with inspiration—and less with external trappings") than it is with technique and monetary profits for Hollywood. "The sad truth is that we have not learned much about Puritanism or New England from any of the Hollywood versions of *Letter*. We have learned more about the pitfalls of moviemaking from them than about American history or human nature."

847 Hewitt, Elizabeth. "Scarlet Letters, Dead Letters: Correspondence and the Poetics of Democracy in Melville and Hawthorne." *Yale Journal of Criticism* 12 (1999): 295-319.

Explores the tendency of Hawthorne and Herman Melville "to use postal letters as a trope to represent the larger issues of literary production and social communication" in both their literal correspondences to each other and in their fiction, suggesting that Melville's "dead-letter" stories "Bartleby, the Scrivener" and "The Encantadas" developed after he disagreed with Hawthorne's own "model for testing the limits of a democratic poetics" in "The Custom-House" and *Letter*. Both authors used the figure of the letter to engage, albeit in radically different ways, a fundamental literary and political problem of American democracy: how to communicate in a way that avoids "authorial tyranny" on the one hand and "interpretive anarchy" on the other. Hawthorne's solution to the problem seems to lie in modifying the possibility of interpretive freedom "into a design for consensus" ("choosing tyranny and calling it freedom," in other words, as Sacvan Bercovitch has demonstrated before—in 635). Melville offers a more compromising view of democratic poetics that takes the middle ground between authorial tyranny and interpretive indeterminacy (just as his letters to Hawthorne did—oscillating

420

"frantically between demanding union with and separation from Hawthorne"), a view "in which union depends on separation and therefore, perhaps, provides us with a language of democracy that will yield neither tyranny nor anarchy."

848 Johanyak, Debra.   "Romanticism's Fallen Edens: The Malignant Contribution of Hawthorne's Literary Landscapes." *College Language Association Journal* 42 (1999): 353-363.

Having determined that Puritan history provided Hawthorne with "ideal plots and settings for the age-old conflict between good and evil," Johanyak examines the Edenic motif and forest settings in three "conflict-laced love stor[ies]": "Young Goodman Brown," "The May-Pole of Merry Mount," and *Letter*—all of which feature a romantic couple whose "shared moral flaw or spiritual weakness blocks their enjoyment of a true or joyous marriage." Hawthorne does not always use the forest to signal celebration and joyful release from social restraints, though; he sometimes depicts through the forest "the evil characteristics and threatening gestures of menacing invaders." In *Letter*, it is the woodland setting—in all of its neutrality, its lack of social structure and Puritan mores—that provides the climax of the tale for Hawthorne's Adam (Dimmesdale) and Eve (Hester). Ironically, however, although the forest sanctuary "provides a bower setting for refueling the lovers' ardor," it also "paradoxically seals their tragic doom."

849 Kreger, Erika M.   "'Depravity Dressed Up in a Fascinating Garb': Sentimental Motifs and the Seduced Hero(ine) in *The Scarlet Letter*." *Nineteenth-Century Literature* 54 (1999): 308-335.

Challenges critics who view *Letter* (and Hester) as radical, because when the novel is placed in the historical context of literary debates on morality and gender in the 1840s and 1850s (in which it was argued that authors were expected to uphold moral standards while avoiding "intrusive, didactic remarks"), it holds a conservative moral position that "affiliates it with, rather than distinguishes it from, the best-selling domestic novels of the era." Hawthorne "carefully guides his middle-class audience to the 'right' ethical conclusion" through his depiction of the central characters—all of whom ultimately "underscore the narrator's conservative lesson about the need for self-denial and social responsibility." Aware of the type of fiction that sold well, Hawthorne adapted conventions of the seduction novel and domestic novel to create his characters. Dimmesdale exemplifies the "socially unacceptable qualities" of passivity and hypocrisy that were associated with eighteenth-century seduction novels (since he is physically "as weak and drooping as the seduced heroine," and morally "as hypocritical and deceptive as the seducing villain"), and Hester (the so-called "fallen woman") embodies the positive cultural ideals of strength, selflessness, and humility of heroines in nineteenth-century domestic novels. Hawthorne's readers would have sympathized, therefore, not with Dimmesdale's suffering and weakness, but with Hester's trials and sacrifices.

850 Nordlund, Marcus. "Across the Canon: Hawthorne, Morrison, and the Freedom of a Broken Law." *Orbis Litterarum* 54 (1999): 45-59.

While several studies have traced intertextual affinities between Hawthorne's *Letter* and Toni Morrison's *Beloved* (see 668, 755, 792, 803, and 841), Nordlund claims to be the first to establish such a connection between *Letter* and Morrison's *Sula* (1973), noting that both pieces are about "transgressive sexuality, and the resulting clash or tension between the individual and the community." Morrison "exuberantly" reinscribes Hawthorne's classic novel by "grafting" key aspects of its "white canonical narrative" into her own "black feminist novel" (particularly *Letter*'s quest for the "absent father," which is "radicalized" in *Sula* to the extent that "the father is expelled, ostracized, and does not seem to be missed"), thus enhancing *Letter* "without enshrining it" and simultaneously exploring "the ways in which issues of race, gender, literary history, and the symbolic are closely interwoven." Morrison's novel thus becomes "both an expression of genuine love for Hawthorne's work *and* a simultaneous expulsion of the literary Father, the one who kept his repressive silence on the question of slavery and turned Hester's tragedy into Dimmesdale's." The happy result of Morrison's literary endeavor, according to Nordlund, is that "that which was written out can be recovered and written back into the text."

851 Sheriff, John K. "A Prospectus for a Pragmatic Reading of Hawthorne's *The Scarlet Letter*." *REAL: Yearbook of Research in English and American Literature* 15 (1999): 75-92.

Reprising material in his 1997 essay on the same subject (see 800), Sheriff claims to "elaborate more fully the scarlet letter's mode of meaning." As with the earlier piece, he applies the semiotics of Charles Peirce (which stress the importance of experiencing signs in a feeling way) to the interpretive behavior of the main characters, showing that their fates are inexorably bound to their perceptions of and responses to signs (Chillingworth looking for truth in empirical evidence, Dimmesdale looking for truth in social convention, and Hester choosing to be guided by her feelings of love). The ideal way to respond to signs, Sheriff argues, is as Hester does—with a receptive, loving heart. Sheriff's "companion

422

argument" remains consistent with his prior essay in its condemnation of all critical approaches to the novel that suppress its artistic context. Sheriff compares such New Historicist and post-structuralist interpretations to the novel's Puritans who were similarly incapable of "feelingly" valuing "the function of art and aesthetic experience."

852 Solmes, Jennifer. "The Reverse Cavalry: The Indian Subplot of Roland Joffé's *The Scarlet Letter* (1995)." *West Virginia University Philological Papers* 45 (1999): 116-122.

Defends Roland Joffé's heavily criticized film adaptation of *The Scarlet Letter* (1995) and praises its efforts to update Hawthorne's tale "to speak directly to [the film-going audience of] our own age." The movie's plot and character revisions actually comprise "a fascinating study in the filmmaker's desire to respond to the demands of the marketplace" in the mid-nineties. The invented Indian subplot, in particular, was devised specifically to "capitalize on a proven Hollywood formula [as in the box office hits *Dances With Wolves* (1990) and *The Last of the Mohicans* (1992), both of which portray Native Americans sympathetically], rework the story to a new resolution more conducive to the medium, and reshape Hawthorne's characters through a symbolic shorthand developed by the nineties phenomenon of the 'Indian picture.'" In fact, Joffé ironically presents a more realistic, "truer sense" of Native Americans and their relationship between colonists than Hawthorne did with his "stony and dehumanized" Indians who only appear on the periphery of the Boston community. While Joffé *does* "build a paranoia around the Native American [that is] reminiscent of traditional Westerns," he only does so to capitalize on the "new paradigm" of the contemporary "Indian picture." Further, the film ingeniously connects Hester and Dimmesdale to the more "reasonable" (referring to an "open-minded" sense of sexuality and morality) Native culture, "thereby divorcing their descendants, current Americans, from the inheritance of an anachronistic, love-obstructing Puritan world-view." Since the "updated" protagonists believe they have sinned only against society and not God, the lovers are permitted a "happy ending" since they are justified in their guilt-free, triumphant, and defiant leave-taking from Boston.

2000

Books

853 Barlowe, Jamie. *The Scarlet Mob of Scribblers: Rereading Hester Prynne.* Carbondale: Southern Illinois UP, 2000. 189 pp.

Building on ideas first presented in a 1997 article in *American Literary History* (see 804), Barlowe reacts to what she claims is an "absence or tokenism" of women's literary criticism in the mainstream scholarship of *Letter.* Such pervasive exclusion called for an "empirical examination of all of the scholarship," the findings of which convinced her of an exclusionary, patriarchal tradition in the criticism on the novel—as well as a conservative, limiting interpretation of the text itself. Barlowe theorizes in her introductory chapter on reasons for the "absent presence" of women's scholarship and criticism in the mainstream body of scholarly and critical work on *Letter*, finding it ironic that while the male-dominated scholarship often claims the text as radical, progressive, and even woman-centered, it yet excludes the vast majority of women scholars (the "academic Other") from its focus and engagement. Chapter two, "What's Black and White and Red/Read All Over?: Hester-Prynne-ism," illustrates how the concept of "academic Othering" applies to the recognized body of scholarship on the novel, as well as explains the lingering dangers in our own society of "Hester-Prynne-ism," the "relentlessly functioning cultural dichotomy of the good woman vs. the bad but desirable woman who needs instruction or punishment." Chapter three, "The Scarlet Snub," re-reads the mainstream body of scholarship of the novel (starting with the 1950s) as a text in itself, and demonstrates the ways in which it has functioned in relation to women's scholarship. Chapter four, "The Scarlet Woman and the Mob of Scribbling Scholars," presents a "destabilized re-reading" of the novel that is informed by over 230 readings by women scholars and critics, and regards Hester in the context established by those readings, as "spectacle, the consequence of the patriarchal gaze." Chapter five, "Demi's Hester and Hester's Demi(se): *The* (New) *Scarlet Letter* and Its Spectators," examines the 1995 film version (in the context of the earlier cinematic versions) and argues that it "rewrites Hawthorne's text and re-envisions Prynne rather than sexualizing her." It is the critics who re-inscribe Prynne as the sexualized object of their gaze, this time in the person of Demi Moore. Chapter six, "Conclusion: Implications of Hester-Prynne-ism and Rereading Women," considers the implications of Barlowe's recontextualization and rereading, warning against the perpetuation of the limiting, sexist cultural practice of Othering that has determined both the critical analyses of Hester and the scholarship on the novel—and that continues to have negative consequences for academic women's scholarship. [Barlowe's book includes a lengthy bibliography that contains a listing of never-before-compiled twentieth-century women's scholarship on *Letter* (pp. 147-162), as well as an equally long general bibliography on the novel (pp. 162-178).

854   Van Kirk, Susan. *Cliffs Notes, Hawthorne's The Scarlet Letter.* Foster City: IDG Books Worldwide, 2000. 120 pp.

Contains information on the life and background of Hawthorne; an introduction to the novel that includes a list of characters and "character map"; summary of and critical commentary on each chapter—with a glossary of vocabulary words at the end of each; analyses of the four primary characters; discussions of symbolism, the Puritan setting, *Letter* as Gothic romance, and structure; a "Cliffs Notes Review" section that tests understanding of the text with multiple choice questions and answers, quote identification, essay questions, and practice projects; a "Resource Center" of useful books, magazines, journals, video, and internet websites; and an index.

Essays and Studies in Books

855   Bloom, Harold. *"The Scarlet Letter." Nathaniel Hawthorne.* Broomall: Chelsea House Publishers, 2000. 14-40.

Part one of this "comprehensive research and study guide" on three of Hawthorne's four romances (*Blithedale Romance* excluded) is on *Letter* and contains a plot summary, a list of characters, and eleven extracts of "critical views" by Anthony Trollope (EC33), Henry James (EC15), Mark Van Doren (EC36), William Bysshe Stein (22), Charles Child Walcutt (28), Roy R. Male (56), Richard Harter Fogle (15), Frederick Crews (182), Michael Colacurcio (289), Sheridan Baker (423), and Terence Martin (437).

856   Crain, Patricia. "The Story of A: Alphabetization in *The Scarlet Letter*." *The Story of A: The Alphabetization of America from The New England Primer to The Scarlet Letter.* Stanford: Stanford UP, 2000. 173-209.

Examines the evolution of the "alphabetization" of American culture (which refers to practices surrounding the internalization of the alphabet) from nursery and schoolroom primers to adult institutions that involve conceptions of literacy and ways of reading. *Letter* is a "foundation epic of American literacy," an influential primer in its own right that adapts "the story of A." Crain first takes up Hawthorne's own apprehension of the letter "A" prior to writing the novel, and then analyzes his allegorical mode and the "poetics and erotics of alphabetization" within the text (where the letter's removal from the alphabetical system parallels Hester's own isolation). "Both as a literary artist and as a fellow traveler within New England's pedagogy of literacy network, Hawthorne finds in the alphabet an artifact that reflects his sense of how people move through and are shaped by what he calls 'the world's artificial system.'" In Hawthorne's world, "the A has grown up—with a vengeance."

857   Duvall, John N. "Cross-Confessing: Updike's Erect Faith in *A Month of Sundays*." *Straight with a Twist: Queer Theory and the Subject of Heterosexuality*. Ed. Calvin Thomas. Chicago: U of Illinois P, 2000. 122-145.

Calls upon a modernist psychoanalytic approach to *Letter* to examine Updike's *A Month of Sundays* (1974) because similar instances of "uncertain masculinity" and "feared homosexuality" are detected in both texts. Although Updike insists that Hawthorne is an "instinctive heterosexual," "the triangulated desire of Arthur, Hester, and Roger [in *Letter*] is yet another instance of transhistorical Oedipal conflict." What's more, "Updike's construction of Hawthorne constantly is undone by a web of intertextuality that simultaneously overwhelms Updike's desire to fix our gaze on *Letter* and fills his texts with queer possibilities." In other words, despite Updike's insistence on the heterosexuality of *Letter*, an undercurrent of homoeroticism exists not only in Hawthorne's novel (in the relation of Chillingworth and Dimmesdale), but also in Updike's retelling of Hawthorne's novel, which retelling is equally shaped by "homosexual panic" in the relation of Roger Lambert and Thomas Marshfield. The homoeroticism of Updike's male characters also oddly parallels Updike's relationship to Hawthorne's text—in Updike's desire to know, penetrate, and master the effeminate Hawthorne.

858   Martin, Laura. "Silent Rebel: Nathaniel Hawthorne's *The Scarlet Letter*." *Narrative Feminine Identity and the Appearance of Woman in Some of the Shorter Fiction of Goethe, Kleist, Hawthorne and James*. Lewiston: Edwin Mellen Press, 2000. 109-151.

In keeping with her feminist, comparatist approach to female heroines in nineteenth-century German and American literature who "speak and act with more independence and authority than their male authors [. . .] seem prepared to acknowledge," Martin discusses *Letter* with reference to Hawthorne's apparent duplicity and subversiveness in his morally ambiguous presentation of Hester and her femininity. Acknowledging the wealth of conflicting critical feminist interpretations of Hester, and dismissing any masculine "Dimmesdalian" readings that view the minister as the hero of the story (deeming such interpretations as "missing what is most interesting in the story"), Martin traces similarities between *Letter* and Kleist's *Die Marquise von O*, noting that both non-moralizing works are about "strong, maternal women who through an excess of 'femininity' (in its positive sense of being loving and nurturing) commit a crime that society finds it cannot forgive them for." She briefly compares *Letter* with Goethe's "Die pilgernde Törin," emphasizing that both stories are "stolen"

426

by main male characters who are often sympathized with by misguided critics. Character analyses of Hester and Dimmesdale, steeped in acknowledgments to previous critics, conclude this study of Hawthorne's contradictions and pervasive ambiguity. Hawthorne subtly applauds Hester's feminine role/radicalism even at the end and purposely undermines the novel's moral lesson, inasmuch as "patriarchal possession of women and children is "what caused the original conflict in *Letter* to begin with."

859   Watson, James G. "Father's Will." *William Faulkner: Self-Presentation and Performance.* Austin: U of Texas P, 2000. 183-197.

"A predecessor and likely model" for Faulkner's depiction of "the American artist as disinherited outcast" in *Go Down, Moses* (1942) is Hawthorne (pp. 192-197), in whose *Letter* Faulkner would have found "a profoundly personal resource for sustaining his own threatened sense of himself as an artist and man." "Many points of similarity [exist] between the two writers in their respective centuries, biographical as well as textual." Of the biographical correspondences, Watson cites analogous personal and professional experiences (such as mind-dulling threats to each artist's imagination, a shared "two-sided duty" to family, and a similar sense of alienation from mainstream America). The textual connection is apparent when one compares Faulkner's novel to "The Custom-House," since both are concerned with custom houses, the ancestral past, the "will" of fathers, and stories "of hidden sin in which an unwedded mother is the sexual and political prisoner of the patriarchy." Faulkner "must have found in Hawthorne's great story of love and bondage both a model and a mode of artistic self-presentation for his own story of historical wrongs."

860   West, Michael. "Wordplay, Romantic Irony, and the Forms of Antebellum Fiction." *Transcendental Wordplay: America's Punsters and the Search for the Language of Nature.* Athens: Ohio UP, 2000. 291-333.

While the chapter as a whole focuses on wordplay in the fiction of several nineteenth-century American authors (Washington Irving, James Fenimore Cooper, Edgar Allan Poe, Hawthorne, and Herman Melville), a subchapter entitled "The Spell of a Scarlet Letter" (pp. 315-323) discusses Hawthorne's lighter side that is often overlooked in favor of his brooding, darker aspects. Intrigued—as was Sophia Hawthorne—with "verbal high jinks" and fanciful grammatical games, Hawthorne created a sort of punning language that led to the playful construction of "etymological aliases" and an interest in theoretical approaches to language (especially as they suggest the relativism of human values and a plurality of meanings).

Letter is a "vastly expanded etymological pun, where various meanings of A can simultaneously be true." Indeed, the letter is something of a riddle that cannot be solved and comes to signify "both change and continuity, both nature and culture, both gloom and gaiety." Above all, it is a sign of tolerance and accommodation in the "almost" bleak tale: "In its glowing shadow Dimmesdale learns to show mercy to himself and dies penitent; with the dowry left her by old Roger Chillingworth a humanized Pearl marries happily; and in a spirit of reconciliation Hester and the Puritans are transformed, accepting their mutual dependency, each embracing on faith what neither can understand in the other."

Journal Essays and Notes

861   Al Madani, Yusur. "Male, Female Expressions of Heathen Love: Brontë's Heathcliff and Hawthorne's Hester." *International Journal of Arabic English Studies* 1 (2000): 313-330.

In studying *Letter* and Emily Brontë's *Wuthering Heights* (1848) from a cross-cultural perspective, Al-Madani notes similarities and differences between Hester's and Heathcliff's expressions of "heathen" love (specifically defining a "heathen" as one who is "areligious, asocial, amoral, acultural" and whose nature-worshipping life acknowledges only those codes of conduct inspired by his own impulses and drives). According to Al Madani, both characters are "true heathens" by this definition and are considered "subordinates" and outcasts in their social and cultural contexts, Hester because she oversteps moral boundaries and patriarchally-prescribed gender roles and Heathcliff because he breaches social decorum and economic class. The two are "strikingly" similar. "Their intense experience of love and their unshakable longing for union with the other constitute their religion and ultimate code of ethics, which, in turn, confer meaning and substance to their existence." Yet whereas Heathcliff achieves personal salvation and triumph in his "defiant masculine expression of heathen love" by uniting in death with the spirit of Catherine, Hester is not able to over-ride her social and religious constrictions, and her female expression of heathen love is "subverted and muted forever by a restrictively male-dominated culture."

862   Bell, Millicent. "The Prophecy of Hester Prynne." *New York Times Book Review* 11 (2000): 39.

Written in anticipation of a meeting of members of the Nathaniel Hawthorne Society in Boston, Bell's essay refamiliarizes readers with Hawthorne's novel by addressing the main reason for its continued popularity and endless interpretations: Hester's enigmatic character and elusive nature. Bell notes that Hester was most likely modeled after Anne Hutchinson and Margaret Fuller, although awareness of these sources certainly does not fully solve the mystery of Hester's character. The only thing Bell claims certainty of is that Hester returns to America to "recover the prophetic mission she once put aside for her small child's sake."

863   Boudreau, Kristin. "*Is* the World Then So Narrow? Feminist Cinematic Adaptations of Hawthorne and James." *Henry James Review* 21 (2000): 43-53.

By way of addressing (and condemning) the contemporary feminist celebration of female sexuality and "absolute freedom," Boudreau reviews two recent film adaptations that clearly share and celebrate a feminist bent that promotes the trivialization of "the just claims of the community": Roland Joffé's *Letter* (1995) and Jane Campion's *Portrait of a Lady* (1996). What both heroines discover in the novels, of course, is that "the world *is* narrow," because "one must find a way to reconcile herself to the unromantic realities of social obligations." Recognizing and fully accepting the noble compromise between self and society, Hester returns to New England to counsel wayward women and Isabel returns to Rome to counsel Pansy. Both cinematic adaptations of these two novels, however, "refuse to recognize either the limitations of the individual or the just claims of society, celebrating instead heroines who thumb their noses at convention and constraint." What they do is to turn Hawthorne's and James's sensitive novels into "adolescent soap opera[s]." Contemporary feminists, like Joffé and Campion, fail to understand the chief idea of both novels: "that identity is historically and socially constituted"—and that personal fulfillment *should* take a back seat to the more mature, larger principles of the human community. To reject Hester's and Isabel's commitments to social responsibility not only trivializes the just claims of the community, but also speaks to our own pleasure-seeking, selfish culture's narrowness.

864   Harper, Preston. "Puritan Works Salvation and the Quest for Community in *The Scarlet Letter*." *Theology Today* 57 (2000): 51-65.

Hawthorne "looked to the Puritan experience not as a detached observer as some critics have posited but as a devout seeker for answers to questions about the possibility of love and acceptance in a human community, one where evil was understood to be the universal malady and the Bible was the guide to overcoming it." In *Letter*, Hawthorne uses Puritanism (softened a bit) not only to arrive at a concept of universal community that was foreign to his blandly righteous contemporaries but also to demonstrate how sin alienates one from community and "to understand how love, not works, enables return." Dimmesdale achieves salvation through long years of "good works" (which are in themselves essentially selfish, performed to receive absolution) and through and by "the love of Hester, a love that [gives] him the strength to recognize how to respond to his awareness that he is part of the sinful brotherhood of mankind." Anyone, Hawthorne implies, can experience "a kind of redemptive love" if he "love[s] and live[s] honestly, keeping no vital secrets from the community." Most important to Hawthorne is keeping one's name on "the roll of mankind" to avoid breaking "the magnetic chain of humanity." Harper's good will does not extend to Hester, who at the end "must continue to suffer toward an impossible resolution" because she never quite assimilates herself into the community. Dimmesdale's brief gesture of brotherly love before death is more sincere than Hester's "loveless" "good works" or her devoting the rest of her life to counseling those in need of help.

865 Hull, Richard. "Sent Meaning Versus Attached Meaning: Two Interpretations of Interpretation in *The Scarlet Letter*." *ATQ* 14 (2000): 143-158.*

Letter depicts a "historical crossing from one kind of interpretation to another," a shift from the Puritan tradition to Enlightenment thought whereby signs are no longer interpreted as having been "sent," but rather take on subjective meaning that is attached by interpreters. "*Letter*'s many interpretations, then, fall into two classes," Puritan interpretations that insist natural phenomena are messages from God and Enlightenment interpretations that dismiss natural signs as "meaningless natural occurrences." "Central points in *Letter*—Dimmesdale's interpretation of a meteor and Hawthorne's finding a rag worthy of interpretation, Hester's interpretation of her child, and Pearl's claim that she has no Heavenly Father—revolve around this shift." A third layer can be added to the shift if one considers Surveyor Pue's Enlightenment attitude as something of a "buffer" between the seventeenth-century Puritan story and the narrator's Post-Enlightenment, romantic interpretation of the story's events. Whereas Dimmesdale and Hester consider the meanings they attach to things to be "meant" by a sender, both the Enlightenment narrator and Pearl deny that such meanings are sent. But the narrator does not dismiss faith or reduce any signs to one subjective interpretation. Hull adds a metaphysical and hermeneutic spin by suggesting that Hawthorne employs what is now known as the Kantian and Derridean concept of "negative theology" in the novel, interpreting the plurality of signs not as a rejection of faith in God but as a skeptical welcoming of multiple discourses with and about God. [For another treatment of Enlightenment thought in *Letter*, see John Arthos (159).]

*For Hull's earlier study on how signs are interpreted differently in *Letter*, see 600.

866 Lee, Sohui. "The Guillotine and the American Public: A Godwinian Reading of *The Scarlet Letter*." *Symbiosis: A Journal of Anglo-American Literary Relations* 4.2 (2000): 152-172.

Detecting continuities between political crises in late eighteenth-century England and political discourse on radicalism in mid-nineteenth-century America, Lee carefully traces the politics of *Letter* beyond the frequently cited Custom House dismissal, arguing that "Hawthorne situates his experience among deeper institutional problems that shape existing American polity, and that his treatment is analogous to William Godwin's critique of British government in [. . .] *Caleb Williams* (1793)." Hawthorne was uneasy with Jacksonian politics,* as seen in his playful, satiric use of radical, left-wing "Locofoco" rhetoric in "The Custom-House" where he connects the French Revolution with his dismissal (decapitation) from his position. He was attracted to Godwin's "ambivalent representation of political rhetoric and public justice" in *Caleb Williams*, as well as the latter's interpretation of the French Revolution as "institutionalized political persecution." Hawthorne's allusion to the guillotine in "The Custom-House" sheds light on his similar "critical view of partisan politics and the rhetorical manipulation of public consensus." Yet more than "a warning against consensual language manipulated by the partisan elite, or the problem of inherent conflict in a democracy," *Letter* is also "a story of misguided radicalism caused by the lack of real political reform." Hawthorne does not permit Hester in her solipsistic radicalism to gain "legal sanction to speculate, discuss, and even challenge the existing orthodoxy," since "her speculation on reform degenerates to an advocacy of anarchism."

*Lee's argument builds on Sacvan Bercovitch's 1991 study (see 635) on Hawthorne's uneasiness with Jacksonian politics.

867 Wardrop, Daneen. "Hawthorne's Revisioning of the 'Little Cherub': Pearl and Nineteenth-Century Childrearing Manuals." *Nathaniel Hawthorne Review* 26.2 (2000): 18-32.

To demonstrate that Pearl is a believable child character whose function far exceeds symbolic status, Wardrop places Pearl within Hawthorne's historical antebellum context, analyzing her behavior not only in connection to Hawthorne's own impish, energetic daughter Una, but also with reference to nineteenth-century childrearing manuals. When viewed in this latter context, Pearl "exceeds the idealization of childhood behavior" by "failing to encompass the sentimental norm of the angelic cherub." Such guidebooks would approve of controlling (although not altogether stifling) Pearl's unpredictable excesses and willful exuberance, and they would have little sympathy with Hester for taking on the entire burden of childrearing herself, since children's salvation rested upon the purity and goodness of their mothers alone.

PART IV

Resource Guide

The following collection of resources is broken down into six categories: special critical editions of *The Scarlet Letter*, collections of criticism, general student introductions to the novel, teaching aids and guides, bibliographies, and biographies. A few of the sources in the first four categories overlap, applicable to more than one category. Numbers in parentheses refer to the annotation numbers of individual entries in the bibliography.

A: Special Critical Editions and Sourcebooks

Bradley, Sculley, Richmond Croom Beaty, and E. Hudson Long, eds. *The Scarlet Letter by Nathaniel Hawthorne: An Annotated Text, Backgrounds and Sources, Essays in Criticism.* New York: W. W. Norton, 1961, 1978. (102 and 353—the first and second editions)

Elbert, Monika M. *The Scarlet Letter.* By Nathaniel Hawthorne. 1850. New York: Washington Square, 1994. (723)

Gross, Seymour [L.], Sculley Bradley, Richmond Croom Beatty, and E. Hudson Long, eds. *The Scarlet Letter: An Authoritative Text, Essays in Criticism and Scholarship.* Third edition. New York: W. W. Norton, 1988. (557)

Lynn, Kenneth S. *The Scarlet Letter, Text, Sources, Criticism.* New York: Harcourt, Brace, and World, 1961. (103)

Murfin, Ross C., ed. *Case Studies in Contemporary Criticism: Nathaniel Hawthorne: The Scarlet Letter.* Boston: Bedford Books of St. Martin's Press, 1991. (637)

The Scarlet Letter in *The Centenary Edition of Works of Nathaniel Hawthorne.* Vol. 1. Ed. William Charvat et al. Columbus: Ohio State UP, 1962.

Scharnhorst, Gary. *The Critical Response to Nathaniel Hawthorne's The Scarlet Letter.* New York: Greenwood Press, 1992. (670)

Spector, Robert Donald, ed. *The Scarlet Letter: Special Aids.* New York: Bantam, 1965. (164)

B: Collections of Criticism

Barbour, James, and Thomas Quirk, eds. *Romanticism: Critical Essays in American Literature.* New York: Garland, 1986. (509)

Bloom Harold, ed. *Modern Critical Interpretations: Nathaniel Hawthorne's The Scarlet Letter.* New York: Chelsea House, 1986. (507)

Bloom, Harold, ed. *Hester Prynne.* New York: Chelsea House, 1990. (609)

Bloom, Harold. *"The Scarlet Letter." Nathaniel Hawthorne.* Broomall: Chelsea House Publishers, 2000. 14-40. (855)

Bradley, Sculley, Richard Croom Beatty, and E. Hudson Long., eds. *The Scarlet Letter: An Annotated Text, Backgrounds and Sources, Essays in Criticism.* Norton Critical Edition. New York: W. W. Norton, 1961 1978. (102 and 353)

Cady, Edwin H[arrison], and Louis J. Budd, eds. *On Hawthorne: The Best from American Literature.* Durham: Duke UP, 1990. (612)

Cohen, B. Bernard. *The Recognition of Nathaniel Hawthorne: Selected Criticism Since 1828.* Ann Arbor: U of Michigan P, 1969. (234)

Colacurcio, Michael J., ed. *New Essays on The Scarlet Letter.* New York: Cambridge UP, 1985. (481)

Crowley, J. Donald, ed. *Hawthorne: A Collection of Criticism.* New York: McGraw-Hill, 1975. (328)

Feidelson, Charles, [Jr.], and Paul Brodtkorb, Jr., eds. *Interpretations of American Literature.* Oxford: Oxford UP, 1959. (81)

Gerber, John C., ed. *Twentieth-Century Interpretations of The Scarlet Letter: A Collection of Critical Essays.* Englewood Cliffs: Prentice-Hall, Inc., 1968. 1-15. (214)

Gross, Seymour L., ed. *A Scarlet Letter Handbook.* Belmont: Wadsworth Publishing Company, 1960. (86)

Harding, Brian. *Nathaniel Hawthorne: Critical Assessments.* Robertsbridge: Helm Information, 1998. (819)

Kaul, A. N., ed. *Hawthorne: A Collection of Critical Essays*. Englewood Cliffs: Prentice-Hall, 1966. (186)

Kennedy-Andrews, Elmer, ed. *Nathaniel Hawthorne: The Scarlet Letter*. New York: Columbia UP, 1999. (829)

Kesterson, David B., ed. *Critical Essays on The Scarlet Letter*. Boston: G. K. Hall, 1988. (558)

Morey, Eileen, ed. *Readings on The Scarlet Letter*. San Diego: Greenhaven Press, 1998. (816)

Murfin, Ross C., ed. *Case Studies in Contemporary Criticism: Nathaniel Hawthorne: The Scarlet Letter*. Boston: Bedford Books of St. Martin's Press, 1991. (637)

Scharnhorst, Gary. *The Critical Response to Nathaniel Hawthorne's The Scarlet Letter*. New York: Greenwood Press, 1992. (670)

Swisher, Clarice, ed. *Readings on Nathaniel Hawthorne*. San Diego: Greenhaven Press, 1996. (775)

Turner, Artlin. *The Merrill Studies in The Scarlet Letter*. Columbus: Charles E. Merrill, 1970. (249)

White, Sidney Howard. *Barron's Simplified Approach to The Scarlet Letter*. Woodbury: Barron's Educational Series, 1967. (199)

C: General Student Introductions to the Novel and Study Guides

Baym, Nina. *The Scarlet Letter: A Reading*. Boston: Twayne, 1986. (506)

Bloom, Harold. "*The Scarlet Letter*." *Nathaniel Hawthorne*. Broomall: Chelsea House Publishers, 2000. 14-40. (855)

Cady, Edwin Harrison, Frederick J. Hoffman, and Roy Harvey Pearce, eds. "Notes on Reading *The Scarlet Letter*." *The Growth of American Literature: A Critical and Historical Survey*. Volume 1. New York: American Book, 1956. 463-466. (45)

Feidelson, Charles, [Jr.], and Paul Brodtkorb, Jr., eds. *Interpretations of American Literature*. Oxford: Oxford UP, 1959. (81)

Gale, Robert L. *"The Scarlet Letter." Plots and Characters in the Fiction and Sketches of Nathaniel Hawthorne.* Hamden: Archon Books, 1968. 136-144. (215)

Gross, Seymour L., ed. *A Scarlet Letter Handbook.* Belmont: Wadsworth Publishing Company, 1960. (86)

Jaffe, Adrian, and Herbert Weisinger, eds. *"The Scarlet Letter." The Laureate Fraternity: An Introduction to Literature.* Evanston: Row, Peterson, 1960. 261-263. (91)

Johnson, Claudia Durst. *Understanding The Scarlet Letter: A Student Casebook to Issues, Sources, and Historical Documents.* Westport: Greenwood Press, 1995. (741)

Leavitt, Charles. *Review Notes and Study Guide to Hawthorne's The Scarlet Letter.* New York: Monarch Press, 1966. (153)

Lynn, Kenneth S. *The Scarlet Letter, Text, Sources, Criticism.* New York: Harcourt, Brace and World, Inc., 1961. (103)

Martin, John Stephen. Introduction. *The Scarlet Letter.* By Nathaniel Hawthorne. 1850. Peterborough, Ontario: Broadview Press, 1995. 11-64. (742)

Mizener, Arthur. "Nathaniel Hawthorne: *The Scarlet Letter.*" *Twelve Great American Novels.* New York: New American Library, 1967. 9-18.

Morey, Eileen, ed. *Readings on The Scarlet Letter.* San Diego: Greenhaven Press, 1998. (816)

Murfin, Ross C., ed. *Case Studies in Contemporary Criticism: Nathaniel Hawthorne: The Scarlet Letter.* Boston: Bedford Books of St. Martin's Press, 1991. (637)

O'Brien, Frank. *Pennant Key-Indexed Study Guide to The Scarlet Letter.* New York: Bantam Books, 1966. (181)

Pennell, Melissa McFarland. *"The Scarlet Letter." Student Companion to Nathaniel Hawthorne.* Westport: Greenwood Press, 1999. 67-87. (842)

Scholes, James B. *Nathaniel Hawthorne's The Scarlet Letter: A Study Guide.* Bound Brook: Shelley Publishing, 1962. (121)

Sheldon, Sara. *Nathaniel Hawthorne's The Scarlet Letter*. Woodbury: Barron's, 1984. (452)

Spector, Robert Donald, ed. *The Scarlet Letter: Special Aids*. New York: Bantam, 1965. (164)

Stewart, Randall, and Dorothy Bethurum. "Nathaniel Hawthorne: *The Scarlet Letter*." *Living Masterpieces of American Literature*. Vol. 2. Chicago: Scott, Foresman, 1954. 55-175. (30)

Swisher, Clarice, ed. *Readings on Nathaniel Hawthorne*. San Diego: Greenhaven Press, 1996, (775)

Telgen, Diane. "*The Scarlet Letter*." *Novels for Students: Presenting Analysis, Context, and Criticism on Commonly Studied Poetry*. Detroit: Gale Research, 1997. 306-328. (802)

Van Kirk, Susan. *Cliffs Notes, Hawthorne's The Scarlet Letter*. Foster City: IDG Books Worldwide, 2000. (854)

Weber, J. Sherwood, Jules Alan Wein, Arthur Waldhorn, and Arthur Zeiger. "Hawthorne: *The Scarlet Letter*." *From Homer to Joyce: A Study Guide to Thirty-Six Great Books*. New York: Holt, 1959. 200-209. (82)

White, Sidney Howard. *Barron's Simplified Approach to The Scarlet Letter*. Woodbury: Barron's Educational Series, 1967. (199)

D: Teaching Aids and Guides

Bryson, Norman. "Hawthorne's Illegible Letter." *Teaching the Text*. Ed. Susanne Kappeler and Norman Bryson. London: Routledge and Kegan Paul, 1983. 92-108. (435)

Butler, John F. "Hawthorne: *The Scarlet Letter*." *Exercises in Literary Understanding*. Chicago: Scott-Foresman, 1956. 18-22. (44)

Gibson, William M. "The Art of Nathaniel Hawthorne: An Examination of *The Scarlet Letter*." *The American Renaissance: the History and Literature of an Era*. Ed. George Hendrick. Frankfurt am Main: Diesterweg, 1961. 97-106. (105)

Gross, Seymour L., ed. *A Scarlet Letter Handbook*. Belmont: Wadsworth Publishing Company, 1960. (86)

438

Josephs, Lois. "One Approach to the Puritans." *English Journal* 50 (1961): 183-187. (115)

Leavitt, Charles. *Review Notes and Study Guide to Hawthorne's The Scarlet Letter.* New York: Thor Publications, 1964. (153)

Lynn, Kenneth S. *The Scarlet Letter, Text, Sources, Criticism.* New York: Harcourt, Brace and World, Inc., 1961. (103)

Male, Roy R. "Hawthorne's Allegory of Guilt and Redemption." *Emerson Society Quarterly* 25 (1961): 16-18. (117)

Marcus, Fred H. "The *Scarlet Letter*: The Power of Ambiguity." *English Journal* 51 (1962): 449-458. (131)

Poe, Elizabeth Ann. "Alienation from Society in *The Scarlet Letter* and *The Chocolate War.*" *Adolescent Literature as a Complement to the Classics.* Ed. Joan F. Kaywell. Norwood: Christopher-Gordon, 1993. 185-194. (698)

Poe, Elizabeth Ann. *A Teacher's Guide to the Signet Classic Edition of Nathaniel Hawthorne's The Scarlet Letter.* New York: Penguin USA, 1991. (638)

Putzel, Max. "The Way Out of the Minister's Maze: Some Hints for Teachers of *The Scarlet Letter.*" *Die Neueren Sprachen* 9 (1960): 127-131. (101)

Ridout, Albert K. "*The Scarlet Letter* and Student Verse." *English Journal* 55 (1966): 885-886. (194)

Roth, Margaret Ann, ed. *A Teacher's Guide to The Scarlet Letter: A Four-Part Television Drama Produced by WGBH Boston.* Boston: WGBH Educational Foundation, 1979. (367)

Scholes, James B. *Nathaniel Hawthorne's The Scarlet Letter: A Study Guide.* Ed. Walter Harding. Bound Brook: Shelley Publishing, 1962. (121)

Sheldon, Sara. *Nathaniel Hawthorne's The Scarlet Letter.* Woodbury: Barron's, 1984. (452)

Sweeney, Susan Elizabeth. "The Madonna, the Women's Room, and *The Scarlet Letter.*" *College English* 57 (1995): 410-425. (763)

Tanner, Bernard R. "Tone as an Approach to *The Scarlet Letter.*" *English Journal* 53 (1964): 528-530. (163)

E: Bibliographies

The bibliographies cited below were reviewed in addition to the annual bibliographies (such as MLA International Bibliography) and the annual essay reviews that can be found in *American Literary Scholarship: an Annual*, the *Nathaniel Hawthorne Journal* (1971-1978), *the Nathaniel Hawthorne Society Newsletter* (1975-1985), and the *Nathaniel Hawthorne Review* (1986-present). For comprehensive annotated bibliographies of Hawthorne scholarship after the year 2000, consult the annual bibliography that is published in the *Nathaniel Hawthorne Review*. Summaries for several works are provided below since annotated entries for bibliographies are not included in Part III of this study.

Barlowe, Jamie. "Rereading Women: Hester Prynne-ism and the Scarlet Mob of Scribblers." *American Literary History* 9 (1997): 197-225. (804)

Following Barlowe's essay is a bibliographic collection of women's scholarship on *Letter* from 1882 through 1996 (pp. 216-223).

Barlowe, Jamie. *The Scarlet Mob of Scribblers: Rereading Hester Prynne.* Carbondale: Southern Illinois UP, 2000. (853)

Presents a bibliography of never-before-compiled twentieth-century women's scholarship on *Letter* (pp. 147-162), as well as an equally long general bibliography on the novel that includes men's scholarship on the novel (pp. 162-178).

Beebe, Maurice, and Jack Hardie. "Criticism of Nathaniel Hawthorne: A Selected Checklist." *Studies in the Novel* 2 (1970): 519-587.

The first part of this collection of criticism and scholarship focuses on general Hawthorne studies, and the second half is divided into discussions of individual works. The *Letter* bibliography covers pp. 573-582.

Blair, Walter. "Hawthorne." *Eight American Authors: A Review of Research and Criticism.* Ed. Floyd Stovall. New York: Norton, 1956. 100-152. (43)

Boswell, Jeanetta. "Nathaniel Hawthorne." *The American Renaissance and the Critics: The Best of a Century in Criticism.* Wakefield: Longwood Academic Press, 1990. 205-292.

This alphabetically arranged, generously annotated five-part bibliography aims "to show variety and representation over a good spread of time." As the chapter title indicates (other chapters annotate criticism on Ralph Waldo Emerson, Henry David Thoreau, Herman Melville, and Walt Whitman), the bibliography is not exclusively limited to *Letter*.

Boswell, Jeanetta. *Nathaniel Hawthorne and the Critics: A Checklist of Criticism 1900-1978*. Metuchen: Scarecrow Press, 1982.

One of the "Scarecrow Author Bibliographies," this volume completes a series on American Renaissance authors (which also reviews Ralph Waldo Emerson, Walt Whitman, Herman Melville, and Henry David Thoreau). This 273-pp. volume includes an alphabetical listing of Hawthorne criticism, a co-authors/editors index, and a subject index.

Browne, Nina E. *A Bibliography of Nathaniel Hawthorne*. Boston: Houghton Mifflin, 1905.

Includes primary and secondary materials and contains a chronological list of Hawthorne's works, pseudonyms used by Hawthorne, bibliographies of Hawthorne, complete works, separate works, translations, dramatizations, biography and criticism, an alphabetical list of Hawthorne's works, and an index.

Cameron, Kenneth Walter. "The Hawthorne Secondary Bibliography, 1838-1950." *American Great Ones: Hawthorne, Emerson, Thoreau*. Hartford: Transcendental Books, 1997. 5-151.

Clark, C. E. Frazer, Jr., ed. *Hawthorne at Auction, 1894-1971*. Book Tower: Gale Research Company, 1972.

A compilation of the most significant Hawthorne collections described in auction sale catalogues published between 1894 and 1971.

Clark, C. E. Frazer, Jr. *Nathaniel Hawthorne: A Descriptive Bibliography*. Pittsburgh: U of Pittsburgh P, 1978.

This comprehensive primary Hawthorne bibliography includes sections on separate publications, collected works, first-appearance contributions to books, pamphlets, magazines, and newspapers, special material, selected bibliographic material, and prose and verse material attributed to Hawthorne.

Frank, Frederick S. *Guide to the Gothic: An Annotated Bibliography of Criticism*

Metuchen: Scarecrow Press, Inc., 1984.

The section on Hawthorne contains 51 items, pp. 261-268.

Gordan, John D. *Nathaniel Hawthorne, The Years of Fulfillment, 1804-1853: An Exhibition From the Berg Collection. First Editions, Manuscripts, Autograph Letters.* New York: New York Public Library, 1954.

Gross, Theodore L. "Nathaniel Hawthorne." *Hawthorne, Melville, Stephen Crane: A Critical Bibliography.* Eds. Theodore L. Gross and Stanley Wertheim. New York: The Free Press, 1971. 1 100.

The chapter includes an introduction, a chronology, a list of editions, evaluations and lengthy annotations for bibliographies and biographies, as well as criticism for each of the novels and a concluding bibliographical index.

Gross, Seymour. "Selected Bibliography." *The Scarlet Letter.* 3rd edition. New York: W. W. Norton and Company, 1988. 435-440.

Contains 19 items on "The Custom-House" and 152 on *Letter*.

Idol, John L., Jr., and Melinda M. Ponder, eds. *Hawthorne and Women: Engendering and Expanding the Hawthorne Tradition.* Amherst: U of Massachusetts P, 1999.

Contains a selective bibliography on the debate over Hawthorne and the "woman question" (pp. 301-305). "Master of ambiguity that he is, Hawthorne is hard to pin down, appearing to some readers to present Hester as a challenge to patriarchal dominance, seeming to others to force Hester back into a role of domestic subservience."

Jones, Buford. *A Checklist of Hawthorne Criticism, 1951-1966.* Hartford Transcendental Books, 1967.

This helpful work offers brief annotations for 906 bibliographic entries.

Nilon, Charles H. *Bibliography of Bibliographies in American Literature.* New York: Bowker, 1970.

The section on Hawthorne, covered on pp. 92-95, includes primary and secondary materials.

Phillips, Robert S. *"The Scarlet Letter*: A Selected Checklist of Criticism, 1850-1962." *Bulletin of Bibliography* 23 (1962): 213-216. (134)

Ricks, Beatrice, Joseph J. Adams, and Jack O. Hazlerig. *Nathaniel Hawthorne: A Reference Bibliography, 1900-1971*. Boston: G.K. Hall, 1972.

Scharnhorst, Gary. "Selected Bibliography." *The Critical Response to Nathaniel Hawthorne's The Scarlet Letter. Critical Responses in Arts and Letters, Number 2.* New York: Greenwood Press, 1992. 255-262.

Scharnhorst, Gary. *Nathaniel Hawthorne: An Annotated Bibliography of Comment and Criticism Before 1900*. Metuchen: Scarecrow Press, 1988.

Stewart, Randall. *Nathaniel Hawthorne: A Bibliography*. New Haven: Yale UP, 1948.

Stock, Ely. "Some Recent Books on Hawthorne." *Nineteenth-Century Fiction* 25 (1971): 482-493.

Tashjian, Nouvart, and Dwight Eckerman. *Nathaniel Hawthorne: An Annotated Bibliography*. New York: William-Frederick, 1948.

Turner, Arlin. "Nathaniel Hawthorne in American Studies." *College English* 26 (1964): 133-139.

Turner, Arlin. "Recent Scholarship on Hawthorne and Melville." *The Teacher and American Literature.* Ed. Lewis Gaston Leary. Champaign: National Council of Teachers of English, 1965. 95-109.

Ulysses Sumner Milburn Collection of Hawthorniana. Canton: Special Collections, St. Lawrence U, 1989.

Wilson, James C. "An Annotated Bibliography." *The Hawthorne and Melville Friendship: An Annotated Bibliography, Biographical and Critical Essays, and Correspondence Between the Two.* Jefferson: McFarland & Company, Inc., 1991. 40-74.

This bibliography involves major discussions of the Hawthorne-Melville relationship.

F: Biographies

Arvin, Newton. *Hawthorne.* Boston: Little, Brown, 1929. (EC1)

Erlich, Gloria. "The Access of Power." *Family Themes and Hawthorne's Fiction: The Tenacious Web.* New Brunswick: Rutgers UP, 1984. 1-34. (459)

Gorman, Herbert. *Hawthorne, A Study in Solitude.* N.p.: George H. Doran, 1929. 83-90. (EC10)

Herbert, T. Walter. *Dearest Beloved: The Hawthornes and the Making of the Middle-Class Family.* Berkeley: U of California P, 1993. (695)

Hoeltje, Hubert H. "A Tale of Sorrow." *Inward Sky: The Mind and Heart of Nathaniel Hawthorne.* Durham: Duke UP, 1962. 240-296. (125)

James, Henry. "The Three American Novels." *Hawthorne.* London: Macmillian, 1879. 83-115. (EC15)

Lathrop, George Parsons. *"The Scarlet Letter." A Study of Hawthorne.* Boston, 1876. 210-225. (EC17)

Mellow, James R. *Nathaniel Hawthorne in His Times.* Boston: Houghton Mifflin, 1980. (392)

Author Index

Numbers refer to the annotation numbers of individual entries,
not to page numbers.

A

Abbott, Anne W., ER 5
Abel, Darrel, 10, 16, 24, 25, 46,
  239, 266, 284, 559
Abrams, Robert E., 728
Adams, Michael Vannoy, 439
Alkana, Joseph, 791
Al Madani, Yusur, 861
Allen, M. L., 108
Allen, William Rodney, 469
Anderson, Douglas, 610, 652
Anderson, Quentin, 259
Andola, John A., 285
Arac, Jonathan, 508
Arden, Eugene, 109
Armour, Richard, 87
Arora, V. N., 333
Arthos, John, 159
Arvin, Newton, EC1, 1
Assmann, Aleida, 830
Atkins, Lois, 31
Auchincloss, Louis, 719
Austin, Allen, 110, 126, 127
Autrey, Max L., 334
Axelsson, Arne I., 309

B

Baker, Larry, 453
Baker, Sheridan, 423
Balakian, Anna, 358
Bales, Kent, 454
Banting, Pamela, 518
Barbour, James, 509
Baris, Sharon Deykin, 455
Barlowe, Jamie, 804, 853, 805
Barnes, Daniel R., 310

Barnett, Louise K., 440, 690
Barker-Benfield, Ben, 286
Barszcz, James, 672
Bartley, William, 653
Baskett, Sam S., 111, 112
Baughman, Ernest W., 204
Baumgartner, Alex M., 267
Bayer, John G., 397
Baym, Nina, 252, 311, 339, 406,
  419, 424, 434, 470, 506,
  777
Beatty, Richard Croom, 102,
  353, 557
Becker, John E., 260
Bell, John M., 240
Bell, Michael Davitt, 261, 386,
  482
Bell, Millicent, 425, 862
Bellis, Peter, 746
Ben-Bassat, Hedda, 729
Benoit, Raymond, 287
Bensick, Carol M., 483, 702, 831
Benstock, Shari, 639
Bercovitch, Sacvan, 560, 575,
  576, 635, 691, 778
Bergman, Herbert, 253
Bergeron, David M., 241
Bergmann, Harriet, 413
Berlant, Lauren, 636
Berner, Robert L., 375
Bernstein, Cynthia, 703
Berryman, Charles, 368, 832
Berthold, Michael Couson, 441
Bethurum, Dorothy, 30
Bewley, Marius, 47, 54
Bier, Jesse, 40

Subject Index

of/relation to/vision of, 154, 213, 219, 259, 260, 344, 354, 356, 393, 444, 454, 56, 479, 515, 531, 540, 615, 636, 664, 677, 691, 721, 728, 743, 838

America and England, the relation between (*see also* New World *and* Old World), 200, 261, 348, 539

American culture, history, and identity (*see also* Comparison of 17th- and 19th-century America), 139, 154, 158, 189, 213, 244, 335, 356, 404, 409, 416, 454, 455, 463, 517, 531, 539, 540, 542, 560, 575, 582, 588, 590, 591, 601, 606, 636, 640, 664, 673, 687, 721, 728, 778, 821, 856

American fiction (as a distinct, national literature), Hawthorne's writing of, 29, 165, 227, 272, 404, 422, 488, 708

American ideology (Hawthorne's participation in and/or criticism of), 356, 508, 513, 560, 575, 635, 677, 727, 728, 732, 746, 778, 782, 788

American literature, as redefined (because of political and social interests), 314, 318, 417, 586, 677, 708, 752

American Renaissance (*see also* Hawthorne in relation to his contemporaries), EC20, 105, 321, 368, 432, 504, 570, 582, 603, 648, 708, 833

American vs. English fiction (*see also* "Novel vs. Romance"), EC14, 55, 89, 259, 263, 307, 314, 586, 587

Androgyny (*see also* "Dimmesdale as effeminate" *and* "Hester as masculine"), 303, 361, 585

Antinomianism/Antinomian Controversy (*see also* Anne Hutchinson), 286, 289, 472, 618, 741

Anxieties, Hawthorne's
Authorial (*see also* Authorship), 211, 340, 395, 512, 513, 533, 569, 583, 620, 627, 632, 648, 699, 711, 718, 727, 749, 760, 793, 797
Class, 620, 693
Domestic/Filial/Parental, 716, 646, 824
Gender, 512, 581, 620, 647, 693, 749, 755, 793, 827, 857
Identity, 693
Race, 508, 594, 620, 660, 664, 708, 732, 755, 792, 850
Readership (*see* Reader)
Sexual (including homosexuality and homophobia), 89, 513, 727, 747, 857
Vocational (*see* Authorship)

Arac, Jonathan (*see also* in Author Index), 576, 651, 652, 660, 708, 755, 779, 811

Archetype (*see also* Critical Approach Index), 238, 333, 385, 743, 770

Art, Hawthorne's (*see also* Authorship), 247, 311, 407, 420, 464, 479, 729, 757
as distinguished from popular literature, 513, 760, 797
as distinguished from women's inferior domestic "scribblings," 492, 799
as establishing "an intercourse with the world," 343, 644, 648
as feminine (or aligned with female writers), 620, 632, 654, 749, 812
as masculine, 799
the commercialization of (*see also* "Literature as commodity" *and* Marketplace), 434, 479, 488, 513, 718, 760, 797

*For more on whether Dimmesdale is "damned" or "saved" at the end, refer above to "Dimmesdale, the confession of" or below to "Election-Day Sermon." Many of the essays imply damnation or salvation in their interpretations of Dimmesdale as either defeated or triumphant in the final scaffold scene.

verbal trickery in (*see also* Wordplay), 365, 464, 683

D

"Damned mob of scribbling women" (*see also* Sentimental Novels/Novelists *and* Women), 536, 804
Dark ladies, EC24, 237, 261, 284, 340, 467, 468, 589
"Dark necessity," 24, 42, 59, 98, 119, 146, 350
Death (including resurrection from), 399, 546, 595, 716, 781, 841
Deconstructionism (*see also* in Critical Approach Index), 616, 766
"Deeper psychology," EC15, 47, 57
Democracy,
    Hawthorne's celebration of/commitment to, EC20, 30, 282, 560, 654
    problems with, 847, 866
Desire, 518, 616
Divine Maternity (Madonna and child), 173, 191, 240, 294, 324, 436, 454, 724, 763, 795
Doubt(s), Hawthorne's, 15, 239, 456, 464, 513, 514, 519, 654, 720, 768, 796, 832, 836
Drama (*see also* Opera, Play, Greek tragedy), 59, 75
Dreams, 238, 369, 444

E

Eagle (of the Custom House), 399, 524
Early reviews (*see* ER1-ER10 and the note that follows ER10)
Eden myth (*see under* Myth)
Editions of *The Scarlet Letter* (*see also* First Edition, Preface to the Second Edition, *and* Translations), 93, 122, 123, 124, 148, 180, 562, 584, 652, 657, 661, 679
Editions, introductions/forewords/prefaces to, EC28, 1, 2, 57, 78, 88, 92, 93, 122, 123, 124, 141, 200, 220, 233, 262, 370, 410, 434, 460, 464, 537, 618, 723, 742, 844
Election Day, 580, 707
Election-Day Sermon, Dimmesdale's, 198, 267, 276, 323, 376, 378, 405, 477, 512, 534, 554, 673, 711, 793, 820, 838
Embroidery, Hester's, 83, 682, 794
Emerson, Ralph Waldo (*see under* "Sources and Influences" *and see also* "Hawthorne, as influenced by Emersonian ideals"), EC20, 21, 72, 80, 150, 207, 220, 235, 259, 287, 321, 374, 401, 488, 495, 544, 648, 650, 653, 672, 684, 808, 818
Ending, 246, 289, 304, 398, 412, 447, 477, 521, 571, 585, 625, 626, 677, 704
    as ambiguous, 307, 621, 677
    as appropriate, 221, 674

I

See also "Hawthorne as part of (or initiating) literary tradition" *and* "Sources"

Interpretation, 432, 865
Introductions (*see* Editions, introductions to)
Irony, EC21, EC37, 30, 51, 91, 113, 117, 133, 143, 159, 163, 175, 180, 196, 216,
    242, 262, 265, 274, 275, 308, 313, 315, 329, 365, 371, 376, 391, 414, 443,
    476, 482, 487, 526, 534, 554, 570, 572, 606, 643, 651, 696, 707, 713, 731,
    742, 755, 780, 804, 820, 848, 852, 853, 860

J
James, Henry (*see also under* Comparisons *and* Influence *and* in Author Index),
    EC17, 13, 30, 47, 50, 55, 57, 59, 74, 88, 97, 132, 208, 244, 259, 344, 441,
    490, 510, 511, 541, 653, 766, 768, 779, 819

K
King's Chapel burial ground (*see also* Tombstone), 118, 530
Knowledge, problems of, 196, 551

L
Landscape, EC14, 78, 241, 245, 428, 515, 723, 728, 848
Language (*see also* Silence, Speech, *and* Voice), 56, 69, 264, 365, 391, 405, 408,
    431, 432, 440, 443, 445, 453, 460, 462, 464, 473, 482, 496, 516, 518, 551,
    588, 592, 616, 619, 620, 643, 653, 658, 672, 673, 690, 715, 726, 761, 791,
    818, 821, 847, 860
Last line of novel ("On a Field, Sable, the Letter 'A' Gules"), 73, 228, 292, 313,
    320
Law/legal Issues, 492, 522, 751, 771, 776, 811, 826
Lawrence, D. H. (*see also under* Influences *and* in Author Index), 12, 54, 97, 174,
    189, 306, 449, 556, 686
Lee, William (*see also* Permanent Inspector *under* Characters), 257, 273, 629
Levity (*see also* Humor *and* Carnival/the carnivalesque), 357, 707
Literary devices (*see* Techniques *and* separate entries for Allegory, Ambiguity,
    Archetype, *and* Irony)
Literature (*see also* "American Fiction," American Literature," "American vs.
        English Fiction," "Hawthorne as 'classic' writer," *and* "*The Scarlet
        Letter* as a classic novel"),
    as commodity, 488, 718,
    as social authority, 704
    classic, 89, 409, 416, 417, 570, 571, 582, 594, 638, 670, 698, 727
Love, EC33, 7, 107, 135, 157, 246, 303, 626, 786, 861, 864

Truth (*see also* "Moral, including but not limited to the concluding moral
              sentiment, 'Be True!'"), EC4, 21, 40, 47, 56, 117, 136, 142, 157,
              229, 230, 235, 239, 298, 356, 384, 401, 407, 431, 445, 446, 468,
              474, 488, 492, 499, 503, 533, 538, 543, 544, 565, 571, 579, 616,
              621, 626, 628, 699, 723, 733, 745, 749, 756, 766, 818, 823, 851
      the apprehension of, 56, 621, 626, 851
      the arbitrary or subjective nature of, 178, 239, 321, 389, 404, 419, 432,
              440, 546, 590, 614, 621, 640, 683
      moral, EC29, 10, 238
      religious, ER7, 106, 150, 179, 286, 425, 443, 544, 573, 626
      the unknowability of, 425, 484, 546, 551, 640
      "Typical illusion," 343, 590
      Typology, 462, 551

U

Una Hawthorne, EC13, 10, 581, 582, 646
Unity, 23, 78, 136, 375, 361, 446, 525, 541, 545, 599, 617, 675, 728, 752, 818
Upham, Charles Wentworth, 33, 257, 273, 363, 574, 604
Upham, Thomas C., 41
Utopia, 210, 411, 474, 486, 580, 636, 716

V

Vision (*see* Hawthorne's dark vision, positive vision, *and* tragic vision)
Visuality, 473, 545, 649, 685, 692
Voice (*see also* Language, Narrative Voice, *and* Tone), 163, 462, 487, 551, 726,
      748
Voyeurism (*see also* Gaze), 415, 533, 685, 686

W

Whitman, Walt, EC20, 21, 72, 165, 259, 287, 488, 549, 648
Witchcraft (including background on the Salem witchcraft trials), 106, 151, 298,
      301, 446, 480, 591, 596, 741, 772, 843
Women in the Nineteenth Century (including the conception of the "new
      woman"), 553, 655, 666, 751, 752, 764, 798
The Woman Question, 32, 172, 284, 569, 642, 820
Women, Hawthorne's view of, including his attitude toward and portrayal of
      women (*see also* Gender, Sexual Politics, *and* "True Womanhood, the cult
      of") 32, 284, 286, 303, 419, 467, 505, 519, 535, 536, 541, 553, 569, 581,
      585, 591, 594, 614, 620, 647, 656, 655, 666, 695, 712, 716, 734, 764, 770,
      787, 812, 820, 823, 831, 834, 844

Critical Approach Index

Numbers refer to the annotation numbers of individual entries, *not* to page numbers.

CRITICAL APPROACHES

Morality Studies

Like religious studies, morality studies are concerned with Hawthorne's handling of sin and morality in *The Scarlet Letter*. Because Hawthorne's narrator resists didactic commentary, critics have had difficulty determining where Hawthorne stands in his dramatization of the conflict between social responsibility and individual freedom, whether he sides with Dimmesdale (who adds hypocrisy to sin by outwardly conforming to sanctified behavior) or Hester(whose dedication to a life of good works masks the fact that she lives in a "moral wilderness" defined by intellectual lawlessness), neither, or both. (There appears to be little disagreement about Chillingworth's status as the "Unpardonable Sinner" in the novel, however, whose violation of "the sanctity of the human heart" is condemned by the narrator. Most critics also agree that Pearl, whose own amoral nature is transformed when she is "humanized" by Dimmesdale's public acknowledgment of her, functions as an agent of salvation or redemption for her parents.) Conservative critics typically argue that Hawthorne condemns his characters' immoral actions (although they usually cite Dimmesdale as the main character and claim that his unflagging dedication to and internalization of the strict principles of Puritan morality necessarily make his suffering more intense than Hester's), and liberal critics generally argue that Hawthorne condones their rebellious, natural, and individualist acts of freedom (frequently arguing that Hester is the leading character because she outshines Dimmesdale in her demonstrated ability to determine her own moral code). Although many early critics of the novel often question Hawthorne's devotion to the principles of morality, later critics—even when having difficulty discerning the "true" moral of the story (which most agree relates to the importance of being true, recognizing the sinful nature of all of mankind, and living honestly)—generally find ample evidence in both "The Custom-House" and the novel to prove that Hawthorne advocates moral and social responsibility over the self-interested gratification of personal desires. Hawthorne appears to these critics to demonstrate the absolute importance of self-denial and self-sacrifice for the greater communal good and to imply that personal suffering ennobles and promotes moral regeneration. He also seems to imply that it is a moral imperative for each sinning individual to participate in the "united effort of mankind," never isolating himself and losing hold of the "magnetic chain of humanity" that binds all sinners together. But because there is no sure guide through which to interpret the views of the two main characters, many critics make convincing arguments to support Hawthorne's identification with his wayward heroine. Critics who emphasize Hawthorne's

498

romantic or radical leanings continue to question Hawthorne's true allegiance to conventional morality, detecting a subtly subversive undercurrent in the novel that aligns itself with Hester's moral independence and promotes the free expression of the self's desires over restrictive Puritan orthodoxy.

Early Reviews (ER1-ER10), D. H. Lawrence (EC18), Darrel Abel (10, 25, 559), Marius Bewley (47), Roy Harvey Pearce (57), Barbara Garlitz (62), James W. Mathews (63), Larzer Ziff (76), Seymour L. Gross (95), Max Putzel (101), Lauriat Lane, Jr., (116), Allen Austin (126), W. R. Moses (133), Austin Warren (178), Johannes Kjørven (187), Lawrence W. Hyman (192), Quentin G. Kraft (244), Leo B. Levy (245), R. W. Butterfield (262), Walter Shear (277), Harold Kaplan (282), Richard H. Brodhead (300), Dan Vogel (308), Elaine Tuttle Hansen (337), Janis P. Stout (341, 553), Michael Dunne (360), Maureen Quilligan (372), Donald Darnell (377), J. Jeffrey Mayhook (391), Edward Stone (395), Terry L. Oggel (401), Claudia Durst Johnson (407), Gretchen Graf Jordan (414), Linden Peach (422), John P. McWilliams (463), Lester H. Hunt (474), Ellen Moers (477), Carol M. Bensick (483), Donald J. Greiner (490), Virginia Hudson Young (556), Kenneth Marc Harris (565), Sacvan Bercovitch (575, 576, 691), Ronald Emerick (579), Janet Gabler-Hover (616), Catherine H. Zuckert (622), Franklin R. Rogers (649), William Bartley (653), Kenneth D. Pimple (715), Eric Cheyfitz (732), Lisa Herb Smith (789), Joseph Alkana (791), Nancy Roberts (798), Donna D. Simms (823), Erika M. Kreger (849), Laura Martin (858), and Yusur Al Madani (861). (*See also* Hawthorne as moralist, Hawthorne's moral philosophy, the Moral, Morality, Moral Ambiguity [*under* Ambiguity], "moral blossom," *and* "*The Scarlet Letter*, the moral nature of" in the Subject Index.)

Religious/Theological Studies

A great many critics grapple with Hawthorne's elusive theological/spiritual views and examine his obsession with sin and guilt, as well as speculate about his interest in the moral and religious character of man. Religious studies often consider the novel as Hawthorne's attempt to dramatize the battle of good vs. evil or to re-enact the Fortunate Fall through the sinning characters of Dimmesdale and Hester (often viewing Pearl as the agent of her parents' moral and spiritual redemption and the demonic Chillingworth as the "Unpardonable Sinner" whose vengeance Dimmesdale escapes through confession during the final scaffold scene). Most religious studies argue that *The Scarlet Letter* is essentially Dimmesdale's story, made all the more tragic because, as a conservative minister, he is deeply committed to the Puritan code of morality and its religious tenets and doctrines. Imagining himself the most polluted sinner on earth for failing to confess his affair with Hester and acknowledge Pearl as his own child while simultaneously fooling his parishioners by wearing the outward mask of visible sainthood, Dimmesdale suffers perhaps more deeply than Hester(who feels guilt and shame but does not seem to internalize her punishment), especially because he is unable to recognize the underlying hypocrisy of a religion that preaches

Original Sin and Universal Depravity and yet ironically refuses to permit sin among its "elect" members. Many studies question whether Dimmesdale is saved or damned at the novel's end after his confession and death (see specific categories under "Dimmesdale" in the Subject Index), and several consider whether Hester redeems herself after her (apparently) penitent return to Boston at the end by dedicating her remaining years to the "good works" of counseling wayward women. Religious criticism also examines Chillingworth's role in the novel (sometimes explaining his function as ironically instrumental to Dimmesdale's salvation) and his fatalistic assertion to Hester that his diabolic actions are a "dark necessity" that are predestined and thus not in his power to prevent. The "true" crime or sin in *The Scarlet Letter* is debated with regularity, but the majority of critics argue that the worst sins of all, according to Hawthorne, stem from individuals separating themselves from others, from cutting their ties to the "magnetic chain of humanity" that unites all sinners in a common bond of sympathy.

Leonard J. Fick (36), Hugh N. MacLean (42), Anne Marie McNamara (50), Randall Stewart (58, 72), Harold J. Douglas and Robert Daniel (60), Henry G. Fairbanks (61), Joseph Schwartz (71 and 146), Horton Davies (77), François Mauriac (79), Abigail Ann Hamblen (96), Joseph T. McCullenand John C. Guilds (98), Joseph Schwartz (146), Neal B. Houston (191), Nicholas Canaday, Jr., (206), Raymond Benoit (287), Preston M. Browning (288), Betty Kushen (294), Dan Vogel (308), Charles E. May (324), Robert Geraldi (342), Michael T. Gilmore (344), Charles Berryman (368), Leland Ryken (373), James Ellis (398), Gretchen Graf Jordan (414), Dorena Allen Wright (433), Harold P. Simonson (438), Sharon Deykin Baris (455), John P. McWilliams (463), Agnes McNeill Donohue (487), Richard Forrer (514), Ursula Brumm (519), Hugh J. Dawson (545), June McMaster-Harrison (549), Reiner Smolinski (552), Kenneth Marc Harris (565), Donald J. Greiner (599), Catherine H. Zuckert (622), John Gatta (626), Evans Lansing Smith (634), P. G. Rama Rao (700), Jenny Franchot (724), Matthew Gartner (750), John Reiss (762), Lisa Herb Smith (789), John Gatta (795), Alfred Kazin (796), Charles Berryman (832), Judie Newman (839), James Plath (843), Preston Harper (864), and Richard Hull (865). (*See also* Calvinism, Catholicism, Christianity, Confession, Hawthorne's secular faith, Religion, Puritan religion/theology, *and* Spirituality in the Subject Index.)

Language Studies
Many critics of the 80s and 90s examine Hawthorne's ambiguous language in *The Scarlet Letter*, considering what it means for Hawthorne's narrator to use highly suggestive, vague, or symbolic language to describe events and characters' actions—the result of which adds complexity and richness to the novel, as well as suggests Hawthorne's awareness that man's perception of reality is limited and that there can be no single objective or universal conceptions of truth and meaning. Critics also explore Hawthorne's and Dimmesdale's deceptive or

500

manipulative uses of language, finding that both exploit the arbitrary, ambiguous nature of language to confess sins while simultaneously protecting themselves from the threat of detection. In addition to examining Hawthorne's devices of ambiguity and the novel's multiplicity of conflicting meanings, language studies also investigate Hawthorne's wordplay or verbal trickery, the novel's shifting tones, the differences implied between speech and writing, and the numerous places in the novel where Hawthorne illustrates the damaging effects of silence or communication failures.

Roy R. Male (56, 408), John T. Irwin (321, 389), William Bysshe Stein (365), Viola Sachs (404), Michel Small (405), Mark Kinkead-Weekes (420), Millicent Bell (425), Michael Ragussis (431), Louise K. Barnett (440, 690), Dennis Foster (443), Gordon Hutner (445, 566), Larry Baker (453), Allen Gardner Lloyd-Smith (462, 551), Stephen Nissenbaum (464), David B. Downing (473), Michael Davitt Bell (482), Michael T. Gilmore (488), John T. Matthews (493), David Van Leer (496, 592), Charles Swann (584), Janet Gabler-Hover (616), Mary Jane Hurst (619), James M. Mellard (643), William Bartley (653), James Barszcz (672), Michael P. Kramer (673), Kenneth D. Pimple (715), Alessandro Portelli (726), Scott Harshbarger (733), Craig Milliman (758), Margaret Reid (821), Michael West (860), and Sohui Lee (866). (*See also* Language, Narrative Voice, Silence, Speech, Tone, Voice, Wordplay, *and* Writing in the Subject Index.)

Law Studies

Because *The Scarlet Letter* illustrates the tensions between freedom and the law, crime and punishment, and emphasizes the harshness of Puritan punitive sanctions by highlighting the centrality of both the prison and the scaffold to the Puritan community, several critics have examined Puritan and nineteenth-century laws, legal issues, and punishments as they relate to the novel. Law studies examine the legal history of adultery, marriage and divorce laws, misogynist law, and even laws pertaining to slavery and American citizenship rights. Several explore the Puritans' zeal for dictating laws, administering punishments, and determining God's will with self-righteous certainty, while others compare the seventeenth century's practices of enforcing humiliating public punishment with the punitive sanctions of today's contemporary society, especially as those sanctions relate to the problem of unmarried women with children.

G. Harrison Orians (19), Lester H. Hunt (474), Peggy Kamuf (492), Hugh J. Dawson (522), Monika M. Elbert (597), Janet Gabler-Hover (616), Elizabeth Aycock Hoffman (628), Deborah Gussman (751), Elizabeth Perry Hodges (771), Garry Wamser (776), Nancy Roberts (798), Laura Hanft Korobkin (811), Shira Pavis Minton (826). (*See also* Law/legal Issues, Puritan civil laws, *and* Puritan punishments in the Subject Index.)

THEORETICAL APPROACHES

New Criticism
New Criticism, also referred to as "formalist" or "practical" criticism, flourished in America from the late 1930s to the mid-1950s* and developed during a time in American academia when the field of literary criticism was struggling to be considered a respectable and serious discipline. Armed with a scientific sense of objectivity and detachment, New Critics reacted against the subjective, "belle-lettristic" kind of content-oriented responses to art that had gone before and emphasized instead the close reading of texts, viewing works of art in isolation from their authorial, historical, and political contexts and considering them to be self-contained, self-reflexive "objects" that possessed a harmonious organic unity and universal meaning that any reader could discover if he followed New Critical methods. The "words on the page" were all that mattered, and their one true meaning could be discovered through close, objective scrutiny of a text's various tensions, paradoxes, ironies, and ambiguities—all of which became resolved and integrated by the text's "poetic" unities and solid structure. New Critics, who express a conservative, often Christian-oriented ideology, typically stress coherence, structure, language, and symmetry, as well as metaphor and symbol, in their analyses of how the parts of a work relate to form a unified, artistic whole. They also tend to focus on the symbolic, allegorical, and mythic aspects of literature (see Archetypal/Myth Criticism). As Elmer Kennedy-Andrews notes (in 829), "The Scarlet Letter, with its highly symbolic narrative method, its careful aesthetic patterning of images and ideas, and its concern with narrative point of view and the relativity of truth, len[ds] itself well to New Critical treatment" (24). New Critics pay especial attention to matters of form, to symbols like the wild rosebush, the prison, and the cemetery, to the ways in which the three scaffold scenes structure the novel, to how Hester's scarlet "A" offers an overall unifying presence, and to color symbolism and images of light and dark—most often considering how images of darkness predominate and illustrate Hawthorne's tragic vision.

John C. Gerber (EC9), Gordon Roper (EC25), Leland Schubert (EC26), Richard Harter Fogle (15, 236), Hyatt H. Waggoner (38, 140, 220), Hugh N. MacLean (42), Robert F. Haugh (48), Marius Bewley (54), Roy R. Male (27, 56), Roy Harvey Pearce (57), Alexander Evanoff (128), Fred H. Marcus (131), Lawrence E. Scanlon (136), G. Thomas Tanselle (138), Michael L. Lasser(209), John C. Stubbs (251), Robert Stanton (258), Arne I. Axelsson (309), Robert Penn Warren (315), J. A. Ward (326), Sanford Pinsker(364), Marianna Torgovnick (412), Barbara Price (418), Mark Kinkead-Weekes (420), and Andrew Hudgins (428).

*Several critics writing during this time period do not fit neatly into this category because they employ aspects of New Criticism in addition to drawing on biography, examining the novel in relation to Hawthorne's other works, and/or placing Hawthorne within his historical context or within a larger literary tradition. These include D. H. Lawrence (EC18), F. O. Matthiessen (EC20), Hyatt H. Waggoner (EC37), Newton Arvin (1), Charles Feidelson, Jr., (21), Richard Chase (55), Harry Levin (70), Charles Feidelson, Jr., (81), Richard Joseph Coanda (207), Robert L. Berner (375), and Darrel Abel (239).

Archetypal/Myth Criticism

Archetypal/myth criticism, very similar to New Criticism in its focus on the text itself, investigates and analyzes archetypal, mythical, epic, and folk narrative patterns, as well as examines character types, themes, imagery, cultural myths, rituals, and motifs in literature. These critics of *The Scarlet Letter* emphasize not only the importance of uncovering larger cultural myths (such as the garden of Eden, the myth of America/the new world, the fall of man and the "Fortunate Fall," the lawless forest wilderness, the isolated hero on a dark journey pitted against a hostile environment, the Faustian myth, the Madonna and child, witchcraft and superstition, the power of blackness, the nature of man, iron men, and dark ladies), but also the relevance of discovering the personal mythology of Hawthorne, focusing on Hawthorne's tragic vision or dark imagination. Rudolph Von Abele (14), William Bysshe Stein (22), R. W. B. Lewis (37), Roy R. Male (56), Harry Levin (70), Richard B. Sewell (80), Leslie A. Fiedler (89, 184) Daniel Hoffman (106), Grace Pleasant Wellborn (120, 151, 152, 179), Richard Joseph Coanda (207), Viola Sachs (213, 393, 404), David W. Noble (219), Hugo McPherson (237), Joel Porte (238), Robert E. Todd (297), Charles E. May (324), V. N. Arora (333), Judith Fryer (340), Donald Darnell (377), Ronald J. Gervais (378), Paul Lewis (384), Leland S. Person, Jr., (385), Jane Donahue Eberwein (387), CarlandaGreen (399), Earl R. Hutchison, Sr., (400), Donald A. Ringe (411), Gretchen Graf Jordan (414), Judith Ruderman (449), Agnes McNeill Donohue (487), Chester Wolford (517), Pamela Banting (518), Henry J. Lindborg (526), Elizabeth Hanson (564), Monika M. Elbert (598), Donald E. Hardy (663), Klaus P. Stich (667), James Barszcz (672), James A. Schiff (686), Nancy Tenfelde Clasby (705), Nina da Vinci Nichols (743), Gil Haroian-Guerin (770), Edward J. Ingebretsen (772), John Gatta (795), Robert S. Friedman (835), and Debra Johanyak (848).

Structuralism

Structuralism, which gained popularity in the early 1960s and derived from the application of ideas explored by structural linguist Ferdinand de Saussure, attempts a more scientific approach to literature than New Criticism does in that it focuses narrowly on language and views language as a system of arbitrary signs (each made up of a "signifier" and a "signified," or a sign and the arbitrary referential meaning that is attached to it) that cannot be comprehended by itself but only by analysis of its respective place within a larger system. In other words, structuralists attempt clinically and objectively to analyze the structure of and relation between signs, isolating the laws by which the signs are combined into meanings. They attempt to demystify literature by positing that it is like any other product of language and is thus a construct whose inner workings may be classified and analyzed like the mechanisms, conventions, and codes of any other science. Like New Critics, structuralists examine a text in isolation from the material conditions in which it was written; but unlike the New Critics, their focus is on the constructedness of human meaning and the "sign systems" that are collectively imposed through language to communicate perceptions of reality. Structuralists examine the larger, abstract structures at work in *The Scarlet Letter* to show textual unity and coherence, attempting to identify and isolate universal features as they appear throughout—such as structure, symbol, design, parallels and patterns, echoes and reflections, oppositions, inversions and contrasts—so that the narrative becomes highly schematized. Structuralist studies are often accompanied by diagrams to reinforce their detached and "scientific" findings, examining the subjective and arbitrary creation of meaning, signs, and Puritan sign systems in the novel, most often focusing on the multiple meanings of the key symbol, Hester's symbolic scarlet letter, but also considering the numerous meanings generated from the appearance of the supernatural letter "A" that glows in the sky on the evening of Dimmesdale's midnight vigil. Hawthorne's symbolic method is closely considered, as is his presentation of how symbols shape the way the Puritans interpret their world and determine meaning. Darrel Abel (239), Gabriel Josipovici (264), John T. Irwin (321, 389), Reed Sanderlin (338), Marjorie Pryse (371), Roy R. Male (408), Louise K. Barnett (440, 690), David Ketterer (446), Kent Bales (454), David B. Downing (473), Franklin R. Rogers (649), Kramer, Michael P. Kramer (673), and N. Natarajan (714). (For similar studies, *see* Semiology/Semiotics directly below and *see* Epistemology, Meaning, Reality, *and* Signs in the Subject Index.)

Semiology/Semiotics

Closely linked to structuralism, semiology is the formal and systematic study of signs. It is widely believed that semiotic (sign) theory, founded by Charles Sanders Peirce (and influenced by Ferdinand de Saussure), developed in reaction to a modernist sense of alienation and despair, with its critics attempting through the study of sign systems, human codes, and conventions in the language of a text to give readers the "key" to be able to read and understand it. Semiology studies on *The Scarlet Letter*, like structuralist studies, consider the "plurality" of signs in the novel, which includes shifting meanings of Hester's scarlet letter, the multiple ways the Puritan community interpret that letter, Hawthorne's symbolic method in the novel, and his tendency to refuse singular interpretations of symbols or events.
John T. Irwin (321, 389) Viola Sachs (404), Mark Kinkead-Weekes (420), Millicent Bell (425), Allen Gardner Lloyd-Smith (462, 551), Richard Hull (600, 865), John K. Sheriff (800, 851), Margaret Reid (821), and Keith Polette (815).

Post-Structuralism

Post-structuralism, which has more of a philosophical background than structuralism and emerged in France in the late 1960s (led by Roland Barthes, Jacques Derrida, Michel Foucault, and Jacques Lacan), approaches language, knowledge, and meaning skeptically. It developed as a reaction against structuralism, out of a desire to deconstruct and replace it. If structuralism recognizes the arbitrary nature of signs, post-structuralism carries that implication one step further to question the stability of any meaning or any language—sometimes going so far as to suggest that nothing can ever be known for certain because classical notions of truth, certainty, reality, meaning, and knowledge cannot be trusted since they rest on a naively representational theory of language. Post-structuralists emphasize writing and textuality, reading texts "against the grain" to look for underlying systems of logic or centers of meaning and then to collapse them by showing that they were unstable in the first place. They also look for internal evidence of gaps, breaks, and discontinuties to show that the text is at war with itself, a house divided. This is particularly the tactic of deconstructive criticism (see directly below), which can be defined as applied post-structuralism (or as an important element of post-structuralist theory used in literary practice), although it has been argued that true deconstruction—aside from the more extreme American brand of it—does not deny the existence of relatively determined truths, meanings, identities, intentions, or historical continuties. Post-structuralist critics tend to rely heavily on the jargon of literary theory and to be emotive, with an urgent tone and flamboyant, self-conscious style. Their titles often contain puns or witty allusions, and their arguments—which are characterized by a dense style and vocabulary—are frequently based on a pun or word-play of some kind. Post-structuralist critics of *The Scarlet Letter* essentially do the opposite of what the New Critics do in that they show the disunity that underlies the text's apparent unity. They argue that Hawthorne is concerned with the arbitrary nature of language, problems of interpretation, and with the subjectivity of all determined meanings, frequently focusing on the narrator's unreliability, Hawthorne's moral uncertainty, and narrative and linguistic imprecision in the novel.

William Bysshe Stein (365), Maureen Quilligan (372), John Dolis (457, 824), Itala Vivan (480), Evan Carton (484), David Van Leer (496), Christine Brooke-Rose (543), Earl Rovit (582), Richard Hull (600, 865), Sam B. Girgus (617), Brian Harding (618), Gerald Doherty (623), John N. Duvall (659), and Michael West (860).

Deconstruction

Deconstruction (an applied type or feature of post-structuralist criticism), which became popular in the United States in the 1970s and 1980s and was strongly influenced by French philosopher Jacques Derrida, focuses on rhetoric and the self-referential aspects of language and posits the undecidability or indeterminacy of meaning for all texts. Critiquing and undermining the hierarchical oppositions and logocentrism that make up the foundations of Western logic and metaphysics, it bases its readings on the fact that there is no solid ground structuring a text or giving it meaning since words and language are arbitrary constructs that have no inherent, fixed meaning in themselves. Deconstuctionists point out that texts consistently contradict themselves, and they imply multiple (if not limitless) possibilities for the construction of meaning out of what appear to be single and straightforward meanings. *The Scarlet Letter* lends itself well to deconstructionists for several reasons, a few being that Hawthorne discredits singular meanings of Hester's scarlet letter, he encourages multiple interpretations of key events, and his narrator makes frequent contradictory assertions. Deconstructionists also argue that Hawthorne "deconstructs" or "destabilizes" the Puritan system in the novel, undermining the stability of Puritan values by depicting characters whose inner realities contradict their outer appearances and by offering multiple, often contradictory, interpretations of events—both of which present mystery, uncertainty, and doubt as comprising the true condition of life and illustrate the impossibility of any one person or group of persons to "fix" meaning or know anything for certain.

Millicent Bell (425), Michael Ragussis (431, 516), Paula K. White (432), Norman Dryson (435), Dennis Foster (443), John Dolis (457, 692), Peggy Kamuf (492), John T. Matthews (493), Ralph Flores (546), Christopher Newfield (603), Brian Harding (618), Steven C. Scheer (621), Catherine H. Zuckert(622), Emily Miller Budick (654, 768), John Dolis (692), Samuel Kimball (713), N. Natarajan (714), Peter Bellis (746), Terence Martin (756), Emily Miller Budick (768), Caroline Woidat (803).

Reader-Response Criticism

Reader-response theory emerged during the late 1960s and early 1970s as New Criticism was fading, focusing on readers' varied and biased responses to texts and emphasizing the different ways a reader participates in the course of reading a text and in the general reading process itself. Reader-response critics are concerned primarily with the reader's contribution to a text, to his role and function (instead of that of the author or the text), and they challenge text-oriented theories of criticism that ignore or underestimate the reader's role. Like other post-structuralists, reader-response critics (or "reception theorists"—those reader-response critics who are concerned with a larger group's general response to literature) focus on the gaps, blanks, and ambiguities in texts, but unlike post-structuralists and deconstructionists, reader-response critics assert that it is the reader's job to interact with these inconsistencies and vagueries and compose meaning as he/she reads, because texts demand that the reader actively engage in the process of producing meaning out of the text's plural, diffuse, and unsettled meanings. These critics find that *The Scarlet Letter* is a particularly "open" text with which to work out their ideas for several reasons. Hawthorne is self-consciously concerned with the reaction his text will elicit from his reader, seeming to establish through various methods a relationship with a certain type of reader and appearing throughout "The Custom-House" and the romance to be "coaching" his audience into a sympathetic reading. Furthermore, Hawthorne refuses didactic commentary and consistently foregrounds contradictory or multiple points of view (largely through the creation of an unreliable narrator who frustrates the reader's attempts to generate firm meanings), both of which invite diverse, even irreconcilable readings and encourage the reader to choose for himself from any number of possible interpretations of events.

Richard Brodhead (300), Kenneth Dauber (343), Arie Staal (345), Michael Dunne (360), John G. Bayer (397), Paula K. White (432), Gordon Hutner (445, 566), David Leverenz (447, 641), Itala Vivan (480), Stephen Railton (648, 699), William Bartley (653), Thomas R. Moore (683), Cynthia Bernstein (703), Joan Burbick (721), Matei Calinescu (731), Scott Harshbarger (733), Sylvie Mathé (735), T. Walter Herbert (752), Susan Elizabeth Sweeney (763), Gloria Erlich (781), and Karen L. Kilcup (784).

Historicism

The historical approach to literature restored to classic works of literature the historical, social, and political context denied by New Criticism. Asserting that art is referential, referring to the world outside it and influenced by it, historicists combine the close reading of a text with an examination of the text's historical framework—both the historical sources and the historical issues at the center of a literary work's concerns. As traditional historicist criticism became increasingly informed by modern critical theory from the 1970s onward, it began to reflect a skepticism about traditional notions of history and literature, the result of which was New Historicism (see directly below). The majority of critical studies of *The Scarlet Letter* are historical in approach, providing background on the history of Puritanism and transcendentalism, suggesting crucial links between the moral, intellectual, and religious climates of nineteenth-century and seventeenth-century New England, locating Hawthorne's potential literary and historical sources, examining Hawthorne within his nineteenth-century American social and political milieu, considering him in relation to his contemporaries, demonstrating ways that Hawthorne appropriated the romantic form and/or diverged from the historical romance tradition (and other popular literary traditions that he borrowed from), exploring the historical accuracy of his recreation of the Puritan past, and offering historical referents for the "The Custom-House" and for the novel's characters, themes, plot devices, and symbolic actions and events.

Edward H. Davidson (11), Chester E. Eisinger (12), G. Harrison Orians (19), Hubert H. Hoeltje (33), Alfred S. Reid (35, 53, 65), Marvin Laser (41), Joseph Schwartz (71), Charles Ryskamp (83), Charles Boewe and Murray G. Murphey

(94), John J. McAleer (118), Charles Feidelson, Jr., (154), Roy Harvey Pearce (158), Johannes Kjørven (187), Marshall Van Deusen (196), Thomas F. Walsh (198), Howard Bruce Franklin (200), David Levin (201), Ernest W. Baughman (204), Matthew J. Bruccoli (205), John McElroy (217), John C. Stubbs (227), Kathryn Whitford (231), Nina Baym (252), Benjamin Lease (257, 273), Quentin Anderson (259), John E. Becker (260), Michael Davitt Bell (261, 386, 482), David J. Hirsch (263), Clifford M. Caruthers (269), Walter Shear (277), Ben Barker-Benfield (286), Michael Colacurcio (289, 481, 486), Isani, Mukhtar Ali Isani (291), Karl P. Wentersdorf (298), Peter L. Hays (302), Leo B. Levy (305), Clifford Chalmers Huffman (312), Charles Swann (314, 651), John T. Irwin (321, 389), M. X. Lesser (323), Louis Owens (330), Ursula Brumm (335, 519), Kenneth Dauber (343), Michael T. Gilmore (344, 488, 693), Patricia Marks (347), Frederick Newberry (348, 539, 550, 602), Hugo McPherson (354), Henry Nash Smith (356), Stephen Nissenbaum (363), Charles Berryman (368), J. Jeffrey Mayhook (391), Edward Stone (395), Lawrence Buell (442), Clark Griffith (444), Melinda B. Parsons and William M. Ramsey (448), Mona Scheuermann (465), Sargent Bush, Jr., (471), Sarah I. Davis (472), Lester H. Hunt (474), Carol M. Bensick (483), David Van Leer (496, 592), Larry J. Reynolds (504), Hugh J. Dawson (522, 524), Fritz Oehlschlaeger (528), Thomas Pribek (529), Laurie N. Rozakis (530), James M. Cox (533), George Dekker (534), Donald Pease (540), Zelda Bronstein (542), Reiner Smolinski (552), David S. Reynolds (570), Thomas Woodson (574), William Ellis (586), Aladár Sarbu (590), Gabriele Schwab (591), David C. Cody (595), Monika M. Elbert (597, 614), Evans Lansing Smith (634), Leland S. Person, Jr., (646), Douglas Anderson (652), William Bartley (653), Eileen Dreyer (658), Klaus P. Stich (667), Samuel Chase Coale (678, 722, 817), Carol M. Bensick (702), Claudia Durst Johnson (711), Jenny Franchot (724), Robert E. Abrams (728), Scott Harshbarger (733), Joseph Alkana (791), Franny Nudelman (813), Harvey L. Gable (818), Thomas R. Mitchell (820), Margaret Reid (821), and Daneen Wardrop (867). (For many more historical studies, *see* "Background on the nineteenth century [forming influences and historical context]," Influences, Puritanism, *and* Sources in the Subject Index.)

New Historicism
New Historicism (the term for which was coined by American critic Stephen Greenblatt in 1980 and is called "Cultural Materialism" in England) is an anti-formalist movement that began in America in the early 1980s as a "corrective" response to historicist criticism (*see* Historicism directly above). It seeks—with a political edge—to destabilize established conceptions of what history and fiction are, viewing written history (or "histories") as a kind of narrative fiction and fiction as an account of history because it is filled with political and ideological implications. Like historicism, this school of thought is in large measure a reaction against the tendency in much modern criticism, starting with the New Critics and extending through deconstruction, to concentrate on the language of

isolated texts and to ignore the cultural, historical, and political circumstances that produced them. Unlike historicists, however, New Historicists (sometimes also called "New Americanists") combine the urge to reconnect texts to their real-world referents and sources with an interest in contemporary language-centered theories (particularly post-structuralism) in order to create a reinvigorated notion of literature as a historically and culturally grounded form of expression. New Historicists typically parallel literary and non-literary texts of the same historical period to show how literary works express the values and interests of the dominant social group. They view *The Scarlet Letter* less as a novel than as a historical and cultural artifact of the nineteenth-century period in which Hawthorne lived and wrote, and they suggest that Hawthorne's aesthetics reflect the concerns and biases (the liberal ideology) of nineteenth-century American culture. Sacvan Bercovitch and Jonathan Arac, for instance, both of whom are big names in New Historicist studies on Hawthorne, view *The Scarlet Letter* as an analysis of antebellum American cultural history in which Hawthorne participates in the dominant middle-class ideology of his day that affirmed social compromise and consensus over radical reform and revolution. They show how his literary techniques such as irony, symbolism, paradox, and ambiguity—which may appear to indicate cultural conflicts and Hawthorne's radical or subversive tendencies— actually illustrate Hawthorne's fear of conflict and rebellion, signaling instead his political passivity and belief in compromise and a gradualist accommodation of progressive ideology. New Historicists often have a Marxist or feminist orientation and focus on issues of oppression, inequality, and injustice that they believe are marginalized in or hidden within the text.

Gretchen Graf Jordan (414), Robert Clark (456), Ellen Moers (477), Jane Tompkins (495), David Stineback (505), Jonathan Arac (508), Emory Elliott (513), Myra Jehlen (515), Louise DeSalvo (535), Donald E. Pease (540), Mary Suzanne Schriber (541), Sacvan Bercovitch (560, 575, 576, 635, 691, 778), Cynthia S. Jordan (588), Jean Fagan Yellin (594), Richard Hull (600), Christopher Newfield (603), Elizabeth AycockHoffman (628), Jon B. Reed (632), Lauren Berlant (636), Stuart Hutchinson (640), Lucy Maddox (642), Leland S. Person, Jr., (646), Joel Pfister (647), Emily Miller Budick (654, 677, 768), Gillian Brown (655), Jennifer Fleischner (660), Rita K. Gollin (661), Deborah L. Madsen (664), Richard H. Millington (674), Laurie A. Sterling (687), T. Walter Herbert (695), Stephanie P. Browner (704), Jay Grossman (708), Adrianne Kalfopoulou (712), Eric Savoy (716), Sandra Tomc (718), Joan Burbick (721), Eric Cheyfitz (732), Deborah Gussman (751), Michael Newbury (760, 797), Nina Tassi (764), Jill Lepore (785), Nancy Roberts (798), Caroline Woidat (803), Laura Hanft Korobkin (811), Elizabeth Hewitt (847), Erika M. Kreger (849), Sohui Lee (866).

Psychoanalytical/Psychological Criticism

Psychoanalytical/psychological criticism adapts the ideas of psychoanalytic theorists Sigmund Freud, Carl Jung, Jacques Lacan, and others (such as I. A. Richards and Kenneth Burke) and is primarily concerned with establishing connections between an artist's inner life and his works of art. Interested in the natures of the conscious and unconscious mind, these critics often focus in texts on what reveals the dual nature of the mind, examining characters' repressed feelings and unconscious motives as they emerge in dreams, fantasy, language, art, and neurotic behavior. Special emphasis is also paid to the psychoanalytic significance of objects or events in a text, as well as to the images, symbols, emblems, and metaphors that might reveal more about the unconscious desires, nature, and/or purposes of the author or of the characters depicted in a particular work. Psychoanalytic critics tend to view *The Scarlet Letter* as the product of Hawthorne's struggle with a complex personal problem or Oedipal complex, often reading the novel in light of classic Freudian terms and concepts, such as the libido, sex drive and sexual repression, phases of emotional and sexual development, sublimated or unconscious desire (heterosexual, homosexual, and/or incestuous), and/or the id, ego, and superego. They often pay close attention to the doctor/patient relationship between Chillingworth and Dimmesdale and view the love triangle relationship between Hester, Dimmesdale, and Chillingworth in Oedipal terms. Psychoanalytic critics also commonly address Hawthorne's tremendous knowledge of human psychology and the maddening split between the private and public self that is explored most prominently in the romance through the self-tortured, sexually repressed character of Dimmesdale. This conflict also plays out in "The Custom-House," as well, where Hawthorne implies that writing the novel is his way of cathartically working out several problems: the private dilemma of the alienated artist who seeks reunion with society, feelings of ancestral guilt, personal humiliation after being fired from the Custom House, and crushing loss after the death of his mother.

Herbert Gorman (EC10), Llewellyn Jones (EC16), Régis Michaud (EC21), Philip Rahv (EC24), John E. Hart (5), Donald A. Ringe (6), Howard Brand (17), Joseph Levi (26) Lois Atkins (31), Rudolph Von Abele (39), Marvin Laser (41), Leslie A. Fiedler (89, 184), Eugene Arden (109), Grace Pleasant Wellborn (120), Frederick Crews (170, 182), William S. Marks, III (174), Leon Edel (183), Nina Baym (252, 311), Betty Kushen (294), Robert E. Todd (297), Richard H. Brodhead (300), Allan Lefcowitz (322), V. N Arora (333), John Franzosa (361), Stephen Nissenbaum (363), Rita K. Gollin (369), Thomas L. Hilgers (380), John T. Irwin (389), William C. Spengemann (394), Michel Small (405), James R. Mellow (410), Leonard F. Manheim (415), NinaBaym (424), Harold P. Simonson (438), Michael Vannoy Adams (439), Dennis Foster (443), Gordon Hutner (445, 566), Carmine Sarracino (450), Gloria Erlich (459), Philip Young (468), Robert Shulman (479), Michael T. Gilmore (488), Elissa Greenwald (489), Albert J. Von Frank (497), Lois A. Cuddy (520), Clay Daniel (521), Edward A. Kearns (525), Leon Chai (532), June McMaster-Harrison (549), Rae Carlson (561), Rita K.

Gollin (563), James M. Mellard (568, 643), Richard D. Rust (572), Joanne Feit Diehl (578), Christopher Newfield (603), Harold Bloom (611), Sam B. Girgus (617), James M. Mellard (643), Edwin Haviland Miller (644), Leland S. Person, Jr., (646), Richard H. Millington (674), Samuel Chase Coale (678), Monika M. Elbert (723), T. Walter Herbert (752), Alison Easton (769), Robert Milder (787), Donna D. Simms (823), Elizabeth N. Goodenough (836), John N. Duvall (857)

Feminist Criticism

Feminist studies, which developed in the 1960s as the direct result of the women's movement and have burgeoned steadily ever since, describe, interpret, and often re-interpret women's nature and experience as depicted in various kinds of literature in an attempt to question long-standing, dominant, phallocentric ideologies, patriarchal attitudes, and male interpretations of literature. Some feminist critics rediscover works of forgotten women writers who were overlooked by a male-dominated culture and revalue women's experience, while others revisit books by male authors and review them from a woman's point of view to understand how they both reflect and shape the prejudices, assumptions, and attitudes that have restricted women. In general, feminist criticism examines texts to critique their masculine forms of authority and to show how they reflect a masculine ideology, especially when the texts cast women in stock character roles or prescribe what their male authors perceive to be legitimate "feminine" goals and aspirations. Feminists rethink the canon, point out limitations of male-centered critical approaches to literature, challenge representations of women as "other," examine power relations and the role of language, and explore issues of gender and male/female identity. While feminist critics have had no difficulty in citing *The Scarlet Letter* as an example of a patriarchally committed, male-authored text that stifles or silences an unconventional heroine, neutralizing her radical potential through the "saving" grace of maternity and "domesticating" her to submit to patriarchal authority and assume the identity of a conventional, nineteenth-century self-abnegating "angel of the house," there have been still other feminist critics who find that Hawthorne distances himself from the masculine world of patriarchal tyranny, linking his art to "feminine" writing and/or female authors. These critics argue that Hawthorne identifies intensely with Hester, claiming that he, like his radical heroine, is a subversive artist alienated from society, intimately concerned with women's oppression and with dismantling the repressive, creativity-negating patriarchal system of authority. Because feminism grew more eclectic in the 1980s, drawing upon the findings and approaches of other kinds of criticism, it is not unusual to find feminist approaches to *The Scarlet letter* that can also be classified as New Historicist, deconstructionist, or psychoanalytic. Also, because feminist criticism itself has headed in so many different directions since the 1990s, I have recognized the subcategories of "black feminist studies," "gender studies," and "family studies" directly below feminist studies. The first subcategory contains criticism that examines *The Scarlet Letter* in reference to issues of race and slavery and mostly in connection to African-American fiction. The second contains numerous studies that consider Hawthorne's complex handling or reversal of gender roles in the novel, and the third grouping includes examinations of *The Scarlet Letter* that treat the novel as a "family romance" or that concern marriage, domesticity, maternity, paternity, or the parent/child relationship.

Ben Barker-Benfield (286), Carolyn G. Heilbrun (303), Judith Fryer (340), Paul Lewis (384), Nina Baym (406, 419), Harriet Bergmann (413), Kristin Herzog (436), Lee R. Edwards (458), Joyce W. Warren (467), Peggy Kamuf (492), Lois A. Cuddy (520), Louise DeSalvo (535), Amy Schrager Lang (536), Mary Suzanne Schriber (541), Janis P. Stout (553), Charles Swann (554), Margaret Olofson Thickstun (573), Anne French Dalke (577), Cynthia S. Jordan (588), Gabriele Schwab (591), Jean Fagan Yellin (594), Monika M. Elbert (598, 614, 624, 834), Christopher Newfield (603), Jennifer Fleischner (625), Shari Benstock (639), Lucy Maddox (642), Joel Pfister (647), Emily Miller Budick (654, 656, 720), Cheryl Parulis (666), Naomi Segal (675), Carol Wershoven (701), Adrianne Kalfopoulou (712), Susan K. H. Kurjiaka (734), Rod Phillips (737), Nancy Walker (745), Deborah Gussman (751), Susan Elizabeth Sweeney (763), Nina Tassi (764), Gil Haroian-Guerin (770), Adrianne Kalfopoulou (773), Carolyn Duffey (780), Karen Jackson Ford (794), Jamie Barlowe (804, 805, 853), T. Walter Herbert (809), Suzan Last (812), Leland S. Person, Jr., (814), Thomas R. Mitchell (820), Claude Richard (822), Donna D. Simms (823), Shira Pavis Minton (826), Carol M. Bensick (831), Elizabeth N. Goodenough (836), Laura Martin (858), and Yusur AlMadani (861).

Black Feminist Studies
Jan Stryz (668), Mara L. Dukats (748), Charles Lewis (755), Carolyn Duffey (780), Jane Cocalis (792), Caroline Woidat (803), and Marcus Nordlund (850).

Gender Studies
Darrel Abel (284), Hugo McPherson (354), Harriet Bergmann (413), Daniel Cottom (427), Lawrence Buell (442), David Leverenz (447), David Stineback (505), Scott S. Derrick (512, 747, 793), Pamela Banting (518), George Dekker (534), Leland S. Person, Jr., (569), T. Walter Herbert (581), Andrew J. Scheiber (583), James J. Waite (585), Christopher Newfield (603), Douglas Anderson (610), Monika M. Elbert (614), Brian Harding (618), Robert K. Martin (620), Joel Pfister (647), Marilyn Mueller Wilton (676), Michael T. Gilmore (693), T. Walter Herbert (695), Ken Egan, Jr., (749), Nina Tassi (764, 827), Karen L. Kilcup (784), Nancy Roberts (798), Lora Romero (799), Suzan Last (812), Donna D. Simms (823), Nina Tassi (827), Carol M. Bensick (831), Claudia Durst Johnson (837), Erika M. Kreger (849), and John N. Duvall (857). [*See also* Gender,

512

Homoeroticism/Homosexuality, "Women, Hawthorne's view of," "Sexual Politics," *and* "True Womanhood, the cult of" in the Subject Index.]

Family Studies
Gloria Erlich (449, 781), Michael Ragussis (516), Joanne Feit Diehl (578), Douglas Anderson (610), Mary Jane Hurst (619), Monika M. Elbert (624, 834) Lucy Maddox (642), Edwin Haviland Miller (644), Leland S. Person, Jr., (646), Emily Miller Budick (656, 720), Naomi Segal (675), Claudia Durst Johnson (837), Franny Nudelma (841), Marcus Nordland (850), and Daneen Wardrop (867).

Texts or Essays on Hawthorne that Examine Critical Approaches and Trends in Scholarship on *The Scarlet Letter*

Cohen, B. Bernard. *The Recognition of Nathaniel Hawthorne: Selected Criticism Since 1828.* Ann Arbor: U of Michigan P, 1969. (234)

Colacurcio, Michael J. "The Spirit and the Sign." Introduction. *New Essays on The Scarlet Letter.* Ed. Michael J. Colacurcio. New York: Cambridge UP, 1985. 1-28. (485)

Garlitz, Barbara. "Pearl: 1850-1955." *PMLA* 72 (1957): 689-699. (62)

Kennedy-Andrews, Elmer, ed. *Nathaniel Hawthorne: The Scarlet Letter* New York: Columbia UP, 1999. (829)

Kesterson, David B. Introduction. *Critical Essays on Hawthorne's The Scarlet Letter.* Ed. David B. Kesterson. Boston: G. K. Hall, 1988. 1-18. (567)

Murfin, Ross C., ed. *Case Studies in Contemporary Criticism: Nathaniel Hawthorne: The Scarlet Letter.* Boston: Bedford Books of St. Martin's Press, 1991. (637)

Scharnhorst, Gary. *The Critical Response to Nathaniel Hawthorne's The Scarlet Letter.* New York: Greenwood Press, 1992. (670)

Shaw, Peter. "*The Scarlet Letter*: The Heretical Temptation." *Recovering American Literature.* Chicago: Ivan R. Dee, 1994. 23-47. (727)

Walcutt, Charles Child. "*The Scarlet Letter* and Its Modern Critics." *Nineteenth-Century Fiction* 7 (1953): 251-264. (28)

Works Consulted

Barry, Peter. *Beginning Theory: An Introduction to Literary and Cultural Theory.*
New York: St. Martin's Press, 1995.

Cudden, J. A. *Dictionary of Literary Terms and Literary Theory* Third edition.
New York: Penguin Books, 1992.

Eagleton, Terry. *Literary Theory: An Introduction.* 2nd edition. Minneapolis: U
of Minnesota P, 2001.

Hawthorn, Jeremy. *A Concise Glossary of Contemporary Literary Theory.*
Second edition. London: Edward Arnold, 1994.

Spikes, Michael P. *Understanding Contemporary American Literary Theory.*
Columbia: U of South Carolina P, 1997.

STUDIES IN AMERICAN LITERATURE